Exploring Society

PATHWAYS IN SOCIOLOGY

GARY PARKINSON
Douglas College

ROBERT DRISLANE
British Columbia Open University

THOMSON
NELSON

Australia   Canada   Mexico   Singapore   Spain   United Kingdom   United States

Canadian Cataloguing in Publication Data

Parkinson, Gary, 1940–
  Exploring society

Includes bibliographical references and index.
ISBN 0-7747-3133-8

1. Sociology.   I. Drislane, Robert.   II. Title.

HM51.P37   1996   301   C94-932448-5

Publisher: Heather McWhinney
Editor and Marketing Manager: Daniel J. Brooks
Projects Manager: Liz Radojkovic
Projects Co-ordinator: Megan Mueller
Director of Publishing Services: Jean Davies
Editorial Manager: Marcel Chiera
Supervising Editor: Semareh Al-Hillal
Production Editor: Laurel Parsons
Production Manager: Sue-Ann Becker
Production Co-ordinator: Carol Tong/Sheila Barry
Copy Editor: John Eerkes
Cover and Interior Design: Opus House
Typesetting and Assembly: Bookman Typesetting Company
Printing and Binding: Webcom Limited

Cover Art: Brian Jones, *Centre of the Universe* (1992). Oil on canvas. 6' × 9'. Photo courtesy of Nancy Poole's Studio, Toronto. Reproduced with permission of the artist.

♾ This book was printed in Canada on acid-free paper.

3 4 5   04 03 02

PREFACE

. . . .

. . . .

Before writing this book, we became convinced that there was a need for an intro-ductory text with a focus different from the usual one. We agree with Howard Becker and William Rau: "Sociology in the 1990s is so hopelessly fragmented that it is increasingly difficult to define its subject matter and to find a common voice in the babel of competing theories and specialities" (1992: 70). What we intend is to recover the common voice in sociology and make it visible to readers. We have resisted the temptation to follow an encyclopedic approach. There is much left out of this book, but we think our approach has allowed us to make the central ideas of sociology more apparent. To be too inclusive overwhelms the reader and often endangers coherence. Sociology has a very wide literature, and we hope students will do some of the sug-gested reading to broaden their understanding.

Like many others, we think the common theme in sociology was, and continues to be, the desire to understand the modern world that arose with the industrial rev-olution. Our commitment to using sociology for this purpose leads us to give explicit consideration to the historical development of modern societies and to an inquiry into their special characteristics. We identify capitalism as the common foundation of modern societies, and we focus on this type of society, especially Canada.

We have titled this book *Exploring Society* to express our belief that the main goal of an introductory text should be to help understand society rather than to display all the "bells and whistles" of sociology. With this in mind, the reader can use the book as a map of society. Sociology is the vehicle we use for exploration. This book maps only the major routes, leaving the reader to investigate the interesting byways.

Since we have focussed on the "major routes," the text is in many ways a per-sonal view of what sociology is, or should be. Others might map a different route. We anticipate some disagreement and hope that teachers will use these disagreements as an opportunity to discuss the many opposing viewpoints within both sociology and society.

Some of these opposing viewpoints are presented in this text. For example, both functionalist and critical analyses aid in the understanding of society, but the dis-cerning reader will see that we favour critical ideas.

A note about our use of newspapers is necessary. We have used them extensively to illustrate our discussion. We could have relied on "academic" sources, but we believe that newspapers are a vital tool for understanding society. All the major soci-ological ideas and debates appear from time to time in their pages. Sociology supplies the linkage, or the analysis, that holds the stories together. However, although newspapers can provide an essential learning resource and classroom tool, one must be careful not to accept their information at face value. It is necessary to be critical and ask questions such as: how did the newspaper get the information? Were its observations carefully made? Does the newspaper represent a particular point of view?

Organization of the Text
• • • • • • • •

We have tried to develop an account of sociology that has a clearly connected and logical structure. The chapters of this book build on the preceding chapters and are designed to present the reader with an overview of sociology as an attempt to comprehensively understand society. Each chapter should be seen as a building block of the whole and should not be considered in isolation.

We begin by introducing sociology as the study of society, something which in Émile Durkheim's words is external to the individual and constraining on individual lives. Since society shapes our lives, the second chapter examines socialization, the process by which society shapes individual consciousness. To understand socialization, and society itself, more fully we must look at the concepts of culture and social structure, the topics of Chapters Three and Four. Culture, social structure, and socialization have not always been the same, so Chapter Five offers a brief history of the emergence of western capitalism as a type of society. Here we see the importance of looking at society as a connected whole and why sociology as a discipline emerged during this social change. Chapter Six provides an overview of the way three classical sociologists (Karl Marx, Max Weber, and Émile Durkheim) began to understand this new society and its consequences.

The remainder of the text examines modern capitalist society. Sociology has been fascinated with inequality and great differences in individual income, wealth, and power, and this is the topic of Chapter Seven. Subsequent chapters examine the Canadian economy, the role of the state, the organization of work, the role of education in society, and the organization of the modern family. All of these substantive chapters are essential to understanding deviance, the focus of Chapter Thirteen. Chapter Fourteen, while it focusses on the media, also draws together the principal themes of this book. It discusses the ways in which communication in modern capitalist society puts pressure on culture itself, creating a consumer culture that many believe is inadequate for giving meaning to individual lives or providing direction for the community.

Throughout this examination, issues of multiculturalism, gender conflict, globalization, economic change, politics, and the growing inequalities of society are introduced. The qualities of sociology itself are examined throughout this text. After an initial discussion of research methods in Chapter One, we provide many instances of how sociologists use evidence to support their arguments as well as examples of probing criticisms of sociological research.

Readers should note that although there is no single chapter on women, the topic is handled extensively throughout the book. Chapter Six addresses the issue of male sociologists and the realities of women, while Chapter Eight discusses women in the structure of inequality. Chapter Nine examines gender and the state, and the following chapter discusses women and work. Marxism and feminism — two central critical approaches — are discussed at length in Chapter Twelve. Special attention is also given to women and education in Chapter Eleven and to violence against women in Chapter Thirteen.

Features and Ancillaries
• • • • • • • •

Each chapter includes a list of key concepts and phrases, an introduction and conclusion, further reading suggestions, and questions to consider. The text is further enriched by thought-provoking boxes featuring material from contemporary newspaper and magazine articles. Charts, graphs, and photographs further enhance the book. A detailed glossary, name and subject indices, and a reference section appear at the back of the book.

Instructors' Manual

An instructors' manual accompanies this book. This resource contains multiple-choice questions, ten short essay questions, two comprehensive essay questions, suggested classroom projects, and recommended videos for each chapter.

Acknowledgements

The authors wish to acknowledge the encouragement of Douglas College and the British Columbia Open University. We also thank Jonah Goldstein and Helga Jacobson, whose sociology courses, designed for the British Columbia Open University, provided us with insights and influenced our thinking. We are grateful for assistance from the librarian at *The Globe and Mail*. Harcourt Brace and Company Canada were very patient with us as our writing timetable became prolonged. Particular thanks to Heather McWhinney and Dan Brooks for encouraging the project and to Megan Mueller for her attention to the details of turning a manuscript into a book. We also appreciate the comments and suggestions made by several anonymous reviewers as well as the main reviewers: Helen Douglas of Okanagan University College, Ken Hatt of Carleton University, Noga Gayle of Capilano College, and Richard Gilbert of John Abbott College. While we adopted many of their suggestions, we of course remain responsible for the final content of the book.

Much information in the tables and boxes was provided through government sources. Readers wishing additional information on data provided through the co-operation of Statistics Canada may obtain copies of related publications by mail from Publications Sales, Statistics Canada, Ottawa, Ontario K1A 0T6, or by calling (613) 951-7277 or toll-free 800-267-6677. Readers may also facsimile their order by dialing (613) 951-1584.

Publisher's Note

Thank you for Selecting *Exploring Society: Pathways in Sociology*, by Gary Parkinson and Robert Drislane. The authors and publisher have devoted considerable time to the careful development of this book. We appreciate your recognition of this effort and accomplishment.

BRIEF CONTENTS

· · · · · · · ·

· · · · · · · ·

CONTENTS

. . . .

10
WORK

1 INTRODUCTION SOCIETY AND SOCIOLOGY

INTRODUCTION

This chapter introduces the sociological way of looking at society and explains why this distinct way of thinking about society emerged. The ideas and concepts of sociology can be used to analyze the character of any society, but the focus of this book is modern capitalist societies, especially Canada. This chapter looks at the special characteristics of social structure (the way social relationships between people are organized) and at culture (shared values, knowledge, beliefs, and norms of behaviour). While these two concepts are very useful as a way to think about society, they should not be considered entirely separate. An individual's experience of society is shaped simultaneously by the structure of social relationships and by the values and norms that guide individual beliefs and behaviour in these social relationships.

Sociology is included among the social sciences. Although most sociologists would agree that its status as a science is arguable, sociology does follow aspects of the **scientific method** in making its claims about how society works. While this general set of rules for making claims is held in common by sociologists, they differ widely on how to interpret society. There is great debate about the value of the various perspectives used to analyze society.

Society cannot be studied apart from the actions of individuals who are part of it. At the same time, however, these actions are shaped by the society in which the individuals live. Social interaction has patterns and is regulated in some way by shared expectations. These patterns in social interaction demonstrate the presence of society. Dramatic events sometimes can visibly demonstrate the power of this abstraction we call society to shape human values and behaviour. A glimpse of society is offered in the following story.

THE *TITANIC* SINKS

On the night of April 14, 1912, the White Star ocean liner *Titanic*, more than 500 kilometres from Newfoundland, slammed into an iceberg. It was just before midnight, and the ship was travelling at almost full speed. The iceberg was not seen until the ship was only 500 metres away, too late to avoid collision. The ship sank within three hours, at 2:20 A.M. on April 15th.

The *Titanic* was on its maiden voyage and had many rich and influential passengers, including the multimillionaires John Astor and Benjamin Guggenheim. Although there were 2201 people aboard and the total capacity of the lifeboats was 1178, only 712 passengers survived the sinking. It was difficult to fill the lifeboats as the ship sank bow-first into the ocean.

We can see society reflected in people's behaviour during this disaster. Public inquiries into the sinking established that as the ship began to sink, there was no violence, no fighting for a chance to escape, no pushing aside of the weak and elderly, no trying to buy access to the safety of the lifeboats (United Kingdom, 1912).

Both Astor and Guggenheim were drowned. Passengers were saved according to the tradition of the sea — "women and children first." While 70 percent of the women and children aboard were saved, only 20 percent of the adult males survived. Half of these males were crew members needed to row the lifeboats.

Why did people not fight for their lives? Why did Astor or Guggenheim not try to buy a place in the lifeboats? Why were most women and children saved, while the great majority of men perished? Benjamin Guggenheim was reported to have said to a steward, "Tell my wife ... if you are saved, tell her I played the game out straight and to the end. No woman shall be left aboard this ship because Ben Guggenheim was a coward" (Wade, 1980: 90).

The people on board the *Titanic* did not make up the rule that women and children should be saved first. This rule formed a part of the culture they had inherited from their society as they became socialized. The beliefs and behaviour of the crew and passengers were deeply influenced by society.

WHAT IS SOCIETY?

Students beginning the study of society often assume that a society *reflects* the beliefs, tastes, and behaviours of its members. Their feeling is that a society gets its characteristics from the people who are part of it. Sociology, in contrast, starts from the assumption that society, though composed of individuals, is separate from those individuals. Society is something in itself.

The starting point in exploring society is to understand that society has the capacity to shape the lives and minds of individuals. French sociologist Émile Durkheim (1858–1917), a founder of sociology, said that society is "external and coercive" (1964: 2). It is something over and above the individuals who compose it and exerts an influence that affects those individuals: it shapes their entire experience of life.

One way to see how society can be a thing in itself is to think of the difference between individual and choral singing. Choral singing is not just individual singing added up. A choir is not just a number of individuals singing simultaneously. Uncoordinated singing would simply be an unmusical chaos of individual voices. To move from individual singing to choral singing demands that each individual shape what he or she is doing to the singing of others. In addition to its members mastering individual singing, a choir needs rules governing how those members will sing together.

The operation of society is analogous to that of any organized activity. In any sport, for example, people playing or participating simultaneously do not necessarily make up a "team." Instead, the team arises only when the individuals begin to act in relation to each other.

· · · · · · · ·

Dale Sanders / MASTERFILE

Choirs also need social organization, in which individuals are grouped as sopranos, altos, tenors, and basses.

One cannot sum up the concept of choir simply by saying, "It's a group of individuals singing." Though composed of individuals, a choir depends for its workings on rules and social organization that do not apply in individual singing. A group of individuals have come together and created a social structure with a set of rules that arises from them, yet becomes a thing in itself.

The same point can be made about any organized activity. In hockey, six people playing simultaneously do not make up a team. A team arises only when individuals begin to play in relation to each other, according to the rules and organization that have been established for the game. The transition from individual play to team play requires each individual to do more than he or she would do purely as an individual. The individuals must now act according to the expectations of the others, that is, follow the rules. They will also follow an organizational structure in playing the game: one will play in goal, two will play defence, and three will play forward.

A group of individuals involved in a social activity create, or apply, rules that govern how they will relate to each other. These rules reflect the **norms** (rules of behaviour appropriate in different situations) and **values** (broad principles of behaviour and moral standards) of the group. They must also create a way of co-ordinating who does what by placing individuals in organized positions, or **roles**, and directing the activities of the group.

Societies, like teams or choirs, are assemblages of individuals, and they too are more than the sum of their parts. The analogy of the team or choir provides a simple practical illustration of the truth of Durkheim's claim that society is external to individuals. It differs from individuals not just in quantity, but in quality: it has components not found in the individual. But what of Durkheim's claim that society is coercive?

It is commonly accepted that a society is able to shape individual behaviour: every day individuals act within a framework established by their society and experience social pressures if they do not. Society has special organizations — the police, the law courts, probation officers, and jails — to enforce conformity to the norms and values of society. Parents, friends, co-workers, and neighbours influence individuals by remonstrating, shaming, ridiculing, or rejecting those whose public behaviour departs from the norm upheld by the society or group.

The coerciveness of society is not limited to direct external control over individual behaviour. The "police" in society are also inside individuals: they are the norms and values that individuals have absorbed during a process of **socialization**, when they encounter social ideas about what beliefs and behaviours are right or wrong, appropriate or inappropriate, normal or abnormal, and natural or unnatural.

It is this absorption of societal norms and values that gives the other dimension to society's coercive character. Rules imposed on people from without can often be evaded, but the rules they have absorbed cannot be evaded. People cannot break them without feelings of guilt, and often individuals will hold to them even at considerable cost to themselves. The behaviour of the passengers and crew on the *Titanic* reflects the society they were all part of.

An individual is born into a complex society. The new entrant soon learns how this society is structured and what behaviours are expected. Sophisticated learning is required; although humans are biologically almost identical in all societies, human societies vary considerably. As a result, humans do not depend to a great extent on instinct to guide how they think and act. Their thoughts and actions must be shaped by society: humans are essentially and inevitably social beings. Human learning can only take place if there is some way for people to communicate with each other; sophisticated learning demands the use of language.

This is why sociologists and social thinkers say that people become fully human only in society: without society there is no language, and without language, people cannot think in abstract ways. It is the cultural development of a symbolic system of language that makes humans unique among animals.

People acquire a language through their exposure to society. But language is not just something neutral used to express individual thoughts, it embodies particular ways of thinking about the world and viewing the world. Individuals' ways of thinking, including their way of thinking about themselves, is shaped by the society around them. As they understand more about social life, they understand more about their personal lives. This makes social inquiry both fascinating and disturbing.

WHAT IS SOCIOLOGY?

To discuss society and explore how it works requires special language and special concepts. This special language and the concepts that go with it have been developed within sociology, the area of study that focusses on the analysis of society. Sociology is, of course, not the only avenue of insight into society. It is allied to anthropology, which focusses on the analysis of traditional societies outside the western, industrial world. In more recent times, anthropologists have given increasing attention to the study of contemporary western society. As a result, the two disciplines are converging and are difficult to separate. Disciplines like history, psychology, linguistics, and economics are also important to the study of society (see Box 1.1).

Psychology tends to study processes internal to the individual, such as cognition, learning, memory, and motivation. This allows insight into the individual sources of

Box 1.1
One Categorization
of the Academic
Disciplines

SOCIAL SCIENCES
anthropology
communications
economics
geography (cultural)
political science
psychology
sociology

HUMANITIES
fine arts
history
languages
literature
philosophy

SCIENCES
biology
chemistry
ethology
physics

INTERDISCIPLINARY STUDIES
Canadian studies
criminology
environmental studies
women's studies

behaviour. Social psychology examines group influences on human behaviour and, as such, overlaps to a considerable extent with sociology. Economists study the processes of producing, distributing, and consuming goods and services. Literature, visual art, architecture, music, and dance are all forms of cultural expression that provide a deeper understanding of society. Sociology borrows from all of these disciplines to draw together ideas about how societies work. For this reason, sociology is often described as a synthesizing discipline.

Sociologists see societies as composed of two sets of features, broadly labelled culture and social structure. These are considered the two most important concepts in sociology.

Culture can be defined as the way that a group of people live. It includes language, art, religion, knowledge, ideas, and beliefs. The natural environment has a profound effect on the culture that a people develop. For example, the Inuit of northern Canada have created many words to distinguish different conditions of snow, and the Native peoples of the Pacific Northwest have elaborate myths, religious beliefs, and rituals that accord legendary exploits and magical powers to the wildlife on which their survival depends. However, although cultural worlds are located in the natural world, nature does not fully determine the way people think and behave. Ways of thinking, behaving, and living are products of history, tradition, and experience.

Social structure describes the way that social life is organized and the ways that people relate to each other. For example, a society in which people have no notion of private property and live communally will have a very different social structure from one that stresses private ownership, inequalities of wealth and income, and widely differing individual status.

BECOMING AWARE OF SOCIETY

Although both culture and social structure occur everywhere, it is possible to be unaware of their existence. People do not usually notice when they act in culturally prescribed ways; they simply take their actions for granted. Their attention is immediately riveted, however, by conduct that radically departs from their own ways of thinking and behaving. Many non-Hindu Canadians became aware of their own values when they read about the funeral planned for Rajiv Gandhi, a former prime minister of India.

> *From ancient times, Hindus have practiced a cremation ritual virtually unchanged except for the introduction of electric crematoriums. Most Hindus prefer the time-honoured cremation by wood fire, although some find it hard to witness.*
>
> *If tradition is followed, Mr. Gandhi's son, Rahul, would light the pyre of his late father near the head.*
>
> *Hindus do not use a coffin to transport the body to cremation. It is wrapped in white linen and tied to a bamboo stretcher. The son leads the procession carrying a fire pot and throwing coins and sweets for the poor... .*
>
> *Before putting the body on the pyre, a priest performs rites invoking some of the millions of Hindu deities and seeking celestial blessings to release the soul.*
>
> *The body is given a final bath and placed on the pyre.*
>
> *If a woman has died, the fire is lighted at her feet. If it is a man, it is lighted near his head. The son and male relatives walk seven times around the pyre and pour on clarified butter to help the fire engulf the body.*
>
> *Cremation attendants keep watch on the skull. If it does not burst from the heat, they break it with a blow from a cudgel.*
>
> *Hindus believe the soul is locked in the skull, and can become trapped. The soul, said to live for eternity, must be released for the cycle of rebirth.*
>
> *After the body has completely burned, relatives and mourners return home and take a ceremonial bath for purification.[1]*

Canadian Hindus find it impractical and illegal to carry out all these steps. However, Hindus and Sikhs in the Vancouver area joined together to build a crematorium that houses many of the symbols important to the ritual. After the funeral, many families return the ashes of family members to India to be scattered in a sacred river.

If you have difficulty understanding the cultural meanings behind this ceremony, consider the following Canadian ritual. When former prime minister John Diefenbaker died in Ottawa in 1979, his body was placed on a train and transported more than 3000 kilometres to be buried in Saskatoon. His wife's body (she had died 3 years earlier) was then exhumed and taken to Saskatoon to be buried next to that of her husband. What beliefs about life after death, about the body, and about marriage make this set of events meaningful?

Just as people tend to overlook the existence of culture, they are often unaware that social life is structured. It is considered simply *normal* to go out to work or to learn formally in school. When they leave home to go to work, they do not usually notice that they have entered a distinct and different social structure. At school, too, the roles of students, teacher, principal, and school board are considered as given and natural. However, encountering a social organization that radically departs from their own experience leads people to recognize the existence of social structure.

For example, the delivery of health care is organized in radically different ways around the world. Among the Azande of southern Sudan, medical diagnosis is done in public; it is a local event likely to draw neighbours and friends. In the society of the Maya in Belize, the patient may move in with the medical practitioner during the course of treatment. In many societies, dreams are considered an important means for the recruitment and training of medical practitioners (see Howard, 1986). Although there is an obvious cultural component in each of these examples, there is also a structural component: the acutely different ways of organizing a life event and of defining the relationship between the medical practitioner and the patient.

What focusses a person's consciousness of culture and social structure is the experience of having unspoken assumptions challenged. This disruption causes people to notice what was invisible, what they took for granted, what they did not even recognize as being created by their society.

Sociological thinking — asking questions about why a society is like it is — begins when people realize that their own society is not founded on some unchallengeable and inevitable law of nature. This realization occurs when there is contact between groups or societies that have different norms, values, and ways of social organization.

Once people realize that their ideas about such things as love and marriage, caring for children, private property, authority in the community, and the purpose of work are not shared by others, sociological thinking can begin. People may indulge in biased thinking, which simply justifies their society's ideology as best, most natural, and most advanced. But they cannot, for long, avoid recognizing that things could be different. Once people recognize that things could be different, they may begin to ask questions (see Box 1.2) about their society.

THE EMERGENCE OF SOCIOLOGY

If sociological thinking arises when one group encounters a very different culture and social structure, sociological thinking must have a long history. The origins of sociology are unknown, but a sociological style of thought, addressing some of the above topics, was a preoccupation of the ancient Greeks.

By the time of Plato (428–347 B.C.) and Aristotle (384–322 B.C.), one key concept had been established in Greek thinking — the contrast between physis (nature) and nomos (law or cultural convention). The recognition that nomos varied greatly from society to society compelled Greek thinkers to recognize that behaviour was not founded on some given and invariable natural law. They recognized that the laws and conventions of the Greek city-state were social products created by people for people. As such, they needed to be justified on rational and moral grounds and could not be explained by an appeal to "nature" (Sinclair, 1951).

Box 1.2
The Central Questions of Sociology

1. How is this society structured? How are its various aspects related? How is it different from other societies?
2. Where does this society fit in human history? How is it similar to and different from societies of the past? Are there forces within it that cause it to change? What are the ways in which it might change?
3. In what ways does this society shape human personality? What qualities does it encourage in the individual? What forms of human behaviour does it support, and what forms does it suppress?

SOURCE: Adapted from C. Wright Mills, *The Sociological Imagination* (New York: Oxford University Press, 1959).

Questions about society are also provoked during periods of rapid social change. All societies change over time, but their pace of change is very different. Some societies seem to have maintained similar central features of group organization and economic activities for hundreds, perhaps even thousands, of years. These slow-changing societies tend to have a simple social organization and limited technology. Their members live off the land and the resources of nature. They hunt and gather and do not alter, or re-order, the natural world to any great extent.

However, other societies, primarily western, have changed rapidly and continually, especially since the eighteenth century. Today, much of the world is swept up in rapid change, including economic globalization, Third World urbanization, and the transformation of traditional social relationships. Although it is easy to overstate the stability of societies in the past, it is accurate to say that no society has ever experienced the comprehensive and rapid change that western society has experienced in the past 250 years.

Any broad measure used to judge the pace of change supports this view. People worked at much the same tasks, in much the same way, for more than a thousand years, from the collapse of the Roman empire to the first stirrings of industrialization in Europe. Certainly, towns grew and technical improvements occurred in agriculture, metal work, engineering, building, and manufacturing, but the most common life situation for people throughout this period was working on the land, living in small rural settlements, and leading a life focussed on kin and community.

The pace of change quickened immensely in the eighteenth and nineteenth centuries, when western society moved from having an agricultural subsistence basis to an economy dominated by trade and manufacture. The new style of life that emerged was dominated by urban settlement and an economy in which people worked for wages. These changes affected the culture and structure of society. Work that had been organized around the seasons and subsistence needs became organized around a clock and for the creation of profit. The social divisions of worker and entrepreneur were created. The roles of women in economic production and the family were substantially altered. The relatively simple social organization of the village gave way to the complex organization of city life. Cultural importance was ascribed to individualism, personal achievement, freedom, and democracy.

The first nation to experience the transforming force of industrialization was England. It was soon followed by Germany, France, the United States, and, a little later, Canada. All these societies encountered massive social change. In 1790 the working population of rural England was twice that of the urban areas; 50 years later the proportions were reversed. Towns grew with unparalleled speed. The population of the cotton city of Manchester increased from 90 000 in 1801 to 400 000 in 1861; Bradford's increased from 13 000 to 104 000 in the same period (Cole and Postgate, 1961: 305). The total population of England also rose rapidly, from under 9 million in 1801 to 16.5 million by 1831.

In nineteenth-century Canada, change in population size and location was also rapid. The population rose from under half a million in 1806 to almost 2.5 million in 1851 and more than doubled again by 1901, to 5.7 million (Marr and Paterson, 1980: 151). In 1851 only about 13 percent of Canada's population lived in urban settlements; by 1901 this figure had risen to 35 percent, and by 1931 more than 50 percent of all Canadians lived in urban settlements (p. 186).

In this new society, self-sufficiency was virtually impossible. Almost everyone worked for money, and it was money that *bought* the necessities of life. Wage work was different from the work of pre-industrial society. Though not always more unpleasant, it was almost always more intensive and extensive — six 12-hour days per week was typical.

As western Europe experienced massive changes in social organization and cultural ideas, there was a growing focus on trying to understand how and why society was being transformed. Newly formed academic disciplines emerged in response to questions about society. Among these, the social science of sociology emerged in response to questions such as the following:

- How do people's roles in society change?
- What are the effects of industrialization on the way people live?
- How is work changing? How does this affect family life and individual happiness?
- What new cultural values are emerging?
- How is this society shaping human personality?

Along with the new ways of living came new ways of thinking, including science.

Auguste Comte (1798–1857), often regarded as the founder of modern sociology, distinguished between past societies dominated by the "theological–military" power of king and church, and the newly emerging "scientific–industrial" society with its practical thinking and elected governments (Aron, 1968).

The contrast between the "theological–military" and "scientific–industrial" societies was striking. In the theological–military society of pre-industrial Europe, the dominant ideas came from religion and tradition. Society was culturally integrated by the immense authority of the church and the power of kings, queens, and lords. Explanations of natural phenomena and of the sources of ethical and political values came from the mystical and supernatural sources of religion, magical belief, and tradition. Political authority was drawn from the claim that God anointed an aristocracy to rule over earthly kingdoms. The military power of aristocrats was used to maintain order and suppress revolt.

In scientific–industrial society, which coincided with the industrial revolution, this past was rapidly swept away. In Europe and the United States, new ways of thinking about the rights of individuals uprooted the old order. Political power once exercised by authority from God, was now considered to be given by the authority of the people, through elected representatives. Magical and religious ideas lost their influence, and the emerging new culture upheld rational, calculating, and scientific ways of thinking. A stress on materialism, commerce, and profit-making accompanied the harnessing of the natural world and its resources to economic expansion and development.

A new culture had emerged, with new ways of looking at the world and of acting upon the world. Part of this new cultural atmosphere was the development of sociology.

SOCIOLOGY AS SCIENCE

Scientific thinking also suggested a new model for thinking about society. This model assumed that society could be understood in much the same way that the natural world could — through the discovery and application of scientific laws. Auguste Comte summed up much nineteenth-century thinking when he claimed that sociology, the emerging discipline of the study of society, would come to replicate the natural sciences of biology, chemistry, and physics. In Comte's opinion, sociology would uncover laws of social development, just as biology and chemistry were uncovering the natural laws of organic development. It would also be able to define laws of social organization, just as physics was able to define the laws that regulated the natural world — the laws of gravity, energy, and mechanics.

The rise of a culture focussed on the practical and rational, rather than on the mystical and religious ways of the past, encouraged the assumption that the new science of sociology would allow for the planned shaping of the social world in much the same way that the disciplines of the natural sciences aided the understanding and manipulation of the natural world.

Few modern sociologists believe, as Comte and others after him did, that there is a body of discoverable social laws (similar to the law of gravity or laws of electrical resistance) waiting to be revealed by the researches of social scientists. But rejecting the search for laws does not remove the possibility of coming to understand how society is organized or identifying its central cultural values. Social scientists do believe that sociology can be systematic, rigorous, and factual in its analysis of society. It can, in short, follow the general framework used to develop and test theories in the natural sciences: a scientific method.

Scientific Method

· · · · · · · ·

What is scientific method? There is a complex debate about this, and considerable literature exists on the topic (Giere, 1984). An outline of some of the basic principles follows (see Box 1.3).

First, and most fundamentally, scientific method demands that researchers keep personal opinions and biases out of their sociological investigations. It is not scientific to ignore evidence that points away from conclusions one would like to reach. Thus, sociological arguments and propositions must strive for ethical neutrality and objectivity. Sociological researchers must separate their political opinions from their investigations. Since it is the task of sociology to accurately describe the social world, comments on how the social world *ought* to be cannot be treated by scientific method and cannot be derived from statements of fact. Sociologists might note, for example, that the divorce rate has risen dramatically in Canadian society in the past 30 years, but they should not set out to argue that divorce, in itself, is morally right or wrong.

Sociologists wear two hats: as citizens they can have moral and political values that affect their views on what they see around them, but as students of society they try to analyze and describe, not judge. This demand for neutrality is difficult to achieve fully, but it must be attempted.

Second, sociological arguments should, ideally, flow from observation. From observing some fact about the real world — for example, a rising number of single-

· · · · · · · ·

Box 1.3
Key Features of the
Scientific Method

· · · · · · · ·

- Ethical neutrality
- Careful and systematic observation
- Demand for replication of findings
- Argument must be falsifiable
- Attention to empirical questions
- Scrutiny by others

· · · · · · · ·

parent families — sociologists develop a theory to help explain why this social trend has occurred. Sometimes the process works in reverse; sociologists begin with a hunch, based on some general assumptions, that something might be true, and then look for evidence that either confirms or refutes that idea. For example, one might assume that Canadian Roman Catholics have a lower divorce rate than do other Canadians because of their church's opposition to divorce. One must then look at the real world to see if the assumption is true. In this case, statistical evidence shows that the assumption is not true; in fact, Quebec, where the population is about 90 percent Catholic, has Canada's third-highest provincial divorce rate (Statistics Canada, 1990b).

Working from observations toward general theories or arguments is called inductive reasoning. Working from a general hunch or hypothesis and then locating evidence that confirms or contradicts the hypothesis is called deductive reasoning. Often, sociological theories and arguments result from a combination of these approaches, as theories and observations influence each other in a two-way process.

Third, sociological arguments must be supported by further observation. This element of scientific method is known as replication. If observation reveals an apparent pattern in social life, a similar pattern should be apparent in further observations. For example, if we discover that all our financially well-off neighbours have university degrees, it appears likely that income and education are linked. This observation needs to be checked (replicated) by further research in other communities before we offer it as a factual statement about the relationship between education and income in Canadian society.

Fourth, and in some ways most important, a sociological argument must be falsifiable: it should be expressed in terms sufficiently clear and concrete that it is easy to define the sorts of evidence that will lead to its rejection. This is a fairly simple point, but a central one. Sociology cannot analyze and therefore should not advance claims like "Crime is caused by evil influences." The problem with such a claim is that it is not susceptible to examination. Alleged "evil influences" cannot be observed, measured, or demonstrated. Although it is possible to assume that a murderer was influenced by extra-human forces, it is not at all clear how such a claim could be disproved. Such a statement could, therefore, never be considered a sociological argument.

Sociological analysis is, however, possible if the statement is changed to: "Crime is produced by inequality." That argument is clear and definite enough to be tested. Indicators of inequality can be identified, crime rates for societies with a low degree of inequality can be established, and comparisons can be made with societies in which inequality is more pronounced. If the argument is correct, evidence will emerge in the data: there will be a link between the amount of crime and the wealth or poverty of different societies. To be certain of a connection, the researcher would compare the findings with those of similar studies (replication), and the evidence gathered would either lend support to the argument or lead to its rejection.

The requirements of scientific method restrict the sorts of questions that can be asked and the sorts of conclusions that can be reached. The method limits researchers to empirical questions — those that can be answered by an appeal to *measurable evidence*. For example, the question "Are First Nations children less likely than their parents to be able to converse in an aboriginal language?" can be answered by asking First Nations respondents in a survey to describe and assess their competence in an aboriginal language. The information gathered will answer the question. (The answer is yes: 36 percent of adults can carry on such a conversation, but only 21 percent of children can [Statistics Canada, 1993a].)

Sociologists use many methods to gather evidence. In addition to using the survey method, they use experiments, case studies of individuals or events, interviews, content analyses of documentary materials (such as newspaper stories and advertisements), direct observation of events (either as direct participants or as non-participating observers), and evidence gathered by data-gathering organizations such as Statistics Canada. The methods that produce numerical accounts are called quantitative methods, while those that produce narrative accounts are called qualitative methods.

Since sociologists often have strong moral and political views, there is an inevitable blending of fact and values in the development of sociological arguments. Scientific method does not apply in all important questions asked about society, but its principles must be kept in mind when deciding what sort of argument — empirical and factual ("is"), or evaluative ("ought") — is being put (see Box 1.4).

Sociology of Science

Many sociologists question the extent to which science can ever be neutral and claim that it is partly a product of society. They subject science to sociological analysis, in an area called the sociology of knowledge. According to this view, science must be understood as a set of concepts and practices whose origin is in the social world. The emergence of science, its growing dominance, and its relationships to politics and economics are all obviously sociological matters.

A more radical sociology of science questions the very assumption that scientific claims have special status as objective truth. Claims to the possession of knowledge and the empirical evidence given to support and evaluate these claims are seen as social products. It is argued that the influences of moral beliefs, class, gender, and ethnic identity inevitably become features of science, in two ways: by influencing the researcher to choose particular topics or by becoming part of the cognitive content of knowledge.

MacKenzie (1981), for example, argued that the interests of the professional middle class entered into the very content of statistical theory. This class supported the assumptions of the eugenics movement, which envisioned a social hierarchy with professionals at the top. In order to demonstrate that there were associations between variables, statisticians developed statistical theory and procedures. It was the interest of certain statisticians in showing that personal qualities like intelligence were inherited that led to the development of particular statistical tests.

Did they do bad science or good science? Should their work be judged by the intentions they brought to their work or by the internal standards of science itself (the scientific method)? While sociologists accept a substantial domain for the sociology of science they also accept Chalmers's (1991) argument that science should be understood internally (by its aims and purpose) rather than externally (by intentions that might be shaped by class or gender). The standards of science themselves are not fixed, however, and must also be seen as social products (see Box 1.5).

Even when sociologists agree on basic methods of gathering evidence and the testing of arguments, they still often disagree about the conclusions that should be drawn. Sociology is an argumentative discipline. Why do sociologists often disagree and propose contradictory and incompatible ideas and theories? There are two key reasons: the facts, and their interpretation.

First, there is simple disagreement about the facts. For example, is crime more likely to be committed by working-class than by middle-class people? This is a straightforward question, but the answer is not straightforward. Certainly the statistics for crim-

Box 1.4
An Attack on Women
Masked by "Science"

• • • • • • • •

Many advantages of the scientific method are revealed in the controversy that arose over the publication of an opinion by chemist Gordon Freeman in a scientific journal.

Based on informal conversations with students, Dr. Freeman said that "about 50 percent of students whose mothers worked outside the home had a strong tendency to cheat" on examinations, a figure that he said was "five times higher than for the general population."

He then argued that the mental states that drove students to cheat on examinations were part of a larger pattern of aberrant behaviour that produced embezzlement, infidelity, political and business corruption, drug use, teen-age sex, and "the murder of 14 female engineering students at L'Ecole Polytechnique in Montreal."

The paper lacked most of the usual features of social science. It did not report precisely how many students were studied, how many of them had mothers that worked, or when those mothers started working. The same questions were not asked of all participants. There was no formal control group of students with non-working mothers to compare with the supposedly psychologically damaged offspring (Stephen Strauss, "Journal Offers Apology for Article by Chemist," *The Globe and Mail*, July 31, 1991 p. A9).

While one can fault Freeman's science, it is also important to notice the political side of his argument. Freeman blames women for the ills of society and implies that women should stay in the home, caring for their children. Some, however, argue that there is no definite division between science and politics. German sociologist Max Weber, though advocating value-free (ethically neutral) sociology, himself admitted that what sociologists choose to analyze is itself inevitably shaped by their personal values and beliefs (Keat and Urry, 1975: 196–227).

While Weber thought that sociologists could be objective in their analysis once they had chosen a subject for investigation, others claim that sociology is not and should not be separated from political and moral values. They criticize the central claim that sociology can be value-free (Gouldner, 1964). One way this criticism is advanced is to ask if science itself, let alone social science, is in reality neutral and objective.

• • • • • • • •

inal *convictions* in Canada are quite clear: working-class people are disproportionately represented. But identifying the people who actually *commit* crime is significantly more difficult. Some sociologists point out that working-class people are more likely to be arrested and charged than are middle-class people, even for the same sort of crime. Middle-class people will sometimes simply be cautioned by police (which doesn't show up in official data) for offences for which people judged "less respectable" will be taken to court (Wilson and Herrnstein, 1985: 27–28). In Canada, a young, dishevelled person standing on the corner of a business intersection is more likely to be suspected of illegal activity than is a corporate executive standing on the

· · · · · · · ·

Box 1.5
Traditional
Knowledge

· · · · · · · ·

Postmodernism sees a plurality of claims to knowledge. Science is only one of them and it is not given a privileged place (Lyotard, 1984). This perspective has stimulated a new interest in traditional forms of knowledge, particularly in relation to environmental issues.

In the past, scientists described spiritual explanations as superstition and dismissed the emotional or subjective aspects of traditional knowledge because it values objectivity and seeks to distance the researcher from the object of study.

Martha Johnson defined traditional environmental knowledge as

a body of knowledge built up by a group of people through generations of living in close contact with nature. It includes a system of classification, a set of empirical observations about the local environment, and a system of self-management that governs resource use. The quantity and quality of traditional environmental knowledge varies among community members, depending upon gender, age, social status, intellectual capability, and profession. With its roots firmly in the past, traditional environmental knowledge is cumulative and dynamic, building upon the experience of earlier generations and adapting to new technological and socioeconomic changes of the present.

Many questions are raised by accepting traditional knowledge as valid. Can it be integrated into scientific knowledge? Should science appropriate traditional knowledge and use it in ways that do not benefit indigenous peoples? Should traditional knowledge, like much scientific knowledge, become a commercial product to be bought and sold in the marketplace of ideas? If traditional knowledge and scientific knowledge disagree, which should be accepted?

· · · · · · · ·

SOURCE: Adapted from Martha Johnson, *Lore: Capturing Traditional Environmental Knowledge* (Ottawa: IDRC, 1992).

· · · · · · · ·

same corner. They may, of course, both be engaged in criminal activity: one selling drugs, the other embezzling company funds.

Statistics on convictions, then, might tell more about the likelihood of people of differing social statuses being prosecuted than they tell about the actual commission of crime by members of different social classes.

Second, and more complex, even if there is agreement on the actual facts of a situation, there may be argument about how the facts should be interpreted. It is on the issue of interpretation that sociologists ally themselves with different perspectives on society. Sociological perspectives are quite varied, but two main ways of looking at the social world have been central to modern sociology: functionalist and critical.

Functionalism is also known by other names, such as structural functionalism, systems theory, consensus perspective, and order theory. **Critical perspectives** are sometimes referred to as conflict theory. Marxism and feminism are forms of critical sociology. In Canada, the political economy perspective, another form of critical theory, is commonly discussed.

PERSPECTIVES ON SOCIETY

· · · · · · · · ·

Functionalism

· · · · · · · · ·

The functionalist approach can be described in a very simple way. It starts with one central judgement: the survival of social life depends on a certain degree of order and stability. Thus, stable societies are in everyone's interest.

From this initial judgement, functionalism develops an understanding of society that considers it analogous to a complex organism. For example, the human organism must perform certain functions if life is to be maintained. The heart is needed to pump blood to the body tissues: life cannot continue without this process of circulation and renewal. In turn, the blood must be oxygenated to perform its function of supporting the body tissue. Organs like the kidneys and liver are also essential in processing body wastes and detoxifying the blood.

To describe what the heart or the lungs actually do, their function is considered part of a physical system that acts to maintain life. Their role is explained in terms of the end result — the maintenance of the body — to which they contribute.

This analogy provides the two foundations of the functionalist approach to understanding society: people share an interest in living in a stable, smoothly functioning society, and societies are best understood as systems (like the human body) that have requirements for effective functioning to which all of their components contribute. From a functionalist point of view, an examination of any aspect of the society should start with the question: What part does this aspect of society play in maintaining the smooth operation of the whole system?

The way this question is posed gives functionalism a reputation for conservative thinking. The question assumes that the current state of society is a given and that the qualities of any functioning society need not be questioned. It is merely necessary to evaluate what part any feature of the society plays in helping the whole system work.

Functionalists are not blind to the fact that some parts of society may not contribute to its smooth operation; there may well be elements that disrupt its workings and detract from its stability. These elements are labelled dysfunctional. While a society can tolerate some dysfunctional aspects (just like the human body can put up with minor ailments), it cannot tolerate a continued disturbance of its basic needs without either disruption or change. Thus a society that is being disrupted will change until it can cope with the disruption and re-establish stability.

Functionalism is capable of showing how the parts of a society fit together and of providing an overall sense of how society works. Consider, for example, why Canada and its provinces have such imposing parliamentary and legislative buildings. Visitors to Regina are struck by the grand scale of the European-inspired legislative building with its massive central dome, marble pillars, and opulent construction in Tyndal stone. The building was constructed in 1909, when Regina was without a sewage system and had a small population gleaning a sparse living from agriculture and the railway. Why was this massive building constructed in such a modest setting?

Functionalists might point to the fact that all societies need a system of authority, in which some person or institution can lay down rules and be obeyed. Without some agreed way of making decisions and settling public issues, societies would function as police states, using force to compel order. This authority has to seem special in some way; it must have a quality that commands respect and makes people feel that obedience is appropriate. It is no accident, then, that the legislatures of Canada and its provinces have grand architecture and impressive formal settings. They are built, as are churches and cathedrals, to impress and suggest, as churches symbolize the authority of God, the authority of the state.

Consider a more down-to-earth example: the division of household labour by sex. Women typically perform family and household roles that are different from those performed by men. A functionalist would tend to see this division as a positive one, arguing that it contributes to the stability of marriage and family relationships by creating mutual dependency. Because household duties are divided, men and women must rely on each other, thus creating a stable foundation for their relationship and for the raising of children.

A key criticism of functionalist theory is that the questions it poses already presuppose the answers. To ask "What is the function of a given feature of society?" assumes that it must have a positive purpose. If something can be shown to help society function, it must be positive, since a smoothly functioning society benefits everyone. Thus functionalism can, and often does, merely explain and justify whatever exists: it upholds the status quo.

Critical Perspectives

All critical perspectives share the view that there are *always* alternatives to the way any given society is organized. It is therefore never enough simply to say that a part of society is justified because it supports society functioning in its present form; society could function in a different form.

Critical perspectives also share a second view: the benefits people derive from the way society works are very different. Some people do very well as a result of certain cultural values and social structures, and others do less well. Those who do less well might be better served by societies that were organized on a different basis.

Critical approaches stress the point that society does not have independent "interests." An element of society that contributes to social stability is not justified on that ground alone, since the maintenance of an existing state of affairs may be good for some people but not for others. Critical sociology, therefore, "rocks the boat" — it shows who benefits from existing social arrangements (and who doesn't) and takes a sceptical view of the status quo.

Consider the earlier example of legislature architecture. A critical approach would reject the argument that it is in everyone's interest that the state should be respected and obeyed, since all people benefit from an ordered society. Instead, it would maintain that the purpose of such buildings is to suggest that government is neutral and above special interests: it works for everyone. Glorifying the state through these great buildings is one way of keeping people from looking behind the stage-set and noticing that the state seems to uphold *particular* interests, not those of everyone in society.

What of the other example — the division of labour by sex? A critical perspective might note that women tend to perform tasks that have less cultural value and give women less power in the household. The particular division of tasks may well contribute to women's dependency on men and to a subordinate role in society.

Notice that the functionalist view concludes that the state's authority and the sexual division of labour are neutral matters by claiming that they benefit us all, whereas the critical approach views respect for the state's authority and the specific division of labour as something that can serve special, not general, interests. This perspective provides an explicit political edge to the critical perspective.

Two examples of critical perspectives are **Marxism** and **feminism**. Marxist perspectives assume that divisions over the ownership or control of economic resources provide the key for understanding other aspects of society. Feminist perspectives acknowledge the subordination of women in society, are interested in identifying the dynamics of this subordination, and hope to stimulate political action to transform society. Marxism focusses on class inequality, while feminism is concerned with the nature and sources of gender inequality. These two approaches challenge people to think about different ways to construct society, and a detailed discussion of both these perspectives appears throughout this book.

Microsociology

This text focusses on the functional and critical sociological perspectives because both discuss the structure of society and provide a way of seeing it as a unified whole. There are other sociological perspectives, however, such as symbolic interactionism, ethnomethodology, conversational analysis, phenomenology, and cultural studies. These perspectives tend to examine individual action and interaction as a way to understand society. These forms of analysis can be called "microsociology," in contrast to the "macro" perspectives examined in this text.

The microperspectives are valuable. Although societies may be thought of as external to and constraining on the individual, they do not act or make decisions in themselves. It is *individuals* who act, and this individual action makes the culture and structure of society visible. It is through daily actions and interactions that individuals produce society. This does not mean, however, that society can be reduced to the characteristics or interests of individuals or that these individuals can create society anew every morning. The behaviour of the passengers on the *Titanic* makes it clear that society permeates and governs the actions and interactions of individuals.

Society is clearly a powerful force. Nevertheless, society coexists with personal uniqueness; it does not eliminate it. The next chapter introduces the topics of personal autonomy, the individual shaping of social life, and variations in individuals' definitions of situations and of social values.

CONCLUSION

This introductory chapter can be summarized as follows.

First, society is external and coercive to the individual. It is more than the sum of its parts — the individuals who make it up. Society has a culture and a social structure that shape peoples' thought, beliefs, and behaviour.

Second, sociology developed because people wanted to understand and describe differences between societies and how and why societies were changing.

Third, sociological ideas, like other ideas, are shaped by the surrounding society. The origins of modern sociology coincide with the development of industrialization in western society and the rise of scientific and rational thought.

Fourth, sociology, influenced by scientific–industrial society, adopts a way of looking at the social world based on the scientific method. Although sociology cannot be strictly scientific, the following principles of the scientific method can be used to arrive at statements about the social world: ethical neutrality, careful observation of the social world, replication, and falsifiability.

Fifth, two main theoretical perspectives in sociology — functionalist and critical — influence the questions sociologists ask about society and the way they interpret their observations of society. The same facts can be interpreted quite differently, depending on the model of society adopted — that it works in the interests of all, or that it works for the benefit only of some people.

Although sociology is clearly not a hard and fast science, it does bring forward support for arguments that are advanced about society. These arguments are inherently political and controversial, but they do not consist merely of one opinion competing against another. The student of sociology must apply the scientific method to evaluate various arguments and theories, to decide whether an argument is logical, whether it seems to be inspired by bias or **ideology**, or whether it appears to be an honest attempt to be objective. Is the evidence in support of an argument fair and adequate, or slanted and insufficient? Has an argument gone through a process of checking by replication? Is it clear enough that it can be regarded as a testable proposition about the social world?

As you progress through this book, you will begin to notice the assumptions from which arguments are advanced, and the approaches — functionalism or critical perspectives — that lie behind them. You will begin to judge which arguments about society have the best correspondence between their claims and the evidence. You will also find new ways of understanding your own experiences and of using them to assess the validity of arguments and theories about society.

Welcome to sociology, the study of society and, through it, the study of ourselves.

SUPPLEMENT ON RESEARCH METHODS

DOING SOCIOLOGICAL RESEARCH

KEY CONCEPTS AND PHRASES

aggregation	levels of measurement
causation	negative correlation
concepts	positive correlation
control variable	statistical significance
correlation	statistics
dependent variable	theory
frequency distribution	units of analysis
hypothesis	variable
independent variable	

Auguste Comte and Émile Durkheim, two important founders of modern sociology, based their work on the assumption that society could be scientifically investigated. They assumed that society was patterned by laws and cause–effect relationships similar to those that governed the natural world. Durkheim developed this approach to society in his work on suicide, which was dedicated to establishing sociology as a scientific discipline. Although there is now substantial debate about the possibility of a truly scientific study of society, it is important to understand the approach Durkheim advocated and its influence on the development of sociology. What follows is a brief guide to this "scientific" way of thinking about society.

UNITS OF ANALYSIS

Any researcher who initiates a project of study must first ask: What kinds of units am I investigating? Will I focus on individuals, groups, or some other unit? If the researcher is studying individuals, the focus must be on looking for variations in the behaviour or social situation of individuals and striving to understand the reasons for this variation. If studying groups, the researcher must focus on variations between groups of people and trying to account for this variation.

Durkheim was not interested in studying individual behaviour; he left the examination of the reasons for individual suicides to others. He was interested in describing the variation in suicide rates among groups of people in different societies and communities. His ultimate goal was to develop a theory to explain this variation.

VARIABLES

When looking at individuals or groups, social researchers use variables to structure their analysis. A variable is a category (relevant for describing individuals or groups) that can take on more than one value. (If it takes on only one value, it is a constant.) Suicide rates, for example, are a variable: they can range anywhere from low to high. Similarly, the religious affiliations of individuals have many potential values (e.g., Hindu, Christian, Muslim). These variables take on additional importance when they are linked to concepts.

Concepts are not material things; they are ideas (e.g., democracy, beauty) that help people think about the world. However, researchers often look for instances of behaviour or social organization that might illustrate the concepts they have developed. So, while they begin by thinking conceptually, to actually study and use these concepts for analysis they select variables that are linked to them. Durkheim, for example, considered divorce rates to be a variable indicating levels of social integration.

ASSOCIATION

When the relevant variables have been defined, they can be linked to a unit of analysis. One can describe an individual, for example, as a Buddhist (a religious affiliation variable) or a society as having a low suicide rate (a behavioural variable). To discuss groups, however, these observations require aggregation. This results in a description of frequency distribution: for example, X percent of individuals in a study are Sikh (and other percentages for other religious affiliations), or Y percent of countries have high suicide rates (and other percentages have low or medium rates).

This initial description of a study population (of individuals or group) is the first step in investigating what social scientists are interested in learning: how variables are associated in a population. They might ask: Is there a pattern to the variations that occur between two variables? If variation is found in suicide rates and divorce rates in the populations of various countries (see Table 1.1), a sociologist might ask: Is the variation of one unit associated with variation in the other? Social scientists call this association between variables a correlation.

For example, the fifteen countries in Table 1.1 can be ranked according to their suicide rates (1 being the highest and 15 being the lowest rates). These countries can also be ranked by their divorce rates (from 1 to 15). If they had identical ranks on both variables, as shown in Figure 1.1, there would be a perfect positive correlation of the ranks for the fifteen countries.

Figure 1.1 shows a direct relationship between two variables: as one variable increases, the other also increases. Thus, if we know the divorce-rate ranking of a country, we can predict its suicide-rate ranking. The correlation could be expressed as a number, +1.00. A perfect negative correlation would be revealed if, as divorce rates went up, suicide rates went down. This is depicted in Figure 1.2. This correlation would be expressed as –1.00.

If there was no association between the variables, when one variable changed (took on differing values) there would be no change in the other variable. This is depicted in Figure 1.3.

In a real research situation, it would be very unusual to find either a perfect correlation or no correlation between variables. In addition, correlations are not usually

	Divorce Rate[a]	Suicide Rate[b]
Norway	0.5	73.0
England–Wales	1.3	68.0
Russia	1.6	30.0
Italy	3.1	31.0
Finland	3.9	30.8
Bavaria	5.0	90.5
Belgium	5.1	68.5
Netherlands	6.0	35.5
Sweden	6.4	81.0
Baden	6.5	156.6
France	7.5	150.0
Wurttenberg	8.4	162.4
Saxony	26.9	229.0
Denmark	38.0	258.0
Switzerland	47.0	216.0

Table 1.1

Comparison of European Divorce and Suicide Rates, Compiled from Data for Various Years from 1870 to 1880

· · · · · · · ·

[a]Per 1000 marriages.

[b]Per 1 million population.

SOURCE: Adapted and reprinted with the permission of The Free Press, an imprint of Simon & Schuster, from *Suicide* by Émile Durkheim, translated by John A. Spaulding and George Simpson. Copyright © 1951, renewed 1979 by the Free Press.

immediately evident. Take a few minutes to rank the fifteen countries in Table 1.1 for each of the two variables and see if any pattern is immediately evident. It is usually necessary to perform a statistical operation on ranks (or data) to discover whether a correlation exists. Statistics refers to a collection of tests or tools used to describe or make decisions about research data. The particular statistic used to determine if there is a correlation will depend on the levels of measurement used, as well as on assumptions about the normalcy of the distribution. All social science measurement has as its goal the differentiation of individuals or groups.

Levels of measurement are simply the qualities of the particular indicator used to do this differentiation. For example, Table 1.1 used suicide rates as a variable and indi-

Figure 1.1

A Positive Correlation between Divorce Rates and Suicide Rates

· · · · · · · ·

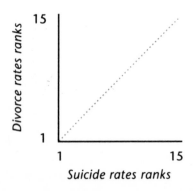

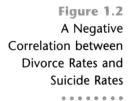

Figure 1.2
A Negative
Correlation between
Divorce Rates and
Suicide Rates
● ● ● ● ● ● ● ●

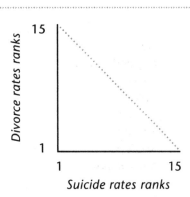

cated the number of suicides per million people in various European countries. Is this indicator just a set of categories, thus making the most basic differentiation among the population? No, it does more than that. Does the measurement establish rank order? Yes, this is the level of measurement developed by ranking each of the countries. Does the measurement allow users to determine the actual difference between one society and another? Yes, Table 1.1 does this; for example, Bavaria has 60 suicides per million population more than does Russia. Does it allow us to establish ratios among the study units? Yes, the figures in Table 1.1 also allow one to, for example, conclude that Bavaria has three times as many suicides per million population as Russia. These levels of measurement are the nominal, ordinal, interval, and ratio levels of measurement, respectively.

In statistical analysis it is assumed that a certain amount of association between the variables may occur by chance. Using probability theory, mathematicians are able to determine the frequency of certain occurrences. Researchers can then make an arbitrary decision about the "level of significance," a specified probability that something will happen. Typically, researchers will use a .05 level of significance, suggesting that this occurrence would happen by chance 5 times out of 100. If they find an occurrence that they would expect only five times out of a hundred by chance, the finding is said to have statistical significance and a decision is made that the two variables are associated. They are confident (95 percent confident) that the finding did not occur by chance.

Figure 1.3
No Correlation
between Divorce
Rates and
Suicide Rates
● ● ● ● ● ● ● ●

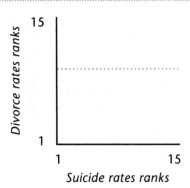

CAUSATION   Researchers are seldom content to merely describe a relation between variables as a correlation. A more powerful description would be obtained if it could be shown that one variable *caused* the other or, more accurately, if a change in one variable caused a change in the other. For example, does smoking cause lung cancer? Does a high divorce rate cause a high suicide rate?

Three conditions must be met before it can be asserted that one variable caused another. First, there must be a correlation between the two variables. (Note that although causation implies correlation, correlation itself does not imply causation.) Second, it must be clear that the causal variable occurred prior to the effect variable. (The causal variable is identified as the independent variable, and the effect variable is called the dependent variable.) This frequently requires the researcher to engage in two periods of observation, known as longitudinal research, which is most easily accomplished through an experimental design in which the researcher can ensure that the dependent variable is not present, and then introduce or manipulate the independent variable to see if the dependent variable occurs. Sociologists do not use the experimental design very often but try to accomplish this separation of variables by manipulating the data. Third, the researcher must be confident that the correlation cannot be eliminated by allowing a third variable to be introduced. If the correlation can be explained away, the relation would have been spurious.

Removing spuriousness is a key element of sociological research. It requires attention to third variables, called control variables or "confounding variables." To examine control variables, consider the research undertaken in Halifax by Clairmont and Barnwell (1989) to determine whether the race of criminal defendants influences the sentences imposed by judges. The research hypothesis, based on an assumption of racial discrimination, was that Black defendants would receive harsher sentences than would non-Black defendants. The researchers' initial data appears in Table 1.2.

In this table, the sentences of Black defendants are compared with those of non-Black defendants; there is a difference of 11 percent when the two groups are compared for high sentence severity. Is this grounds for believing that the courts are biased? Is this apparent association spurious? What other variables might influence how a judge decides on a sentence? Is it possible, for example, that the judge is taking prior criminal conviction into account? What about the relative seriousness of the offence or the poverty of the defendant? These should each be control variables.

The researchers found that defendants with three or more prior convictions did in fact receive harsher sentences, that 58 percent of their sample of Black defendants had three or more prior convictions, and that 40 percent of the non-Black sample had three or more prior convictions. It is clear that prior convictions must be controlled for.

TABLE 1.2
Sentence Severity
by Race

		Race of Offender	
		Black	Non-Black
Sentence severity	High	55%	44%
	Low	45%	57%
		n=51	*n*=170

SOURCE: Donald Clairmont and Winston Barnwell, "Discrimination in Sentencing: Patterns of Sentencing for Assault Convictions," in *The Royal Commission on the Donald Marshall, Jr., Prosecution.* Vol. 4 (Halifax, January 1989).

Table 1.3			2 or Less Prior		3 or More Prior	
Sentence Severity by Race, Controlling for Prior Convictions (N=215)			Black	Non-Black	Black	Non-Black
	Sentence Severity	Low	71%	72%	24%	35%
		High	29%	28%	76%	65%
			(*n=21*)	(*n=99*)	(*n=29*)	(*n=66*)

SOURCE: Donald Clairmont and Winston Barnwell, "Discrimination in Sentencing: Patterns of Sentencing for Assault Convictions," in *The Royal Commission on the Donald Marshall, Jr., Prosecution*. Vol. 4 (Halifax, January 1989).

When researchers "control for" a variable, they hold it constant; it is not allowed to vary. Table 1.3 shows how the researchers accomplished this.

The first half of Table 1.3 holds prior record constant; everyone has two or fewer prior convictions. Now the percentage difference found for Blacks and non-Blacks has disappeared: there is only a 1 percent difference for those receiving high sentences. It now appears that the relationship between race and sentence severity is minimal. However, the right side of the table (three or more prior convictions) indicates that a greater proportion of Black offenders receive severe sentences. This could perhaps be explained by considering other variables (employment status, for example, might influence judges), or perhaps the difference would remain and it could then be concluded that Black offenders were treated differently. Clairmont and Barnwell did not find statistically significant correlations, however, because their sample sizes were small.

THEORY AND RESEARCH

Researchers may undertake a study in order to explore a matter about which not much is known or for which there is, as yet, no theory. Usually, however, social science research is directed or guided by theory. Rather than examining variables in some haphazard way, the research is guided to variables made relevant by a theory. Theory is an integrated body of assumptions, propositions, and definitions connected in such a way as to provide a conceptual model of some aspect of the social world. A good theory provides a model that explains things in the real world.

To determine if a theory is adequate or not, however, requires testing. This is achieved by making observations in the real world. The phenomena that should be observed will be determined by the theory. Researchers will deduce a hypothesis (an empirical assertion about the real world that may or may not be true) from the theory, determine what indicators they could use to measure the concepts stated in the hypothesis, and then gather data to see if the hypothesis is true or false. If it is true and has been logically deduced from the theory, it can be assumed that the theory itself is true or adequate.

It is also possible for a theory to be created after research observations; it can be constructed to explain the patterns found in the research. This, however, is not in itself a test of theory. An independent test would then have to be conducted with further observation.

This supplement has presented the traditional method of doing science; it captures the essence of what Durkheim and others have done. There are, however, many philosophical problems embedded in this way of doing research. Sociologist Harvey Sacks stated that "in terms of the history of sociology nothing is more tragic than that Durkheim's *Suicide* should be conceived as a model investigation" (Cuff and Payne, 1984: 215). The shortcomings of the scientific method will become apparent by the end of this text.

· · · · · · · ·

NOTES
· · · · · · · ·

1. Excerpted from Dilip Ganguly, "Hindu Funeral Ritual Follows Ancient Form," *The Globe and Mail*, May 24, 1991, p. A9. Reprinted with permission of the Associated Press.

· · · · · · · ·

FURTHER READING
· · · · · · · ·

Chalmers, Alan. *Science and Its Fabrication*. Minneapolis: University of Minnesota Press, 1991. A useful review of some critiques of science provided by the sociology of science, and a defence of the idea that science must be judged according to its aims and the point of the activity.

Collins, Randall. *Three Sociological Traditions*. New York: Oxford University Press, 1985. A helpful guide to essential differences in sociological perspectives.

Jaggar, A.M., and Paula Rothenberg. *Feminist Frameworks: Alternative Theoretical Accounts of the Relations Between Women and Men,* 2nd ed. New York: McGraw-Hill, 1984. A useful introduction to the various streams of feminist thought.

Keller, Evelyn Fox. *Reflections on Gender and Science*. New Haven: Yale University Press, 1985. Interesting reflections by a scientist who found herself asking: Is the nature of science bound up with masculinity?

Mazlish, Bruce. *A New Science: The Breakdown of Connection and the Birth of Sociology*. New York: Oxford University Press, 1989. A helpful history of sociology that sees it emerging from the kind of social change discussed in this chapter.

Nisbet, Robert. *Sociology as an Art Form*. New York: Oxford University Press, 1976. A brief and very readable introduction to the history of sociology and its main concerns. Interesting because it focusses on a way of thinking (the art of sociology) rather than on the use of science.

Tucker, Robert. *The Marx–Engels Reader*. New York: W.W. Norton, 1972. Includes the *Manifesto of the Communist Party*. The preface to the 1883 German edition, included in this book, provides a clear one-page statement of the central materialist theme of Marxist sociology.

Wilcox-Magill, Dennis. "Paradigms and Social Science in English Canada." In J. Paul Grayson, ed., *Introduction to Sociology*. Toronto: Gage, 1983. A helpful introduction to some early Canadian sociologists: Carl Dawson, Leonard Marsh, John Porter, Harold Innis, and Samuel Clark.

· · · · · · · ·

STUDY QUESTIONS
· · · · · · · ·

1. How would you respond to the argument that it is impossible to study society objectively because we are all influenced by our own experiences and personal values?
2. "The whole is more than the sum of its parts." How can this saying be applied to society?
3. Why did sociology first develop in western societies?

4. What are the basic assumptions of the functionalist perspective on society?
5. What are the basic assumptions of the critical perspectives on society?
6. How would you use Durkheim's method to study domestic violence? Create independent, dependent, and control variables and describe how you would obtain the information (data) required to study the topic.
7. How does sociological argument differ from ordinary differences of opinion?

$\mathcal{2}$ ▬ SOCIALIZATION
THE INDIVIDUAL
IN SOCIETY

· · · · · · · · ·

INTRODUCTION
· · · · · · · ·

Society is separate from individuals, but only individuals can create society, through their actions and interactions. Yet those actions and interactions are not random; human behaviour is influenced by social norms and values. How are social norms and values absorbed by individuals? Sociologists answer this question with the concept of socialization, the process by which individuals learn and internalize the culture of their society.

This chapter considers socialization mainly by reviewing the work of George H. Mead, Erik Erikson, and Philip Slater. If the self originates in society, as Mead argued, do societies with differing cultures or social structures create different types of individuals? Erikson showed how cultural values shape child-rearing techniques and, as a result, the personality of children. Slater argued that modern capitalist societies produce distinctive kinds of individuals.

There is some disagreement about how to understand socialization. It emerges most clearly in relation to the way individuals are socialized for their place in society, particularly for places in a structure of inequality. From a functionalist perspective, one can ask how individuals are prepared to fill necessary roles in society. From a critical perspective, one can ask whether society indoctrinates individuals to accept and uphold the existing structure of inequalities.

· · · · · · · · ·

What gives pattern to social behaviour? How do regularity and predictability become present in human interaction? Chapter One tried to show that all humans are born into an ongoing society, and that this society has both a distinct culture — language, knowledge, ideas and beliefs — and a distinct social structure — a way of organizing social life. To secure stability in society, new members must learn how to live and work with other people. They have to learn shared norms and values and go through an experience of education and training that fits them for a place in the society. How does society become part of the individual?

SOCIETY AND THE INDIVIDUAL
· · · · · · · · ·

Sociologists refer to the way in which individuals become societal members as the process of **socialization**. Individuals' behaviour is not shaped only by outside constraints; they do not follow norms simply from fear of negative consequences if they do not. Rather, society becomes a fundamental part of individuals, so that it becomes impossible for them to understand themselves apart from society. Individuals become carriers of culture and of social structure.

The claim that all people are social members and that society is a fundamental part of everyone prompts the questions: just what is an individual? Where does the influence of society end and unique personality begin? Sociologists talk about these concerns as questions of *identity* or of *self*. Most people know that they are somewhat unique; they have identifiable tastes and preferences, distinctive appearances, and personal ways of doing things and thinking about things. Although sociologists are not primarily concerned with investigating what makes individuals distinct, any theory of identity they develop must be compatible with this fact.

Sociologists observe that people see themselves in relation to others. Knowing how individuals relate to others is an important component of human identity. People often think of themselves as if viewed from the outside — not just as unique individuals, but as people in definite positions in society: daughter or son, wife or husband, mother or father, student or teacher, worker or employer. They think of themselves and others in relation to social roles, and assume and expect some consistency of behaviour among sons and daughters, or wives and husbands.

But, however individual they might think they are, it is difficult to imagine their self-conception being wholly individually created. Can one ever make up "from scratch" an image of who one is? Of what one is like? Or is it easier to imagine oneself by using the resources that culture makes available? The language individuals use, the beliefs they hold, and the values they share are essential ingredients in fashioning a sense of themselves.

Chapter One's account of the sinking of the *Titanic* vividly shows the link between the individual and society. Faced with certain death, passengers accepted their fate and men gave priority to women and children. Individuals cannot easily abandon their socially derived sense of self, even at the cost of unimaginable personal stress. The passengers were not autonomously creating their lives; the way they thought about their situation and the rules they felt they must follow were shaped by society.

This link between the individual and society is not only recognized in sociology. It is assumed in everyday life and in the way individuals make sense of the world. They understand events, and each other, by trying to link personal beliefs and behaviour to a social context. This was demonstrated during a 1990 human rights hearing in which the Moncton school board, accused of tolerating hatred toward Jews, argued that its anti-Semitic students should be understood as society's victims. The lawyer for the school board described the students who shouted obscenities, drew swastikas, and insulted Judaism as coming from "totally deprived backgrounds," ranging from poverty to drug abuse and inadequate parents.[1]

Although the lawyer's explanation of the youths' behaviour cannot erase the students' responsibility, there is some justification for trying to understand people's behaviour in light of their family backgrounds and social circumstances. When

Photo 2.1
Sociologists observe that people see themselves in relation to others. People visualize themselves as, for example, mothers and daughters, husbands and wives, students and teachers.
. . . .

Andy Cox / TONY STONE IMAGES

young people offend cultural norms, it is common to try to understand what it is about their relation to society that gives rise to this conduct. They are often seen as somehow uncared for or displaced and lacking the sense of opportunity and self-worth that might commit them to society. At the same time, "normal" youths are understood in the same way, but as the products of other, more positive, social environments. Most people try, at times, to understand individuals by imagining their experience in society.

From a theoretical perspective, this way of thinking is associated with functionalism and the assumption that deviant conduct occurs when socialization has failed. A critical perspective would examine poverty and exclusion in society and the role of cultural stereotypes in creating prejudice and hostility.

THEORIES OF SOCIALIZATION
. . . .

Having focussed on the importance of the link between individual and society in creating a sense of identity, it is time to examine how it comes about. How do individuals become members of society? There are two questions here. First, how does learning what is expected in society occur? People must learn to fit into society by observing other societal members — learning by example — and by becoming aware of social norms and values. There are many ideas about how this learning takes place. Second, how does what one learns about the expectations of society become part of one's sense of identity? Why do people accept and obey the social norms and values they have been introduced to even when others do not monitor them? This issue is one of how culture is internalized, about how it gets inside individuals and becomes part of them.

The processes of learning and internalization are reviewed in the following discussion of the theories of George H. Mead, Erik Erikson, and Philip Slater.

George H. Mead: Becoming a Socialized Being

· · · · · · · · ·

An important aspect of the process of socialization is that it continues throughout an individual's lifetime. Just as lives move through a natural cycle of birth, maturation, adulthood, and death, so do the ways individuals relate to society. Their age and position in society affects what they have to know and what they must do. As infants, individuals begin to learn what is, and is not, expected of them as they observe the reactions and understand the language of other people close to them. As children, they learn that expectations of their behaviour are different from those attached to the infant. As young adults, they meet the challenges of independence, self-direction, and self-support.

If they marry, they encounter another set of responsibilities and personal and cultural expectations. Those who have children encounter another role definition — parent. As people age, they again encounter societal norms that suggest appropriate behaviour for older people. From the moment of birth, then, and throughout life, people are exposed to the expectations of others: the cultural norms and values that shape individual beliefs and conduct.

These stages of life are not separate "slices" of experience; rather, they overlap and interweave with each other. For example, while individuals certainly learn much about being a parent from actually having children, they have also learned a lot (perhaps most) about being a parent from being a child and having a parent themselves. So, at all times, even when they are not actually playing a particular role in society, they observe how that role is performed and the sorts of expectations that accompany it.

Preparation for the performance of social roles begins in earliest childhood. It can be clearly observed in children's play. For example, children often act out parenting roles, when they play with dolls or the family pet, by giving directions and commenting on behaviour. Their first acquaintance with social rules comes when they experience the reaction of others to their behaviour.

Initially, children are conditioned to control their behaviour: they do not recognize abstract rules but do know that some actions will generate disapproval or punishment. This realization occurs at a very early age: psychologists point to the breast-fed infant's control of the biting reflex during feeding, which must be accomplished to avoid withdrawal of the breast, as the first example.

As individuals become more aware of our social surroundings, they prepare to take part in society by looking at what others are doing. They notice and copy discrete actions, for example, some of the activities of housework. Then they move beyond imitating individual acts and begin to play at being someone else, by imitating their role behaviour. Finally, individuals realize that there are some general social rules that seem to govern the way most people relate to each other. They see people act according to some established pattern of behaviour, and they comprehend that social life has rules that are like the rules of a game.

George H. Mead (1934), whose work on the formation of social identity is central to sociology, explained that the process of becoming a social member through socialization has three stages: the preparatory stage, play stage, and game stage.

The Preparatory Stage

· · · · · · · · ·

Mead's starting point was that thought is not possible without some form of language. Language, for Mead, included facial expressions and gestures as well as sounds and words, which are all symbolic in that they represent something. A clenched jaw may symbolize anger; an outstretched hand may symbolize a greeting. Words, of course, are a complex symbolic system and can represent an infinity of things, concepts, emotions, values, and beliefs.

Mead claimed that an individual's emergence as a conscious, thinking being depends on the use of symbols. He argued this claim by saying that a mind cannot come into existence outside a social context. People can develop a consciousness of themselves only when they are able to see themselves from the outside, when they are able to imagine how others see them. In imagining how other people see them, people are also able to see themselves, to get a sense of themselves, for the first time. This imagination of how others see one is possible only when one is able to communicate with others.

Communication is possible only through a shared understanding of symbols of expression, gestures, or words. Until this is accomplished, it is impossible for people to express and share their thoughts and feelings. People who want to interact with others must first come to grips — at least in part — with the relevant symbolic system. For example, in parts of West Africa, it is a friendly greeting to shake your fist at someone you meet (Bowen, 1964: 1). When receiving a gift, one must extend both hands cupped. To take a gift with one hand is to suggest that the gift is inadequate; to use the left hand is to insult both giver and gift (p. 7). In Thailand, it is considered offensive to seat oneself on the ground with one's feet pointing toward another person. In Pakistan, a woman should not make eye contact with adult males outside her family.

Westerners might easily send, or receive, the wrong message in one or all of the above contexts. Communication is not possible until the meaning of gestures is mutually understood (see Box 2.1). What is true for gesture and expression is equally true

· · · · · · · ·

Box 2.1
A New Identity for
the Deaf Individual
· · · · · · · ·

For many years deaf individuals have been given, and frequently accepted, a stigmatized identity. They have been perceived by the hearing community to have a medical handicap that makes them inferior. Not being able to participate in the culture of hearing, they have faced enormous obstacles to participation in social life. They have often accepted this perception of inferiority and thought it "natural" that they would receive less education than hearing individuals.

Recently, however, the deaf community have begun to propose a new way of understanding themselves and are asking the hearing community to transform its perceptions. Rather than being seen as a handicapped group, they wish to be seen as a cultural community. They have a distinctive language and a unique set of values. In this respect, they ask to be considered in the same manner as other language groups, such as Italian-Canadians. Thus, an identity based on "infirmity" is replaced by one based on being a language minority. This provides a positive identity for the deaf and makes it possible to see that education and success should be natural and desirable expectations for the deaf individual.

· · · · · · · ·

SOURCE: Adapted from Harlan Lane, *The Mask of Benevolence* (New York: Alfred A. Knopf, 1992).

· · · · · · · ·

for words and sounds: people must know this verbal language before they can enter into deliberate and directed social interaction with others. A consciousness of society occurs only when the infant begins to understand the language of others.

The Play Stage

In the play stage, children begin to play at being another person and acting out how they behave. A three-year-old girl plays at being her mother, and casts the family cat in her own role: she feeds the cat and tells it not to be messy and to eat its food. She does, however, not yet see that there is a general pattern to what her mother does, and she moves from one identity to another — mother to storekeeper, police officer to doctor — quite freely and impulsively as she plays.

The Game Stage

During the game stage, children develop an ability to see that there is consistency in the way people behave and that general rules and expectations govern this behaviour. They learn that social norms govern how, when, and where people do certain things and what they think and believe. Rather than just playing one part, children recognize that society and social relationships are shaped by abstract, but definite, rules.

"Game" is a revealing word for this last stage in the general socialization of the child — a game arises only when those involved have recognized that their actions and those of other participants are governed by rules. To guide their conduct in society, children must absorb its rules just as they must absorb hockey rules to play hockey. Once they have done this, something happens to them at the deep level of personal identity: they have developed an ability to apply norms and rules to evaluate their own thoughts and behaviour. The foundations of primary socialization are completed. The child can now encounter a situation and know what is expected, according to social rules. The game has become possible because all players generally observe the rules. They use an external standard of judgement to evaluate both their conduct and that of others.

Mead calls this use of an external standard the recognition of a **generalized other**. Children now examine and evaluate their actions from the standpoint of other people. At this point, individuals have "absorbed" society: they use cultural standards to guide and evaluate their own conduct. No longer is it sufficient to say "I want this." Instead, the question becomes "What are other people going to think of me if I do this?" Mead calls this internal dialogue **reflexive role-taking.** Children now look at their actions from others' point of view.

Mead examines a central problem in understanding society: how to account for personal uniqueness and conformity. He accounts for conformity by showing how children go through stages in their entry to the social world. He accounts for uniqueness by using a metaphor that the self — the personality in society — consists of two components: an **I**, the inner ego; and a **me**, the individual's understanding of the expectations of society. What individuals want as ego-centred beings is always reviewed by the part of them that has absorbed the norms of the surrounding society; what individuals decide and how they act is always conditioned by the society within them, but society does not always *determine* how they will act or what they will think.

Although society guides individuals and shapes their thoughts and actions, the unique inner self has the capacity not only to conform, but to cut loose from the expectations of others. Mead theorized that people's emotional commitment to social norms and values — their internalization of these norms and values — arises because they become socially conscious as they become conscious of themselves. Their emergence into self-consciousness is the same as their emergence into social consciousness.

Erik Erikson: Child-Rearing Techniques and Personality Patterns

Erik Erikson was not a sociologist, but rather a psychologist trained in the analytical tradition founded by Sigmund Freud (1856–1939). As a Freudian, Erikson was convinced of the crucial importance of earliest childhood experiences in the formation of personality. He argued that the way in which the infant is treated creates predispositions that shape all subsequent social and emotional life. Freud argued that there are three crucial psychological–physiological stages through which all infants pass: the oral, anal, and genital stages. Each stage can be handled by the adults who care for the child in different ways, with quite different psychological results.

The Oral Stage

At the oral stage, the newborn infant is focussed entirely on securing oral satisfaction for physical comfort and security. The newborn infant "lives through and loves" with the mouth (Erikson, 1963: 72). Women in some societies, responding to all demands from the infant, practice prolonged and unlimited breast feeding. In other societies, stress is put on the early weaning of babies and feeding occurs according to some plan or routine.

The Anal Stage

At the anal stage, the focus of the developing infant's sensual and emotional interest moves from the mouth to the anus and bowels. In some societies, no great control of the bowels is expected in the infant and no attention is paid to toilet training. Children simply learn control as they develop and eventually emulate the older children around them. In other societies, toilet training is given great attention and strong expectations exist about early control and regularity.

The Genital Stage

At the genital stage, the child (at around age three) develops an intense awareness of the physiology and sensations of the genitals. In many traditional societies there is little adult censoring of child's play, and children of three or four will engage in mock sexual intercourse in playful imitations of adults. Often there is no attempt to discourage masturbation, and children are assumed to be passing through a natural stage of development. In other societies, there is a contradictory mix of denial and horror of the sexuality of children. It is denied that children have natural sexuality; any manifestation of it is assumed to be pathological and is discouraged.

Psychology and Society

Erikson moved between psychology and sociology, between individual and society, by arguing that there is an observable pattern to variations in the handling of these stages in different societies. These variations exist because societies' child-raising techniques encourage particular paths of emotional development in children that are linked to traits needed or desired in adults.

To develop his argument, Erikson claimed that the three stages of development are each connected to important emotional outcomes. The oral stage influences whether an individual will be either trusting (encouraged by freely receiving the comfort and satisfaction of the breast) or distrustful (linked to the withdrawal, or fear of withdrawal, of the breast). The anal stage shapes the personality traits of either confidence and generosity or shame and doubt. Societies that allow the child to control the activity of the bowels are said to encourage confidence and generosity. Feces are initially precious to the child; they are something the child is proud of having made. When there are rigid expectations about toilet hygiene, the child can experience shame and doubt, tension about bowel control, and fear of disapproval or disgust. The genital stage is about initiative (the expression of desires and their confident pursuit) versus guilt (anxiety that desires, if expressed, will be censured).

These opposing experiences of trust and mistrust, autonomy and shame or doubt, and initiative and guilt, brought forth during the infant's handling and nurturing, lend shape to the way adult personality will emerge. The personality formation at each stage is shaped by the society the child is born into. In responding to the developmental process of the child, the society also influences the emerging personality.

Societies in which the group is all-important and in which people rely heavily on each other in order to survive in a hostile environment direct child raising in quite different ways from those that stress self-reliance, self-control, and individualism. Erikson discussed the example of the Sioux, who do not actively wean children from the breast but nurse them until they lose interest of their own accord. This practice encourages the development of trust, first toward the mother and then toward the other members of the tribe. Neither are the Sioux systematic about toilet training; they simply let the older children lead the toddlers into the bush. Gradually, the child develops control as he or she wishes to be more like the older children. According to Erikson, this practice encourages generosity toward other members of the tribe because it supports confidence about releasing the bowels, about giving and "letting go." The Sioux also ignore the genital explorations of children, especially males, which Erikson linked to the development of the energy and aggressiveness needed for the hunter.

In contrast, Erikson viewed the child-raising patterns of modern western society as encouraging a very different kind of character structure. The early weaning of western babies from breast or bottle encourages an eagerness to get and grasp onto private possessions, since the babies do not have the experience of generous feeding and the comfort of being held. The stress on early control of the bowels, which Erikson claimed is characteristic of western culture, arises from a desire to develop orderliness and punctuality in the child and prepare them for routine and disciplined life styles. This is linked to "the spread of middle-class mores and of the ideal image of a mechanized body" (Erikson, 1963:81). Inhibition of the exploration of genital sensations, which is common in western cultures, may instil a lack of direction and purpose and encourage a passive reliance on direction from others.

Erikson was careful not to be mechanical: there is no simple relationship between child-handling and the personality traits that are important in adult society. Rather, the child-raising system merely encourages or discourages the development of certain energies and values rather than others (pp. 137–138).

Freud's theory of developmental stages, as outlined by Erikson, is controversial and has received vigorous criticism.[2] One might ask, for example, if it is the child's growing genital awareness or the sex-differentiated treatment received from earliest infancy that is the main shaper of behaviour (Kessler and McKenna, 1978: 90–91). Although there is disagreement, the ideas Erikson put forward provide a general explanation of the psychological and physical stages of maturation and of how these stages are linked to the process of socialization, especially the internalization of culture. Erikson's observation that different societies handle children in different ways helps to clarify why the resulting adults have very different ways of relating to the society around them.

Philip Slater: Being Shaped for a Mobile, Changing Society

· · · · · · · · ·

Philip Slater (1976) offered another perspective on the link between society and personality by distinguishing patterns of socialization in traditional "simple, stable, and familiar" societies from those in modern "complex, shifting, and strange" societies. He argued that these two distinct types of societal organization require people to be prepared in different ways for adult participation. Thus, at a deep level of traits established in the personality, individuals in different kinds of society are different (see Box 2.2).

Box 2.2
The Rise of
Individualism

While North Americans say the squeaky wheel gets the grease, in Japan the maxim is "The nail that stands out gets pounded down."

And while Western children who won't finish their food are given stern warnings not to waste it, Japanese children are told, "Think how bad the farmer who raised the food for you will feel if you don't eat it."

Such contrasts have emerged from a rapidly growing body of scientific studies that show how deeply individualism runs in most Western cultures, and how shallow that vein is in most others.

The new cross-cultural studies are confirming what many observers have long noticed: that the cardinal North American virtues of self-reliance and individualism are at odds with those of most non-Western cultures.

They also suggest that the nature of individualism has been changing toward a greater emphasis on raw self-interest, and that the rise of individualism in a society goes hand in hand with economic growth.

The work contrasts individualism with "collectivism," in which a person's loyalty to a group like a family or tribe overrides personal goals. Recent studies say this outlook predominates in most cultures of Asia, Africa, the Middle East, and Latin America.

The late Raoul Narrol, a professor of anthropology at the State University of New York at Buffalo, found in a 1983 study that such societies have among the lowest rates of homicide, suicide, juvenile delinquency, divorce, child abuse, and alcoholism. They also tend to have lower economic productivity, though as countries like Japan become more affluent, they also tend to become more individualistic.

The collectivist cultures make up about 70 percent of the world's population, according to the studies. But virtually all the data of modern psychology and most other social sciences come from the most individualistic cultures, like the United States.

As a result, some social scientists say, many Western assumptions about the universals of human behaviour actually apply to a minority of people, albeit those in the most advanced economies. ...

The loyalty of individualists to a given group is very weak; they feel they belong to many groups and are apt to change their membership as it suits them, switching churches, for example, or leaving one employer for another.

In such cultures, people subscribe to values like "Winning is everything" and "To be superior, a man must stand alone."... In collectivist cultures ... family integrity is of the utmost importance. People strongly believe, for instance, that children should live at home with parents until they get married, and that aging parents should live at home with their children.

SOURCE: Daniel Goleman, "The Group and the Self: New Focus on a Cultural Rift," *The New York Times*, December 25, 1990. Copyright © 1990 by the New York Times Company. Reprinted by permission.

Taking America as his example of modern society, Slater drew attention to some characteristics that distinguish it from most others. Americans are less apt to engage in public displays of emotion than are other peoples. Although television frequently shows scenes from other societies where people loudly, publicly, and without apparent control, express their grief, anger, and joy, Americans are much more likely to appear expressionless and cold, even during times of grief or joy. American attitudes and behaviour exist in the context of a rapidly changing society that values individualism, self-control, careful planning for the future, and the ability to discipline one's urges and desires.

According to Slater, modern societies encourage traits of competitiveness, uninvolvement, and independence. Rather than valuing co-operation and group work, these societies admire individual effort and accomplishments. Direct involvement in social problems and difficulties is discouraged; counsellors are hired, money is "thrown at" the problem — or an attempt is made to control or intimidate offending people. The aim is to "flush" the problem from view. Dependence on others is discouraged, and independence and self-reliance are praised.

Traditional, slow-changing societies, in contrast, require children to be shaped for community, engagement, and dependence. Their social life is built around a trusting and co-operative relationship with others and in a community where people are encouraged to express their feelings, trusting that the community will help to both support and control them (Slater, 1976: 9). There is no deep division between one's private emotions and public expressions. Socialization encourages the development of connection and a commitment to group life.

Slow-changing societies require different traits in adults from those required by modern societies, and this is reflected in their patterns of early socialization. Slater suggested that socialization in more stable societies stresses *external* controls, while modern societies rely on *internal* controls.

In a traditional society, the community is always with the individual and thus is able to exert control directly. The expression of impulses and desires only go as far as the community wishes. The individual learns to be dependent on the community. However, in a modern society the idea of community is weak and a division is maintained between private and public life. People are expected to be individually responsible for their lives and to be prepared for personal independence. The responsibility to control one's conduct, after childhood, is the individual's: to face it, they must be equipped with self-control. Thus, young people in modern society must become their own police. Cultural values must be internalized so that they become their own controllers.

External controls are those imposed on individuals by the community. They work only when there is a strong and stable community life in which people are intimately associated with each other. When social life is less directly lived with the community, individuals are more responsible for controlling their own behaviour. They must become committed to the moral standards and regulation of conduct upheld by the society: they must develop internal controls.

According to Slater, internal control is accomplished by the western emphasis on "love oriented" techniques of child raising. These techniques encourage children to incorporate the values of parents (representing society) in order to avoid losing the parents' love and approval. The acceptance of parental norms and values is created not by instilling fear of punishment, but by reasoning with children and offering encouragement and love in return for compliance. Successful socialization results in compliance motivated by a fear of the loss of love.

In modern societies, the loss of individual control is to be avoided at all costs. This results in people having great difficulty in expressing spontaneous emotion. They fear losing control, so they repress their joy and fear. The exercise of internal control has a great price; sometimes people react against the burden imposed on them by giving their responsibility to fascist governments, authoritarian religious cults, and other external authorities. At other times, the reaction is to seek a way of breaking through their control mechanisms and get "in touch" with themselves through counselling, psychotherapy, encounter groups, or psychoactive drugs.

SOCIALIZATION AND PERSONAL UNIQUENESS

It is now clear that socialization is the process by which individuals learn and internalize the culture of their group. It is the process of becoming a social being. As a result of socialization, the behaviour of people in any identifiable community will exhibit some consistency and predictability.

However, the discussion so far has assumed a standard pattern of socialization in any given society and that the child, in contacts with parents, caregivers, neighbours, and teachers, encounters a common set of norms and values. In reality, social life is much more complex. Socialization is uniquely shaped by the individuals involved and varies according to the beliefs and values of distinct groups within society. This section considers these aspects of socialization in more detail.

Socialization as Shaped by Individual Experience

As noted by George H. Mead, individuals are not just socially determined units. They have a unique identity — the "I" — that responds to, reflects on, is influenced by, but is not necessarily governed by their internalization of culture — the "me." Any individual who experiences socialization is therefore involved with other individuals, whose version of the society's culture is shaped by their experiences and temperaments. There is always individual variation in the socialization experience. People are not just subjected to socialization; they are actively involved in the process. Thus, socialization is a two-way street: the people acting as socializers and those being socialized influence each other and shape the outcome. Individuals create, as well as act out, norms for defining and structuring their social interaction. These ideas are associated with the sociological perspective of symbolic interactionism.

Piaget: Application of Social Rules

One way to think of the role of the individual in creating and recreating norms and values is through the work of Swiss developmental psychologist Jean Piaget (1952). Piaget's work focussed on the development process of children and is based on direct observations of children in an institute for child development that Piaget directed, for much of his life, in Geneva, Switzerland. His work has great importance for understanding children's distinct stages of mental development.

Piaget suggested that children do not start out with an adult mental structure and simply fill it with learning and knowledge as they mature. Instead, the structure goes through stages of development, especially *moral development*.

Up to the age of four or five, a child, according to Piaget, is a stickler for rules: rules are inviolable and must always be applied. The child has no sense that rules can change from context to context. Thus, stealing groceries to feed a family is just as wrong as stealing for fun. Between the ages of five and ten, children begin to realize that rules may be interpreted and applied with judgement. For example, they may notice that grabbing toys or making a mess at the dinner table is more tolerable from their young sibling than from them. For them, the rules are no longer an absolute, but a guide. This emerging sense that rules are not absolute culminates in the stage that

Piaget called "moral relativism." Now, the child, like an adult, is capable of seeing that rules are subject to interpretation and that their applicability is linked to context.

Piaget showed that there is a mental development in individuals that takes them beyond the mere mechanical application of learned rules and places them in a situation in which they subject these rules to individual and circumstantial judgement. As a result, there is a dialogue between individuals in a social situation whereby they arrive at a definition of the situation and interpret or develop the rules or expectations that they will apply to that situation.[3]

Socialization does not flow only from adults to children, but also flows the other way. In traditional societies, where there is considerable stability and where children are destined largely to repeat the experiences of their parents, the flow of influence is chiefly from parents and elders to children. In modern societies, where there is rapid social change, children may represent the present more than their parents do and adults may look to children for information and advice. Canadian parents of the present generation, for example, are often behind their children in their knowledge of a common technology, computers. A generation ago, parents were challenged to adjust their sexual norms to those of children who assertively entered early and open sexual relationships (Mead, 1970).

Socialization Shaped by Group Variations of Culture

· · · · · · · ·

Societies clearly differ in the ways they socialize individuals and in the values they transmit. The values and expectations about the organization of social life imparted by the socialization of children in rural India will be very different from what is imparted in Toronto. Socialization, therefore, is not merely about the induction of individuals into culture, but into specific cultures in specific societies.

For example, not everyone in Canada shares in the overall culture of the society to the same extent. Canadians of Chinese descent may have an experience of socialization in the family that is different from that of aboriginal Canadians; Canadians in Newfoundland get a cultural message different from the one received in Montreal.

Sociologists discuss cultural variations among groups within a society by using the concept of **subculture** — a culture within a culture. The idea of subculture recognizes that each group within a society has norms and values that differ from those of other groups. Subcultures can be linked to a variety of groups that are distinguished in some way from others, for example, Afro-Canadian subculture, youth subculture, gay or lesbian subculture, drug users' subculture, criminal subculture. Children of immigrant parents may learn a unique combination of values and have experiences different from those of other children. Box 2.3 illustrates the importance of subcultures and reinforces the point that socialization is two-way.

SOCIALIZATION FOR A PLACE IN SOCIETY

· · · · · · · ·

What are people being fitted for when they are socialized? The sociological term for a part played by an individual in a society or group is a **role**. While society does not give its members a fixed script, it does shape individuals for existing patterns of social life.

The expectations attached to social roles are encountered at birth. The debut role of baby already has quite a job description: to be cared for, to bring emotional rewards to parents and grandparents, and to generate new roles as parent, grandparent, sister, or brother for others.

People continue to encounter roles as they age, and each role requires a process of socialization. Sociologists refer to the continuation of socialization as secondary socialization. Socialization can be broadly directed to shape social behaviour on the

Box 2.3
Multiculturalism and
Socialization

I am Korean-Canadian. But the hyphen often snaps in two, obliging me to choose to act as either a Korean or Canadian, depending on where I am and who I'm with. After 16 years of living in Canada, I discovered that it's very difficult to be both at any given time or place.

When I was younger, toying with the idea of entertaining two separate identities was a real treat, like a secret game for which no one knew the rules but me.

I was known as Angela to the outside, and as Sun-Kyung at home. I ate bologna sandwiches in the school lunch room and rice and kimchee for dinner. I chatted about teen idols and giggled with my girlfriends during my classes, and ambitiously practised piano and studied in the evenings, planning to become a doctor when I grew up. I waved hellos and goodbyes to my teachers, but bowed to my parent's friends visiting our home.

I could also look straight in the eyes of my teachers and friends and talk frankly with them instead of staring at my feet with my mouth shut when Koreans talked to me.

Going outside the home meant I was able to relax from the constraints of my cultural conditioning, until I walked back in the door and had to return to being an obedient and submissive daughter.

The game ended when I realized that it had become a way of life, that I couldn't change the rules without disappointing my parents and questioning all the cultural implications and consequences that came with being a hyphenated Canadian.

Many have tried to convince me that I am a Canadian, like all other immigrants in the country, but those same people also ask me which country I came from with great curiosity, following with questions about the type of food I ate and the language I spoke. It's difficult to feel a sense of belonging and acceptance when you are regarded as "one of them." "Those Koreans, they work hard. ... You must be fantastic at math and science." (No.) "Do your parents own a corner store?" (No.)

Koreans and Canadians just can't seem to merge into "us" and "them."

After a lifetime of practice, I thought I could change faces and become Korean on demand with grace and perfection. But working with a small Korean company in Toronto proved me wrong. I quickly became estranged from my own people. ...

I was expected to accept my inferior position as a woman and had to behave accordingly. It was not a place to practise my feminist views or be an individual without being condemned. Little Korea [the author's workplace] is a place for men (who filled all the senior positions) and women don't dare to speak up or disagree with their male counterparts.

The president (all employees bow to him and call him Mr. President) asked me to act more like a lady and smile. I was openly scorned by a senior employee because I spoke more fluent English than Korean. The cook in the kitchen shook her head in disbelief upon discovering that my cooking skills were limited to boiling a package of instant noodles. "You want a good husband, learn to cook," she advised me.

(continued)

- - - - - - - -

(continued)

In less than a week I became an outsider because I refused to conform and blindly nod my head in agreement to what my elders (which happened to be everybody in the company) said. A month later, I was demoted because "members of the workplace and the Korean community" had complained that I just wasn't "Korean enough," and I had "too much power for a single woman." My father suggested that "When in Rome, do as the Romans." But that's exactly what I was doing. I am in Canada so I was freely acting like a Canadian, and it cost me my job.

- - - - - - - -

SOURCE: Excerpted from Sun-Kyung Yi, "An Immigrant's Split Personality," *The Globe and Mail*, April 2, 1992. Reprinted with permission from the author.

- - - - - - - -

basis of age and sex; people learn the roles of child, teenager, young adult, adult, wife, husband, parent, grandparent. Alternatively, it can be narrowly focussed, shaping individuals to perform very specific roles, such as social worker, lawyer, teacher, logger, plumber, or cook.

Socialization for Age Roles

- - - - - - - -

Some socialization processes are experienced by everyone, but not necessarily in the same way. The most striking fact about social roles connected to age is that they are not entirely determined by individual age-related natural qualities and capacities: they are culturally created and culturally variable. Since they are culturally created, "acting one's age" is not a natural process. It is a result of specialized effort and social learning.

Ariès: The Creation of Childhood

- - - - - - - -

One of the most interesting perspectives on age roles was developed by the French cultural historian Philippe Ariès (1962). Ariès's work deals with changing views of the "child" in western society over the last 500 years. Ariès argued that a society in which children simply join in the life and work of adults, as they are able to, can manage without any cultural notion of a "childhood" stage or of distinct roles for children. Ariès and others argue that the social roles of the young and the form and function of the modern family emerged together. Although the timing of these changes is uncertain, the transition, according to Ariès, is as follows.

Beginning in the fifteenth century and increasing in the two following centuries, the growth of trade and small manufacture spurred the development of an urban middle class of merchants and professionals. Increasingly, this group developed a sense of separate social status from the common people who lived and worked around them. The sense developed in an increasingly separate and private domestic life. Middle-class women withdrew from work outside the home and focussed increasingly on the domestic world and the care of children. Religious ideas that the parents had a moral duty to mould the child were linked to revival of the ancient Greek belief that the child must be prepared for the adult world. Accordingly, the child was provided with special treatment and training until able to take on adult roles.

Thus began the process of isolating young people from adults and segregating them in special institutions such as schools and the myriad of age-graded groups and agencies devoted to the development of citizenship. The family was the centre of these changes and underwent significant transformation. It became more than an agency through which names and property were transmitted; it became a vehicle for moral training and socialization. The modern family, Ariès argued, in focussing on children, created rigid boundaries between private life and the outside world. This revolution in the life of the middle-class family — becoming a private institution focussed on child socialization — gradually spread to both lower- and upper-class families.

Ariès argued that the concepts of child, teenager, and adolescent, of great significance to the modern family and around which a unique culture has emerged, are historically specific. These age-stages have not always existed and may not always exist; they are a social creation. The socialization of new members of the society was transformed, and in the process new identities were created for those members. What were the implications of this new process of socialization for the family?

First, the family became a private institution. It withdrew behind walls into a private world where it could concentrate on its central task of socializing the child. Previously the family had been enmeshed in the flux of social life; the household had been open to extended family, servants, and the community. Thus there had been little separation of the private from the public sphere of life.

Second, the family withdrew into a community of its class. Led first by the middle class, there was a development of life styles exclusive to each class. This was allied to the concept that individuals should conform to the appropriate social type; previously the society had been marked by a free intermingling of classes.

Third, as the family became a more private institution, with a focus on child rearing, gender roles were reshaped. The domestic roles of women in particular were changed, leading to a focus on mothering and the separation of women from the public world. Women were left to deal with children, household maintenance, and the emotions of the private world.

Fourth, the family became the principal agent in socializing the child. A period of quarantine became necessary to prepare the child for the adult world. Previously, the child had been allowed to grow up as the natural companion of adults, taking on adult roles as its capacities developed.

In this discussion, what is commonly considered an ordinary stage of development appears in a new light. Childhood is a social distinction with a unique history. Occupants of this social role are related to in specific ways (family roles had to change to accommodate the new importance given to childhood) and experience particular expectations and obligations. Beyond that, of course, a particular culture arises as a result of separation from the adult world. A world of children's games, children's literature, comics, youth music, and distinct styles of dress emerges.

Ruth Benedict and Margaret Mead: Adolescence
· · · · · · · · ·

Whereas Ariès's main concern was with the social shaping of childhood, two famous anthropologists focussed on the later stages of childhood, the period during which sexual maturity arises and the child makes a transition to adult roles and behaviour: adolescence. Is this transition, associated in western society with individual emotional turmoil and socially troublesome behaviour, a natural, universal stage, or is it too socially shaped and created? Both writers were convinced that adolescence was a social category, not a natural life stage.

Ruth Benedict (1973 [1938]) argued that "adolescence" was a social creation. It was unrecognized in many non-western societies because these societies avoided "discontinuity in cultural conditioning." Although many societies did stress passage through age-grades, they did it through rituals and ceremonies that maintained a clear and supportive link between the individual and the community. As a result, youths were aware of their place in the society and able to establish a clear sense of social identity. In western society, there was great ambiguity about the adolescent stage. Was it one of growing independence and autonomy, or one needing direction through iron discipline and close adult supervision? Did the western pattern confusingly deny autonomy and personal responsibility while at the same time demanding it?

Benedict concluded that the upheavals of adolescence were not hormonal or based in some universal need for a stage of youth rebellion against adults; they were a creation of modern society. This attitude was shared by Margaret Mead (1928). Mead travelled to Samoa to investigate the coming of age of youth in that society. What she discovered confirmed the views of Benedict: adolescence was unknown to the Samoans, who grew smoothly and responsibly into adult roles. Although Benedict's and Mead's research has been criticized (Freeman, 1983) for taking a one-sided stand in favour of the importance of socialization — nurture — against the role of biology — nature, it clearly established the important influence of societies in shaping the intermediate stage between child and adult.

Socialization and Gender Identity

Ariès, Benedict, and Mead viewed childhood or youth to some extent as a socially constructed category that is very different from society to society and that may even be unrecognized in some societies. Age, rather than being a purely objective, factual characteristic of the individual, is given quite different meanings from place to place and time to time.

Sociologists and anthropologists have also focussed on what various societies and historical periods have made of another apparently objective characteristic: sex. The physiological differences between males and females clearly cannot account for all divergencies between the sexes. Physiological difference does not explain why 126 years elapsed before Canada had a female prime minister or why only one in nine Canadian members of legislatures are women. It is hard to see how sex difference alone can explain why Canadian women's average wages are only 70 percent those of men, or why women make up only a tiny fragment of the total number of corporate directors and senior executives. Many stark differences exist between the social and economic positions of men and women that cannot be explained simply as a result of physical differences.

To make it possible to discuss what differences between the sexes are based on physiology and what differences rest on cultural ideas and social organization, social scientists have developed a somewhat special language. The term **sex** is applied to the biological distinction between females and males, and **gender** refers to the cultural elaboration placed on sex. While "male" and "female" are words that have a physiological meaning, "masculine" and "feminine" have a cultural meaning. This usage is common in everyday speech: it is male (*sex*) to have a penis, it is considered masculine (*gender*) to enjoy riding a motorcycle; it is female (*sex*) to have a vagina, it is considered feminine (*gender*) to enjoy romance novels.[4]

The difference between sex and gender is often confused by a tendency to use the terms interchangeably. Accurately used, however, these terms serve a vital purpose in directing attention to the ways in which societies make sex into something far beyond simple physiological distinctions and capabilities.

Sociologists are most interested in the differences that arise from society or culture rather than from physiology. They therefore concentrate on gender. But a comment on the physiology of sex differences is useful here.

Primary Sex Differences

There is a chromosome difference between females and males: females carry two X chromosomes, and males carry an X and a Y chromosome. There is also a difference in hormonal balance. In women, the dominant hormones are estrogen and progesterone. The dominant sex hormones in males are androgens, the most powerful of which is testosterone. Females are equipped with ovaries, clitoris, and vagina; males with penis, testes, and scrotum. Only females can give birth. There is abundant evidence that females generally are healthier and more robust than males. They suffer from far fewer hereditary diseases and have a better chance of recovering from serious illnesses. The death rate of girls under age one is considerably less than for boys.[5]

Secondary Differences

Considerable overlap exists in the secondary differences between men and women. On average, however, men are taller and heavier than women, and a greater percentage of their body weight is muscle. Females have lighter skeletons, different shoulder–pelvis proportions, different pelvic bone shapes, and different socket shapes at the hip and shoulder. Physical strength is greater in males than in females, which is reflected in athletic performance. The differences between women and men in a variety of athletic tests are not very great, as Table 2.1 shows.

Even apparently fixed physiological differences are socially influenced. Over the last several decades, as women have increasingly participated in competitive athletics and organized sports, their performance has converged toward men's. Male and female physical capacities show dramatic divergence only in tests of sheer strength; for example, the male weightlifting record is about twice that of women.

Features of Gender

Sociologists, of course, are not talking about physiological distinctions when they refer to males and females as *socially constructed*. Rather, they refer to the social and cultural expectations based on these biological differences. These expectations are culturally specific: although women are biologically similar in all parts of the world, the social roles they play vary widely and are shaped by the society's definition of gender. Gender consists of much more than the physiological differences between males and females. It is clearly a social construction in which cultural baggage is added to the physiological differences, as the following illustration from the African nation of Burundi shows.

Table 2.1
World Athletic Records, 1994

Event	Male	Female
100 metres	9.85 seconds	10.49 seconds
1500 metres	3.28.82 minutes	3.50.46 minutes
3000 metres	7.25.11 minutes	8.06.11 minutes
High jump	2.45 metres	2.09 metres
Long jump	8.95 metres	7.52 metres
1500 metre freestyle swim	14.41.66 minutes	15.52.10 minutes

SOURCE: Courtesy of Athletics Canada.

The Rundi conception of the innate differences between men and women is ... well defined. ... To begin with, it is believed that women are better suited by nature than men for manual labour. They work better and longer in the fields than men. The Hutukazi (Hutu women) are able to carry on their heads burdens twice as heavy as those which men can carry. ... Stronger than men, women are thought to be less agile. Consequently, in domestic battles, the husband can vanquish the wife. He must, nevertheless, be on his guard if she becomes very angry. For even though men (as superiors) are able to control their anger, women (as inferiors) are likely to lose their heads. She can take a knife and kill her husband, says the Hutu; she will poison her husband, says the Tutsi. Furthermore, women are regarded as less coura-geous than men in the presence of enemies; they are more easily discouraged when there is misfortune; they cry more easily and do not conceal their emotions. No attention whatever is paid to any evidence which might contradict this stereotype (Albert, 1971: 192–193).

When a child is born, the eyes of the mother and the helpers check the genitals and a category is applied: boy or girl. Why is sex so important? Although sex differences are significant, the sexes are more alike than different, aside from their reproductive specialization. There are differences in strength, but there is little evidence of difference in innate capacity to perform most tasks and no difference in general intelligence. Sex is given importance because it will shape the child's life destiny: males and females are assumed to be headed toward quite different places in the organization of society.

For a female, society assumes the development of personal qualities of caring, support, nurturing, and consideration for others. These traits are expressed in a female life career that encompasses roles as daughter, sister, wife, mother, and grandmother and in occupational and social roles that have tended to be quite different from those of men. For a male, society assumes the development of toughness, aggressiveness, determination, and independence. These traits are expressed in a male life career that encompasses roles as son, brother, husband, father, and grandfather and occupational and social roles different from those of women.

Life careers so different, based on the identification of individuals by biological sex, are reflected in a socialization that is also very different. From birth a female child, whatever the reality, is seen through lenses shaped by assumptions about gender. She is assumed to be (or want to be) pretty, delicate, sweet, and loving. The male child is seen as being (or wanting to be) rugged, strong-willed, and independent.

Characteristics that are culturally defined as appropriate to females and males are automatically ascribed to infants on the basis of their sex. Culture results in the different treatment of boys and girls, different techniques of child raising, different relations with parents and relatives, different toys, different games and sports, different hobbies, different education, and different jobs (see Box 2.4).

Research suggests that baby boys are initially talked to more than girls. From the second year on, however, girls are interacted with more often, encouraged to stay close to their caregiver (usually the mother) and are held more than boys. Boys are more likely to be left alone and are more frequently punished (Mackie, 1987).

Socialization rapidly becomes a two-way street: girls identify themselves as female (like sister, like mother, like grandmother, like day-care worker); boys identify themselves as male (like brother, like father, like bus driver, like construction worker); and each takes up the rudimentary role play of the appropriate sex. From age three to about five, gender play is often inconsistent, but thereafter it becomes quite strict and

Box 2.4
Gender Development
and Children's Play

A considerable body of research has focussed on sex differences in children's toys and play styles. The results show that, during the preschool years, children prefer sex-role-stereotyped toys and activities and reject cross-sex-stereotyped toys and activities. Specifically, boys play in a more aggressive, rough-and-tumble fashion and play more actively than girls. As they grow older, children continue to prefer same-sex activities, although girls show an increasing interest in cross-sex activities.

Lora Moller, Shelley Hymel, and Ken Rubin, of the University of Waterloo, added to this research interest by examining differences in the play styles of girls and boys to determine whether a child's popularity is influenced by his or her play style. Their results showed distinct sex differences in play behaviours across the years of childhood. It appears that these sex differences are greatest by grade four. Generally speaking, male-preferred play was characterized by greater involvement in group games with rules, while female-preferred play included a greater frequency of peer conversation.

They also found that the grade four boys who were most popular among males were those engaging with greater frequency in "masculine" or male-preferred play styles. The boys who were most popular among girls displayed a greater frequency of "feminine" or female-preferred play. There appeared to be no association between popularity and sex-typed play for girls.

SOURCE: Adapted from Lora Moller, Shelley Hymel, and Ken Rubin, "Sex Typing in Play and Popularity in Middle Childhood," *Sex Roles* 26 (1992): 331–353.

deviations from appropriate gender behaviour become the subject of joking or discomfort (Mackie, 1987: 128–129). Sex becomes linked to cultural ideas about gender. It thus becomes an organizing concept in the child's mind.

The child is steeped in the world of gender. Gender identity is shaped by noticing who does what in the family, the behaviour of parents, observations of people in social roles, and cultural messages about the roles and emotions of the sexes.

We know, in an instant, which sex does what: Who digs holes in the street? Who runs day-care centres? Who pilots planes? Who nurses at the hospital? Who conducts the symphony orchestra? Who does clerical work at the doctor's office? We know, in an instant, who behaves in what way: Who is likely to confront another? Who is likely to attempt quiet negotiation? Who is likely to drive the car aggressively? Who is likely to be cautious?

Just posing these questions and noting the automatic responses suggests a society fixated on gender, a society in which sexual identity has great consequence for all individuals (see Box 2.5).

A Review of Slater

One must be careful in generalizing about the socialization process of children. Does Slater, with his focus on socialization for independence and autonomy, offer an account more fitted to the experience of one sex than another? This is something suggested by Nancy Chodorow (1978) in her argument that while males are socialized

Box 2.5
Saturday Morning
Television

When ABC announced [the fall 1991] schedule for Saturday morning children's programming, Jennie Trias, the U.S. network's vice-president for children's programs, had some bad news for girls: their favorite Saturday morning show, *The New Kids on the Block*, the cartoon adventures of the rock band with an enormous pre-teenage following, would be gone.

"Only girls were watching the show," Trias said. "And you have to have boys watching a show for it to succeed."

Next season, the landscape of Saturday morning will not be merely dominated by programs featuring male characters; it will be an exclusive male preserve. ... "It is well known that boys will watch a male lead and not a female lead," Trias said. "But girls are willing to watch a male lead."

... Network executives said the reluctance to accept female characters was so ingrained in boys that it was difficult to resist. Judy Price, the CBS vice-president for children's programs, said CBS had used focus groups of children to help make judgements about children's shows and characters.

"We had to segregate the groups by both age and sex," Price said. "The older kids didn't want to be seen liking the things the younger kids liked, and the boys certainly didn't want to be seen liking the things the girls like."

"Barbie is the most popular character for young girls, probably of all time, but she would never succeed as a Saturday morning show," she added. "The boys would refuse to watch her."

Trias said ABC employed a child psychiatrist who had suggested that "boys between 6 and 11 go through a period of time when they want to separate from their mothers."

"Any time the boys see a female in charge, they reject it," Trias said. "They still want their mothers to tuck them in at night, of course, but they do have this desire for separation."

Price said: "The daddies have something to do with it, too. They instil a certain expectation in boys. The boys resist being associated with girls. There's peer pressure not to be considered a sissy."

Price also pointed out that no stigma was attached to girls trying such traditionally male activities as sports or camping or even wearing boy's clothing, and it had been fashionable for girls to wear their father's clothes.

"Can you imagine the reaction if a boy said he wanted to wear his mother's clothing?" Price said.

SOURCE: Bill Carter, "Children's TV, Where Boys are King," *The New York Times*, May 1, 1991. Copyright © 1991 by The New York Times Company. Reprinted by permission.

for separation and differentiation from their mothers, girls are socialized for identification and connection (see Box 2.6).

Assumptions about gender are central to western culture and social organization. Gender, therefore, is a topic that is referred to and analyzed throughout this book.

Box 2.6
Chodorow on
Mothering

The work of Nancy Chodorow has become important for many feminists in understanding the differences between men and women. These differences lie in the fact that most children are raised by their mothers. Girls can remain attached to their mothers as they establish their identities. Males, on the other hand, must separate themselves from their mothers in order to develop a male identity. Accordingly, women find comfort in attachment and fear separation, while men find comfort in separation and fear attachment.

According to some feminists, everything in women's lives as well as men's lives flows from this: men make war, women make peace; men like hierarchy, women like co-operation; men are aloof and unemotional, women are emotionally and personally involved. There is now a vast literature about the wide gulf between men and women; much of the literature considers the gulf to be natural (although Chodorow considers the distinctions as arising from the social arrangements of child rearing).

More recently, feminists have begun to identify female attributes as desirable and male attributes as "the problem." This is a reversal of centuries of discussion that considered female characteristics as "the problem" since they deviated from the male norm. While supportive of valuing female characteristics, C. Travis is not supportive of continuing to focus on the division between men and women. This, she argues, is what some social scientists do when they attempt to make feminine values more important than masculine values or to see gender differences as natural.

SOURCE: Adapted from Nancy Chodorow, *The Reproduction of Mothering* (Berkeley: University of California Press, 1978), and C. Travis, *The Mismeasure of Women* (New York: Simon and Schuster, 1992).

Its many ramifications must be considered in an analysis of how many aspects of society work.

For example, this discussion has so far assumed a heterosexual world. The fact that a significant number of people are homosexual makes the study of socialization for sexual identity more complicated. What is it like to grow up in a society that socializes people for a narrow range of sexual identities and restrictive gender identities?[6] Janice Raymond (1979) explores these and other questions in a study of transsexuals — people who wish, and sometimes achieve the wish, to be the opposite sex.

Saying that socialization is influenced by an individual's assumed destination, based on his or her sexual identity and age, also says something about socialization itself. It is not only about the reproduction of culture — its transmission to new members of society — but also about the reproduction of social structure, the creation of individual role-players who will fit into the existing framework of roles in society. Understanding socialization as partially concerning the reproduction of social structure, including the reproduction of relations between sexes and classes, allows the process to be examined from both a functionalist and a critical perspective.

PERSPECTIVES ON SOCIALIZATION

Is it in everyone's interest for the existing structure of society, its structure of sexual and economic hierarchy, to be reproduced?

Socialization and Functionalism

According to the functionalist perspective, every member of society benefits from its stable maintenance. Since individuals must be members of society, a smoothly functioning society is best for all, and a smoothly functioning society can exist only when people are able and willing to perform necessary roles. Society ensures a supply of people with appropriate attitudes, knowledge, skills, and capacities for various positions via the process of socialization. Socialization, therefore, can be understood as the matching of supply (individuals) to the demand (roles) that arises within any organized society.

This account of socialization remains quite neutral about the qualities that exist in the society for which the individual is being socialized. If a society requires landowners and agricultural labourers for its economy to work effectively, then it is the task of socialization to provide them. A successful process, serving the needs of society, will shape appropriate numbers of individuals to perform and accept the various required roles.

Socialization and Critical Perspectives

Critical perspectives assert that there are alternative ways to organize social life. No social structure and no cultural norms and values should be upheld simply because they support an existing form of social life; it could always be otherwise. There is no natural or given way that a society must be. Socialization, as a process that reproduces a particular society, also upholds existing values and social arrangements, which advantage some and disadvantage others. Critical accounts of socialization therefore maintain that socialization could equally well be called indoctrination: it shapes people to accept and uphold existing social arrangements, even when those arrangements confer very different statuses and rewards on individuals. Feminist social scientists, in particular, have stressed the importance of socialization in maintaining a society that has pervasive sexual inequality (Chodorow, 1978).

This opposition between functionalist and critical views of the socialization process is made clear in their differing views of the roles of the various institutions through which socialization is carried out. They have, for example, very different views of the role of the family: does it socialize males and females to fill natural sex-appropriate roles, or does it inculcate men and women into a hierarchy of dominance and inferiority that exists both within the family and in society at large? Does the education system simply socialize individuals for particular types of occupations and roles, according to their intrinsic talents and capabilities, or does it uphold a pattern of unequal opportunities and rewards based on people's sex, status, or class? Are the mass media, particularly television, instruments for expressing the values of a culture, or do they socialize individuals into a culture of consumerism? These topics are examined in subsequent chapters.

CONCLUSION

This chapter has answered the fundamental question in understanding society: how can social order be fashioned from human individuals who are each, to some extent, unique? All societies have a mechanism — the process of socialization — through which individuals are shaped by the norms and values (culture) of their society and by which they are prepared to take up roles within their society (social structure), thus creating and recreating an organized social life.

This process can be described and understood in many ways. The role of language is fundamental because language includes ways of looking at the world, the names of things, the categories of things, and the concepts used to understand, describe, and evaluate what people see around them. To enter into language is to enter into culture. Language also gives individuals the capacity to think about themselves as if from the outside and to consider other points of view.

The work of George H. Mead, has shown how socialization can both create the conformity necessary for ordered social life, and preserve a measure of personal uniqueness and spontaneity. Individuals are not simply processed by society; but socialization is an interactive process in which people are the shapers as well as the shaped.

Finally, although it is clear that socialization reproduces culture and social structure, socialization into sex, age, and class or status roles is not a neutral process but serves particular forms of society and social arrangements.

· · · · · · · · ·

NOTES

1. "Racist Youths Called Victims," *The Globe and Mail*, December 15, 1990, p. A6.
2. Particularly controversial is Freud's view of the differing infantile development of the two sexes (Mitchell, 1974).
3. Piaget considered the process of moral development as being linked to the way that the human mind is biologically structured. The process of development is shaped by social context, but not caused by it; rather, these stages reflect the underlying structure and developmental process of the mind itself.
4. These are examples of stereotypes from western culture.
5. Canadian data for the period 1980–88, based on two-year intervals, shows an average of 952 deaths per 100 000 males under age one and an average of 750 deaths per 100 000 females under age one (Statistics Canada, 1990a: 41–42).
6. Clear evidence of the oppressive character of normative heterosexuality is apparent in Canadian suicide statistics suggesting that up to 30 percent of teen suicides involve gay and lesbian youth ("Social Studies: Troubled Teens," *The Globe and Mail*, June 4, 1991, p. A20).

· · · · · · · · ·

FURTHER READING

Chodorow, Nancy. *The Reproduction of Mothering*. Berkeley: University of California Press, 1978. An attempt to combine psychoanalytic theory, sociology, and feminism in order to show how mothers produce different experiences for sons and daughters and, in so doing, maintain the social structure.

Erikson, Erik. *Childhood and Society*. New York: W.W. Norton, 1963. An exploration of the link between early childhood handling and training and the development of adult personality and gender identity.

Sennett, Richard, and Jonathan Cobb. *The Hidden Injuries of Class*. New York: Vintage, 1973. An insightful discussion of the experience of growing up in the lower class.

Shattuck, Roger. *The Forbidden Experiment: The Story of the Wild Boy of Aveyron*. New York: Washington Square Press, 1980. An engaging account of the nineteenth-century case of a child apparently raised in isolation from humans. Can he be civilized? Can he learn language? This story was also depicted in Francois Truffaut's 1970 film, *The Wild Child*.

Travis, Carol. *The Mismeasure of Women*. New York: Simon and Schuster, 1992. A critical review of research that considers female development and characteristics inferior because they do not fit the male norm and of research drawing a sharp and natural dichotomy between women and men.

Weeks, Jeffrey. *Sexuality and Its Discontents*. London: Routledge and Kegan Paul, 1985. A study of the way in which western society has dictated the channelling of conventional sexuality, and an argument for the acceptance of variety in human sexual expression.

. . . .

STUDY QUESTIONS

. . . .

1.   Interview a friend or relative raised in a non-western society on the following topic: "What are your thoughts about the differences between your experience of growing up and that of contemporary Canadian youth?"
2.   How do sociologists explain both the conformity of behaviour and the existence of individual uniqueness in society?
3.   Why did George H. Mead insist that language is essential to the emergence of "self"?
4.   Why do sociologists argue that age is a cultural as well as a physiological concept?
5.   What is the difference between sex and gender? Why is this distinction helpful?
6.   Is the socialization of girls and boys different or similar? Illustrate with examples.

3 SOCIETY AND CULTURE

· · · · · · · ·

**KEY CONCEPTS
AND PHRASES**
· · · · · · · ·

androcentrism
beliefs
cultural crisis
cultural variability
culture shock
ethnicity
ethnocentrism

hegemony
ideology
nations
norms
race
racist ideology
values

INTRODUCTION
· · · · · · · ·

This chapter introduces culture as the first of two major concepts for understanding society. The emphasis is on appreciating cultural variability and considering whether a distinctive Canadian culture exists. Ideology, a central idea of critical perspectives and a particular aspect of culture, is also introduced and will become a key concept in subsequent chapters.

· · · · · · · ·

Chapter One presented sociology as the study of society, an abstraction made concrete by the analogy of the hockey team or choir. Each of these organizations is characterized by rules or expectations about people's values and behaviour and a pattern of social relationships within which these rules or expectations are brought to life. Sociologists say that each organization has a culture and a social structure — two concepts that provide a useful way to analyze any society. The study of society must start with an understanding of these two concepts. The notion of culture is discussed in this chapter.

CULTURE
· · · · · · · ·

Although culture is a concept central to sociology, it can be difficult to grasp because it is all-encompassing. It includes all that is learned by the people in a society. Culture gives shape both to society and to the individual.

An example of culture is necessary before continuing. British Columbians read with horror the story of a son visiting his mother in hospital and learning that although his mother's co-patient had been dead for several hours, the body had not been removed from the room. Reactions varied: it wasn't fair to the living patient to leave a corpse in the same room; more respect should be shown to the dead. The reactions were based on a number of rules about aspects of behaviour toward the recently deceased: appropriate persons to view the dead, respectful conduct around the dead, reactions expected from relatives of the dead, authorized persons to pronounce death, acceptable ways to dispose of dead bodies, and so on. Some of these rules are laws; others are customs. Both kinds of rules, and the meanings behind them, are, in part, what sociologists mean by culture.

Since culture is so central to the way one understands the world, a way to analyze it is necessary. Three elements of culture — what people believe; what rules regulate social behaviour; and what social and economic values exist in the society — are discussed below.

Beliefs
. . . .

Members of a society or group share a number of beliefs about their world; they have common understandings about the way things are. People have beliefs, for example, about the origin of the universe, the causes of childhood colds, the sources of unemployment, the effects of nuclear war on the environment, or what happens to them when they die. Beliefs may be either factual truths or merely assumptions about what is true.In developed societies, for example, high-rise buildings often have no designated thirteenth floor because thirteen is believed to be an unlucky number.

The Bemba, an African society, do not aim to accumulate surplus or reinvest in their productive activity. They believe the environment is like a reservoir whose goods may or may not be released by the ancestors; shortages result from ancestral intentions. Economic success therefore can be influenced by humans pleasing the ancestors (Gudeman, 1986). This stands in sharp contrast to North American beliefs about ways to ensure economic success.

The Mistassini Cree of northern Quebec believe that animals are not caught and killed during a hunt; rather, they offer themselves to humans. Hunting is a form of exchange; in return for their success in hunting, humans owe respect and gratitude to the animals and their guardians. This is reflected in the special ways the animal is taken home, announced to the community, and displayed (Tanner, 1979). The idea that success in hunting indicates something about the relationship between humans and animals contrasts with mainstream Canadian beliefs in luck or individual skill.

Subcultures
. . . .

Clearly not everyone in Canadian society shares the same beliefs. To account for some of this disagreement, sociologists use the concept of subculture — a culture within a culture, or the culture of an identifiable segment of a society. Ethnic groups may be referred to as subcultures (Chinese-Canadians, Italian-Canadians) to the extent that they share beliefs (as well as values and norms) that set them apart from the majority society (see Box 3.1). Many other groups also qualify as subcultures: youth culture, gay or lesbian culture, criminal culture, drug culture, and so on.

At what point does a group become a subculture? Although that point cannot be clearly defined, a degree of self-sufficiency can be proposed as a criterion for identifying subcultures; persons are part of a subculture if they can interact with, be entertained, and find mates among those who share common beliefs and expectations.Box 3.2 provides a glimpse of a subculture within Canada.

Native Canadians:
Subcultures
or Nations?
. . . .

While the Native peoples of Canada can properly be thought of as ethnic groups and subcultures, many assert that they are nations — people with common characteristics and constituting a distinctive political community (see Box 3.3). Having never surrendered their sovereignty under treaties (some Native peoples, mostly in British Columbia, never signed treaties), they retain political autonomy. As a result, many

Box 3.1
Canada as an
Immigrant Society

In 1991, 16 percent of Canadians reported that they were immigrants. About 28 percent of them arrived in Canada during the decade 1981–91. The places of birth of these last arrivals are as follows:

Asia	48%
Europe	25%
Central and South America	10%
Caribbean	6%
Africa	6%
USA	4%
Oceania	1%

The first language learned by Canadians was as follows:

English	63%
French	25%
A non-official language	12%

Among the last group (non-official languages), 1.9 percent learned Italian, 1.8 percent learned Chinese, and 1.7 percent learned German.

SOURCE: Adapted from Statistics Canada, *Mother Tongue: The Nation*, cat. no. 93-313, and *Immigration and Citizenship: The Nation*, cat. no. 93-316 (Ottawa: Statistics Canada, 1993). Reproduced by authority of the Minister of Industry, 1994.

Photo 3.1
A subculture is a culture within a culture. Ethnic groups, such as Chinese-Canadians or Italian-Canadians, can be referred to as a subculture to the extent that they share beliefs, values, and norms that set them apart from the majority.

Andrew Sacks / TONY STONE IMAGES

- - - - - - - -

Box 3.2

Feng Shui: Some
Chinese Won't Buy a
House Without It

- - - - - - - -

When Judy and Abbott Fong bought their new townhouse, they had more to consider than location and good value. Cultural concerns were also important. ...

Although the Fongs were born in Canada and grew up unconfined by strict Chinese tradition, neither completely discounts the old ways. And, like many other young Chinese, they respect their parents' demands that no matter how many bells and whistles there may be in a new house, it must also have good *feng shui*.

The words *feng shui* translate to wind and water, the two cornerstones of Chinese geomancy. More than mysticism, Chinese geomancy is a combination of geography and climatology.

In essence, *feng shui* stands for the power of the environment, the power that willfully makes and breaks the family fortunes in an agrarian society.

Passed on verbally from one generation to the next, the dictates of *feng shui* cannot be found in a single reference. Instead, there are geomancy experts who make a career of study and of advising architects, builders and home buyers. ...

Bad fortune can flow from numerous sources, according to Vancouver architect Andrew Cheung, who recently designed a new house for his brother on Vancouver's west side. By chance, the house already had a good street address (two eights, which bring good luck). But Cheung says the belief in lucky numbers is nothing more than superstition. ...

When it comes to talking about *feng shui*, however, Cheung's face turns serious as he explains his interest in the science. ...

"First we look at the surroundings of a site, where the ponds and the hills are located. And then we look at the street and how it is related to the house. Even the rooflines of the neighboring houses are considered," Cheung says.

"These things can be good or they can be very bad. You also have to look at the orientation of the house itself. We measure the orientation of the building by means of a geomancy compass."

The red and black compass, ornate with gold symbols, helps the architect design a house with good *feng shui*. If the building lot is prone to evil forces, architects can be employed to deflect them.

Front and back doors must not align for fear that money will come in one door and head straight out the other. Similarly, the base of a staircase must not face the front door of a house. And a house must never be situated at the end of a street where evil spirits have nowhere to go, except into the house.

There are ways to thwart evil spirits, however, and some Chinese buyers will still buy a house if they believe they can avoid its bad luck, says Abbott.

"One remedy is to put mirrors on the front door, then the evil spirits will be reflected away," he says. "Another thing you can do [is] put a goldfish pond in the front of the house and the fish will eat up the evil spirits."

- - - - - - - -

SOURCE: Susan Balcom, "Feng Shui: Some Chinese Won't Buy a House Without It," *The Vancouver Sun*, May 14, 1988, pp. C1–C2. Reprinted with permission.

- - - - - - - -

Box 3.3
Aboriginal Ancestry

Until the 1991 census, Canada has not had an accurate count of the number of its aboriginal peoples. Many Native peoples boycotted the census process in the past, and many may have been reluctant to report aboriginal ancestry for personal reasons. It has now, however, become politically advantageous for the Native community to have an official measure of its size. In 1991, 1 002 675 people reported that they were North American Indian, Métis, or Inuit, either as a single response or in combination with other origins. This group represents 3.7 percent of the Canadian population. It is distributed among the provinces and territories as follows:

Newfoundland	13 110
Prince Edward Island	1 880
Nova Scotia	21 885
New Brunswick	12 815
Quebec	137 615
Ontario	243 550
Manitoba	116 200
Saskatchewan	96 580
Alberta	148 220
British Columbia	169 035
Yukon	6 390
Northwest Territories	35 390
Canada	1 002 675

When asked if they identified with their Native ancestry, 626 000 people affirmed that they did. Native Canadians have demographic features that distinguish them from the majority society. For example, only 6–7 percent are over the age of 55; the comparable figure for Canada is 20 percent. Similarly, 38 percent of the Native community are under 15, compared with 21 percent of the whole Canadian population.

SOURCE: Adapted from Statistics Canada, *Aboriginal Peoples Survey 1991: Language, Tradition, Health, Lifestyle and Social Issues*, cat. no. 89-533 (Ottawa: Statistics Canada, 1993). Reproduced by authority of the Minister of Industry, 1994.

"First Nations" argue for recognition of their continuing right to self-government (see Engelstad and Bird, 1992).

Values

Values are broad social definitions of what is good, right, or preferred. A set of values consists of principles or goals that can be appealed to in making difficult choices. Values are not often discussed in Canadian society and become apparent mainly in times of crisis. For example, the scandal surrounding the use of performance-enhancing drugs in sports during the 1992 Summer Olympics highlighted Canadian values about honesty and fairness in competitive athletics.

Disastrous forest fires in northern Manitoba during 1989 raised other questions about values. After deploying resources to protect human life and community property, the Manitoba policy appeared to protect only forests that had commercially valuable timber. Native communities objected because their relationship to the surrounding forest was not captured by the concept of resource values. They would have protected forests on the basis of different values, such as spirituality and traditional usage.

Consider another example: sharing the fruits of one's labours. In many hunting societies the game is entirely distributed, with specific parts of the animal going to those having particular social status. The collectivity is valued much more than the individual. In industrial societies, however, how are people perceived when they give away all the fruits of their labour? Members of a religion that vowed perpetual poverty might be able to give away all their earnings, but otherwise their friends or family might well encourage them to see a psychiatrist.

Norms

· · · · · · · · ·

While values are general principles of social behaviour, **norms** are relatively precise rules that specify permitted and prohibited behaviours, thoughts, and feelings. Previous examples included norms about the treatment of the dead and of animals killed during the hunt. Further examples are helpful.

The ideal village among the Dobu (an island people who live northeast of New Guinea) is a circle of huts facing inward to a central area, which is the village graveyard. The situating of houses and of graveyards is a normative matter, expressing the villagers' enduring links with their ancestors, their fear of outsiders, and their communal privateness. Contrast this to the location of urban Canadian graveyards, most Canadians' feelings about being in a graveyard, or the practice of disposing of the ashes of a loved one in their favourite spot.

In Mistassini Cree society it was expected that hunters should smear animal fat on the walls of their houses, doorposts, and guns, as well as on the head, to promote thoughts, dreams, and enhanced contact with animals. This normative behaviour is understandable in light of Cree beliefs about the relationship between hunters and their prey.

Canadian society has tremendous opportunity for normative conflict, as differing cultures meet and mingle. Consider the tension that arises when Canadian women interact with Iranians: Iranian norms stress the segregation of women from men and require behaviour like veiling of the face (see Box 3.4).

While the cultural variability demonstrated in the previous examples is interesting, for the sociologist the phenomenon is important for a more fundamental reason. Culture, in the earlier examples of the hockey team and the choir, represents a shared understanding about the purpose of the organization, the direction of its development, and the meaning attached to participation and to the activities carried out. Without some common understanding of these matters, co-ordinated activity is impossible. The possibilities for lack of understanding are endless. Some members may think the purpose of the sports team is to play football, others hockey; some may think the meaningfulness of participation comes from the exercise, others from contributing to national unity; some may think the emphasis is on teamwork, others on individual performance. In any society, culture provides an element of predictability and coherence to social interaction.

Agriculture Canada will stop sending female grain inspectors aboard Iranian ships after one Iranian crew refused to allow a woman on board until she put on a veil.

A federal official described the policy as the only way to resolve an extremely sensitive cultural and religious situation.

But a woman's organization said it reinforces discrimination against women under the guise of being culturally sensitive.

Kingsley Chong, Agriculture Canada's district manager, said, "Whenever there is an Iranian ship in port, operational requirements permitting, then we will avoid sending women aboard."

"My own position? I don't think that we should have to comply with their cultural-religious practices. They should comply with Canadian regulations. That is my own feeling."

In Ottawa, George Blouin, deputy chief of protocol for external affairs, said there is no easy solution.

"We cannot defend their practice, but we cannot force our own people to wear a veil. The only thing we could do was to find some compromise: Send a man rather than a woman. But I agree it is not right."

"We cannot force a woman to go aboard a ship without a veil if the captain does not accept her. When it touches on religion, these issues are very delicate."

He said diplomatic officials in Ottawa often face a similar problem with the Iranian ambassador, who refuses to shake a woman's hand.

SOURCE: Kevin Griffin, "Women Inspectors Face Iran Ship Ban," *The Vancouver Sun*, November 17, 1990. Reprinted with permission.

Culture is equally important for the individual. In the above examples, sharing in a common culture makes individual action meaningful, provides a sense of personal identity, and binds individuals to the community and to their social roles.

In most societies, religion plays a central cultural role because the values and beliefs it transmits deal with the fundamental questions of human life: the meaning of life, ideas about good and evil, and visions of the future. For this reason, the dominant values of the various cultures have been religious values. For the past few hundred years, however, most western societies, have seen a decline in the centrality of religion. Religious values have become more and more like museum pieces.

Although 27 percent of Canadians reported that they "attended church in the past week" (Bibby, 1990: 84), their religious values seem quite separate from their everyday lives. For example, the fertility rate for Roman Catholics is now much like that of non-Catholics.[1] Nineteenth-century sociologists were concerned about the decline of religion, but many anticipated the development of strong secular values that would serve the community as well as the past religious values. Has this happened? Do economic values like profit, efficiency, and pragmatism, anchor Canadians and provide them with a sense of belonging?

CANADIAN CULTURE?

· · · · · · · · · ·

The concept of culture is most frequently used to describe societal groups or nation-states; thus, one can talk about American culture or Chinese culture. It seems reasonable to wonder how sociologists might describe Canadian culture. Canadian culture has been the object of much speculation within Canada. Some argue that there is no distinctive Canadian culture, others find it in literature, and others create caricatures, such as "the Great White North."

Sociological debate about Canadian culture in the 1950s and 1960s was influenced by the work of Talcott Parsons, who dominated American sociology for a quarter of a century. Parsons and his students were interested in contrasting modern and traditional societies and in characterizing the prerequisites for modern economic development (capitalism). In answering these questions they emphasized cultural differences: modern society is culturally different from a traditional culture, and certain cultural features are required for modern economic development to occur.

Parsons (1951) captured these cultural characteristics with *pattern variables*: a set of concepts for talking about culture, best understood as choices that must be made in everyday relationships. These value alternatives are summarized in Box 3.5.

- Affectivity — Affective neutrality: These terms describe a relationship that is personal and emotional on the one hand, or impersonal, instrumental, or bureaucratic on the other. In many of their relationships people try to control their emotions and reveal little of how they actually feel. (Family and friends usually are exceptions to this.)
- Diffuseness — Specificity: These terms describe a relationship that is personal on the one hand, or businesslike on the other. They represent a choice between dealing with people in a very broad or holistic way or dealing with them in terms of specific roles. Relations between most people are specific; for example, people deal with the cashier, the teacher, or the bank manager. They share only a part of their personality with any person. (Again, family and friends usually are the exception to this.)
- Particularism — Universalism: These terms describe a relationship in which people make decisions about others, taking into account the others' membership in a particular group, or universal criteria. In most aspects of their lives, people believe they should be judged on universal criteria: favouring one's family in hiring, lying to protect one's friends, and excluding members of other racial groups are all considered wrong.
- Ascription — Achievement: These terms describe relationships in which the other is judged according to certain qualities they possess (like their skin colour, accent,

· · · · · · · · ·

Box 3.5	**TRADITIONAL, STABLE SOCIETY**	**MODERN, CHANGING SOCIETY**
Parsons's Value	Affectivity	Affective neutrality
Alternatives	Diffuseness	Specificity
· · · · · · · · ·	Particularism	Universalism
	Ascription	Achievement
	Collectivity	Self

· · · · · · · · ·

or social position of their family) on the one hand, or on their demonstrated ability to perform tasks. A policy that allowed people to enter university simply because their parents had attended would uphold ascription. Basing university entrance on demonstrated school performance, in contrast, would uphold a system of achievement.

- Collectivity — Self: These terms describe the orientation one chooses in a relationship. The choice is between orienting one's actions toward the group or the relationship itself on the one hand, or toward one's self-interest on the other. In Canada, most people are urged to consider their self-interest; they are not expected to maintain a relationship with their insurance agent at the expense of finding the best policy to meet their interests. There are exceptions to this; people are expected to be more altruistic with family and friends than with strangers.

The pattern variables classified under the heading of a "modern, changing society" in Box 3.5 most accurately capture the relationships urban Canadians encounter at school, at work, at the department store, and in dealing with government. However, there are some exceptions, mostly having to do with family and friends. In more traditional societies, all relationships tend to resemble those with our family and friends.

Parsons argued that modern economic development must be accompanied by cultural change away from the pattern variables of traditional values and toward those of competitive individualism. He maintained that if a society remained tied to the values of ascription, diffuseness, collectivity, particularism, and affectivity, its economic development would be severely hampered. Although Canada is an economically developed society and demonstrates "modern" value patterns, sociologists influenced by Parsons's analysis have raised some questions about Canadian culture. They argue that Canadian culture is less modern than others, notably the United States. A great deal of the discussion about Canadian culture has developed from a comparison with American society and an attempt to articulate the ways Canada differs from that society. Some analysts have identified a number of fundamental differences and used these to make inferences about Canadian culture. Consider the following observations.

The homicide rate in Canada in 1991 is 2.8 per 100 000 population, while in the United States it is 9.8 per 100 000.[2] In Canada, 85 percent of the unemployed received government assistance in 1987, while only 25 percent of the American unemployed did so. Virtually every Canadian citizen is provided with free medical care, while approximately 30 million Americans are without any coverage at all, and only 40 percent of medical funds come from the public purse. Approximately 20 percent of American households own stocks, while only 13 percent of Canadian households do so (Chawla, 1990: 4.6). In the United States, between 30 and 50 percent of eligible voters cast a ballot in national elections, while in Canada the comparable figure is 75 percent or higher. Further, more American youth aged 20–24 enrol in postsecondary education than do Canadian youth. Canada grants an annual average of five patents for every 100 000 citizens, while the United States grants sixteen (Economic Council of Canada, 1989). Finally, Canadians give a substantially smaller part of their personal income to charity than do Americans.[3]

What are we to make of these comparisons? Some sociologists interpret these facts as support for a claim that Canada has less fully accepted the values of modern society than has the United States. In other words, as a culture Canada is more traditional.

Even the fact that Canadians give less to charity is ascribed to their reliance on government to respond to social problems on their behalf. They expect a communal rather than a personal response — evidence of a collectivity orientation rather than a self-orientation. The fact of fewer young people participating in postsecondary education is offered as evidence that Canadians are more likely to accept their status in society (ascription) than are Americans. The fact that they invest less in the stock market is evidence that they are not as motivated by self-interest. Canada's low homicide rate is evidence that Canadians are more respectful of authority and value order and stability more than the Americans do (Lipset, 1990).

This comparison, of course, is highly biased. The whole analysis has been hotly disputed (Baer, Grabb, and Johnston, 1990; Hardin, 1974; Lenton, 1989), but the idea that Canada's culture is more traditional, more conservative, and less entrepreneurial remains a powerful image of the country.[4] While not wanting to accept this assessment of Canadian culture, without developing the concept of social structure it is difficult to say more. The topic of Canadian culture will be discussed in the next chapter in order to develop another view of Canadian values.

FEATURES OF CULTURE
· · · · · · · · ·

When culture is defined to include a body of beliefs, values, norms, knowledge, meanings, and expectations, it is defined as being symbolic. The symbolic component of society makes behaviour meaningful, gives meaning to a way of life, and provides direction to a society. To say that culture is symbolic suggests that it is largely a way of thinking; it does not become observable until it is embodied in art, the production of goods, and individuals' behaviour.[5]

To assert that culture is symbolic and largely a matter of thought implies that it is learned. This claim rejects any notion that human behaviour or social arrangements are the sole product of instincts or some innate feature of humans. Human behaviour differs over time because people have learned different things; societies differ through history because societal members have acquired different ideas. Although sociologists do not deny that a human being is also a biological organism, with biological needs and drives, they do argue that the satisfaction of these needs and drives is not self-directed; rather, it is directed by culture. For example, dog flesh and human flesh can fulfil human needs for food, but many people might choose to starve rather than eat them.

The claim that humans are best understood in terms of their culture rather than their biology is the subject of ongoing debate regarding race (see Box 3.6) and gender. Are the social differences between men and women the outcome of different learning patterns or different biologies? It is difficult to disentangle social and biological influences, to separate nature from nurture. Sociologists rely on two research methods to attempt this separation. First, they carry out cross-cultural studies. How do men and women behave in different societies? Are there variations in their behaviour across cultures? Variation suggests a social basis to behaviour; consistency suggests a biological basis. Second, sociologists rely on historical studies. Does behaviour vary over time? If it does, a social basis to behaviour is demonstrated.

To suggest that culture is learned also suggests that it is learned from others and that it is transmitted. This implies two central features of culture. First, culture is a public rather than private entity; it is shared. Thus, one cannot have a private culture, since the very concept of culture implies sharing. This also means that everyone is "cultured" since one cannot participate in human society without some sharing in a culture. Second, language, a shared symbolic system, is essential for the

Box 3.6
Race

The term **race** first appeared in the English language in about 1500. It was not until the eighteenth century that the word was used to indicate a division of humans with certain physical characteristics in common. As science developed in the western world there was a movement to classify all living things. Carolus Linnaeus (1701–78) was the first scientist of his time to take on the task of classifying all creatures. The ideas of "species," "genus," and so on date from this period. Johann Friedrich Blumenbach (1752–1840) identified five races: Caucasian, Negro, Mongol, Malayan, and American Indian. Several other classification schemes emerged later.

It is important to note that these first efforts to classify humans were made by Europeans. They wished to compare the peoples they were beginning to read about and encounter in their explorations with themselves. Many scientists of this time wished to arrange the races (assumed to be rigid divisions) in some hierarchical order ranging from the "primitive" to the "civilized." This led to the development of **racist ideology**, a belief that humans can be classified as superior or inferior according to physical features. Racism, then, is an attitude or behaviour based on the belief that there is a fixed hierarchy of races.

While there is no scientific basis for these beliefs, some people (even scientists) continue to assume that inferiority or superiority can be associated with the physical diversity of humans. Some, for example, believe that differences in intelligence are attributable to racial influences. There is no credible evidence to support this claim, since it appears impossible to measure intelligence in an objective manner and it is difficult to untangle the influence of heredity and environment.

Although the concept of race has little scientific interest for social scientists, it is clearly an important *social* classification. Social scientists are interested in studying the social relationships between peoples with differing physical characteristics, the locations of groups of people within the social structure, cultural beliefs about physical differences, and so on.

Ethnicity, on the other hand, refers to divisions within the human community based on cultural heritage. It may be important to our sense of our ethnic identity to associate ourselves with a geographical territory, with a set of cultural beliefs and practices, or with a particular national origin.

SOURCE: Adapted from David Hughes and Evelyn Kallen, *The Anatomy of Racism: Canadian Dimensions* (Montreal: Harvest House, 1974).

transmission of culture. Language becomes the storehouse of culture. To learn a language is to become a cultural member; to become a cultural member is to learn a language (see Box 3.7).

Culture Shock   What are the implications of *not* sharing the culture of the dominant group? People may experience this sense of cultural non-belonging when they travel internation-

Box 3.7
Aboriginal Languages
Survive!

O f the aboriginal peoples who identify with an aboriginal group, 36 percent of adults say they can speak an aboriginal language; 6 percent report they have lost the ability to speak their Native language, and 55 percent state they have never been able to speak a Native language.

Among children ages 5–14, 21 percent report they can speak a Native language. Among adults who identify themselves as Métis, 18 percent report they can carry on a conversation in an aboriginal language. Among adults who identify themselves as Inuit, 75 percent report they can carry on a conversation in an aboriginal language.

SOURCE: Adapted from Statistics Canada, *Aboriginal Peoples Survey, 1991: Language, Tradition, Health, Lifestyle and Social Issues*, cat. no. 89-533 (Ottawa: Statistics Canada, 1993). Reproduced by authority of the Minister of Industry, 1994.

ally; immigrants often experience it. Not knowing the common language and not appreciating the dominant customs and laws leaves people feeling uncomfortable, lonely, and increasingly unsure of who they are and of what is going on around them. Their world becomes unpredictable because old cultural rules no longer apply. This experience is known as culture shock (see Box 3.8).

Ethnocentrism

Ethnocentrism is another possible outcome of cultural variability. If people learn to interpret the world according to cultural instructions, then any event or practice that doesn't fit with instructions presents a challenge. What is an observer from a free-enterprise, wealth-seeking culture to make of groups that expect people to give all their wealth away? One frequent approach is to consider the practice (and the group) as inferior or deviant. One considers one's own culture to be natural and therefore judges the other's practice to be unnatural. Ethnocentrism is an attitude that one's culture is inherently superior (see Box 3.9).

Imagine a more everyday example. A person from a culture in which arranged marriages are the norm comes to Canada and witnesses Canadian young people falling in love and deciding to marry without thinking it necessary to ask their families' permission. What might the newcomer think? Perhaps, that the parents had neglected their duties toward their children and were not very loving or concerned. Or that the children, having neglected the interests of their parents, were disobedient or selfish. In either case, it would be quite normal to see the Canadian family as inferior; this would, however, be an ethnocentric view.

Although ethnocentrism is inevitable, it is not considered acceptable in Canadian society; respect is necessary to maintain harmony in a society in which different cultures exist side-by-side. This is why Canadian elementary-school students learn about cultural variation. They are encouraged to see themselves as members of a cultural group and to be aware of other cultures, both in their own society and in the rest of the world. This knowledge of cultural variation makes them less likely to mistake the cultural for the natural or to adopt an attitude of superiority. Understanding the

Box 3.8
Elderly Immigrants
Suffer Most from
Culture Shock,
Isolation

In 1988, more than 42 000 people arrived to be reunited with their parents, siblings, and children in Canada. In many cases, the separation ended only after months or years of frustrating delays.

Counsellors who work with new immigrants agree that social isolation has become the most serious problem for aging parents, particularly women, who have uprooted themselves to live here with their adult children.

The problem cuts across all ethnic lines. ... When the separation has been too long, family members may have outdated information and images of one another, says Lisa Chen of Chinese Family Life services in Toronto.

"They see their children as more westernized and having abandoned traditional values. There is a culture shock and a cultural strain."...

Elderly parents, struggling with a new and difficult language and unused to the cold climate, essentially become housebound or reluctant to leave their immediate neighbourhood. They may be pressed into service to look after young grandchildren while their daughter or daughter-in-law works outside the home.

Because of the self-imposed restrictions on their mobility, the women tend to have few friends. Starved for companionship, they look to their children, and cannot understand why they have little or no time for them. Fearful that moving out might be misinterpreted as having been thrown out, they continue to live with their children but feel like a burden.

Csilla Nagy, a social worker at the Family Service Association of Toronto, says that, especially among older men, who expect to be consulted but whose advice may be out of step, "there is a real power loss. In the old country, the elderly are the most important people in their family. Here they find themselves really dependent on their children."

SOURCE: Adapted from Dorothy Lipovenko, "Elderly Immigrants Suffer Most from Culture Shock, Isolation" *The Globe and Mail*, January 5, 1989, p. A5. Reprinted with permission.

concept of culture helps overcome the inevitable consequence of the phenomenon of culture.

Androcentrism

Feminist scholarship has raised the following question: does Canadian culture represent the experience and creative participation of all peoples (all voices), or is it dominated by the voice of men? Feminists have pointed out that most cultures present a male-dominated view of the world as if it were the only view. People must be aware of **androcentrism**, the habit of talking and thinking as though the world contained only men. They argue that these cultures are created largely by men and that there has been an active exclusion of women from the culture-creating process. To become a cultural member, then, suggests that one learns to view the world through "male eyes." If so, women may become culturally invisible.

....

Box 3.9
The Potlatch among
Northwest Coast
Native Peoples

....

Native groups in much of British Columbia practised the potlatch which was central to the culture and social structure of the communities. The potlatch was used to celebrate initiation, to mourn the dead, to mark the rise of a new chief, and to establish claims to names, power, or status. During the potlatch, wealth in the form of material goods such as blankets, boxes, food, fish and canoes that had been accumulated for years, was given away to community members or even destroyed during a substantial and significant ceremony.

Europeans saw this behaviour as totally alien to their values of individualism, materialism, and the importance of private property. Accordingly the practice was considered "uncivilized," "irrational," and "barbaric." It was always assumed that the Native peoples would become "civilized" over time if values appropriate to modern society were promoted and traditional values suppressed. With this in mind, the potlatch was outlawed from 1884 to 1951. Its suppression, however, destroyed community identities, disrupted local economies, and disturbed the system of stratification.

....

As a result the perspectives, concerns, and interests of only one sex and class are represented as general. Only one sex and class are directly and actively involved in producing, debating, and developing its ideas, in creating its art, in forming its medical and psychological conceptions, in framing its laws, its political principles, its educational values and objectives. Thus a one-sided standpoint comes to be seen as natural, obvious, and general, and a one-sided set of interests preoccupy intellectual and creative work (Smith, 1987: 20).

The "naturalness" of looking at the world through male eyes was demonstrated in the separation of a set of Siamese twins.[6] Their physical attachment was such that radical surgery was necessary to separate them. Since they also shared genitals, a decision had to be made regarding the sex of the children. One child was left with male genitals. The doctors appeared to assume that without a penis the other child must be a girl. They surgically fashioned a vagina and placed the "girl" on hormones to enhance the development of other female attributes. The implication of the decision was that a woman is a person without a penis. Clearly this definition leaves much to be desired. The concept of woman might include having the ability to bear children and the ability to derive pleasure from one's vagina. Neither of these abilities would exist in the "woman" created by surgery. Would the decision about this sex change have been different had the doctors been women?

Further instances of androcentrism occur in magazines, on television, and in daily interaction. It is most frequently identified by the use of language — using male language (e.g., he, his) as though it were descriptive of both sexes; having men's views represented as the universal, providing little public space for women's activities or interests, and so on.

Many differences exist between male and female ways of making sense of things (Belenky, 1986; Segal, 1987; Tannen, 1990). This fact prompts an interesting question: are women a subculture in society? To answer this, one must try to identify women's distinctive beliefs, norms, and values. Lakoff (1990) considers the distinctive features of women's language — always a good indication of subcultural status — as arising from their subordinate position in the power structure. Note that this does not imply that men too are a subculture; rather, they represent the dominant culture.

PERSPECTIVES ON CULTURE

Having introduced a number of concepts related to culture and noted cultural differences among groups, the social scientist searches for explanations. For example, why do some cultures have rules against eating pork? Why do some cultures instruct men to act like fathers to their nieces and nephews rather than to their own biological children? Answers to these questions are provided by theories. A theory explains a particular thing by locating it within a model of some aspect of the world (e.g., culture). A model asserts that some aspect of the world is "like this": it is assumed that the world corresponds to the model. If the real world works as asserted by the model — if the theory is confirmed by evidence — then one can begin to understand the particular thing of interest. Chapter One of this book indicated that sociologists do not agree on interpretations of facts; they also disagree on theory (or models). While social scientists agree that religiously observant Jews do not eat pork, they argue about how to interpret this. They have conflicting theories.

Functionalism

Structural functionalism asserts a shared, cultural basis to society. It explains the parts of culture by showing how they contribute to the overall stability or survival of the society in which they occur. Bronislaw Malinowski (1954 [1925]) provided an example of this approach in his study of the Trobriand Islanders of the southwestern Pacific. Malinowski noted that every aspect of ocean fishing among the islanders was surrounded by an elaborate system of magic. He then asked: Why do they believe in magic? In answering his own question, he noted that ocean fishing is an extremely uncertain activity: fisherman have no control over the weather; the location of fish is uncertain; the activity is dangerous. Given these facts, it was difficult for the fishermen to undertake the activity day after day. Magic, however, provided them with a sense of control over the environment and allowed users to undertake dangerous and uncertain activity without reluctance. The belief in magic, and its use, contributed to the stability and survival of the society. It served the general interest.[7]

Talcott Parsons was perhaps the greatest exponent of structural functionalism. Recall his suggestion that culture (particularly "traditional" values and beliefs) could be an obstacle to the development of modern economy. Parsons thought that a modern economy must be preceded by the acquisition of modern values, such as individualism, liberty, rationality, and progress. What this suggests is a functional relationship between culture and the rest of the society — a kind of integration. A particular kind of society (modern and changing) must have a particular culture (one adopting the values of achievement, self-interest, and so on). Some argue that Canadian culture does not serve Canadians well because it creates an impediment to full economic development. In this view, Canadians would all benefit from a culture that placed more emphasis on the values of achievement, self-interest, and universalism.[8]

Critical Perspectives

Although critical approaches to matters of culture also see a definite link between culture and the rest of society, they do not see society as being in a state of equilibrium and having a consensus about its direction and purpose. They assume instead that there is a basic, unavoidable conflict among people. Inequality is at the root of this conflict. Since a central feature of a critical perspective is the assumption that there are always alternative ways of doing things, culture does not reflect a social consensus but, rather, the interests of some groups of people at the expense of others. Culture produces one version of society but may at the same time make it difficult for people to appreciate other ways of organizing society. Although cultural beliefs and values may stabilize society, they also support and legitimize particular social arrangements from which particular groups benefit.

Critical theorists tend to discuss **ideology**, an aspect of culture, rather than culture itself. An ideology is a pattern of linked beliefs that help to uphold, explain, and justify certain social values and social arrangements. While this definition seems to overlap with that of culture, it is more specific because it focusses on the role of particular beliefs and values in justifying social arrangements. For example, from the earliest times slavery was associated with racist beliefs that asserted the mental and moral inferiority of the slave in comparison with the enslavers. Or think of the ways in which the rewards of society, such as food and housing, are distributed. In Vancouver and Toronto, some people stand in line to receive supplies from a food bank, while others are greeted by an attendant at the door of an expensive restaurant. How do Canadians justify this arrangement?

Culturally justifiable explanations can be provided, although one might not entirely accept them. A common view is that people succeed according to their own hard work and enterprise. People who have wealth deserve it, and their initiative should be rewarded. Thus, too much income redistribution (through progressive income taxes) might undermine the incentive to work hard. Sociologists would characterize such ideas as an ideology. The dominant ideology (a liberal-individualistic ideology) justifies the status quo. A contrasting ideology (a radical ideology) would justify some new state of affairs, and in doing so would criticize the existing inequalities. This ideology might believe that the rich should be taxed more heavily, that all citizens should be guaranteed a reasonable standard of living, and that public funds should be spent to improve community life.

Consider the following examples.

Jackie Solway, an anthropologist, observed a change in Christmas customs in Botswana.[9] The traditional celebration of Christmas focussed on one or two communal feasts, during which much of the community came together. More recently, however, the celebration focussed on many small feasts, based primarily on kin groupings. The new pattern of celebrating Christmas was most obvious among a group of farmers who had taken on a free-enterprise kind of business. Rather than using their cattle for ploughing, for milk, or for lending to other community members, they sold them on the cattle market. This limited their social relations. The smaller networks of friendship (and fewer attendant obligations) enabled them to share their resources with fewer people.

For the rich people — those who owned cattle — changing the Christmas customs was a reflection of their new interest in their cattle. This economic change did not serve everyone's interest, since the rich were now less willing to lend their cattle to non-owners and less willing to use the cattle for milk that could be distributed to others. There was an inherent conflict over the use of the cattle, and the new Christmas custom would legitimate the interests of the owners; one only had obligations to kin, not to the wider community.

Barbara Ehrenreich (1988) discussed changes in western beliefs about work, from considering it as an indignity to seeing it as a sign of character. She suggested that this cultural shift occurred during the industrial revolution, when it became necessary for large numbers of people to work long and hard, for low wages, while others did little or nothing at all. The shift represented the interests of the industrial capitalist and ignored an inherent conflict over the nature of work, the distribution of profits, and the kinds of goods and services produced.

Both these examples portray social relationships as the foundation of society. Social relationships that are unequal create tension and inevitable power struggles and conflict. Culture plays a supportive role in maintaining these unequal relationships, and cultural change occurs when the needs of the dominant group change. When there is inequality, there can be no consensus regarding cultural beliefs and goals.

Hegemony
· · · · · · · ·

When there is stability in societies that have unequal social arrangements, it is obtained either through coercion or through the ability of the dominant group to gain consent, even when it goes against the interests of less powerful groups. In modern capitalist society, the state and its agencies have the sole right of coercion. The state achieves consent, in contrast, by having people see social arrangements as legitimate and desirable. This situation is achieved through ideology, supported by education, the media, religion, family life, and even language and the meanings given to it. This encompassing set of influences tending to uphold existing social arrangements is known as **hegemony** (Gramsci, 1971). Hegemonic rule by a group is the ability to exert force through the state and, more importantly, is legitimized through a wide range of social practices.

**CULTURAL
CRISIS**
· · · · · · · ·

Since culture provides communal direction and gives individuals a sense of belonging, it is impossible to imagine a society without culture. Many sociologists, however, express concern about the adequacy of contemporary culture to provide meaning to community life and to give individuals a sense of identity. Although many are concerned about a **cultural crisis**, they disagree about how best to interpret the origins of this crisis. Some tend to think of culture as autonomous, separate from the way the society is organized, and therefore seek for the origins of the crisis within the culture (Bellah, 1985). Others are more likely to see this crisis in the context of changes in the way society is organized, since culture is a product of a particular pattern of social relationships (Schiller, 1989). This is an ongoing debate: in understanding society, should priority be given to culture or to social structure? Which is the more important factor in shaping society? The next chapter investigates this issue by discussing the concept of social structure.

CONCLUSION
· · · · · · · ·

This chapter introduced the concept of culture — a complex set of rules and expectations that make the world meaningful. These rules and expectations include beliefs, values, and norms.

A preliminary discussion of values and Canadian culture demonstrated pattern variables. Culture was characterized as being a symbolic (rather than material) entity, as being learned from others, shared with others, and distinguishing one group of people from another.

Two significant concerns arose from the discussion of cultural variability: ethnocentrism and culture shock. One may believe that one's own culture is superior to others, and by implication that members of other groups are inferior. But appreciating the concept of culture makes it possible to eliminate or control this ethnocentric view of the world. One can learn to see differences among the world's peoples as cultural rather than moral. The concept of culture shock provides a useful tool for understanding the experience of immigrants to Canada.

Many cultures exclude the perspectives of women, so learning about a culture may result in one's assuming that it contains only men's perspectives. Androcentrism presents an important challenge for everyone, but particularly for men.

Functionalist theory and critical theory were applied to cultural facts to demonstrate the ongoing debate between these two viewpoints. The concept of ideology was introduced as describing aspects of culture that justify a particular set of social arrangements (e.g., inequality).

Finally, the possibility of a culture emerging that is unable to give meaning to people's individual lives or to give purpose to social life was introduced. Although it is a significant concept, a discussion of cultural crisis must await the development of a more thorough understanding of society.

NOTES

1. Interestingly, Italy (at 1.3 births per woman during her lifetime) has one of the lowest fertility rates in the world and Quebec (at 1.72) the second-lowest provincial fertility rate in Canada (1992 rates). Between 1987 and 1990, Quebec's fertility rate rose by 20 percent. New Brunswick has the lowest rate.
2. *Juristat Service Bulletin*, Statistics Canada, 10 (14).
3. Alistair Lawrie, "Why Are Canadians Such Tightwads?" *The Globe and Mail*, October 26, 1990, p. A13.
4. Two interesting discussions of Canadian culture are Hardin (1974) and Bell and Tepperman (1979).
5. Some social scientists draw a distinction between material culture and symbolic culture; material culture includes all the things produced — art, industrial goods, and so on. This distinction is not important here, but "symbolic culture" includes the material if the material is considered as the embodiment of beliefs, values, knowledge, and so on.
6. This story benefits from a letter to the editor written by Sylvia Hale, *The Globe and Mail*, August 11, 1984.
7. Cultural materialism as represented by Harris (1975) is a form of functionalism. Harris argued that cultural elements emerge as a rational response to the environment. Jews don't eat pork, he argued, because it was irrational to husband pigs in an arid environment like the Middle East.
8. Structuralism as represented by authors such as Piaget and Levi-Strauss presents another theory of culture. This theory considers culture as a representation of the deep structure of the mind, a structure that is in-born. Since this theory does not explain society in social terms, it is not discussed in this book. Gardner (1972) presents a readable review of these ideas.
9. This story is discussed in "Class, Culture, and Cuisine" aired on CBC, *Ideas*, October 10–24, 1983.

FURTHER READING

Berton, P. *Why We Act Like Canadians: A Personal Exploration of Our National Character.* Toronto: McClelland and Stewart, 1982. An attempt to describe the uniqueness of Canadian culture.

Bibby, Reginald W. *Mosaic Madness*. Toronto: Stoddart, 1990. An interesting discussion of the consequences of the values of individualism, relativism, and pluralism for Canadian society.

Harris, Marvin. *Cows, Pigs, Wars and Witches: The Riddles of Culture*. New York: Vintage Books, 1975. Delightful reading about some of the cultural patterns that have puzzled social scientists.

Henley, Nancy, and M. LaFrance. "Gender as Culture: Difference and Dominance in Nonverbal Behavior." In A. Wolfgang, *Nonverbal Behavior* (pp. 351–371). Toronto: C.J. Hogrefe Inc., 1984.

Jacobson, Helga E. *Speaking From the Shadows: An Introduction to Feminist Thinking in Anthropology*. Ottawa: Canadian Research Institute for the Advancement of Women, 1989. A useful introduction to the challenge feminism presents for the inclusion of women into anthropological accounts.

Lane, Harlan. *The Mask of Benevolence: Disabling the Deaf Community*. New York: Alfred A. Knopf, 1992. An argument proposing that the deaf be seen as a cultural group rather than a medically "handicapped" group.

Lipset, Seymour M. *Continental Divide: The Values and Institutions of the United States and Canada*. New York: Routledge, 1990. A useful discussion of the cultural differences between Canada and the United States. A briefer presentation of these ideas is found in his article "Historical Traditions and National Characteristics: A Comparative Analysis of Canada and the United States," *Canadian Journal of Sociology* 11 (1986): 113–155. For some counterarguments, see D. Baer, E. Grabb, and W. Johnston, "The Values of Canadians and Americans: A Critical Analysis and Reassessment," *Social Forces* 68 (1990): 693–713.

Malcolm, A.H. *The Canadians*. Toronto: Fitzhenry and Whiteside, 1985. Another recent attempt to identify what it is to be Canadian.

STUDY QUESTIONS

1. Define and distinguish "racism" and "ethnocentrism."
2. Interview a member of a visible minority to discover if he or she has experienced racism. On the basis of your subject's experiences, how would you define racism?
3. Is it helpful to describe women as members of a subculture?
4. After a period of listening to the radio, watching television, or reading newspapers or magazines, describe how androcentrism affects one of these media.
5. Interview a friend or relative from a non-western society to have them identify values, beliefs, and norms that contrast with western or Canadian values, beliefs, and norms.
6. Interview some adult members of your family or neighbourhood and ask them what "Canadian culture" means to them. Prepare a brief report about their responses.

4 SOCIETY AND SOCIAL STRUCTURE

INTRODUCTION

This chapter introduces social structure, the second major concept for understanding society. An understanding of social structure can be developed through role analysis, institutional analysis, and an examination of types of society. The chapter examines the relationship between social structure and culture by assessing the connection between the structure of capitalism and the cultural belief system of liberalism. Do capitalist societies provide equal opportunity, individual freedom, choice, and democracy, as suggested by liberalism? Or is liberalism, as suggested by critical perspectives, principally an ideology that legitimizes capitalist society's class and gender relations?

The previous chapter examined culture, one of the two concepts used to describe and analyze society. Culture, thought of as the community's shared ideas, is the symbolic component of society. These shared ideas make behaviour meaningful and predictable, give society a sense of direction, and provide a sense of identity for individuals. Society, however, is not just a pattern of beliefs; it has a concreteness as well. It is the result of real people behaving in particular ways, interacting in relationships, and engaging in various social practices. This aspect of society is highlighted by the concept of **social structure**.

Every society has a social structure, a way of organizing who does what and of directing the activities of the group. The way an activity is organized affects the experiences of those engaged in it. People experience quite different social relationships in a society in which food is produced by a collective hunt or communal gathering of plants and fruits from one in which people work for wages under the management and direction of others.

Social structure can be thought of as regular, orderly, and patterned relationships in which people engage. At its most primary level, social structure is about social roles, positions in society governed by social norms that outline prescribed ways for performing them. The way roles are linked to each other in any organized group also tends to be patterned. Regarding a sports team, for example, one could ask if the players hire and fire their coach. Do players own their equipment? Do they get paid the same amount for performing the same roles? Do they take turns playing in goal? Do they have a union? Whatever the answers to these questions, there is a stable way of organizing the team's activities. To understand the team (or the game), this organization must be understood.

The team may be located in a league that is organized in a particular way, with franchises, a system of league competition, and rules about recruitment and transfer of players. At this level one might ask, who gets first choice at recruiting new players? How is the revenue received: from television royalties or from the box office? How is the league commissioner chosen?

There are a number of levels of analysis. The first level concerns the roles of individuals, such as players, coach, manager, franchise owners, and stadium staff. The second level is that of the team, where the individual roles are integrated into an organization of players and support personnel. Third is the league, where the individual teams are linked to each other in a defined system of competition. Each of these levels of analysis provides a structural analysis of sports. These levels are also found in society generally: the individual playing a role (e.g., mother); the institution within which the role is performed (e.g., family); and the type of society in which the group is located (e.g., capitalist). Examining any of these levels provides a structural analysis of society that is narrowly focussed at the level of role, wider at the level of group or institution, and widest at the level of the overall society.

SOCIAL STRUCTURE

Individuals' lives are lived within social structures. People occupy social roles and work in an institutional environment that is organized in a particular way, and both roles and institutions are set in a society that itself is organized in a distinct fashion. These social structures must be understood as separate from the individuals who live in them and must be seen as constraining on their lives. The roles people are required to perform are, to a great extent, determined by the structure of organizations in society.

People's experiences are shaped by whether education is formal and compulsory or occurs through family and community activity. Their experience of the work they do is shaped by whether they work for themselves or are employed for wages. These simple examples show why sociologists focus on people's location in a social structure: location indicates a great deal about the individual.

Role Analysis

Members of any society are socialized to perform social roles. Consider, for example, age and gender roles, both of which are shaped by socialization. Although age is a biological characteristic, it has different meanings from society to society and from time to time. Every society has a set of age-related norms (expectations about acting one's age), and age is clearly important for understanding how many activities are organized.

There is age segregation in contemporary schools, for example. Although schools are thought to be organized around achievement levels, school grades are to a consider-

Social structure can be thought of as a regular, orderly, and patterned relationship. At its most primary level, social structure can be broken down into social roles and positions in society (such as parents, teachers, doctors, and police), which are governed by social norms.

. . . .

Bruce Ayres / TONY STONE IMAGES

able extent age groups. Children start school at roughly the same age, and there is some concern for keeping them with their age mates from then on (see Box 4.1). Until the age of approximately 15, young people are required to attend school and are prevented from participating in most adult activities. For example, they may not vote or enter into most legal contracts, they can't marry or have sex with adults, they are restricted in the amount of work they can be required to perform, and they frequently have distinct wage rates. Even the intimate decision to marry is socially shaped by age-related expectations: generally people marry others who are roughly their own age, and there is often gossip about those who stray too far from this pattern.

Age is also significant at the other end of the life cycle. We find that "seniors" are frequently treated differently from other age groups: they may receive free ferry or bus passes or special government grants, and they may be isolated from other age groups in "homes for the aged," seniors housing, or retirement villages. Thus, whether one likes it or not, one occupies an age role, which plays an important part in shaping one's life.

Gender roles are also an important organizing concept in Canadian society. There are normative expectations for men and women, and people are often criticized or ridiculed for not acting in ways that are expected of a woman or a man. In addition to cultural expectations, there are also structural components of gender: many aspects of people's lives are organized around it. As with age, there is sex-based segregation. In some schools, boys and girls form separate social groups and activities may differ — girls rarely play football, for example, and boys rarely learn to sew or bake. There are some entirely separate schools for boys and for girls. Although there are many exceptions, there is also a tendency for gender to influence employment: some occupations are predominantly female and others predominantly male. For

Box 4.1
Age Groupings Are
Pervasive

· · · · · · · ·

The Girl Guides of Canada provide clear evidence of the growing segregation of age groupings. This organization now makes the following divisions:

> *Spark* (ages 5–6)
> *Brownie* (ages 6–9)
> *Guide* (ages 9–12)
> *Pathfinder* (ages 12–15)
> *Ranger* (ages 15+)
> *Cadet* (ages 15+)
> *Junior leader* (ages 15+)
> *Leader* (adults)

Manuals on child rearing also provide evidence of extensive age grading. For example, Burton White (1975), in a well-used parents' guide, outlines age groupings that relate to infant development: from birth to 6 weeks, from 6 weeks to 3 1/2 months, from 3 1/2 months to 5 1/2 months, from 5 1/2 months to 8 months, from 8 months to 14 months, from 14 months to 24 months, and from 24 months to 36 months. Each division is thought to correspond to a stage of physical development, but the stages are also associated with social expectations, which take on cultural significance. Parents can exchange comments about their children and check to see if their child is progressing satisfactorily or not.

· · · · · · · ·

example, in 1991, 95 percent of dietitians and nutritionists were women and 92 percent of civil engineers were men.

One also notices that men tend to dominate group discussions (see Box 4.2); women tend to do most child care; women are likely to be poorer than men and to have less power in society as measured, for example, by membership in Parliament, status in the workplace, or numbers of corporate directorships. Is this a coincidental pattern? Is family life organized so that everyone has an equal chance of pursuing a career and sharing the unpaid work? Or is it organized in such a way that women carry the main responsibility for maintaining the family and are therefore constrained in job opportunities and other life choices?

In short, gender shapes lives in profound ways. The social roles one is born into may become oppressive in many ways. This oppression can, of course, be resisted but only if one imagines other ways of organizing social life.[1]

**Institutional
Analysis**

· · · · · · · ·

The term **institution** generally refers to social practices that are continuously maintained by social norms. An institution is a more general unit than a role; it is a complex of interrelated roles. The family as an institution, for example, incorporates several roles (such as mothers, fathers, daughters, and sons) and specific norms (for example, children must be cared for; parents must introduce their children to expected social behaviours).

Sociologists have developed many ways to discuss key institutions in society, but there is general agreement that five large institutional areas can be identified: *economic*

Box 4.2
Language and
Women's Social Role

Professor Robin Lakoff has developed a fascinating analysis of women's and men's differing use of language. These differing forms of speech can be understood in relation to the social roles of women and men. Since it appears quite reasonable that the two sexes are characterized by differences in clothing, mannerisms, interests, and capabilities, why not distinguish forms of speech as well? Lakoff identifies 14 special characteristics of women's language use (while noting that not all women use them, and none use all of them).

1. Women often seem to hit phonetic points less precisely than men do; for example, they may lisp or obscure vowels.
2. Women's intonational contours display more variety than men's contours do.
3. Women use diminutives and euphemisms more than men do.
4. Women make use of expressive forms more than men do; for example, "lovely" or "divine."
5. Women use forms that convey impreciseness; for example, "so" or "such."
6. Women use "hedges" of all kinds ("it could be suggested"; or "perhaps we might think that") more than men do.
7. Women use intonation patterns that suggest questions rather than statements, indicating uncertainty or need for agreement.
8. Women's voices are breathier than men's.
9. Women are more indirect and polite than men.
10. Women won't readily commit themselves to a strong opinion.
11. In conversation, women are more likely to be interrupted and are less likely to introduce successful conversational topics.
12. Women's communicative style tends to be collaborative, seeking to reach agreement and consensus, rather than being competitive.
13. More of women's communication is expressed non-verbally, through gesture and facial expressions.
14. Women are more careful to be "correct" when they speak, using better grammar and fewer colloquialisms than men do.

Where do these features of social roles come from? Are they an expression of natural differences, such as hormones or brain function? Or are they accidental and without consequence? Lakoff argues that they are of great consequence and are to be understood as arising from differing locations in the structure of power in society. Men's language is the language of the powerful. "Women's language developed as a way of surviving and even flourishing without control over economic, physical, or social reality. Then it is necessary to listen more than speak, agree more than confront, be delicate, be indirect, say dangerous things in such a way that their impact will be felt after the speaker is out of range of the hearer's retaliation."

SOURCE: Adapted from Robin Lakoff, *Talking Power* (New York: Basic Books, 1990).

institutions (providing and distributing goods), *political* institutions (regulating power and managing conflict), *kinship* institutions (linking people by blood descent and marriage), *stratification* institutions (allocating positions and rewards in society, e.g., schools and universities), and *cultural* institutions (e.g., the media).[2]

The institutions that compose social structure are not always patterned in the same way. Consider some examples of variance in institutions. In some societies, men have more than one wife: a marriage form known as **polygyny**. In other societies, women may have more than one husband (**polyandry**) and there is sometimes a social rule that the husbands be brothers. Among some Inuit of the Canadian Arctic there is a practice of families giving up their biological children for adoption and then adopting children themselves.[3] In Burundi, an African society, the heavy work is done by women, while in other societies it is done by men. Each of these practices represents ways of organizing family and gender relations.

A few workplaces have been organized to give workers more control over what they do. This often results from the withdrawal of private capital from the plant and workers pooling their resources to buy ownership and preserve their jobs. Workers hire and fire, decide on the purchase of equipment, and have access to financial records, learn to read income statements, and set profit goals. In these workplaces, work is organized much more democratically than in traditional factories.[4]

In churches, denominations may be organized so that the rules and procedures are set by someone in a position of authority, such as the bishops or the pope, or the congregation itself may set the rules and procedures and hire its own clergy. Authority may derive from above or below; thus, a religion may be hierarchical or congregational — two structural terms.

The above are all examples of variations in the social structure of institutions. Sociologists have an extensive vocabulary for describing the differing ways in which aspects of life are organized: the patriarchal (male-dominated) family, the conjugal family, centralized power, co-operative work, egalitarian education, the free-enterprise economy, the congregational church, division of labour, differentiation of roles, and so on. These terms capture the essentials of how aspects of social life are structured.

Types of Societies

The various parts of society cannot be put together in just any fashion. The way any one part is organized may reflect other aspects of life in that society. In recent years, for example, Japan has found that its **fertility rate** (the average number of children born to a woman in her lifetime) has fallen to 1.7 per woman (down from 2.0 in 1960), the lowest rate in its history (UNICEF, 1993b: 85). To keep Japan's population stable (excluding immigration), it is estimated that a fertility rate of 2.1–2.2 is needed (Popenoe, 1988: 299). Sociologists do not assume that this decline is simply a random result of women and men deciding to behave in a different way. Rather, the change in the fertility rate is assumed to result from changes in other aspects of the society, such as the way work is organized. Many Japanese women now have careers and are required to work long hours, leaving little time for family life. Further, housing has become expensive, day care is inadequate, and living costs are high. No wonder women and men decide to limit the size of their family or to not have children.

In contrast to the Japanese experience, Swedes are noticing an increase in their fertility rate, placing Sweden in a class almost of its own in the industrial world. The rise in the fertility rate to 2.0 (up from 1.6 in 1980) is attributed to a more "family-friendly" atmosphere in Sweden. The government pays a fixed allowance to all parents with children, provides widespread public child-care services, and through a parent-insurance program allows either parent to take well-paid leave after the birth of a child (with a longer leave after the birth of a second child).[5]

Since there are linkages between family life, work, education, and the economy, there must be some compatibility between these aspects of society. This recognition of the inevitable interlocking of the parts of society prompts the highest level of structural analysis, where society is considered as a connected system. This connection is clear in cases where developing nations experience a weakening of their traditional family systems or where developed societies have specialized schooling systems and no longer rely on learning from the family. Talcott Parsons was talking about society as a connected system when he said that cultural patterns must fit with economic and social organization: modern, changing societies demand different values and social relationships from those of traditional, stable societies.

There is an extensive sociological vocabulary for describing and distinguishing different types of societies. For example, there are hunting and gathering societies, pastoral societies, agrarian societies, feudal societies, and capitalist societies.[6] To appreciate societal differences and the subsequent discussion of capitalist society, it is useful to analyze the evolution of human society.[7] There are various schemes for doing this, but the usual way to classify societies is to identify types of major institutions, usually those related to technology and economic organization. For example, Sanderson (1988) uses as a category "levels of technology" and identifies hunting and gathering, simple horticultural, intensive horticultural, agrarian, pastoral, and industrial societies. He also analyzes contrasting systems of ownership and distribution of economic products (see Box 4.3).

• • • • • • • •

Box 4.3
Types of Societies, Using Three Criteria: Level of Technology, Forms of Ownership, and Forms of Economic Distribution

LEVEL OF TECHNOLOGY
Hunting and gathering
Simple horticultural
Intensive horticultural
Agrarian
Pastoral
Industrial

FORMS OF OWNERSHIP
Communism
Lineage (kinship) ownership
Ownership by chiefs
Seigneurial (including feudal) ownership
Lineage or private ownership
Private ownership

FORMS OF ECONOMIC DISTRIBUTION
Reciprocity (balanced or generalized)
Redistribution (pure or partial)
Surplus expropriation
Market dominated
Command (modern communism)

SOURCE: Adapted from S.K. Sanderson, *Macrosociology* (New York: Harper and Row, 1988), with the exception of the notion of "command" economies, which comes from Robert L. Heilbroner, *The Making of Economic Society*, 8th ed. (Englewood Cliffs, NJ: Prentice-Hall, 1989).

These systems fit together in various ways. For example, hunting and gathering societies also have communistic forms of ownership and reciprocity as a form of distribution (each person gives to others and either keeps track of the obligations created or knows there is a generalized obligation created). Similarly, feudal societies have an agrarian level of technology, a seigneurial form of ownership (a few individuals own vast tracts of land), and a form of surplus expropriation (owners compel producers to give the surplus to them). Finally, capitalist societies are characterized by an industrial level of technology (the production of goods is dominated by the use of machines) and private ownership, and the market dominates the distribution of goods and services. Each of these types of society also has a distinctive form of stratification, power, and family structure.

There is a danger of oversimplification when classifying whole societies because mixtures of the types often occur as one society merges into another. However, these models of societies (or ideal types) capture the essential features of a pure example of a type. Toward the end of this chapter a model of capitalist society is presented, and in the next chapter a model of feudal society is described.

Hunting and Gathering Societies
· · · · · · · ·

It is helpful to have an example in mind when discussing a society as a connected system. Stanley Diamond's (1974) discussion of **hunting and gathering societies** is useful for this purpose.[8] Hunting and gathering societies have a simple organization in which family ties are the central bond and the economy and everyday life are organized around a narrow range of hunting and gathering activities. Relationships are always personal and direct; there are no impersonal institutions, and the individual is wholly integrated into the community. This joining of individual and society results from the way the community is organized (see Box 4.4).

Generally, the aboriginal societies of Canada fit into this pattern, though there are complex variations among them. Some, like the Montagnais-Naskapi of Labrador and Quebec, were egalitarian and had little division in social and sexual status. Others, like the Sioux, emphasized leadership and men were clearly dominant. In the Pacific Northwest, where there were considerable forest resources and fish and game, the Haida developed a hierarchical society that bestowed considerable power and authority on hereditary chiefs, and conquered tribes were sometimes forced into slavery. Unlike some hunter–gatherer societies, among the Haida there would often be a seasonal division of the community into small kin-based groups for hunting, trapping, or fishing.

In hunter–gatherer society the close bond between individual and community, necessary for economic success and physical security, is supported by the absence of significant private property, the central role of kinship, little recognition of privacy, and the freedom for individuals to express their emotions in everyday life. There is a patterned relationship between the parts of this society that allow us to characterize it as being of a particular type.

Canadian Culture Revisited
· · · · · · · ·

This example of how to view society as a connected whole prompts questions about the way other types of society are organized. A recent immigrant to Canada might notice that his or her family is structured in a different way from those of other Canadians and that the family values are different. It might be expected that grandparents live in the same home as their children and grandchildren. The senior generation might exercise considerable influence and authority; parents, for example, may choose the marriage partners of their children, in contrast to the usual Canadian

Box 4.4
Diamond's Model
(Ideal Type) of a
Hunting and
Gathering Society

1. *There is a communalistic economic base; subsistence comes from the shared resources of nature.* There is little sense of private property, and work is co-operative. Little surplus is produced, and no profits are made. There is extensive gift-giving.

2. *Power is dispersed.* It is held by the community itself or shifts among members on the basis of particular talents or skills. There is general material equality, and conflict is resolved in ways that involve all community members, but with men usually playing the most prominent roles.*

3. *There is no formal law and no institutionalized law enforcement.* Traditional customs and community sentiment guide all social life, and these are slow to change.

4. *The community is thought of as a large kinship group.* There is little separation of family life from other aspects of the group life, and it is difficult to determine where the family begins or ends.

5. *There is little division of private and public life.* The community will intervene on any matter, intimate or not. For example, some societies have norms against husbands and wives having sexual intercourse when the wife is still nursing a child. Breach of the rule brings community comment and ridicule.

6. *All experiences within the community are emotionally charged and of a personal nature.* Everyone participates fully in community life; there is little division of labour and no isolation of individuals from other aspects of social life.

7. *Art, religion, and the experiences of daily life are fused.* People's aspirations, needs, and anxieties are expressed in art and ritual, and these expressions bond the individual to the culture and the society.

*There are some exceptions to this generalization about hunting and gathering societies. Descriptions of egalitarian societies exist in Leacock (1977) and an interesting account of the !Kung can be found in Reiter (1975).

SOURCE: Adapted from Stanley Diamond, *In Search of the Primitive* (Chicago: Transaction Books, 1974).

practice of free choice in marriage partners. It is reasonable to ask whether the immigrant family organization is likely to change in a different society.

This initial understanding of social structure prompts a review of a question encouraged by the previous chapter: What is the link between culture and social structure? How do they combine to shape a society? One way to explore this linkage is to ask which is the primary influence on the nature of society: culture or structure? Is social structure a reflection of cultural ideas and beliefs? Or are ideas and beliefs a reflection of social structure?[9] One way to look at this issue is through the sociological debate about the character of Canadian society. Some give priority to the influence of culture and others to social structure. Both approaches are efforts to understand society as a connected system.

Canadian culture has been described as tilting toward a traditional/stable set of pattern variables. Thus, Canada emphasizes ascription over achievement and a collective orientation over a self-orientation. Canadian culture, because it contains some traditional values that clash with a modern business-centred economy, has been held responsible for the nation's weak industrial–technological development, compared with that of the United States. The proponents of this view obviously place great emphasis on the concept of culture. They see culture as shaping social structure, especially the structure of Canada's economy. If its cultural values were more modern, they would argue, Canada's economic structure would also be more advanced.

The alleged more traditional quality of Canadian culture is identified in Canadians' apparent strong reliance on government (e.g., government-owned corporations and regulated markets). Canadians' collective orientation is said to place value on the community rather than on individuals and to lead to government programs like medicare, public ownership of resources and utilities, public broadcasting, and economic support for depressed regions. In short, governments play an important part in the society, and Canadians pay for this through high taxation. These public policies are considered an expression and outcome of Canada's culture; thus, critics argue, Canada must modernize its culture if it wants a dynamic and efficient economy. Self-reliance and initiative must be given more value. Advocates of this view argue that Canada ought to privatize many of its crown corporations, reduce government involvement in the economy, and encourage private initiatives. Proponents of continental free-trade adopt this argument.

Where does this Canadian approach to organizing social life come from? Seymour Lipset (1986; 1990) attributes priority to culture and says that, unlike the United States, Canada never had a revolution against a central colonial authority. The United States had a war of independence from Britain that overturned the existing authority structure and shaped that country forever, making it mistrustful of authority and committing it to the values of individualism and personal initiative. Canada, on the other hand, was strongly affected by those who fled America during the war of independence (1776–83). The United Empire Loyalists brought with them values that were respectful of authority and of the British imperial system. Their arrival stamped a traditional set of values on Canada and shaped the nation's destiny. Lipset, however, did not link Canada's culture to its conditions and experience; he only suggested that it was imported by the United Empire Loyalists. Their immigration is seen as the key event in the shaping of our society.

Is there another reason why Canada has a more collective approach to economic and social problems than does the United States? Could more importance be given to Canadian social structure and physical and economic geography? Perhaps. Prior to Confederation, Canadian parliamentarians and business leaders had a constant fear that the United States would take over the small and distant Canadian market, or even invade the land, as they did in 1812 and threatened to do on subsequent occasions. For Canada's political and business leaders, the nation's vulnerability came from its economic development being different from that of the United States. In order to develop or protect markets and to provide necessary capital, the colonial government was encouraged by business institutions to regulate the market and develop resources. This government involvement resulted in projects like the Welland Canal and the financing of the transcontinental and regional railway systems.[10] By the end of the nineteenth century, the strong regulation of the market through the National Policy provided tariff protection for Canadian manufacturing.[11] This analysis of Canada's situation provides a structural account and suggests that culture is a response to conditions of social organization, not a cause of them. Canadians organized society and social policy to adapt to the geographic and political realities of Canada, and from these responses a culture of public enterprise emerged.[12]

This chapter began by defining social structure as enduring and predictable relationships among parts of a society. It focussed on the role of the individual (in a specific position, such as parent); on the institution, such as the family (a set of linked roles), and on the society as a whole (the complex of institutions and cultural values). These levels of analysis are like photographs taken by cameras with different lenses. The widest-angle lens provides a panoramic view of the society, the intermediate lens shows an institution like a team or a family, and the narrowest-angle lens provides a portrait of a particular social role. The portrait is interesting in itself, but it is part of the panoramic background and cannot be fully understood outside that background. It can, however, promote a deeper understanding of society when it is placed in social context.[13]

Most of this book provides a brief examination of the way various aspects of life are organized in Canadian society: work, political power, social and economic inequality, family, the media and the economic system. In every case it is important to see the topic against the backdrop of the wider society. The discussion of hunting and gathering societies identified them as a societal type. All societies can be classified into a range of types. The most important characteristic of Canadian society is that it is a capitalist society. This, of course, does not distinguish Canada from the United States, Britain, France, Germany, and many others; they are all capitalist societies.[14] However, viewing Canada as a capitalist society provides a useful way to understand it. The concept of a capitalist society provides a panoramic view of society and the context for everything that can be observed about Canadian society.

Capitalist Society

Describing a society like Canada as capitalist typically refers to the way the economy is organized. This is clear in the characteristics outlined in Box 4.5. Notice that economic organization has consequences for other aspects of society; thus capitalist society, too, is a connected system.

The features of capitalism developed here are somewhat sketchy and abstract (this is only a model) but are sufficient to provide an easy way to clarify what is meant by capitalism. This discussion begins by focussing on the structural aspects of this model and proceeds to examine the cultural aspects.

Box 4.5
Key Features of a Capitalist Society

1. Productive resources are privately owned.
2. The motive force in economic activity is self-interest.
3. Formal legal equality exists for all citizens.
4. It is possible for individuals to change their class position.
5. The economy rests on a competitive market.
6. Price and wages are set by the forces of supply and demand.
7. There is a pronounced division of labour.
8. Economic growth is fuelled by the reinvestment of profit.
9. The government usually is a democratic political system.

The key structural characteristic of the Canadian economy is that the great majority of the society's productive resources are privately owned or, like its natural resources, mainly under private control. This means that decisions to start businesses, accumulate capital, and make investments are a private responsibility, as are decisions about the kinds of goods produced and the locations of production. This key feature of capitalism contrasts it with other modern economic systems in which the state owns resources and makes central decisions about the production of goods, services, and investment.

The structure of the economy rests on a competitive market system that is constantly driven to achieve greater efficiency as suppliers of goods and services strive against each other to secure market position. The economy is centred on the production of goods and services for sale on the market, rather than on the immediate needs of the producers, as was typical in pre-industrial times.[15]

The prices of goods and services, including wages, are largely determined through the market forces of supply and demand. The market also determines the distribution (or allocation) of rewards — goods, wealth, and income. Individual achievement, rather than ascription, determines personal social and economic success. The market mechanism is assumed to be the best way to allocate economic resources, and governments are expected not to excessively distort market forces.

The pursuit of efficiency in the use of resources leads to a pronounced **division of labour**. This technique of work organization breaks production down into highly specialized tasks in order to enhance the productivity of labour.

The competitive market also ensures that economic growth is fuelled by a constant reinvestment of profit. Most of the profit goes back to the business for expansion and technical development. The business must maintain its competitive position by continuous scientific and technical advancement.

In summary, capitalism is a way of organizing the economy; the focus is on individuals as economic actors, and the economy is dominated by the market. The purpose of production is private profit. The allocation of resources (what is produced) and the distribution of income (who gets what) is done through the market mechanism. There is a complex division of labour and specialization of roles and institutions. In principle, capitalism is self-regulating through the interplay of market forces.

CAPITALISM AND DEMOCRACY • Underlying this organizational structure is the idea of individuals making free choices that maximize their personal satisfaction. The fundamental belief that citizens should be as free as possible to act rationally in their self-interest demands formal legal and political equality. Therefore, capitalist societies have a special affinity with electoral political systems (democracy) that confer equal legal and political status on adult citizens. There is a very close link between capitalism and electoral democracy. Today, all economically mature capitalist countries have electoral political systems.[16] Conversely, almost all nations that might be termed democratic have capitalist economies. Although there is a tendency for developing capitalist countries to undergo periods of dictatorship and repression, such situations are rare in developed capitalist societies.[17] Of course, extending the vote to all adult citizens in capitalist countries takes considerable time. Only since 1960 have *all* adult Canadians had the right to vote. In the past, those without property were excluded, as were women, Native peoples, and citizens of Chinese and Japanese ancestry.[18]

Classical liberal theorist Milton Friedman (1962) argues that the association of capitalism with electoral systems of government is not accidental, because capitalism both creates and sustains democracy. The central task in preserving freedom and democracy, he claims, is to be mindful of the need to sustain capitalism:

> It is widely believed that politics and economics are separate and largely uncon-
> nected; that individual freedom is a political problem and material welfare an eco-
> nomic problem; and that any kind of political arrangements can be combined with
> any kind of economic arrangements ... such a view is a delusion ... there is an inti-
> mate connection between economics and politics, ... only certain combinations of
> political and economic arrangements are possible, and ... a society which is socialist
> cannot also be democratic, in the sense of guaranteeing individual freedom.
>
> The kind of economic organization that provides economic freedom directly,
> namely, competitive capitalism, also promotes political freedom because it separates
> economic power from political power and in that way enables the one to offset the
> other.
>
> Historical evidence speaks with a single voice on the relation between political
> freedom and a free market. I know of no example in time or place of a society that
> has been marked by a large measure of political freedom, and that has not also used
> something comparable to a free market to organize the bulk of economic activity.
>
> The basic problem of social organization is how to co-ordinate the economic
> activities of large numbers of people. Even in relatively backward societies, extensive
> division of labour and specialization of function is required to make effective use
> of available resources. In advanced societies, the scale on which co-ordination is
> needed, to take full advantage of the opportunities offered by modern science and
> technology, is enormously greater. Literally millions of people are involved in provid-
> ing one another with their daily bread, let alone with their yearly automobiles. The
> challenge to the believer in liberty is to reconcile this widespread interdependence
> with individual freedom.
>
> Fundamentally, there are only two ways of co-ordinating the economic activities
> of millions. One is central direction involving the use of coercion — the technique of
> the army and of the modern totalitarian state. The other is voluntary co-operation of
> individuals — the technique of the market place.[19]

While it was earlier suggested that capitalism is a way of organizing the economy, it is now clear that capitalism implies something about the way other parts of the soci-ety are organized. First, there is political equality, suggesting that power is equally dis-tributed throughout the society. The system of representative government is the chief mechanism for organizing this power. Second, the above features imply something about the organization of inequality. Since all individuals act as free individuals and make decisions about their property and interests, the society should be an **open-class society**. Third, work is organized around the private ownership of the resources of production and an extensive division of labour. Fourth, capitalism has an identi-fiable cultural belief system — liberal philosophy, or liberalism.

LIBERAL PHILOSOPHY • All societies have a set of ideas that makes the structure of the society seem right, natural, and moral. The values of **liberalism** uphold capitalism as an ideal form of social organization (see Box 4.6).

Some version of liberalism is characteristic of all mature capitalist societies. Three central ideas are embodied in liberal thought: individualism, liberty, and utilitarianism.

. . . .

1. Focusses on liberty for the individual, in the form of freedom from constraint.
2. Individuals express their freedom through choice in a free market.
3. Governments should interfere only minimally in individual life and in economic activity.
4. A democratic state will control the abuse of economic power.
5. Allowing individuals to maximize their self-interest will also maximize social benefit.

. . . .

The focus of liberalism is individual freedom. The best society, according to liberalism, is one in which people are free to pursue their individual interests. It values **individualism** rather than communalism. Liberalism asserts that all people are born free and all have equal rights. This was the central idea in the Declaration of Independence, adopted by the American colonists in 1776: "We hold these truths to be self-evident, that all men are created equal, that they are endowed by their Creator with certain unalienable Rights, that among these are Life, Liberty and the pursuit of Happiness." This was a new view of the balance of rights and duties between individual and society.

Earlier ideas of community, tradition, hierarchy, and ascriptive status were undermined by the rise of a market economy. A decisive historical change took place: the longstanding hierarchy of society that was found in chiefdom, monarchy, and aristocracy was overturned and individualism was born. Individualism could only be supported by a focus on liberty. Liberty implies that society has rights and authority over the individual only so far as necessary to protect the enjoyment of liberty by others. This notion of liberty is contained in the Canadian Charter of Rights and Freedoms (see Box 4.7).

According to this view, a moral society must rest on the value of individual freedom. A society based on this value must be open. It must be possible, in principle, for any individual in the society to rise to the highest social and economic positions. This belief in the importance of individual liberty also applies to citizens as economic actors. It is implied in discussions about free markets and limiting the intervention of government in the market. These ideas are captured well by Terrence Corcoran:

> *The real magic of a free market is that it gives individuals more power and control over their lives than anything else. More, even, than democracy. ...*
> *... The virtues of free markets go hand in hand with the magic. The principle virtue is an absence of coercion. Every government action that interferes with a free market is an act that forces people to do things that they would rather not do, or that prevents them from doing things that they would rather do. It is the latter, preventing consumers from doing what they would rather do, which is the most insidious and dangerous of the economic alternatives to free markets.*
> *We are not talking here of preventing people from engaging in immoral or violent behaviour or fraudulent acts. ... The economic alternatives to free markets are found in more subtle and seemingly innocent activities like subsidies, trade and business barriers, regulated monopolies, and other measures that only states can impose by force.[20]*

Box 4.7
The Canadian
Charter of Rights
and Freedoms

The Canadian constitution has a number of provisions protecting the freedom of the individual from the constraints of society.

2. *Everyone has the following fundamental freedoms:*
   (a) freedom of conscience and religion;
   (b) freedom of thought, belief, opinion and expression, including freedom of the press and other media of communication;
   (c) freedom of peaceful assembly; and
   (d) freedom of association.

The following legal freedoms are also guaranteed:

7. *Everyone has the right to life, liberty and security of the person and the right not to be deprived thereof except in accordance with the principles of fundamental justice.*
8. *Everyone has the right to be secure against unreasonable search and seizure.*
9. *Everyone has the right not to be arbitrarily detained or imprisoned.*
10. *Everyone has the right on arrest or detention*
    (a) to be informed promptly of the reasons therefor;
    (b) to retain and instruct counsel without delay and to be informed of that right; and
    (c) to have the validity of the detention determined by way of habeas corpus and to be released if the detention is unlawful.

The Canadian Charter of Rights and Freedoms allows, in a minor way, the rights of the community to override those of the individual. This is consistent with the liberal idea of constraint being justified if it is necessary to enhance the freedom of others. Section 1 states, "The *Canadian Charter of Rights and Freedoms* guarantees the rights and freedoms set out in it subject only to such reasonable limits prescribed by law as can be demonstrably justified in a free and democratic society." Just how this is to be interpreted will be determined by Supreme Court decisions.

The Charter also allows provincial legislatures or Parliament to override some of its provisions (section 2 and sections 7–15), perhaps allowing collective rights to take precedence over individual rights. Quebec used this provision in 1989 to restrict the rights of individual businesses to display signs in languages other than French. It should also be noted that section 35 of the Constitution Act, 1982, contains a notion of group rights. Section 35(1) states, "The existing aboriginal and treaty rights of the aboriginal peoples of Canada are hereby recognized and affirmed."

How can this stress on individual choice be reconciled with community interests and values? How can the social good be served when people work toward realizing their self-interest? Liberalism asserts that when individuals, in a free society, maximize their own satisfaction, then the overall result must be that the greatest happiness is secured for the greatest number. This is the concept of **utilitarianism**: the society that allows individuals to maximize their own satisfactions at the same time maximizes overall social benefit. Individualism creates social advancement and does not oppose it. For example, the proper care of children is a community concern. It is important for a healthy, stable community that children be nurtured, loved, and adopt co-operative behaviour. The best way to achieve this, according to liberal thought, is for parents to make decisions about child care that make them happy and satisfy their interests. Ideally these decisions should be made within a market of child-care resources. The accumulated decisions of Canadian parents becomes the best social decision. Canada achieves its social goals by allowing parents to make individual choices about their children.

PERSPECTIVES ON CAPITALIST SOCIETY

An appreciation of the structure and cultural ideas of capitalist society makes it possible to develop an analysis of this type of society, particularly the form it takes in Canada. The two comprehensive sociological perspectives, functionalist and critical, can be used to analyze this type of society.

Functionalism

Functionalism does not begin with a vision of an alternative society, but mainly seeks to comprehend the forces that maintain effectiveness and stability. It assumes that the parts of this society must function in a harmonious manner in order to fully develop and maintain it. Each of the parts of the society can be examined to determine how it contributes or detracts from the society's well-being.

Terrence Corcoran's analysis, above, argued that economic well-being is directly proportional to the degree that markets are free within a country. He argued further that trade barriers (tariffs) and government subsidies to corporations are examples of the market being constrained by government policies and that these policies are dysfunctional for producing economic well-being.

The functionalist argument can also be used to defend the extent of inequality in Canada. It can be argued that people deserve to be rich because they have worked hard to achieve, and that the benefit they receive encourages their initiative and produces benefits for others in the form of jobs. Inequality, from this point of view, is functional for the society: it motivates people to work hard, and the hard work of some benefits everyone. Parsons (1951) noted a functional link between capitalist social structures and liberalism: "modern" social values must be adopted before the economic and social structures of capitalism can flourish.

Critical Perspectives

A critical perspective, on the other hand, begins with the belief that alternative societies are always possible. It begins by noting that not everyone derives equal benefit from a capitalist society, or from any society with social inequalities. The way society is organized may chiefly benefit those with money or property (e.g., capital), or it may benefit men or people of white European descent. A critical perspective sees the education system as allowing those with privilege to maintain this position in society; government policies (e.g., taxation) as benefiting the rich and powerful; the family structure as maintaining a mobile and reserve labour force and protecting male domination in society; the division of labour as placing control of the work process in the hands of owners and managers; and electoral democracy as restricting the range of voices heard in political decisions.

Critical perspectives are particularly hard on the cultural aspect of capitalism found in liberal thought (see Box 4.8). It is seen as **ideology**: as providing the moral justi-

Box 4.8
A Critical View of
Liberalism: A
Summary

1. Liberal thought does not satisfactorily explain how social needs that transcend individual self-interest will be taken care of in a market system. When the market is seen as virtuous and capable of serving community interests through individual decisions, the ability of the community to act collectively on its own behalf becomes weakened.

2. Liberalism fails to recognize that there is a great inequality of influence among individuals, both in the marketplace and in the political system. Is it really a society of equal individuals?

3. Liberal philosophy fails to systematically examine whether economic power and political power complement, rather than offset, each other. Do corporations have more power than the individual or the local community?

4. Liberalism fails to recognize the extent to which social status is based on ascription rather than achievement as the advantages and disadvantages of wealth, education, and social connections are transmitted from generation to generation.

5. Although liberalism explains why political democracy is important, it does not properly value democracy in the workplace. Why are some types of decisions that affect people's whole lives — if and when they work, the jobs they do, the rewards they receive — taken by individuals and businesses over whom there is little social control?

6. Liberalism fails to recognize the way in which citizens' liberty is compromised by the relatively autonomous power of large corporations. Why does government pose a bigger threat to individual freedom than do privately directed giant corporations? Doesn't corporate economic power and the ability to exercise control pose a threat to individual liberty and well-being?

7. Liberalism overstates the degree to which capitalist countries have achieved representative democracy. Is there an open and democratic direction of government?

8. Liberalism locates power in the market and the state and consequently neglects the family as a site of women's oppression. Thus feminists argue that understanding women's position in society means that patriarchal structures and social values that oppress women must be analyzed and understood.

fication for a particular way of organizing society that benefits the few. As ideology, liberalism justifies the status quo and prevents people from seeing an alternative vision of society.

There is some common ground between critical and functionalist perspectives. Critical theorists agree that culture and social structure are not assembled together at random: there is a patterned integration of the various institutions of capitalist society. However, rather than seeing the integration of parts as simply contributing to stability they use the concept of hegemony (see Chapter Three) to show how the broad fit among institutional areas is essential for reproducing class domination or male domination. In addition, the functionalist assumption that a normal state for society is harmony and balance is completely rejected. On the contrary, there is a constant struggle between contending interests and contending values. This struggle might focus on class, status, gender roles, or ethnic groups: it is present in all complex societies. Critical theorists also accept the idea that societies can be subject to violent and transformative change as one group of interests becomes dominant over another and discards the cultural values and social structures of the old society.

Capitalism as a Global System

Critical theorists consider capitalism a world system. Wallerstein (1974) has been influential in relating this tradition to the rapid developments taking place in the modern world. Rather than seeing capitalism as concerning the economic relationships among citizens of a single nation, critical theorists view it as a system of economic relationships among nations. Examples include the farmers of Botswana becoming integrated into the international market for cattle and the importance of economic links between Canada and the United States.

In world systems theory, some core nations are dominant and are described as metropolis nations, while other peripheral nations are subordinate and are called hinterland nations. From its first beginnings capitalism has been a world system in which some nations had the power to shape (or restrict) the development of other nations as markets or as sources of resources and labour. Core nations tend to have a different economic base from that of peripheral nations (being fully industrialized rather than primarily resource-based), different labour requirements (more skilled labour than unskilled), and different education systems. Critical theorists tend to see Canada as a hinterland nation in relation to the American metropolis. The relationship is considered to be one of subordination, and Canada's economic development is thought to have been restricted through either coercion or ideologically produced consent (e.g., Canadians seeing themselves as inferior).

Placing Liberal Philosophy

Liberalism can be understood as an account of modern capitalist society provided from the heart of that society. It can be thought of as a cultural belief system functionally necessary for the development of modern society or as an ideology that justifies the social inequalities found in all such societies. While this book tends to treat it as ideology, it is important to see that liberalism itself is not a sociological theory. However, functionalism has many similarities with liberal thought and, especially as developed in the United States, has become the academic justification of modern capitalist societies. For this reason, subsequent chapters often discuss liberalism and functionalism together.

CONCLUSION

This chapter introduced the second sociological concept used to describe any society — the concept of social structure. While culture is the symbolic component of society, social structure captures the way society is actually organized. Every society has relatively stable ways of organizing who does what and of directing the activities of the group.

Every society differentiates among people and assigns them roles: this is the most primary level of social structure. Some people are women, some are men; some are teachers, some truck drivers; some are mothers, some sons. The roles that a society creates and the expectations that accompany these roles regulate individuals' lives to a large extent.

These roles, however, are performed within particular areas of social life, which are organized in identifiable ways: this is the intermediate level of social structure. The church may be congregational, the family patriarchal, the workplace undemocratic, power centralized, marriage relationships monogamous, ownership of resources collective, and status and rewards may be accessible through open competition. The way any area of life is organized affects the roles available to people and shapes individual experience in profound ways.

The final level of analysis focusses on society as a whole. The parts of a society are connected in identifiable ways, enabling a discussion of types of society. The type of society one lives in affects the way areas of social life are organized and thus affects the roles available and the nature of one's experience.

In examining the relationship between culture and social structure, two distinct positions are taken. The first gives priority to culture and sees the way social life is organized as reflecting culture. The second gives priority to social structure and sees culture reflecting and supporting the way social life is organized. These ideas were brought together in the discussion of capitalist society and liberal philosophy, its cultural element.

The chapter concluded with a return to two broad sociological perspectives: functionalism and critical perspectives. Functionalism tends to justify the status quo by seeing the way the society is organized and the cultural values as necessary for maintaining the society in a harmonious state. Critical perspectives tend to be critical of both the way the society is organized and of the culture, seeing the cultural component of liberalism as an ideology seeking to justify the social structure and existing inequalities.

· · · · · · · ·

NOTES

· · · · · · · ·

1. The male role could also be considered oppressive. Evidence for its tensions and stresses includes the facts that men are more likely to commit suicide than their female counterparts (this may be the result of the differences in methods used by the two, however); are more likely to be arrested for drug or alcohol abuse; are more likely to be homeless; are more likely to die from homicide; and die younger, on average, than women.

2. Giddens (1990) identifies four large institutional dimensions of modernity: capital accumulation (capitalism), transformation of nature (industrialism), control of information and social supervision, and control of the means of violence.

3. Matthew Fisher, "Inuit Way of Adoption Continues to Flourish," *The Globe and Mail*, January 2, 1989, p. A1.

4. Sharon Cohen, "Everyone's a Boss," *The Globe and Mail*, December 17, 1990, p. B6.

5. Sweden was one of the first nations to reduce its fertility rate to what we now consider modern levels. This decline in fertility occurred at the same time as the welfare state was being developed with a range of "family friendly" social policies (see Popenoe, 1988). Italy now has the lowest rate, at 1.3.

6. There are many accounts of these types of society. Fried (1967) provides an analysis that reflects the point being made here. Giddens (1989: 42–56) also develops a useful societal classification.

7. It has long been assumed that the concept of evolution makes sense of social change or history. This has been a powerful image for social science, but not all accept this image any longer. If we reject this image, we also reject the notion of history having a unity and of there being unifying principles of social organization and social change. Like Giddens (1990: 6), however, we do not believe, if one rejects evolution, "that all is chaos or that an infinite number of purely idiosyncratic 'histories' can be written." In order to have a historical sociology,

we must accept that there are definite episodes of historical transition and that generalizations can be made about this transition.

8. Diamond, being an evolutionist, uses the term "primitive society" rather than hunting and gathering. He supports his use of the term by noting that the word means "primary" or "first of its kind." Unfortunately, it has also come to mean "uncivilized" or "backward." Most social scientists are reluctant to use this term because it appears to evaluate the societies as culturally inferior. We have therefore adopted the designation "hunter–gatherer."

9. Those who give priority to culture are sometimes called "idealists," and those who give priority to social structure are called "materialists."

10. For an interesting account of these early developments of Canadian public enterprise, see Hardin (1974).

11. Laxer (1989) points out that the National Policy actually encouraged foreign ownership of Canadian manufacturing because it focussed on obstacles to importing manufactures into Canada and not on foreign ownership of manufacturing within Canada.

12. For an account of how Canadian sociologists shifted their focus from culture to social structure, see Brym and Fox (1989).

13. The notions of portrait and panorama come from Nisbet (1976).

14. There is some debate about whether it makes more sense to refer to these societies as capitalist or as industrial, postindustrial, modern, and so on. This disagreement goes to the heart of sociology. Marx thought of modern societies as capitalist, since he gave priority to the form of ownership. Durkheim and, to some extent, Weber thought of modern societies as industrial, since they gave attention to the level of technology (the division of labour). Berger (1986) sides with Durkheim and argues that we think of modern society as industrial. Giddens (1990) takes the argument forward somewhat by arguing that this dichotomy has hampered our analysis. He argues that capitalism and industrialism are simply two equal dimensions of modern society. He identifies four institutional dimensions.

15. Heilbroner (1989) contrasts a market economy with a command economy, one in which a central authority commands the economy to produce specified types and quantities of goods. The now- abandoned communist regimes of eastern Europe were examples of this system.

16. Countries like South Africa test this claim. While South Africa does have an electoral system, the majority of citizens were unable to vote until 1994.

17. The association of capitalism and electoral democracy is very close, but some capitalist societies in the process of development, like Taiwan and Korea, exhibit a combination of authoritarian, military-supported politics and capitalism. Historical experience so far is that electoral democracy is the normal political system in mature capitalist societies.

18. Canada was not alone in taking considerable time to extend the vote to all adults: in Great Britain, for example, only 4 percent of adults could vote in 1832, and by 1911 less than 30 percent of the total adult population could vote.

19. Excerpted from Milton Friedman, *Capitalism and Freedom* (Chicago: University of Chicago Press, 1982), pp. 7–13. Reprinted with permission.

20. Terrence Corcoran, "The Magic of Free Markets is Bananas in Canada in January," *The Globe and Mail*, January 9, 1990, p. B2.

. . . .

FURTHER
READING
. . . .

Girvetz, Harry K. *The Evolution of Liberalism*. New York: Collier, 1963. A valuable introduction to the origins and transformation of liberalism.

Hostetler, J.A., and G.E. Huntington. *The Hutterites in North America*. New York: Holt, Rinehart and Winston, 1965. A functionalist view of a group of people, a community, as a connected whole.

Lee, Richard B. *The !Kung San: Men, Women, and Children in a Foraging Society*. New York: Cambridge University Press, 1979. A thorough study of a hunting and gathering society.

Luxton, Meg. *More Than a Labour of Love*. Toronto: Women's Press, 1980. A community study from a critical perspective, feminism.

Marchack, P. *Ideological Perspectives on Canada*, 3rd ed. Toronto: McGraw-Hill Ryerson, 1988. An account of competing ways to think about Canadian society.

Scott, James C. *The Moral Economy of the Peasant*. New Haven: Yale University Press, 1976. An absorbing study of peasant economic life.

Wolf, Eric. *Europe and the People Without History*. Berkeley: University of California Press, 1982. A good discussion of the impact of capitalism on precapitalist societies that became absorbed into the capitalist system.

. . . .

STUDY
QUESTIONS
. . . .

1. Choose an example of a social role that you occupy and list the main norms that suggest how it should be performed.

2. Provide a brief statement of the link between culture and social structure.

3. Outline the debate between those who adopt a culturally focussed versus a structurally focussed account of the characteristics of Canadian culture.

4. Describe the social structure of your workplace or educational institution by identifying the roles and describing the relationships among them.

5. Interview a friend or relative raised in a non-western society. Is liberal thought evident in the society in which he or she grew up? If not, what were the central values of that society?

6. What do you think liberal thought would say about arranged marriages? Authoritarian governments? Pornography? The criminalization of non-medical drugs?

7. Speak to a person of the other sex and discuss the language usage of men and women. Prepare a brief report.

8. Explain why the critical perspective describes liberal thought as an "ideology," even though it is such a central value or belief system in Canadian society.

. . . .

5 THE DEVELOPMENT OF MODERN SOCIETY

. . . .

KEY CONCEPTS
AND PHRASES
. . . .

affinal relationship
feudalism
kinship
manor
medieval period

nation-states
patriarchal
seigneurial system
vassalage

INTRODUCTION
. . . .

Sociology developed as a way to understand the nature of the rapidly developing capitalist societies of the nineteenth century. These societies represented a revolution in both culture and social structure: a new world of human relationships. The changes that capitalism represented can only be grasped by studying the nature of past societies. This chapter provides a historical outline of the development of capitalism and discusses the rise of feudalism and its decline as capitalist society developed in England.

. . . .

Societies are always changing, but they change most rapidly when new types of social relationships and new economic resources become dominant and the obstructions posed by older social values, traditional institutions, and economic structures are pushed aside. The seeds of modern capitalism, developed over several centuries in Europe, created a global revolution. Today the flow of capital and investment is increasingly mobile and unanchored in any particular nation-state.

Sociologists assume that all societies that encounter the influence of capitalist development experience similar changes in their culture and social structure. The experiences are not the same, since each blend of old and new cultural ideas and social structures is unique, but there are some patterns to the social changes that take place. Understanding the origins of capitalism is required to gain a perspective on the modern world and the global transformation that is driven by this new form of society.

THE RISE OF
FEUDAL SOCIETY
. . . .

Sociologists assume that the first human societies were organized around **kinship**. Kinship is the web of links between individuals created by sharing common blood descent, or by **affinal relationships**, the ties established with other families by marriage. In *all* traditional societies analyzed by social scientists, the founding principle of social structure is this web of relationships based on connections of blood and intermarriage. Unity was rarely a problem, since society was founded on intimate bonds that existed between individuals. When there was need to set and enforce some rules

Photo 5.1
Both Canadian and American societies are fundamentally capitalist. The New York Stock Exchange, perhaps the best-known symbol of North American free-market capitalism, is pictured here.

L.E. Frank / FIRST LIGHT

for social behaviour it was the community itself, sometimes embodied in a chief or elders, that performed this role. Diamond's comments on hunting and gathering societies (see Box 4.4) provide an outline of these early ways that humans lived together.

The social change from kin-based societies to larger units was a prolonged process. Today's nation-states arose slowly and unevenly from the tribal or community basis of traditional society; ethnic divisions sometimes reverse this process and break states down, once more, into smaller divisions. Larger units emerged as some tribes gained territory through conquest or spread their influence through alliances and intermarriage.

Outside the bonds of kin-based society, social life was unpredictable. Local wars might erupt, marauding bands might raze a community, or social life might be transformed by conquest and the setting up of empires. Empires, like those of Greece and Rome, rose and fell under waves of military assault and economic dislocation. Defence was the first priority, and social organization was often founded on the leadership of a military chief or band of armed warriors.

For about 700 years, from about 200 B.C. to A.D. 500, Europe was largely dominated by the military–economic system of the Roman empire. Roman power was constantly challenged during the period of empire, and control of territory shifted back and forth between the Roman armies and many military opponents. Finally, in the fifth century, the empire was overthrown by successive waves of assault from the so-called Barbarian invasions. Rome itself was sacked (looted and burned) in both 410 and 455. The western Roman empire had virtually collapsed by 476 (Grant, 1985: 85). Though there were periods of revival in Roman power, the fifth century marked the end of the relatively centralized imperial system that had shaped much of Europe. The roads and coinage system created by the Romans had supported extensive patterns of trade and economic development, but now social anarchy and economic dislocation engulfed Europe.

Waves of armed invaders swept into Europe as the Roman system declined. Western Europe was attacked from the south by Persians, from the east by Hungarians, and from the north by Scandinavians. The invasions from Scandinavia were prolonged, widespread, and unpredictable as the raiders penetrated deep inland along the navigable rivers of England, Belgium, Germany, the Netherlands, and

France. Some towns, still surrounded by the fortifications built by the Romans, were able to resist the invaders, but many trading centres along river routes were looted and burned and their inhabitants carried off into slavery. As late as 861 the merchants of Paris, attempting to escape the invaders by taking to their boats in the river Seine, were overtaken by the Scandinavian ships and carried off as prisoners (Bloch, 1961: 39).

Historian Marc Bloch suggests the state of European political disorder in a quotation from an assembly of the bishops of the French province of Rheims in 909:

> *You see before you the wrath of the Lord breaking forth. ... There is naught but*
> *towns emptied of their folk, monasteries razed to the ground or given to the flames,*
> *fields desolated. ... Everywhere the strong oppresseth the weak and men are like fish*
> *of the sea that blindly devour each other* (1961: 3).

Feudalism: A
Military–Economic
System
· · · · · · · ·

The collapse of empire destroyed centralized power and encouraged the development of **feudalism**. The security and order of communities could now only be established by the development of localized means for the defence of community and the protection of resources. A system of social organization that could equip, feed, and support a class of trained, skilled warriors had to be created. The classic form adopted in feudal times was the feudal manor, in which a warrior chief and his retinue were supported by the produce and revenue created by working the manorial lands (Bloch, 1961: 443). The economy of the manors was based on land rents, dues of produce, and often the labour of unfree serfs.

Serfs, who were bonded labourers, were the foundation of the system of manorial farming. They were bound to the lord and the manor by a variety of obligations and some rights. They were not slaves, because they were not treated as human commodities that could be bought and sold in the marketplace; but they were not legally free, because they were subject to compulsory labour duties on the lord's land and did not own land in their own right. They could not leave the estate and take up other employment.

Serfs were protected, however, against gross abuse because, though subject to the lord of their particular manor, they were also the subjects of superior lords or of a king. Unlike slaves, they could own personal property and were free to buy and sell anything except the land they occupied under the lord. They had some legal rights because the lord's domination over them was restricted to demands for agricultural work and regulated by legally enforceable customary rules (Lipson, 1945: 34–46). A common arrangement was for the lord to maintain a central farm, worked for him by the serfs, while the serfs had holdings scattered around the estate.

The lords also had obligations. They must defend and protect their serfs, provide food in times of scarcity or famine, and grant rights to the use of their resources, including horses and cattle, for agricultural work on the serf's own holding. The relationship of lord and serf therefore involved reciprocal rights and obligations that were regulated by law and custom.

This localized form of social organization was a response to the ruin of larger-scale political and economic systems (Coulborn, 1965: 4–11; Bloch, 1961: 443). It was also shaped by changes in military organization. Increasingly, armed horsemen replaced foot soldiers as the foundation of military power. The mounted, heavily armoured, horseman was an overwhelming opponent to the foot soldiers. Battle was transformed into a highly professional pursuit that demanded extensive training of the mounted warriors.[1] From perhaps the age of 12, boys of knightly rank and special ability would be schooled in the techniques of horseback battle. Horses were especially bred for use in battle, and expensive equipment was needed. These specialized warriors were supported by economic organizations capable of producing a surplus to sustain them (Coulborn, 1965: 7–9).

The manors in a whole region might be dominated by one leader with whom subordinate leaders would form alliances. The pledges of service and loyalty involved in this arrangement between leader and subordinate, relationships of military service and obedience, were a special form of relationship found in feudal society whereby a man became "the man of another man." This was the feudal institution of vassalage. Vassalage, the homage of one man to another and usually based on a duty of military service, appears in all recorded historical examples of feudalism, not only in Europe, but in China, Russia, and Japan (see Coulborn, 1965). Women were never directly involved in the military aspect of vassalage because all medieval cultures regarded them as incapable of military activity. Therefore, women were not generally permitted to inherit lands granted to male relatives in return for military services (Bloch, 1961: 220).

The social relationship of vassalage was a semi-religious bond: Imagine two men face to face; one wishing to serve, the other willing or anxious to be served. The former puts his hands together and places them thus joined, between the hands of the other man — a plain symbol of submission, the significance of which was sometimes further emphasized by a kneeling posture. At the same time, the person proffering his hands utters a few words — a very short declaration — by which he acknowledges himself to be the "man" of the person facing him. Then chief and subordinate kiss each other on the mouth, symbolizing accord and friendship. Such were the gestures — very simple ones, eminently fitted to make an impression on minds so sensitive to visible things — which served to cement one of the strongest social bonds known in the feudal era (Bloch, 1961: 145–146).

Society and Religion

Just as capitalist societies have a common cultural component, liberal ideology, European feudal societies also had a common cultural element, Roman Catholicism. The Catholic church existed side-by-side with the feudal structures of vassalage and the manor. Christianity had spread throughout Europe and the Middle East after the death of Jesus and by the fourth century it was adopted as the official religion of the Roman empire. The church became a parallel political and administrative system to the empire (Grant, 1985: 83). The church's religious organization, however, survived the decline of the empire. Many of the manors were ecclesiastical — run by the church — and the church was supported by local production and religious taxes. There was a close union of church and military–political authority. The church used its spiritual influence to uphold and legitimate the rule of lords and kings and was a foundation of the medieval political system.

Relationships of power and authority in feudal society were deeply personal and direct and were made sacred by the cultural solemnity in which they were held. It was a society bonded at the all-important local level by ties of tradition, family, and custom. It was a system of social organization that could remain stable only so long as economic and social life remained localized and simple.

The Decline of Feudalism in England

The feudal system had periods of fragmentation, when local organization was most important, and times of increased centralization, when regional domination might be established. More elaborate political systems sometimes emerged when lords became subordinate to others and recognized one leader or king. Kingship provided

Box 5.1
Feudalism in Canada?

The landholding system of France had a strong influence on the early settlement of French Canada, an area composed of parts of modern Nova Scotia, New Brunswick, Quebec, and Ontario. Although there was never a fully developed Canadian feudal system, with serfs and the system of vassals, there was a seigneurial system of landholding, introduced in 1627. At its greatest extent, it covered most of the land between the principal settlements of Montreal and Quebec.

Land was granted to nobility, to the church (to support the provision of hospital and educational services), and to military officers and government administrators. The holders of these seigneuries granted tenancies to individual small farmers ("habitants"). There were some features of feudal obligation in this relationship: the seigneur could establish a court of law, operate a mill (and require that the habitants pay taxes to grind their grain at the mill), and claim part of the habitant's crops. After 1700, there were also demands for labour services to the seigneur.

The crucial difference between the seigneurial system and the European system was that the habitants were not in any way bound to the land and were quite free to enter or leave landholding contracts. Because there was no legal subordination of habitant to seigneur (as in feudal lord-and-serf relationships), the obligations and duties were not extensive. It was common, because of the relative scarcity of people and plentiful supply of land, for seigneurs to out-bid each other in minimizing rents and other requirements in order to attract settlers to their land.

With the rise of British domination of Canada (after 1763) the seigneurial system ceased to expand and began to be seen as an obstacle to economic development. It was finally abolished in 1854 by a law that gave tenants rights to claim land they had traditionally held.

SOURCE: Adapted from William L. Marr and Donald G. Paterson, *Canada: An Economic History* (Toronto: Gage, 1980), pp. 76–82.

the foundations for the emergence of nation-states — clearly bounded territories, linking together people with some common history, customs, language, or religion. Areas with centralized authority were the first to secure the political foundations for the development of complex economies, trade, economic growth, and the beginnings of modern social organization.

England was one of the first coherent nation-states to emerge, and this was a key reason why it became the first industrial capitalist nation in the world. At a time when much of Europe was still in the throes of civil wars and foreign conquest, England was a relatively peaceful and secure kingdom, where trade and commerce could be carried out in fairly well-regulated and predictable circumstances (Elton, 1955). England was also the first European society to experience the breakdown of feudalism.

The Seeds of Capitalism in England
....

English medieval society was not uniformly feudal. While an area might be predominantly organized around the military–economic system of the manor, there were social statuses other than lords, military retainers, and serfs. Many individuals held land within estates as free tenants and freemen, a status sometimes granted by lords in recognition of faithful military service. Sometimes free status persisted from local traditions and custom; or areas may not have a manorial organization at all, but be based on free village settlements, in which land was farmed and owned outright by small farmers. There were free towns or cities in regions under the authority of royal charter, outside the social relationships of the feudal manor, and beyond the jurisdiction of the feudal lords.

Feudal social relationships, anchored in traditional authority and binding one person to another through labour services and military duties, existed parallel to relationships that were more modern in form: those of employer and wage employee, in which free contracts, rather than the traditional statuses of lord and servant, were the foundation of the relationship. The precise balance of feudal versus non-feudal relationships in English society in the medieval period (about 1000–1500) is not known, but it is clear that wage employment, and payments in cash for both work and rents of land, were important features of the economy (Kosminsky, 1962). Social change came from these non-feudal seeds within the society.

The most important single event in directly uprooting feudalism and serfdom in England, and paving the way for an economy of employers and workers engaged in production for trade, was the Black Death of the 1340s. This devastating plague killed at least a third, and perhaps half, of the total population of England. Its immediate effect was to transform the relative power of landowners and serfs: it dramatically increased the demand for labour at the same time as it created a surplus of agricultural land. Rents for land and demands for labour services began to fall, and serfs began to drift away from their traditional manors and move to other areas where they were usually welcomed, without questions, by other landlords eager to rent out land to them or employ them as wage labourers. By 1500, serfdom had become virtually extinct. The lower social classes were now small-holding peasant renters or wage labourers, and often a combination of both. So great was the relative change in the value of labour that real wages appear to have reached levels in 1450–1500 that would not be matched again until the second half of the nineteenth century (Brown and Hopkins, 1962: 179–196).

THE GROWTH OF TRADE
....

By 1500, England was both internally and externally a trading nation. The importance of trade in developing capitalism is why Wallerstein (1974) argued that capitalism was always a world system rather than strictly a national system. Major export commodities included tin, leather, carvings, grain, salt, dairy products, preserved fish, and — most important of all — raw wool and finished woollen cloth. Finished cloth soon became the most important trading commodity of all and the foundation of the first phase of England's development as an industrial nation. On the import side, silk, velvets, furs, spices, wine, gold, silver, and jewels were important.

As trade developed, the infrastructure for trade developed too. Most important was the growth of trading centres and urban development, and specific industries greatly expanded to service trade itself, especially shipbuilding. As towns developed at an accelerated pace, the number of people dependent on agricultural production, yet not direct food producers themselves, rose and encouraged the growth of more commercially directed farming.

Wool and woollen cloth were the most important trading commodities. Though not such a big employer as agriculture or building, the wool industry was, by far, the dominant manufacturing industry. Its early growth was based on a domestic system of organization. Merchant clothiers bought the raw wool and then "put it out" to home workers, at piece rates, for spinning, weaving, dyeing, and finishing. Both men and women were involved in this home-based production. Although women tended to specialize in spinning and men in the weaving and dyeing operations, there was no rigid division of labour. In addition, food production (of both crops and animals), dairy production, and brewing were crucial parts of the home economy. These activities were generally female dominated (Oakley, 1974).

Weaving was a fairly localized activity, but spinning was carried on over a wide area, since it took about six spinners to keep a single weaver supplied. There were some weaving workshops, employing perhaps six or more journeymen (graduate apprentice) weavers under a master weaver, but the typical form of production was for weavers to work for themselves in their home.

Woollen products had important characteristics as a mass trading commodity. Raw material was easily available; there were local manufacturing skills; the product was neither perishable nor breakable; and it was easy to transport. In addition, demand was guaranteed, because clothing was an essential. These factors all favoured woollen goods as the foundation of the first wave of the industrial revolution.

Woollen cloth had limits as a trading commodity: it was unsuitable for the rich markets opening up in Africa and the Arab societies of the Middle East. There was some development in the techniques of woollen cloth making in the mid-1500s that led to new, lighter cloths, but they were still of limited value in hot countries, and this inhibited the growth of the international mass market. However, these limitations did not prevent the woollen industry, other manufactures, shipbuilding, and military expenditures allied to trade from stimulating economic growth and the rise of a commercial economy.

INDUSTRIAL CAPITALISM: THE WORKSHOP AND FACTORY ARISE

The woollen industry established only the very beginnings of an industrial economy based on centralized mass production. The spread of that form of economic organization demanded a product that lent itself to mass markets and mass production on a factory scale. This product, the foundation of modern capitalism and the industrial revolution, was cotton cloth.

The cotton industry was the first to take on the centralized form of factory production. Its growth, under the impact of a buoyant internal and international mass market, was a new historical phenomenon. Towns and cities associated with the industry experienced extraordinary growth. Manchester, for example, experienced a tenfold increase in its population in only 70 years (Hobsbawm, 1969: 56). The cotton industry, from its beginnings in England, was associated with trade to Africa and Asia. It was always an export industry, following in the footsteps of British exploration and military conquest. In Africa it immediately became associated with the slave trade. Ships left England carrying cotton goods to Africa. There they loaded a human cargo of slaves for transport to the cotton plantations of the Caribbean and, later, the southern United States. From those regions, ships carried back raw cotton for manufacture in England.

The ancient exploitation of slavery, combined with new techniques of industrial production, created opportunities for immense profits to finance re-investment in the cotton industry. Many other industries, transportation, iron and steel, coal, and building also experienced massive expansion under the impact of this cotton-led economic growth. The sheer size of the cotton-based economy is impressive even today: it is estimated that just prior to the American Civil War (1860) there were *four million* slaves in the southern United States, almost all of them working in cotton-linked activity (Thistlethwaite, 1961: 151). In England, at the other end of the cotton trade, there were more than a half-million jobs directly in cotton manufacture in the mid-19th century.

Technological innovation was quite rapid. In the 1780s, spinning was revolutionized by the invention of a steam-powered spinning mule that served to overcome the traditional bottleneck of unmechanized spinning. After 1815, power looms were rapidly developed. They quickly ended the decentralization of the weaving industry and brought it into a factory-centred form of organization. The growth of machine technology and the displacement of small-scale, localized manufacture was rapid and irreversible and spread from industry to industry and to new industries, seemingly created overnight. English historian Eric Hobsbawm writes that the new economic system led to the rapid application of innovations as capitalist factory owners applied a "rigorous rationalism to their methods of production" (1969: 60).

The systematic application of technology and the rational organization of work to enhance human labour power and pursue maximum productivity was a new phenomenon in history. The economies of the past had focussed on securing subsistence and self-sufficiency. Production for trade and exchange, though always present, was secondary. Now production for the purpose of trade was the central dynamic behind economic activity and the goal of securing profit, in order to re-invest and expand the capacity to produce, drove the system onward. With the spread of factories and the general development of a market-directed system of production, there came about "a new economic relationship between men, a new system of production, a new rhythm of life, a new society, a new historical era" (Hobsbawm, 1969: 65).

With the industrial revolution, society entered a continuous cycle of "self-sustained economic growth by means of perpetual technological revolution and social transformation" (Hobsbawm, 1969: 34–5).

The Capitalist Revolution

The development and full emergence of capitalism as the primary mode of economic organization marked a complete revolution. Individuals were no longer bound to each other by tradition, custom, and complex webs of obligation and service. Instead, the relation of person to person in the economic activity of everyday life was typically that of employer to employee — a relationship based on the formal legal equality of individuals. The bond, such as it was, in the new economic relationships was primarily that of contract: an agreement by which one person would provide labour to another in return for wage payment. Unlike the social relationships of the past, this one was not overlaid with ties of permanence and special obligations. It was founded in the market-exchange of labour for wages and would last only as long as economic advantage continued for the parties. The employee, if offered higher wages or more appealing work elsewhere, could, and did, leave and go to work for someone else. The employer, as soon as it was advantageous to do so, could simply terminate the worker's employment and, without responsibility of any kind, end the wage contract.

New Social Values

In the marketplace for goods and services, it was now expected that individuals would act according to their own interests and seek to gain the maximum personal benefit from their dealings. This was true of all market exchanges. No longer were people's economic acts and decisions seen as having non-economic, or moral, dimensions: the marketplace of selling and buying was considered morally neutral.

To buy a commodity for the purpose of selling it later at a profit was seen as rational, enterprising, and sensible. In feudal society and right up to the emergence of capitalism as the dominant economic system, it had been seen as outright exploitation. In pre-capitalist Europe, it was regarded as quite immoral that people should seek to control supply and take advantage of induced shortages to charge higher prices. A key influence in creating and upholding these attitudes to trade and commerce was the Roman Catholic church. In Catholic theology, strivings for profit and advantage were a distraction from the eternal purpose of human life: the glorification of God. To derive a profit from market transactions that went beyond the just compensation for one's cost and labour was an offence to God's moral order. Many towns passed local laws to regulate conduct in their marketplaces and attempted to compel merchants to sell at a "just price," fair to both buyers and sellers (Lipson, 1945: 299). Those who engaged in what is now called wholesaling — buying production in bulk for retail sale in the marketplace — were said to be "a manifest oppressor of the poor and a public enemy of the whole commonality and country" (Lipson, 1945: 301).

In the newly emerging society, where market transactions rapidly became the dominant form of economic exchange, old bonds of tradition, reciprocal responsibility, and service were steadily eliminated. The ties that bound members of the society together, ties of personal loyalty and obligation, made concrete by being based in the land or in military or household service, were now replaced by the principle of contract. People were now bound to each other only insofar as their relationship promoted their mutual self-interest or provided access to the only means of livelihood.

Community and the New Society

The transformation from societies chiefly bonded together by tradition and status to those focussed on the theoretically voluntary bonds of contract was profound (see Maine, 1960 [1861]):

> *Modern societies are perhaps the first in history, not just to change, but also to be aware of change as the very nature of society. While in most past societies the ideal image was of an established and unchanging order, the ideal image of modern societies is of a steady economic growth involving constant upheavals in the social organization* (Aron, 1968: 13).

This awareness of the depth and range of social change underlay the classic sociology of the nineteenth century.[2] The most important work of this period is concerned with comprehending how the newly arising capitalist societies that were overthrowing the traditional order would provide a new basis for social integration and harmony. Could the individualism and self-interest that characterized capitalism provide the necessary foundations for community life? Understanding how the capitalist revolution was affecting, changing, and perhaps threatening social life must be the paramount concern of a purposeful analysis of society.

CONCLUSION

This chapter travelled a long distance in time in a few pages to provide the briefest sketch of the historical changes that led to today's society. The sketch makes clear why the first modern sociologists were so concerned with the question of how to preserve social unity and order. They were trying to make sense of a revolution in ideas, beliefs, social organization, and the economy. This revolution continues today. As a result, many of the ideas that were important to nineteenth-century sociology remain central to analyzing Canada and other modern societies.

Feudal society, centred as it was on military and political life, removed women from power and influence. Feminist sociologists, over the past 20 or more years, have sought to re-examine the earlier portrayal of history and recapture the previously neglected roles and activities of women. Much of this analysis has focussed on the patriarchal character of past societies (Lerner, 1986). Women's lives and work were profoundly affected by the emergence of capitalist society. The causes and consequences of these changes will be examined in subsequent chapters.

NOTES

1. In societies in which the basic form of military organization was an armed peasantry, the system of feudalism and the manor did not generally arise, since there were no great distinctions between the military capabilities of social classes and there was no group of military professionals. Parts of the Netherlands, Scotland, and Scandinavia are examples of those societies (Bloch, 1961: 248–444).

2. Giddens (1990) argues that even sociology, with its theories of the "evolution" of modern society, has often failed to grasp the profoundness of the change experienced during this period. He uses the term "discontinuities" to capture this change and argues that the discontinuities associated with modernity were and are more substantial than those of any previous period. He discusses three types of discontinuity: the pace of social change, the scope of social change, and the nature of modern institutions.

FURTHER READING

Anderson, Bonnie S., and Judith P. Zinsser. *A History of Their Own: Women of Europe From Prehistory to the Present.* Vols. 1 and 2. New York: Harper and Row, 1988. A much-needed resource for recovering women's history and writing history with women in mind.

Heilbroner, R. *The Making of Economic Society,* 8th ed. Englewood Cliffs, N.J.: Prentice-Hall, 1989. An accessible account of the modern market society's rise from the economic systems of the past.

Hobsbawm, E. *Industry and Empire.* London: Pelican Books, 1969. An account of the industrial revolution in England, skilfully weaving historical, political, and sociological analysis. Contains many useful graphs and charts of key social and economic statistics.

Holton, Robert J. *The Transition from Feudalism to Capitalism.* New York: St. Martin's, 1985. A review of the attempts to explain the transition from feudalism to capitalism.

Marr, William L., and Donald G. Paterson. *Canada: An Economic History.* Toronto: Gage, 1980. A survey of the economic development of Canada and an analysis of the unique patterns of economic growth that emerge from Canada's economic and political geography. Contains an extensive bibliography of sources in Canadian economic and social history.

STUDY QUESTIONS

1. Outline the relationship in feudal society between social structure and cultural values.

2. In what ways was the growth of trade a threat to feudal society?

3. Why did England become the world's first capitalist industrial society?
4. Are "contrasting pattern variables" an accurate picture of the differences between feudal society and capitalist society?
5. Why does capitalism stimulate continual technological development and economic growth?

6 SOCIOLOGY AND THE NEW SOCIETY

INTRODUCTION

The previous chapter outlined the emergence of modern capitalist society; this chapter reviews the response of three classical sociologists to this new society. Karl Marx, Max Weber, and Émile Durkheim each looked at modern society as a connected whole. They considered its culture, its social structure, and the relationship of the two. Marx's central ideas are the concept of **alienated labour** and **materialist understanding of history**. Weber developed the concepts of **rationalization** and **bureaucracy**. Durkheim's work focussed on the idea of **anomie**. These three authors and these key ideas will be encountered again in subsequent chapters.

The coming of capitalist society produced a challenge to social thinking. How was such a radically new culture and social structure to be comprehended? This chapter introduces some of the sociological ideas that emerged in the effort to understand the new society. It focusses on the work of Karl Marx, Max Weber, and Émile Durkheim. The remainder of this book demonstrates how their ideas, and others, can be applied in the study of Canadian society.

THE LOSS OF COMMUNITY

. . . .

Modern sociology originated in France with Henri de St. Simon (1760–1825) and Auguste Comte (1798–1857). France was a troubled society during their lifetimes, undergoing violent political revolution, war, and economic transformation. These two men began a discipline devoted to understanding society and argued that it could improve society. Comte, however, developed the new field of sociology (he coined the word) farthest.

Comte: A Positive Role for Sociology

. . . .

Comte's central concern was not "the perception of the new but, rather, an anguished sense of the breakdown of the old, and of the anarchy which day by day envelops society as a consequence. The ghost of traditional community hovers over all his sociology" (Nisbet, 1966: 57).

Traditional community was a powerful and appealing vision for people troubled by the disorder of their own society. Past societies seemed to have the solid foundations of traditional and intimate bonds between individuals. The intellectual authority of religion and the church shaped and unified the culture and regulated social values. Social life was based on the natural rhythms of the seasons and the age-old activities of agriculture and crafts. Comte described these past societies as theological–military societies, founded on the authority of the church and the military power of warrior lords.

The new societies appeared to have much more fragile foundations and to be threatened by weak community bonds and social disorder. Industrial revolution generated constant social and economic transformation and promoted a new culture of scientific and rational thinking. Comte called this new type of society scientific–industrial society.

Comte believed that sociology could guide society through the transformation it was undergoing. Sociological analysis would make it possible to uncover laws governing the functioning of society, and people could use this knowledge to purposefully shape the social world (Aron, 1968: 69). Just as physics and chemistry had uncovered the laws that govern the natural order of the world, sociology could reveal the laws that underlay ordered society.

Comte was optimistic that the new "positive" scientific discipline of sociology could lead to enlightened government and constructive measures to improve society. Others were more negative; their sociological ideas drew a very unfavourable contrast between traditional and modern society.

Tonnies: A Distinction That Has Become Central

. . . .

Ferdinand Tonnies (1855–1936), a German sociologist, was also important in shaping the central concerns of sociology. Tonnies contrasted the "Gemeinschaft" of the past to the modern "Gesellschaft."

Gemeinschaft means community. It is a social life in which individuals are bonded together by face-to-face interactions, have widely based ties of kinship, friendship, and mutual obligation to each other, and are caught up in the collective life of the group.

Gesellschaft means society or association. Individuals are focussed on their self-interest, and community bonds are weak. Social relationships are generally formal and entered into for specific, narrow purposes. For example, work is structured by contracts limited to the exchange of payment for labour and does not involve broad moral commitments or obligations. Individuals are primarily involved with others to reach defined ends or goals, and not for the sake of a social relationship itself.

Tonnies thought that the individualism of the new capitalist society would undermine community, weaken the family, and create impersonal and anonymous social relationships. He called for a resuscitation of family and community life, describing it as a "moral necessity" and arguing that co-operatives and other small associations must be created to revive community within the modern Gesellschaft (1963[1887]: 197). The image Tonnies presented of contrasting forms of social life continues to influence modern sociology.

THE SOCIOLOGY OF CAPITALISM The following sections of this chapter introduce the ideas of the three most important founders of sociology: Karl Marx, Max Weber, and Émile Durkheim, all of whom developed comprehensive sociological analyses of capitalist society. Their work continues to influence modern sociology, and many of the central concerns of the discipline can be traced directly back to their very divergent views of capitalist society.

KARL MARX

THE REVOLUTIONARY

Marx was before all else a revolutionist. His real mission in life was to contribute, in one way or another, to the overthrow of capitalist society (Engels 1968[1883]: 436).

BORN
Trier, Germany, May 5, 1818
DIED
London, England, December 2, 1883
WORK
Political journalist and editor in Germany, France, and Belgium, 1842–1849
Exiled from Germany and banished from France, 1849
Research, writing, and political organization in England, 1849–1883
MAJOR WRITINGS
The German Ideology (with Frederick Engels), 1846
Manifesto of the Communist Party (with Frederick Engels), 1848
Wage Labour and Capital, 1848
Capital, 1863–1867
The Civil War in France, 1871
Critique of the Gotha Programme, 1875

Karl Marx Karl Marx never described himself as a sociologist, yet his ideas are a foundation of modern sociology (see Box 6.1).[1] His social and economic analysis was directed to the overthrow of capitalist society and its replacement by a democratic and co-operative society based on common ownership of productive resources. There is no ethical neutrality in Marx's work. Instead, we encounter a condemnation of capitalism and a theory of revolutionary liberation.

- Alienated labour
- Class
- Class struggle
- Class-for-itself
- Contradictions of capitalism
- Exchange value versus use value
- Materialist conception of history

Marx thought that capitalist society had not brought democracy and individual freedom, but was just a new form of domination by few over the many. Like the class-divided societies of the past, capitalism rested on mass oppression. The mass of the people were denied the opportunity to develop themselves freely and fully and to express themselves in shaping and controlling their daily lives.

The Materialist Conception of History

Marx's analysis of capitalism, and his approach to social analysis in general, rested on a materialist understanding of society. While pluralistic theories of society claim that society is shaped by a complex of influences and that no single influence is dominant, Marxist ideas insist that the social and technological organization of production, the mode of production, is the key force in shaping society.

> *In the social production of their life, men enter into definite relations that are indispensable and independent of their will, relations of production which correspond to a definite stage of development of their material productive forces. The sum total of these relations of production constitutes the economic structure of society, the real foundation, on which rises a legal and political superstructure and to which correspond definite forms of social consciousness. The mode of production of material life conditions the social, political and intellectual life process in general. It is not the consciousness of men that determines their being, but, on the contrary, their social being that determines their consciousness* (Marx, 1968[1859]: 182).

Understanding the social and technical organization of the economy in any society provides insight into its social organization and cultural ideas. This applies as well to understanding institutions like the state, law, education, the values and structure of the family, and the dominant social and political ideas in the society.

Marx did not claim that history and social change are shaped solely by material forces. He warned against trying to turn the materialist view of history into a "master key" that could explain all historical experience. All historical situations must be analyzed separately to be fully understood. Individuals and ideas can and do have an impact on history. People make their own history, but they must do so in conditions that have been given to them (Marx, 1968 [1852]: 95).

Materialism and Social Life

Marx distinguished types of society by their differing modes of production. He speculated that in the beginning of human social life, people lived together in a state of **primitive communism**. They worked together in the creation of their means of life, gathering plants and fruits and hunting animals for food and useful materials. In these earliest societies, there was no concept of private property, since the resources of nature were equally open to all. Production took place entirely for need; there was no accumulation of resources and wealth. Individual's powers to produce were not much in excess of their needs for subsistence: a day's work produced a day's living, and little else.

Between 15 000 and 20 000 years ago, pastoral and horticultural societies emerged. Pastoral society was based on the domestication of animals, horticulture on the growing of crops. Instead of simply living off the resources of nature, humans now added to nature. The result was a great increase in the productivity of labour and the wealth of societies. It became possible for people to elaborate their cultural activities, to spend time shaping tools, making baskets and boxes, and creating furnishings and pottery.

The development of an improved material basis for social life had other consequences. For the first time it became consistently possible for individuals to produce more than they needed for immediate survival: humans became capable of creating a surplus of production over need. The accumulation of wealth became possible, and inequality soon began to appear as some people gained control of economic resources and excluded others.

The Emergence of Social Inequality

Perhaps the earliest inequality to emerge in these pastoral and horticultural societies was between men and women. Inequality developed because individual humans, now able to produce more than they needed for subsistence, themselves became economic assets. Women had children and became producers of producers: they created the labour power that was the source of wealth. Men exerted domination over women as a way to control the production of producers. A new emphasis in human culture was placed on separating kinship from community, so that specific individuals became linked in stable relationships and obligations to other specific individuals. The concept of "family wealth" emerged. Men dominated the producers of producers (women) and took power and authority within the kinship system (Lerner, 1986: 46–53; Engels, 1968[1884]). The resulting subordination of women is called **patriarchy**, a form of culture and social structure in which women are placed in inferior statuses and their role in society is restricted and devalued.

The growth of sexual inequality was accompanied by other divisions in wealth and status. Since producers are economic assets, there was wealth and power to be gained by those who controlled the producers' labour. Originally, the rights to another's labour were directed through the kinship system. But it could also be exerted through new types of relationships — slavery, serfdom, and, of course, the wage system of modern capitalism.

With the rise of surplus production there grew also an unremitting contest between groups for the control and possession of this surplus. Marx referred to these groups as **classes** and believed that, with the exception of primitive communism, "the history of all hitherto existing society is the history of class struggles" (Marx and Engels, 1968 [1848]: 35). Capitalism was just a new form of this class domination, disguised by the fictions of legal equality and freedom of contract.

Class Society

Surplus production makes class-divided societies possible. Two common forms of class society emerged before capitalism. In ancient societies, individuals were divided into two great classes, citizens and slaves. Citizens had legal freedom and lived off the surplus production of subjected slaves. Slaves had no legal rights and, generally, no security of person. They were treated as instruments of labour, traded like a commodity in the marketplace, and valued only for their capacity to produce goods and services for their citizen masters. Marx called this system the ancient mode of production. The second common form was the **feudal mode of production** in which the central class division is between landlords and a serf class of bonded agricultural labourers. Here, the ownership and control of land allowed a group of landlords to dominate a class of unfree serfs and seize control of their surplus production. The feudal form of society broke down for many reasons, chiefly linked to the rise of trade and the development of markets for goods and services. In its place emerged the capitalist mode of production.

Marx and Engels devoted a lifetime to studying and analyzing the capitalist mode of production. They began by observing that capitalism, too, is a system in which the social organization of production allows one class of people to dominate others and to seize control of the society's surplus. In capitalist society, all individuals are formally free and equal; no one is physically forced into economic relations with another. Relations between worker and employer are voluntary and entered into on the basis of contract, not force. But capitalist societies have private ownership of the means of production, and the vast majority of the population does not own the means of production. They must exchange their labour power for wages in order to survive.

In fact, capitalist society only develops when the worker who produces is separated from ownership and control of the means of production. Most of the population lose independent access to land, equipment, or machinery, from which they can make a living. In agriculture, the feudal system breaks down and is replaced by a system based on landowning and wage labouring. Many subsistence producers are forced off the land by termination of their rights to use common lands ("enclosures") or by direct eviction from customarily held land. In manufacturing, individuals who spin or weave on their own equipment in their own homes are forced from independent production and marketing by larger-scale systems dominated by merchant clothiers. Later, spinning and weaving, and many other home-located occupations, are relocated in centralized factories and workshops.

The Growth
of Capitalism

• • • • • • • •

Once manufacturing was centralized and specialized and a rigorous **division of labour** had been established, human productivity rose beyond anything ever imagined before. The great classical economist Adam Smith (1723–1790) explained and illustrated the process in relation to the production of pins:

One man draws the wire, another straightens it, a third cuts it, a fourth points it, a fifth grinds it at the top for receiving the head; to make the head requires two or three distinct operations; to put it on is a peculiar business, to whiten the pins[2] is another; it is even a trade by itself to put them into the paper; and the important business of making a pin is, in this manner, divided into about eighteen distinct operations. ... I have seen a small manufactory of this kind where only ten men were employed, and where some of them consequently performed two or three distinct operations. ... They could, when they exerted themselves, make ... among them upwards of forty-eight thousand pins a day. ... But if they had all wrought separately and independently ... they certainly could not each of them have made twenty, perhaps not one pin in a day (Smith, 1937[1776]: 4–5).

No home-based craft could survive against competition from producers using such a systematic division of labour and an increasing level of technology. In the social organization of production under capitalism, the main beneficiary of this rise in labour productivity was the capitalist. Though unions developed quite quickly with the onset of capitalism, they were initially very weak, faced legal obstacles and outright suppression, and had little bargaining power because of constant competition for work from large numbers of unemployed. Therefore wages tended to be close to the bare minimum necessary for the physical maintenance of the worker. The additional wealth generated by rising productivity was captured by the capitalist owner of the workplace and, under the force of the competitive dynamics of the capitalist economy, was quickly re-invested in the enlargement and technical development of the means of production. In this process, technical development was unending, and sector after sector of the economy was brought into the framework of capitalist organization (see Box 6.2).

The Capitalist Machine

The most distinctive feature of capitalist production is that it is carried out for the purpose of producing something for exchange rather than for immediate use. The capitalist starts with money and resources of land, materials, and labour, and puts these to work in the production of an object — a commodity — which is then sold for money. If the capitalist has conducted the transactions wisely, the original money investment and all costs have now been recaptured, with a profit, by the subsequent sale of the commodity. The capitalist has realized a surplus value and now has increased amounts of money with which to start the process again of converting this money, via the manufacture of a commodity, into a larger sum of money. It is this money–commodity–money circulation that is the driving dynamic of the whole capitalist system.

Production is carried out for profit; profit is reinvested to expand or technically advance production. This leads to "self-sustained economic growth by means of perpetual technological revolution and social transformation" (Hobsbawm, 1969: 34–35), a unique characteristic of capitalist economies. Observing the extraordinary inventiveness and dynamism of capitalism, Marx and Engels wrote that capitalist industry had revolutionized the productive capacity of society. In less than 100 years the new system had created more economic development than had all the preceding generations of human history (1968[1848]: 39–40).

Capitalism generated a revolution in the productive capacity of society, but the structure of private ownership excluded the mass of the population from an equal share in the benefits. The capitalists paid the workers less than the value of the workers' production, thus gaining control of the surplus and accumulating wealth. And work, a fundamental human activity, was directed and controlled by someone other than the worker. The worker was put to work for a number of hours at a task defined by someone else and in a way planned by someone else. In a work process of this sort, there could be little involvement of the individual and little satisfaction found in the work. For Marx, this was the root problem of capitalist society: it developed and intensified alienated labour.

Alienated Labour

Alienate means to transfer ownership, withdraw, or estrange. In withdrawing, estranging, and taking the title to the products of labour, capitalism, said Marx, divorced humans from something essentially human: self-expression in work. The uniqueness of humans as living creatures lies in the fact that they are conscious beings and that this consciousness expresses itself in a desire to produce and create. Humans express

Box 6.2
Engels on the Loss
of Community

Frederick Engels also expressed the classic theme of nineteenth century sociology — the loss of community and the fear that the growth of capitalism, with its polarization of rich and poor, threatened unified social life. At the age of 24, while visiting London, Engels wrote about the threat to social unity posed by the new industrial capitalist age.

The hundreds of thousands of all classes and ranks crowding past each other, are they not all human beings with the same qualities and powers, and with the same interest in being happy? And have they not, in the end, to seek happiness in the same way, by the same means? And still they crowd by one another as though they had nothing in common, nothing to do with one another, and their only agreement is the tacit one, that each keep to his own side of the pavement, so as not to delay the opposing streams of the crowd, while it occurs to no man to honour another with so much as a glance. ... And, however much one may be aware that this isolation of the individual, this narrow self-seeking is the fundamental principle of our society everywhere, it is nowhere so shamelessly barefaced, so self-conscious as just here in the crowding of the great city. The dissolution of mankind into monads, of which each one has a separate principle and a separate purpose, the world of atoms, is here carried out to its utmost extreme ... people regard each other only as useful objects; each exploits the other and the end of it all is, that the stronger treads the weaker under foot, and that the powerful few, the capitalists, seize everything for themselves, while to the weak many, the poor, scarcely a bare existence remains. ... Everywhere barbarous indifference, hard egotism on one hand, and nameless misery on the other, everywhere social warfare, every man's house in a state of seige, every-where reciprocal plundering under the protection of the law, and all so shameless, so openly avowed that one shrinks before the consequences of our social state as they manifest themselves here undisguised, and can only wonder that the whole crazy fabric still hangs together.

SOURCE: Frederick Engels, *Conditions of the Working Class in England in 1844* (London: George Allen & Unwin, 1897[1845]), pp. 24–25.

their consciousness and their intellects through work. Other animals produce — beavers build dams, birds make nests — but they do so instinctively. Human work, however, is a creative process because it is carried out not only for function, but also for beauty and artistic expression. Humans gain satisfaction and meaning from creating things that embody their artistic and emotional personality: they see their own reflection in a world that they have constructed. If work as a form of self expression is replaced by work motivated solely by profit, then it becomes alienated from the worker and disconnected from personal identity.

The Sociology
of Revolution

Marx not only criticized capitalism, he predicted its revolutionary overthrow. Revolution, he claimed, would be generated by the dynamics of capitalism itself, by the laws of motion of the capitalist mode of production.

The laws of motion of capitalism led to an intensification of class conflict and to radical economic instability. Class conflict must grow because of the nature of capital accumulation in competitive conditions. Under competitive conditions, there is a tendency for factories and workshops to grow larger as more non-human capital is used in production. Companies not current with technological innovations are forced out of the market, and the winners become increasingly large and centralized.

The centralization and growing scale of production has two consequences that propel capitalist society toward revolutionary social change. First, it alters the whole social situation of workers. Instead of working in isolated small-scale workshops or in domestic industry, they are drawn together in urban concentrations. Social communication becomes more intense. It becomes possible to develop workers' organizations (unions and political parties) that were previously held back by lack of class identity. Instead of simply existing as a class of workers, sharing a social situation but not conscious of common interests (a **class-in-itself**), the workers come to see that they have common interests that unite them in common opposition to capitalists (a **class-for-itself**). Worker organizations make it possible to demand a different distribution of the revenue from production (between labour and the accumulation of capital) and to have some control over the conditions of work.

Capitalist organization of the economy creates the **proletariat** — the workers who have no other resort for economic survival than to sell their labour for wages (to the **bourgeoisie**, the owners of the means of production) in the marketplace. Marx assumed that unceasing competition between capitalists would tend to drive down the level of wages. There would be a constant search to cut labour costs and to substitute more productive machine technology for human labour. Real wages would fall, and a great mass of people would live in such miserable conditions that they would have "nothing to lose but their chains. They have a world to win" (Marx and Engels, 1968[1848]: 63).

Workers and capitalists form two antagonistic classes locked into a permanent battle. The workers organize to promote good wages and conditions; the capitalists seek to promote higher profit through the intensification of work and lowered wages. Workers increasingly come to believe that collective ownership and control of the means of production will create a more just and satisfying social life. **Class consciousness** leads to a complete rejection of the capitalist system by the great mass of the people.

Class consciousness and political struggle also express a contradiction within the structure of the capitalist economy. Marx argued that capitalist economies are ultimately destroyed by the capitalist economic system itself, by its own internal logic.

In previous societies, individuals produced within a limited framework of specialization and exchange. Individuals, families, and small groups in workshops were the typical units of production. But in capitalist society, production is carried out on a massive scale. It is a system in which the capacity to produce is constantly expanded as industrial organization and technology advance.

Production has a society-wide character; it requires great numbers of people to work together and complex chains of interdependency between different industries and economic sectors. But the structure of private ownership leads to an increasing polarization of wealth, as large capitalists squeeze out the small and use their economic dominance to keep wages low.

The accumulation and concentration of capital strengthens the capacity of the capitalist to increase profit and weakens the ability of the workers to maintain their wages. Productive capacity expands, but the capacity to consume is reduced. Masses of goods and services are produced, yet the majority of people cannot afford them.

Capitalism, by its nature, cannot reconcile the enormous scale of production with the private purpose of production. This dislocation of the economic system — the "anarchy" of capitalist production — leads to mass unemployment, increasing poverty, and finally into revolutionary working-class action to transform the economic and political system.[3] In creating the proletariat, capitalism creates the agent for its own destruction.

Post-Revolutionary
Society
· · · · · · · · ·

Marx theorized an economic and social revolution but was quite sketchy and vague about the type of society that would follow this revolution. He always stated that it was not possible to foretell the lessons that would be learned in a society that had not yet been accomplished.

He assumed that postrevolutionary society would be without classes and class exploitation. In the process of capitalist development, the working class becomes the vast majority of the population, and its revolutionary seizure of political power and of the means of production simply realizes democracy: true democracy. In a society where the means of production are held in common, there will be no exploitation of one class by another and no private interests to divert the people from administering the society for the collective benefit. Though the work of production will still remain a necessity, people will have much greater control over it and will be freely able to choose alternative activities. In political life, the state and the government will be transformed into institutions that directly serve the majority of the society, rather than instruments that uphold the class rule of capitalism (Marx 1968[1875]: 330). Marx had little to say about the institutions of the new society, though he praised direct democracy, with its recall of delegates, rather than the representative parliaments of capitalist society. And, importantly, the mode of production would itself become democratic — managed and directed by the workers themselves in the collective interest.

Marxism has been a major cultural influence in society, not only in politics but also in the way people have come to see and understand the rest of human activity. Marxism provides the student of society with a radically alternative view to the liberal ideology of individualism and private enterprise. It proposes a very different understanding of capitalist society, and its ideas will be used to cast many familiar parts of modern society in a very unfamiliar light throughout this book.

MAX WEBER
· · · · · · · · · · · · ·

THE PESSIMIST
· · · · · · · · · · · · ·

The fate of our times is characterized by rationalization and intellectualization and, above all, by the "disenchantment of the world" (Gerth and Mills, 1970: 155).

· · · · · · · ·

BORN
Erfurt, Germany, April 21, 1864
DIED
Munich, Germany, June 14, 1920

(continued)

(continued)
WORK
Law professor, Berlin, 1892
Professor of Political Economy, Freiberg, 1894
Professor of Economics, Heidelberg, 1896
Research, writing, administration, 1896–1920
MAJOR WRITINGS
Methodological Essays, 1902
The Protestant Ethic and the Spirit of Capitalism, 1904
Economy and Society, 1910–1914
Sociology of Religion, 1916

Max Weber

Max Weber, like Karl Marx, brings a very different perspective to understanding capitalist society from that suggested by liberal ideology. Unlike Marx, Weber had no definite political program. Although he had progressive views, he always insisted that sociology should not be concerned with the promotion of values. The task of sociology was to understand society, not to develop a political program for its transformation. Weber did not have a general theory, and he considered the materialist conception of history too narrow to provide an effective analysis of society.

Weber insisted that a whole range of factors, in addition to the social organization and technological base of the economy, influenced the development and qualities of society: religion, cultural values, political and military power, geography and external relations, and the actions of individuals (see Box 6.3). It was never possible, therefore, to adequately analyze a society within the confines of materialism.

Weber's Sociology of Capitalism

What caused the rise of capitalism? Weber's answer was that there was no single cause. History is complex. At any time in the history of a society there are many cross-cutting forces influencing how people live, how they think, and what they believe. There were many societies whose *potential* for undergoing a rapid transformation to industrial capitalism was no less than that of western Europe. They had similar economic endowments and levels of political order, yet they did not make a transformation to capitalism. Capitalism arose only in some countries of western Europe; in the rest of Europe and the world there was no internally generated break with tradition, no industrial revolution, no rising of a scientific age.

What special additional factors in some areas of western Europe were absent elsewhere? Weber observed that in Europe there was a distinct pattern to levels of capi-

Box 6.3
Key Ideas of a Weberian Sociology

- Rationalization
- Bureaucracy
- Protestant ethic
- Status groups
- Types of authority

talist economic development. In Catholic–dominated countries, capitalist economic development was generally far behind those areas where Protestantism was dominant. Religion also appeared to affect individuals' social roles. Most of the leading capitalists and skilled industrial workers of Europe were Protestant. The Roman Catholic upper class, in contrast, favoured education in humanistic studies — rather than sciences, applied sciences, economics, or commerce — and tended to steer clear of business pursuits. The Catholic working classes were much more likely to remain in their traditional crafts than to take up wage employment in the factories (Weber, 1958[1904]: 35–39).

Weber concluded from these observations that "Protestants ... have shown a special tendency to develop economic rationalism which cannot be observed to the same extent among Catholics. ... The principal explanation of this difference must be sought in the character of their religious beliefs, and not only in their temporary external historico–political situations" (1958[1904]: 40). Analyzing the economic and material foundations of differing societies could provide only part of the explanation of their pattern of social change and economic development. A full account needed to comprehend the independent role of culture, specifically religion, in influencing individuals' beliefs and behaviour.

Religion and the
Rise of Capitalism

Rationalism and rationalization are concepts that provide the foundations of Max Weber's sociology of capitalism. For Weber, rationalization had two meanings. First, it involved the rise of a way of thinking that insisted that every phenomenon in the world was, in principle, understandable and open to a non-mysterious explanation. For example, science explained weather patterns through the laws of physics, while old ideas explained weather as the expression of the pleasure or displeasure of the gods. Rationalization of ideas led to the retreat of supernatural and religious beliefs about the world before the steadily advancing methods and scope of scientific enquiry and explanation. Weber described this process of the rationalization of thought as involving the expulsion of magical ideas from human culture: the **disenchantment of the world.** Second, rationalization was a process by which social institutions were structured on a formal and disciplined basis and by which their administration was directed to the efficient achievement of precise goals.

Rationalized institutions adopted methods that allowed for rigorous record keeping and the effective execution of their role. The modern capitalist business corporation provides a classic example: the quantifiable goal is profit, and rationalization is rigorously adopted in pursuit of it (Weber, 1958[1904]: 76). But rationalized institutions are not exclusive to capitalist society; they were found, for example, in ancient Rome, in its military administration and in the administration, practice, and formal content of Roman law. Some ancient eastern and middle eastern societies developed complex administration systems to control and direct agricultural irrigation.

In capitalist society, however, rationalized institutions become the dominant form of social organization. Not only are they present in the private world of business, they also permeate the world of public administration: federal and provincial governments, municipal governments, schools, colleges, universities, hospitals, and government-owned corporations. All these institutions require systematic administration, calculating, and rigorous direction and effective cost accounting.

What is the connection between these processes of rationalization and the growth of capitalism? How is religion connected with this process of social change? The first aspect of rationalization is that it leads to the disenchantment of the world, to the elimination of magic. The Roman Catholic religion, according to Weber, was itself a bastion of non-rationalized, mystical ideas where the priests had special powers of absolution and a mysterious communication with God.

THE PROTESTANT ETHIC • Protestantism, especially its Calvinist variant, differed radically from Catholicism. There was no authoritative priest, as the agent of God, to forgive sins. The God of Protestantism was a severe one, a judge and condemner of the weakness of humanity. Yet this God offered the prize of salvation to those whose life and work exhibited, and constantly refreshed, a commitment to God's design for the world. The design itself was a divine mystery, not knowable to woman or man, but individuals must nonetheless play their role in it. To this end, God endowed all with different capacities and abilities, and these capacities and abilities shaped the roles individuals were to perform.

All individuals must take upon themselves the task to which God had appointed them and carry it out with diligence and commitment. This was a person's calling. The calling could be exalted or lowly, richly rewarded or a meagre subsistence, yet it was work for the glory of God and for the certainty of one's election by God for the gift of grace. In practice, the idea of calling was linked to occupation. It was the work that one became placed in, by social opportunity and fortune. It was therefore God's will that worldly work be done diligently, energetically, and without letup.

Weber argues that this concept of a worldly calling provided a cultural component necessary for the growth of capitalism. It preached ceaseless work for the glory of God. Yet because the work was for God's purpose, its product should never be squandered or casually and indulgently consumed. What should not be casually consumed must be either used with responsibility or accumulated and invested. This set of moral directives showed that

a specifically bourgeois economic ethic had grown up ... the bourgeois business man, as long as he remained within the bounds of formal correctness, as long as his moral conduct was spotless and the use to which he put his wealth was not objectionable, could follow his pecuniary interests as he would and feel that he was fulfilling a duty in doing so. The power of religious asceticism provided him in addition with sober, conscientious and unusually industrious workmen, who clung to their work as to a life purpose willed by God (Weber, 1958[1904]: 176–177).

Thus Protestantism contributed a peculiar compulsiveness to work and enterprise that was culturally unique. The Protestant ethic was a crucial factor in changing traditional forms of trade and manufacture into a modern capitalist system characterized by systematic organization and endless dedication to effort, hard work, and the restrained and calculated use of wealth.

Bureaucracy So far the idea of rationalized institutions has been presented at a rather abstract level. What did they actually look like? Weber's approach to understanding social institutions begins with the creation of an abstract model that embodies the pure characteristics of contrasting types. Often Weber constructed his models by imagining one set of characteristics and then developing a model of their direct opposites: he created polar types. At one extreme of social organization, for instance, there are social institutions that are guided by the power of tradition and are deeply conservative and personal. In Tonnies's Gemeinschaft, social institutions were not primarily, or even mainly, shaped by the desire to achieve specific goals as effectively as possible. Traditional cultures do not focus their economic life on efficiency, but on social process:

> The values which they put upon their food do not consist simply in its capacity to satisfy hunger, but in the use they can make of it to express their obligations to their relatives-in-law, their chiefs, their ancestors; to show their hospitality; to display their wealth; to initiate or marry off their sons. The value that is put on a canoe is not to be measured only in terms of the capacity of the vessel to carry goods and passengers, and of the fish that are to be caught from it, but also by the way in which it is a symbol of craftsmanship in wood, an object of artistic carving and decoration, a reminder of traditional voyages, and even the resting place or embodiment of a God. … The whole economic system of the people is run with this complex set of values in mind (Firth, 1958: 64–65).

At the opposite pole are institutions constructed in order to achieve desired results as effectively as possible. The focus is on achieving goals, rather than celebrating of cultural values. These institutions coincide with the forms of society that Tonnies described as Gesellschaft. The classic form of this type of organization is the rational bureaucracy, which is,

> from a purely technical point of view, capable of attaining the highest degree of efficiency and is in this sense formally the most rational known means of carrying out imperative control over human beings. It is superior to any other form in precision, in stability, in the stringency of its discipline, and in its reliability. It thus makes possible a particularly high degree of calculability of results for the heads of the organization and for those acting in relation to it. It is finally superior both in intensive efficiency and in the scope of its operations, and is formally capable of application to all kinds of administrative tasks (Weber, 1966[1947]: 336).

Rational bureaucracies are characterized by formality, hierarchy, carefully specified division of roles, administration by specialized experts, appointment and promotion on the basis of technical competence and seniority, and the fact that the occupation is a person's full-time career. They are systematically ordered for the planned and calculated performance of specific roles. Weber depicts these rationalized institutions as entirely objective and mechanical in their actions. The way they are structured, and their disciplined division of functions among personnel, makes them passionless (see Box 6.4). Weber suggests that among the essential characteristics of this form of organization are the following features. Again, the contrast between Gemeinschaft and Gesellschaft is reflected.

Bureaucratic Essentials

1. Officials are subject to the discipline of the organization only when at work duties. *Alternatively*: They could be subject to general control and domination, like a serf.
2. There is a clearly defined hierarchy of jobs. *Alternatively*: There could be argument and negotiation over who directs, as occurs in a community meeting.
3. Each official's job has a clear area of responsibility and authority. *Alternatively*: Each individual could take on tasks as they come up, with no recognized limits to one's role.
4. The official is chosen by free selection and appointed by contract. *Alternatively*: The official is appointed from a defined group and appointed for life.

Box 6.4
Rules Are Rules

The nature of bureaucracy is demonstrated in the small details of life. In 1993, a Calgary police officer was killed while on duty. His funeral, the largest in Calgary's history, demonstrated an outpouring of community sympathy and rage. Rules created barriers, however, when it came to burial. The local community, where the burial was to occur, had a set of rules regarding the size of grave markers: they must not be larger than 14 inches in height. A family that had violated this rule in the past had been required to reduce the size of the gravestone. The justification for this rule was the need to make it easier for workers to tend the grounds. The family of the slain police officer wished to place a large marker on the grave, in the shape of a police officer's badge. The local council, however, would not bend the rules.

SOURCE: "Calgary Police Mourn Slain Officer," *The Toronto Star*, October 9, 1993, p. A12.

5. Appointments are made on the basis of the candidate's skills and ability. *Alternatively*: Appointments are made on the basis of traditional entitlement or personal relations with members of the organization.

6. Officials are paid by fixed salaries established by contracts and a salary scale. *Alternatively*: The individual receives gifts and privileges at the discretion of the organization's head.

7. The official is a professional worker, whose office is his or her main occupation. *Alternatively*: The individual might be employed irregularly by the organization and gain his or her chief income elsewhere.

8. The job is located in a career hierarchy: there is a system of promotion according to seniority, proven ability, or both. Promotion depends on the judgement of superiors. *Alternatively*: Jobs are given, changed, or withdrawn without any systematic rules. Promotions depend on random selections during religious ceremonies.

9. The official does not own the administrative organization, nor is possession of the position based on ownership. *Alternatively*: The individual provides the means and personnel for administration and, once appointed, is recognized as sole legitimate owner of the job.

10. The official is subject to strict control and discipline in the conduct of the job. *Alternatively*: There are no clear criteria that outline how the job is to be done, and there is no organized supervision of the individual.

Weber knew that few, if any, bureaucratic organizations possessed all of the formal characteristics outlined above. An organization that did would be an example of an ideal type bureaucracy. Most organizations would have specifically non-rational elements. For example, appointments and promotions might be based on social contacts, appearance, accent, ethnic background, sexual attraction, mutual private business dealings, or an exchange of favours. These occurrences were not denied by Weber; he simply argued that they occur less often as an organization becomes focussed on precise goals and optimal ways to achieve them.

Organizations that have a complex of tasks that must be smoothly fulfilled must develop some aspects of rational bureaucracy: "The decisive reason for the advance of bureaucratic organization has always been its purely technical superiority over any other form of organization. The fully developed bureaucratic mechanism compares with other organizations exactly as does the machine with the non-mechanical modes of production" (Gerth and Mills, 1970: 214). This is a striking statement. Older forms of organization work like a system of handicraft — each decision or action is made individually and has its own special character. The rational bureaucracy, in contrast, is like a decision-making and administrative factory. It processes decisions through a standard set of procedures and according to fixed criteria.

Rationalization and Social Life

· · · · · · · · ·

For Weber, understanding the culture and dynamics of modern society meant grasping the process of depersonalization through the mechanization of social relationships and understanding that capitalism is a potent force for the rationalization of society:

> *Today, it is primarily the capitalist market economy which demands that the official business of the administration be discharged precisely, unambiguously, continuously, and with as much speed as possible. Normally the very large, modern capitalist enterprises are themselves unequalled models of strict bureaucratic organization. ... Bureaucratization offers above all the optimum possibility for carrying through the principle of specializing administrative functions according to purely objective considerations. ... The "objective" discharge of business primarily means a discharge of business according to calculable rules and "without regard for persons." "Without regard for persons" is also the watchword of the "market" and, in general, of all pursuits of naked economic interests* (Gerth and Mills, 1970: 215).

In capitalist society, there is an inexhaustible growth of scientific and technological knowledge and economic development. This growth is accompanied by a profound change in the way people experience their social life. Social interactions, aside from those in the intimate gatherings of family and of friendship, become increasingly shorn of their emotional component and replaced by formal, regulated relationships undertaken for practical purposes. The personal and spontaneous quality of human community life is increasingly extinguished, and emotions retreat to small and intimate circles and personal situations (see Box 6.5).

Weber believed that capitalism promotes a culture of acquisition, instrumentalism, and rationalism. Although capitalism is a rational economic system, it limits and reduces human experience and imprisons all members of society in an "iron cage" of compulsive material relationships. "Man is dominated by the making of money, by acquisition as the ultimate purpose of his life. Economic acquisition is no longer subordinated to man as the means for the satisfaction of his material needs" (Weber, 1958[1904]: 53). From the viewpoint of personal happiness and satisfaction, this rationalized society has irrational consequences: people now exist for the sake of business, rather than business for the sake of people. It is easy to recognize parallels with Karl Marx in these ideas.

The Future of Capitalism

· · · · · · · · ·

Although there is some agreement between Marx and Weber about the alienating characteristics of capitalism, there is complete disagreement about capitalism's future and about the relationship between a capitalist economy and social class. Weber did not envisage the division of society into two great opposed classes, the proletariat and the bourgeoisie. On the contrary, he saw a continuation of a very complex social

Box 6.5
Rationalized
Neighbourhoods

The landscape of Canada changed forever in 1952 with the building of a new suburban development named Don Mills. Built on over 800 ha of land and designed to provide homes for 30 000 people, this planner's dream was the first of countless planned neighbourhoods and suburbs across Canada.

The land for Don Mills was assembled by financier E.P. Taylor, and the project was designed by Macklin Hancock. The rational planning of towns is a long way from the organic growth common to traditional community building and expansion; while Don Mills appears to have been very well thought out and implemented, its critics say it was a "brilliant expression of bad ideas."

Many of the suburban problems that large numbers of Canadians live with are evident in Don Mills and its imitators. It is too spread out to support public transit; the street system is confusing; the separation of living, working, and shopping is too rigid; the walkways are unsafe and everyone has to drive.

SOURCE: Adapted from John Barber, "Don Mills," *The Globe and Mail*, May 29, 1993, p. D1.

structure in which there were important divisions of status (honour or respectability) as well as class. While agreeing with Marx that economic situation was a most crucial aspect in shaping a person's social situation, Weber also considered influences such as sex, race, occupation, education, and religion as part of a complex matrix of factors contributing to an individual's social situation. He therefore did not anticipate a growing class polarization that would tend irresistibly toward social revolution.

Weber, who was himself caught in a short-lived communist revolution in the state of Bavaria, had no doubt that there might be social revolution. However, he thought it neither inevitable nor even probable. Even if there were to be a revolutionary upheaval in capitalist society, leading to a collectivist socialist society, it would not lead to democracy and a reinvigoration of collective community life. On the contrary, argued Weber (securing a reputation as a prophet of the experience of Soviet-style communism), any attempt to exert direction over the economy and bring it under the realm of co-ordinated control would inevitably spread the bureaucratic mode of social institutions. Socialism would not defeat the emotionless domination of bureaucracy, but entrench it.

Domination and the Politics of Modern Society

Surveying human history, Weber saw that society was always founded on some form of authoritative direction: a system of **domination** — a way in which some person, group of persons, or set of institutions was endowed with the **authority** to command the obedience of individuals in the society. Authority is not merely **power**. People who submit to directions for the sole reason that non-compliance will damage their interests are being subjected to power. In contrast, those who follow directions because the person or institution doing the directing is believed to be rightly empowered to give them is submitting to authority. Where power directs, people obey because they fear force or negative consequences if they do not. Where authority directs, they obey because they accept the claim to obedience as rightful or legitimate.

Though Weber was well aware that many human societies had been dominated by raw power, he was much more interested in how domination had been exercised within a framework of **legitimate authority** in various human societies. As a sociologist, he believed that the different forms of political domination, an aspect of social structure, were linked to definite cultural ideas. Weber examined the nature of legitimate authority by using his method of constructing ideal types. He proposed that there were three possible pure types of authority. First, and most common in human history, is **traditional authority**. This was followed by rational–legal authority and, finally, charismatic authority.

In the magical and pre-rational world, authority was usually founded on tradition. In simple societies, traditional authority was exercised by family heads, chiefs, and sometimes through the collective acts of the community itself. In more complex societies, the usual forms of traditional domination would be hereditary royalty. Social control was maintained by traditional beliefs. People obeyed the elders, the chief, the lord, prince, or king because that was the way it had always been. The system of authority in the society was transmitted from the past, supported by a mythology of the past.

Systems of traditional rule are usually linked to, and depend on, the notion of the shared kinship of ruler and ruled. A traditional ruler gains legitimacy — the title to rightful authority — through representing the communal past of the society: a king or queen is both separate from the community because of special authority and at the same time the embodiment of the community.

Feudalism is an example of a traditional form of domination. It was not compatible with the rise of a market economy. Nation-states ruled by monarchies were much more compatible with capitalism. In England and Germany, for example, the outer form of traditional aristocratic rule had been preserved, yet beneath this outer appearance the system of state power had become highly rationalized and bureaucratized.[4]

The traditional forms of domination changed as the rise of capitalism was accompanied by liberal ideas about individual rights. Even where kings or queens remained, their authority was either formal, as in England, or regulated by law and public opinion, as in Germany. Authority was no longer vested in a claim to rightful obedience because that was how it had always been, but on the basis of **rational–legal authority**. This modern form of domination rested on a system of legal and administrative rules that applied to all members of the society. Authority now rested on the claim of rightful obedience to rules and laws made legitimate through some special procedure. The law was made superior to all individuals: people obey the edicts of law, rather than specific individuals.

Authority became completely depersonalized. Though exercised by individuals it was not possessed by them, but was granted and regulated by laws that all members of the society are subject to. Thus the nature of authority in modern capitalist society, the structures and goals of organizations, and human thought itself, all became drawn into a pattern of calculated impersonality. The culture of rationality, in law and public authority, was simply another social embodiment of the bureaucratic organization that pervades society.

Weber did, however, envisage a social force that could act as a counterweight to the suffocating routine of bureaucracy. He insisted on the important role of the individual in shaping history. Throughout history, he maintained, there had been great leaders who unleashed major forces of cultural and political change. These individuals possessed **charismatic authority**. Human history showed that masses of people could be brought into action through the exceptional force of creative, inspiring, and mystical leadership. This leadership rested not on tradition or law, but on the special magical qualities and driving mission of the leader. This potential for the eruption of charismatic leadership existed in all societies and provided the possibility of a great wave of social upheaval and transformation in people's consciousness.

Weber's conception of charismatic leadership is an important one to understand. The force of this leadership can be seen in recent religious leadership, especially in the Islamic world, and in the political leadership of individuals like Napoleon Bonaparte, Vladimir Lenin, Adolf Hitler, Mohandas Gandhi, Mao Zedong, and Fidel Castro. But Weber did not expect the charismatic upheaval of the modern rational–bureaucratic state to be a common pattern. On the contrary, he thought that the whole orientation of culture and of social institutions in such societies was a profound barrier to such experiences.

Weber's vision of capitalist society was a bleak one, unlightened by the prospect of revolutionary transformation and progress. The material standards of society undoubtedly would rise. The principles of rationality, calculation, and legal authority would conquer the world as the market-driven application of science and technology and the refined techniques of bureaucratic administration eliminated traditional forms of economic organization and social life.

A great machine moves compulsively toward ever-greater routinization and systematization of life. Meanwhile, human life in all its emotional depth and complexity, in its passions and imagination, retains its hold only at the level of intimate social relations. In new world of rationality, private and public life are strictly divided, and emotions, expressible only with a small circle of family and friends, are rigorously segregated from daily life.

This concludes the portrait of Weber's sociology of modern society. His ideas are a way to understand capitalism as a type of society with distinct cultural and structural characteristics. Competitive capitalism, allied with a culturally sanctioned acquisitiveness and driven by calculated pursuit of profit, is only at surface a rational form of society. Beneath the appearance of dispassionate practicality is a deep and suppressed conflict between human imagination, creativity, and emotion and the mechanical regulation of daily life.

ÉMILE
DURKHEIM

. . . .

THE
FUNCTIONALIST

. . . .

Man is only a moral being because he lives in society, since morality consists in solidarity with the group (Durkheim: 1984 [1893]).

. . . .

BORN
Epinal, Alsace, France, 1858
DIED
France, 1917
WORK
Teacher of philosophy, 1882–1887
Professor of Education and Sociology, Bordeaux and Paris, 1897–1917
Research, writing, and editing of journal *L'Annee Sociologique*, 1898–1917
MAJOR WRITINGS
The Division of Labour in Society, 1893
Rules of Sociological Method, 1895
Suicide, 1897
Elementary Forms of the Religious Life, 1912

Émile Durkheim
. . . .

Émile Durkheim created a very different world of ideas from those of Marx and Weber. He looked at society as a physician might look at a patient. In Durkheim's view, the patient is society itself and good health is shown by a state of ordered stability (see Box 6.6). Durkheim followed Comte in believing that a careful and objective analysis of society would create sociological knowledge that could be used to improve social life.

Durkheim's concern with the health of society was no accident. He had been born in a century of turmoil for French society. When he was thirteen, France was overwhelmingly defeated in a short and disastrous war with Germany (1870–71). At the end of the war, a revolutionary movement of French communists, both workers and soldiers, seized control of Paris. They immediately became embroiled in a civil war with the army of the French government. The war was soon decided in the government's favour, yet the legacy was bitter: hundreds of those who were captured or surrendered were shot in mass executions. In all, up to 30 000 Parisians were killed in the brief struggle of French against French (Cobban, 1965: 212–215). It is no surprise, then, that Durkheim's goal was to understand how social unity was created and maintained and how it could be strengthened.

Social Order:
Functionalism
. . . .

Durkheim did not believe that sociologists should develop wide criticisms of modern society or of any society, for that matter. Sweeping criticism of whole social orders, like Marx's condemnation of capitalism, was just value judgement and ideology. In Durkheim's work, a much cooler climate prevails: capitalism was a fact of social organization; thus, understanding, not revolution, was the business of sociologists. The most important question to be asked about capitalist society was simply: how can it provide for peaceful and ordered social life? Durkheim assumed that social stability and peace were the basic goals of any human community. He considered society as a moral good in itself. Societies fulfilled their purpose when they effectively sustained a rich social life, which attached individuals to each other through shared values and activities.

Social Bonds and
the Individual
. . . .

Durkheim assumed, like Comte, that past societies had been strongly integrated, and he too developed a sociological model to express the contrast between societies of the past and the present. He believed that the central distinction between past and present was that past society was unified by **mechanical solidarity**, while modern society was characterized by **organic solidarity**.

Mechanical solidarity was found in societies where the ties that bound individuals to each other were obvious, directly encountered in daily activity, and constantly reinforced by community life. The connections between aspects of social life and

. . . .

Box 6.6
Key Ideas of a
Durkheimian
Sociology
. . . .

- Anomie
- Organic solidarity
- Forced division of labour
- Integration
- Social bond

. . . .

between one individual and another were evident and unhidden: people shared the same beliefs and activities, they naturally co-operated with each other in work. Their personal relationships were anchored in close ties of kinship and intermarriage and links of clan, tribe, and region. Mechanical solidarity was a solidarity of resemblance: people were essentially alike, thought much the same thoughts, and were joined together in a daily life of common activities. There was very little specialization and almost no sense of any divide between public and private life.

The characteristics of organic solidarity are, in most respects, opposite to those of mechanical solidarity. There is great difference between individuals, considerable specialization, a wide range of beliefs and values, and a pronounced division between private and public life. Durkheim used the word "organic" in a biological sense. He thought that modern society, like a living body, was composed of specialized parts that were interconnected and must work together to maintain the system. In the body, for example, the heart, lungs, liver, kidneys, and brain all play an essential role in maintaining life. They are distinct from each other and have entirely separate functions, yet life cannot continue unless they each effectively perform their roles (Aron, 1970: 22).

The same was true of modern society. Although it was marked by great specialization and a division of the spheres of life — public/private, economic/political, religious/secular — it was, beneath the surface, acutely interdependent. Individuals may have absolutely no contact with the people who supply their homes with water or gas or those who grow the food they eat, but that does not mean that interdependence does not exist. The modern citizen depends on anonymous others, just as traditional village dwellers depend on their neighbours for economic and social co-operation.

The need for social solidarity in interdependent modern society was acute, but creating and sustaining solidarity in the conditions of modern society was a complex problem. Solidarity would not necessarily occur spontaneously. The interconnection and mutual dependency of people was far from obvious. A highly specialized and complex social life might disguise or obscure the ties of individual to individual, and people might become indifferent to the public life of the society. Durkheim called this state of affairs a condition of anomie, where individuals feel rootless, disconnected, and unsure about any guiding rules for social life. There was an absence of the shared norms and values essential for unifying and regulating a society.

The Healthy Society

A healthy society, according to Durkheim, is founded on strong bonds between people and a strong commitment to shared values. Ideally, a society should have a dominant set of generally supported norms and values possessing great authority. Without this collective conscience, or moral culture, social stability would be impossible. Societies also must have a dense network of institutions binding individuals into forms of social co-operation with others. People must come together in a myriad of different groups to share joint activity toward common purposes. Only in that way can the individual really become bonded to society and a true member of it.

These two types of social bonds — shared norms and values, and shared participation in social institutions — Durkheim termed normative integration and structural integration (Durkheim, 1951[1897]: 151–216; 241–276). Between these two types of social bonds there is no definite separation, since people define, learn, and internalize norms and values within the institutional structures of group life. But the separation Durkheim suggests is useful in thinking about how societies are (or are not) bonded together into a common social life.

Normative integration was generally not a problem in most precapitalist societies, because their culture was traditional and stable and the young were socialized by the old. A lack of normative integration — anomie — can, however, arise when a society is rapidly changing and the values of the past no longer seem relevant to the present or future. The problem can be especially acute when there is weak social regulation of important areas of social life, such as work and family life.

Structural integration is also not a problem in traditional and more stable societies. There is little separation between public and private, since such societies have "natural" economies based on the land. As a matter of course, people intermarry within a restricted group of individuals, the ties of kinship are richly interwoven, and people work, celebrate, and practice rituals together. In more complex societies, like nation-states, structural integration must be provided by a myriad of social institutions that fill the space between the level of the individual and that of the nation-state. These intermediate associations can be enormously varied. Most important are the ties of family and kinship, which link individuals at the most intense levels of emotion. But any social association with others enriches structural integration. Tennis club, Boy Scouts, Girl Guides, Lions' Club, Canadian Legion, trade union, environmental group, political party, church, neighbourhood association, and many other organizations provide for this structural integration of individual and social life.

The Individual and Society

Durkheim's sociology clearly focusses on a concern for the health of social bonds. This concern came not only from a fear of the social anarchy that might erupt if social bonds were weakened, but also from a fear of internal war within the individual. Durkheim believed that individuals who were not directed by definite social norms and who had weak social links with others could easily begin to find life meaningless and pointless and become self-destructive. The individual needed to be wrapped in the security of society.

Durkheim's fundamental claim that the individual can only be stable and healthy within the folds of strong social values and ties is most fully argued in his famous study of suicide.

SUICIDE • The idea that there can be a sociological understanding of suicide is, at first, shocking. It is more common to think of suicide in relation to the most private feelings and experiences. It is the outer expression of private pain.

In general, Durkheim agreed that suicides in modern society were directly caused by very individual and personal factors.[5] But he claimed that social influences were also very important. The social influence in suicide could be demonstrated by the fact that different societies and different groups had very different rates of suicide. Durkheim reasoned that individual experiences of personal misfortune and sadness must be of approximately the same frequency in any comparable type of society. People in Italy did not get less sick, or lose fewer relatives, or suffer less economic deprivation, than people in France, Germany, or Denmark. Yet these societies, at the time Durkheim wrote, had very different rates of suicide and the rates were strikingly consistent over periods of time. Italy, for example, experienced a suicide rate that was one-quarter of that in France, one-fifth of that in the German state of Prussia, one-ninth of that in Denmark, and one-tenth of that in the German state of Saxony (Durkheim, 1951[1897]: 50).

Assuming that individual circumstances predisposing people to suicide were more or less the same among comparable societies, these differences were remarkable.

Societies themselves must play a role in protecting individuals from translating a personal crisis into the act of suicide. Some societies did this much more effectively than others. Why? The explanation must lie in concrete characteristics of different societies. There must be some features of their culture and social structure that caused variations in their capacity to sustain individuals who were suffering private despair.

Durkheim took up the inquiry by examining the suicide data for different countries and regions to try to detect some link between suicide rates and the surrounding society. A definite link was discovered: individuals were far less likely to commit suicide where the surrounding society upheld strong traditional norms and values. They were also far less likely to commit suicide where they were strongly integrated into family, group, and community.

Durkheim concluded that, in general, people with family ties, especially when married with children, committed suicide far less than others. He argued that this was because married people with children have strong social expectations placed on them: their role is clear, and the norms that guide it are definite. He also argued that Roman Catholics were far less likely than Protestants to commit suicide, because they were members of a strong authoritarian church that encouraged submission to religion, as revealed by the pope and priests. Protestants, in contrast, were responsible for their own faith and for their own conduct in the eyes of God. They had to regulate themselves; the Catholic was more regulated from outside. Jews also had a low rate of suicide, and again a social reason could be uncovered. The Jews were a minority in all societies and subject to discrimination in many; they therefore found strength in their own community and meaning in their distinct culture and traditions.

Low suicide rates were consistently found in societies and groups that had strong cultural values and norms and dense linkages of family and community.[6] The conclusion drawn from this analysis upheld Durkheim's fundamental belief about individual and society: people need to have a strong social integration, and the direction of clear social norms, in order to maintain psychological stability.

Integration into social life by family ties, church, and community associations gave people a sense of attachment and meaning that could not otherwise be achieved:

Social man presupposes a society which he expresses and serves. If this dissolves, if we no longer feel it in existence and action about and above us, whatever is social in us is deprived of all objective foundation. ... Thus we are bereft of reasons for existence. ... The incidents of private life which seem the direct inspiration of suicide are in reality only incidental causes. The individual yields to the slightest shock of circumstance because the state of society has made him a ready prey to suicide (Durkheim, 1951[1897]: 213–215).

It was therefore inconceivable, as the analysis in *Suicide* demonstrated, to think of people experiencing a rewarding and satisfying life outside the bonds of a well-regulated and richly integrated society. It was the task of sociology to act on that knowledge.

The Foundations of Moral Authority

Moral order in society could exist only when people were committed to shared values and disciplined by those values. This commitment could be developed only in the process of socialization. Durkheim was not much concerned with the process of primary socialization, which was focussed in families, but with secondary socialization, which was focussed in the public institutions of society, such as schools and workplaces. It was there that individuals must become connected to social values and develop a full sense of moral regulation in social life. In a complex society, the kinship system could not provide a sufficient socialization. In the new society, it was school, not large kin groups and an intimate community, that socialized the individuals and introduced them to complex social relationships with others.

A successful education, from the point of view of society, therefore inculcates the child into moral regulation and into attachment to society and social groups. It requires enlightened discipline, which stresses the moral responsibility of the child, rather than just a subjection to commands, and it requires that the child come to know and be committed to the society. Ideally, the teaching of sociology itself might give the child a sense that society is "real, alive, and powerful" (Durkheim, 1961[1902]: 275). But in practice, in the lower grades, the study of society's history best accomplishes an understanding of and sympathy for the traditions, morality, and culture that surround the child and shape experience. It is through understanding the past of their society that children absorb the "collective consciousness" of the group and become part of it. Only this strongly founded identification of individual and society can protect and advance moral regulation and social order.

Capitalism and Collective Consciousness

It followed from Durkheim's deep concern with social order and solidarity that his chief preoccupation with capitalist society was understanding how it might accomplish these goals. His book *Socialism and Saint-Simon* (written in 1895) set the central theme of his analysis of capitalism. He viewed the rise of socialism, with its radical rejection of capitalism, as a symptom of stress in society. The tremendous influence of socialism on the working classes of Europe was a sign of profound division over social values.

Capitalist society, according to liberal thought, would maximize social welfare by the dynamic process of free-enterprise, individualism, and initiative. Social welfare would result from individuals having the freedom to make the decisions that suited their own interests best. Socialist theory rejected this claim entirely. It proclaimed that both rationality and morality demanded that economic life be made subject to conscious and democratic social control. The values and assumptions of liberalism and capitalism were completely rejected.

Socialism could therefore be viewed as a symptom of social imbalance and distress, but what was the illness that underlay it? Why did the current state of society produce such a stark division in social values? An analysis of the condition of the patient — society — was needed.

Organic Solidarity and the Division of Labour

Durkheim had no wish to repair the stresses of modern society by attempting to return to the past. He argued that the rise of a complex modern society had supported an enormous flowering of culture and of opportunity for personal growth and development. Societies of the past, founded in mechanical solidarity, had, he claimed, imposed a suffocatingly uniform life on their members. But in modern society the division of labour had greatly increased the range and variety of people's activities and made choice and individualism truly possible (Durkheim, 1984[1893]: 336).

The division of labour demanded, however, quite different bonds of solidarity from those in primitive and traditional society. In a complex society the connective tissue could not be the simple links of mechanical solidarity, but must arise from a state of highly intricate interdependency: organic solidarity.

The problem with organic solidarity was that individuals were absolutely reliant on others without this necessarily being apparent. Where people did not form social attachments, except within the narrow confines of family and friendship, social solidarity was threatened. If the new relationships of a complex society were not structured in binding ties between individuals and regulated by principles commanding social consensus, then the moral order itself would be in question.

It was therefore essential that people comprehend the division of labour as creating acute interdependency among all members of society. Thus understood, individuals would always be aware of their dependence on society and of the checks and constraints it placed on them.

Capitalism and Community

· · · · · · · · ·

Durkheim well understood that capitalist economies were deeply affected by class conflict and that there were important divisions in people's ideas and beliefs. His view of socialism was that it was a sign of disturbances in the social and moral tissue of society; indeed it was *caused* by those problems.

Durkheim diagnosed capitalist society as suffering weaknesses in the connective tissues of structural and normative integration. Individuals were too weakly integrated into groups and insufficiently attached to clear norms and values.

The crisis in structural integration was created by the collapse of traditional forms of social association. Premodern societies, such as feudalism, had a rich texture of social associations. Individual life was interwoven with kin and community from birth to death. Family association was solid and seemingly permanent, rooted in shared work and the passing of land down the generations. Much trade and manufacture was organized through guilds of craftspeople (there were women guild members and guilds of women) whose function was both economic and social. They controlled the quality and prices of goods, and they regulated the conduct of their members. They took concrete form in social gatherings and activities focussed in great halls in the towns of Europe.

As the modern state and the modern economy arose, these local social associations were weakened as regional and central power developed. In France, in particular, the revolution of 1789–1815 created an entirely new political structure. The old provinces of France were forcibly dissolved, and new administrative divisions of government, which had no genuine historical or social basis, were artificially created. At the same time, the traditional occupational associations, including guilds, were weakened and soon destroyed: "All secondary organs of social life were done away with. Only one collective form survived the tempest: the State. By the nature of things this therefore tended to absorb all forms of activity which had a social character" (Durkheim, 1951 [1897]: 389).

Therein lay the great problem of modern society. Individuals were no longer subject to the collective influence of community-based social organization, but only to the state. Yet the state was too remote and abstract to create a sense of social integration or to exert strong social regulation.

Somehow, society itself must be strengthened so that its members could not escape its influence. To do this it was necessary to revive intermediate associations that could have a direct effect on individuals. The central problem with capitalism was that it lacked a system for bringing individuals within the various occupations together. In premodern society, occupational association was a rich soil for the development of collective bonds because it united people by geographical origin, by culture, and by the nature of their work (Durkheim, 1951[1897]: 378). Occupational life, people's work, was absolutely central to their social experience, and it was untenable that it should be left without institutions for mutual association:

> *The absence of any corporative institution therefore creates, in the organization of a people such as ours, a vacuum the significance of which it is difficult to overestimate. We therefore lack a whole system of organs necessary to the normal functioning of social life. Such a structural defect is plainly not some local affliction limited to one segment of society; it is a sickness ... that affects the entire organism* (Durkheim, 1984[1893]: LV).

Normative integration was also a significant problem. In the past, work had been subject to very definite regulation. In the guilds of premodern Europe, for example, members had been very strictly regulated in craft standards and in maintaining integrity and honesty in trade. In modern European societies, in contrast, occupational life was almost without regulation. Durkheim again proposed occupational corporations as the answer to this problem. These corporations would include both employers and employees within a given occupation, and their role would be to provide a framework of rules for regulating working conditions and mediating disputes. Mutual agreements between all parties would prevent the strong from unduly exploiting the weak and give individuals a sense of common purpose (Durkheim, 1951[1897]: 380). The occupational corporations would serve the end of both structural and normative integration: "Thus the social fabric, the meshes of which are so dangerously relaxed, would tighten and be strengthened throughout its entire extent" (1951[1897]: 381).

Capitalism and Anomie

Anomie arises from a state of disconnection between individual and society. In capitalist societies, the potential for such disconnection was enormously increased by the complexity of the division of labour and the resulting abstractness of social relationships. In addition, capitalist forms of production fragmented the labour process:

> *It has often been accused of diminishing the individual by reducing him to the role of a machine. And indeed, if he is not aware of where the operations required of him are leading, if he does not link them to any aim, he can no longer perform them save out of routine. Every day he repeats the same movements with monotonous regularity, but without having any interest or understanding of them. He is no longer the living cell of a living organism. He is no more than a lifeless cog* (Durkheim, 1984[1893]: 306–307).

Such a situation was fertile soil for anomie. It was crucial to develop occupational association, so that people could become conscious of the state of organic solidarity that existed between them.

Not only does capitalism create the possibility of anomie through the organization of production, through disconnection from others and lack of a sense of regulation, it can threaten it also where the division of labour — the social and economic placement of individuals — appears to be a forced division of labour.

In a modern secular society, social structure that exhibits inequality cannot be justified by an appeal to tradition or religious values. It must be justified by some set of rational beliefs: it must appear to be legitimate and right. In capitalist society that source of justification comes from liberal ideology. This ideology claims that one's placement in social structure — where an individual fits in relation to income and status — is determined by ability and effort. Durkheim took the view that this was a necessary belief in modern society in order to give legitimacy to the division of labour.

It was therefore essential that the division of labour be a spontaneous division of labour, where "social inequalities precisely express natural inequalities" (Durkheim, 1984[1893]: 313). If it became apparent that power, privilege, and inheritance were the keys to social status and economic position, then there would be anomie because there could be no consensus about the allocation of rewards. At times, Durkheim claimed that the social conditions of individuals would have to become more equalized so that all had comparable resources. The social structure would then simply reflect inequality of talent and application, rather than the use of power and advantage. It might even be necessary to restrict the inheritance of wealth so that true equality of opportunity could be created.

Thus Durkheim's analysis of capitalism led back to the fundamental theme of his sociology: the necessity for social solidarity. Modern capitalism challenged social solidarity because it failed to unite people in their occupations. It lacked normative legitimacy because it tended to maintain inequality based on privilege, not the morally justifiable distinctions of talent and hard work. Evident disturbances of social order and of social integration in the contemporary world showed how necessary it was to mobilize society to attend to the repair of its connective tissue and secure the foundations of harmonious social life.

Durkheim and
Functionalism
· · · · · · · ·

Of the two general perspectives in sociology, functionalist and critical, Durkheim was definitely in the first camp. He was concerned with the stabilization of society; accordingly, his sociology was dedicated to inquiring how the functional needs of social stability could be produced. But Durkheim is very distinct from many more modern functionalist theorists: he does not simply assume that harmony and stable integration are normal and natural. Although he claimed that society had essential functional needs, including a normative system about which there was consensus, he did not claim that those needs were actually being fulfilled. Although he argued that the structure of inequality could only be normatively supported when merit, not privilege, determined placement, he did not go on to claim that placement by merit was actually the case in the social world.

Later sociologists who adopted Durkheim's functionalist model often forgot that Durkheim's approach to capitalism was analytical and inquiring and not simply a circular justification of any existing state of society.[7] For Durkheim the symptoms of social sickness were real and apparent, and the capacity of capitalism to generate collective sentiments was extremely weak. Only by purposive social policy would it be possible to invest the new society with a secure basis for normative and structural integration.

Durkheim can best be appreciated as having presented a challenge — not a challenge to imagine a completely different world, but to understand the dependence of people on society and to grasp how society must be purposefully shaped to realize human needs.

MALE
SOCIOLOGISTS
AND THE
REALITIES OF
WOMEN
· · · · · · · ·

The foundations of modern sociology rest on the work of three men. Did the sex of the writers affect their understanding of the place of women in society? Must their theories be supplemented by additional ideas in order to grasp the wholeness of a society with two sexes?

The short answer to both questions is yes. The rest of this book applies ideas from feminist sociologists who have, in many ways, altered sociologists' understanding of the social world. Feminism is not a unified set of theories or concepts, but a broad orientation that stresses the unique cultural and structural factors that affect women's experiences, roles, and status within society. It is a corrective to the intentional and unintentional denial of women's different social experience. However, a thorough account of feminist ideas, areas of focus, theories, concepts, and major areas of debate demands a book in itself. The rest of this book is able only to touch on some of the major ideas feminists have brought to sociology.

It is important to indicate some of the areas in which women sociologists in particular have found the ideas of the male "founding fathers" of modern sociology to be lacking in a consciousness of the social world of women.

Marxism is criticized for its limited understanding of the distinct place of women in society, which is entirely separate from the issue of their class location. Although Marxism stresses the analysis of social structure in relation to economic class, it excludes a comprehensive analysis of women's unique roles in reproduction, mothering, and housework. Consequently, the assumption in Marxism that women will become emancipated when they hold equal places in the economy with men glosses over the demands on women to do domestic work and ignores the strength of patriarchal ideology. Women's entry into the paid labour force may simply result in a double burden of paid *and* domestic work (Sydie, 1987: 89–123).

Weber's work gives an account of history in which women's place and situation is largely overlooked. He uses the concept of a patriarchal family as a basic way to understand the social organization of a traditional society and tends to assume that this is a product of the natural roles of women in reproduction and the sexual division of labour. His account ignores the fact that patriarchy occurs even where women play important public social and economic roles. He fails to provide an analysis of the foundations of the cultural idea that women are inferior to men (Sydie, 1987: 51–87).

Durkheim can fairly be said to be strongly chauvinistic. He viewed women as less intelligent and less culturally developed than men. Yet, at the same time, he saw these culturally shaped organic differences as positive for society. The intellectual inferiority he attributed to women suited them to the restricted life of the household, and this anchored the family system and society itself. The special qualities of women, as creatures of the domestic world, complemented the external roles of men. Men and women were naturally divided in their roles, and this role division had the effect of compelling them to depend on each other: men on women for domestic life, psychological retreat, and the care of children; women on men for economic support and social protection. His analysis led him to criticize social movements promoting the equality of women. He saw this as destabilizing for society and not in the best interests of women (Sydie, 1987: 13–49).[8]

The rest of the book attempts to compensate for some of these prejudices and blind spots while drawing on the sociological ideas of these three authors.

CONCLUSION This chapter outlined a sociological tradition that examines society as a connected whole and seeks a comprehensive view of culture and social structure. It is now possible to see where the two sociological perspectives central to this book have come from. Marx is the primary source of the critical conflict theory of society; Durkheim is the advocate of functionalism. Max Weber is less easy to place, but on the whole he offers a perspective deeply critical of the culture of capitalist society.

Although these three authors provided the foundation for sociology, they did not anticipate some modern developments, and, to some extent, this narrowness has restricted debate within sociology. For example, while Marx and Weber clearly saw the dehumanizing effects of modern forms of work organization they did not foresee the systematic degradation of the environment associated with industrialism and private profit. A sociological understanding of the relationship between humanity and the environment is only now being developed.

These three authors were, however, central figures in drawing attention to the importance of comprehensively examining the structure of modern society. And we build on their approach in the following chapters.

· · · · · · · · ·

NOTES

· · · · · · · ·

1. Throughout his work, Marx collaborated with Frederick Engels. Many of the important works of Marxist theory, including the *Manifesto of the Communist Party*, were written jointly with Engels. Engels also developed Marxist theory in some areas largely overlooked by Marx, especially the family. Marx was, as Engels himself stated repeatedly, the deeper and more original thinker of the partnership; for that reason, the corpus of ideas associated with Marx and Engels are usually simply designated as Marx's. We have followed that practice in this discussion.

2. That is, to polish the steel pins.

3. Marx wrote: "Centralization of the means of production and socialization of labour at last reach a point where they become incompatible with their capitalist integument. This integument is burst asunder. The knell of capitalist private property sounds. The expropriators are expropriated. The capitalist mode of appropriation, the result of the capitalist mode of production, produces capitalist private property. ... But capitalist production begets, with the inexorability of a law of Nature, its own negation. This does not re-establish private property for the producer, but gives him individual property based on the acquisitions of the capitalist era, i.e., on co-operation and the possession in common of the land and of the means of production" (Marx, 1954: 715).

4. Japan and Germany were leading historical examples of the emergence of highly sophisticated systems of government and administration within semi-traditional authority structures.

5. The words "in modern society" are important. We do not explore the topic here, but Durkheim argued that there were types of suicide very directly caused by society itself. He described two types: altruistic and fatalistic, both mainly associated with traditional societies. Roughly, altruistic suicide was committed to uphold social values and for the good of the society, and fatalistic suicide was linked to people's despair about their position in society (e.g., it was common among slaves).

6. There is considerable debate about the correctness of some of Durkheim's analysis, which we do not examine here; see Douglas (1967). It is fair to say, however, that his broad claims about the link of suicide rates to the characteristics of the surrounding society have now become generally accepted by sociologists and a new group of specialists — "suicidologists" — who are directly concerned with the understanding and prevention of suicide.

7. The article on inequality by Kingsley Davis and W.E. Moore (1945) examined in the next chapter exhibits this tendency.

8. More modern versions of these arguments can be found in Parsons and Bales (1955).

∘ ∘ ∘ ∘ ∘ ∘ ∘ ∘

FURTHER READING

∘ ∘ ∘ ∘ ∘ ∘ ∘ ∘

Although numerous secondary sources about Marx, Weber, and Durkheim exist, some of their original work should be read. The *Communist Manifesto* by Karl Marx and Frederick Engels is accessible, as are Max Weber's *Protestant Ethic and the Spirit of Capitalism* and Émile Durkheim's *Suicide*.

Abbott, Pamela, and Clare Wallace. *An Introduction to Sociology: Feminist Perspectives.* London: Routledge, 1990. A useful corrective to some of the oversights of the classical sociologists.

Giddens, Anthony. *The Consequences of Modernity.* Stanford: Stanford University Press, 1990. A brief introduction to Giddens's work on developing a theory of society as a connected whole. While building on the classics, it goes beyond the early foundations.

Sydie, R. A. *Natural Women, Cultured Men.* Toronto: Methuen, 1987. An important re-examination of many theoretical works in the social sciences that critiques the view of women presented in them.

∘ ∘ ∘ ∘ ∘ ∘ ∘ ∘

STUDY QUESTIONS

∘ ∘ ∘ ∘ ∘ ∘ ∘ ∘

1. Why did Marx praise capitalism but call for revolution?
2. Explain the argument that Max Weber thinks of culture as more independent from social structure than does Marx.
3. Prepare an organization chart of a bureaucracy you are familiar with, such as your workplace or the educational institution you attend. Include the bureaucracy's job titles, and arrange the various positions by rank.
4. How does Durkheim explain the variations of suicide rates among societies and among different religious groups?
5. Classify Marx, Weber, and Durkheim as either pessimists or optimists about the future of society. Provide reasons for your choices.
6. Contrast the views of Marx, Weber, and Durkheim on the prospects of socialism.
7. Compare and contrast the views of Marx and Weber.
8. What are the consequences of modern society, in the opinions of Marx, Weber, and Durkheim?

7 INEQUALITY

INTRODUCTION

This chapter begins the examination of Canadian society and offers an initial assessment of liberalism as a way to understand society. According to liberalism, access to positions in capitalist society is equally open to all. While there will be inequality of condition, there will also be equality of opportunity. Thus, the economic situation of children should not affect their life chances.

It is clear, however, that economic situation is often passed on from parents to children. There is a *pattern* to the social structure that is reproduced over time. If positions in the social structure are, to some extent, being transmitted, Canada may be considered a stratified society. But can it be thought of as a class society? This analysis relies heavily on the views of Karl Marx and Max Weber.

The concept of class does not, however, seem to fully account for the position of women in society. The nature of women's inequality cannot be understood as a product of class. Women can, however, be thought of as a status group, a term developed by Max Weber. Evidence of class and status being ascribed in Canadian society casts doubt on liberalism's claims of equality of opportunity. How then to understand liberalism? Can it be thought of as an ideology?

The last chapter reviewed sociological responses to the historical transformation of western society outlined in Chapter Five. These responses were preoccupied with the problem of social inequality, a pervasive feature of capitalist societies. This is the topic that we examine in detail in this chapter.

IDEOLOGIES OF INEQUALITY

· · · · · · · · ·

With the rise of capitalism, traditional systems of inequality based on ascription and rigid divisions in legal and social status are replaced by a new form of economic inequality arising from the competitive workings of the marketplace. Along with this new foundation for inequality come new cultural ideas that justify and support it. Social inequality, unless it is maintained solely by force, is usually upheld by a set of beliefs — an ideology — that makes the inequality seem just, right, moral, and natural. The ancient Greek philosopher Aristotle (about 330 B.C.) provided an example of an ideology of inequality. He argued that slavery was moral and right because some people were naturally superior to others: "Just as some are by nature free, so others are by nature slaves, and for these latter the condition of slavery is both beneficial and just" (Aristotle, 1948: 17).

In feudal society, inequality was justified by an ideology founded in tradition. Rights, duties, and obligations were transmitted from the past, within strongly patriarchal families and in a web of lasting feudal rights and obligations. Authority was strong because the existing social organization seemed to be a natural way of life.

Box 7.1 outlines yet another form of inequality — a caste system. Notice that the caste system has an accompanying set of ideas that serve to justify it. Inequality in Canada is justified as well, but by a very different ideology.

The justification for the inequality found in India is provided by the beliefs linking various groups to their origins in differing parts of the Brahma's body. The ensuing disparities among groups comes to be seen as natural and right. The government of India has tried to eliminate the caste system and to challenge the beliefs about natural superiority, but these traditions are deeply ingrained and the privilege of the few is a considerable obstacle to change.

In Canada, too, some people believe in the natural superiority of one race, sex, or class over others, or claim traditional entitlement to privilege, but these views are not considered acceptable. Instead, the predominant justification for economic inequality in Canadian society is liberalism, which upholds individual freedom and equality and rejects traditional privilege. People are considered free to compete for rewards and to get what they deserve for their ability and hard work.

Before considering the adequacy of liberalism as an account of social reality and examining theories of inequality, the nature of inequality in Canadian society should be investigated.

DESCRIBING INEQUALITY

· · · · · · · · ·

Equality can take two forms: **equality of condition** and **equality of opportunity**. Equality of condition occurs when everyone has similar wealth, **status** (honour or respectability), and power (the ability to direct other people's lives). This is absent in modern societies; all have considerable inequality of condition. Equality of opportunity occurs when people have similar chances to pursue economic and social rewards. It would be present where inequality of condition does not produce much difference in people's life chances.

Liberalism contends that Canada's level of inequality of condition is tolerable because it co-exists with a reasonable equality of opportunity. Examining that claim will take most of this chapter, starting with a look at inequality of condition in Canadian society.

Inequality of Condition

· · · · · · · · ·

No one claims that there is equality of condition in Canada. We are constantly reminded that some of us are rich and others poor. Raghib Ismail signed a four-year contract with the Toronto Argonauts in 1993 for $26 million; Joe Carter of the

Box 7.1
"Segregation Deeply
Imbedded in India"

Mr. Chowdhury, who lives in Metro Toronto with his wife and three children, is an Untouchable — a member of the lowest rung of Hinduism's rigid caste system in India.

He is among the 500 or so Untouchable families living in Southern Ontario and Vancouver. These days, they are glued to their TV sets, following the mayhem that has engulfed India over Prime Minister V.P. Singh's plan to reserve 50 percent of government jobs for Untouchables and other tribal peoples.

To most outsiders, Mr. Singh's affirmative-action plan makes sense. Since the lower castes make up more than 60 percent of India's 850 million people, it seems fair that 50 percent of government jobs should be reserved for them.

The caste system goes back to the origins of Hinduism — more than 2000 years ago. Originally, there were four castes: Brahmins or priests; Kshatriyas or warriors; Vaishyas or merchants; and Shudras, the menial workers who cleaned human excretion, tanned animal skin, picked up carcasses, carried dead bodies.

In the words of the Hindu scriptures: "In order to preserve the universe, Brahma (the Supreme) caused the Brahmin to proceed from his mouth, the Kshatriya to proceed from his arm, the Vaishya to proceed from his thigh, and the Shudra to proceed from his foot."

Over the years, the castes multiplied into several thousand subcastes, but sanctions, such as the prohibition against Shudras owning land, remained. The effect is still visible today.

... the Untouchable population is well over 100 million or more than one in seven Indians. Yet, half of the Untouchable work force is made up of landless agricultural labourers and more than 71 percent are in debt to upper-caste moneylenders, landlords, and shopkeepers.

As even law enforcement comes under the control of the upper castes, the semi-slavery institution of debt-bonded labour has been permitted to persist. One survey found that Untouchables accounted for more than 62 percent of the 2.6 million reported cases of debt-bonded labour.

Another survey found that in 53 percent of the villages studied, Untouchables were barred from the only well. In 73 percent of the villages, Untouchables were barred from the local Hindu temple.

Dr. B.R. Ambedkar, a British-trained lawyer, Untouchable leader, and a father of the Indian constitution, succeeded in securing guarantees that 22.5 percent of government jobs would go to Untouchables and the tribal peoples of India. Mr. Singh now seeks to increase that figure to 50 percent.

But even if a job is found, promotions are scarce. Mr. Chowdhury trained as a lawyer and worked for eleven years in the Indian Health Ministry under an upper-caste boss. When the time came for promotion, an upper-caste Hindu got the job. Two years later, in 1970, Mr. Chowdhury left for Canada.

SOURCE: Excerpted from Zuhair Kashmeri, "Segregation Deeply Imbedded in India," *The Globe and Mail*, October 13, 1990. Reprinted with permission.

Toronto Blue Jays earned $7 million in one year. Canadian rock star Bryan Adams earned approximately $35 million in 1993. It was recently reported that the highest-paid man in the Canadian corporate world, Lawrence Bloomberg of First Marathon Incorporated, received an annual pay package of $6.9 million.[1] In 1991, Sergio Cragnotti bought 1 172 985 shares of Lawson Mardon Group Limited for $10.25 per share; a cost of $12 023 096. After this purchase he held 8 182 830 shares, a total value of over $80 000 000.[2] Peter Munk, president of American Barrick Resources Corporation, was granted an option to buy corporate shares at $7 each in February 1987. In 1991, he sold these shares for $25.12 each and realized a pretax profit of $36.6 million.[3]

When the rich and famous divorce or contest an estate, we gain a glimpse of their economic situation and lifestyle. When Harold Ballard, the owner of Toronto's Maple Leaf Gardens, died, his wife Yolanda filed a claim with the court handling the estate for an interim monthly payment of $16 050. The details of her claim are of interest: she needed $75 000 a year to purchase clothes, $7600 for personal grooming, $21 000 for cleaning and laundry, and $15 000 to care for her dog. To get away from it all she required $60 000 annually for vacations.[4]

What is life like at the other end of the income scale? The National Council of Welfare (1993) reported that the welfare income of a single parent with one child ranged from a low of $9956 per year in New Brunswick to a high of $16 527 in Ontario. This figure for Ontario was estimated to be 80 percent of the poverty level and only 55 percent of the estimated average income. Being on welfare in Canada is not exceptional. In June 1991, 13.9 percent of Ontarians under the age of 60 were on welfare.[5] Almost a million Canadian children live in poverty. Children from poor families do worse in school and drop out of school more frequently than do those from affluent families (Hudson and Galaway, 1993: 340).

The gap between welfare incomes and those of selected individuals receiving high incomes can be looked at more systematically. Table 7.1 shows the percentage of total before-tax income going to families and unattached individuals by quintile (20 percent groupings) for the period 1951–1992. Note that in 1951 the poorest 20 percent (lowest quintile) of the population received 4.4 percent of the total before-tax income, while the richest 20 percent (highest quintile) received 42.8 percent. Comparing the distribution over time, in 1992 the poorest 20 percent received 4.6 percent of total income, while the richest 20 percent received 43.6 percent of the income.

Although these were decades of increasingly numerous two-income families and of growing transfer payments to individuals and families, the distribution of income remains quite fixed. One would have expected the income distribution to become

Table 7.1

Income Distribution by Quintile, Families and Unattached Individuals, Canada, 1951–1992

Income Quintile	1951	1961	1971	1981	1992
Lowest 20%	4.4	4.2	3.6	4.6	4.6
2nd 20%	11.2	11.9	10.6	10.9	10.3
3rd 20%	18.3	18.3	17.6	17.6	16.7
4th 20%	23.3	24.5	24.9	25.1	24.8
Highest 20%	42.8	41.4	43.3	41.7	43.6

SOURCE: Statistics Canada, *Income Distributions by Size in Canada*, cat. no. 13-207 (Ottawa: Statistics Canada, various years). Reproduced by authority of the Minister of Industry, 1994.

more equal as a result of the rise of the welfare state and income-related taxation, but there was no shift in this direction. There is, however, evidence of growing *inequality* in incomes. As long ago as 1976 the National Council of Welfare (1978) noted that the gap between the average incomes of the richest 20 percent of income earners and the poorest 20 percent of income earners had multiplied by over two and a half times (from $6900 in 1951 to $18 000 in 1976, stated in 1976 dollars). The income hierarchy has stretched, and the distance between rich and poor has grown dramatically.[6]

The lives of Canadians among the lowest income quintile are substantially affected by this position. Poor teenagers, for example, are five times more likely to bear children than are those of the richest quintile. Children born to the poorest group are more likely to have very low birth weight and to die before their first birthday (Wilkins et al., 1991). There is conclusive evidence that poor nutrition, associated with low incomes, is an important factor in reduced educational performance. Research on the causes of death by income quintile shows that the suicide rate among the poorest quintile is twice that of the richest quintile. The homicide rate of the poor is four times that of the richest group, as is the rate of death due to alcoholism. Deaths from lung cancer are 69 percent higher, deaths from mental disorders 132 percent higher, and deaths from bronchitis, emphysema and asthma are 56 percent higher (Wilkins, Adams, and Brancker, 1990).

Economic inequality is not only a matter of income. The distribution of wealth (real estate, bonds, stocks, and other investments) is also important, and it is even more unequal than income. If all Canadians are divided on the basis of their wealth into five groups — each containing 20 percent of the population — interesting facts are revealed. Those in the poorest 20 percent are in debt (they have a negative net wealth), while the next poorest 20 percent have only 2.4 percent of the wealth pie. On the other hand, the wealthiest 20 percent have 69 percent of the wealth and the richest 10 percent have just over 50 percent of the wealth.[7] This distribution of wealth has been relatively stable over time.

Wealth in stockholdings also displays inequality. While only 13 percent of Canadian households hold stocks of some kind (Chawla, 1990) nine Canadian families control 53 percent of the stock in the Toronto Stock Exchange's leading 300 companies (the TSE 300).[8] Ken Thomson, owner of the Hudson's Bay Company and a vast communications empire, is perhaps Canada's richest man and the eighth-richest individual in the world. This empire adds $4.4 million a week into his personal dividend account (Newman, 1991).

Inequality of Opportunity

How do these differences in income and wealth come about? Do they reflect a consensus of views about the importance of some jobs and the need to reward sacrifice? Or are they shaped by the privilege that comes with the rights of private property, the presence of unions, the sex of the worker, and cultural devaluation of certain types of work?

The illustration of caste in India indicated an ideology of inequality justifying rigid stratification. In a caste system, the basis of inequality — its key dimension — is status (honour or respectability). Status is ascribed; people are born into it. The **ascribed status** depends upon the part of the Brahma's body the group is said to have emerged from. Those with high status are identified with the head of the body, and those with low status are identified with the foot. As the various parts of the body each play a part in its overall functioning, so too it is thought do the various status groups of the society each contribute to the preservation of "the universe." A clear consistency of status, class, and power exists. This is demonstrated by the fact that while the untouchables are a large group (about 100 million), they do not own land and are relegated to perform "dirty" jobs. Status groups then are identified with particular economic classes. The untouchables have little power, reflected in their inability to prevent rules being enforced that restrict their ownership of land, use of wells, or attendance at the temple. Power, then, is aligned with status and class groups.

To use a simple analogy, Indian society is like a layered cake; it is stratified. The particular layer in which one is located has substantial consequences for one's life, since practices supporting inequality are diffused into many aspects of society (e.g., land ownership and law enforcement). There is no equality of opportunity. Religious beliefs provide an ideology legitimizing the structure of inequality. As a result, the caste system is reproduced over and over.

Is Canada a stratified society? Canada certainly does not have a caste system of **stratification** that disqualifies individuals from positions on the basis of status. But, as in all industrial societies, Canadians are sharply differentiated by their economic condition. Does this economic differentiation give different shape to people's lives and to their life chances? Does Canadian society have a pattern that, despite having a different foundation, still has results like those in India, where children born to untouchables are the future untouchables? Is inequality transmitted from Canadian parents to their children? Is power aligned with class, so that the rich are more likely to be in positions of influence? Do status groups exist in Canada? These questions are central to investigating inequality and assessing whether Canada is a stratified society.

Social scientists concern themselves with two related questions in studying stratification. First, what determines the rewards allocated to particular positions or occupations in a society? Why do doctors tend to have higher incomes than nurses? Why are presidents of corporations paid so much more than the employees? Why are women's average full-time wages only 70 percent those of men? Second, how are individuals placed in these unequally rewarded positions? What type of people are recruited to particular roles? Who becomes a doctor? Who become directors of large corporations?

Photo 7.1
Social scientists focus on issues such as the unequal pay levels between doctors and nurses, between workers and corporate presidents, and between men and women. It is still against the odds for a woman to acquire a supervisory position in a field, such as construction, traditionally dominated by men.

Peter Poulides / TONY STONE IMAGES

The allocation of rewards creates economic inequality, while the recruitment for specific roles places individuals in this structure of inequality. Although both processes are necessary to a system of stratification, the second process — recruitment for roles — is central to a consideration of inequality of opportunity.

Allocation of Rewards

To examine the reward-allocation process, consider the following example. At the University of Victoria (in British Columbia), a Secretary IV makes $1937 per month while a Groundskeeper I makes $2233 per month.[9] What explains these differences in wages?

FUNCTIONALIST VIEWS • Functionalist perspectives regarding the allocation of rewards build on the central assumption that widespread agreement exists about the necessity of dividing labour and rewarding workers differently. Functionalists like Kingsley Davis and Wilbert Moore (1945) assume that most institutions and social conventions serve useful purposes in society; they claim that inequality is functionally necessary to society. Davis and Moore base their argument on three assumptions:

- Every society requires some division of labour.
- Some jobs are functionally more important than others (i.e., they contribute more to the well-being of the community) and deserve greater rewards.
- Some people are inherently more talented and capable than others and must be given the incentive to develop their talents by being appropriately rewarded.

Davis and Moore argue that society holds out the promise of money, power, and prestige to attract the best people to these functionally important positions. Incentives, they argue, are especially important when a job is particularly demanding or when it requires the skills of specially trained personnel. Thus, doctors in Canadian society are paid more than most other workers because medical work is among the more important social tasks and people must be rewarded to compensate for the sacrifices made during a long training period. High incomes for doctors ensure that talented people are prepared to undergo this sacrifice.

This functionalist argument is directly related to the assumptions of liberalism. It is assumed that differing rewards for jobs reflect the value that society places on them and provide the incentive needed to get people to train for them and carry them out. If this perspective were applied to the earlier example of the secretary and the groundskeeper, one would assume that the secretary required less training and was less essential to the operation of the institution than the groundskeeper.

Melvin Tumin (1953) criticized this view of inequality by pointing out four weaknesses:

- The assumption that some positions are functionally more important than others is vague and extremely difficult to prove. What do Davis and Moore mean by "important"? Is a lawyer more important to society than a day-care worker? Nurturing and socializing young children is essential to the community, but those performing these roles (usually women) are low-paid and enjoy little social esteem. Is a groundskeeper more important than a secretary?
- Are functionalists right to assume that there is consensus in society about what jobs deserve most rewards? Do we all, for example, agree that lawyers deserve more than most other occupations?

- Social inequality does not necessarily support the most effective development of skill and talent in society. It may obstruct it. Those who hold important positions and receive the privilege of these positions are motivated to protect this privilege and attempt to reserve future positions in the privileged group for their children. Also, of course, those with higher incomes are best able to support and encourage their children in the development of their talents, so advantages are transmitted and the most talented are not necessarily discovered and developed.
- The social and financial perks of high-status positions are usually excessive. How great must the rewards be to recruit talented people to important roles? Are unequal rewards the only way to attract people to perform certain roles in society? Are there not other rewards than money that encourage people to strive for particular roles? Many people volunteer for important and demanding roles without having the incentive of money.

Charles Anderson (1974) adds a further criticism when he points out that Davis and Moore neglect to say anything about the most obvious form of economic inequality — ownership of property. To say that inequality in ownership of property is necessary to a society is obviously untrue, since there have been societies without this inequality.

Returning to the above example from the University of Victoria, these criticisms can be applied. Two things are important to note: first, the secretarial position at this university usually requires a grade 12 education and some experience, while the groundskeeper position requires only grade 10 education and no specific experience. The functionalist approach would have predicted the opposite. Second, there is public debate about whether such pay differences are fair; there is no consensus. These points seem to clearly undermine the assumptions made by Davis and Moore.

What alternative explanation might be offered? We note that all of the secretaries are women and most of the groundskeepers are men. Is a different valuation of the work on the basis of the employee's sex apparent here? What does a critical perspective have to say? Box 7.2 illustrates a critical perspective on the role of private charity in combating poverty.

CRITICAL PERSPECTIVES • Max Weber and Karl Marx each offered a non-functionalist analysis. The critical perspective they shared suggests that inequality results from the exercise of power. Marx said inequality is not established by the nature of tasks people perform or on the basis of consensus; it arises from the ownership, or exclusion from ownership, of the means of production. Weber said the structure of inequality in society stems from a general and continuing struggle for wealth and power among numerous economic and status groups. In either case, those who obtain economic and status advantages are able to allocate rewards so as to favour their own group. One group may, for example, restrict others from access to resources and opportunities. An example of this restriction is the legal right attached to private property, which excludes workers from exercising power over the work they do or the results of their labour. Similarly, laws in most provinces give doctors a legal right to exclude other groups from practising medicine. Workers may collectively withdraw or disrupt services through strikes or demonstrations, which are sometimes given legitimacy through labour legislation (i.e., the right to strike).[10] On the other hand, the power of workers can be contained by restricting legal opportunities to withdraw services and by using force against workers when they withhold services. Many of these exam-

Box 7.2
Food Banks: Who
Benefits?

The first food bank in Canada opened in Edmonton in 1981. By June 1991, the Canadian Association of Food Banks reported that food banks were operating or supplying about 1800 food programs in 300 communities. These operations have become an important part of Canada's social safety net. Rather than being funded by governments, however, this safety net relies on volunteers and private charity. How can we understand this development?

One view sees food banks as a functional adaptation to the crisis of public funding in Canada. As governments find it more difficult to respond to public need because of our substantial debt, private charity has risen to fill the new need. Some also see the transfer of responsibility from governments to individuals and community groups as an important way to increase a sense of altruism and instil a sense of community.

On the other hand, 60–70 percent of food donations contributed to food banks comes from commercial outlets. Although they give the food away, there is an economic benefit for business from this gift. The food they give away is already paid for, since the cost of "waste" is built into the pricing system. Further, this waste is normally a cost for the company, since it has to pay to transport the food and there may be dump-site fees. Having the food bank pick up the "waste" reduces the burden on the company.

There has been discussion in Canada of adopting the American system of giving business protection from liability that may be incurred if their gifts cause sickness or harm to the consumer and offering tax credits to food donors. In the United States these policies have contributed to the creation of a vast bureaucracy around food banks and have made them a permanent part of the welfare system.

SOURCE: Adapted from Marlene Webber, *Food For Thought* (Toronto: Coach House Press, 1992).

ples suggest that the law can be a resource to be used by the powerful to enhance their position in the society. There may be a relationship between the legal system and the pattern of inequality.

In the example of the groundskeeper and the secretary, a number of questions arise that are overlooked in functionalist theories. Is the administrative system that sets pay ranges sexist in undervaluing the work of women compared with that of men? Do unions give equal support to the demands of male members and female members, or is the union run by men who give priority to improving some positions and not others? It may not be the task the workers perform that is important in determining their rewards. Other influences connected to power and status may be more important.

In summary, critical perspectives argue that the allocation of rewards, or the structure of inequality, results from the exertion of power. Rather than there being agreement regarding evaluations of worthiness, there are conflicts over access to resources and rewards. Sex and race discrimination, transmission of privilege, and practices of exclusion may each affect the pattern of inequality that develops.

Recruitment for Roles

· · · · · · · · ·

How are people recruited to positions within a structure of inequality? Although liberalism is not concerned about economic inequality among individuals, it does demand that society provide equality of opportunity: this provides the moral justification for inequality of condition. Liberalism offers no support for inequality of opportunity, since barriers to individuals are also barriers to society benefiting from what individuals may have to contribute.

Émile Durkheim, who accepted many aspects of liberal thought, stressed the importance of equality of opportunity when he claimed that normative integration could be maintained only when the allocation of roles (or the division of labour) was spontaneous and not forced. People must accept that inequality justly represents the differing abilities and contributions of individuals, not the exercise of power and privilege. Durkheim feared that if people felt that social roles were not allocated according to natural differences among individuals, they would conclude that the society must be unjust. People's commitment to the normative system would be weakened, and competing value systems, like socialism, would become stronger, as would class conflict and criminal deviance. There are weighty reasons, therefore, to examine the issue of equality of opportunity.

The debate about recruitment can be sketched quite briefly. On one side are those who argue that the social and economic positions people attain as mature adults are mostly determined by features of the individual, such as intelligence, hard work, diligence, thrift, and wise choices. For these theorists there is no social pattern behind who rises and who falls in the social hierarchy. On the other side are those who argue that the best explanation of the varying achievements of individuals lies in the social features of the individual, such as the economic situation of the individual's family, ethnic background, education, and sex. Further, many argue that the social situation of one's parents is the most powerful determinant of one's adult position. People tend to reproduce the economic positions of their parents.

An argument over the usefulness of the concept of class — individuals sharing a similar economic position — underlies this debate. Class is thought to be a useful concept with explanatory power by those who understand inequality in social terms. It is considered an unhelpful concept by those who explain inequality in terms of individual factors.

FUNCTIONALIST VIEWS • The functionalist view, to use the earlier analogy of the cake, is that the social structure is a well-blended mix; women and men from all kinds of family and ethnic backgrounds are evenly distributed throughout the various levels of society. Those at the top of the hierarchy are there because they are more deserving — more intelligent, more talented, more self-controlled, more hard-working. According to this theory, one's economic and status position would not be much affected by that of one's parents. The only pattern apparent in the social structure would be that those who trained longest, had most natural ability, and worked hardest would be at the top.

Functionalists may well acknowledge, however, that the society does not work as it should and that inequality of opportunity denies access to many who are talented and deserving. Social policies (such as free public education, family support, and human rights legislation) may be required to promote equality of opportunity. They would not see anything fundamentally wrong with the way society is organized, but would only see problems of implementation of equal opportunity.

CRITICAL PERSPECTIVES • A critical perspective on recruitment for social roles begins by claiming that society is organized in such a way as to reproduce its pattern of inequality. People's life chances largely depend on the social location of their parents, so there is restricted mobility within the society. For this reason, the location of groups of people does not show much generational change, and this maintains the status quo. As suggested previously, the critical theorists argue that one group may openly or covertly restrict the opportunities (the recruitment process) of other groups and that unequal conditions of groups disadvantage people in accessing opportunities (see Box 7.3).

Critical theorists might examine the workings of the school system, selection and promotion processes in corporations, inheritance rights, government social programs and services, and taxation laws to see if these allow some groups to pass privilege to their children and restrict equality of opportunity for others. An advocate of a critical perspective, for example, would point out some of the apparent benefits the rich receive: the executive who made $36 million through the sale of company stocks, for example, pays capital gains tax at less than the rate of tax most of us pay on our wages. Further, many countries have a wealth tax (rather than just an income tax); why does Canada not have such a tax? In addition Canada does not have a tax on assets gained through inheritance upon the death of a family member.

SOCIAL MOBILITY

· · · · · · · ·

Testing the value of these alternate portraits of the recruitment process in society involves us in the study of **social mobility:** the movement of individuals up or down the social hierarchy. Do people's individual or social characteristics play the greatest role in determining the roles they attain?

In India, the barrier to higher wealth, income, status, and power for those ascribed the identity of untouchables seems almost absolute. What about Canadian society? Is the social structure mixed smoothly, or are there layers to it, not so distinct as in a caste society, yet definitely patterned? Is there random promotion to or demotion from positions in the society? Is there a weak or strong link between social origin and social destination? Is there an association between a person's position on one scale of measurement, such as income, and their possession of status and power? If there is an association, sociologists refer to **status consistency**; if not, they refer to **status inconsistency**.

In considering social mobility, determinations must be made about the degree to which people experience movement away from the social location of their parents. To do this it is necessary to construct some standard of measurement and comparison. Most studies use occupational status as the key variable. Sociologists start with a group of Canadians and determine the occupational classification of their fathers. (Mothers are not yet used in these studies because too few of them were in the labour force to make comparisons feasible.) Then a comparison is made with the position achieved by their grown children. If a large number of sons and daughters have different occupational classifications from their fathers, a high rate of social mobility is indicated. Conversely, if there is little variation, a low rate of mobility is indicated.

A recent study of mobility in Canada has been done by Creese et al. (1991). As indicated in Table 7.2, the highest rate of inheritance for sons was found among those of lower blue-collar fathers (code 8), where 38.58 percent were located in the same occu-

Box 7.3
An Income
Disadvantage for
Visible Minorities?

Using the 1986 census returns, Monica Boyd studied foreign-born Canadians who had immigrated to Canada before 1984. Her research shows the complex interplay of birth status (foreign born or Canadian born), visible-minority status, and gender in shaping the structure of inequality. Does being a visible minority affect earnings? There are a number of variables that are known to be related to earnings: for example, education, work experience, age, region of residence, weeks worked, and full-time/part-time status. To study the effects of visible-minority status on earnings, these factors must be controlled for; they must remain constant in order to see if the two primary variables are linked.

When Boyd did this, she found that foreign-born visible-minority men earned 20 percent below the average wage and salary if they had the same sociodemographic profile as the entire male population. Foreign-born visible-minority women earned 11 percent less. While women appear to be less disadvantaged, the opposite is in fact true; women are doubly disadvantaged in comparison with the entire male population. Mean wages and salary adjusted for the factors identified above are as follows:

Females

Canadian born, not visible minority	$15 234
Canadian born, visible minority	$15 554
Foreign born, not visible minority	$14 882
Foreign born, visible minority	$13 446

Males

Canadian born, not visible minority	$27 455
Canadian born, visible minority	$26 392
Foreign born, not visible minority	$26 595
Foreign born, visible minority	$21 712

Boyd concludes that the data clearly show a pattern of disadvantage: "If all groups had the same socio-economic profile, being foreign-born, a member of a visible-minority group, or female would be associated with lower earnings."

SOURCE: Adapted from Monica Boyd, "Gender, Visible Minority, and Immigrant Earnings Inequality: Reassessing an Employment Equity Premise," Table 3 in V. Satzewich, ed., *Deconstructing a Nation: Immigration, Multiculturalism and Racism in '90s Canada* (Halifax: Fernwood, 1992). Reprinted with the permission of the Social Research Unit, Department of Sociology, University of Saskatchewan.

pational category as their fathers. The highest rate of inheritance for daughters was found among those of lower white-collar fathers (code 7), where 39.47 percent were located in the same occupational category as their fathers. Taking the data overall, 25.6 percent of sons did not move (experiencing occupational inheritance), while 38.8 percent moved up and 35.6 percent moved down. Women experienced less occu-

Table 7.2		Son's Occupation							
Intergenerational Occupational Mobility of the Nonagricultural Labour Force by Sex, Canada, 1986 (Outflow Table- Percentage by Row)	**Father's Occupation**	**1**	**2**	**3**	**4**	**5**	**6**	**7**	**8**
	1	—	15.96	21.08	14.46	—	—	14.46	—
	2	—	**17.99**	14.19	12.42	6.46	9.63	20.53	16.09
	3	—	11.54	**9.38**	7.99	18.42	11.67	13.95	22.71
	4	—	—	—	**15.94**	—	19.70	—	24.05
	5	—	13.89	11.45	8.73	**15.47**	11.74	18.62	15.90
	6	2.65	8.71	6.80	7.77	5.89	**26.45**	11.28	30.40
	7	—	11.43	9.19	13.20	9.07	10.61	**17.68**	24.17
	8	2.47	7.54	7.80	5.52	5.39	20.15	12.55	**38.58**

	Daughter's Occupation							
Father's Occupation	**1**	**2**	**3**	**4**	**5**	**6**	**7**	**8**
1	—	—	—	25.19	—	—	34.04	—
2	—	**14.26**	—	19.80	17.34	—	32.71	8.73
3	—	13.56	—	10.01	20.27	—	39.54	—
4	—	—	—	—	—	—	44.36	—
5	—	11.91	—	12.54	**19.71**	—	35.86	7.47
6	—	6.35	7.03	8.50	21.54	2.56	38.26	13.99
7	—	11.59	—	13.61	16.39	—	**39.47**	11.72
8	—	7.54	4.57	9.73	16.01	—	44.15	**15.54**

Sons n = 4582

Daughters n = 3502

Cells with few cases have been suppressed.

Occupational codes: "White collar" indicates a job that is principally clerical/administrative; "blue collar" a job that is principally manual labour.

1	High management	**5**	Upper white collar
2	Professional	**6**	Upper blue collar
3	Mid-management	**7**	Lower white collar
4	Semi-professional	**8**	Lower blue collar

SOURCE: Gillian Creese et al., Table G, *Ups and Downs on the Ladder of Success: Social Mobility in Canada,* cat. no. 11-612E, no. 5 (Ottawa: Statistics Canada, 1991), p. 46. Reproduced by authority of the Minister of Industry, 1994.

pational inheritance (12.2 percent), and more moved both up (47.6 percent) and down (40.0 percent) than did men.

One might conclude on the basis of these figures that Canadian society is indeed very open. But before drawing conclusions from the data generated by this analysis, two important questions must be answered. First, has change in the structure of the economy itself created apparent social mobility? Second, how much occupational change between generations is needed to provide evidence of mobility?

To answer the first question the data must be adjusted to account for structural mobility, which is caused by changes in the occupational structure of the economy and has little to do with the openness of the class and status structure. If the economy changes so that there are more jobs in services and fewer in the manufacturing sector, there is automatic occupational mobility. Children of industrial workers may now be working in the banking sector or retail trade, but in terms of the occupational structure of the changed economy their relative social position may not have changed. The data in Table 7.3 on the changing distribution of occupations from 1951 to 1990 demonstrate the way the labour market has changed and created apparent mobility. Table 7.3 reveals a great rise in white-collar occupations and a considerable decline in blue-collar occupations. This structural change in Canada's economy necessarily creates apparent social mobility.

Interpreting the figures on mobility is also complicated by the special situation of women. Since there is pronounced occupational segregation by sex, the kinds of occupational opportunities available to women are quite different from those of their fathers. The daughters of blue-collar workers, for example, have quite a low chance of working in manual occupations and are necessarily more likely to move from father's blue collar to their own white-collar jobs. Thus, changes in the occupational structure and sex-based distinctions in occupations create an appearance of mobility that exaggerates the reality of mobility.

A second concern is to analyze the meaningfulness of observed mobility. To do this the concept of occupational distance is useful. How far must individuals travel from the occupational status of their fathers in order to assert that there has been mobility? This distance is measured by comparing the occupational categories classified along a hierarchy.

The study reviewed here divided occupations into eight categories (two agricultural categories were excluded from Table 7.2). A son or a daughter who moved out of the father's occupational category was assumed to have experienced social mobility. The problem with this approach is that the social significance of the mobility can easily be exaggerated. Is there meaningful social mobility when a logger's son works as a bank teller? Does a woman who works in a day-care centre move out of the social status of her truck-driver father? It would, of course, be significant evidence of social mobility if 50 percent of all doctors and lawyers were children of manual workers, but do more minor changes indicate real social mobility?

	1951	1990
Agriculture	18.4%	3.3%
Forestry, fishing, trapping	2.9%	N/A
Mines, quarries, oil wells	1.5%	2.4%
Manufacturing	26.5%	16.1%
Construction	6.8%	6.7%
Transportation, communication, and other utilities	8.8%	7.4%
Trade	14.1%	17.7%
Finance, insurance, and real estate	3.0%	5.7%
Community, business and personal service	18.0%	33.8%
Public administration	N/A	6.4%

Table 7.3
Distribution of Canadian Labour Force, 1951 and 1990
· · · · · · · · ·

SOURCE: For 1951, *Perspectives Canada III* (Ottawa: Statistics Canada, 1980); for 1990, *Labour Force Annual Averages*, cat. no. 71-220 (Ottawa: Statistics Canada, 1991). Reproduced by authority of the Minister of Industry, 1994.

Concerns about occupational distance can be remedied to a certain extent by collapsing the occupational categories into broader classifications. In doing this a more significant move in occupational status is needed before it counts as mobility. It is also possible to calculate the amount of structural mobility and adjust the data to allow for it, though this can be done only in aggregate rather than for individuals. Creese et al. (1991) collapsed the categories to five (combining 1+2, 3+4, 5+6, 7+8, and now including two groups of agricultural workers) and adjusted for the amount of structural mobility. The amount of real mobility (what they call "circulation mobility") was considerably reduced from that suggested by Table 7.2.

Table 7.4 shows that approximately half of the sons and daughters experienced mobility that resulted from the society being open and flexible, thus allowing them to move up or down. Since structural mobility is most likely to be upward, because there has been a growth of white-collar jobs, it is reasonable to assume that a lot of the real — "circulation" — mobility has been downward.

While there is room for debate about the amount of mobility in Canada, the data on social mobility suggest that it is less a fact of Canadian life than most believe. The class position of Canadians is likely to be somewhat similar to that of their fathers.

ELITE RECRUITMENT

Social mobility can also be studied in a second way: examining recruitment to positions at the very top of the economic hierarchy.

The study of social mobility into the highest status groups in society is called the study of elite recruitment. The first substantial Canadian study of this subject was John Porter's *The Vertical Mosaic* (1965). This study was based on an identification of the membership of the dominant elite in Canadian society for 1951 and an examination of their social characteristics. Wallace Clement continued this tradition with *The Canadian Corporate Elite* (1975), based on a 1972 examination of the elite group in private corporations. Both of these studies described the social origin of the elite and demonstrated that membership was very restricted.

Clement, for example, examining the 673 Canadian-born persons who represented the directors and senior executives of the 113 dominant corporations operating in Canada, found that "access to the corporate elite has become more exclusively the preserve of the upper class from 1951 to 1972." He found that 192 members had directly inherited their elite position. A further 123 members had received their advantage from a father's placement in another elite group, from their wife's family or from a father in a substantial business (but not large enough to make the 113 that Clement studied). When added together, these groups account for 47 percent of the corporate elite. A further group of 85 were classified as of privileged background, since they had attended private school, and a further 57 had fathers who were doctors, lawyers, clergy, or managers. An additional group of 177 had attended university,

Table 7.4
Extent of Social Mobility, Adjusting for Structural Mobility and Occupational Distance

	Sons	Daughters
No mobility (inheritance)	33.0%	30.4%
Structural mobility	16.0%	26.6%
Real mobility	51.0%	43.0%

SOURCE: Adapted from Gillian Creese et al., *Ups and Downs on the Ladder of Success: Social Mobility in Canada*, cat. no. 11-612E, no. 5 (Ottawa: Statistics Canada, 1991), p. 51. Reproduced by authority of the Minister of Industry, 1994.

quite unusual for this generation of Canadians. All of these groupings account for 94 percent of the elite group. The remaining 6 percent were classified as of working-class background (Clement, 1975: 189–190).[11]

Clement's data show that social mobility into the highest positions in the economic elite is very limited and, at this level, Canada is clearly a closed-class society.

INEQUALITY OF OPPORTUNITY OR INEQUALITY OF ABILITY?

The functionalist and the liberal views of social inequality are not, however, necessarily refuted by the evidence. Social mobility studies, especially at elite level, do demonstrate closure and thus apparent inequality of opportunity. But it is certainly plausible to suggest that individual factors could still account for this. In particular, does intelligence play a role? Is the apparent status transmission simply the result of the inheritance of the individual talents and capacities that made an individual's father successful? Is intelligence a determiner of income? Does recruitment for roles in a structure of inequality reflect intelligence differences among people?

Inequality and Intelligence

Psychologists have argued that about 80 percent of intelligence (or mental ability) is genetically transmitted. If individuals end up in the same class position as their parents, this may be because they have inherited their parents' intelligence. Evidence supporting this view comes from the following kinds of research: studies of foster children demonstrate that the mental ability scores of natural siblings (those with common biological parents) are more highly correlated than the abilities of foster children and their foster siblings. Further, the occupation of the natural parents is a better predictor of the mental ability of a child than is the occupational status of a foster parent. Finally, studies of identical twins show that the score received by one sibling is a very good predictor of the score achieved by the other. Lest one think that this is because they share an identical environment, studies of identical twins reared apart show that the mental ability of the separated twins is still more strongly correlated than are the scores of non-twin siblings reared together. These facts do suggest a strong hereditary basis to intelligence.

What is the relationship of intelligence to social standing? The few research studies examining this subject have shown a correlation between intelligence scores and occupational categories. When occupations are ranked by prestige or according to conventional categories (professional and managerial, clerical and skilled, semi-skilled, unskilled) there is some correlation between occupational status and intelligence; the average intelligence score for professionals is higher than the average score for skilled workers. Since this research reports only average scores, it is clear that there is still a great deal of variation within each occupational grouping.

All of this research appears to support the functionalist position that inequality of reward serves to attract the most talented to the most important occupational tasks in the society.

What are some of the more cogent criticisms of this research?

Even if it is assumed that intelligence is inheritable, most agree that it is also shaped by environmental conditions. Height, for example, is an inheritable characteristic but any individual's actual height depends in part on diet. Nutrition, especially in early infancy, also appears to have important effects on intellectual development. Environment of the child is important too: it has been found that the intelligence scores of children can improve by 10–15 percent when they are moved to a more stimulating situation. Intelligence is definitely affected by the context the individual lives in.

Researchers have also found that when the data on the linkage of social class and intelligence are looked at another way the issue becomes even more blurred. Bane and Jencks (1976) found that differences in intelligence account for less than 10 percent of the variation in actual job performance. If smarter people were recruited for demanding jobs, more intelligent people would routinely perform those tasks better. This does not seem to be true. The authors claimed that differences in intelligence accounted for only 12 percent of the differences in people's incomes.

There are deeper problems with research into intelligence. The most perplexing is a conceptual problem: no one is quite sure what intelligence is. Herrnstein (1973) and others are content to work with an operational definition: intelligence is that which is measured by intelligence tests. This is quite an unusual problem for science, since good science begins with a concept, usually one with theoretical importance, and attempts to measure the concept. In the matter of intelligence it is noted that the measurement itself becomes the concept and there seems to be no theoretical significance to the concept. No one, for example, has any idea whether there is a gene (or genes) for intelligence. Until this is determined, the quest for knowledge in this area is speculative.

In summary, functionalists and liberals claim that inequality in Canadian society results from the inequality of individual capacities and efforts. Canadian society is assumed to be open, and consequently the concept of class, which assumes distinct layers in the social structure, has little value. If the concept is used at all it is used descriptively, describing arbitrary groupings of people on the basis of income or wealth. In examining the social mobility data presented above, they tend to focus on a positive interpretation and claim a high degree of mobility. Critical sociologists, on the other hand, stress the evidence for closure in Canadian society and find class a useful concept for explaining this situation. Groups of people with common economic interests tend to act together to protect their privilege; the result is a society in which the class structure is reproduced from generation to generation.

CLASS AND STATUS

"Class" and "status" are terms used throughout this chapter, and it is time to take a closer look at them. The concept of class is associated with Karl Marx, and status is associated with Max Weber.

These terms indicate somewhat different ways of looking at social inequality. Class suggests a definite layering of the society and low social mobility: one can predict an individual's destination in the social structure by knowing the economic class position of their parents. Status, in contrast, is determined in a more complex way: people are placed in the social hierarchy on the basis of the social honour or prestige they are accorded. Economic class is just one element in the determination of status. Status may be either closely linked to class or separate from it.

Marx: Class Society

Marx defined class as an economic relationship. A class consists of a group of individuals who have the same relationship to the means of production: the tools, materials, technical expertise, and financial resources to engage in the production of goods. Those who have ownership and control of the means of production are the bourgeoisie, and those who have no alternative but to work for others are the proletariat.

Marx chose to define class in terms of the relations of production because he regarded the relations of production as the fundamental base of human society. Marx argued that the way life is organized around the production of goods — whether co-operative and communal, based on slavery or on feudal or capitalistic relationships — is the main influence shaping a society's social structure, politics, legal system, relations between women and men, and intellectual ideas.

Marx also argued that class situation has a pervasive influence on an individual's life situation: the owners of the means of production enjoy a life of material abundance sustained by the labour of others. The workers, in contrast, are mere units of labour power, commodities bought and sold in the marketplace when and where the capitalist has need of labour. The capitalist system of economy, argued Marx, divorces labour power from the human person who provides that power and treats the workers as a resource of production and profit, like any other commodity or factor of production. In a general way the life situation of workers is identical.

It is important to realize that Marx was not presenting a description of the actual social structure of the capitalist society around him. He was acutely aware of the existence of more than two distinct classes in capitalist society. Among other classes that Marx identified were the **petite bourgeoisie**, a group of small capitalists owning modest means of production and employing perhaps only one or two workers, and the artisans, a group of craftspeople and tradespeople working independently. Marx also recognized the distinct situation of the peasant class of small landholders and of the **lumpenproletariat**, a disorganized underclass never stably employed, whose members are disconnected from the rest of society and drift into crime.

Marx's two-class model of society was based on the expectation that capitalism will lead inevitably toward a **polarization** of the class structure. This process will come about as a result of the dynamic of capitalist competition. In the development of capitalist competition, big capitalists will swallow small capitalists; artisans will become wage labourers as new industrial technologies force out the independent producers; peasants will become wage labourers as farming increasingly develops large scale production. The central division of classes — that between bourgeoisie and proletariat — will become more stark. Marx believed that people would develop a consciousness of their shared class position and act together as a class.

Marx: Are Classes Groups?

• • • • • • • •

The working class, Marx argued, will gradually be transformed from being simply a number of individuals sharing a common class position into a cohesive group sharing class consciousness, a clear sense of their similarity of situation and of their collective interests. When workers were spread out over the countryside, they could not, however similar their economic and social situation, develop any form of class consciousness. Before there was communication among them, they could not see themselves as part of a large unity of individuals. By producing a greater and greater concentration of factories in large urban areas, capitalism produced the essential context for class unity and class organization. The establishment of working-class sectors of great urban centres made it possible for the working class to develop from a group that has a common identity yet is unaware of it — a class in itself — to something with solidarity and shared purpose — a class for itself.

This growingly self-conscious class can have only one goal in seeking to advance its position: the overthrow of capitalism. Coincident with the rise of capitalism, a commercial class arose and took power from the land-owning aristocracy and, in the process, came to dominate the wage-earning class. But the situation of the working class is different from this. The only way in which the working class can free itself from domination and exploitation is by abolishing the division of society along class lines entirely: by moving to a classless society. Its goal can only be the revolutionary overthrow of capitalist society and the replacement of private ownership of the means of production with public (collective) ownership. A free society of equal individuals — free from class conflict and class division — will emerge.

Marx's vision of a classless society is too unrealistic for many people, but this brief description does show how the concept of class is central to his general historical approach. It also reveals a critical view of society. Since the way people organize themselves to produce goods is central to all societies, at the moment when one group of individuals is able to take control of the means of production and organize society around this act of power, the interests of the dominated and the dominating are forever in conflict, and this conflict is fundamental to understanding the society.

Marx's concept of class has explanatory power; it allows him to explain people's motivation, their life chances, their interests, and the process of social change and collective action. Marx would call on the concept of class to answer our earlier question: how are people recruited for social roles? The answer is that their placement in the class structure is largely determined by their parents' placement. Those who subsist on the rewards from labour are not able to gain access to the rewards of society that fall into the laps of those who own and control capital. The dominant economic class is also able to exercise political and cultural domination. Their view of the world becomes the ruling view in society and dominates consciousness until it is challenged, and finally overcome, by the class consciousness developed by the workers in their struggle against the capitalists.

Weber:
The Basis of
Social Inequality

In talking about all societies, Weber defined class as "a number of people having in common a specific causal component of their life chances, in so far as this component is represented exclusively by economic interests in the possession of goods and opportunities for income, and is represented under the conditions of the commodity or labour markets" (Gerth and Mills, 1970: 181). Put more simply, a class is composed of a group of individuals with an economic situation in common.

Weber stressed the centrality of economic situation when he stated that property and lack of property are the basic categories of all class situations. This approach is underlined further by his claim that "the kind of chance in the market is the decisive moment which presents a common condition for the individual's fate. 'Class situation' is, in this sense, ultimately 'market situation'" (Gerth and Mills, 1970: 182). Weber's primary emphasis on economic situation in his definition of class places him very close to Marx.

There is a difference, however: Weber used the term "market situation" rather than referring to relations of individuals to the means of production. Weber's concept of class is more complex; it suggests that there can be differing "market situations" for individuals within the capitalist class and within the proletariat. For example, bankers may be distinguished from manufacturers, and transportation owners from owners of mining resources. Similarly, teachers may be distinguished from engineers, and engineers from carpenters (or secretaries from groundskeepers).

Although there are multiple possible class locations, Weber did believe that common elements in class situation may provide a basis for classes taking collective action.

Weber: Are
Classes Groups?

Like Marx, Weber acknowledged that classes can and do become conscious of their class interest and do engage in collective action to enhance those interests. As in the writings of Marx, class action is not automatic but only arises under specific conditions. Among other things, class action depends on the "transparency of the connections between the causes and the consequences of the 'class situation'" (Gerth and

Mills, 1970: 184). That is, when individuals can clearly see that their life chances result from the present distribution of property or the structure of the economic order, collective action may be taken to alter these things. Classes may organize to obtain power to effect these changes.

Status Groups

Weber does not agree with Marx that class is necessarily the most important distinction between groups in a society. In India, status, as exhibited in the caste system, is the central feature of social stratification. An untouchable may, like Mr. Chowdhury, become a lawyer, but he remains an untouchable. The central hierarchy is a status hierarchy. Status is based not on economic power but on the quality of social honour, or lack of it, adhering to the individual's social origin and role within society. It is this acute sense of the importance of status differentiation that gives Weber's understanding of social inequality its special richness and value in social analysis (Gerth and Mills, 1970: 69). In insisting that class position and status position do not always coincide, Weber gave a more pluralistic explanation of stratification than did Marx. Most of the time, according to Weber, class and status are linked. But class position does not always match one's status position. A white construction worker and a Black construction worker have the same class position, but in some societies they do not have the same status.

When status and class do not coincide, class divisions are blurred and group, or class, consciousness does not fully emerge. It may be this complexity of class/status division that makes it difficult for men and women to work together on economic matters. Weber argued that class has historically been the predominant force of social division in periods of political and economic upheaval, but that status regains importance when there is a slower rate of social change. Where status divisions within classes are important, they lack coherence and unity.

Finally, Weber completely rejected the notion that a **classless society** is possible. He insisted that no society can survive and function without a clear hierarchy of co-ordination and relations of domination and subordination. The idea that collective ownership of the means of production (i.e., socialism) will lead to an elimination of social inequality is an illusion. Socialism will not be able to overcome the technical indispensability of domination and bureaucratic administration. Indeed, in seeking to make society and the economy more "rational," socialism will have to interfere in social life more and more.

These two critical views of social inequality both share the view that *in modern capitalist society* the key source of inequality is economic. In addition, both support the idea that not just income, but status and life opportunities in general, can be linked to position in the system of economic inequality. Weber's ideas are more pluralistic and stress the importance of status (which has various sources, including class) as a principle of social inequality. Both views vary from the functionalist and liberal views by suggesting that class and status inheritance, rather than equal individual competition, are crucial aspects of society, and that class, status, and power are usually consistent.

WOMEN IN THE STRUCTURE OF INEQUALITY

If status reflects class position, primary attention need only be given to class. However, when class and status diverge, a more complex analysis is required of the roots of social inequality, and a synthesis of the ideas of Marx and Weber is useful. Canadian society does exhibit some structures of inequality that are not reducible to class. The most central one is inequality between men and women.

Throughout this book it has been claimed that Canadian women experience pervasive inequality. Some evidence was presented in support of this. Sociologists are confronted with challenging questions: how can they best understand this inequality? What is the basis of gender inequality? Does the concept of class properly capture women's position in society? Is the basis of women's inequality economic ownership? Feminists have answered the last two questions with a resounding No.

Evidence of Inequality
. . . .
Inequality of Power and Authority
. . . .

Four indicators of social power and authority are examined here: membership in the House of Commons, judicial appointments, senior positions in the federal civil service, and corporate directorships. In each of these categories, women are significantly under-represented.

The 1993 federal election sent 53 women to the 295-member House of Commons; thus 18 percent of the seats in the House were held by women.

In 1990–91 women made up 52 percent of the undergraduate enrolment in law schools. However, as of January 1990, of the 850 federally appointed judges only 73 (8.6 percent) were women (Maille, 1990).

Although women made up 42 percent of the federal civil service in 1987, they held only 8 percent of executive positions and 13 percent of senior management positions. It should be noted that the federal government is the biggest single employer of women in Canada (Morgan, 1988).

In 1985, all of the chief executive officers of the top 500 companies in Canada were men. The numbers of the boards of directors of all major corporations were almost all men (Peitchinis, 1989: 64).

Economic Inequality
. . . .

In terms of the distribution of income, there is clear evidence that women receive less income than men. Consider first the 1991 data on poverty: 41.4 percent of all single adult women are poor, compared with 31 percent of adult men (Statistics Canada, 1992c). Furthermore, 47.6 percent of female single-parent families are poor, compared with 16 percent of male single-parent families. (The figure for two-parent families with children is 9.2 percent).[12]

Economic differentiation by sex is also evident among the elderly poor. One elderly Canadian in five lived below the poverty line, but the risk of poverty was significantly higher for aged women than men.

The occupational location of women and their earnings also indicates a measure of inequality. The 1991 census reveals that while women account for 39 percent of full-time, full-year workers, they represent 72 percent of such workers in the lowest-paying occupations and only 20 percent of those in the ten highest-paying occupations.

In light of the above facts, it is not surprising that the average earnings of women working full time in 1992 were 71.8 percent of what men earned. For every dollar a man earned, a woman earned 71.8 cents. Table 7.5 shows that there has been some improvement in this earning ratio over the past two decades, but progress has been slow.

While it is clear that the differing locations of women in the labour force account for some of these differences — a higher percentage of women being in the poorest paid jobs — this does not account for all of the difference. A significant difference is evident even when considering income differences *within* the same occupations (see Table 7.6).

It is clear that an understanding of women's lower earnings compared with those of men must begin by understanding their differing locations in the labour force. In

Table 7.5		
Women's Earnings as a Percentage of Men's for Full-Time, Full-Year Workers, 1971–1992	1971	59.7
	1976	59.1
	1981	63.7
	1986	65.8
	1989	65.8
	1991	69.6
	1992	71.8

SOURCE: Statistics Canada, *Earnings of Men and Women*, cat. no. 13-217 (Ottawa: Statistics Canada, various years). Reproduced by authority of the Minister of Industry, 1994.

addition, women's different relationship to children and child care as a contributing factor is suggested by the fact that single women who have never married and worked full-time earned 99 percent of their male counterpart's earnings in 1992, rather than the 66.6 percent for married women. Finally, women's different role in the family may be important. All these topics are considered in later chapters.

Although sociologists favour a social explanation for gender inequality, there is an alternative approach. In the same way that apparent transmitted inequality is sometimes explained by alleged differences in inherited intelligence, sexual inequality is sometimes explained by biological theories.

Biological Theories

Biology has frequently been used to explain the social inequality that exists between men and women. The apparent differences in the nature or constitution of the two sexes are thought to explain the social and cultural arrangements built around them. Sociologists, of course, do not accept this analysis for two reasons: they demand that social factors be used to explain human social behaviour, and they do not accept the conservative implications of biology. If biology explains inequality, for example, can inequality be changed? Should people try to change it? Sociologists would tend to see biological explanations as part of an ideology that helps to maintain the structures of inequality. Nevertheless, this type of analysis needs to be examined as part of the debate over gender inequality.

Table 7.6	Women	Men
Average Employment Incomes by Occupation for Full-Time Workers, Women and Men, 1991		
Physicians	$61 606	$107 433
Lawyers	$50 012	$80 082
University teachers	$49 000	$53 725
Geologists	$43 480	$48 882
Accountants, auditors, financial officers	$32 716	$45 479
Social workers	$31 355	$30 811
Bus drivers	$21 719	$26 622
Sheet metal workers	$22 617	$28 283
Barbers, hairdressers	$16 785	$21 985
Cashiers, tellers	$17 243	$10 101

SOURCE: Statistics Canada, *Employment Income by Occupation*, cat. no. 93-332 (Ottawa: Statistics Canada, 1993). Reproduced by authority of the Minister of Industry, 1994.

Generally speaking, biological theories of gender inequality begin by assuming that human beings have strong sexual and aggressive drives and that men are generally bigger and stronger than females, who are made additionally vulnerable by bearing and caring for children (Eichler, 1980: 93). Through coercion, men dominate women and a society characterized by inequality between men and women is developed.[13]

There are many problems with sociobiological theories of gender inequality. For the most part they are errors of history, logic, and conceptualization. Consider errors of history. If gender inequality is a natural and inevitable product of male physical dominance, it is reasonable to assume that such inequality must have existed in all previous societies. Although there is still debate over the historical and anthropological evidence, it is clear that male domination was not universal (Sacks, 1979). Anderson (1987) argued, for example, that women in seventeenth-century Huron society had equal social standing with men. Leacock (1981) claimed that women of the Montagnais-Naskapi, a hunter–gatherer society in Quebec and Labrador, were not subordinated to men until colonialism undermined traditional culture. Frederick Engels (1968[1884]) also assumed that women were not subordinated at an early point in history. The domination of women occurred with the development of private property and men's seizure of its control.

A biological explanation of inequality between the sexes would also lead one to expect a consistent division of gender roles in the world's societies. There is some evidence of this: women take chief responsibility for child care and almost never make weapons or do metalwork. But variation is more apparent than any clear pattern. In some societies, women do the heavy work and are the most important producers of food and household supplies. In other societies, for example, the Montagnais–Naskapi (Leacock, 1981), the !Kung (Reiter, 1975), and the BaMbuti pygmies (Turnbull, 1961), men as well as women play prominent roles in the care and nurturing of children. In all these societies too there is little evidence of female subordination. Cultural variation is apparent in all these examples: there is no consistent cross-cultural pattern as predicted by biological theories.

Sociobiologists also claim that there are parallels between animal and human patterns of dominance and aggression. A vast literature has claimed that the natural dominance of males in the animal world demonstrates the naturalness of male domination in the human world. Critics claim that this argument ignores the difference between humans and animals: the existence of consciousness and of culture.

The animal observations on which biological theory is based have also been questioned: there is a growing body of literature that suggests dominance behaviour even among animals may be *learned* and not natural (Sayers, 1982: 74). Hunting among animals is taken as an indicator of aggressiveness, and it is assumed to be a male activity. Among lions, however, the female hunts.

Biological approaches to explaining gender inequality appear to be unconvincing, but this does not mean that biology, in another sense, is unimportant. Women's roles in childbearing and nursing an infant clearly reduce their ability and opportunity to develop their careers, further their education, or compete for resources. But does society adequately respond to this inequality of opportunity? (See Box 7.4.) Finally, the assumption that the lower economic and status levels of women is biologically related does not seem to account for the fact that there is now little real difference in the educational levels attained by the two sexes. To the extent that there are differences, there is clear evidence that they are being reduced.

Box 7.4
Maternity Leave for
Working Women

Western European countries provide paid maternity leave for all working women. The woman's job and benefits are guaranteed, and she receives a significant portion of her income while on leave. The leave period ranges from three months in Portugal to a full year in Sweden. The benefit level varies from 50 percent of previous salary to 90–100 percent in Sweden and Denmark. Some countries provide some form of parental leave for fathers.

In the United States, only unpaid maternity leave is provided. In Canada, women are offered a 15-week benefit period at 57 percent of previous earnings plus an option of a further 10 weeks of parental leave for the father or mother.

SOURCE: Excerpted from L. McQuaig, *The Wealthy Banker's Wife* (Toronto: Penguin, 1993), pp. 73–75.

For the reasons reviewed above, sociologists reject simple biological explanations of gender inequality and look to society itself for an explanation. The role of culture and social organization in creating and maintaining inequality is explored in subsequent chapters.

Women: A Class or Status Group?

Although it is clear that the concept of class (ownership of economic resources) is helpful in understanding the situation of individual women, can it explain the situation of women as a group? Are women a class?

The answer to this must be no. Women cannot be said to form a class because the notion of class implies the possibility of movement out of a class. One can change one's class situation, but biological sex is fixed. The concept of class would become meaningless if women corporate presidents were placed in the same class as supermarket cashiers.

Eichler points out that when women and men are compared on scales of inequality, it is clear that women are consistently placed lower. For example, when men and women have equivalent educational qualifications, women still have lower-placed jobs than do men; when jobs are similar, women still earn less than men; when women dominate an employment sector, it is most often low paid. Sex appears to work independently of all other aspects of the person and reduce women's position in society (Eichler, 1980: 97). To understand the social situation of women therefore requires the concept of status because there is a hierarchy even within economic classes that tends to place women in subordinate positions.

Women are less valued as a group than men are and this devaluation affects all aspects of their lives. Although their class positions may vary and create competing interests, women share a common status position. They are a status group, as are many other groups (see Box 7.5). This devaluation has brought women together, and the women's movement has mobilized women to transform their social situation. The women's movement is affected by the other social divisions within society, however; it is frequently accused of being too middle class and too white.

Box 7.5
The Politics of Status

W omen are not the only Canadian status group. There are a number of other such groups in Canada. The past, and indeed the present, treatment of many ethnic and racial groups is evidence of their devalued position in Canadian society. Some of these groups occupy distinct economic positions and have varying degrees of power, but past treatment has become a strong symbol of low or stigmatized status. As a result, they have become politically active to demand an apology or compensation for past devaluation.

First Nations groups provide numerous examples of marginal social position; Afro-Canadians in many parts of the country feel their personal and collective existence is wrapped in negative stereotypes; Chinese-Canadians see the head tax and the Chinese Exclusion Act of 1923 as discriminatory; Ukrainian-Canadians were interned during World War I; Jews remember the Canadian government's refusal to take Jewish immigrants who were attempting to escape Nazi Germany; Sikhs remember the *Komagata Maru* being turned away from Vancouver harbour in 1914, and, of course, Japanese-Canadians recall their internment and loss of property during World War II.

Japanese-Canadians in 1989 were successful in obtaining a public apology for their treatment, individual compensation for survivors, and public funds for community development. Other groups have not yet had these successes. In 1993, the Canadian government agreed to make an "omnibus apology" and construct a "Nation Builders Hall of Record" to commemorate the contributions of immigrant groups to Canadian society. This offer was not accepted, however, and the politics of status continue.

CONCLUSION

This chapter raised as many questions as it answered. For example: what role does the government play in creating or maintaining inequality? What role does the school play in providing equality of opportunity? Does the school prepare men and women differently for the work force? How is the labour force organized for men and women? Do the differing roles of men and women in the family contribute to their inequality? What is a patriarchal family? These questions are taken up in subsequent chapters.

The chapter also introduced the concept of class, suggesting its use as an explanatory concept. By thinking of groups of people with common economic interests as a class, it is possible to imagine them acting collectively to change the society or to maintain the status quo. Inequality may then be thought of as shaped by the exercise of class power. Class is used by critical sociologists as a powerful concept for examining the role of the state and understanding the Canadian economy — topics discussed in the next chapters.

Functionalist and critical perspectives on social inequality were examined through an inquiry into social mobility. The functionalist perspective believes there will be high rates of social mobility in society, while the critical perspective believes society to be quite closed and with low rates of mobility. The data on general mobility, while open to some interpretation, do suggest that Canadian society has a moderate level of class inheritance. The data on elite recruitment is quite definite: it clearly supports a closed-society thesis. This debate is important for Canadians because liberalism claims that Canada is open and that it provides reasonable equality of opportunity for all citizens.

Although the concept of class is useful for understanding inequality in Canada, it does not provide an adequate explanation of the position of women. Weber's concept of status and status groups was explored and found to be more useful.

This chapter began an examination of the structure of contemporary Canadian society. Its structure is similar to a layer cake. The concepts of class and status, distinct divisions between groups in both economic and social position, reflect this metaphor and are a useful tool for understanding society.

Society is more than a system of inequality, however; it consists of various parts, such as the economy, the state, the family, and educational institutions. The book now turns to an examination of how these parts of society are themselves structured.

· · · · · · · ·

NOTES

· · · · · · · ·

1. Brenda Dalglish, "Are They Worth It?" *Maclean's*, May 9, 1994, p. 35.
2. "Insider Trading," *The Globe and Mail*, June 27, 1991, p. B11.
3. Allan Robinson, "Munk to Make $36.6-Million on Sale of Barrick Stock," *The Globe and Mail*, August 30, 1991, p. B1.
4. D. Downey, "Yolanda Ballard Seeking $16,050 a Month in Support," *The Globe and Mail*, October 2, 1990, p. A7.
5. Sean Fine, "Welfare Weaves Its Way into Ontario's Fabric," *The Globe and Mail*, April 3, 1992, p. A1.
6. Charles Murray (1991: 17–18) reports that this is also true for the United States. He says that in the 1950s, fewer than one family in every 1000 had an income of $100 000 or more, but by 1989 one in every 25 had an income that great. In addition, he notes that in 1980 a male college graduate made 30 percent more than a male high-school graduate; in 1988 the college graduate made 60 percent more. This is clear evidence of the growing gap between rich and poor.
7. A. Michalos, "Taxation Justice for All? Base It on Personal Worth," *The Globe and Mail*, February 6,1989, p. A7. These figures underestimate the degree of concentration of wealth because they do not include all forms of wealth.
8. "Report Cites Danger in Family Holdings," Vancouver *Sun*, March 19, 1985, p. D1. Note: These figures are derived after the shareholdings of the banks are removed.
9. "Equity: Scaling the Ivory Tower," *The Martlet*, October 18, 1990, p.1.
10. Unionized workers have higher wages than do non-unionized workers doing similar work (Women's Bureau, Labour Canada, 1990).
11. There is a debate over the adequacy of Clement's research that is worth reading; see Ogmundson (1990) and Clement (1990).
12. These figures represent low incomes using the 1986 base. For a discussion of methods of measuring poverty, see Spector (1992).
13. These kinds of arguments can be found in Wilson (1975), Goldberg (1973), and Tiger (1969).

· · · · · · · ·

FURTHER READING

· · · · · · · ·

Curtis, Bruce, D.W. Livingstone and Harry Smaller. *Stacking the Deck: Streaming of Working-Class Kids in Ontario Schools*. Toronto: Our Schools/Our Selves Education Foundation, 1992. A thought-provoking examination of one of the mechanisms for the reproduction of the structure of inequality in Canadian society.

Francis, Diane. *Controlling Interest: Who Owns Canada*. Toronto: Macmillan of Canada, 1986. For those interested in identifying the capitalist class that owns much of Canada, this is an essential guide written by a journalist generally supportive of big business.

Gould, Stephen. *The Mismeasure of Man*. New York: W.W. Norton, 1981. An important and readable critique of science, particularly the study of intelligence.

Grabb, Edward. *Theories of Social Inequality: Classical and Contemporary Perspectives*. Toronto: Holt, Rinehart and Winston, 1990. A thorough discussion of the sociological interpretations of inequality.

Gunderson, Morley, L. Muszynski, and J. Keck. *Women and Labour Market Poverty*. Canadian Advisory Council on the Status of Women, 1990. A useful theoretically informed discussion of women's economic situation.

National Council of Welfare. Many of this organization's publications are helpful for staying in touch with the condition of poverty and policies affecting that condition. See, for example, *Poverty Profile, 1988* (April 1988); *Women and Poverty Revisited* (Summer 1990); *Welfare in Canada: The Tangled Safety Net* (November 1987).

Satzewich, Vic, ed. *Deconstructing a Nation: Immigration, Multiculturalism and Racism in '90s Canada*. Halifax: Fernwood, 1992. A worthwhile collection of readings examining some of the more important cleavages in Canadian society.

STUDY QUESTIONS

1. Explain the importance of the idea of equality of opportunity in functionalist theories of inequality.
2. What are the main obstacles to equality of opportunity in Canadian society?
3. In what ways does class shape people's lives?
4. How would you relate functionalist and critical perspectives to individual versus social explanations of inequality? Explain your answer.
5. Are ethnic groups best understood as classes or as status groups? Discuss.
6. Women's inequality must be thought of as both structural and cultural. Discuss.
7. Describe the placement of women in your workplace or your university or college. How would you explain this placement?
8. What precautions must be taken in interpreting social mobility studies?

8 THE CANADIAN ECONOMY

INTRODUCTION

This chapter continues to evaluate the liberal model of society through a discussion of the Canadian economy. While this model depicts an open, competitive economy, examination reveals that competition is restricted by the concentration of ownership, substantial family wealth, and a high degree of foreign ownership. Although Canada is a wealthy nation, its economy has many unique and troubling features. Compared with those of other mature capitalist societies, its economy is "distorted"; it has characteristics of a much less developed nation. How has this situation come about, and why does it persist?

The previous chapter demonstrated that considerable inequality exists among Canadians and, more importantly, that a strong argument could be made for using the concepts of class and status to understand this inequality. Liberalism argues that capitalism provides for individual freedom and fairly equal opportunity. The evidence, however, suggests that Canada is a relatively closed society. This is particularly noticeable among the economic elite. This chapter explores a related question: does the structure of the Canadian economy correspond to the beliefs of liberalism?

THE LIBERAL MODEL OF THE ECONOMIC SYSTEM

A liberal free-market economy is believed to have the following five characteristics: first, the economy consists of many competitive suppliers of goods and services. Second, no individual or corporation can control the market. Third, prices are set by the marketplace through the forces of supply and demand. Two related characteristics follow from these three: in order to maintain competition, the ownership of economic resources should be widely distributed throughout the society; and a nation's economic resources should be responsive to control by its residents — economic independence should be tied to political independence.

This chapter provides an examination of the correspondence between these liberal ideas and the realities of Canada's economy.

CHALLENGES TO THE LIBERAL MODEL

· · · · · · · ·

Large Multinational Corporations

· · · · · · · ·

In the distant past, goods and services were produced by a large number of small businesses, often owned and operated by family members. It was possible for many people to start a business because the initial investment was quite small and the competitors were also small businesses. The dispersion of economic power prevented co-ordinated pressure from being exerted on governments, so political power was not directly linked to economic power.

Now, however, large corporations dominate the economy, and these corporations operate in a number of countries. Historians see three periods of significant growth in the concentration of capital and multinationality of companies. The first period occurred during the last two decades of the nineteenth century; the second in the 1920s and 1930s; and the final period from 1960 to the present (Teichova, 1990). While small producers continue to provide most employment in Canada, the largest producers have great economic power and perhaps pose a challenge to political power. For example, a select group of 600 international corporations, each with annual sales of more than $1 billion, produce an astonishing 25 percent of everything made in the world's market economies (Mittelstaedt, 1989: 75). Although responsible for 25 percent of the goods produced, they employ only 3 percent of the world's work force.[1]

Table 8.1 lists the ten biggest non-financial corporations in Canada in 1992. This table does not reveal the true size of corporations, since many of the large corporations listed in it are owned by other corporations; they are the subsidiary operations of much larger, perhaps multinational, companies. General Motors of Canada, for example, is 100 percent owned by General Motors Corporation of Detroit. Similarly, Exxon of New York owns 69.6 percent of Imperial Oil of Canada, and Brascan owns 45 percent of Noranda, while 49 percent of Brascan is owned by Edper Enterprises. Behind these corporations, then, there are even larger conglomerates.

General Motors (GM) is the largest company in the world, with sales of $127 billion (U.S.). If the wealth of corporations like GM were compared with that of nations and the combined list ranked, GM would have the world's twentieth-largest economy. If the top 100 economies are examined, there are 53 nations in this exclusive

Table 8.1

Ten Biggest Non-financial Corporations, by Revenue, Canada, 1992

· · · · · · · ·

	Revenue ($millions)
Bell Canada Enterprises	20 784
General Motors of Canada	18 347
Ford Motors of Canada	14 443
George Weston	11 599
Chrysler Canada	9 453
Alcan Aluminum	9 183
Canadian Pacific	8 963
Noranda	8 538
Imasco	7 989
Imperial Oil	7 968

SOURCE: *The Financial Post 500* (Summer 1993): 100. Reprinted with permission.

list and 47 corporations. In 1980 there were 61 nations and 39 corporations in this group.[2]

These facts reveal that a significant portion of the world's wealth and productive capital is owned and controlled by a few large corporations. This is strong evidence of the concentration of capital in a few megacorporations.

Concentration of Economic Power

· · · · · · · · ·

The concentration of capital and of economic power raises important questions for any society:

> *In democratic societies the terms corporate concentration and corporate power often evoke a series of images coloured with economic, political, and social implications. It starts with the classical economic perception of individual corporations controlling the price and quantity of products and services, thereby reducing consumer surplus and impeding efficiency. It continues into the political realm, where it is perceived that through their economic power such corporations have the ability to influence government policy and legislation. Ultimately, the impact of increasing corporate concentration extends to the social fabric of society, as large corporations demand loyalty from their employees and through the means of mass communications shape the tastes and attitudes of consumers. It is this image of a somewhat sinister force at variance with democratic principles of "equality" that has caught the public eye and motivated researchers in many disciplines to study the concentration of corporate power* (Krause and Lothian, 1989: 3.14).

The concentration of economic power may be a threat to the principles of a democratic society with serious implications for the economy, political life, and social life in general. The extent of corporate concentration in Canada is therefore an important issue. The significant degree of concentration in Canada has two related problems: more than that of other western industrial societies, Canada's economy is concentrated in family hands; and an unusually significant part of the Canadian economy is foreign dominated.

There are two related ways to examine economic concentration in any economy. The first method uses the individual company as the unit of analysis, while the second uses the conglomerate (or enterprise) as the unit of analysis. For example, one could look at Brascan itself or at all of the companies controlled by Edper Enterprises.

Using the first method, researchers are able to construct a concentration ratio. This ratio is the portion of the assets or revenues in a sector of the economy controlled by the top four companies. (This is the CR4 index.) Liberalism suggests that competition is good, ensuring the proper working of the market and avoiding too much corporate power in politics. Some sectors of the Canadian economy do correspond to the competitive model, but not all of them.

The concentration ratio (CR4) for 1986 in selected industries is presented in Table 8.2. The figures in this presentation indicate that in the production of tobacco products, for example, the four largest companies own 99 percent of the assets in that sector. This kind of concentration also occurs in the automobile industry, where the majority of automobile production is controlled by three large companies. In another 20 manufacturing industries (not singled out above), four companies control 75 percent of the production.

There is also considerable concentration in the financial sector. The concentration ratio (CR4) in the trust industry in 1984, for example, was 75 percent, up from 55 per-

Table 8.2
Concentration
Ratios for Selected
Industries,
Canada, 1986

Tobacco products	99.0%
Rubber products	66.0%
Primary metals	61.2%
Petroleum and coal products	67.8%
Transportation	57.4%
Storage	70.4%
Communications	72.0%
Utilities	73.8%
Metal mines	58.7%
Transportation equipment	43.1%
Paper and allied products	39.2%
Yarn and cloth	39.2%
Electrical appliances	38.5%
Beverages	30.3%

SOURCE: A. Mayrand, *Concentration in the Canadian Financial Sector: The Situation in 1987.* Working Paper (Ottawa: Economic Council of Canada, 1990), p. 60.

cent in 1950 (Richardson, 1988).[3] The concentration ratio (CR4) for banking assets was 45.4 percent (Mayrand, 1990). There is clear evidence of concentration of economic power in Canada. The above data also ignores the fact that many corporations are merely subsidiaries of other corporations; they are part of a conglomerate. A conglomerate is illustrated in Figure 8.1, which shows one corporation controlling a large number of other corporations. Taking this corporate integration into account reveals a higher degree of concentration than is apparent in the first analysis. A recent analysis shows that 10 percent of the nation's enterprises (conglomerates) own approximately 90 percent of its corporate assets (Krause and Lothian, 1989). The 25 largest conglomerates have also been growing at a more rapid pace than have other enterprises. Between 1975 and 1986, their share of assets, sales, and profits grew by approximately 190 percent, compared with 95 percent for other enterprises.

This kind of concentration is not only a concern for researchers; the corporate class also worries about the trend. Bernard Ghert, president of Cadillac Fairview Corporation, expressed his concern about the impact on society if a handful of conglomerates, as few as three or four, dominated the economy. "They would wield enormous power in a country the size of Canada. That power would be sufficient to influence significantly the political process itself and ultimately our political freedoms."[4] Ghert clearly considered economic concentration as posing a threat to the free market and democracy; it may result in inefficiency in economic activity; it may lead to higher prices; and it may result in economic power being immune to political power.

James Gillies, founding dean of York University's Faculty of Administrative Studies, claims that "the degree of concentration, or in other words the lack of competition, in many markets in Canada is the greatest in the world and concentration of economic power is enormous" (1991: 19). Sandy Peel, chairman of a forest resources commission in British Columbia, raised concerns about concentration in the forest industry by noting that 75 percent of the trees taken from the province's publicly owned forests are cut by ten companies. He went on to say that if "you have that control of the resource by that few companies, you don't have any free-market determination at all."[5]

This kind of concentration is also readily evident in the food industry. The number of beef packers in Ontario fell from nineteen in 1988 to 10 in 1993. In 1961, there were eighteen pork buyers; in 1993 there were three. In 1985, the province had 596 dairy buyers; in 1993 there were 97. Three companies grade up to 75 percent of all the eggs produced in Ontario, and 40 percent of all broiler-chicken farmers sell to the same company that supplies their chicks and feed.[6] Farmers worry that the lack of competition hurts their incomes. The consequences of this increasing concentration of ownership and the vertical integration of industries (a single corporation owning or controlling all phases of the production, delivery, and sale of a good) has wider effects. Box 8.1 provides an account of concentration's effects on the experience of grocery shopping and life on the family farm.

Concentration is an inevitable consequence of a market economy; it is not an indication of the system not working properly. When Central Guaranty Trustco sold its corporate trust operations to its rival, Montreal Trust, it explained this action by referring to its inability to be as competitive as its rival because of its relatively small size, which made it unable to benefit from economies of scale.

During the 1980s this process of concentration occurred in many industries, including automobile tire manufacturing. Michelin bought Uniroyal–Goodrich, Bridgestone purchased Firestone, Continental acquired General Tire, Pirelli bought Armstrong, Sumitomo bought Dunlop, and so on. At the end of this activity, six companies were estimated to control about 80 percent of the world market for tires.[7]

In the early 1980s there were seven major confectioners in Canada; after a period of rationalization there were four. George Weston (of the Neilson brand) bought the Cadbury line, Hershey Foods took the Lowney brand, Nestle SA bought the rights to Rowntree, and Mars began importing U.S.-made bars to Canada.[8]

Concentration clearly has its economic advantages, and this is why it is pursued. However, it also raises a number of concerns: is it possible for nations or consumers to control the actions of companies through political action or consumer action? Does concentration provide consumers with the widest choice of products? Does it guarantee competition and consequently the lowest price? Does economic concentration allow a few firms to manage the market to their advantage?[9]

Although concentration is inevitable, Canada's position is somewhat unusual. In explaining the high degree of concentration in Canada, James Gillies maintained that government policies in Canada have been designed to prevent competition and that "Canadian businessmen have never wanted or encouraged competition. Indeed, the reaction of many to competitive inroads has been to sell the business; as a result there is a higher percentage of foreign ownership in Canada than in any country in the world" (1991: 19). Business leaders have argued that the Canadian market is too small for a completely free market and have pressured for a degree of market domination (limiting competition) to compensate for this. Governments have complied by providing only weak enforcement of the Competition Act and allowing markets to be structured to ensure concentration.

Powerful Families

When examined at the enterprise level as well, there is a great deal of concentration in the Canadian economy. The impact of this might be less serious if the ownership of these powerful conglomerates was widely held. If a large number of Canadians owned voting shares (stocks) in the corporations, it could be argued that real corporate control was widely dispersed in the hands of citizens. What are the facts concerning ownership of these large companies?

Figure 8.1
The Bronfman
Family's Holdings

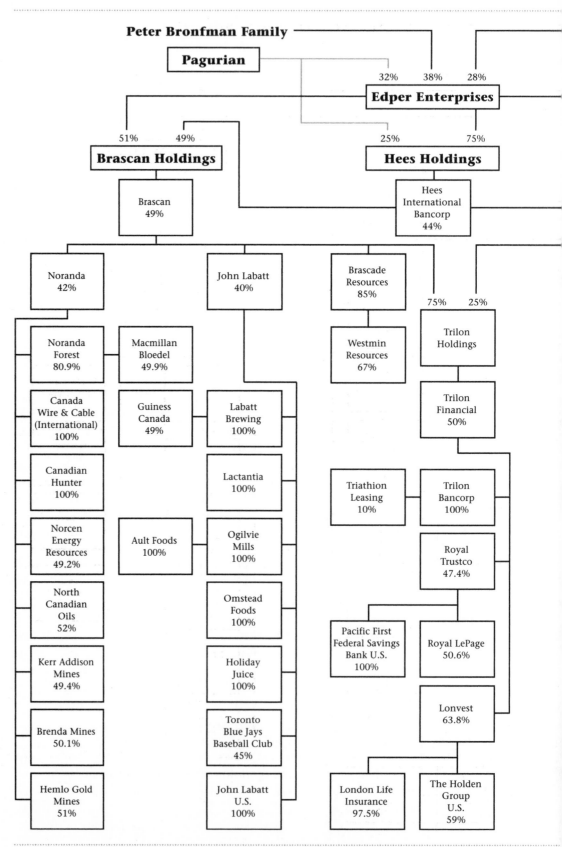

SOURCE: *The Financial Post 500* (Summer 1990): 170–171. Reprinted with permission.

Edward Bronfman Family

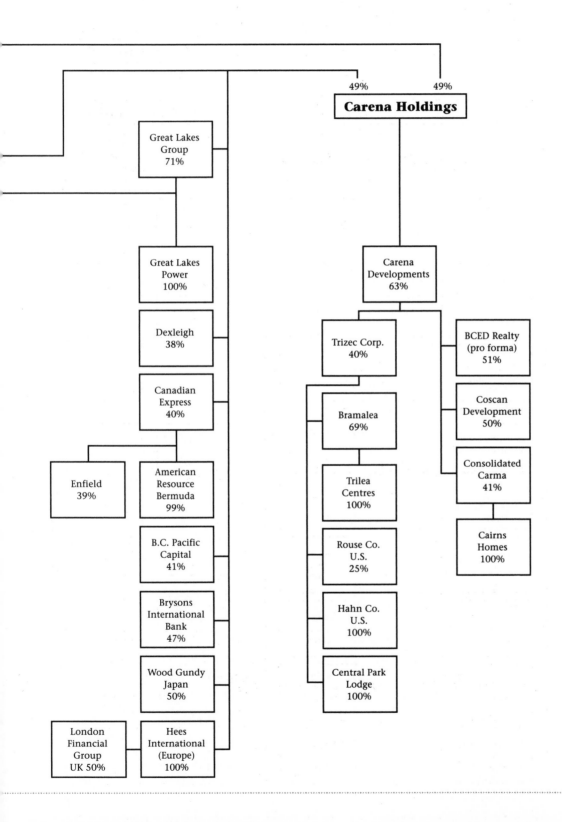

Carena Holdings — 49% / 49%

Great Lakes Group 71%

Great Lakes Power 100%

Dexleigh 38%

Canadian Express 40%

Enfield 39%

American Resource Bermuda 99%

B.C. Pacific Capital 41%

Brysons International Bank 47%

Wood Gundy Japan 50%

London Financial Group UK 50%

Hees International (Europe) 100%

Carena Developments 63%

Trizec Corp. 40%

Bramalea 69%

Trilea Centres 100%

Rouse Co. U.S. 25%

Hahn Co. U.S. 100%

Central Park Lodge 100%

BCED Realty (pro forma) 51%

Coscan Development 50%

Consolidated Carma 41%

Cairns Homes 100%

Box 8.1
Concentration Affects
the Supermarket

The retail food sector is verging on an unprecedented wave of merger activity. Over the past two years the food giants have feverishly attempted to outdo each other in lowering costs and shutting down smaller, less profitable stores with higher labour costs relative to sales.

These mergers are bound to have an impact on a broad segment of Canadian society. Consumers, food processors, their labour force, farmers, and the communities that depend upon processing and related farming are being placed in jeopardy by the corporate shuffling in the Montreal and Toronto boardrooms.

In Canada, retail food chain stores have expanded their control of supermarket sales dramatically, from 23 percent in 1950 to more than 75 percent today. This would not be so worrying if there were a substantial number of competing chains in the marketplace, but this is not so.

At the local or city-wide level, the relevant market for most consumers, some Canadian cities had reached the point by the 1970s where four or fewer chain stores controlled 75 percent or more of the retail food sales.

The completed and impending takeovers of the Provigo, Steinberg, and Super Carnival food empires by the remaining food giants, in this case Loblaws and the Maritime-based Sobey's Stores, will reduce consumer options to levels unacceptable in a free-market society.

More than consumers and retail workers are at risk, however. In recent years many food processors, especially the smaller firms, have had their brands squeezed off the supermarket shelves. Many of those that remain in business depend heavily on sales under the private labels of the supermarket chains.

While the chains have little choice but to stock the major, nationally advertised brands produced by the biggest processing companies, they can shop around among food processors for the lowest price for the supermarkets' private-label products.

In Canada's food system, the bulk of supermarket purchases are funnelled through only four wholesale buying organizations, controlled by the chain stores themselves.

Therefore, the food retail giants have considerable leverage in deciding what they are willing to pay processors for private-label merchandise, which now accounts for the majority of sales for some products.

Even fewer chain stores will mean the smaller processors without well-known brands will be more vulnerable to the whims of the chain-store buyers. With already slim profits in the very competitive processing industry, more of these firms will be forced out of business by the pressure from the retail giants.

Recently, research has indicated that in fruit and vegetable production, for example, the smaller food processors are the most willing to deal with small farmers, who often have no alternative for selling their products.

Moreover, research suggests that small farms support development of healthy and vibrant rural communities. ...

SOURCE: Excerpted from Anthony Winson, "Shakeups in Supermarkets Spread Beyond the Shelves," *The Globe and Mail*, June 30, 1988. Reprinted with the permission of the author.

Box 8.2
Who Owns Canada?
Families with
Substantial Influence
on the Canadian
Economy

Irving	Eaton	Campeau
McCain	Roman	Wolfe
Sobey and Jodrey	Love	Richardson
Molson	Jackman	Singer
Bronfman	Weston	Mannix
Desmarais	Black	Ghermezian
Webster	Bronfman	Belzberg
Ivanier	Reichmann	Southern
Steinberg	Mann	Pattison
Bata	Thomson	Bentley
Posluns		

SOURCE: Diane Francis, *Controlling Interest: Who Owns Canada?* (Toronto: Seal Books, 1986).

Ownership patterns in Canada are quite distinct. Corporate power is not widely dispersed through the mechanism of voting shares but is concentrated in the hands of very few people. In fact, it is concentrated in the hands of a few Canadian families. These are not just rich families; they control the corporate wealth and power of the country (see Box 8.2). "Canada has become a collection of family dynasties and management fiefdoms, with more billionaire families per capita than the United States" (Francis, 1986: 2). Only 20 of Canada's 400 largest public corporations have widely dispersed share ownership; 380 of the corporations have a shareholder with at least 15 percent of the stock; and in 374 of these, controlling interest of 25–30 percent is held by a Canadian family or conglomerate (Francis, 1986). The nation may be witnessing the emergence of "a Canadian conglomeracy — a closely interlocked group of 37 conglomerates, 32 of which are family owned" (Richardson, 1988: 18). Even the corporate world is worried about these developments.[10]

In 1985, the president of the Canadian Bankers Association said that "the [amount of] concentration is dangerous."[11] A survey by the association stated that if the chartered banks were removed from the calculation, nine families controlled 53 percent of the Toronto Stock Exchange's widely watched list of 300 companies known as the TSE 300. The report did not specifically name the families, but the *Toronto Star* said they included the empires of Kenneth Thomson, Edward and Peter Bronfman, Edgar and Charles Bronfman, Paul Desmarais, Galen Weston, Conrad and Montague Black, and the Reichmann family, as well as Ron Southern and the Seamen brothers of Calgary.

Antoniou and Rowley (1986), in researching 247 of the largest Canadian-owned corporations in 1979, confirmed the importance of the family-owned firm. They found that almost 37 percent of the companies were majority owned (one owner had more than 50 percent of the shares), and in 68.4 percent of the companies one owner had at least 20 percent of the shares. This research challenged the notion that there had been a dispersal of corporate ownership in Canada. Francis (1986) claimed that Canada is somewhat unique in this regard; only 75 of the companies included in the American Standard and Poor's 500 stock index have a large shareholder.[12]

Ownership versus Control

· · · · · · · · ·

Why are sociologists interested in whether the corporate sector is dominated by large shareholders or even by families? It was assumed that as western economies expanded and new capital was required for expansion, most corporations would seek new investors. They placed shares in their company on the public stock exchange, and ordinary citizens were able to invest their savings. In theory, this process would reduce the number of single owners and disperse ownership. Corporations would no longer have single owners, but instead would have many shareholders who entrusted the business to corporate managers and executives. There would be a separation of ownership and control.

Some writers assumed that managers would operate corporations in a manner different from that of owners. They would be freed from the goal of short-term profit and focus instead on responsible long-term growth, a good corporate reputation, and responsiveness to a wide range of interests. They would give the corporation more "soul" (Kaysen, 1957). American studies, however, have shown that there is little difference between manager run and owner run corporations. Managers typically have a large financial interest in the success of the corporations they run; the mixing of ownership of shares and management of a company is considered good for business. Consider the following:

> H.J.Heinz Co. chairman Tony O'Reilly earned nearly $40 million last year and was a bargain at that price, according to actuary Ken Hugessen's calculations.
>
> Mr. Hugessen uses that example in his argument that Canadian companies are far too conservative in their attempts to pay senior executives by performance.
>
> That conservatism means they are not really encouraging their executives to increase the value of their companies, the managing director of William M. Mercer Ltd. consultants told a conference on executive employment contracts organized by Lexium Educational Services.
>
> Executives of U.S. companies often get much more of their compensation in the form of stock options, he said. For example, Mr. O'Reilly in one recent year was granted options on four million shares valued at nearly $30 each.
>
> Calculating in a way similar to how actuaries work out the current value of someone's pension, Mr. Hugessen estimated those options were worth about $36 million when they were granted.
>
> That is on top of a base salary of $708 000 and bonuses of $2.6 million, for a total package approaching $40 million.
>
> He acknowledged his calculations are rough, but his point is that a person with an option on $120 million of equity in a company is more likely to care what happens to its share price than a typical Canadian executive with stock options worth maybe $500 000 to $2 million.[13]

If corporate ownership was dispersed and senior corporate positions were achieved by merit, this would promote a breakdown of rigid class boundaries based on ownership and inheritance. Social stratification would become more open and be based on achievement and occupation, guaranteeing a high degree of social mobility. Since Canada's economy continues to be dominated by owner-capitalists, it can be argued that Canada's class system is more closed and more rigid than that of other western capitalist societies.

Family corporations abound in Canada. In New Brunswick, for example, the Irving family has some 400 companies, and 25 percent of the province's gross domestic product is produced by Irving companies. One of every twelve employees in the province works for Irving. The McCain family, another large conglomerate, is also located in New Brunswick. There is another dimension to economic ownership in Canada, however, which again makes Canada somewhat unique: the extent of foreign ownership of its corporate assets.

Foreign Ownership Concern about foreign ownership of the economic resources of Canada is almost as old as the country itself. In 1972 a Government of Canada study report said: "The degree of foreign ownership and control of economic activity is already substantially higher in Canada than in any other industrialized country and is continuing to increase" (Canada, 1972: 5). In 1983, a United Nations survey found that the value of direct foreign investment was higher in Canada than in any other country in the world (Laxer, 1989: 225). Direct foreign investment is money invested in order to gain control of a corporation, while portfolio investment is used to gain interest or dividends. Direct foreign investment leads to the development of a branch-plant economy: the parent company is located outside the country, and the branch-plant provides goods and services to the national market or for the parent. Not surprisingly, branch plants and the managers of these operations are an important group of people in Canada.

> *The branch-plant class, instead of being an exotic little splinter group as it is in London or Milan, constitutes the single most important force within our business population. In 40 years its relative size has almost tripled. ... The branch-plant class is an acutely Canadian phenomenon. There are, of course, local employees of foreign firms in every country. But in the other 20 or so developed nations, they are a much smaller portion of the private-business population: about 5% in places such as France and Germany, up to 15% or so in small countries like Belgium. In Canada, where the calculation is arbitrarily done on the basis of majority share holding, the figure is 25% (Saul, 1988: 82).*

Of the 500 largest companies in Canada in 1990, 54 percent were entirely foreign owned; another 88 firms were partially foreign owned. The previous decade was a time of frenzied merger activity by large companies, and this increased the presence of foreign ownership in Canada. Foreign firms (mostly American) do not typically come to Canada to start new business; rather, they buy existing companies. In 1987, approximately 50 percent of the profits in the manufacturing sector went to foreign companies. Indeed in 1992, 29 percent of revenue received by companies in Canada went to foreign-controlled firms. Hurtig claims that for the period 1946–90, U.S. direct investment in Canada amounted to $6.631 billion. From this investment American investors were able to withdraw $69.460 billion from Canada in the form of dividend payments, and the book value of the investments made increased to $76.710 billion (1991: 63).

During the recession of the late 1980s and early 1990s, domestic firms were hit harder than were foreign-controlled firms. This allowed foreign-controlled firms to increase their share of revenue, by expanding their ownership, from 25.4 percent in 1988 to 27.6 percent in 1992. Recently the managers of foreign-controlled firms complained that their powers were reduced as more decision making was transferred to the parent corporation. Linked to this complaint was the decision of an increasing number of foreign-controlled firms with publicly traded stocks to buy out the minority shareholders (typically Canadians). These decisions make foreign-controlled firms less accountable to Canadians and imply that the Canadian division is really just a "domestic" division of the corporation rather than a "foreign" division.[14] In short, the Canadian border is becoming less meaningful to foreign corporations.

While there may be strictly nationalist arguments for worrying about a high degree of foreign ownership, there are also economic reasons. Foreign ownership, it is argued, contributes to the weakness of Canada's economy in many ways. First, since nearly a quarter of the economy is foreign controlled, parent companies do little of their research and development in Canada. Rather, they import the technology to the branch-plant. The result is an overall weakness in Canada's research and development, a process that should lead to the development of new products and increased efficiencies to increase Canada's competitiveness.

Second, the other implication of the relationship between parent and branch plant is that a significant portion of Canadian trade consists of intercorporate transfers. The parent exports goods or services to the Canadian branch plant or imports them from the branch plant. These transfers account for approximately 75–80 percent of Canada's trade and due to its special nature this trade is not responsive to the same kind of market pressures as are other transactions. This also means that foreign firms create fewer jobs in Canada than do Canadian-controlled firms.

A third issue is implied by the above concerns: branch plants frequently operate in a different manner from their indigenous counterparts. Since they are largely controlled by the parent company, they are not encouraged to compete with it. Their role is not seen as one of innovation and expansion to a world market. Rather, they are designed to serve the Canadian market or to meet the needs of the parent company.

This suggests the final concern: parent companies frequently remove profits from Canada for other investments or in order to purchase a larger share of the Canadian economy. This is done through the payment of dividends and through transfer pricing.

Transfer pricing is the practice of increasing corporate profits in countries with the lowest tax rate and decreasing profit where there is high tax. This can be done by setting the price of goods and services provided to the branch plant at artificially high levels, which reduces the amount of tax the Canadian government is able to collect. It has been estimated that more than half of Canada's imports and exports involve transfer pricing (Hurtig, 1991: 67).

Conspiracy, Collusion, Bid-Rigging?
• • • • • • • •

A free market demands that no single player or small group of players can exert dominant market influence. There are government departments set up to monitor the marketplace to ensure that it remains competitive. The Canadian Competition Tribunal enforces the Competition Act, which is designed to "encourage competition in Canada in order to promote the efficiency and adaptability of the Canadian economy, in order to expand opportunities for Canadian participation in world markets … and in order to provide consumers with competitive prices and product choices."

The Competition Act recognizes that it is not uncommon to have competitors collude to limit competition and ensure price stability in the marketplace. This works best in those areas where there are a few producers and communication and co-operation between them are made easier. Conspiracy to manage the market (and make it less than free and open) costs Canadians millions of dollars annually.

The Canadian market for compressed gases, for example, is controlled by five firms who control 90 percent of the market. There have been numerous allegations that these firms have colluded to keep prices unusually high. Clients of these companies were contractually bound to their suppliers. When notified of a price increase they had 15 days to find another firm offering a lower price. They were, however, never able to find a lower price, so they remained tied to their initial supplier.[15] Similar allegations have been made about the road-paving firms in Ontario. They reportedly met to divide up the work and made uncompetitive bids on work they had agreed would go to one of their "competitors."[16] Much of this kind of activity remains concealed from the public, so there is no way to know the extent of the problem. A regular examination of newspapers indicates a significant number of cases, however.

Working Together or Working in Competition?

A more ordinary issue, and one that can be closely monitored, is the nature of links between corporations. This is usually studied through an examination of interlocking directorships: the extent to which companies that might be competitors have common directors on their boards. The assumption is that companies in real competition with each other will want to keep their business activities and financial situation secret from others. Thus they would not be expected to share directors.

Carroll et al. (1982) investigated this by examining the boards of directors of the 100 largest Canadian firms (20 financial companies, 10 merchandising firms, and 70 industrial firms). What they discovered confirms earlier findings of a high degree of connection among these boards: "97 of the 100 firms are found to constitute a single connected subnetwork." Further, their research found that nearly two-thirds of all pairs of firms could reach each other through one intermediary board at most. This means that if the 100 firms were divided into pairs (and there would be a large number of possibilities), in two-thirds of the cases one end of the pair could be in touch with the other end through one other board.

This discovery indicates a very close connection among the group, but what is more important is that this network was not organized in a way for outsiders to identify competitors: there did not seem to be an effort to stay further away from one's competitors. The significance of the finding is summed up by Carroll et al.: "large-scale capital in Canada is socially integrated ... providing a structural basis for the co-ordination of the process of capital accumulation and for social solidarity" (1982: 44–45).

The importance of these studies is to show that capital is socially organized (either through illegal conspiracy or through the perfectly legitimate means of sharing directors) and that this organization contains the possibility of reducing the competitiveness of the marketplace. This potential must of course be added to the earlier facts: the presence of large multinational corporations, the "Canadian factor" — a few families controlling a significant part of the economy — and a substantial portion of foreign ownership. All these factors may reduce the competitiveness of the market and contradict the liberal model of how the economy works.

A DISTORTED ECONOMY

Although the issues raised above are significant, Canadians, sociologists included, have been more preoccupied with what appear to be distortions in the Canadian economy. There has been a great deal of effort to document these distortions, and an intense debate revolves around how to best understand them. Is the problem with the Canadian economy a product of Canada's particular culture, or can it be understood in structural terms?

Research and Development

In order to identify some of the more significant features of the Canadian economy, the best starting place is with a topic raised above — research and development. For a corporation or a country to remain competitive, it must devote some of its resources to researching new products, new services, and new technologies and to developing these for use. When applied to the local economy, these new technologies ought to make the company or nation more productive than its competitors (at least until they catch up). This issue can be examined in two ways: the amount of money Canada spends as a nation on research and development, and the extent to which it imports or exports technology.

Canada has devoted less of its national resources to research and development than most other industrial countries, and this situation is not improving (see Table 8.3).[17] The Economic Council of Canada (1989) reported that among a group of eight industrial countries (the United States, West Germany, France, Sweden, the United Kingdom, the Netherlands, and Japan), Canada ranked lowest in the number of scientists and engineers in the labour market by population. Canada's overall performance in graduating engineers is quite low. In Belgium, for example, 36.1 percent of degrees awarded to men in 1988 were engineering degrees, as were 8.2 percent of degrees to women. In Canada, by contrast, the figures were 13 percent and 1.4 percent, respectively (Oderkirk, 1993: 10).

Further, Canada ranked lowest in the number of international patents granted by population; lowest in terms of gross research and development expenditures as a portion of gross domestic product; lowest in industry-funded research and development as a portion of gross domestic product; and middle in terms of government-performed research and development as a portion of gross domestic product. The Canadian pulp and paper industry spent 0.3 percent of sales on research in 1988, while Sweden, Japan, and Finland spent 0.8–1.0 percent. Unless Canada begins to spend more on research and developing competitive technologies, it will remain behind other nations in productivity. Why is relatively little research and development carried out in Canada?

An Exporting Nation

Canada's small population makes it essential that it be a trading nation: its internal market is too small to support a comprehensive range of manufacturing activity. Approximately 50 percent of Canada's gross domestic product (GDP) is involved in trade: it exports 26.8 percent of its GDP and imports an additional 22.8 percent, compared with a combined total of 30.4 percent for Australia and 16.6 percent for the United States. Canada is indeed a trading nation. In 1986, 77.8 percent of its exports went to the United States and 69.5 percent of its imports came from the United States. No other country is so dependent on one trading partner. But what is the nature of Canada's trade?

Table 8.3

Research and Development as Percentage of Gross Domestic Product for Selected Countries, 1981 and 1989

	1981	1989
West Germany	2.41	2.88
Switzerland	2.29	2.8
Japan	2.14	2.85
United States	2.45	2.82
France	1.97	2.32
United Kingdom	2.41	2.20
Canada	1.21	1.33
Australia	1.01	1.24

SOURCE: Economic Council of Canada, *Pulling Together*, cat. no. EC22-180 1992E (Ottawa: Minister of Supply and Services, 1992), p. 35.

	Exports			Imports	
Coal, minerals	30%		Electrical equipment	28%	
Iron and steel	19%		Mechanical equipment	18%	
Wood pulp	11%		Vehicles and parts	18%	
Organic chemicals	10%		Footwear	11%	
Aluminum	6%		Leather goods	7%	
Ores, slags, ash	5%		Clothing knitted	5%	
Fertilizers	4%		Textiles	4%	
Raw hides	2%		Rubber	4%	

Table 8.4

Exports and Imports for First Half of 1991, between Country A (Mature) and Country B (Less Mature)

· · · · · · · ·

SOURCE: Statistics Canada, *Imports by Country, 1992* (cat. no. 65-006) and *Exports by Country, 1992* (cat. no. 65-003) (Ottawa, Statistics Canada, 1992). Reproduced by authority of the Minister of Industry, 1994.

Consider the trade figures above for two unnamed countries. Country A is a mature, developed nation, while country B is developing. Examine Table 8.4 to determine whether the trade data are for the mature economy or the developing economy.

The exporter/importer in these figures is Canada, and the trading partner is South Korea. The character of the exports and imports in this list suggests a developing nation, one without an established industrial sector producing finished goods. While these figures are in part a reflection of South Korea's import restrictions, they do reflect something of the nature of the Canadian economy: low value-added products exported, high value-added manufactures and technology imported.

By far the largest part of Canada's total export trade is in raw or semi-finished products. In 1988, for example, 18.4 percent of its trade was in energy materials, 12.8 percent in metals and minerals, 7.8 percent in pulp and paper, 4.2 percent in lumber and saw mill products, and 5.5 percent in chemicals and fertilizers (Economic Council of Canada, 1989: 10). A further 20 percent was accounted for by automobiles and parts, leaving 21.6 percent for other manufactured goods. The automobile industry, however, is dominated by foreign companies who operate in Canada under the Auto Pact, thus ensuring that Canadian companies do not really compete with their American parent. For the most part, they import research and technology. The other large areas of Canada's export trade are less dependent on research and technology, and much of what is required is imported. Although Canada has 10 percent of the world's forests, it is difficult to find finished wood products that are made in Canada.

The nature of its exports leaves Canada in a very vulnerable position: when oil prices decline, Alberta has financial and employment problems; when fish quotas are cut, the Maritime provinces are in trouble; when the price of minerals drops, many single-industry communities in Canada receive a severe blow; if wheat prices fall, Saskatchewan experiences rural depopulation; if a cheaper source of wood pulp is found, British Columbia will lose a substantial part of its provincial economy.

This vulnerability raises significant questions: why has Canada not been able to diversify its economy more quickly? Why has Canada been unable to develop a manufacturing sector around its resource base? For example, it could produce fine papers from its forests, make furniture from its trees, or start manufacturing around its mineral base. These questions became urgent in the 1990s, as manufacturing appeared to be on the decline in Canada (the deindustrialization of Canada) and the resource sector transformed itself in order to produce more product with fewer workers. These changes accompanied a rapid move to a service economy, raising doubts that wages or skill levels would remain as high as in the manufacturing sector.

PERSPECTIVES ON THE ECONOMY

· · · · · · · · ·

Concerns about Canada's economic development focus on the question whether Canadians produce enough of what they use every day. Are they depleting their resource base and creating international debt in order to support purchases from others? Measures of strong industrial development include a favourable balance of trade in finished goods, domestic ownership and control of productive enterprises, and internal access to advanced technology (Laxer, 1989: 37). This chapter review of each measure has found weakness in all these areas.

Canada's period of initial industrialization occurred between 1870 and 1914, somewhat behind that of Britain (1760–1830) and the United States (1825–1860). Canada is part of a group referred to as "late-followers" (along with Australia, Japan, Russia, and Sweden), and is the only one of the group not to develop a mature, independent industrial economy. In light of Canada's pre-Confederation history this conclusion seems unpredictable, since Canada had begun to develop a strong industrial base.

At Confederation, Canada was the eighth-largest manufacturer of industrial goods in the world and, by 1900, the seventh-largest. It had a reputation for innovation and a skilled labour force. For example, Massey's light binder (for agricultural use) won a special trophy of honour at the Paris Exposition of 1889, and the company went on to export harvesters, mowers, and ploughs to over 40 countries. By 1900, however, it was clear that Canada was relying more and more on foreign direct investment and that ownership of its productive capacity was falling into the hands of non-Canadians: Canada was becoming a branch-plant economy.

What went wrong? Several theories attempt to explain the development of Canada's state of dependency on foreign capital and technology.

Critical Perspectives

· · · · · · · · ·

Staple Thesis

· · · · · · · · ·

Developed by Harold Innis[18] in the 1920s, the staple thesis considers Canada as a hinterland to a colonial metropolis (in the early period of its history, Canada was a colony of France and then of Britain). This theory argues that economic development in the hinterland is determined by the demand for goods and the level of technology in the metropolis. In addition, of course, development is affected by geography and the supply of resources. As cultural tastes change, demand changes, (e.g., the demand for the beaver pelt hat), and energy goes into applying technology and developing government policy to extract this resource for the metropolitan area.

According to this view, Canada's history is one of extracting furs, fish, wheat, coal, hydroelectricity, minerals, timber, and pulp. The colonial powers that Canada was linked to shaped its development, ensuring that it would remain a source of raw materials for economic and technological development elsewhere. Industrial development was stunted because Canada's energy and resources went into basing an economy and society on the extraction of resources. Thus Canadians remained dependent on the colonial power for technology and markets. While this is a useful way to examine Canada, it fails to explain adequately how Canada became part of the American empire (and thus "hewers of wood and drawers of water" for them). It also fails to acknowledge the positive development of Canada's economy in the nineteenth century.

Elites Theory

· · · · · · · · ·

Developed by authors such as R.T. Naylor (1975) and W. Clement (1975), this approach derived from a form of Marxism that considers the owners of capital as exerting unusual power in society and as being able to shape political policy. Some sectors of the Canadian economy are dominated by Canadian owners and have a prominent place among the large corporations of this society. Banks and transportation companies (and, later, utilities) are largely Canadian owned (often as a result of laws restricting or excluding foreign ownership). These groups gained their importance early in Canada's development, and elites theory argues that their unusual prominence allowed them to distort the nation's economic development. They developed those areas of the economy that were of benefit to them (building the railways, encouraging large government projects such as canals, and so on), but were reluctant to invest in other areas of the economy. American capital and branch plants came to Canada to fill the gap left by these large holders of capital.

This theory, although interesting, does not explain how this small group was able to exert so much power during a period of expanding political franchise. Neither does it explain why other groups with business interests were unable to influence Canadian policies. It also fails to explain the adoption of tariffs in the latter part of the nineteenth century as a way to protect the Canadian manufacturing sector — a policy that many think did not work because it encouraged foreign capital to develop branch-plant manufacturing in Canada in order to avoid the tariff.

Class Theory
· · · · · · · ·

Laxer (1989) developed an alternative explanation whose strength lies in its revelations of the relationships between classes in Canadian society. He argued that Canadians must understand their economic history as developing out of their own political situation. In examining other industrial societies, Laxer argued that rule by the wealthy (the growing commercial class) was quite usual. But their power was usually counterbalanced by a politically strong agrarian class of farmers and landowners.

According to Laxer, agrarian classes tend to have three key interests: they want to reduce the power of centralized banking systems and create easier credits for small farmers; they favour strong military policy to protect land and perhaps expand borders to allow for growth (military development also leads to technological development); and they oppose high government expenditures because they fear high land taxes (which were at one time a key source of tax revenue).

In some countries, an agrarian class (perhaps in co-operation with workers) did gain power. Three things are noticeable about the goals they pursued: the development of a competitive and decentralized banking system to improve access to capital; support for technological development (perhaps a spin-off from military development); and a low level of government expenditure, thus allowing for capital to be used by other sectors of the economy. But this did not happen in Canada, where the agrarian class failed to achieve power. Why was this?

Laxer's answer to this is quite detailed and reviews significant signposts in Canadian history. In summary, he argued that ethno-national divisions (French and English) impeded the development of common class interests and prevented an agrarian movement (or other movements for popular democratic control) from gaining power. As a result, Canada remained politically dominated by the commercial class.

Public policy reflected this outcome. The banks retained their conservative lending policy, starving small enterprises and farmers of capital; the government overdeveloped the railways (and other public infrastructure) and built them at great cost; and access to land was restricted. The government paid for the railways by massive grants of land to the rail companies. This tied up much accessible agricultural land. The new farmer was faced with the choice of paying the rail company for land or crossing the border to the United States and getting homestead land free of charge. Many settlers chose to leave Canada, and the loss of population retarded the growth of industry to service the expected settlers. These policies all reduced domestic economic activity and increased the need for foreign capital. In addition the Canadian policy of relying on Britain for defence and military technology (and markets) thrust Canadians along a path of technological dependence. Finally, Canada's national divisions weakened any resistance to the growing dependence on foreign capital and technology.

Laxer's explanation for Canada's failure to develop an independent industrial economy is formulated in terms of conflicting class interests and the failure of one group (or class) to attain a measure of power sufficient to offset the interests of the commercial class. This failure leads to a dependence on foreign ownership and a branch-plant economy.

Liberal Views

Liberal views regarding Canada's economic development focus on conditions that impede competition or distort the free market. These conditions include the fact that Canada's cold climate increases the costs of production; the size of the country increases transportation costs; strong unions increase labour costs; a developed welfare state leads to higher corporate taxes; import tariffs encouraged the survival of uncompetitive industries; and the labour force has limited skills.

From this perspective, a set of changes to Canadian society that would make the economy more competitive include narrowed social programs, more stress on training a skilled labour force, reduced tariffs (e.g., the free-trade agreements), lower corporate taxes, the transfer of government-owned corporations to the private sector (e.g., Petro Canada), decreased regulatory requirements on services and products, and a strengthened Competition Act.

The above list makes it clear that the majority of the public debate about the Canadian economy over the past decade — the deficit, free trade, privatization, social programs — has been framed by liberal thought, and much of Canada's economic policy reflects this perspective (see Box 8.3).

Functionalist Theory

Functionalist theory is quite similar to liberalism in identifying features of Canadian life that appear to impede the development of a modern economy. Functionalists may look at structural problems — the absence of a national education system, for example, reduces Canadians' ability to have a common goal for education that will serve the nation. More likely, however, functionalists will identify the culture of Canada as the stumbling block. Canada's collective orientation, for example, may have impeded the development of the entrepreneurial individual.[19] Its years of colonial experience may have created an attitude of self-defeat, encouraging Canadians to pull down those who begin to show signs of success. Years of clerical domination of Quebec, with religious support for tradition, community, and family, have undermined a modern individualistic achievement motivation.

This approach to understanding Canada's economy was reflected by American economist Michael Porter (1991), who suggested that Canadian consumers are generally less sophisticated than those in other countries. For example, Nintendo delayed release of its new game in Canada because many Canadians had not yet tried the old version.[20] Because consumers are cautious, Porter reasoned, Canadian businesses are less aggressive and innovative than foreign firms. Further, Canadians make half as many complaints to the Better Business Bureau as do Americans. Finally, they do not have a strong consumer lobby (like Ralph Nader's organization, for example).[21] Gillies also made a functionalist argument in claiming that "the culture of the

Box 8.3
Understanding Debt
and Deficit

Government debt and the deficit have become central issues in Canadian politics. The *deficit* is the gap between governments' revenues, from taxes and charges, and their expenditures, on programs, infrastructure, and debt financing. The projected total deficit for Canada's federal and provincial governments in 1993 was $52 billion. *Debt* is the total amount owed by governments to lenders who have bought bonds and Treasury bills sold by governments to cover past deficits and operating expenses. The 1993 debt was $624 billion. There is little agreement about the significance of these figures.

One view is that governments have overinflated their role in society with social programs, capital spending, regulation, and bureaucratic administration and have created the debt crisis. From this perspective, governments must cut back their role. There must be a functionally necessary adaptation to the realities of a competitive world and a globally based economy. Canada already has a larger government sector than do many of its competitors, so it is time to reduce government and let the market system operate with less hindrance.

A contrasting view is that the deficit and the debt have grown in size relative to the economy because governments are taking in too little revenue. As corporations have found themselves squeezed by new competitors and cheaper labour markets, they have pressured governments to reduce corporate taxes and transfer more of the tax burden to individuals. There has been a decline in the taxation of rich individuals and corporations. It is also pointed out that Canada's economy is weakened by the substantial transfer of corporate capital out of the country to multinational parents and by transfer pricing. Finally, critics of the cut-government view point out that Canada's federal government does not run a deficit but a small surplus, if only program expenditures are counted. The deficit is created by interest payments on current and past government debt.

nation, since the time of the United Empire Loyalists, has led to the development of a 'social compact' among various sectors of society rather than to the embracing of a tough, hard competition" (1991: 19).

This discussion completes the examination of the structure of Canada's economy and the competing ways of understanding its characteristics. There is, however, one other feature of Canada's economic structure that must be mentioned: its regional nature.

REGIONAL DISPARITY

The above sections presented the national economy of Canada as having serious distortions. However, another distortion exists in the Canadian economy, resulting in distinctive regional politics and regional disparities. Canada does not have a national economy; it has a set of distinctly regional economies. Canadian provinces, for example, have surprisingly little trade with each other. Manufacturing is concentrated in central Canada; 78 percent of the manufacturing dollars are created in Ontario and Quebec (54 percent in Ontario alone) and 21 percent of the jobs in both Ontario and Quebec are located in the manufacturing sector (compared with 12 percent in British Columbia). The Maritimes depend on fishing, the Prairies on grain and mineral extraction, and British Columbia on forestry.

Table 8.5		
Average Employment Income by Province, 1991	Newfoundland	$18 098
	Prince Edward Island	$17 711
	Nova Scotia	$21 033
	New Brunswick	$19 871
	Quebec	$23 441
	Ontario	$26 454
	Manitoba	$21 257
	Saskatchewan	$19 859
	Alberta	$24 037
	British Columbia	$24 801

SOURCE: Statistics Canada, *Employment Income by Occupation*, cat. no. 93-332 (Ottawa: Statistics Canada, 1993). Reproduced by authority of the Minister of Industry, 1994.

These regional differences create visible differences in the lives of individual Canadians. Central Canada tends to be wealthier than other regions. Although Ontario has only 36 percent of all Canadian households, it has 48 percent of households among the highest 20 percent of income earners. The average incomes for each region are reported in Table 8.5. Unemployment also takes on a regional pattern (see Table 8.6). The provincial differences result from many factors, but a key factor is that provincial economies that are less diversified are more susceptible to fluctuations in market demand for resources, and this susceptibility results in a less stable economy. This is reflected both in the numbers of unemployed for each province and in the numbers living below the poverty line (see Table 8.7). Saskatchewan is something of an exception here: in recessions, rapidly rising out-migration tends to keep unemployment levels down.

Canada has a national policy of using equalization payments and program transfer payments from the federal to provincial governments to offset variations in the wealth of regional economies. These payments allow the provinces to provide health, welfare, and education services at close to the national level.

Just as the provinces do not have equal economic power, neither do they have equal political power. The tension created by these factors is intense. Concerns about western alienation, the isolation of the Maritimes, and the disquiet of Quebec are

Table 8.6		
Unemployment by Province, 1992	Newfoundland	20.2%
	Prince Edward Island	17.7%
	Nova Scotia	13.1%
	New Brunswick	12.8%
	Quebec	12.8%
	Ontario	10.8%
	Manitoba	9.6%
	Saskatchewan	8.2%
	Alberta	9.5%
	British Columbia	10.4%

SOURCE: Statistics Canada, *Canadian Economic Observer, July 1993*, cat. no. 11-010 (Ottawa: Statistics Canada, 1993), Table 2.1. Reproduced by authority of the Minister of Industry, 1994.

Table 8.7 Families below Low-Income Cut-Offs, by Province, 1991 · · · · · · · · ·	*Newfoundland*	15.8%
	Prince Edward Island	9.8%
	Nova Scotia	12.4%
	New Brunswick	12.1%
	Quebec	13.9%
	Ontario	9.7%
	Manitoba	15.1%
	Saskatchewan	13.4%
	Alberta	11.4%
	British Columbia	9.2%

SOURCE: Statistics Canada, *Income Distribution by Size in Canada, 1991*, cat. no. 13-207 (Ottawa: Statistics Canada, 1992). Reproduced by authority of the Minister of Industry, 1994.

long-standing. While each region has an economic elite representing the strongest sectors of the regional economies, there is also a national corporate economic elite located almost entirely in central Canada. While regional interests are often in competition with each other, the national elite has been able to manage the national internal tension. It is, however, becoming increasingly difficult to achieve consensus or compromise among the regional interests of Canada.

Sociologists are interested not only in documenting regional disparities but in understanding them. How did this internal pattern of economic development occur? What are the processes by which the uneven development is reproduced from generation to generation? There are competing ways to understand these regional economic patterns.

Liberalism
· · · · · · · ·

Adherents of classical liberalism tend to believe that regional distortions in Canada's economy result from interference in the market. Since the market is thought to be self-regulating, if it were allowed to run its course unimpeded the adjustments necessary to ensure a sound economy would occur. Liberal thinkers would argue that government interference has prevented this from happening. A typical argument would be that government spending on unemployment insurance (which many of the poorer regions depend on) distorts the labour market. For example, less generous unemployment insurance payments would have encouraged out-migration and consequently lower unemployment in Newfoundland. Individual workers are able to hold out for higher wages or remain without jobs because of the backup provided by unemployment insurance. This tends to keep wages high and therefore keeps capital from the region. If wages were allowed to find their natural level, capital would flow into the region and economic development would occur.

Functionalist Perspective
· · · · · · · ·

Functionalists adopt a position that is not too distant from that of liberalism. They tend to focus on the culture or central institutions of a depressed region and argue that these aspects of society are not modern enough to sustain a modern economy. They might describe the culture as too parochial (or, in the case of Quebec before the 1960s, as too controlled by the church and therefore too traditional), or as too resistant to risktaking.

A version of this theory that fits with liberal thought is the belief that years of dependence on government support have made the people of a region psychologically dependent. This is a form of the "culture of poverty" thesis, which sees the psychological response to poverty as part of the problem itself. Thus, in order to change the psychology of dependence, social policies (such as unemployment insurance) would have to be changed. This is the link to liberalism.

Critical Perspectives

A critical perspective takes quite a different view of these matters. It considers the underdevelopment of some regions as serving the interests of the central or dominant region. This perspective is known as the **metropolis–hinterland theory** and derives from the theory of imperialism. The assumption is that as capitalism develops, there is an inherent need for geographic expansion. This expansion allows for the importation of new resources, the domination of new markets, and the inflow of new capital. The new territories are brought within the orbit of the stronger economy, and the relationship between the two regions itself creates a state of dependency. The underdeveloped region becomes dependent on consumer goods produced in the centre and on the central markets to purchase its resources. The region is not able to develop fully, however, because capital is not accumulated in the region but is drained off to the centre, and economic development is driven by the needs and interests of the centre.

This state of dependency is reproduced through economic policy. Canadian transportation policy has long reflected regional disparities. In 1883, for example, freight rates for western wheat were three times higher than rates for goods shipped comparable distances in eastern Canada. Although the Crow's Nest Pass Agreement of 1887 significantly reduced freight rates for western wheat, it also reduced rates on manufactured goods travelling to the West. This latter policy helped impede the development of secondary industry in the West because it was cheaper to ship goods from central Canada (Brodie, 1990: 114–115).

The Maritime region was not always the poor cousin of central Canada. At the time of Confederation, the Maritimes were the manufacturing centre of the country. Economic and political power was located there, but as Canada developed the Maritimes found themselves at the end of a very long transportation system. Confederation had forced regions such as the Maritimes to shift their focus from trade with Britain and the American states toward the centre of Canada. The more important factor in the decline of the Maritimes, however, was the National Policy, a tariff and duty policy affecting goods coming into Canada. By making it more expensive to import goods, it was thought that Canadian production would be stimulated, thus strengthening the Canadian economy and keeping Americans from dominating the emerging Canadian market.[22]

The consequence, however, was that American producers soon realized they could reduce the effect of this tariff policy by developing their plants inside Canada to serve the Canadian market. This led to the domination of the Canadian economy by foreign companies and to the development of economic power in central Canada, as the new industrial sector flourished in this region and declined in the East. (Notice that this view of regional disparity is allied to the staple thesis, which explains Canada's economic development as a whole in relation to metropolis–hinterland relationships.)

CANADA IN THE GLOBAL CONTEXT

While Canada attempts to grapple with a "distorted economy" and a high per capita national debt, it must also act within a global context that is also undergoing substantial changes. These changes are putting considerable pressure on Canada and create significant obstacles to economic growth and the maintenance of living standards.

This new global context can be described briefly as follows. First, as the economies of more nations begin to mature, Canada is exposed to enhanced competition, often from parts of the world with much cheaper production costs than Canada's. The economies of developing nations are expanding much more rapidly than those of mature industrial nations. In order to ensure access to markets for resources, countries have moved to establish trade agreements (as Canada has done with the United States and Mexico) that remove trade barriers between co-operating countries, ensure market access, and often allow business from the "foreign" country "national status" in the second country and attempt to create a "level playing field" for companies in participating countries.

Second, trade policies such as NAFTA (the North American Free Trade Agreement) and GATT (General Agreement on Tariffs and Trade) further restrict the ability of governments to intervene in their economies. This further exposes companies and their workers to the pressures of the international market.

Third, technological developments in telecommunications and computerization mean that companies are less tied to a national base than ever before. Work can easily be moved to foreign contractors who perform the work with low-wage labour: for example, many Canadian-based hotel chains use reservation systems and personnel based in the United States.

Fourth, capital itself has become very mobile, seeking the highest rate of return without regard for national obligations.

Fifth, as competition among companies increases, the race for new technologies also increases, and marketing pressure to adopt these technologies speeds up the pace of work and social life in general.

Finally, the general philosophy behind much of this development is a faith in the ability of the market, operating with fewer regulations than in the past, to create wealth and contribute to the social welfare of citizens. In short, liberal ideology is fostered, and this puts pressure on the social-welfare states that have emerged in much of the western world in the last 50 years.

These six pressures not only restrict the actions of governments, they have immediate effects on the citizens. As major sectors of the Canadian economy find themselves less competitive than foreign competitors, Canada's unemployment rate increases and many workers are forced into lower-paying jobs. Businesses scramble to find a niche in the economy where they can be competitive and find profits. Hopes are placed on "high technology" and on the production of goods and services requiring high degrees of skill. As a result, new pressures are placed on schools in the attempt to develop the intellectual skills necessary for the emerging workplace. Family life is placed under major stress by the unemployment of family members, loss of income, pressures to stay in or return to school, and a less optimistic future for the children.

CONCLUSION This chapter presented an initial description of the structure of the Canadian economy. In detailing this structure, five central characteristics were highlighted: the concentration of economic ownership, the family basis of corporate ownership, the extent of foreign ownership, the relative weakness of the economy, and regional disparities in economic development. To understand these features is to begin to understand Canada.

Many of these features were contrasted with liberal thought and shown to challenge that philosophy. The economy is not as open as is believed; regional access to capital and to economic opportunity is not equal; economic ownership is not widely dispersed; national control of the economy is restricted. Each of these shortcomings has consequences for Canadians: a tendency to have a high rate of unemployment and lower-quality jobs. Job training is not easily accessible or well developed. The economic power of corporations is not easily offset by political power. There are regional differences in standards of living and job opportunities. Enormous amounts of wealth leave the country through dividends and intercorporate transfers, necessitating an expanding sale of resources and high taxes. Restricted competitiveness results in the prices of many goods being higher than they need be.

Some argue that as free trade with the United States becomes more fully implemented, these costs will be more pronounced (see Hurtig, 1991). Jobs will leave the country to find cheaper labour and lower taxes; the standard of living will decrease, placing increasing pressure on families and individuals; and as the tax base diminishes, there will be pressure to reduce government expenditures on social programs. The alternative view is that a freed-up market system will ensure a better allocation of resources, a more productive Canada, and, ultimately, higher standards of living.

Competing ways of understanding the Canadian economy were presented. Liberalism sees the economy simply as having failed to develop a free-market economy. The market has been hindered by government regulations, provincial trade barriers, a weak training and education system, and a distorted labour market. From this perspective, Canada's economy can be improved by more fully implementing liberalism. This might require the elimination of interprovincial trade barriers, encouraging corporations to spend more on training their workers, making education and training programs more responsive to market demands, strengthening the Competition Act, encouraging ordinary Canadians to invest in the stock market to raise capital for Canadian companies, and encouraging Canadians to take economic and financial risks.

A critical perspective focusses on the natural tendency of economic wealth and power to become concentrated in a capitalist society. Capital is also believed to have a natural tendency to flow outward to expand markets, develop new resources, and increase profit.[23] In light of these two developments, it is not unusual that economic power is concentrated and that there is foreign ownership of economic assets in Canada. The extent of each of these is unusual, however, making Canada somewhat unique. Given these two features of the Canadian economy, a critical perspective would be concerned about the ability of the market itself to balance the economic power of corporations and to limit foreign ownership. The only power that can perhaps balance the economic power of corporations is the collective power of the people as expressed in our government.

A critical perspective would look to the government to play a more active role in limiting economic concentration, in restricting foreign ownership, and in reducing the ability of foreign companies to use Canadian savings to buy up Canadian resources. It would expect the government to prevent the abuse of transfer pricing and the transfer of profits out of the country. It might claim that corporations who wish to use Canada's resources and sell to the Canadian market make a commitment to the social welfare of the workers and the country.

· · · · · · · ·

NOTES

· · · · · · · ·

1. It should be noted, however, that many large corporations in the mature industrial nations are "downsizing" and eliminating thousands of jobs worldwide.

Factory workers as a percentage of all workers are in decline in many countries. In the United States, factories employed more than 23 percent of U.S. workers in 1979; they now employ only 16 percent of workers.

2. Peter Cook, "Companies Prove Bigness is Better," *The Globe and Mail*, December 26, 1991, p. B2.

3. Mergers in 1991 left two trust companies dominating the market: Murray Oxby, "Central Guaranty Paring Operations," *The Globe and Mail*, December 17, 1991, p. B1. In 1993 the Canadian Imperial Bank of Commerce reported discussions aimed at acquiring the two remaining independent trust firms, Montreal Trust and National Trust: John Partridge, "CIBC Looking for Acquisitions," *The Globe and Mail*, October 7, 1993, p. B9.

4. Dan Westell, "Bronfman Director Speaks Out Against Corporate Concentration," *The Globe and Mail*, May 7, 1986, p. B1.

5. Ben Parfitt, "Concentration Kills Free Enterprise in Forests, Peel Charges," Vancouver *Sun*, June 11, 1991, p. C1.

6. John Muggeridge, "Just a Cog in a Vast Food Line," *The Globe and Mail*, October 2, 1993, p. D2.

7. Madelaine Drohan, "Pumping Up a Flat Industry," *The Globe and Mail*, September 17, 1991, p. B19.

8. Jacquie McNish, "Weston Adjusts to 'Cruel World,'" *The Globe and Mail*, August 19, 1991, p. B1.

9. Corporate retailers may be able to keep the prices of commodities high by keeping manufacturer's discount stores out of the country. They can do this by refusing to handle the manufacturer's product if they distribute directly to the Canadian public.

10. Jeffrey Simpson raised this issue in *The Globe and Mail*: "The upper echelons of the Canadian economy remain dominated by foreign-controlled firms, Crown corporations and companies controlled by the Five Families (Bronfman, Desmarais, Irving, Weston, Reichmann)." He goes on to suggest that the control of so much by so few has become a non-subject in Canadian public debate: "All in the Families," *The Globe and Mail*, June 4, 1988.

11. "Report Cites Danger in Family Holdings," Vancouver *Sun*, March 19, 1985, p. D1.

12. Zeitlin (1974), however, claims that nearly two-thirds of major American corporations are owner-controlled and that family capitalism is alive and well in the United States.

13. Margot Gibb-Clark, "Firms Rapped for Low Executive Pay," *The Globe and Mail*, January 16, 1991, p. B3. Reprinted with permission.

14. John Saunders, "Head Office Flexes Its Might: Branch Plants Lose Clout," *The Globe and Mail*, January 18, 1994, p. A1.

15. Jock Ferguson, "Gases Cost $80-Million a Year Too Much," *The Globe and Mail*, October 11, 1990, p. A1.

16. Jock Ferguson, "Paving Firms Rigged Tenders for Ontario Roads," *The Globe and Mail*, October 10, 1990, p. A1.

17. Foreign-owned companies spend less on research and development than do Canadian-owned firms, and Canadian corporations spend less on research than does the Canadian government.

18. Innis wrote a number of books and articles, but his early work *The Fur Trade in Canada* (1970) remains a classic.

19. Canada has more billionaires per capita than does the United States.

20. "Nintendo Held as Example of Our Caution," Vancouver *Sun*, January 4, 1992, p. A7.
21. Evidence that the corporate sector would like to have it both ways: Terrence Corcoran, a clear spokesman for liberalism, suggested that Ralph Nader stay away from Canada: "Goodbye, Ralph Nader; Markets Work," *The Globe and Mail*, March 13, 1991, p. B6.
22. The National policy was the third of a set of policies developed to enhance the position of the emerging entrepreneurial class in Canada. The other two were Confederation itself, creating a nation state with the ability to dominate the territory, and the building of the railway which would allow for the movement of immigrants to the undeveloped regions and the transportation of goods and resources against the pull of the north-south magnet.
23. As of 1988, 12 percent of America's manufacturing base was foreign-owned and Americans became concerned about the growing presence of Japanese capital (Phillips, 1990: 141).

· · · · · · · ·

FURTHER READING

· · · · · · · ·

Brodie, Janine. *The Political Economy of Canadian Regionalism*. Toronto: Harcourt Brace Jovanovich, 1990. An excellent discussion of the problems of regional development in Canada.

Burrill, Gary, and I. McKay. *People, Resources, and Power*. Fredericton: Acadiensis Press, 1987. A collection of articles examining the underdevelopment of Atlantic Canada from a critical perspective.

Hurtig, Mel. *The Betrayal of Canada*. Toronto: Stoddart, 1991. A very readable examination of the Canadian economy. Hurtig is very critical of the extent of foreign ownership in Canada.

Kneen, Brewster. *Trading Up*. Toronto: NC Press, 1990. Exposes the way a major multinational, Cargill, is transforming Canada's system of agriculture.

Laxer, Gordon. *Open For Business: The Roots of Foreign Ownership in Canada*. Toronto: Oxford University Press, 1989. A clear sociological account of the emergence of foreign ownership in Canada.

Laxer, James. *False God: How the Globalization Myth Has Impoverished Canada*. Toronto: Lester, 1993. An important book, due to Laxer's challenge to what he calls the "globalization myth." A useful critique of the flood of claims about the new economy.

· · · · · · · ·

STUDY QUESTIONS

· · · · · · · ·

1. What main features of Canada's economy depart from those of a competitive model?
2. Can Canada's "regional tensions" be related to its economic structure?
3. What arguments can be advanced against the policies of Prairie governments that attempt to maintain the "family farm"?
4. Compare a cultural critique and a structural understanding of Canada's relatively low level of industrial manufacturing and technological research and development.
5. Select ten food packages from the store shelf. Identify the manufacturer (or distributor). Do some library research to determine how many of these companies

are separate and how many are part of the same conglomerate. The librarian may be helpful in your research.

6. Identify a prominent company in your area and do library research to determine if it is wholly Canadian owned, partly Canadian owned, or wholly foreign owned. (For example, research the major telephone company in your region or determine the ownership of the publisher of this textbook.)

9 SOCIETY AND THE STATE

....

INTRODUCTION
....

One of the central values of most capitalist societies is the idea of democracy. Democracy suggests that individuals will have the right to contribute to decisions about how their society should be governed and the values that will be upheld in social life. The ideal is that political power be dispersed. In Canada, however, economic power is not widely dispersed. It is, in fact, highly concentrated. Therefore, it is important to ask: Does political power offset economic power? Can the community, acting through democratic government, radically influence the structure of its society? This chapter outlines how political sociology has debated this key question about the reality of democracy in capitalist society.

....

This chapter is about the role of the state in capitalist societies. How does an economic system founded on inequality co-exist with a political system founded on democracy? Can society control corporate power through political institutions?

By the end of this chapter it should be clear that the democratic political systems of capitalist societies operate within strict constraints. There are obstacles to the effective representation of the views and interests of citizens, and government in these societies works within a framework of ideas — liberal philosophy — that sets limits on the legitimate role of the state.

INEQUALITY AND THE ROLE OF THE STATE: A PARADOX

· · · · · · · · ·

In Canada, the top 20 percent of income earners receive almost ten times more income than the bottom 20 percent. The top 20 percent of wealth holders have 69 percent of the wealth, while the bottom 20 percent are in debt. This structure of inequality is common to all advanced capitalist societies. In the United States, the richest 0.5 percent of U.S. households own 26.9 percent of private wealth. The top 1 percent of Americans have more net worth (wealth) than do the bottom 90 percent (Phillips, 1990: 11–12). In Britain, the top 1 percent of the population own about 28 percent of the total wealth; the bottom 50 percent own about 4 percent of total wealth (Giddens, 1989: 216).

Polarization of income and wealth is not something that has happened in the last few years. In Canada, there has been no significant change in economic inequality in 40 years; the welfare state has had almost no impact on income distribution. During the 1980s and early 1990s, there appears to have even been an increase in inequality.[1]

Inequality is not only a matter of money. What about the status of women in society? Women have less wealth, earn less, are much more likely to be poor, and are much more likely to be bound to tasks of family and child care.

Why does economic and gender inequality persist when adult voters — the majority of whom are women — could elect governments to promote equality? Why is the concentration of economic power not more vigorously challenged by democratically elected governments? Why has gender inequality been so slow to change, even though women have voted for more than 70 years?

Photo 9.1

The state itself is an abstraction: it cannot act directly. However, people and agencies can act in its name. In Canadian society, state agencies include the federal and provincial governments; government ministries, boards, and commissions; the courts; the police, the Royal Canadian Mounted Police, and the military.

· · · · · · · · ·

Kevin Miller / TONY STONE IMAGES

THE FOUNDATIONS OF STATE POWER

· · · · · · · · ·

All but the simplest societies have some formal system for communal government. In all modern societies, this system is the state.

The state is itself an abstraction: it cannot act directly, but people and agencies can act in its name. In our society, state agencies include the federal and provincial governments, government ministries, boards, commissions, and law courts, and the police and military who work under their direction. These institutions all share in the right to give commands that must be lawfully obeyed.

Max Weber defined the state as "a human community that successfully claims *the monopoly of the legitimate use of physical force* within a given territory. ... The state is the sole source of the right to use violence" (Gerth and Mills, 1970: 78; emphasis in original). The words "successfully claims" are important, since success can be based on force as well as consent: not all state systems are democratic.

Sociologists and political scientists often study societies in which state power is founded principally on force, but the main focus of interest has been on societies in which consent is important. In these societies, cultural ideas uphold the system of state power as a form of **legitimate authority**. Legitimate authority is present where people — enough people — believe in the rightful authority of those who claim to exercise state power.

Max Weber pointed out that societies usually have a set of cultural ideas that uphold the state's authority to exercise power. He distinguished three ideal types, or classic forms, in which these ideas have been found.

The most common form of state rule in past societies was **traditional authority**. Most often, traditional systems of rule were based on myths and rituals, and rulers were seen as embodying the shared history, experience, and identity of the members of the society.

Also common in history is **charismatic authority**. This is authority possessed by exceptional leaders who inspire followers with complete faith in their mission and their destiny. Charismatic leadership is not, however, characteristic of modern capitalist society.[2]

In western capitalist societies, the idea of **rational–legal authority** gradually replaced traditional rule. In rational–legal systems, the power of government is regulated by law; no individual is above this law, and there is some representative institution that is the source of the law and of the right to use state power. Rational–legal authority is usually supported by the idea of **democracy.**

DIRECT DEMOCRACY

· · · · · · · · ·

Democracy is a concept that originated with the ancient Greeks. "Demos" is Greek for "people," and "democracy" meant rule by the people. In the ancient Greek world, political systems were based on city, rather than nation-state, organization. In the period 500–400 B.C. the city-state of Athens developed the most complete form of democratic government by the people. Here is a description of this democracy:

> *No constitution has ever given more weight to the decisions of the ordinary man*
> *than did the Athenian. This constitution was a direct democracy, in which policy,*
> *even in matters of detail, was decided by an assembly of all adult male citizens;*
> *executive officers were appointed either by lot or by vote and their performance in*
> *office was carefully vetted by this same assembly. It met at a minimum forty times*
> *a year and as often besides as the chief executives thought fit. Proposals were intro-*
> *duced only by these executives or by members of the council, but the assembly had*
> *full powers of debate, of amendment from the floor, and could even at times instruct*

the Council to introduce some specific proposal at a future meeting. The Council itself ... consisted of 500 members chosen annually by lot from all parts of Attica. ... Thus Athens was run by ordinary Athenians (Forrest, 1966: 17–21).

For Athenians, therefore, democracy was naturally and inevitably participatory democracy. To participate in government was the expression of citizenship itself. Democracy was not just about elections; it was a social process of direction and decision making in which citizenship itself came alive.[3]

REPRESENTATIVE DEMOCRACY

. . . .

The concept of democracy current in modern society is quite different from the original Greek system: it is founded on the idea of representation, rather than direct citizen involvement. This transformed concept of representative democracy emerged as traditional systems declined and there was a new cultural emphasis on individual freedom and political equality. In the nineteenth century, democracy meant the right of socially and economically successful citizens to take part in choosing their government. The threat of the poor mass of people taking over government and using it to radically transform the inequalities of society was avoided by restricting political rights to the middle and upper classes of society. Voting rights were extended very slowly to the mass of the people in western "democratic" systems.

A common justification for the denial of equal political rights was that citizenship was something that all should be equally free to *earn*. It was common for nineteenth-century capitalist democracies to impose economic tests for voting rights. The assumption was that a limited franchise (right to vote) preserved political **power** for those who had a responsible commitment to society. The Canadian government boasted in 1874, for example, that "the evils of universal suffrage were avoided" by the limited franchise (Trade Union Congress, 1874). In the United States, a rule persisted for many years that restricted the vote to men owning real estate with a set annual rentable value. Women were excluded from voting on equal terms with men until 1920.

In Canada, the federal government of John A. Macdonald actively resisted Ontario's leadership in widening the right to vote (1874–1888) by imposing property ownership qualifications to keep the federal voters' list restricted (McInnis, 1969: 416). Women were refused the federal franchise until 1918 (see Box 9.1). In Britain, the general enfranchisement of men waited until 1885 and was not complete until 1918. Women could not vote at all until 1918 and not on equal terms with men until 1928 (Taylor, 1965: 262). For Germany, historian Erich Eyck refers to "the undiluted plutocratic character" of the Prussian suffrage laws that permitted plural voting for rich property owners and that persisted from 1869 to 1919 (Eyck, 1962: 9, 24–25).

The combination of capitalism and democracy was relatively natural, so long as the propertied classes (and those just below who aspired to join them) exercised political domination. Reconciling capitalism and democracy became more problematic when the franchise was extended to everyone in society and the poor had formal political power to control the state through majority vote.

How could a system of social and economic privilege withstand the assault of democracy? We now have one answer to this: in the early stage of capitalism, the right to vote was severely restricted. The right to vote is now spread very widely in Canada, and there is evidence that democracy has become a more powerful tool. Modern capitalist societies now have social programs, state-subsidized education up to high school, and more progressive systems of taxation. There are constraints on political action, however, and one important limitation is the view of government found in liberal philosophy.

Box 9.1
Chronology of
Federal Suffrage
in Canada

1868	First federal general election held; only men who owned a specified amount of property allowed to vote.
1885	Electoral Franchise Act defined a "person" as a male, excluding a person of Mongolian or Chinese race.
1917	Wartime Elections Act disenfranchised Canadian citizens born in an enemy country and naturalized after March 31, 1902, as well as those whose "mother tongue" was the language of an enemy country, regardless of country of birth.
1918	Wives, sisters, and mothers of servicemen won the franchise; extended to all adult women later the same year.
1948	Franchise extended to Canadians of Japanese ancestry.
1950	Inuit, explicitly excluded in the 1934 Dominion Franchise Act, become eligible to vote.
1960	Indian Act amended to extend the franchise to Native Canadians living on reserves.
1987	Judges become eligible to vote.
1988	People with mental disabilities granted the franchise.
1992	Voting rights extended to prison inmates.

SOURCE: Statistics Canada, *Canadian Social Trends*, cat. no. 11-008E (Ottawa: Statistics Canada, Winter 1992), p. 4. Reproduced by authority of the Minister of Industry, 1994.

LIBERALISM AND DEMOCRACY

Liberalism argues that the society that works best, in helping individuals to satisfy their diverse needs and desires, is the one in which people are as free as possible to make their own choices. It is individuals who know best what they want and who are best placed to make decisions for themselves that maximize their satisfaction.

Liberalism starts from a "conception of the individual as essentially the proprietor of his own person or capacities, owing nothing to society for them" (Macpherson, 1962: 3). The individual is the possessor of all rights and freedoms, and no group can have rights in itself: there can be no collective rights that are superior to individual rights, except the right to be free from constraint. Since it is quite clear that any government action invades the sphere of individual freedom, it follows that such invasions need a very good justification indeed: they must be justified as protecting, more than limiting, the rights of all. Liberalism, in upholding the sacred quality of individual rights to freedom and choice, is a natural ally of the principle of democracy. If people are to be restrained, then they must be restrained by and through their own consent. Since all are inherently equal, all should have an equal right to decide what sorts of freedoms are to be given up.

The liberal stress on the primacy of individual rights can evidently come into conflict with democratic ideals. If rights of individuals come first, democracy, a community process, cannot generally be used to limit individual rights that are natural and inherent. In its insistence on individual rights, liberalism upholds democracy and, at the same time, places profound limits on the role of that democracy.

This is another important part of the answer to the question of how political democracy and economic inequality can exist together. The liberal ideology associated with capitalism greatly restricts the scope of state activity; it must not interfere too much with individuals' liberty to own and control resources and to buy and sell in accordance with their own wishes. At the same time, there are demands in any complex society that the market system in itself has not proven capable of fulfilling, and it is because of them that the state has grown despite an ideology that calls for its limitation.

THE RISE OF THE WELFARE STATE

While classical liberalism would suggest that the state adopt a minimal role, the principle of **laissez-faire**, it is quite clear that modern states play a very extensive role in society. In Canada, for example, it is estimated that government (federal, provincial, and municipal) expenditures account for 35 percent of the total value of all goods and services produced (the gross domestic product) (OECD, 1986). This is typical for other capitalist societies too. (Recently, however, there has been a trend for government expenditures to go to debt servicing and not to new programs.) Why did this broadened role for the state emerge? What are the functions of the modern state?

In the nineteenth century it became evident from social unrest and the growth of socialist and labour movements that private capitalism would persist only if there was social reform. The British politician Joseph Chamberlain, for example, challenged the upper classes (of which he was a member) to recognize that a "ransom" had to be paid by those who wanted to keep their privileges and that this ransom must include free education, good housing, and fair rents for ordinary working people (Cole and Postgate, 1961: 410). In Germany, Chancellor Bismarck, as part of a struggle to reduce the appeal of socialism, introduced (in 1881–1889) progressive social programs, including a system of social insurance (Taylor, 1968: 157–161; Ashworth, 1962: 141–142).

The rise of democracy and the fear of political instability were contributors to the rise of the modern "welfare state" throughout Europe, Canada, and, less fully, the United States. The growth of Canada's social programs is outlined in Box 9.2.

To understand why the state has grown so large, its functions must be analyzed. What do states do that cannot be encompassed by other institutions or by unregulated market forces? Canadian political scientist Leo Panitch (1977) argued that the state performs three linked functions. First, the state engages in capital accumulation, by developing infrastructure like roads and sanitation and by expanding human capital via state-provided education. This function supports the process of *private* capital accumulation: it provides essential services to business. Second, state activity legitimates the political and social order with measures that promote social harmony. These **legitimation** measures include the regulation of conditions of labour and the provision of social welfare. Last, the state acts as the final guarantor of social order through the **coercion** function it possesses as the sole source of the legitimate right to use force.

Capital Accumulation

In a society of towns and cities that trade extensively internally and internationally, some agency must develop and maintain social infrastructure, including water and sanitation, urban planning, and transportation. The state stepped in where the market drew back and was deeply involved in the provision of this essential infrastructure for a developing industrial economy.

The state also played a role in the accumulation of **human capital**, chiefly through education. There was no effective private alternative for educating people so that they could play a useful and productive role in the economy. Private investment

Box 9.2
The Rise and Fall of
the Welfare State

1914	Ontario Workmen's Compensation Act becomes the first provincial legislation to assume that some injuries on the job are inevitable and that compensation should be provided without regard for responsibility.
1916	Manitoba becomes the first province to pass a Mother's Pension Act to assure a small income for widows and divorced or deserted wives with children to support. (By 1921, all provinces had such legislation.)
1927	First government-sponsored old-age pension program for those 70 years of age and over; with a means test.
1940	Unemployment Insurance Act passed.
1944	Family Allowance Act passed.
1951	A universal old-age pension system for those 70 years of age and over; no means test.
1957	Federal government agrees to share the cost of provincial hospital-insurance programs. By 1961, provinces had introduced hospital-insurance programs to ensure access to hospital care.
1965	Canada Pension Act provides an occupational pension plan for all workers as a method for improving old-age pensions for many Canadians.
1966	Medical Care Act brings universal medical care to all Canadians.
1966	Canada Assistance Plan is introduced, committing the federal government to sharing 50 percent of the costs incurred by other levels of government in meeting social assistance and welfare needs.
1967	Guaranteed Income Supplement program provides an income-tested supplement to pensioners with little or no income other than their old-age security pension.
1973	Family Allowances are subject to taxation.
1983	Federal legislation passed to block extra-billing for health care.
1989	Universality of old age pensions (OAS) eroded by legislation imposing a tax on this pension for those earning more than a specified income.
1990	Legislation passed to eliminate the role of government in funding unemployment insurance.
1991	Canada Assistance Plan amended to limit the amount that Ottawa will share with the richer provinces on a 50/50 basis.
1992	Family allowances eliminated and replaced with policies targeted at the poor.
1993	Eligibility rules for unemployment insurance tightened.

makes sense only where the benefits can be captured by the investor: in the case of education, there could be no control of where an educated person would work and thus no private interest in educating him or her. Instead, the state took on the responsibility of investing in the educational training of the population as productive workers. As capitalism developed, higher levels of literacy and numeracy were demanded in work: it was the state that met these demands.

Legitimation Legitimation makes social arrangements seem right, proper, moral, and rational. In capitalist societies, this legitimation must come from rational ideas, since there can be no appeal to religion and tradition. In capitalist societies the culture becomes, as

Max Weber put it, "disenchanted." Religious ideas lose their central role in upholding and justifying the social structure. There must be a new way of binding people to support the social order. At a minimum, this demands that people have some stake in society; there must be some social welfare. Although individuals might be left to starve, this cannot happen to whole classes of people without social turmoil.

In a purely free-market capitalist society, with inevitable cycles of economic expansion and contraction, large numbers of people can be pushed down to and below the barest levels of subsistence. Where people have nothing to lose and are given no support by society, they cannot be attached to it. At such an extreme level of inequality, capitalism and democracy are often not compatible and military or fascist dictatorships tend to emerge. However, liberal-democratic capitalism, in which state force remains in the background, demands that society generally provide the means of life.

Legitimation and the Growth of Modern Liberalism

In the later nineteenth and early twentieth centuries, the state became increasingly viewed as the guarantor of reasonable equality of opportunity. The word "liberal" itself became connected to the view that the state needs to be active to ensure individual freedom and opportunity. Canada's former prime minister Pierre Trudeau linked the principle of individual freedom to an active role for the state:

> *I recognized early on that the concepts of justice and of the freedom of all individuals to fulfill themselves to the best of their ability, to which I attach such fundamental importance, have little practical meaning in the absence of economic opportunity. Where is the justice in a country in which an individual has the freedom to be totally fulfilled, but where inequality denies him or her the means? Absolute freedom, in fact, tends to create inequality because there are the strong and the weak, the sick and the healthy, and the rich and the poor* (Trudeau, 1993: 186–187).

This idea that the state must ensure reasonably equal opportunity — "positive liberalism" — became the dominant view of how capitalist societies should work. It was adopted by almost all political parties in western societies, from the non-communist left to the conservative right.

Recently, there has been a revival of support for more purely free-market capitalist society, with less of the "liberal" intervention that has grown up within it. This revival of classical liberalism has made an impact on public debate and the shaping of government policy. It has not, however, much changed the scale of modern government.

Coercion

The coercive function of the state lies in the background in most modern capitalist societies. It acts ultimately as a guarantee of the preservation of social order. In capitalist societies, coercion is connected, of course, to the preservation of the assumptions on which capitalism itself is based: the protection of the right to individual ownership and use of property. Although a systematic resort to force against whole classes of individuals has not been typical in western societies, all have, at some time, selectively resorted to it to put down challenges to the social and economic order. When the resort to force becomes frequent and is directed against large groups democracy itself begins to crumble and military or fascist regimes arise. Usually, effective legitimation demands that this function of the state be a matter of ultimate rather than frequent resort.

The Stabilization of Society

....

There is another important role for the state, linked to legitimation: the stabilization of the economy (Panitch, 1977: 4–5). Economist John Maynard Keynes first provided a developed theory of how government actions could moderate the inevitable recessions and depressions in capitalist economies that resulted from inherent cycles of business activity. He argued that it was consumption — demand — that provided the support for an economy. In times of recession, governments should become active in supporting investment and upholding consumption, perhaps by undertaking public works or income support programs. Unless such government intervention occurred, it was certain that large numbers of people would be pushed to and below the level of subsistence until economic balance was restored.

This is a point of deep significance today, when Canada *typically* functions with an official unemployment rate in the range of 8–12 percent. It has been estimated that this "official" rate, comprised of those known by labour surveys to be actively seeking work, may disguise a rate of up to 5 percentage points higher because many people have simply given up on the search for employment. Government support helps maintain legitimation, but it also supports consumption and the process of capital accumulation. The federal government in 1993 spent 41 percent of its operating budget on direct income transfers to individuals (Canada, 1993).

A common pattern was evident wherever industrialization and urbanization developed: governments expanded their role into labour regulation, social programs to support minimal subsistence, and the administration and capital development of public health projects, sewers, water provision, and public housing. These interventions were all made necessary, in part, by the need to even out levels of economic activity and prevent the social disruption of widespread unemployment and poverty. Often they were responses to the threat of social unrest. The role of the state, then, can be considered not so much a policy to promote equality but one to support economic growth and maintain a reasonable level of social harmony.

THE ROLE OF THE STATE: COMPETING PERSPECTIVES

....

The **state** in modern capitalist society must perform several related functions if the economy and society are to work effectively and command popular support. It is in the very nature of the state, therefore, for it to play a somewhat independent role in society. But how do state agencies act? Does "democratic government" mean that the state is simply a servant of society, directed by individuals popularly chosen? Does it mean that the state is free of control by any single group in society and neutral in responding to social needs and demands? Or is it part of a dominant power system wedded to a *particular* structure of society that its actions (and inactions) protect and promote? Various views provide differing answers (see Box 9.3).

Functionalist Views of Democracy

....

Functionalists assume that the state manages society's collective needs and mediates between the various interests and demands of all members of society. Politics is a process of adjustment and compromise in which state institutions, politicians, citizens' organizations, and a whole complex of representative groups from business, labour, low-income groups, women, ethnic minorities, and other sectors influence the purpose and direction of public policy. Although not perfectly responsive to majority opinion, governments holding the state power are part of a system of **pluralistic politics** in which power is widely distributed throughout the society. This wide distribution of power is upheld, first of all, by the institutions of democracy itself, the majority-elected parliaments that are subject to popular choice (see Table 9.1).

Box 9.3
Conflicting Views on
the Role of the State:
A Summary

1. Functionalism suggests that the state simply gives society necessary order and direction; critical theorists argue that the state acts to preserve a *particular* form of social and economic order.
2. According to functionalism, legitimation arises from the existence and maintenance of cultural ideas that validate a form of government and a purpose for government on which most people agree. In critical theories, the state is a part of a particular social order in which there is ideological and structural domination by the economically powerful.
3. Functionalists consider the state's role in capital accumulation (though they would not use the term) as something that benefits everyone; critical accounts examine this role of the state as a way of requiring all members of society to pay for capital accumulation processes that make private profit possible (O'Connor, 1973).

To gain control of state power, any group must, by definition, offer a program and a set of values that appeal to a large number of people. Those gaining power are likely to be representative of the society as a whole. The programs and values that people favour are themselves shaped by a wide debate in the society, promoted by a free media, independent universities, research foundations, and various interest groups, all influencing public opinion within a framework of guaranteed freedom of debate and expression.

Some people and some organizations will undoubtedly be more influential than others. Generally, however, the democratic basis of government, operating in a context of open public debate and a participatory political process, will guarantee government based on the promotion of societal benefits as a whole, rather than for one group or class.

It is important to notice that this argument applies only to rational–legal systems of government based on electoral consent. It would not be applied to dictatorships. But liberal democracies realize the essence, if not all the details, of societies in which personal freedom is guaranteed and in which each individual, both alone and in groups, has an opportunity to influence the course of politics.

Table 9.1
Average Voter
Turnout in Canada
and Other
Democracies

Australia	94%*
Italy	90%
Sweden	89%
Germany	87%
Israel	79%
United Kingdom	74%
Canada	**73%**
Japan	71%
United States	54%

*Compulsory voting: a fine is levied on those who do not complete a ballot.
SOURCE: Statistics Canada, *Canadian Social Trends*, cat. no. 11-008E (Ottawa: Statistics Canada, Winter 1992), p. 5. Reproduced by authority of the Minister of Industry, 1994.

The functionalist argument is the prevailing picture of government in capitalist societies that is offered in the media and in much academic and public discussion. An important writer on the state in capitalist societies puts the point as follows:

> Most western "students of politics" tend to start, judging from their work, with the assumption that power, in western societies, is competitive, fragmented and diffused: everybody, directly or through organized groups, has some power and nobody has or can have too much of it (Miliband, 1969: 2).

In summary, functionalists see a system of pluralistic politics, of representative democracy, and of the state managing society's collective needs.

Critical Views of Democracy

. . . .

Critics argue that the functionalist model does not apply to the reality of Canadian political experience or that of other developed capitalist democracies. They claim that politics is dominated by upper- and middle-class males of European origin. It is worthwhile examining this claim with some information about the social background of Canadian politicians, particularly those in government.

Federal Politicians and Canadian Society

. . . .

The backgrounds of Canada's federal politicians are much more exclusive and upper-class than is warranted by the social makeup of the population as a whole. The ordinary members of the House of Commons display a distinctly elite character, but this is even more true of the most important of those members: the members of the federal cabinet, who actually direct the government.

There has been a considerable amount of research into the backgrounds and affiliations of Canadian politicians since the pioneering work of John Porter in *The Vertical Mosaic* (1965). Porter concluded that Canadians were ruled by a group of

Photo 9.2
Critics argue that the functionalist model of politics does not apply to the reality of the Canadian political experience. These critics claim that politics is dominated by upper- and middle-class white males

. . . .

Mario Bartel, Photographer

politicians dominated by a few occupational backgrounds (especially lawyers) and originating from the upper and middle class. This statement is still accurate today. The most recent research shows that there has, in fact, been an increase in the proportion of members of Parliament who come from the highest socio-economic groups in the population. In 1965, 77.3 percent of members were from the two highest categories of socio-economic status; in 1985, this had risen to an astonishing 87.9 percent. How does this compare with the population as a whole. In the 1980s, 6.9 percent of Canadians were either owners or self-employed professionals, yet this group held 52.7 percent of the seats in the House of Commons. Professionals and middle managers were 12.6 percent of all occupations, yet 35.2 percent of MPs. On the other hand, 20 percent of the working population was blue collar, yet only 1.2 percent of MPs came from that background (Guppy et al., 1987).

An interesting result of recent research is evidence that the New Democratic Party, which might be assumed to be more representative of ordinary Canadians, has contributed to, rather than counteracted, the elite composition of the House of Commons. In the federal cabinet, this inequality of representation becomes more extreme. In the 1980s, just under 0.2 percent of adult Canadians were lawyers, yet they comprised 35.1 percent of federal cabinet ministers. A further 26.7 percent came from corporate backgrounds (Guppy et al., 1987). Clearly, Canada is governed by a restricted group of individuals from a few specific occupations and the highest socio-economic background (see also Clement, 1977; Olsen, 1980).

Class, of course, is not the only division in Canadian society. Sex is important too, and here again a marked discrepancy exists between the composition of the House of Commons and sex ratios in the population as a whole. The 1993 election sent a significant number of women to the House of Commons, but women still make up only 18 percent of all MPs (see Table 9.2). This is a long way from equality in sexual representation, though there was definite progress in the 1980s and early 1990s. But rising female representation in the House of Commons has done nothing to counter the elite character of that body: just over 90 percent of women MPs come from the two highest socio-economic statuses. They are an even more elite group than male MPs, for whom the corresponding figure is 83.2 percent (Guppy et al., 1987).

Table 9.2
Women Candidates
in Federal Elections,
Canada, 1921–1993

Election Year	% of Women Candidates	% of Women Elected
1921–1967	2.4	0.8
1968	3.5	0.4
1972	9.4	3.4
1979	13.8	3.6
1980	14.4	5.7
1984	14.5	9.6
1988	19.2	13.2
1993	22.0	18.0

SOURCE: For 1921–1988, Chantal Maillé, *Primed for Power: Women in Canadian Politics* (Ottawa: Canadian Advisory Council on the Status of Women, 1990), p. 9; reprinted with permission. For 1993, Elections Canada.

Politics and Corporate Affiliation

· · · · · · · ·

The above examination of the social origins of Canada's federal politicians found overwhelming corporate and professional predominance. But this topic can be examined from another angle: what happens to leading politicians when they leave office? Again, there is evidence of a social situation quite different from that of other Canadians. Typically, senior politicians return to ordinary life to become corporate directors. They are prized as corporate board members and directors because of their influence and potential for shaping public policy (see Box 9.4).

The Professional State Elite

· · · · · · · ·

Politicians, of course, are not the only people guiding and exercising state power. Actual government policy development and administration is performed by the state bureaucracy of civil servants. Are the senior state bureaucrats socially representative? The federal bureaucratic elite is more reflective of the social composition of Canada than is the political elite, yet it still bears the imprint of class origins different from those of the rest of society. Definite gender stratification is evident as well.

Regarding the social origins of the state bureaucratic elite, a survey based on 1973 data concluded that the bureaucratic elite (defined as those of deputy minister rank in the federal public service and a sample of four provinces) was "predominantly middle class in its origins" (Olsen, 1980: 78). Although the civil service is theoretically based on the merit principle of placement and promotion, only 15 percent of the professional elite group could be described as of working-class origin. It was also found that even where individuals of working-class origin had gained access to the elite, they were usually placed in its bottom ranks (p. 79).

· · · · · · · ·

Box 9.4
Corporate Appointments of Former Premiers and Prime Ministers

· · · · · · · ·

HONOURABLE WILLIAM BENNETT (Social Credit, British Columbia): Canadian Pacific Forest Products Ltd., Imasco Ltd., Prime Resources Group Inc., Teck Corp.

HONOURABLE WILLIAM DAVIS (Progressive Conservative, Ontario): Bramalea Ltd., Canadian Imperial Bank of Commerce, Corel Corp., Fleet Aerospace Corp., Ford Motor Co. of Canada Ltd., Hemlo Gold Mines, Honeywell Ltd., Magna International, Power Corp. of Canada, The Seagram Co. Ltd.

HONOURABLE PETER LOUGHEED (Progressive Conservative, Alberta): Bechtel Canada Inc., Bombardier Inc., Brascan Ltd., Canadian Airlines International, Canadian Pacific Ltd., Norcen Energy Resource Ltd., Northern Telecom Ltd., PWA Corp., Royal Bank of Canada.

HONOURABLE DAVID PETERSON (Liberal, Ontario): Industrial Alliance Life Insurance Co., National Trust Co., Rogers Cantel Mobile Communications Inc., Unitel, Victoria and Grey Mortgage Corp.

RIGHT HONOURABLE JOHN TURNER (Liberal, Canada): Curragh Resource Inc. (resigned 1993), Empire Life Insurance Co., Noranda Forest Inc., Purolator Courier, Beatrice Foods Inc., Dominion of Canada General Insurance Co.

RIGHT HONOURABLE BRIAN MULRONEY (Progressive Conservative, Canada): Horsham Corp., American Barrick Resources Corp., Archer-Daniels-Midland Co.

· · · · · · · ·

SOURCE: *The Financial Post Directory of Directors, 1993* (Toronto: The Financial Post Company, 1992). Reprinted with permission.

· · · · · · · ·

The senior state bureaucracy also fails to reflect the sexual composition of society, even the sexual composition of the bureaucratic workforce itself. In 1987, women made up 42.4 percent of the permanent employees of the federal public service. At senior levels, the proportion of women declined drastically: they made up 8.7 percent of the executive category and 13.2 percent of the senior management positions (Morgan, 1988: 1).

While social origins and sexual composition suggest an unrepresentative character for the state bureaucracy, there is also the question of its affiliations. With what socio-economic interests are state bureaucrats associated? One comprehensive study concluded that there were substantial links between the senior personnel of state and state-supported institutions and private corporations. The authors of this research used the method of calculating how many ties were possible in principle between each area of the state sector and the private sector and then calculating how many ties there were. The example they cite to explain their method is the 19 crown (government-owned) corporations and the 34 leading firms in the private financial sector. The possible ties here are 19 times 34, that is, each crown corporation and each financial firm could be linked for a total of 646 ties. In fact, 166 ties were observed. This leads to a ratio of 166 ties from a possible 646, or a density of 257 actual ties per 1000 possible ties. In relation to ties between the senior level of the state bureaucracy and corporate organizations, the authors found there were 61 ties — a density of 202 per thousand (Fox and Ornstein, 1986).

A number of interesting examples lie behind these dry statistics. For example, the most important civil servant in Ottawa is the clerk of the Privy Council, the secretary and chief executive officer for the cabinet. This position was held, for most of the period from 1974 to 1984, by Michael Pitfield. After leaving the position in 1984, Mr. Pitfield joined the boards of Cadillac-Fairview Corporation, Great-West Life Assurance Co., Power Financial Corporation, and Montreal Trustco Inc. For the first year of the Progressive Conservative government elected in 1984, the clerk of the Privy Council was Gordon Osbaldeston, who later became a director of the American transnational corporation DuPont Canada Inc.

The second most central position in the federal public service is the deputy minister of finance. From 1970 to 1975, this position was held by Simon Reisman, who later became chairman of Ranger Oil and a director of George Weston Ltd. as well as holding other corporate appointments. From 1982 to 1985, the deputy minister of finance was Marshall Cohen, a tax and securities lawyer from New Jersey. Mr. Cohen joined the Department of Finance in the early 1970s and became deputy minister of finance. From the Department of Finance, Mr. Cohen moved to Olympia and York Developments, owned by the Reichmann family, and from there to Molson breweries, where he became president and chief executive officer. Following Marshall Cohen at finance was Stanley Hartt, who later became chief of staff to Prime Minister Brian Mulroney. In 1990, he was appointed chairman of Campeau Corporation.

These anecdotal examples suggest some very close affinities, at senior levels, between the public service and the corporate sector.

Elitism and Pluralism

Leading politicians and the most important state bureaucrats are obviously not a socially representative group. In addition, there is a strong connection between the leading positions in the state and the corporate sector. Does this matter? Does it compromise the extent to which the state reflects the broad spectrum of interests in society? The pluralist–functionalist view of politics is that it does not (Presthus, 1973).

Generally, pluralist theorists argue that the process of decision making by state institutions is affected by a wide range of representative groups who advocate diverse interests and encourage compromise and balance. It is true that this process does not usually involve large numbers of people, but it does involve the representation of most interests in society through the leaders of formal group organizations. "This group process," argues one author, "represents not only the whole substantive spectrum of national interests, but subcultural and economic interests as well, and often simultaneously" (Presthus, 1973: 10). The outcome of this process of group-influenced political decision making is assumed to be a "process of bargaining and compromise upon which the stability of the system rests" (p. 7).

In this picture of politics in Canada, one broadly applied by functionalists to all democratic capitalist societies, the elite class origins and affiliations of many important people in the state organization is not an obstacle to democratic government. People in government, however elite their origins and affiliations, are subjected to pressures from a comprehensive range of interest groups. These competing influences shape public policy, and as a result government produces generally consensual politics based on compromise and balance between the diverse claims and interests.

Corporate Political Influence

Critical views of the state in capitalist society reject the pluralist account and see democracy as frustrated by an alliance of the state and the capitalist economic system. Many examples can be found of how this alliance shapes public policy. Examinations of two instances follow: the forest industry in British Columbia, and the federal government's regulation of the tobacco industry.

British Columbia's Forest Industry

The forest industry in British Columbia has been very controversial for many years. Environmental and other groups have argued against the forest companies' harvesting methods (clear cutting) and have claimed that the management of the resource fails to expand job opportunities and support economic development through adding value to the harvested lumber. The industry is accused of neglecting the environment, non-sustainable harvesting, and using up the resource without contributing adequately to the industrial development of the province. In relation to the last point, the federal government forestry service confirmed that British Columbia has a particularly low level of jobs created in relation to the amount of timber harvested (Jacques, 1988). It has also been claimed that the provincial stumpage rates (government charges for cutting timber on public land) were for a long time too low and did not represent an appropriate return to the public.

Given the "hot" political issues in this industry, the role of the state (at the provincial level) seems to demand the maintenance of arm's-length relationships with the industry, so that independent decision making might be possible. But government–industry ties have actually been close and collaborative. A former premier of British Columbia, William Bennett, (premier 1975–86) had close personal ties to important forest industry companies. He was, subsequent to his premiership, a very large investor in Doman Industries, an important forestry company, and a close personal friend of its founder, Herb Doman. In 1988, after stepping down as premier, Mr. Bennett was appointed to the board of Canadian International Paper (subsequently merged with Canadian Pacific Forest Products), one of Canada's leading forest products companies. In 1992, subsequent to the electoral defeat of British Columbia's Social Credit government, the former minister of forests, Claude Richmond, was appointed chairman of the Western Environment and Development Taskforce, a lobby group working on behalf of the forest industry.

There are also ties between the forest corporations and non-government state sectors. In 1986, it was announced that David Strangway, president of the University of British Columbia since 1985, had accepted appointment to the board of Macmillan Bloedel, a leading corporation in the province's forest industry. This appointment is of interest because the University of British Columbia forestry faculty is the chief source of professional personnel for the industry and for the public service. It has been closely allied with the industry and has played a prominent role in counteracting criticism of the industry and supporting industry policy and procedures.

These links indicate very close ties both between government and the industry and between the publicly funded University of British Columbia (which might be expected to be a source of independent advice and analysis) and the industry.

The Tobacco Industry

It has been known conclusively for over 30 years that cigarette smoking directly causes an array of fatal diseases, including lung cancer and heart disease. Yet the state has left the industry free to market and promote cigarettes and tobacco products, and only in the last few years have restrictions on advertising and the inclusion of health warnings on tobacco packaging been legislated.

The history of tobacco industry and state dealings has been long (in 1957, for instance, defeated Liberal prime minister Louis St. Laurent was appointed to the board of Rothmans) and complex, so only a few issues are discussed here. For example, the government proposed in July, 1988 to strengthen the printed health warnings on tobacco products packaging. Leading the industry side, in seeking to influence the shape of any regulations, was William Neville, president of the Canadian Tobacco Manufacturers Council and previously principal secretary to former prime minister Joe Clark. Mr. Neville was also a prominent director of the Conservative party's 1988 election campaign. Details of negotiations about the new regulations show that "the strength of warnings about the effects of tobacco use to be included on tobacco products packaging was reduced after a series of private interventions by William Neville," and that "health groups lobbying for the changes had been kept unaware that there was negotiation over the regulations".[4] In 1993, the government once more postponed the implementation date of its new warning label on tobacco products.

In 1991, the Canadian government proposed an export tax on Canadian-made cigarettes. The tax was designed to frustrate the smuggling of duty-free cartons back into Canada. It was abandoned by the Conservative government after pressure from the tobacco industry. William Neville was again chief lobbyist for the industry, and he was able to get junior finance minister John McDermid to set up meetings with the minister of finance for senior executives from Imperial Tobacco Ltd., RJR-MacDonald Inc., and Rothmans Benson and Hedges Inc. Mr. Neville was believed to earn $400 000 a year for his efforts on behalf of the Canadian Tobacco Manufacturers Council.[5]

Critical theorists argue on the basis of this sort of evidence that it is not correct to depict a plurality of interests outside government as democratizing the decision making process. The structure of power outside the state system does not contradict but corresponds to the structure inside it: there is a systematic linkage of the state and state institutions with private capital. The state is not something standing above and independent from private capital, but rather is intimately connected to it.

This chapter has considered some evidence of the *general affinity* of the political and state elites with the leading ranks of the capitalist class in Canadian society. But this is not conclusive evidence that the state is allied with the *particular interests* of that class. Pluralists insist that the process of government is best understood as a competition of interests and values within a democratic electoral framework. In a democratic society, government can be changed. Political parties forming governments that fail to represent people will be rejected. Democracy in capitalist societies is said to create consensual politics reflecting popularly held norms and values. This view of politics is supported by the fact that no capitalist democracy has ever freely elected a government seeking to radically transform society.

The absence of revolutionary political movements in mature capitalist societies leads pluralists to argue that critical theories of the state are mistaken: people have the legal right to express political choice, but they have generally done so for parties and groups that support the basic characteristics of those societies. This suggests that there is genuine consensus in the society.

Consensus: Genuine or Manipulated?

Critical theorists have several answers to the view that elections guarantee political choice and reflect public opinion and public values. First, there is argument about facts: is it true that capitalist democracies have experienced only consensual politics? Has state violence been used to restrict political choice? Second, is it true that politics in capitalist societies is a process of equal competition? Or is electoral choice and public debate structured by inequality in the power to influence and communicate? An answer to these questions must consider the state's use of violence and the role of the media and universities in creating genuine debate.

State Violence

Critical theorists' examination of the capitalist state includes a very different account of the relationship of the state to violence or force. In functionalist theory, any complex society demands an ultimate source of social control. The state uses its power of violence as a last resort and to uphold the laws and values agreed on by the society. On the contrary, according to critical views, the law and law enforcement can be best understood as a system of domination upholding a society divided by class, gender, or race.

In this view the state acts as a guarantor of a particular kind of social order — one that supports the right of private ownership and use of capital — a patriarchal order, or one of racial or ethnic subordination. If there is little political opposition to the rule of dominant groups, the coercive role of the state remains in the background. If a challenge does develop, then the state power is used to control and suppress it. In Canadian history, events like the Winnipeg general strike of 1919, the Regina riots of 1935 (see Box 9.5), the asbestos strike in Quebec in 1949, the FLQ crisis of 1970, and the Oka crisis of 1990 are considered occasions on which the coercive power of the state was used to suppress dissent and uphold the social and political order. In critical views, the state in a capitalist society is always ready to resort to violence to protect the interests of capital.

The Media and Public Opinion

If "information is power," then that power is very concentrated in Canada. Without information, people cannot gain an accurate appreciation of how the society around them is working, cannot make informed judgments, and cannot make decisions based on a knowledge of available choices. In localized traditional societies, the community itself is an adequate and effective means of transmitting information and providing the knowledge to exercise choice. In modern societies, which are marked by both complexity and impersonality, the transmission of information and the shaping of public debate is a specialized activity.

● ● ● ● ● ● ● ●

In 1935, the RCMP buckled under to heavy pressure from the Conservative government of R.B. Bennett to make a series of arrests on flimsy charges for political reasons. It was this that caused the notorious Regina Riot of July 1, 1935, in which one city policeman was killed and 100 people hospitalized.

The situation in Regina was tense that summer. Eighteen hundred jobless men from the relief camps of the three western provinces poured into town by boxcar on June 14 on the famous On To Ottawa Trek. Their purpose was to go on to the capital and lay their grievances before the prime minister. They wanted union wages instead of 20 cents a day, their so-called "slave camps" closed, and they wanted the right to vote in federal elections.

Bennett had refused all their demands. But the public was enthusiastically on their side. And the Canadian Pacific Railway co-operated fully. It allowed them to ride the freights and even held the trains so they could wash up and eat en route.

The trek was organized by Arthur (Slim) Evans, a longtime Communist who might have stepped directly out of a Dos Passos novel of the thirties. Bennett, who had a pathological fear of the Communist revolution, determined to stop the movement cold at Regina, headquarters of the RCMP. However, the RCMP was contracted out as Saskatchewan's provincial police force and Jimmy Gardiner, the province's tough Liberal premier, took a different view.

To get control of the police, Bennett pressured both railway presidents to write Gardiner that the trek constituted a menace. That allowed him to invoke the Railway Act, a national statute.

With the RCMP under his thumb, Bennett immediately gave orders that the force patrol the railway yards and prevent the trekkers moving east. ...

Since there weren't enough police in town to stop the trek, Bennett opted for delay. He sent two cabinet ministers to "negotiate" with the trekkers. ... The confrontation in Ottawa solved nothing. ...

Evans returned to Regina to announce that the trek would continue east by highway; hundreds more were waiting in Winnipeg to join in. Again Bennett panicked. The assistant commissioner of the RCMP, Colonel S.T. Wood, was ordered to stop and arrest them. He was told — and apparently believed — that a special order-in-council had been passed, allowing the government to take emergency action under the "peace, order and good government" clause in the Relief Act.

There was no such order-in-council. Nothing of the sort could be passed when Parliament was sitting. But peaceful citizens were about to be denied the use of the King's highway.

Wood also announced that Regina citizens who helped the trekkers in any way — with food, shelter or transportation — would be arrested. That preposterous statement, which had no basis, was carried in the press and believed. Aid for the trek dried up.

A token convoy of three vehicles, led by the Reverend Sam East, attempted to move. They were stopped by a cordon of steel-helmeted Mounties. ...

Bennett still believed the country was facing a revolution. R.J. Manion, one of the ministers sent to Regina, told him the communists were trying to force

(continued)

(continued)

one. Actually, the Communists were trying to negotiate an end to the affair. But Manion said that strong measures were needed to curb them, that "somehow the leaders should be got at."

Bennett acted. On June 28, Wood got his orders. The government wanted the strike leaders arrested — urgently. The handiest section of the criminal code — section 98 — was to be invoked. Under it, any trekker believed to be a Communist could be arrested. ...

Over the objections of Regina's chief of police, the RCMP decided to make the arrests at 8 that night during a public meeting called by the trekkers in Market Square. More than 100 steel-helmeted RCMP and city police would surround the square and advance on it while a flying squad of plainclothesmen made the arrests.

The crowd, composed of Regina citizens with a few hundred trekkers, was unaware of what was happening. When they saw the helmeted police apparently attacking them, swinging clubs and batons, people panicked. ...

One of the worst civilian riots in Canadian history began at that moment, leaving the hospitals and jails full and downtown Regina in shambles. A royal commission blamed the Communists. But the real culprit was Bennett.

SOURCE: Pierre Berton, "When Mounties Were Manipulated, the Riot Began," *The Globe and Mail*, January 1, 1990, p. A7. Reprinted with the permission of the author.

How is this specialized activity of communication structured in modern society? At first sight, multiple channels of communication exist in Canada and other capitalist societies: a number of television channels, radio stations, newspapers, magazines, and so on. But beneath this apparent array of choice and variety lie some major limitations to pluralism. First, the media is dominated by a few major corporations, with a substantial interlocking of shareholders and directorships. Second, the media are themselves major business corporations, tending naturally to define the world from a business perspective. Third, the purpose of the media is not primarily the discovery, analysis, and reporting of news and public affairs, but the provision of entertainment that will generate a large audience.

What exactly are the goals of media corporations? Many people carry a mental image of the press — which they extend to television and radio — of editors and reporters seeking out the news and trying to expose the truth about public and political events. They think, perhaps, of the American movie *All the President's Men*, where reporters fearlessly expose wrongdoing during the Watergate scandal. Or they think of how the Canadian press and electronic media took up the story of David Milgaard and aroused public opinion to demand an open review of his conviction for murder.

But is this role of information and criticism what the media is principally about? The answer to this question begins with the fact that, except for public broadcasters, the media are corporately owned and the purpose of corporations is profit. There is

The purpose of the media is not only to discover, analyze, and report news and public affairs. The media also provides an element of entertainment that will generate a larger audience.

· · · · · · · ·

Len Wagg, Photographer

an ethic of journalism, in which reporting and analysis is a professional pursuit and a moral commitment, but although this plays an important role in the media, it usually occurs in the context of corporate business.

Since profit is the motivation for corporate activity, what are the consequences of corporate ownership of the media? Smythe (1981) provides a useful suggestion to help understand the issues. He argues that the media, like any other corporation, is selling a product, but this product is not quite what one would expect. It is not newspapers or programs that are the central product of media corporations; their primary product is an audience.

Typically, newspapers derive about 20 percent of their revenue from readers' purchases and about 80 percent from advertising (Frank and Durand, 1993: 21). Advertisers, chiefly other corporations, buy space in newspapers to sell their products to the readers. The value of the newspaper space to the advertiser depends on the size of the readership and on its socio-economic characteristics. The newspaper or magazine corporation, therefore, is primarily concerned with the development of readership that it can sell as an audience (the product) to the advertiser, who is the chief source of revenue. The same holds true for radio and television, except in this case the advertiser is usually the sole source of revenue.

This perspective on the media opens up an entirely different understanding of their goals: they are not primarily about news, analysis, and comment, but about the creation and maintenance of a marketable audience. Their chief source of profit lies in selling access to this audience to other corporations. Thus, programming has two central goals: it must maintain, not offend, the audience; and it must harmonize with the sort of products being advertised.

The links of media corporations to the rest of the corporate structure are also important. A close relationship suggests limits on the independence of media news coverage and comment. In the early 1970s, 51 of 105 important media owners and directors for whom data was available were also members of the corporate elite. An additional 21 held positions in important corporations that were not, however, among the largest in Canada. In total, 69 percent of the media elite were also holders of important corporate positions, and a further 10 percent were closely related by kin connection to the corporate elite (Clement, 1975: 325).

The channels of public communication are corporately owned, and these media corporations are themselves integrated into the corporate structure of the economy. The corporate elite have channels to communicate with the public, but the public have few resources to communicate with each other.

What about the role of publicly owned media? In Canada the Canadian Broadcasting Corporation (CBC), established in 1936, has a mandate to provide Canadians with distinctly Canadian programming and news focus. Yet the CBC too relies heavily on the corporately owned news services provided by the various press agency associations and private broadcasters. The pressure, especially in television, to maintain an audience for sale to advertisers is also strong at the CBC. However, the CBC does provide a service to Canadians that is different from that provided by private broadcasters. In 1988 it was reported that the CBC, although it had only half of the audience of private television stations, accounted for 60 percent of the spending on Canadian made television programs. The French-language division of the CBC, Societé Radio Canada, with an audience comparable to that of the private stations, accounted for 76 percent of all spending on original French-language programs.[6]

Public, rather than corporate, ownership of the media clearly does make a difference in the content of programs and attention to Canadian life and culture. In recent years, the resources of the CBC have been cut back and with this the attention to Canadian issues and to the creation of programs reflective of Canadian life and experience has been under siege. Corporate control of the media, cross-ownership of newspapers, radio, and television, and integration of media into the structure of corporate Canada all cast doubt on the pluralist view that information and debate is open and varied in Canadian society.

Universities and Public Debate

What role do the universities — conventionally thought of as bastions of learning and criticism — play in modern society? Do they foster open and critical information about society? Until recently, it was thought that universities in a democratic society were a source of detached and open inquiry and criticism. People spoke of "academic freedom," the right and duty of professors and researchers to seek knowledge free from the pressures of political service or financial inducement. Today, this view is rarely proposed. The relative autonomy of the universities, as sources of independent and objective knowledge and criticism, is less valued than is their functional role in society and, more specifically, the economy.

Universities have begun to focus much more directly on the specific development of trained human capital. For example, a Ph.D. in the sciences once implied a generalized training that would be shaped later into the specific vocational knowledge required in the workplace. Today, universities maintain an intimate association with the corporate sector so that graduates will already be, to a large extent, functioning workers immediately on entry into employment. Whole new faculties with direct reference to the corporate world have developed in the universities: schools of industrial relations, public administration, and business administration, each articulated very closely with the specific vocational requirements of corporate and public-sector employers.

As the university–vocational link has strengthened, so have university–corporate ties become more evident. The authors of a study on state–corporate ties found that universities were especially marked by close links to the corporate world (Fox and Ornstein, 1986: 482). Lloyd Barber, president of the University of Regina and chair of the Corporate–Higher Education Forum, in commenting on this forum said: "If you sat around the table and listened to the discussion and didn't know, you'd be hard-pressed to know who was a university president and who was a corporate president" (Newson and Buchbinder, 1988: 7).

How might one interpret this observation? Functionalists might ask, "What's the problem?" The function of universities is surely to provide society with a supply of educated people for important social roles and occupations. This job is best accomplished when universities are directly linked to the corporate world, in which most of their graduates will be employed.

From a critical viewpoint, there *is* a problem, and it is a deep one for a democracy. Universities are not just about providing people trained for occupations; they have a role in providing society with debate, criticism, analysis, and information. This is a vital role in a democracy, where informed debate is essential for rational public policy. Evidence of the integration of universities into a functional relationship with corporate capital suggests an ideological integration too. Can competing views of society and of the world be effectively represented in universities that are so strongly linked to particular interests?

Whatever view one takes of the social value, or social cost, of this integration, it is evident that universities cannot simply be portrayed as independent institutions standing outside the power structure of the corporate world. To the extent that the universities are reduced in independence, the pluralist view of their role in society and politics is undermined.

A STRUCTURALIST APPROACH: MARXISM REVISITED

Discussion about the state from critical perspectives has largely concentrated on the empirical analysis and demonstration of the close ties between the state and state institutions and the corporate world. These ties are seen as binding the state to a corporate definition of politics and social values.

Some critical theorists, however, see the analysis of interpersonal and interinstitutional ties of state and private capital as being interesting but not really explanatory of the role of the state. They suggest that the ties that do exist are not a cause of the close integration of state and corporate capital, but merely a symptom of it. They argue that the state in a capitalist society can work only within the context of maintaining capitalism. This view stresses that a capitalist economy demands capitalist politics too: the investment and capital growth on which capitalism rests must be protected by the state and by any government. This argument, known as structural Marxism (Miliband, 1976: 66–74), contrasts with a more instrumental view of the state (Marchack, 1985).

This structural view of the state was discussed earlier in this chapter, when it was argued that the state is "captured" by the structure of existing society and must work to reproduce the economic and social order. To achieve this, it performs the central functions of capital accumulation, stability, and legitimation. Not only does the state contribute to the economic requirements of capitalism, it also plays a role in maintaining and upholding a legal system that reflects the ideological system of capitalism. For example, the state supports corporate power by a legal framework that bestows legal personality on corporations and accords them the rights that attach to individuals. Private rights are enshrined. Public rights, in contrast, are left undefined, vague, and difficult to assert both in politics and in law.

There has been a lively debate about the value of the instrumental versus structural analyses of the state, and it is now generally agreed that they are both valuable. They both provide a useful way to grasp the constraints on the role of the state in capitalist societies. However, they tend to present the state's role as fully determined by the capitalist economic system. History shows that politics does matter.

Relative Autonomy of the State: The Realm of Politics

• • • • • • • •

The study of the close links between private capital and the state system and the understanding of the state as part of a system that must serve the needs of capital suggests that politics is a very limited affair. But this picture does not fully reflect the experience of politics in capitalist societies. The policy directions of the state are clearly shaped by the electoral process, by political parties, and by public opinion. The role of the state is not simply dictated by corporate interests and the economic requirements of a capitalist economy.

Sweden, the United States, and Canada can all correctly be called capitalist societies, but they have very different degrees of government involvement in economic regulation and have developed differing forms of the welfare state. These three different combinations of capitalism and politics show that the state cannot be understood as completely subject to corporate dictatorship or as trapped in a completely controlling economic structure. The state can play a role that is, to some degree, independent of the structure of economic power in a capitalist society.

How is this relative independence or autonomy of the state best understood? In a famous comment about the state, Karl Marx and Frederick Engels wrote that the state "is but a committee for managing the common affairs of the whole bourgeoisie" (capitalist class) (Marx and Engels, 1968[1848]: 37). As Miliband points out, this statement implies that if there are "common affairs," there must be particular ones as well (Miliband, 1976: 67). There are not only class interests; there are also interests of individuals within that class. Even if all large corporations want to stimulate trade and the movement of goods, railway owners will want it to take place on the railways, while trucking company owners (and truck makers) will want to have governments develop the road network. While steelmakers want to encourage the use of cans, glassmakers favour the use of more bottles.

It is in the nature of capitalism itself that, *to the extent that it remains competitive,* there are conflicting interests between various segments of industry and services and between the various factions of the corporate class associated with these economic sectors. It is inevitable, in this light, that the state will play a role in mediating these conflicts and in judging between competing and conflicting interests within corporate capital itself. The state must therefore, to some degree, stand above the particular interests of any one group and play a role in determining the interests to which state institutions will actually respond (Miliband, 1976: 68). This role as referee between conflicting corporate interests becomes less meaningful, of course, when capital is under the control of relatively few conglomerates, as is the case in Canada. The state's role as arbiter contracts as corporate interests become more monolithic. But the state has certainly played roles in Canada, for example in the North American Free Trade Agreement, that favoured some sections of private capital — such as energy producers and forestry companies — against others.

A relatively independent role for the state also arises from the wider democratic political process in which the electorate and various interest groups place their demands and goals on the political agenda. A Co-operative Commonwealth Federation government introduced medicare in Saskatchewan and created a public demand that forced its rapid adoption for all of Canada. The minority Liberal federal government, dependent on New Democratic Party support (1972–74), intervened in the economy to increase Canadian ownership and control of oil exploration, recovery, refining, and marketing. Some Canadian governments have decided that higher taxes on corporations and well-off individuals are necessary to produce social programs that will integrate and support poorer members of the community. The role of the state involves a wider and more long-term perspective than private interests are able to develop.

In some ways, the critical approach to understanding the state accepts something of the pluralist model: the state does indeed mediate between conflicting interests and, depending on the degree of political activism in the society, does respond to a diversity of pressures and demands. But this mediating role is not neutral or independent; the state system is closely integrated into the system of economic power in society. What the state possesses is **relative autonomy**: though not commanded by unified interests of private capital, the state does act to maintain and preserve a particular social structure and to uphold a particular set of values. Reform is minimized and democracy is contained.

GENDER AND THE STATE

Feminist critical theories have added to the scope and concepts of sociology generally; what has feminist analysis added to the understanding of the state? Is there something in the state's role that relates directly to the maintenance of gender relations? Critical sociologists have employed the concept of "social reproduction" (Dickinson and Russell, 1986) to more fully examine the role of the state in society. Social reproduction means more than simply reproducing the social relations of production. It also highlights the most fundamental and primary social process of all: the sexual reproduction and nurturing of human individuals.

Marx observed: "The maintenance and reproduction of the working class is, and must ever be, a necessary condition to the reproduction of capital." He also claimed that "the capitalist may safely leave its fulfilment to the labourer's instincts of self-preservation and of propagation" (Marx, 1954: 537). But was this true? Perhaps this "instinct" may not be sufficient to maintain physical reproduction of the working class in the living conditions of early capitalism. Britain's Children's Employment Commission of 1842 records:

We find that instances occur in which children are taken into these mines to work as early as four years of age, sometimes at five, and between five and six, not infrequently between six and seven, and often from seven to eight, while from eight to nine is the ordinary age at which employment in these mines commences (Trades Union Congress, 1968: 23).

Working-class children were placed in physical jeopardy by the degraded conditions in mines and factories. And so were society's physical reproducers — women. The wholesale and indiscriminate use of children and women in the production process was perilous to family life. Not only was health compromised, but so was the upbringing and physical preservation of the youngest children, often left to their own resources as parents and older siblings were forced by economic necessity into the work force. The tendency of unregulated market capitalism to establish low wages and conscript all sectors of the population to the labour force undermined the essential processes of physical reproduction. Far from being able to "safely leave" the process of reconstituting the labour force to individual families, it seemed that the generalized capitalist exploitation of all possible labour endangered this process.

The state acts to arrest the unlimited draining of labour power and takes on this central role of "balancing of the productive–reproductive needs of society" (Ursel, 1986: 164). In all capitalist societies, it regulates and restricts the work roles of women and children. It also, where necessary, provides economic support to maintain families at minimal levels of subsistence. These policies, however, have tended to support and perpetuate a particular role structure in the family: women as custodians of the home and children, and men as the principal wage earners. A domestic role for women becomes culturally normalized, and legislation to "protect" women as reproducers leads to women as workers becoming something less than men. They are segregated into service and other jobs requiring a relatively low level of education and training. In seeking to protect the family and the health and welfare of women and children, the state reinforces a social division between men and women and defines women into subordinate positions in the private sphere of life. The balancing of production and reproduction is structured on the restriction and subordination of women. Women who work outside the home are also pushed into dependency by the lower wages resulting from a segregated labour market (Ursel, 1986: 188).

GLOBALIZATION AND THE MARGINALIZATION OF THE STATE

In the last few decades, the international economy has witnessed intensifying "globalization." Capital has become increasingly mobile. A writer in the *Wall Street Journal* describes the new world economy:

> *Across increasingly meaningless lines on the map, entrepreneurs rush huge and turbulent streams of capital, manufacturing components, product sub-assemblies, in-process inventories, research and development projects, royalties, software programs, technology licences, circuit board schematics and managerial ideas. Many of the most important transactions consist of electronic or photonic pulses between branches, subsidiaries, contractors and licencees of particular companies and defy every calculation of national debt and exchange.[7]*

With this internationalized economy, nation-states experience a reduction of their power. Governments of independent countries increasingly lose political autonomy as social and economic policies pressure them toward international "harmonization." Individual state policies must be set in a competitive context in which large corporations may demand that nation-states provide equal opportunity for the accumulation of capital and, consequently, equalize taxation, social policies, and standards of labour and environmental regulation. (A mere 600 corporations now produce about 25 percent of everything made in the world's market economies.)

Policies of regional and sectoral economic development and social welfare are increasingly constrained by competition against other states in which capital is allowed to operate less hindered and with a lesser burden of demands from the public authorities. Citizens' democratic choice is reduced and the international power of corporations enhanced. The tension between the inevitable inequalities of capitalism and the principles of political democracy are expressed in a new form, where private capital increases its power over the political systems of individual nation-states.

CONCLUSION

This chapter has drawn attention to processes and structures that restrict the democratic responsiveness of the state and impede society's ability to use the state to foster values of community. It began by showing that liberal philosophy itself is a limiting influence, since it insists that government should not interfere with individual liberty and free enterprise. More important, perhaps, is the fact that in modern society democratic government refers to representative, rather than participatory, democracy. This limits the kind of control citizens have over the content of political debate and the decisions of governments.

Elected members of government tend to be socially unrepresentative, and research shows marked affinity with the corporate sector. In addition, the corporate sector has a tremendous ability to manipulate public opinion through the concentrated ownership of mass media and a corporate–public university link that can restrict the range of voices heard in democratic debate. The current globalization of capital reduces the relevance and independence of individual states and provides less community control of vital economic and social decisions.

Now some answers can be put to the two important questions posed at the beginning of this chapter. First: how are economic inequality and legal political equality reconciled in modern society? Supporters of a pluralist theory of the state argue that a broad spectrum of interests are represented in decisions of state institutions and that economic inequality in the wider society is counterbalanced by political equality. Capitalism and democracy co-exist in an atmosphere of compromise and mediation. The critical view claims that the reconciliation comes from restricting the meaningfulness of political equality: equality operates within a very narrow field, and for most purposes the inequality of the economic order is reproduced in the political order. Democracy is constrained.

The second question is this: can society use state institutions to control the tremendous economic power of corporations? A pluralist would respond with a yes. The political process is sufficiently open to allow all groups to have a political impact and exert community control over corporate power. From a critical perspective, communities are significantly restricted by the alliance of state and corporate power.

NOTES

1. According to Phillips (1990), the United States has squeezed past France to become the nation with the most uneven distribution of income.
2. As with all ideal types, there may be a blend of different types of authority. Hitler, for example, was a charismatic leader who also claimed a rational–legal basis for his exercise of power.
3. First Nations peoples also had traditional forms of democracy that stressed active participation and involvement; these are now being recovered by their communities.
4. Graham Fraser, "Group Says Tobacco Warning Weakened," *The Globe and Mail*, June 26, 1989, p. A1.
5. "Threats Derailed Tobacco Tax," *The Globe and Mail*, May 22, 1992, p. A1.
6. Hugh Winsor, "Private Broadcasters Scolded," *The Globe and Mail*, June 10, 1988, p. A4.

7. G. Gilder, cited in "Worth Repeating," *The Globe and Mail,* April 26, 1988, p. B6.

. . . .

FURTHER READING

Bashevkin, Sylvia B. *Toeing the Lines: Women and Party Politics in English Canada.* Toronto: Oxford University Press, 1993. Everything you ever wanted to know about women's participation in the political process.

Brodie, M.J., and J. Jenson. *Crisis, Challenge and Change: Party and Class in Canada,* 2nd ed. Toronto: Methuen, 1991. A standard guide to party politics in Canada.

Lee, Robert Mason. *One Hundred Monkeys.* Toronto: MacFarlane, Walter and Ross, 1989. A very readable introduction to the exercise of political power in Canada.

MacKinnon, Catherine. *Toward a Feminist Theory of the State.* Cambridge: Harvard University Press, 1989. A welcome and substantial effort to rethink the role of the state from a critical feminist perspective.

Martin, Lawrence. *Pledge of Allegiance: The Americanization of Canada in the Mulroney Years.* Toronto: McClelland and Stewart, 1993. Clearly a political book, but an engaging account of how one Canadian government handled its relations with a foreign state, the United States of America.

York, Geoffrey, and Loreen Pindera. *People of the Pines.* Toronto: Little, Brown, 1991. A recounting of the Oka crisis of 1990, an important incident in Canadian history, in which the government turned its ultimate coercive force, the army, against its own peoples.

. . . .

STUDY QUESTIONS

1. How can the principle of individual rights be used to argue both for and against democratic politics?
2. What is the main claim of a pluralist view of politics?
3. How would someone taking a pluralist view of politics explain the development of unemployment insurance? How would this explanation differ from a critical perspective?
4. Does the development of a global economy necessarily conflict with democracy?
5. Consult the biographies of your region's members of Parliament or members of the provincial legislature. What is the class composition of this group?
6. Would the presence of more women in Parliament or your provincial legislature make a difference? Discuss.
7. Using the computer access to newspaper files in your library, research the history of government attempts to regulate the tobacco industry. Prepare a brief report.

10 WORK

INTRODUCTION

The modern workplace has organized work in a manner profoundly different from the manner in traditional societies. To understand this new organization, classical sociologists developed three key concepts: alienation, rationalization, and anomie. All workplaces, whether they are aware of these sociological concepts or not, must respond to the fact that many workers are alienated, dislike the impersonality and routinization of work, and have a weak social bond to the workplace. Women appear to experience the additional problem of gender-based disadvantage in the workplace. Women's wages are lower, their jobs less secure, and their employment conditions poorer.

Functionalist and critical perspectives interpret these problems very differently and advocate markedly different workplace policies. An examination of modern work organization reveals a substantial gap between people's roles as citizens and workers. As citizens they expect to have some say in how their society is organized, but as workers they are typically subservient to the authority of an employer. Unions can be partly understood as worker associations that attempt to reduce the contrast between people's roles as citizens and workers.

Work is a social activity central to most people's lives. They spend a great deal of time preparing to do it, wondering when they will find it, purchasing clothing and supplies to carry it out, actually doing it, unwinding from doing it, and dreaming about being without it. Does the way society organizes work affect people in significant ways? Would they find more meaning in work if it was organized in other ways? How has the nature and organization of work changed over time? How

Work is a social activity central to most of our lives. We spend a great deal of time preparing to do it, wondering when we will find it, purchasing clothing and supplies to carry it out, actually doing it, unwinding from doing it, and dreaming about being without it.

· · · · · · · · ·

Cathie Archbauld, Photographer

have those changes affected social life? A sociological view of work suggests that the organization of such a basic human activity must have far- reaching consequences, both for individuals and for society.

WORK IN MODERN SOCIETY

· · · · · · · · ·

Traditional peoples produce for immediate use and stockpile supplies for the future. They do not produce just for the sake of trade, profit, or the accumulation of wealth. Work in these societies is not only an activity of production; it also expresses cultural celebration and community solidarity. In modern capitalist enterprises, in contrast, work has an entirely different foundation. It is almost always carried out in formal organizations in which some people exercise general authority to direct the work while others carry out its various steps.

Modern work is often specialized and involves a complex division of labour. Productivity and efficiency, not personal satisfaction or community celebration, are the central aims of work. The goal is to produce goods and services that can be sold for profit. The organization of work for the narrow aim of efficiency and profit has important effects on the ways in which it is experienced.

Tensions in the Workplace

· · · · · · · · ·

The central premise of liberal philosophy is a society of choice, in which individuals can make decisions that enhance their freedom and contribute to their self-fulfilment. People may choose to live a subsistence life and produce only for their own immediate needs, but most work with (and usually for) others. When people enter the workplace they remain free people, bound only by a narrow contract of employment; they can choose to enter that contract or not to enter it.

There is a shared interest between workers and employers in maintaining a profitable business that can provide jobs. But there are also fertile grounds for conflict. There may be disputes over job content, methods of work, strictness of management direction, and the overspecialization of work, and there may be problems resulting from boredom.

Women experience the additional problem of gender-based disadvantage in the workplace. Women's wages are lower, their jobs are less secure, and their employment conditions are poorer.

Bruce Ayres / TONY STONE IMAGES

One of the main conflicts in the workplace is about how much work should be performed for the wage earned. Most individuals have some commitment to the work ethic of a "fair day's work for a fair day's pay." Max Weber suggested that the development of capitalism was dependent on a transformation of social values. New values were created that made work, in itself, seem like a moral pursuit to be carried out with energy and diligence.

But workers and employers can have different ideas about commitment and effort. Workers want to maintain their jobs, but it is rare for them to have the same interest as their employers in maximizing productivity. How do employers try to ensure that their workers are efficient and productive?

Scientific Management and Mass Production

Scientific management, developed by F.W. Taylor at the end of the nineteenth century, was one of the early systems for increasing workplace discipline and enhancing productivity. Taylor's main aim was to give management the tools to analyze the work process and organize it for maximum efficiency (Taylor, 1919).

Taylor's management system was designed to overcome the tendency of workers to collude to restrain the speed and effort they put into their work. He began by recognizing that piece-work payment (linked to quantity of work output) is not a satisfactory way of inducing workers to produce as much as they can manage. Workers know that if they make more than a certain wage on piece rates then those rates will be cut and more work expected. Workers have to produce more to maintain their wages. Piece workers recognize that it is in their common interest to restrict production, so they establish their own group norms for production considerably below the potential output.

Taylor accepted that output restriction by workers is rational. "Systematic soldiering," as he called it, is an effective technique for restraining the pace of work. Scientific management sets out to undermine this worker control over the pace, methods, and quantity of work and to enhance management direction and control.

Three linked steps are involved in scientific management. First, management must gain possession of the workers' knowledge. This is done by systematic analysis of the steps involved in the work: how they are performed, how long they take. Time and motion study is used extensively in this process. The aim is for management to be able to specify precise rules and methods for the organization and performance of the work.

Second, the design of the work should be separated from the process of carrying it out. This "division of conception and execution" allows the work itself to be carried out *automatically*: the process of production is uninterrupted by decision making or by moving between tasks.

Third, the knowledge gained by management is used to completely control the pace and methods of work.

The knowledge and increased control over the work process gained by management makes it possible to fragment the work. More highly paid skilled workers can be used only for skilled tasks, and simpler work can be left to the unskilled or semi-skilled.

The idea of **deskilling** is central here. A craftsperson understood all phases of the work process in a unified craft. But scientific management showed that maximum cost efficiency could only be achieved by rationalization and fragmentation of the labour process. The division of labour is intensified and the integrated work, practised by the craftsperson, is fragmented (Braverman, 1974).

Bureaucratic Rationalization: Public and Corporate Administration

The division of labour and precise specification of the mode of work can also be applied to management and administration. As "scientific management" leads to the fragmentation of production, so does what Max Weber calls "bureaucratic rationality" lead to the fragmentation and specialization of administrative work. In production, the assembly line becomes characteristic of the work process; in administration, highly rationalized **bureaucracy** becomes the order of the day.

Administration is broken down into specialized components in the same way as is production. Max Weber's model of highly specialized bureaucracy parallels Taylor's scientific system for manufacturing production. Rational bureaucracy also embodies specialized work according to precisely defined rules and administration by experts. Procedures are designed to permit the orderly management of problems; they are classified and assigned an identification number. Routinization and impersonality give modern bureaucracy a special efficiency. Although bureaucracies do not often achieve this dispassionate machine-like efficiency (Weber was advancing an ideal type), they are still greatly superior to other methods of complex organization. In administration, just as in manufacturing, the rise of specialization and the division of labour uproot older methods of working in an integrated way. They also affect leisure (see Box (10.1).

SOCIOLOGICAL RESPONSES TO THE MODERN WORKPLACE

Marx: Alienation

How did this new stress on productivity and profit affect the social experience of modern work? The classical sociologists gave diverse answers to that question.

Marx argued that humans are unique among animals because they work for self-expression, not just to satisfy direct needs. Even in simple low-technology societies, there is a great stress on making objects of production beautiful and expressive of cultural ideals. Here, for example, is a description of the making of bark loincloths among the pygmies of Zaire:

Box 10.1
Where Has
Leisure Gone?

Juliet Schor argues that thirteenth-century estimates for the work time of peasant families were approximately 150 days, or 1400–1500 hours, a year. A mid-nineteenth-century worker in England or North America may have put in an annual work time of 3150 to 3650 hours. Capitalism has a built-in dynamic to increase productivity and the work time of the work force. In the early days, the conflict over work time focussed on the introduction of the clock and the keeping of a new (and then considered unnatural) time schedule. In the late nineteenth and the twentieth centuries unions were able to stop and even reverse the increase in work time. The eight-hour day was introduced and holidays and rest days increased.

Schor suggests that in North America there has been a gradual erosion of these worker gains and that work time for the average worker has expanded. This has been accomplished in a number of ways. During the 1980s employers were able to demand more work: more overtime, shorter vacation periods, and fewer rest breaks. Those paid on an hourly basis often found that their real wage had decreased. These workers now must work an additional 245 hours just to reach their 1973 standard of living. Salaried workers did not receive a pay reduction, but subtle pressures were placed on them to work harder, and in some cases the competitive atmosphere of the workplace drove people to greater productivity. Women's entry into the labour force also increased their work time, since this amounted to new work added to housework. The result is that average Americans own twice as much as they did in 1948 but have less free time.

The productivity gains of the past three decades could of course have been diverted to increased free time. This has happened much more clearly in Europe, where laws support 4–5 weeks of paid vacations (France and Sweden provide 5 weeks by law) and many negotiated agreements give workers 5–8 weeks of paid leave. In Canada and the United States, it is more typical to find the minimum period of 2 weeks' paid vacation.

SOURCE: Adapted from Juliet B. Schor. *The Overworked American* (New York: Basic Books, 1991).

There are several vines that yield a suitable bark. ... Then it is either soaked in water or mud, the mud giving it a bluish colour, or softened by smoking it over a fire. After that it is spread over a fallen tree trunk and beaten with an ivory tusk. It spreads out into a soft, supple cloth, the texture varying with the type of bark. There are many fashions in bark cloth, not only in the choice of a particular bark, but in the way it is dyed or decorated, and also in the way it is worn. The women nearly always do the decorating, using nkula *bark to make a red paste, or the gardenia fruit,* kangay, *for black dye. ... Then, using a finger, she daubs the fresh cloth, which may be white, fawn, brown, or blue, with bright splotches of red. If she is using the fruit juice she carefully collects it in a cup made from the hard shell of some forest fruit, and with little twigs she draws fanciful patterns of straight lines, crisscrossing the cloth with unconventional pygmy geometry (Turnbull, 1962: 130-131).*

The most simple item of clothing thus becomes an artistic creation, expressing the culture of the tribe and the personality of its producer.

This traditional approach towards work, according to Marx, is inherent in human psychology and personality. Humans express themselves and find meaning in a world they create and where they recognize their own reflection. But how is work related to the producer in modern society? Marx suggests that the very purpose of work, the making of profit for the capitalist, leads to a transformation in how work is organized and experienced. The unity of work and personal expression is broken. Work loses its meaning for the individual and becomes alienating.

There are four elements to this **alienation** from work. First, workers are alienated from ownership of the product of their labour. Their work becomes the property of the capitalist. The profit made from the work increases the wealth of the capitalist and the strength of capital in the workplace and in society. Second, workers are alienated from control over the process of production. Their work is directed and controlled by the employer: workers become mere objects in the production process. Third, they are alienated from their individual human capacity for creativity and self-expression in work: the work is imposed. Last, the competitive conditions of the workplace and the central goal of private profit disconnect work from human social involvement and community: workers are forced to see each other as competitive threats.

Capitalism, in bending work to the private purpose of profit, destroys the unity of work and worker. This is an inevitable consequence of the structure and goals of the capitalist workplace. Alienation can be overcome, and the unity of work and worker restored, only by co-operative socialism, in which workers, in free association, both own and control the means of production.

Weber:
Rationalization

· · · · · · · ·

Weber's analysis of work in formal institutions has much in common with Marx. It is fair to say that Weber's depiction of modern bureaucracy is, in itself, a description of an organization in which people are alienated from personal self-expression and creativity in the work process. In fact, rationality and efficiency *depend* on the rigorous separation of work from the personal emotions of the worker. Weber, unlike Marx, did not envisage a revolutionary upheaval by the working class and the abolition of domination in the workplace. He did not agree that management and direction were simply parasitic. He saw rationalization as an indispensable basis for effective organization:

> The ruled, for their part, cannot dispense with or replace the bureaucratic apparatus of authority once it exists. For this bureaucracy rests upon expert training, a functional specialization of work, and an attitude set for habitual and virtuoso-like mastery of single yet methodically integrated functions. If the official stops working ... chaos results, and it is difficult to improvise replacements from among the governed who are fit to master such chaos. This holds for public administration as well as for private economic management. More and more the material fate of the masses depends upon the steady and correct functioning of the increasingly bureaucratic organizations of private capitalism. The idea of eliminating these organizations becomes more and more utopian (Gerth and Mills, 1970: 229).

Weber did not link alienation and the impersonality of work simply to capitalism. He saw alienation as an inevitable consequence of the complexity and specialization of work in modern society. But he was hardly less critical than Marx of the psychological and sociological effects of this imposed work, driven by the economic machine of modern capitalism:

> *The Puritan [i.e., Protestant] wanted to work in a calling; we are forced to do so. For when asceticism was carried out of monastic cells into everyday life, and began to dominate worldly morality, it did its part in building the tremendous cosmos of the modern economic order. This order is now bound to the technical and economic conditions of machine production which today determine the lives of all the individuals who are born into this mechanism. ... Perhaps it will so determine them until the last ton of fossilized coal is burnt* (Weber, 1958[1904]: 181).

Durkheim: Anomie

· · · · · · · · ·

Unlike Marx and Weber, Durkheim did not believe that alienation and impersonality in the capitalist workplace was inevitable. For Durkheim, sociology was a diagnostic science of society, not a political program. The sociologist cannot abolish the modern system of work. But it is right to ask why modern work so often fails to generate personal satisfaction and social solidarity.

He defined two problems: first, people cannot identify with work if they do not understand the importance of their contribution to the whole process; second, there will be anomie when the **division of labour** is forced (based on power and privilege not objective differences in skills) and when there is weak normative regulation of the workplace. Fragmentation of work is not necessarily a problem unless there is also a failure of effective communication and lack of mutual respect between workers and employers.

In reality, argued Durkheim, modern society demands far greater social integration and social interdependency than did any previous society: self-sufficiency is impossible for most people. This complex system of specialized interdependence creates a state of **organic solidarity**. The **mechanical solidarity** of past society joins people by immediate and extensive ties of personal relationship, but the new form of solidarity is more abstract. People may be unaware of how acutely they depend on others. The specialization of the complex modern division of labour leaves people unaware of the ties that bind them to each other. If this division of labour is not clearly regulated and people are not brought into meaningful association with each other, then both the workplace and society as a whole can fall prey to **anomie**, a social condition of normlessness and lack of solidarity.

Durkheim's answer to this problem was not to seek a transformation of the social relations of production (i.e., workers take over the factories and offices), but to strengthen ties between workers, managers, and owners. He proposed the development of occupational corporations. These corporations would have something like the functions of the medieval guilds, bringing workers and owners together in systems of regulated co-operation.

Durkheim was also concerned that the division of labour not appear to be forced: it must not be based on power and ascription. But a division of labour based on merit, where people's roles are allocated on the basis of ability, could become a source of normative integration.

This perspective on work adopts a functionalist view that anonymity and fragmentation can be remedied through institutional means. It is an approach indirectly linked to management theories quite different from Taylor's aim of complete employer domination of the work process. Instead, efficiency and productivity can come from the development of feelings of solidarity among workers and between them and employers. A development proceeding from these ideas is human relations management.

**FUNCTIONALIST
RESPONSES TO
WORKPLACE
TENSIONS**

• • • • • • • •

**Human Relations
Management**

• • • • • • • •

The human relations approach to work management does not replace scientific management, but is added to it (Krahn and Lowe, 1993: 202–203). It is based on the view that one-sided direction of the workplace by management cannot ensure complete control or take advantage of the knowledge and initiative of workers. Scientific management adopts a conflict model of work, assuming that effective work must be forced from the workers; human relations approaches attempt instead to involve and motivate workers. The theory developed from some famous work studies at General Electric's Hawthorne plant in Chicago in the 1920s and 1930s.

The experiments started out from the scientific management perspective. They were intended to explore the effects on productivity of different levels of lighting in the workplace, different temperatures, and different timetabling of rest periods. The intent, of course, was to establish the mix of conditions that would lead to maximum productivity.

Psychologist Erich Fromm provides an account of what researchers *thought* they had discovered.

> *Rest pauses were adopted in the morning and afternoon, refreshments offered during these rest periods, and the hours of work cut by half an hour. Throughout these changes, the output of each worker rose considerably. So far so good; nothing was more plausible than the assumption that increased rest periods and some attempt to make the workers "feel better" were the cause of increased efficiency. But a new arrangement in the twelfth experimental period disappointed these expectations and showed rather dramatic results: by arrangement with the workers, the group returned to the conditions of work as they had existed in the beginning of the experiment. ... To everybody's amazement this did not result in a decrease in output but, on the contrary, the daily and weekly output rose to a higher point than at any time before* (Fromm, 1955: 264–265).

This set of observations led to the conclusion that what had been most important in motivating the workers was the attention they received and the sense of teamwork they developed with management. This outcome has subsequently been termed the Hawthorne effect. As it turned out, later analysts showed that the experiments were flawed, their design was poor, and their results inaccurately recorded (Murrell, 1976). But that was years after the reported results had become part of the folklore of work management. The idea that human relations were the key to motivating work productivity was born.

Of course, the concept of "human relations management" did not win favour just on the basis of a series of flawed workplace experiments. There was a flood of further, more precise, experiments that clearly demonstrated its value. Blumberg (1968) tabulated results from some of the more significant studies since the 1930s and concluded that there is hardly a study in the entire literature that fails to demonstrate increased work satisfaction or other positive benefits from increased worker participation.

The human relations stress on worker involvement in the process of production can take a variety of forms, and there have been many variations. Attempts have been made to enlarge jobs by adding related tasks to the work performed by each individual in order to provide changes of pace and a variety of activities. Other steps have been taken to enrich jobs, by adding to the range and nature of tasks. A worker might take responsibility, for example, for ordering supplies, keeping records, and maintaining equipment. Box 10.2 gives a recent example of this approach to human relations management.

The story also shows the influence of another concept of work management — quality control — that gives workers more responsibility for management at the point of production.

. . . .

Box 10.2
Workers Enjoy Work
Enrichment

. . . .

Most kids love a fresh box of brightly coloured crayons, but few could picture themselves working in a dingy crayon plant for 29 years, like Bonnie Lamb.

"We got ourselves into such a rut," says Mrs. Lamb, 55, who logged most of those years on the same packing machine. Life on the line, she says, was boring.

But that was before the work-team revolution swept Binney & Smith (Canada) Ltd.'s 54,000-square-foot Crayola plant about 18 months ago. "Drastic," is how Mrs. Lamb describes the changes.

Now instead of mindlessly toiling at one machine, "I can do just about anything on the crayon department side. I can do the labellers. I can do the packers. I can do the collator. The only thing I can't do is mold crayons. The racks are too heavy."

In fact most Crayola workers can operate an array of machines — some are even volunteering to drive the fork-lift. "People used to say, 'That's not my job, so I'm not going to do it,'" says Patricia Foerderer, a sprightly woman known as the crayon team leader. "Now, it's a team effort. They get along better, they ask each other questions, they depend on each other."

The Crayola team operates like a mini-factory. It is almost self-sufficient, taking responsibility for every step in the manufacturing process, including production scheduling, inventory and cost management, machine maintenance and quality control. There are 10 such teams, encompassing processes from marker production to customer service. The payback has been greater employee satisfaction, but also a stronger competitive position for this small plant 130 kilometers northeast of Toronto.

... But the biggest issue was compensation. The non-union plant used to operate on a piece-rate schedule, which rewards individual performance but does little to foster the co-operation and creativity the company was seeking. The old system often sparked squabbles on the plant floor, such as when several machines broke down at once and there weren't enough mechanics to fix them.

Now, workers get a straight wage of about $13 an hour. The various teams are expected to meet weekly production targets if they want to avoid weekend work. That means pinch-hitting for each other, helping to fix a colleague's machine, and, in general, putting the interests of the group first.

. . . .

SOURCE: John Heinzl, "Crayon Plant a Brighter Place," *The Globe and Mail*, June 18, 1992, pp. B1–B2. Reprinted with permission.

. . . .

The idea of quality control circles was pioneered in Japan. It was first established in Japan's car industry, with Toyota leading the way. The basic system is for workers to be formed into teams each dealing with some aspect of the production process. For example, where an individual worker might tighten nuts on a starter motor, the team might be responsible for the whole process of installing it. The team, as a group, is then responsible for the quality and speed of the work. Each team has a leader, at much the same level in the workplace hierarchy, who works alongside the others and provides cover for them during breaks or absences and helps when one task in the process gets behind. Typically, each worker within the team is capable of performing all the tasks in their work unit and job rotation, to provide variety, is often practised.

This approach seems to promise a more humanized and less fragmented experience in the workplace, but critical sociologists think it has severe problems. Their key claim is that the system is manipulative and invasive: it seeks to use the workers' solidarity and personal attachment to each other for the purposes of management. Workers become disciplined by their desire not to let down their colleagues or their team leader. They know that any slacking, absenteeism, or lack of care in the work will affect the status of the whole team and impose more work on the other team members. These other members of the team, including the leader, are workers like themselves, not representatives of management. Workers are therefore motivated to work hard to support their immediate workmates. They are disciplined externally by the careful management monitoring of work quantity and quality by each team, and they are disciplined from within by the group solidarity that, in other circumstances, provided a basis for collective resistance to the dictates of management (Kamata and Dore, 1983). Box 10.3 gives a sense of the tensions and conflict surrounding quality control circles in Canada's auto industry.

If the critics are correct in their analysis of quality control, it is an unstable arrangement. Since workers are far from passive in the face of management attempts to increase control and direction over the work process, do they "catch on" to the effects of the new methods and begin to resist management after an initial period of optimism? Three years after the report quoted in Box 10.3, in September 1992, the plant was on strike: 99 percent of the employees had voted in favour of a walkout. During the previous year, 500 grievances had been laid against management by the union, and they were now fighting over money. Workers wanted the same wages as other auto workers were receiving.

> The company attitude is "arrogant" because CAMI has enjoyed a cost advantage for years over other joint-venture plants that pay the same wages as traditional Big Three plants, said CAW president Buzz Hargrove. "As far as we're concerned Suzuki's not going to compete in the future on the backs of its workers," he said in a news release.[1]

The union argued that the blend of Japanese and Canadian management methods had been disappointing to workers because it had not resulted in the greater empowerment of workers.[2]

The first large-scale manufacturer to turn its back on the old-style assembly line and develop the team concept was Volvo of Sweden, with its 1988 plant. In 1991, however, it was considering closing the plant because it had not seen the rise in productivity that it had anticipated. A joint venture by General Motors and Saab Scania had earlier given up on the team concept.

Box 10.3
The Dilemma of
Quality Control
Circles

When the joint General Motors–Suzuki auto plant at Ingersoll, Ont., moves into full production later this year, it will be a Canadian showcase for the Japanese style of work organization known as the "team concept" — a system that is supposed to motivate workers by liberating them from the mind-numbing monotony of assembly-line work.

... A private but hot discussion has been sparked within the union by the plant, which will be producing five GM and Suzuki models by the end of the year and will eventually expand its present staff of about 225 to 2000. The CAW has generally been sceptical of new-fangled work methods and corporate programs emphasizing quality. Many union activists say employees end up identifying with the company and its interests rather than their own interests as workers.

In theory, the plant and its team concept sound almost like a workers' paradise. "People want some fulfillment in their jobs," said James Cameron, CAMIs vice-president for personnel. "We're telling people, 'We're hiring you for your brain as well as your brawn.'"

Employees will work in teams of, say, 12, under a leader who will be a union member, he explained. They will rotate jobs within their teams and to other teams so they can become multifunctional and retain some excitement about their jobs.

After work if they wish, they will attend meetings of "quality circles" — small groups that will talk about problems in the plant and how to improve the quality of the product.

"We're trying to drive the decision-making down to where the expertise is," Mr. Cameron said. "The guys who are putting together the cars know more than time and motion engineers."

But this kind of talk sends shivers up the spines of some unionists, particularly those who start from the assumption there will always be a natural antagonism between the interests of labor and capital.

... In the United States, where Japanese work styles are in place at more than two dozen auto plants and similar programs are moving into such industries as steel and paper, some unionized "team" plants operate nearly the same as non-unionized plants, said Jane Slaughter of Detroit, co-author of *Choosing Sides: Unions and the Team Concept*, a book that is sharply critical of the new methods. ...

She said introduction of the new work methods usually means overburdened workers — something that is impossible to determine yet at CAMI because it is not in full production. "Most of the glowing reports you hear from these plants are from their very early days."

SOURCE: Excerpted from Lorne Slotnick, "Experiment with Quality," *The Globe and Mail*, January 28, 1989, p. D1. Reprinted with permission.

CRITICAL
PERSPECTIVE
RESPONSES TO
WORKPLACE
TENSIONS

· · · · · · · · ·

Workers as
Managers

· · · · · · · · ·

All of the above methods of motivating increased productivity and of using human relations approaches to moderate, or overcome, alienation take the social structure of work for granted. They preserve the private purpose of the work. Other approaches have sought to modify the social relations of the work itself. One such approach is to enable workers to participate in management (see Box 10.4.)

Participation in management has extended to worker representation on corporate boards. Critics, however, argue that worker participation in capitalist enterprises can never be real: the private purpose of the corporation and genuine worker participation cannot be blended. This argument seems too absolute: there might be something between full management direction and control and complete workers' ownership (for example, profit sharing or ownership participation) that could offer meaningful participation and involvement. But for many critics, only one system of working can genuinely overcome the divide of capital and labour: workers' control.

Workers' Control

· · · · · · · · ·

An example of workers' control has been developed in the Basque town of Mondragon, Spain, where 22 000 worker-owners run a range of co-operative industries. The co-operatives are run through elected supervisory boards under the direction of general assemblies of the workers. No worker or manager may receive more than 4.5 times the pay of the lowest-paid worker. Worker-directed management overcomes the division of capital and labour, and its effects are seen in consistently high levels of growth and productivity. Social relations among workers, both in the workplace and in the community, express strong solidarity (Krahn and Lowe, 1993: 300–301; Rinehart, 1987: 204–205).

The former state of Yugoslavia, under a communist government, also developed an extensive system of worker control and direction in state enterprises. The Yugoslav system was in strong contrast to the centralized and bureaucratic systems generally adopted in other former communist countries. There is evidence that this structure helped to make work more meaningful and workers more committed (Blumberg, 1968).

ALIENATION
AND CANADIAN
WORKERS

· · · · · · · · ·

Critical theorists, following Marx's ideas, assume that work in capitalist enterprises will be alienating. The fact that employers adopt work enhancement and improved human relations management to promote efficiency is evidence that alienation does indeed exist. For other evidence, a variety of data sources are possible: employee turnover, absenteeism, and unusually low productivity.

Volvo reported a turnover rate of 16 percent of its employees each year and a short-term absenteeism rate of 12.2 percent in 1990.[3] General Motors said that an average 13.2 percent of its Canadian work force of 37 500 is absent daily for legitimate reasons such as vacations or sick leave. But on any given day, another 5 percent are away for reasons the company lists as misuse of benefits, personal problems, or lack of motivation.[4]

For a more comprehensive view, attitude surveys might provide direct evidence of how workers see their jobs. After all the criticism of the workplace, the result is surprising: most Canadians report that they are satisfied with their jobs. In 1987 a survey for *The Globe and Mail* by Environics Research Group reported that fully 89 percent of Canadian workers were either "very satisfied" (51 percent) or "somewhat satisfied" (38 percent) with their jobs.[5] A 1991 national survey showed similar results: 75 percent of Canadian workers reported general satisfaction with their jobs (Wyatt Company, 1991).

What do critical theorists make of this evidence? They argue that levels of satisfaction depend on expectations. The first point to recognize is that workers are, after

Box 10.4
Workers as Managers

In his 20 years as a transport truck driver, Nick Ellen never dreamed that he and his fellow drivers, rather than the company brass, would decide on how to spend $8 million on new equipment.

"A lot of the drivers had a good laugh," he recalls. "They said the company would go through the motions of picking our brains but then do whatever they wanted."

The drivers aren't laughing anymore. Before the exercise was over, Mr. Ellen and a team of drivers at CP Express and Transport not only had selected the winning bidder, but went to France to kick the tires at the plant where the vehicles were made.

"Before, if you expressed yourself, the response was, 'You're just a truck driver, what do you know?'" said the Toronto pick-up and delivery driver. Now in the wake of the truck purchase, he has come to believe he is participating in a true management revolution. ...

"I don't believe we would be here today if we hadn't made a 180-degree turnabout in our management philosophy," Mr. Thibeault said. ... "Brain power is widely dispersed in the species. It's not a monopoly held by a few managers."...

At the management level, "we had to convince them that we didn't want a boss–servant relationship where the boss knows everything. The boss doesn't know everything. In fact, the boss knows little. We are asking the boss to act in a supportive role and stop judging the individual employee."

While many trade unions are suspicious of or hostile to employee involvement programs, often regarding them as tools for bypassing the union in dealing with workers, the Transportation and Communications Union has given its blessing to Mr. Thibeault's approach.

Jack Boyce, president of the 14 500-member transport union, says the CP Express workers like the challenge that comes with a little authority. "They have more pride in their jobs when they are given a say in their work."

The new attitudes have eliminated confrontation between workers and supervisors, he said, adding that there is no more of the "who can screw who mentality."

Since the changeover, none of the employee-operated terminals has registered a grievance, and country-wide the number of grievances has plummeted. Workers are acting independently to solve problems, improve quality and reduce costs.

SOURCE: Excerpted from Wilfred List, "On the Road to Profit," *The Globe and Mail*, July 10, 1991, p. B1. Reprinted with permission from the author.

all, socialized for the workplace through the family and the educational system. Do individuals shape their expectations as a result of their observations of the work roles of their parents and other adults? Does the education system play a role in adapting individuals, through both explicit and hidden curricula, to the social relationships they will encounter in the workplace?

Second, when workers say they are "satisfied," what do they mean? What is their point of reference? Are they satisfied with their jobs, *given their culturally limited expectations of what working should be like?* If that were the case, a statement of satisfaction might mean very little, if anything (see Rinehart, 1987: 143). Surveys that report high levels of worker satisfaction are often ambiguous. For example, while recording a general satisfaction level of 75 percent, the Wyatt study showed only 39 percent satisfied with the style and quality of decision making at their workplace and only 50 percent satisfied with the quality of work supervision and relations with supervisors. *The Globe and Mail* study showed that 42 percent of workers would choose a different occupation — which casts some doubt on their reported levels of job satisfaction.

Another way to investigate the extent of alienation in the workplace is to look at the quality of human relations at a basic level: do employers always put the life and health of workers above private profit? Or does the conduct of management sometimes show complete indifference to the health and safety of workers? The disturbing report in Box 10.5 suggests how far the alienation of people from each other can be promoted by the division of interests in capitalist enterprises.

The events reported in Box 10.5 are not isolated examples. An exhaustive analysis of the asbestos industry (Brodeur, 1985) reported that up to 270 000 people would die in North America from asbestos-related diseases between 1980 and 2009. Virtually all the asbestos companies suppressed medical evidence of the dangers of asbestos exposure for more than 30 years. In 1948, a Canadian doctor examined workers at Johns-Manville in Quebec and found that of 708 tested, only four had healthy, normal lungs: this information was completely suppressed by the corporation (p. 102).

THE NEW ECONOMY: HAS ALIENATION BEEN ELIMINATED?

Many social scientists, politicians, and economists claim that the Canadian economy has changed so dramatically in the last few years that it has now created a transformation in society itself. This new society is said to have a changed economic foundation, which has, in turn, transformed the nature of work in contemporary society. It is argued that Canada has moved away from a society dominated by the production of physical goods to an economy in which the main activity is the delivery of services and the development of knowledge to support these services. While Canada was once able to create wealth by the export of raw materials (oil, gas, lumber, coal, wheat, fish), this is no longer guaranteed to maintain the standard of living to which Canadians have become accustomed. A new kind of economy, with a quite different labour force, is now required.

There is certainly evidence to support this view. The occupational structure of Canada continues to change in the direction of a **post-industrial society**. Blue-collar occupations have been in decline, while white-collar occupations have been increasing. Between 1981 and 1986, a relatively short period of time, the white-collar occupations accounted for an increase of 134.5 percent in overall employment growth in Canada. Blue-collar occupations, on the other hand, showed a 34.5 percent decrease in employment. Information workers in 1971 accounted for 45.1 percent of the labour force; by 1986, this proportion had increased to 52.4 percent (Economic Council of Canada, 1990: 14).

These figures certainly suggest profound change in the structure of Canada's economy, but there is considerable debate over how it should be interpreted. On the one hand, Bell (1973) argues that increasing technological development and the rationalization of production have ushered in an age in which menial physical work will

The U.S. government says it has found widespread fraud in the coal industry by mine operators who repeatedly tampered with the coal dust samples used to gauge miners' risk of black lung disease.

A 20-month investigation by the Labor Department uncovered 4700 alleged instances of tampering at about 850 underground coal mines, Labor Secretary Lynn Martin said.

About 500 companies are being fined a record $5 million (U.S.) for violations at mines in 16 states, she said. In addition, criminal charges are being pursued.

... The government requires coal-mine operators to take airborne dust using a sealed filter cartridge. Some mine operators had been blowing or vacuuming out some of the dust before submitting the samples, Ms. Martin said. There have also been reports of mine operators placing the cartridges outdoors to ensure a clean sample.

SOURCE: Excerpt from "Coal Dust Tampering Found," *The Globe and Mail*, April 8, 1991. Reprinted by permission of the Associated Press.

be eliminated and greater emphasis will be placed on high-level technical skills and professional knowledge. If this portrait of the economy is correct, there should also have been a rise in the general skill level of the work force and an expansion of the middle class.

As unskilled or semi-skilled work is eliminated, the blue-collar working class is reduced in numbers and the middle class (the designation of the new knowledge and information workers) increases. It is claimed that skilled workers and professionals have more job autonomy than blue-collar workers and that changes in the occupational structure therefore lead to the elimination of the alienating, repetitive, narrow, and unpleasant work discussed by the classical sociologists.

On the other side of this debate, Braverman (1974) argues that the search for increased profit in capitalist enterprises leads to management increasing its control of the work process. This is accomplished, in part, through the rigorous division and fragmentation of the labour process and through an increased reliance on unskilled or semi-skilled labour. This reduces the overall cost of labour in production. As a result, technological change and rationalized work management lead to increased fragmentation of work, more routinization, and greater alienation.

While Braverman is primarily concerned with manufacturing, others have argued that the shift to a service-based, "knowledge intensive" economy has also led to a degradation of work. They reject the claim of the postindustrial theorists that work skills and knowledge have risen and argue that, on the contrary, there has been an increase in lower-paid and less highly skilled workers.

From this point of view, there has been a decline of the middle class and in the general skill level of the work force. If this argument is correct, the class divisions of the workplace will remain or intensify and workers will become more alienated as they lose autonomy and perform increasingly narrow and repetitive work.

As is the case with many sociological debates, this one is not easy to judge. It is difficult to research the conflicting claims, and the evidence is contradictory. There is evidence to suggest that the middle class, defined in terms of income, is in decline, although not at a dramatic rate. If the middle class is defined as those families with 66–133 percent of the median family income, the percentage of all families in this bracket has fallen from 44.4 percent in 1980 to 40.7 percent in 1992.[6] There are several possible explanations for this decline, however, so it is really necessary to look at research on the shifting labour market and on the skill content of jobs and at case studies of particular occupations to reach a firmer conclusion.

The Economic Council of Canada (1990: 13) reported that over half of Canadians are now employed in occupations that are primarily concerned with the creation and use of data. The council also found that the service sector in general, including areas such as health care, transportation, business, retail service, financial service, education, and public administration, grew dramatically. This area accounted for 34 percent of the total employment in 1911, 44 percent in 1951, 59.4 percent in 1967, and 70.9 percent in 1988. Most Canadian workers are in the service sector of the economy, and the trend toward a service-based economy is unabated — 90 percent of job growth since 1967 has been in the service sector. There has also been an accelerating trend in the growth of highly skilled jobs (managerial, administrative, and professional and technical). These categories now make up over one-quarter of all employment.

While this seems encouraging, the council also found that jobs in the service sector became more polarized than they were in the old goods-producing sector. For example, a substantial number of information and knowledge jobs involve repetitive work entering data, and this work may not be any more integrated or less alienating than the old kind of work.

In reality, the service sector continues to produce a large number of low-skill, low-paying jobs as well as a large number of high-skill and high-paying jobs. There is a tendency to polarization in jobs, and the decline in the numbers of the middle class reflects this: some have moved upward and some downward.

What are the educational requirements of the new labour market? In a survey of workers, researchers found that 30 percent reported that they were overqualified for their present job (with somewhat more women than men reporting being overqualified) (Myles and Fawcett, 1990: 17). Further, a full 40 percent reported that they could have learned their present job skills with a short demonstration or with up to 30 days' training. Neither of these pieces of information leaves one convinced that Canadians have become highly trained workers in jobs requiring complex cognitive skills and allowing the opportunity to exercise autonomy and control.

Research such as Braverman's, which focusses on a few case studies of specific occupations, almost always concludes that skills have been downgraded over time. Studies of the printing industry, for example, found a loss of skills (Wallace and Kalleberg, 1982), and Clement's (1981) work on mining showed the same trend.

Studies that attempt to measure the objective knowledge and competencies involved in carrying out a job have generally concluded that skills have been upgraded over time, while those that use a methodology allowing for measurement of worker autonomy and control have generally concluded the opposite (Economic Council of Canada, 1991: 90). The Economic Council of Canada concluded that, on balance, the evidence supports a hypothesis claiming a general upgrading of skills in the work force.

The reader might well conclude that neither of the two positions outlined at the beginning of this section is correct. Or, to be more positive, one might conclude they are both a little bit correct. There has been a polarization of the labour market, with a large number of people in low-skill and low-wage positions and a large number in high-skill and high-wage positions. Those in the middle have been in decline. There is another way to characterize jobs that have been created over the past few years, however: non-traditional employment. This is part-time employment, short-term employment, temporary work, and self-employment. The Economic Council of Canada (1991) found that almost half of the net job growth in the past decade was in non-traditional jobs, so that 33.8 percent of all jobs were non-traditional. It concluded that this growth did not just represent a response to bad times in the business cycle; rather, it represented a fundamental change in the operation of the labour market (p. 88). It is here to stay for the foreseeable future. Non-traditional employment is problematic because the workers in these jobs generally have inferior compensation and job security. Krahn (1992) also reports that workers in non-traditional jobs report less job autonomy, more repetitive work, and lower skill requirements than do workers in standard jobs (p. 107).

The post-industrial society thesis, though there is some basis for it, is too optimistic: Canadians have not become a society of unalienated knowledge workers. The new jobs often do not demand advanced skills and knowledge, but at most a short period of on-the-job training. Being overqualified for one's job leads to boredom and frustration; being in non-traditional employment often means poor working conditions, no benefits, and no employment security. The unskilled or semi-skilled work force in the service sector may be no less alienated than traditional production workers.

Modern methods of working and of information-based management may also have led to increased direction and control of administrative and managerial workers. Workers in these jobs report that the new information age has led to an intensification of demands for productivity and a consequent increase in the monitoring of work. In the banking industry, for example, managers are given performance targets. Daily information is fed through the computer to head office, where managerial performance can be reviewed on a daily basis. If the targets are not met, the manager may be fired; and, if they are met, they may well be set higher for the next month. Although managers are classified as high-skill and high-wage workers, it is clear that increased alienation exists even at this level of employment.

WOMEN AND WORK

Any discussion of work must single out the situation of women. Women do not participate in the employment structure in the same way that men do. There is clear and dramatic evidence for a convergence in the situation of men and women as workers, but there are still distinct differences. The most striking thing about women and employment is the dramatic change in employment participation, which is both cause and effect of changing childbearing and family responsibility (see Tables 10.1 and 10.2).

Although women's participation rates have increased and they now constitute almost half of the work force, there are marked differences from the work patterns of men. The first major distinction is that women make up only 39.2 percent of the full-time labour force but 71.6 percent of the part-time labour force. Second, they still tend to be located in particular sectors of the labour force. In 1990, 57 percent of female workers were employed in just three broad occupational areas: clerical, sales, and service (see Table 10.3). If medicine and health are added, in order to include nurses, the proportion increases to 66 percent. By contrast, 26.2 percent of male workers are in the first grouping and only 28.1 percent in the expanded grouping. Male workers are far less "ghettoized" than women; their jobs are located throughout a range of occu-

Table 10.1	1951	24.0
Women's	1975	44.4
Participation Rate in	1980	50.3
the Labour Market,	1991	58.2
Canada, 1951–1991		

SOURCE: Paul Phillips and Erin Phillips, *Women and Work* (Toronto: James Lorimer and Company, 1993), p. 34. Reprinted with permission.

pations. Third, and obviously linked to the first two differences, women tend to receive lower pay than do men. On average, for full-time work, women make about 70 percent of the level of average male earnings.

How should one understand these linked special characteristics of women in the labour market: over-representation in part-time work; occupational segregation; and lower wages? Following is a brief look at three ways to interpret these facts and at the kinds of policies that flow from each perspective.

Liberal Philosophy

Liberalism adopts explanations that rest on the idea of women workers having different characteristics from men and bringing different skills to the labour market. This approach, sometimes labelled supply-side theory (Gunderson et al., 1990: 39), argues that women workers are less effective revenue producers than men are, and consequently are paid less than men. They are concentrated in low-paying jobs because they have not pursued enough education or training or, perhaps, because they lack the personality characteristics necessary to get ahead in a competitive world. This theory was at one time more plausible than it is now, since for the last twenty or more years women have participated in education as much as men.

Those who still argue that women are paid less because they are less productive as workers are likely to argue that the solution to the ghettoization of women and low wages is to encourage women to pursue an education, to consider training in the well-paid trades, or to become involved in career development counselling. In short, the focus is on changing women's attributes as workers to fit the demands of the labour market. It is argued that as women take steps to break out of job ghettos and extend the range of their training and education, wage and status inequalities between the sexes will automatically disappear.

Dual Labour Market Theory

A different approach entirely is to look at the structure of the labour market itself: at the sorts of jobs that are available and the kinds of skills that are demanded. Demand-side theories often talk about a dual labour market perspective. There are said to be

Table 10.2	1901	13.4
Women as a	1931	17.0
Percentage of All	1961	27.3
Workers, Canada,	1971	34.3
1901–1991	1980	40.0
	1991	45.0

SOURCE: Paul Phillips and Erin Phillips, *Women and Work* (Toronto: James Lorimer and Company, 1993), p. 47. Reprinted with permission.

Table 10.3		Women as % of Occupational Grouping	% of Female Labour Force
Occupational Location of Women, Showing Women as a Percentage of the Work Force in Selected Occupational Categories and Showing the Percentage of the Female Labour Force for Each Category, Canada, 1991	Stenographers, secretaries, typists	98.4	7.5
	Sales clerks	53.9	6.0
	Bookkeepers	84.3	5.3
	Cashiers	88.2	4.7
	Nurses	94.9	3.8
	Food & beverage servers	78.4	3.5
	General clerks	82.4	2.9
	Elementary and kindergarten teachers	81.7	2.6
	Receptionists and information clerks	93.1	2.1
	Child care workers	96.7	2.0
	Janitors and cleaners	45.9	2.0
	Computer operators	78.0	1.7
	Chefs and cooks	48.9	1.7
	Barbers and hairstylists	83.6	1.3
	Nursing assistants	83.0	1.2

SOURCE: Statistics Canada, Occupations: *The Nation*, cat. no. 93-327 (Ottawa: Statistics Canada, 1993). Reproduced by authority of the Minister of Industry, 1994.

two markets for labour. One, the primary labour market, consists of jobs that are more highly paid, have good benefits, are secure, and offer some prospect of career advancement. These jobs are found in the public sector and in private employment in relatively uncompetitive sectors of the economy. They are usually unionized. Jobs in the less competitive area of the economy are usually found in large-scale manufacturing. Manufacturing has initial capital costs that tend to limit competition. Someone can enter the restaurant business with a few thousand dollars, but manufacturing usually demands millions of dollars. Businesses that, like manufacturing, have high capital investment have a cost structure in which wages are often not a major contributor to the final cost of the product. So wage rates can be increased without cutting deeply into profit. It is also easier for large manufacturing firms to pass on wage cost increases to their consumers.

Businesses with high capital overhead also tend to be more captives of their workers: the corporation must meet enormous capital carrying charges even when production is not being carried out. The concentration and large scale of manufacturing also favours the growth of union organization: most manufacturing is unionized in Canada and other industrial countries. Strikes are a strong weapon for the workers, because owners cannot afford to let their capital investment sit idle. The primary labour market, for historical and cultural reasons, tends to be dominated by male workers, and the pattern of recruitment — based perhaps on gender stereotyping — tends to maintain that situation.

Women, in contrast, tend to be located in the secondary labour market, with poorly paid jobs, minimal benefits, and little security. A complex of factors are at work in shaping this situation. First, contrary to the situation in the primary labour market, employers tend to be exposed to fierce competition. Capital thresholds to enter the industry or service are low, making it easy for competitors to start up. Wages, in restaurants and retail sales, for example, tend to play quite a large role in the final cost of the product or service. And, because of competition, wage increases cannot be passed on to customers. This all means that many areas where women tend to be concentrated cannot afford, in a free-wage market, to pay good wages and benefits. Further weakening the economic clout of women workers is the fact that there tends to be fierce competition between women for these types of jobs — often they are the only jobs that fit in with other types of demands placed on women by family responsibility. Because of cultural stereotypes and gender socialization, men and women continue to think of themselves as participating in different aspects of the labour market, and the segregation continues.

These economic dynamics lead critics to argue that pay equity must be produced by government legislation that prescribes equal pay for work of equal value (see Box 10.6). These policies attempt to interfere with the market as the arbiter of wages and appeal to a broad principle of "equal value." This policy may do little to reduce segregation, but it would increase the wages of women. It may have the effect of bring-

* * * * * * * *

**Box 10.6
Pay Equity**

* * * * * * * *

In 1956, Canada's federal government passed a law that required equal pay for equal work for all employees under federal jurisdiction. This made it illegal to pay women less than men for the same or similar work. During the 1960s and 1970s similar legislation was adopted by the provinces. But the impact of these laws was limited because only similar jobs in the same plant or location were subject to pay equalization. Further, artificial distinctions were sometimes built in to job requirements to prevent male–female comparison and wage adjustment. Another problem was that many job areas were totally dominated by women, and historic undervaluations of job worth could not be addressed by comparison: there were few, if any, men in these occupations to whom wages could be compared.

In the 1970s, there was a movement to establish a new principle of pay equity: equal pay for work of equal value. This principle permitted comparison of wages across occupational categories on the basis of educational requirements, skill, and responsibility. It became possible to compare secretaries to groundskeepers, or nurses to the police. Initially, the legislation was complaint-based: a group of workers had to apply for pay-equity adjustment and present a case.

In the 1980s, several provinces moved toward a pro-active pay-equity policy that required specified employers to develop plans to implement pay equity. In 1989, Ontario became the first government in the world to legislate equal pay for work of equal value in the private sector. Continued occupational segregation and, perhaps, some inherent biases in job-value assessment (stress on effort and working conditions) have restricted the impact of the new laws.

* * * * * * * *

SOURCE: Adapted from Paul Phillips and Erin Phillips. *Women and Work* (Toronto: James Lorimer and Company, 1993), pp. 151–152.

* * * * * * * *

ing more men into what has been considered women's work and perhaps reduce the stereotypes and discrimination that exist in the labour market.

Political Economy Perspective
....

Dual labour market theory is expanded upon in what is called the political economy perspective (a critical perspective). This perspective extends the notions of cultural stereotyping and discrimination implicit in the second theory and argues that the broader position of women in society must be understood. Society is still focussed on the roles of men; thus, women continue to bear primary responsibility for child care. While the ability to give birth is a biological fact, being the primary care giver is a social and cultural construction that can be altered. Women's responsibility in this area, it is argued, puts them at a disadvantage in the labour market and influences the decisions they make about their participation. Women who have never married compare very well with similar men in terms of wages (earning 99 percent of what men earn). The family, then, is seen as an important determiner of labour force participation and success.

From this perspective one can understand the importance of society ensuring that affordable and accessible day care is provided for all children and that women have control over their reproduction. If men and women had equal responsibility for child care, this would equalize their employment opportunities.

It is also claimed that what women do in the workplace is automatically considered to be worth less pay than men's work simply because women are doing it. Doctors (men) are among the highest-paid workers in western society; nurses (women) were for a long time among the lower-paid workers. The professionalism of nursing was denied in the wage structure and reflected in a world of health politics, where the doctor was king. The relative devaluation of the work that women do is suggested by other examples cited in this book: the higher rates for male groundskeepers over female secretaries; the lower wages for female day care workers, compared with male workers at zoos or in warehouses. Such wage discrimination proceeds from the assumptions made about the value of jobs women do.

While there is abundant evidence of bias against women in the occupational wage and status system, there is also growing evidence for the merit of some key assumptions in supply-side theories. Women have, as those theories predict, experienced rising status and rising earnings in the labour market as they have begun to conform more to the training, occupational, and participation patterns of men. Although obstacles remain to equal opportunity for women, especially with regard to their unbalanced commitment to family responsibility, current data suggests a clear trend toward these being overcome. Women's concentration in traditional job ghettos has decreased somewhat, and there has been a significant increase in their participation in management and administrative positions (much faster than that of men) and in professional fields such as law, accounting, and social work.

UNIONS
....

Liberal philosophy encourages the view of workers as individuals going into the labour market and, armed with their individual skills and abilities, making free contracts to provide work for wages. Unlike other factors of production, labour, because it is embodied in humans, must generate income in order to subsist. People must work, and they must take the work available: it is work or starvation. In a market economy, labour is, in principle, like any other commodity in having its price determined by supply and demand. But what if there is more labour available than there is demand for it? In a free market, wages would fall to the minimum level necessary to keep employed workers alive — a bare subsistence level — while the unemployed would starve. This has, of course, happened throughout history: the number of people outruns the means of subsistence (either from direct production or through paid work), and large numbers die from starvation.

Workers are unlike other "factors of production" in having consciousness and the capacity for action. They do not simply react passively to whatever the market for labour dictates as appropriate wages; for centuries, they have organized into associations for the purpose of exerting some control over the price paid for labour and the conditions of work. A workers' strike took place in Ancient Egypt, during the reign of Rameses III, in about 1165 B.C. (Mandel, 1969: 176). Throughout history, revolts by slaves, serfs, peasants, and workers have been organized to gain more rights and improved conditions. In medieval times, conditions of work and levels of wages were often determined by negotiation in guild associations consisting of both employers and workers. Usually, in these pre-industrial times, there was no great gulf in wealth and status between master employers and craftspeople, and consensus was easily arrived at (Pelling, 1976: 4).

With the dawn of industrial capitalism, however, production took on a much larger scale and working for wages, rather than for self-sufficiency, soon became the standard situation of the ordinary people. One of the first sectors to feel the influence of organization of workers was the wool-weaving industry in England. There is evidence of extensive activity to form weavers' associations, for the purpose of collective bargaining, in the eighteenth century (Cole and Postgate, 1961: 63).

Essentially, the development of capitalism and the development of trade union organization are parallel stories, with union organization tending to follow quite soon after the establishment and development of industries. In the eighteenth century, worker organization was often created for the purpose of demanding some legal regulation of wages and conditions from the British Parliament. It seems to have been accepted in England that appeals from organized groups of workers for some regulation of their trade were legal, and Parliament frequently responded to such requests. On the other hand, unions in themselves were of "doubtful legality" (Cole and Postgate, 1961: 171) and were specifically forbidden in certain trades by about 40 different acts of Parliament.

With the ascendency of classical liberalism, in the last years of the eighteenth century, government policy turned from ambivalence to outright hostility. The British Parliament passed Combination Acts in 1799 and 1800 that, among other provisions, specified three months in jail (or two months with hard labour) for any worker found guilty of combining with others to seek changes in wages or conditions, or for encouraging another person to leave work, or for refusing to work with another worker (Cole and Postgate, 1961: 173). This repressive attitude to trade unions reached a famous climax in 1834, when farm labourers from the village of Tolpuddle, who had attempted to organize an association, were tried and sentenced (for administering illegal oaths of membership) to seven years' transportation to Australia. This sentence could be equivalent to death, since prisoners very often died during the voyage or during the period of the sentence. Public protest and declining government fear of union-led unrest resulted in a pardon for the offenders in 1836 (Pelling, 1976: 42).

A battleground emerged in the early period of industrial capitalism that can still be recognized today. On one side is the principle of classical liberalism that unions distort the labour market, restrain trade, and assault the rights of owners of capital. On the other side are ideas of group solidarity and class consciousness developed by workers who want to protect and advance their interests. There has been continual struggle between these principles within capitalist societies, and the line between state legal repression and general tolerance of union organization has been redrawn many times.

In Canada, trade unions were illegal prior to 1872 because they were considered to act in restraint of trade. In that year, legislation was passed that gave immunity to trade unions against criminal prosecution for certain actions that would normally be illegal (Panitch and Swartz, 1988: 18). The state responded to trade union activities and demands in an ambiguous fashion — at times, unions might be given expanded rights; at others, the full weight of the state, including the army and the police, might be used to break strikes and weaken unions. Panitch and Swartz (1988) argued that there have been periods when legal acceptance and support of trade unions has advanced, particularly during the 1940s, and times when union rights and activities have been under attack, especially since the 1970s. State policy toward unions is shaped by the interplay of a variety of factors: the political make-up of governments, the strength of union organization, and the state of the economy and of public finance. It is wrong, they argued, to see union organization as something that has been increasingly accepted and encouraged in Canadian society: the pendulum of state policy continues to swing between acceptance and hostility.

Unions are not only about wages. They are about the exercise of power in the workplace. Canada, like most other advanced capitalist societies, had developed a system of social programs, but they often ensure only a minimal standard of living. Canada's unemployment insurance system has been changed to cut off benefits for those who "voluntarily" quit work, a measure that will decrease workers' choices. Even with social programs, most people depend on their jobs in order to live at a reasonable standard. People have to work, and the balance of power with an employer is usually one-sided simply because of that fact. The power position of people who enter the workplace in an individual relationship to the employer is usually very weak. They can easily be dismissed or "laid off" if the employer wishes. They have little control over the conditions, intensity, and demands of work and must rely on the employer's sense of fairness.

Many Canadian employers have voluntarily set conditions and wages that are superior to those usually found in their industry. Often, however, this policy is intended to head off unionization drives, and some "progressive" employers are famous for the ferocity of their opposition to union organization (for example, see Canada, 1978). Superior conditions and treatment are, of course, at the discretion of employers. They are not a right of the workers, and in some ways they increase the worker's dependence on the job.

Union organization in the workplace has the effect of changing the structure of power relations. A Canadian government report noted that the organization of workers into unions for collective bargaining has the effect of narrowing the gap "between the rights of the individual as a worker and his rights as a citizen" (Canada, 1969: 97). Union organization provides for what Durkheim would call the "normative regulation" of the work process: both employers and workers enter into agreements that set the conditions of their relationship. Collective bargaining agreements usually set not only rates of wages and benefits, but specify work conditions and expectations, procedures for the settlement of disputes, and rights to grievance procedures for workers who feel they have been unfairly treated.

About a third of Canadian workers are unionized: in 1990, 34.7 percent of workers were union members (men 38.6 percent; women 30.3 percent) (see Table 10.4). There are marked regional variations in the rate of unionization: in Alberta it is only

Table 10.4		
	1976	32.6
	1980	32.2
	1985	34.4
	1990	34.7

Table 10.4
Union Membership
as Percentage of
Paid Labour Force,
Canada, 1972–1992.

SOURCE: *Annual Report of the Minister of Regional Industrial Expansion under the Corporations and Labour Unions Return Act Part II, Labour Unions,* cat. no. 71-202 (Ottawa: Statistics Canada). Reproduced by authority of the Minister of Industry, 1994.

26.6 percent, while in Newfoundland it is 55.1 percent (Statistics Canada, 1992b). These differences seem to relate to the structure of the economy (unionization is highest in manufacturing and the public sector and lowest in service industries) and to historical and cultural factors (Newfoundland's high unionization rate is attributable to the fishing industry). There appears to be good evidence for the view that unions are especially valuable for promoting the equality of pay for women: women's hourly wage in full-time unionized employment is 85.1 percent that of men, while it is only 71.4 percent of men's in non-unionized work (Women's Bureau, 1990).

Unions emerged initially as a counterbalance to the natural power advantage of employers and have given workers "a measure of dignity, self-respect and security that they would not otherwise have gained" (Canada, 1969: 97).

However, the whole concept of collective organization to promote the interests of workers runs against the assumption of liberal philosophy that only individuals (and individual corporations) are entitled to rights and freedoms. Union organization has become widely tolerated in the modern democratic state (see Table 10.5), because it is a natural outcome of worker's experiences in the workplace and reflects the demands for security, fair treatment, and good conditions that individuals strive for in their work lives. Tolerance of unions has grown as a result of the power they and their members can exercise in society and of the support of public opinion. Legal acceptance of their role is an element in the legitimation of the state as a representative of all citizens, not just the wealthy and powerful.

Although they are tolerated in modern democracies and even officially encouraged in some societies, like Sweden, unions have never achieved full acceptance by business or in liberal thought. In times of political crisis, in Canada and elsewhere, union freedoms have often been among the first casualties. The era of globalization will bring a new chapter to the story of unions and their role in modern capitalist soci-

Table 10.5
Union Membership
in Selected OECD
Countries, 1988

Canada	34.6%
United States	16.4%
France	12.0%
Germany	40.1%
Italy	62.7%
Sweden	96.1%
United Kingdom	46.1%

SOURCE: *OECD Employment Outlook* (Paris: Organization for Economic Co-operation and Development, 1991). Reprinted with permission.

eties. Will unions lose power in the globalized economy, or will national and international labour organizations provide some counterbalance to the eroding power of nation-states to set economic policy and labour standards?

CONCLUSION

This chapter focussed on work in modern capitalist societies, which is work organized for the creation of profit and for efficiency. To maximize profit and achieve efficiency, work is fragmented and control and regulation of the work process is removed from workers. Workers and employers are only bound together by a narrow employment contract, and work and its products are distanced from cultural and social values.

Sociologists have been interested in understanding the personal and social effects of this relatively new way of organizing work. Marx was concerned about the rise of alienation; Weber was concerned about the impersonality of work and the destructive effects of work organized for efficiency and removed from broader social and human values. Durkheim worried about the weakening of social solidarity and the conflict that might arise from the new division of labour. Marx argued that there was reason to be optimistic about a resolution of the problems produced by the new wage economy: removing private ownership, he thought, would transform the social relations of work and eliminate alienation. Weber was thoroughly pessimistic, seeing industrial society's deepening ties to the bureaucratic way of organizing social life: people will remain locked in the "iron cage" of a rationalized social world. Durkheim, like Marx, was optimistic, although for very different reasons. He thought that the structure of the wage economy and the division of labour could be retained as long as rules to provide normative regulation of workers and managers could be developed.

Behind all of this, however, there is a deeper problem: a distinct tension between people's rights as citizens and their rights as workers, which flows from the way work is organized. As citizens they expect to exercise control and autonomy, to be able to make a difference as an individual, to not be coerced, and to not be subject to authority that does not have their approval, and consent. In the modern economy they find their choices limited. They must work in order to live, but they find they have little control over their work or the products of their labour. There is little real democracy in the workplace.

Labour unions can be understood as attempting to narrow the gap between people's rights as citizens and their rights as workers. The collective action of workers can introduce an element of democracy in the workplace and can offset the exercise of power by owners/managers.

The restrictions on women are even greater than those on men. Not only do they experience the above tension, but their choices are limited by prevailing cultural attitudes and socialization. They also find that the unequal distribution of family responsibilities constrains their choices further.

Work is a central component of everyone's life. All are socialized to fit into the way work is organized in the society and to the particular spot in the organization of work that they come to occupy. Schooling, a central instrument of this socialization, is the subject of the following chapter.

NOTES

1. Adapted from V. Galt "No End in Sight for Strike at Cami Automotive Plant," *The Globe and Mail*, September 30, 1992, p. A8; and "GM–Suzuki Strike Tests Plant's New Harmony," Vancouver *Sun*, September 15, 1992, p. D7.

2. See CAW–Canada Research Group on CAMI (1993).

3. Steven Prokesh, "Volvo Experiment on Brink of Failure," *The Globe and Mail*, June 9, 1991, p. B1.

4. Rob Carrick, "Car Makers Target Absenteeism in Talks," *The Globe and Mail*, August 1, 1990, p. B3.

5. Rona Maynard, "How Do You Like Your Job?" *The Globe and Mail, Report on Business Magazine*, November 1987, pp. 112–125.

6. Daphne Bramham and Gordon Hamilton, "Death of the Middle Class," Vancouver *Sun* November 14, 1992, p. A15. This analysis is confirmed by the Economic Council of Canada (1990: 14–15).

FURTHER READING

Armstrong, Pat, and Hugh Armstrong. *Theorizing Women's Work*. Toronto: Garamond Press, 1990.

Heron, Craig. *The Canadian Labour Movement: A Short History*. Toronto: James Lorimer, 1989. An introduction to the history of Canadian unions.

Krahn, Harvey, and G. Lowe. *Work, Industry and Canadian Society*, 2nd ed. Scarborough, ON: Nelson, 1993. An excellent review of work relations in modern society.

Phillips, Paul, and Erin Phillips. *Women and Work*, rev. ed. Toronto: James Lorimer, 1993. A standard reference on women's relationship to the labour market.

Reich, Robert B. *The Work of Nations*. New York: Vintage Books, 1992. A firm believer in human capital theory, Reich gives a spirited account of what work will be like in the "new economy."

Rinehart, J. W. *The Tyranny of Work*, 2nd ed. Toronto: Harcourt Brace Jovanovich, 1987. A brief and engaging examination of work in modern society.

Schor, Juliet B. *The Overworked American: The Unexpected Decline of Leisure*. New York: Basic Books, 1991. An economist provides confirmations of what may already be apparent to you: work absorbs more and more of our time.

STUDY QUESTIONS

1. Ask an older friend or relative who has worked in the same occupation for a number of years to describe the changes in the way his or her occupation is carried out. Does the description support a "deskilling" thesis or show an increased demand for skills and knowledge?

2. In what way can "scientific management" be seen as promoting deskilling?

3. What are the key claims of the postindustrial society thesis?

4. How would you change the representation of women in the work force? Would these changes represent a functionalist, liberal, or critical perspective?

5. Interview workers in a co-operative or worker-owned business. Discuss their views on the advantages and disadvantages of such a workplace.

6. Interview a recent immigrant to Canada to learn about his or her experience in joining the work force. Did the principle of equality of opportunity appear to be present for that person?

7. How would you change your (or a family member's) workplace? Do your proposed changes reflect a functionalist or a critical perspective?

11 EDUCATION AND SOCIETY

• • • • • • • •

INTRODUCTION
• • • • • • • •

Functionalism and critical perspectives have substantially differing views on the role of education in society. This disagreement involves the linkage between schooling and the economy and focusses on two themes.

First, functionalists, who support the liberal belief in equality of opportunity, argue that schooling prepares young people for future roles based on merit. A critical perspective argues that the principle of merit is quite weak in practice. Instead, schooling tends to reproduce existing class and gender divisions and foster an ideology encouraging students to believe that these divisions are natural.

Second, functionalists support the ideas of human capital theory and argue that personal and public investment in education will modernize the economy, enhance competitiveness, and promote economic growth. Critical perspectives suggest that Canada's economic problems are rooted in its history and the structure of its economy. They argue that real job growth in Canada does not lie in the high-technology and information areas assumed by human capital theory. They also raise questions about the commercialization of education.

• • • • • • • •

This chapter considers education and its role in society, furthering this book's analysis of the structure of Canadian society. Many assumptions exist about the part education plays in society. Liberal philosophy assumes that the best society is one in which individuals have maximum freedom to pursue their own interests and goals and are not bound by tradition or ascribed characteristics. The functionalist perspective assumes an open-class society in which individuals rise or fall, depending on their merits. In both these views, the school is assumed to be one of the central aspects of society for identifying merit and rewarding it through grades and degrees in order to prepare people for the demanding roles of society.

FUNCTIONALIST VIEWS OF THE ROLE OF SCHOOLING

· · · · · · · · · ·

Durkheim argued that anomie would be absent in a society with a "normal" (spontaneous) division of labour, one in which the social roles that people fill match their abilities and interests. This spontaneous division of labour can be fostered and achieved through education. He also saw the school playing an important role in establishing solidarity by transmitting a common culture to students. The previous chapter presented an examination of social roles central to most people — their work roles. A functionalist assumes that people need to be prepared for these social roles and that education is a necessary aspect of that preparation. As work roles become more technical and more demanding, more people will be required to attend school and to spend longer periods of time in school. This belief is described as **technological functionalism**. Finally, the examination of the Canadian economy hinted that some people believe that the key to the nation's future economic development, a way out of the crisis, is an investment in educating and training human resources. This belief is also an aspect of the functionalist perspective and is called **human capital theory**.

Both functionalism and liberalism assume that the education system is best viewed as a supplier of socialized, educated individuals for roles in society and the economy. It is believed that education supports the economy of the society, fostering individual enterprise, equality, and the development of necessary human capital.

Functionalists are concerned about the maintenance of integration between education and other spheres of society. For example, they see education changing in focus along with family change. The family — while a centre of economic, religious, health care, and educational activity in the distant past — has given up many of these functions to more specialized institutions with the emergence of modern, urban, industrial societies. One of these specialized institutions is the school. Almost any government inquiry into the role of schooling in society takes up this theme. In

Photo 11.1
Functionalists argue that schooling prepares young people for future roles based on merit.

· · · · · · · · ·

Cathie Archbauld, Photographer

British Columbia, for example, the Royal Commission on Education made the following statements:

> The school as we have come to know it fulfils three major social functions. First, schools provide custodial service; they are valued as places where children can spend time in relative safety and under the care of adults while the adults in their own families work. Second, schools serve to socialize children and adolescents to the norms and values of their society. Although the first agency of socialization remains the family, the school socializes children to a community broader than that of family. In schools, children meet other youngsters from other parts of society and learn attitudes and abilities different from what they learn at home, but necessary for community participation and for entry to the world of work.
>
> Third, the school performs an educational function. In schools children learn the set of basic skills which enable them to continue to learn throughout their lives.[1]

These paragraphs provide the essence of a functionalist analysis of schooling: as the family (and other aspects of society) have changed, the school has had to change in response so that the essential work of nurturing, monitoring, providing security and moral training, instilling tolerance, and fostering the self-development of young citizens is achieved. This new mandate for schooling creates many tensions both within the school and between school and family. For example, what if a family does not want its children to receive sex education? New tasks for teachers may also interfere with the ability of the school to meet its initial mandate to produce a knowledgeable individual with basic competencies in reading, writing, and arithmetic.

The teachers and the public have become acutely aware of this changing role of the school, with its potential for the state to intervene in more aspects of individual and family life.

CRITICAL VIEWS OF THE ROLE OF SCHOOLING

A critical perspective offers a very different approach to education, stressing its role in serving the interests of status or class groups. The school, according to this view, tends to recruit people for future social roles in a largely ascriptive fashion and to promote an ideology that encourages an acceptance of unequal social roles. This chapter presents an assessment of these contrasting perspectives, functionalist and critical, which are central to sociological views of education. This is accomplished through a review of the topics of equality of opportunity and human capital theory.

EQUALITY OF EDUCATIONAL OPPORTUNITY

A few generations ago, prolonged education was largely reserved for the economic and social elite of Canada. It was not an avenue for achieving wealth and power, but an accoutrement of the wealthy and powerful. It was also largely the preserve of men. Since the end of the 1950s however, there has been pressure to democratize education by making it available to the masses. "All over the world, the school reform movements of the last 15 years have taken their point of departure from the demand for equality of educational opportunity for all children, irrespective of their origins, locality, race or sex" (OECD, 1976: 38).

This demand for change was joined by those who thought that economic development could be stimulated by governments investing in the education of the work force. These two powerful forces transformed the Canadian education system: curricula were changed, student loan programs were developed, and new universities and the community college system were established. But has the democratization of edu-

Photo 11.2
The critical perspective, in contrast to the functionalist perspective, argues that schooling tends to reproduce existing racial, class, and gender division. Here, a young Black child reads a book that features only white characters.

Cathie Archbauld, Photographer

cation decreased its exclusivity? An answer to this question will help in assessing the claims made by the functionalist and critical perspectives.

Assuming that talent (merit) is equally distributed throughout society, it is reasonable to assume that if equality of educational opportunity has been achieved, individuals from various ascribed statuses (sex, locality of birth, or race) will be equally distributed throughout the education system. The determinants of transitions from one grade to the next, from high school to university, from an undergraduate program to a graduate program, should be merit rather than identifiable ascribed characteristics. As mass education becomes a feature of Canadian society, there should be a discoverable reduction in the exclusivity of participation in higher levels of education. The evidence is reviewed with particular attention given to the participation of the lower class and of women.

Socioeconomic Status

An Assessment of Functionalism

The education system can be thought of as a hierarchy:

professional and graduate programs in universities
undergraduate programs in university
community colleges
secondary school
elementary school

Every examination of educational participation rates by socioeconomic groups has shown that each step up this ladder results in an increase in the relative participation rate of the higher-income groups. This indicates the present pattern of educational participation, but has the ratio of higher- to lower- income groups changed over time? Is there a historical pattern? Surprisingly, there has been little historical research on this question. Recent research, however, has produced some significant findings. Guppy (1984) approached this problem by using data from a national sample of Canadians and organizing the data according to birth cohorts (those born in particular years) from 1919 to 1952. For each of these cohorts, he determined the socio-economic status of the parents as well as the educational attainment of the respondent. If there had been a democratization of education, the education level of more recent birth cohorts should reveal a significant increase. (This is another way to study social mobility.) What does the data reveal?

The data suggests that there has been a significant increase in high school completion for children from all class backgrounds. Of those born in the 1913–1922 period, 71.6 percent of those from professional or managerial families completed high school. Completion rates for this group rose to 79 percent for the 1943–52 birth cohort. Children from blue-collar families and born in the first time period had a completion rate of 35.4 percent; this rose to 49.5 percent for those born in the last period.

In order to compare these two socioeconomic groups, Guppy used a disparity ratio (the completion rate of the professional group divided by the completion rate of the blue-collar group; for example, 71.6 divided by 35.4). The disparity ratio declines from 2.02 in the 1913–22 period to 1.59 for the 1943–52 period. Thus, in 1913–22 a child from a professional or managerial family was about twice as likely to complete high school as was a child from a blue-collar family. For 1943–1952, this disparity is reduced to just over one and a half. While the distance between the two groups has been reduced substantially, a considerable discrepancy in high school completion continues to exist.

What has happened at the postsecondary level? Using a birth cohort of 1910–14, Guppy discovered that children from professional or managerial backgrounds had a postsecondary attendance rate of 45.2 percent. For the 1944–49 cohort, the attendance rate increased to 65.2 percent. For children from blue-collar families, the respective attendance rates were 19.8 percent and 37.5 percent. The disparity ratio shows a reduction from 2.28 to 1.73. Guppy concluded that "the influence of socioeconomic background on postsecondary attendance has steadily decreased over time." Notice, however, that there is a greater disparity ratio for postsecondary attendance than for high school completion and that the disparity between the two income groups is still rather substantial.

The reduction in the postsecondary attendance ratio is misleading, however. Guppy put it this way: "A comparison ... reveals that the democratization of postsecondary education has not come about because of processes occurring at the university level. In terms of university degree completion, only a minor reduction in socio-economic disparity has occurred. Not only are socio-economic disparities larger at the university level ... but these inequalities have also receded only minimally" (p. 86).

Where did the children of blue-collar families go, then? Guppy argued that they went to community colleges, which emerged in most provinces in the 1960s or later, and into the technical and vocational schools. There is nothing wrong with them going to community colleges or vocational schools. But since there continues to be a relationship between class and education, the location of working-class children in postsecondary institutions outside the university has not had a major effect in reducing the link between class and educational attainment. Although the processes influencing success and location have not been examined here, it is reasonable to conclude that equality of educational opportunity still remains an elusive goal. Significant disparities remain between socioeconomic groups in terms of university degree completion, postsecondary attendance, and high school completion.

A Critical View
• • • • • • • • •
The critical perspective holds a quite different position on education, one that helps us understand the above facts to some degree. The **correspondence principle** is central to most critical perspectives, stating that the location of individuals in the school hierarchy corresponds to their economic and social position outside the school. Using this principle, one would predict that upper-middle-class and upper-class young people would be located disproportionately in the universities and under-represented in the community colleges. The reverse would hold for lower-class young people. This in fact is what Guppy's data, reviewed above, suggests. Rather than being agents for the democratization of society, schools, according to this view, are agents for reproducing the class structure of society.

The school does not perform this task automatically, however. It depends on the actions and decisions of parents, teachers, and students, and on the presence of structural forces that provide advantage to some and disadvantage to others. Students going to school hungry, for example, are less able to concentrate and may do less well in school. Some schools in poorer neighbourhoods avoid scheduling tests after the middle of the month because they know that many children will be increasingly hungry as welfare cheques fail to stretch through the month. Similarly, the fact that schools place great value on communication skills and that all of the teachers are middle class by virtue of their education and income, provides an advantage to children from homes in which reading material is available and a great deal of verbal interaction with the children occurs. These families tend to be middle class. Teachers may form expectations about students on the basis of these cultural indicators of class and begin to treat children differently from their first day at school (see Box 11.1). These expectations are known to foster aspirations that conform to the teacher's expectations (see Rosenthal and Jacobson, 1968).

Not all students fit into the way the classroom is organized, and they often suffer negative evaluation by their teachers. Albert Einstein, who became one of the great scientists of modern times, did not like the disciplined classroom of his time with its emphasis on memorizing names and dates. He thought the teachers behaved like army sergeants or automatons rather than like friends from whom one could freely learn. These teachers thought that Albert was uninteresting and would never amount to much; they said that he did not have a "retentive memory" and lacked "clearness and fluency in expressing himself" (Quasha, 1980).

Classroom dynamics have been examined very closely in order to understand the underachievement of Black students in the United States. It has been found that at every level, from elementary school to graduate school, something depresses Black achievement. This poor performance is constant across social class lines and in spite of preparation as measured by Scholastic Aptitude Test scores.

Black students drop out in greater numbers than do their white counterparts, do less well on average, and fail more frequently. Steele (1992) argued that the best way to understand this performance is with Erving Goffman's concept of stigma, the constant devaluation many Blacks face in American society and schools. He did not refer just to prejudice and discrimination on the part of teachers. Rather, stigma is a result of a general image of society fostered by advertising, school curricula, literature, and public discourse, in which Blacks do not fare well or are invisible. This sets up a particular problem in the school, where all students are subject to lower evaluations if they have difficulty with school work. Black students face compound challenges: ordi-

Box 11.1
Streaming and
the Reproduction
of the Structure
of Inequality

The realities of the Canadian school system are revealed when streaming (the placement of children in particular programs) in elementary and secondary schools is examined. Ontario has 16.4 percent of its elementary school children in some form of "special education" program. The majority of these are in what might be called "normative" programs — classrooms of children diagnosed and placed not on the basis of universally agreed-upon physical criteria but on the basis of observation and evaluation of their classroom behaviour. Who are these children?

An early Toronto study found that children from families existing on welfare or family-benefits payments were 60 times more likely to be in these special programs than were children from professional families. A 1982 Toronto study found that 11.5 percent of low socioeconomic group students, compared with 3.1 percent of high socioeconomic group students, were in special education classrooms. Further, it was found that 34.6 percent of Black students and 18.9 percent of all West Indian students in the city of Toronto were in special education. On the other hand, it has been found that the majority of students in French immersion programs are of middle-class or upper-middle-class background. Not surprisingly, this is an area of education that has received substantial support and resources in the past few years. There has also been a significant growth of private schools, and these are attended almost exclusively by the middle class or upper middle class because of their cost.

One might conclude that streaming is alive and well. This is significant because students placed in special education programs seldom return to the regular classroom, and they leave with lower aspirations and fewer occupational choices than do other students.

SOURCE: Adapted from Bruce Curtis, D.W. Livingstone, and Harry Smaller, *Stacking the Deck: The Streaming of Working-class Kids in Ontario Schools* (Toronto: Our Schools/Our Selves Education Foundation, 1992).

nary problems of learning are linked to negative social stereotypes about the intellectual and social skills of Blacks; as a result, Black students have great difficulty identifying with schools and with academic life (see Box 11.2).

These are concerns for Canada as well. According to a "confidential" report by the Anti-Racist Directorate of the Ontario Ministry of Citizenship, "there is a higher than average dropout rate among racial minorities and Black students in particular are over-represented among high school dropouts."[2] They are also over-represented in vocational schools and under-represented in advanced-level programs. Among other things it is suggested that one cause of this situation is that Blacks still have a very limited presence in the higher status roles in society; they seem not to be part of the fabric of society.

The concept of cooling-out, developed by Burton Clark (1960), has been used to describe the process of shaping students' ambitions to match their probable destination in social status. This process is a response to a dilemma of modern societies:

Box 11.2
Schools, Youth, and
the Police

In some communities the police have become a major presence in the school system in dealing with issues that were traditionally handled by school staff. Increasingly, incidents such as schoolyard fights and scuffles — which have occurred for years — are frequently being upgraded to "assaults" with the laying of criminal charges. The creation by some police services of special police units to counter youth crime and school violence, coupled with the introduction of "zero tolerance policies" for disruptive and criminal activities in the schools, mean that police officers have become more and more involved in maintaining order on behalf of school authorities.

Serious concern has been raised about implications of these developments for Black and other racial minority students. There is a strong perception that the increased police presence has a negative, disproportionate, and unwarranted impact on racial minority youth. Some initial research suggests that school officials and police officers may target Black and other racial minority youth unfairly. Police and school officials react one way to certain behaviours on the part of white students, and differently when those behaviours are manifested by Black and other racial minority students. The research also suggests that some teachers are more afraid of Black and other racial minority students than of white students.

SOURCE: Excerpt from "Schools, Youth, and Police," *Some Key Issues Being Explored* (Toronto: Queen's Printer for Ontario, September 1993), p. 8. Reprinted with permission of the Commission on Systemic Racism in the Ontario Criminal Justice System.

with the democratization of education, everyone is encouraged to have high ambitions. Many set their sights on goals that are higher than they can realistically attain, and these individuals need to become reconciled to more limited goals or "cooled-out." More recent authors use the concept with a more critical edge: those who aspire to a position beyond their class of origin need cooling-out in order to maintain the class structure.

Jerome Karabel (1972) looked at the American community college system in relation to the social class structure and argued that the institution channelled working-class young people into lower-status occupations. He claimed that the community college is a vehicle for maintaining the class structure rather than transforming it by providing an opportunity to everyone to fulfil high aspirations. He argued that this perpetuation of class structure is accomplished through the structuring of opportunity in the community college. Community colleges tend to make visible for the student a number of vocational training programs, rather than professional programs: nursing rather than medicine, dental assistant rather than dentist, and mechanic rather than engineer. As working-class students are cooled-out, they are encouraged to lower their aspirations and are shifted into future destinations more congruent with their origins. (Recall the research by Guppy showing that a great deal of the increase in working-class participation in postsecondary education came from their registration in community colleges.)

Students do not learn just the three R's while in school, however. They experience a powerful **hidden curriculum** as well. The hidden curriculum can be thought of as the style of teaching and the educational and social aspirations that are encouraged (or discouraged) in the student. Does the classroom encourage choice, initiative, and open discussion, or are students closely regimented and their work specified in detail? One style of teaching socializes for leadership and management, the other for subordinate roles. Students also learn a way to understand their present position in the society as well as their future position. The school makes a contribution to the ideological reproduction of society. While students are competing for grades they are learning to believe that rewards are distributed according to personal merit. Those who are successful in this scheme of things are deserving and will be rewarded with higher incomes and more power in the society.

At higher levels of education, students learn to believe that the division between mental and manual labour, between those who can tell others what to do and those who must accept orders, arises because of the nature of the tasks they do and that these tasks require different levels of education. Putting these two together, the student is encouraged to believe that work roles have natural divisions corresponding to the nature of the tasks performed; that these tasks require different levels of education; and that those with the most education achieved that goal according to personal merit. If in fact the way schools assess and counsel students is shaped by the cultural indicators of the student's class of origin (e.g., their language usage), a powerful ideology is transmitted that disguises this process of ascription. Students come to believe that success and failure are linked to individual talent and personal effort, when it may be more strongly linked to their parents' social class.

Gender Socialization
. . . .
An Assessment of Functionalism
. . . .

Historically, women had very low participation rates in postsecondary education (see Box 11.3). This low participation must be understood in terms of formal and informal barriers and socialization that directed women's aspirations away from education. With the democratization of education, women's participation should have approached that of men. Consider the situation in the academic year 1970–71, displayed in Table 11.1. In 1970–71 women accounted for 36.7 percent of students enrolled in an undergraduate or first professional degree program. One is struck by the extent of program segregation. Women dominated traditional female fields such as nursing and household sciences, and were quite under-represented in other professional areas. The majority of female enrolment was in the general area of "arts." In examining the 1990–91 figures, a revolution of sorts is apparent. Women now account for the majority of students in undergraduate and first professional degree programs and are close to parity or above parity in many professional areas. They do, however, remain dominant in areas such as nursing, education, and household sciences. The only areas where they remain under-represented are science and engineering, and even here there has been a remarkable change.

Women, then, have been much more successful than have the lower class in gaining access to university education. They have been in the majority among community college students, and program segregation is more pronounced at this level. In 1990–91, for example, women made up 86.7 percent of those enrolled in social services programs, 90.6 percent of those in educational and counselling services, 96.9 percent of those in secretarial science programs, and 89.2 percent of those in nurs-

Box 11.3
Have the Doors
Always Been Open?

In 1910, the University of Montreal became the first French-language university in Quebec to give a Bachelor of Arts degree to a woman. By 1960, all faculties in French-language universities had opened their doors to women. The Quebec College of Physicians and Surgeons accepted a woman in 1930, and in 1945 a woman received a law degree from McGill University.

Mount Allison University in New Brunswick was the first university in the British empire to grant a Bachelor of Science degree to a woman in 1875. Women were admitted to Dalhousie University in 1882, to McGill University in 1884, and the University of Toronto in 1885. In 1883–84, the University of Toronto and Queen's University established separate medical colleges for women rather than admit them to existing programs. The women's college at Queen's University was closed in 1895, and women were not admitted to the medical faculty until 1942. In 1897, a woman was called to the bar in Ontario — the first woman lawyer in the British Empire.

SOURCE: Adapted from *Report of the Royal Commission on the Status of Women in Canada* (Ottawa: Information Canada, 1970).

ing programs. These four programs alone account for 41.6 percent of all full-time women students in community college. Men account for 83.8 percent of the enrolment in engineering and applied science programs, and this one program area accounts for 42.5 percent of male students.

A Critical View   The figures showing gender-based program segregation in community colleges are understandable in light of the correspondence principle: women enrol in educational programs that correspond to their location in the labour market. Many women are concentrated in lower-paying service-sector jobs; it is reasonable to assume that the education system will reflect this pattern of segregation. A host of factors may help explain this gender segregation in schools, but it would be useful to consider features of the educational programs themselves. Gaskell (1985) identifies issues that may contribute to segregation: the recruitment criteria for programs may exclude women. Programs may offer specialized programs without common core courses, thus cutting their participants off from other alternatives. Social work, for example, is separated from sociology; public health from the physical sciences; secretarial science from the managerial stream. Having a math or science prerequisite may help segregate men and women, since secondary school girls participate in math and science at lower rates than do boys. The lack of support services such as day care and financial assistance may encourage women to enter a narrow range of programs or to discontinue their education.

A critical perspective would also examine the hidden curriculum, to discover factors encouraging gender segregation. Do the textbooks provide stereotypical views of men and women? Do teachers talk to the boys more than they do the girls? Does the classroom atmosphere discourage men or women from participating and succeeding?

	1970–71 (% women)	1990–91 (% women)
Table 11.1 University Enrolment by Women in Selected Fields, Canada, 1970–1971 and 1990–1991 — **Field of Study**		
Commerce and business administration	10.2	50.7
Education	56.4	70.0*
Applied arts	56.8	64.6
Law	12.7	52.1
Sciences	28.0	30.3
Agriculture	10.5	45.5
Engineering and applied science	0.2	16.0
Dentistry	5.6	39.7
Medicine	18.1	45.4
Nursing	97.9	94.6
Pharmacology	49.0	61.6
Household sciences	99.3	90.7
Veterinary medicine	12.2	61.9
Total	36.7	56.7

*If physical education is removed from this group, women make up 74.0 percent of undergraduates.

SOURCE: For 1970–71, J. Gaskell, "Women and Education," in *Towards Equity*, cat. no. EC22-126 (Ottawa: Ministry of Supply and Services, 1985). For 1990–91, *Education in Canada*, 1990–91, cat. no. 81-229 (Ottawa: Statistics Canada, 1992). Reproduced by authority of the Minister of Industry, 1994.

A hidden curriculum is also displayed in the sex composition of the staff in the school system. If women are employed as staff members at the lowest levels and men at the highest levels, students may learn something about gender authority in the society as well as learning something about their own place in society. Consider the location of women as employees in the Ontario education system, as outlined in Table 11.2. This kind of gender stratification also occurs in Canadian universities as shown in Table 11.3. These dramatic examples of status segregation present students with lessons about their own futures and their appropriate expectations.

HUMAN CAPITAL THEORY

Can education play a role in helping the technological development and modernization of the Canadian economy? Many argue that Canada must invest more in education in order to develop the human capital necessary to expand its economy into new areas. Human capital is the skills, knowledge, literacy, and adaptability possessed by individuals. It is an economic resource that people bring with them into their various roles in the economy.

A society can, of course, enlarge its human capital by investing in educational services to give individuals the opportunity to make a personal investment in expanding their skills. The level of education and training possessed by individuals is thought to play a key role in economic development. It is assumed that the expansion of a society's human capital will automatically stimulate the economy.

A number of implications arise from these beliefs about human capital. The first assumption is that workers are paid according to their productivity, the extent to which they add value to the work accomplished. Those receiving a high wage are

Table 11.2
Women as a
Percentage
of Selected
Occupational
Categories in the
Education System,
Ontario, 1991
. . . .

Directors of education	5.1
Assistant directors	11.5
Principals, secondary	15.6
Vice-principals, secondary	27.3
Principals, elementary	26.2
Vice-principals, elementary	43.6
Teachers, grade 13	34.3
Teachers, grades 11–12	43.4
Teachers, grades 9–10	50.3
Teachers, grades 7–8	54.1
Teachers, grades 4–6	68.3
Teachers, grades 1–3	92.1
Kindergarten teachers	97.6
Clerical and secretarial staff	97.2

Note: Figures for teachers represent the public school system only.
SOURCE: *The Status of Women and Employment Equity in Ontario School Boards*, Report to the Legislature by the Minister of Education, 1992 (Toronto: Ontario Ministry of Education, 1993).

assumed to have more "human capital" and therefore make a more substantial contribution to the economic value of the good or service produced than do workers receiving a lower wage. The allocation of wages is thought to be a rational process not affected by non-capital attributes of the worker, such as race, sex, class, or union strength.

This claim is challenged by research showing that women are often paid less than men for doing comparable jobs. It also does not explain why the salaries of management appear to be less responsive to the forces of the market than do those of workers. Management salaries, for example, often increase while those of workers decrease. Further, the gap between the salaries of senior management and workers is typically so great that it is difficult to imagine how this could reflect real differences in the contribution to the value of the product created. The income and benefits of an average American CEO (chief executive officer) exceed the salary of the average worker by 160 times. If the average salary is $30 000, the CEO will receive $4 800 000. The benefits provided to the CEO of Coca Cola makes even this benefit seem paltry. In 1992, he was given a stock package worth $81 million dollars.[3] This was in addition to his base salary of $1.06 million, plus bonuses and incentives that added about $4 mil-

Table 11.3
Full-Time Female
University Teachers
by Rank and Year,
Canada, 1960–61
and 1990–91
. . . .

	1960–61 (% women)	1990–91 (% women)
Full professor	4.2	7.6
Associate professor	9.8	19.6
Assistant professor	11.8	33.4
Rank below assistant professor	24.3	49.5
Total	11.4	20.2

SOURCE: *Teachers in Universities,* cat. no. 81-241 (Ottawa: Statistics Canada, 1993). Reproduced by authority of the Minister of Industry, 1994.

lion more. Before the stock gift, he already owned stocks valued at approximately $140 million.

In Japan the ratio of a CEO's salary to that of the average worker is under 20 to 1, while in the United Kingdom it is under 35 to 1. CEO salaries were not required to be published in Canada until a 1993 Ontario law required companies listed on the Toronto Stock Exchange to disclose the pay of their top executives. Stephen Bachand, president of Canadian Tire, was paid $3.2 million; Peter Munk, CEO of American Barrick Resources Corp., was paid $1.9 million in salary, bonus, and stock options; Edgar Bronfman of Seagram was paid $2 million; and Robert Schultz, Chairman of Midland Walwyn, $2.9 million.[4]

The second implication is that the differences in the economic success of nations (measured in terms of gross domestic product, perhaps) are an indication of different levels of the development of "human capital." If Canada wishes to improve its competitive position in relation to that of other nations, it is assumed the nation must invest more in education. It follows from this that people must spend more time in school because the workplace now requires a greater investment in knowledge and skill. The nature of work has changed so that lower levels of education are of little value to the employer. Numerous examples of this kind of thinking are based on human capital theory (see Box 11.4). The following statement from the Prosperity Secretariat of the Government of Canada sums up this thinking.

> *In this new world, countries with advanced economies like ours have shifted toward the production of high-quality, specialized goods and services. This is not only true of high-technology, leading-edge industries, but also of more mature industries such as automobile and machinery, and of the service sector. In fact, the fastest growth has been in the service sector. It now accounts for 71 percent of all employment in Canada, and business services involving highly skilled and highly paid jobs — like engineering, legal services and management consulting — has been the fastest growing component of the service sector.*
>
> *Taken together these trends constitute a fundamental change in the nature of the way we do business and create wealth. In the past, nations could prosper by processing and selling inherited natural resources. Today's successful economies create value by applying knowledge to goods and services or by inventing better ways of performing old tasks.*
>
> *... The skill and knowledge requirements of most jobs in the economy will rise in the future. Fewer jobs will be available for the unskilled and uneducated, and new workers will require a higher level of skills as they enter the work force* (Canada, Prosperity Secretariat, 1991: 2–3).

Evidence Supporting Human Capital Theory

It is possible to find ample evidence supporting the above evaluation of the new role of education in meeting Canada's economic needs. First, compared with other societies, Canada retains young people in school at a significantly lower rate than do other countries. The participation rate of 17-year-olds in 1989 was as follows: Japan, 94 percent; West Germany, 89 percent; United States, 87 percent; Sweden, 78 percent; Canada, 72 percent (Maynard, 1989: 92). The conclusion is that part of Canada's economic problems stem from its failure to match other nations in raising the educational level of its work force.

What is doubly disconcerting about these facts for Canadians is that as a nation Canada spends more on education than does any other country, with the exception of Japan, yet it clearly appears to do less well at retaining students. It is also of inter-

- "To hold its own in a crowded global marketplace, Canada needs a world-class workforce, and the one we have isn't measuring up." (Maynard, 1989: 88)
- "When the country's wealth lay mainly in rocks and forests, Canada could afford to be complacent about its human capital. But sweaty-brow jobs are disappearing as the forces of the information age conspire to make brain power the ultimate resource. Most of the job growth is occurring in high-skill areas." (Maynard, 1989: 88.)
- "While there are many elements in the challenge to improve our competitive position in world markets, a key factor is the need to raise the quality of our human resources. In the final analysis, it is people who make the difference between inferior or superior products, whether goods or services." (Gordon Simpson, "Training Canada's Competitive Edge," *The Globe and Mail*, February 2, 1991, p. B4.)
- "Shouldn't we be imbuing our school children with the beauty and the social consequences of science so that they will be ready for the challenge of the high-tech world, which is almost here?... The educational standard of all its citizens must be raised across the spectrum of knowledge, but especially in science." (Thomas Walkton, "Rote Learning Not the Panacea," *The Globe and Mail*, December 19, 1988, p. A7.)
- "Japanese students routinely do better than Western-schooled children in mathematics and science. Japanophiles (and Japanophilia has become somewhat of a craze among business thinkers) say that with this kind of education system — rigorous, structured and disciplined — it is no accident that Japan is on its way to dominating the world economy." (Derek York, "Falling Behind in High-Tech World," *The Globe and Mail*, October 7, 1989, p. D4.)

est that Canadian students spend 180–185 days per year in school, while Japanese students spend 243 days (Barrett, 1990: 80).

The abilities to read, write clearly, express oneself, and manipulate figures are key aspects of an increasing number of jobs. There is reason to be concerned about Canada's ability to graduate students with these skills, however. A recent survey of Canadians found that more than one in five could not read, write, or compute well enough to cope with normal working life. More than three-quarters of these functional illiterates were born in Canada, and one-third are high school graduates. A high dropout rate is compounded by large numbers leaving school or graduating who have not mastered what must be basic skills. In a study for the Business Task Force on Literacy, it was estimated that illiteracy costs business at least $4 billion a year in accidents, errors, and lost productivity (Maynard, 1989: 88).

Second, the International Association for Evaluation of Educational Achievement has recently shown that Canadian 17–18-year-olds placed 11th out of 13 nations in biology tests, 12th in chemistry, and 11th in physics (Crocker, 1990). Again, it is assumed that Canada cannot compete as a nation in the competitive world of international business without a work force trained in science.

Third, Canada ranks lowest among a group of eight nations (including the United States, Germany, France, Sweden, the United Kingdom, the Netherlands and Japan) in terms of the number of scientists and engineers in the work force and in terms of international patents granted (Economic Council of Canada, 1989: 15).

Fourth, the real earnings of the average worker have stood still for the past decade (Economic Council of Canada, 1989: 39). It is assumed that worker productivity has not increased because of the failure to increase skill levels. The lack of education affects Canada's productivity.

Fifth, unemployment in Canada during the 1980s was higher than the average unemployment in OECD countries and the average in seven major industrialized nations. Those with higher education have lower rates of unemployment than those with less education, so it is assumed that Canada's unemployment rate could be reduced by developing an educated work force. Canada's productivity has fallen considerably behind that of other nations, creating pressure on its economy because this means that goods and services can be produced in other nations more cheaply than they can in Canada.

Sixth, the government predicts that 40 percent of the new jobs created from now until the year 2000 will require more than 16 years of schooling. If this is so, the nation must do a better job of retaining students, expand the numbers going on to postsecondary education, and increase its investment in education and training.

Finally, Litchfield claims, "If there is any doubt about the relationship between education and economic growth, U.S. studies have shown that, in the period from 1948 to 1982, GNP grew at an annual rate of 3.2 percent. Surprisingly, only 15 percent of the growth resulted from more capital equipment. Fully one-third of the gain came from the increased educational level of the U.S. workforce, and half the growth was from technological innovation and increased know-how" (Litchfield, 1991: 63).

Drawing on these seven points, human capital theory, supported by both liberals and functionalists, calls for a rethinking of Canada's national pedagogy in order to retain students and permit graduation with higher rates of literacy. It also calls for an expansion of investment in postsecondary education and an alignment of that system with business interests. The Porter report on Canada's position in the competitive economic world, for example, urges business to "take a more pro-active approach if they want educational institutions to produce employees with both the general and specialized skills required for competitiveness. Canadian business, like its counterparts in Germany and several other countries, should be providing more direct input into course development at universities, colleges and technical institutes" (Porter, 1991: 78).

Evidence Critical of Human Capital Theory

• • • • • • • •

All of the above discussion is from the functionalist perspective or reflects liberalism. What does a critical perspective have to say about the role of education in society? It seems unwise to be critical of human capital theory, since education is a good thing and more people should be encouraged to pursue it. However, critical theorists do raise some important questions about human capital theory. Their major criticism is that by focussing on investment in education, attention is shifted away from an analysis of the economy. Does it make sense to believe that a more educated work force, by itself, would transform the Canadian economy, or does Canada also need a fundamental change in the structure of its economy? Do Canadians also need to raise questions about the actual nature of jobs in society, about their ability to predict emerging jobs, and about the structures that support a highly skilled work force?

Central to human capital theory is the assumption that the future Canadian economy will require many more skilled workers than are now produced by the schools. Investing in the development of these skills as individuals or as a society is a way to foster economic growth. If this is thought to be an empirical claim about the future rather than simply a statement of the ideal, it is based on our ability to predict the future, and there is ample evidence that Canadians have not been very accurate in predicting their future labour needs. The deputy minister of employment and immigration conceded that "nobody does this really well."[5] He went on to say that even business, which invests in the economy, is unable to predict what will be required very far into the future. "It is anybody's guess what the status of the Big Three automakers is going to be in five years. So how can we predict how many tool-and-die makers we'll need?" No one is able to predict which jobs will be required this year, let alone five years from now. This was demonstrated by the realization that Canada was not training enough physiotherapists and occupational therapists to meet demand in 1992, so it encouraged the immigration of these skilled workers.

The Canadian Federation of Independent Business (1988) (using American data) claimed that the fastest rate of growth of emerging jobs is in areas requiring high skill. The ten occupations showing the fastest rate of growth are: paralegal personnel; medical assistants; physical therapists; physical and corrective therapy assistants; home health aides; podiatrists; computer systems technicians; and employment interviewers.

What the federation did not emphasize, however, was that all the new jobs created in these ten areas did not equal the number created in the one area showing the largest absolute growth: retail salespersons, which showed an increase of 1 200 000 jobs, compared with 777 000 in the previous ten areas. The ten jobs showing the largest absolute growth have a very different character: retail salespersons; waiters; registered nurses; janitors and cleaners; general managers and top executives; truck drivers; general office clerks; food counter workers; nursing aides, orderlies, and attendants. It is evident that the only job category above that promises high-status work — general managers and top executives — is quite small in absolute numbers.

Since 90 percent of the job growth in Canada since 1967 has been in the service sector, it is reasonable to assume that this will continue to be the source of the majority of employment. What is known about these jobs? Between 1981 and 1986, almost 50 percent of job growth was in what the Economic Council of Canada calls non-standard employment — part-time work, self-employment, short-term employment, and temporary-help agency work. The council acknowledges that this form of work may increase the economic insecurity of growing numbers of workers. It also acknowledges that virtually all the recent employment growth has involved either highly skilled, well-compensated and secure jobs, or unstable and relatively poorly paid jobs.

This change is confirmed by studies of wage rates. Between 1981 and 1986, the number of full-time equivalent jobs at the lowest wage rate increased by 275 000, while the increase at the high end was approximately 250 000 jobs (Picot et al., 1990). Kuttner (1983) warned Americans of this new development some time ago: "There is a good deal of evidence that job opportunities in the United States are polarizing, and that as a result, the country's future as a middle-class society is in jeopardy. ... As the economy shifts away from its traditional manufacturing base to high-technology and service industries, the share of jobs providing a middle-class standard of living is shrinking" (p. 60). More recently, Richard Barnett claimed that it was becoming increasingly difficult for all mature capitalist societies to provide good jobs for their citizens. Between 1979 and 1992, the Fortune 500 companies presented 4.4 million of their employees with pink slips (Barnett, 1993: 48).

While there is clearly more demand for high-skill and high-paid labour, the other side of this development must not be overlooked — increased polarization of the work force and a continued need for low-skill and low-paid labour. There are grounds for doubting that the labour market of the future can be accurately predicted, and it is not clear that there is a declining need for low-skilled workers. Labour demand is, of course, shaped by the structure of the economy. What parts of the economy might be expected to generate the demand for highly skilled labour and propel Canada into a high-technology future? One obvious candidate is research and development.

Canada spends less on research and development than do many other industrial economies and even some developing nations. The corporate sector is particularly ungenerous. There are many reasons for this, but the weakness of competition in Canada is an important contributing factor. Some of the characteristics of the economy that contribute to a lack of competition are the extent of foreign-ownership (foreign-owned companies generally spend less on research and development than do Canadian companies); the reliance on resources for which the market demands little value-added production (logs, coal, wheat, minerals); the concentration of capital in relatively few hands; and the presence of regional barriers to trade.

Many features of Canada's economy reduce expenditures on research and development. As a result, Canada had a trade deficit in the area of technology of $7 billion in 1987 alone. It imports significantly more technology than it exports. Canada's share of world exports of high-technology products was 2.6 percent in 1989, dramatically in contrast to the United States (19.7 percent), the European Community (37.6 percent) and Japan (17.65 percent) (Economic Council of Canada, 1989: 7).

Investment in machinery and equipment by the business community was lower in Canada than in most other industrialized nations between 1980 and 1989. It is not only human capital that Canada needs; financial capital is also in short supply. Investments made by Canadian firms in worker training also fall well short of the levels found in other advanced economies. As of 1988, Canada's private sector provided an average of seven hours of in-house training per worker, compared with 170 hours in Sweden and 200 hours in Japan.[6] An argument could be made perhaps that the Canadian business community has transferred the responsibility for educating and training workers to the government, with a resulting increase in government budgets and a growing fiscal crisis for governments. The result is a contradiction between claims made about the importance of education and the financial support being given to education.

At the same time that the government is calling for each citizen to consider his or her own investments in education, the budgets of universities are shrinking. Between 1980 and 1991, full-time enrolment at Canadian universities increased by 43 percent. During this decade, most universities were under extreme pressure to hold down their budgets or even to shrink them. University presidents warn that we are entering an age when only the wealthy need apply to university. Federal and provincial governments are reducing their expenditures on education and attempting to shift the financial burden to the student or to the other level of government. If student fees go up without a corresponding increase in financial assistance for needy students — and some argue they should rise steeply in order to bring a market mentality to the education system — universities will draw their clients from a narrower segment of society and accessibility will diminish even further.

Even if educational access were expanded, it is clear that just producing more university graduates will not address the structural problems of the Canadian economy. For example, 40 percent of Canadian workers claim that their job is not at all related to their education and 25 percent think they are overqualified for their jobs (Krahn,

1992: 16). It must be noted, and this is important, that Canada already has a higher proportion of adults with university degrees than all other OECD countries except the United States (Oderkirk, 1993: 9). Participation in higher education within and outside the university is also more common in Canada than in other OECD countries.

It is also relevant to look at emigration from Canada to the United States. Between 1910 and 1988, 3 062 970 Canadians moved to the United states while 1 601 665 Americans moved to Canada. For almost every decade since 1910, the number of Canadians moving across the border has surpassed the number of Americans. An examination of the Canadians moving shows that as a group they have much more education than those staying at home. In fact, as a group they have slightly more education than the American population (Statistics Canada, 1990b). It may well be, then, that Canada's well-trained and educated workers find employment opportunities greater in the United States; of those who emigrated since 1975, 55.8 percent were employed in skilled and specialized occupations in the United States. Is it education of the work force that is lacking, or is it jobs for educated workers?

This discussion can be concluded with a broader concern. The past decade has seen the globalization of capital and the development of an international market breaking down national markets. The move toward the free flow of capital and commercial goods and services has resulted in a deep restructuring of the economies of most countries. This restructuring has renewed Canada's interest in its labour force and encouraged the stress on "brains, not brawn" to resolve its economic crisis. Globalization, however, will challenge many other Canadian policies, including the regulation of the labour market itself.

If economies can have free flow of capital and goods, why not the free flow of labour? Government regulations now require that employers attempt to find qualified Canadians for job vacancies before they are permitted to hire workers from abroad. This is an attempt to create a national market for labour. There has been growing pressure for the government to moderate this policy. For example, professors in business and some areas of engineering are now exempted from this policy. The growing commitment to the market adopted by all western governments may well create pressure on government to remove regulations entirely to solve any labour shortages. If this were to happen, Canadians would find themselves competing against labour from many other countries. As has happened so often in the past, Canada may choose the option of immigration rather than investing in the training of its own citizens.

Critical perspectives, then, while not discouraging the pursuit of education, do not see the origin of the economic crisis in the undersupply of highly skilled workers, nor the solution as residing in increased expenditures on education and training. The problem is thought to be rooted in many structural features of the economy that reduce levels of technological development and the need for highly skilled workers.

THE COMMERCIALIZATION OF EDUCATION

What are the consequences for education and educational institutions if business is allowed to take control of the postsecondary curriculum in order to achieve the skilled workers required by the economy?

Critical sociologists express concern that following the ideas of human capital theory may push educational institutions, particularly postsecondary institutions, into partnership, real or implicit, with business. Students, the public, the corporate sector, and the institutions themselves may come to believe that education should have a commercial benefit. Students may think education should prepare them for employment; and the corporate world may think university research should have commercial application and that universities should provide trained workers ready for employment. The university may become a clear extension of the commercial basis and business values of the society.

This concern must be understood against a particular view of the place of the university in society. For many Canadians, the value of the university as an institution is its independence from many other areas of society. This independence makes possible the articulation of alternative views on issues of public concern, the development of knowledge for its own sake, and the expression and investigation of values other than those of efficiency. Central to this vision of the university is a pluralist conception of society in which there is space for dissent, variation, criticism, and competing values.

Given the dominance of the idea that education should help the society achieve economic goals, it would not be surprising to find the corporate sector prominent, particularly in postsecondary education. Axelrod (1982), in examining the establishment of new universities in Ontario in the 1960s, found tremendous support for such expansion among the business class but also found that they dominated the new boards (see Box 11.5). Another study of the boards of Ontario's universities in 1974 found that 500 different corporations and financial institutions were represented on the boards of governors. It was noted that 41 percent of board positions were held by members of the economic elite (Barkans and Pupo, 1974: 86).

Box 11.5
The First Board of
York University (1959)

The new board brought an impressive list of corporate associations to the fledgling institution: Robert Winters, chairman of Rio Tinto Mines, became the first chairman of the York board. Also appointed to the board in 1959 were: Allen Lambert, president of the Toronto-Dominion Bank; W.C. Harris, of Harris Partners; John D. Leitch, chairman of Maple Leaf Mills; William Pearson Scott, president of Wood Gundy (Securities); John S. Proctor, executive vice-president of the Bank of Nova Scotia; and Edwin H. Walker, president of General Motors of Canada. Other appointees included David B. Mansur, a financial consultant; Edgar Burton, chairman of the Robert Simpson Company; Mrs. John David Eaton, wife of the president of the T. Eaton Company; F.G. Gardiner, a lawyer and former chairman of the Metropolitan Toronto council; Bertrand Gerstein, president of People's Credit Jewellers; John M. Gray, chairman of Macmillan Company of Canada; J.William Horsey, chairman emeritus of Salada Foods; W.F. McLean, president of Canada Packers; L.G. Lumbers, president of Canada Wire and Cable Company; and A.J. Little, a partner in Clarkson Gordon, all of whom were appointed between 1960 and 1963. ...

Members of the board with links other than in the business community were: William Mahoney, vice-president of the Canadian Labour Congress and national director of the United Steel Workers of America; Senator (and banker) D'Arcy Leonard; Dr. R.F. Farquarson, chairman of the Medical Research Council; and Dr. W.F. James, a consulting geologist.

SOURCE: Excerpted from Paul Axelrod, *Scholars and Dollars: Politics, Economics, and the Universities of Ontario 1945–1980* (University of Toronto Press, 1982), pp. 66–67. Reprinted with permission.

These observations are confirmed historically. Many postsecondary institutions arose from the financing and encouragement of corporate executives. McMaster University, for example, owes its existence to the work and funds of William McMaster, founder and first president of the Canadian Bank of Commerce. Similarly, James McGill, a leading capitalist of his time, left a large endowment for the establishment of McGill University. The corporate sector was also able to shape the curriculum through capital and research grants. For example, William Macdonald (of the tobacco industry) supported various agricultural programs at McGill University, while Colonel A. Gooderham, a prominent distiller, provided funds for a department of zymology (the science of fermentation) at the University of Toronto.

The creation of the University of Waterloo is particularly interesting, since it reveals a large measure of co-operation between the university and the corporate sector. From its beginnings as a university, for example, Waterloo established a program of co-operative education whereby students spent alternating semesters in the classroom and the workplace. This necessitated the establishment of an advisory board of business and industry to comment on the university curriculum and to work with the university in placing and assessing students.

More recently, Simon Fraser University opened a downtown Vancouver campus, which was largely funded by private capital. Walking through the campus, one notices the names of corporate donors on classroom doors, lecture theatres, and other facilities. It seems reasonable that corporate values and interests will be apparent in the curriculum as well and that the private sector will have the ability to influence the development of the campus program.

This kind of relationship between the corporate world and the university is now common as universities find their budgets insufficient to meet operating costs. There has been an intensification of the linkages between the university and corporate sector. The president of the University of Manitoba said "we have to create bridges and relationships with industry."[7] Some of these bridges are apparent in new programs and centres developed for the university. An "associates program" allows corporations to contribute annual fees to the Faculty of Management as a way to "provide the business community with a means to support and encourage the faculty. Contributions were intended to be much more than financial." The Faculty of Management operates three centres: Centre for International Business Studies, Centre for Accounting Research and Education, and Centre for Entrepreneurship.

At the University of British Columbia, a number of new academic chairs were created in 1992 including landscape and liveable environment; food protection; food marketing; Alcan chair in materials processing engineering; Elizabeth Kenny McCann chair or professorship in nursing; Marianne Koerner chair in brain disease; Alcan chair in neuroscience; and fisheries oceanography. The university also created a new Centre of Entrepreneurship and Venture Capital Research.

The University of Waterloo has an office of technology transfer and licensing. The university now generates a substantial fund (about 1 percent of the annual budget) from royalties on scientific or technological inventions. About 20 private-sector firms owe their start to research begun at the university. These kinds of developments are happening across the country. In British Columbia ten companies in the field of biotechnology have been launched by University of British Columbia faculty. Does this strong attention to economic returns on intellectual resources further integrate the university into the business sector?

There is nothing inherently troubling about these developments, but it is important to see how the school and the university become integrated into the business

Box 11.6
Advertising in the
Classroom?

In 1992, Halifax became the focus of a debate that will eventually touch all schools. The largest school board in the province debated the advantages of introducing a classroom news service. This service would bring 12 minutes of television news into the classrooms of the district everyday. Some argued that while teenagers watched 24 hours of television a week, only 4 percent of them regularly watched news and current affairs shows. Perhaps schools had a role to play in shaping the viewing habits of young people and in educating them about world affairs.

There was another side: the 12 minutes of news programing would also include one-half minute of commercial advertising directed at the young audience. This advertising time would help offset the costs of the program service. The students in the classroom would become a captive audience for this advertising, and the school could now be seen to have a new role. It would take a step toward the commercialization of curricula material and bring the powerful consumer culture into the classroom. Rather than developing a critical spirit toward this culture, it would be presented as a legitimate part of most sectors of society.

SOURCE: Adapted from Stephen Godfrey, "Ads in Classroom Cause Furor," *The Globe and Mail*, December 24, 1992, p. A1.

concerns and needs of the society and into the society's specific needs (see also Box 11.6). Recall Michael Porter's advice to the business community that they must take a more pro-active approach if they want educational institutions to produce employees that meet their needs and they must have direct input into course development. There is ample evidence that this is happening.

This input clearly occurs through the funding of specific programs and projects, but it also occurs at a somewhat more subtle level: the integration of university governors and the business elite. It is illustrated in Box 11.5, and it continues to occur. Dr. David Strangway, president of the University of British Columbia, was elected to the board of directors of B.C. Gas Incorporated in 1992. In addition, he was a director of MacMillan Bloedel Limited, the Business Council of British Columbia, the Corporate Higher Education Forum, the Canadian International Institute for Sustainable Development, and Echo Bay Mines.[8]

The most obvious feature of human capital theory is that it focusses attention on individual educational attributes and consequently urges each person to judge their position in society in terms of these individual features. People may come to believe that they are well-off financially because they made an effective investment in education, while others are poor because they did not invest in knowledge and skill. In short, this theory minimizes the social (structural) constraints on mobility, life chances, and success. In this respect, human capital theory is consistent with liberal philosophy and its emphasis on the individual. At the societal level, human capital theory focusses on the supply of labour rather than on the structural characteristics of Canada's economy that limit competitiveness and undermine the development of high quality jobs.

CONCLUSION This chapter considered the role played by education in Canadian society. Considered from a functionalist or liberal perspective, education prepares young people to adopt future social roles in society. It is an important institution of socialization, passing on the culture of society and the knowledge and attitudes required to perform adult roles. It introduces students to the universalistic values of society by demanding that students be evaluated on the basis of their achievements and talents rather than their particular characteristics. This makes possible the selection of the most talented individuals for the most demanding positions in society.

A critical perspective, on the other hand, is sceptical of these claims. Rather than considering that education prepares young people for future social roles and identifying students on the basis of universalistic criteria, education is considered to sort students according to particular characteristics, such as class of origin, ethnic background, and sex. As an institution of socialization, it prepares students for roles of subordination and authority.

This view of education was supported by an examination of the location of the lower class and of women in the education system. Using the principle of correspondence, it was shown that the lower class does not have the same access to higher levels of education and that women tend to be located in institutions and programs that correspond to their subordinate position in the labour market. It was further shown that the hidden curriculum is as important as the overt curriculum of knowledge and skills. Students learn an ideology that allows them to understand and individualize their future positions of subordination.

The idea of human capital theory, a feature of the functionalist perspective and of liberalism, was also examined. First, evidence was considered to support the view that Canada's diminishing economic position in relation to that of other nations is in part an outcome of the nation's failure to develop an appropriate degree of skilled labour. Among other things, Canada does not retain students in postsecondary education to the same degree as do other countries, and it produces fewer scientists and engineers.

This view was challenged from a critical perspective by arguing that many of Canada's problems can better be understood in terms of the nature of its economy rather than the nature of its labour supply. Many workers, for example, think they are overqualified for their jobs; a large number of skilled workers emigrate to the United States; Canada spends less on research and development than do most other developed economies; there is a weakness in the investment of financial capital; and Canadian business invests less in training workers than do their counterparts in other countries.

Finally, the implications of human capital theory for the university were considered. If the logic of human capital theory is followed through, there would be a considerably greater integration of the university with the business sector of society, and business values would be given a much higher place in the university. This would reduce the degree of pluralism in Canadian society.

This chapter has considered an important institution for socializing young people. The next chapter continues this investigation with a consideration of the role of the family in modern society.

NOTES 1. Barry M. Sullivan, Commissioner, Royal Commission on Education, *A Legacy for Learners: Summary of Findings* (Victoria, BC: British Columbia Ministry of Education, 1988), pp. 13–14, 21–22. Reprinted with permission.

2. Satwant Kaur, "Dropout Rate High Among Black Students," *The Globe and Mail*, July 2, 1991, p. A10.

3. "Bonanza for Coke Chief," *The Globe and Mail*, March 20, 1992, p. B16.

4. Brenda Dalglish, "Are They Worth It?" *Maclean's*, May 9, 1994, p. 35.

5. Virginia Galt, "New Skills, But For What?" *The Globe and Mail*, January 11, 1992, p. A1.

6. R.D. Fullerton, CIBC Chairman, "Worth Repeating: When Is Canada Going to Catch Up?" *The Globe and Mail*, February 10, 1992, p. B6.

7. "University Enters the Big Leagues," *The Globe and Mail*, May 31, 1991, p. C5.

8. *The Globe and Mail*, May 22, 1991.

· · · · · · · · ·

FURTHER READING

· · · · · · · · ·

Gaskell, Jane, and Arlene McLaren. *Women and Education: A Canadian Perspective.* Calgary: Detselig Enterprises, 1987. This collection of essays provides good coverage of the many issues raised around women's role and participation in education.

Our Schools, Our Selves. A journal that provides many insights into contemporary issues involving education.

Reports such as John Calam and Thomas Fleming, *British Columbia Schools and Society*, British Columbia Royal Commission on Education, Commissioned Papers, vol. 1 (May 1988), are always interesting. Government reports of this kind provide a good reflection of the school from a functionalist or liberal perspective. See also the report on the New Brunswick education system, *Schools For A New Century* (1992). Saint John: Commission on Excellence in Education. A research report prepared for the Economic Council of Canada, *Education and Training in Canada* (1992), Ottawa: Minister of Supply and Services, is also very useful.

Newson, Janice, and H. Buchbinder. *The University Means Business: Universities, Corporations and Academic Work.* Toronto: Garamond Press, 1988. This short book provides a useful introduction to the growing connection between the university and the business world.

Noble, David. *A World Without Women: The Christian Clerical Culture of Western Science.* New York: Oxford University Press, 1992. A valuable account of the early contribution to education made by women and a detailed examination of the values, politics, and structures that led to their exclusion from the world of education and science.

· · · · · · · · ·

STUDY QUESTIONS

· · · · · · · · ·

1. Drawing on your own educational experience (or the observations of others), describe some experiences that could be considered evidence of the workings of a "hidden curriculum."

2. Outline the arguments both for and against human capital theory.

3. To what extent does the education system encourage people to see occupational success or failure in purely personal terms and deflect attention from social structure?

4. Is the experience of men and women in the education system the same or different? Interview classmates to gather some ideas. Prepare a brief report with illustrative examples.

5. Research your university or college to describe the proportion of men and women in various occupations. What do you think the consequences of this are? (Your institutions may have an equity committee or a report on this matter that will provide much information.)

6. Interview a recent immigrant to Canada to find out more about the experience of fitting into the school system.

12 FAMILY LIFE AND SOCIETY

· · · · · · · ·

INTRODUCTION
· · · · · · · ·

This chapter continues the investigation of the interconnectedness of the principal institutions of society. Although the family is the focus of this chapter, an enormous variety of family structures and value systems exist in Canadian society, and they cannot all be discussed. A sense of the variety of families is provided throughout the chapter, but the primary concern is to provide an analysis of the most common form of family system experienced during the life cycles of Canadians: the **conjugal family** of a couple and their children.

This chapter adopts a narrow interpretation of the word "family" to mean a set of social relationships in which children are reproduced (or adopted) and raised to maturity. It therefore does not discuss the life situation of couples without children, same-sex couples without children, or those living in extended kinship (complex) families or communal households. Some of the sources listed in the "Further Readings" at the end of the chapter will provide a fuller sense of variety in the family than is possible in this single chapter.

One of the most important changes that came with the rise of modern society was the transformation of family life. A new family form emerged: the conjugal family. This family system is founded on individual nuclear families of couples and their children. Its internal bonds are far more important than duties and obligation to extended kin. In other societies, and at other times, nuclear families lack this inward focus and have strong ties to extended kin and the community. They are then not conjugal, but form part of **consanguineal family** systems, which are still the most common form in the world.

Consanguineal and conjugal families can be thought of as ideal types that differ in composition, functions, and central values. The conjugal family first arises in

Europe in the form of a **bourgeois family**. The family lives separately from its extended kin and has bonds of sentiment rather than strict duties and obligations. Stress is placed on the development of private family life and on "modern" values of individualism and love. This family is also characterized by a rigid sexual division of labour. It is rare for wives and mothers to work outside the home; wage earning is done by men who monopolize the public domain of work and political life.

The bourgeois family form was replaced by a new type of modern family, which values equality between partners. It is one in which both partners often work outside the home. Because of the decline in women's dependence on men, there has been a rise in divorce rates, and many men abandon their financial and emotional responsibilities to their families. The increased participation of women in the labour force is associated with a continuing decline in fertility rates and a general narrowing of family functions.

Social theorists offer differing interpretations of the changes that have transformed families and offer contrasting prescriptions for trying to shape family life. Conservatives seek a return to the bourgeois family, with its rigid division of labour and its focus on domesticity, love, and security.

Functionalists see the modern conjugal family as a necessary and constructive adaptation to the needs of contemporary society. Critical theorists tend to view it as an adaptation to the demands of a patriarchal society and a capitalist economy. They link families to the reproduction of patriarchy and class domination. Critical theorists also focus on the situation of women and identify a set of social and personal problems arising from the structure and values of the conjugal family.

• • • • • • • •

Families, say sociologists, are the bridge between the individual and society. They first make visible to the infant the values and organization of a world outside themselves. They physically reproduce society through the birth and nurturing of children, and they socially reproduce society through the transmission of culture and the preparation of children for roles in the social structure.

It might be possible, like Aldous Huxley did in *Brave New World*, to *imagine* a society that maintains itself without the family — a society in which embryos are conceived in laboratory dishes, the fetus grows in an artificial womb, and children are raised in institutions. But in all societies in human history, so far, it is in families that the great majority of children are born, raised, and socialized. It is in families that almost all individuals first encounter society and have their formative emotional and psychological experiences.

Families are formed by groups of individuals linked by **kinship**. Kinship is formed by bonds of blood relationship (child/parent, brother/sister, etc.) or by **affinal relationship** established by law or custom (wife/husband, son-in-law/mother-in-law, etc.)

DEFINING FAMILIES

• • • • • • • •

Family relationships, though they occur in all societies, vary so much that there seems to be no way to give a standard definition of "family" that would apply everywhere. What sorts of links bring "family" into being? Is it formed when two people get married? Or when people live together in a relationship that includes sexual intimacy? Or do couples only become "families" after children are born or adopted? Must a couple be of opposite sex to make up a "family"? What other relatives should we include as part of someone's family?

This chapter treats family relationships as including the roles of reproduction (or adoption), care, and primary socialization of children. In doing this we follow the sociological tradition of thinking of a family as an institution that physically, through

Photo 12.1

The modern family in Canadian society values equality between partners, in principle. Women, who may have stayed home to raise their children in the past, are now working. Conversely, men are taking a more active role in raising their children.

· · · · · · · ·

Dan Bosler / TONY STONE IMAGES

the birth (or adoption) of children, and culturally, through socialization, reproduces society itself.

Families not only introduce children to cultural values and the preliminary experience of social structure, they also deeply shape an individual's personality. Will people be individualistic and ambitious, or closely bonded to family and community? Will people be carefully self-controlled, or will they be spontaneous and open? Will they be aggressive or peace-loving? Will men and women have a similar social identity, or will they be seen as very different? The answers depend on the individual's experience in family relationships, and these, in turn, are shaped by the surrounding society.

Two main themes are stressed in this book: the importance of looking at society as a connected whole, and the comprehensive effects on society of the rise of modern capitalism. Now that the family is in focus it is relevant to ask, how did the comprehensive changes that emerged with modern society transform family life? How are the characteristics of modern family life linked to the culture and social structure of modern society? To answer the questions, it is useful to know how family life can be differently experienced. The discussion begins by looking at the traditional Chinese family as a radically different model of family life.

THE CONSANGUINEAL FAMILY IN CHINA

· · · · · · · ·

Composition

· · · · · · · ·

The European family system, the most common in Canada, is based on **bilineal descent**. This means that in principle, one's relatives through both one's father and mother are of equal importance. In contrast, the traditional family in China is **patrilineal** — founded exclusively on the blood-linked descent of males. Cultural ideas hold that a family consists of all a man's male ancestors and descendants. Females are attached to the family only as the wives, mothers, daughters, and sisters of the male members. Women's central role is to provide men with the sons that will continue the male lineage.

A male is born into his family in a household that might consist of up to five generations of male relatives. He moves through his whole life cycle — son, husband, father, grandfather, great grandfather — within one family and, often, one household. Men bring their wives into the household. A female, in contrast, is destined to a life cycle that takes her out of her father's household when she marries and into another family and household. Her role as a wife is to perpetuate her husband's family by having sons. Having sons will also raise her status. Land ownership passes from fathers to sons: daughters have no right of inheritance, except items of their mother's personal property. If there are no sons, the family will try to adopt a closely related male. Sometimes a daughter's husband will move into the household, and the couple's first son will bear the daughter's family name and descent.

Roles

Family **roles** are inclusive and encompass all tasks associated with child care, maintaining a household, and producing goods and food for household use. The family is a unit of economic production founded on the land. Gender roles vary: in some communities, women work on the land; in others, they work gardens and produce a range of goods. It is not considered appropriate for males to be involved in the running of the household or the care of children.

Values

The supreme duty of a Chinese male is to protect and preserve his patrilineage. Marriage is essential to secure heirs in order to continue his family, but, since duty to the patrilineage comes first, marriage is not decided by individual attraction and emotion. Instead, marriage is arranged by the parents and the couple are not expected to have any great fondness for each other, or even to have met. If it is suspected that affection between an engaged couple has grown too strong, a male's family may abandon the marriage arrangement. Too much intensity of emotion between the couple may undermine the commitment to patrilineal kin.

A woman fulfils her duty to her father's family by marrying out of the household and gains a bride price for her parents. The bride price is an important matter in settling the marriage agreement. The bride's parents will find themselves needing to pay a bride price when her brother marries. When a woman is married, she ceases to be a member of her family of origin: she passes on forever to the family of her husband. Her father slams the door behind her as she departs and pours water on the ground. This symbolizes that she, like the water absorbed into the ground, can never return to her father's house. This is often literally true.

The cultural belief in the importance of family continuity, and the belief that this can be achieved only through males, is associated with a **patriarchal** system. Males are dominant in authority, and women are valued as instruments for the achievement of male goals. However, the status hierarchy between the sexes is not all one way, since age and generation are a source of prestige. Grandfather (or great grandfather) has the highest status because of sex, age and generation, but grandmother, because of age and generation, is due deep respect from father and his generation. A woman is at the low point of her status as a daughter and then as a new wife. Once she has children, especially sons, her status in her husband's family rises and she has more respect and co-operation from her mother-in-law and father-in-law.

In summary, we see that China founded its family system around the principle of the continuity of male lines and respect for elders. The all-inclusive roles of the family unit made family life absolutely central to individual existence. Hugh Baker provides a clear sense of the gulf between Chinese and western ideas of family:

It is perhaps not unreasonable to say that in the West we see the family as an institution which exists in large part to provide an environment in which the individual can be conveniently raised and trained to go out into the world as a full member of society. An indication of the validity of this notion is the break-up of the family when the children reach adulthood. But the emphasis in the traditional Chinese situation was reversed — it was not the family which existed in order to support the individual, but rather the individual who existed in order to continue the family (Baker, 1979: 26).

Links to Wider Society
· · · · · · · ·

The traditional Chinese family is well integrated with the society's economic system. It is generally land-based and almost self-sufficient. Land is transmitted through the generations of male descendants. Since the land lies at the foundation of family life, the descent system, through which access to land is gained, is carefully guarded and protected. This is accomplished through a system of arranged marriages and the separation of women from social association and obligation to their families of origin. In this way the Chinese family is connected to the perpetuation of the values and structure of Chinese society.

The system described above was the cultural ideal for traditional Chinese family life; only a minority of families actually maintained all these characteristics. However, the model — now much transformed by China's exposure to communism and economic modernization — does provide a clear contrast to the families of western society.

CANADIAN FAMILIES
· · · · · · · ·

There is no standard "western" or "Canadian" family. In Canada and other multicultural modern societies, families include an enormous variety of structures and values. There are Canadian families of Chinese origin that retain some similarity to the type described above, and many other families reflect cultural ideals from all parts of the world.

First Nations peoples have varied concepts of family. Some First Nations families are **matrilineal**, where blood relationships through females are most important and children are members of their mother's lineage. In these systems, men have important duties to their sisters' children because it is through them, and not their own children, that their family will be continued. Often, the responsibilities of men as uncles of children are more strictly defined than their roles as fathers. Women, in matrilineal society, usually occupy much higher status than they do in patrilineal systems. They perpetuate family lineage and have an ambiguous relationship to men: bonds of duty and obligation to brothers may be stronger than to husbands. Traditional economic and social roles of men and women are often similar, and there can be marked equality between the sexes. Other First Nations cultures maintain patrilineal descent, stressing the link of respect and obligation between father and son. The status of women is often distinctly lower than that of men. Yet other cultures follow bilineal descent, where paternal and maternal lineage is equally important. Women's status is close to that of men in some of these societies (Leacock, 1977).

Families vary not only in descent patterns, but also in composition. There are multigeneration consanguineal families, conjugal families, homosexual couples with children, single parents, blended families. And in any society family life is varied by a unique blending of cultural patterns and personal interpretations of family life and values. However, it remains true that most Canadians are born into a household that consists, most of the time, of their parents and their siblings. They are most likely to get married (or live common-law) and themselves have children in a conjugal family like the one they were born in.

The Conjugal Family

Composition

In 1986, only two in every 100 Canadian children lived in households that did *not* include at least one parent, and 85 of every 100 children lived with both parents (Statistics Canada, 1990a: 15–16). It is quite common that the parents are not married. In 1977, 11 percent of children were born to unmarried parents; in 1990 the proportion was 23 percent. In Quebec in 1990, 48 percent of all children were born to unmarried parents (Dumas and Perron, 1992). Many couples do become married *after* a child is born, however, so only about one in twelve Canadian children has never-married parents. Another one-in-twelve children lives with a separated or divorced single parent (Dumas and Perron, 1992: 16–17). Figures 12.1 and 12.2 give a sense of the life path of Canadians in their relationship to family.

The composition of the conjugal family is very simple: two adults marry (or live common-law) and have (or adopt) children. The household is composed of the adults and the children. When the children reach maturity they move out of the household and, in most cases, marry (or live common-law) and have children, thus establishing their own conjugal family. The original couple now live in a household alone and generally maintain that structure until the death of one partner. At this point, the remaining partner will usually live out his or her life residing alone, with relatives or with non-relatives. Fewer than 4 percent of Canadian family households have an

Figure 12.1
Life Patterns of Canadian Men

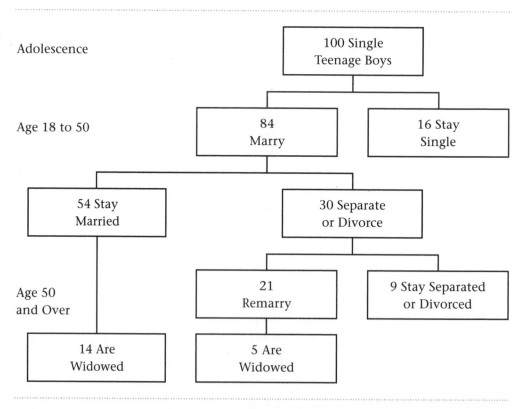

SOURCE: *Women and Poverty Revisited* (Ottawa: National Council of Welfare, 1990), p. 134. Reprinted with permission.

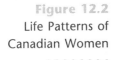

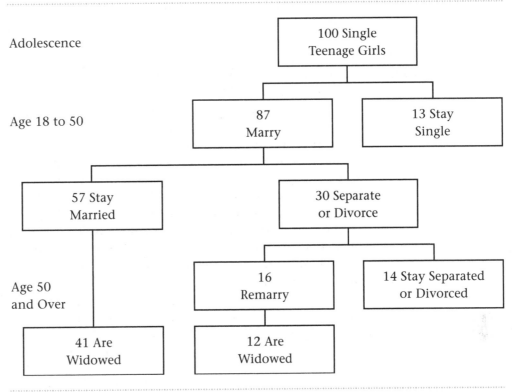

Figure 12.2

Life Patterns of Canadian Women

Adolescence — 100 Single Teenage Girls

Age 18 to 50 — 87 Marry / 13 Stay Single

57 Stay Married / 30 Separate or Divorce

Age 50 and Over

16 Remarry / 14 Stay Separated or Divorced

41 Are Widowed / 12 Are Widowed

SOURCE: *Women and Poverty Revisited* (Ottawa: National Council of Welfare, 1990), p. 16. Reprinted with permission.

elderly family member living with them: as is indicated in Table 12.1, the generationally extended family is rare (Vanier Institute of the Family, 1994: 33). Meanwhile the grandchildren have matured, moved out of the house, and started their own families. The cycle then moves onward.

This structure encompasses only two generations. During the middle third of the life cycle, most individuals are members of *two* nuclear families. One is composed of them, their siblings, and their parents (their **family of origin** or orientation); the other consists of them, their adult partner, and their children (their **family of procreation**).

Table 12.1

Living Arrangements of Canadians 65 Years and Over, 1991

	Men	Women
*With family**	80.7%	55.7%
With relative	1.8%	4.4%
With non-relatives	2.3%	1.8%
Alone	15.2%	38.1%

*Includes just a spouse.

SOURCE: *Families: Number, Type and Structure*, cat. no. 93-312 (Ottawa: Statistics Canada, 1993). Reproduced by authority of the Minister of Industry, 1994.

Roles

....

Family roles in the conjugal family are much narrower than they are in consanguineal families. Families have experienced what functionalists call **structural differentiation** — a process by which families narrow their previous roles and pass them over to other institutions. For example, until the nineteenth century only a minority of children were formally educated. Children learned from their family and from living and working in the community. Family and friends helped women deliver their babies, treated and cared for the sick, and aided the elderly. Families also worked together at trades, or on the land: they were units of production in which everyone had a job. The young often depended on their parents for somewhere to live after marriage and for access to land and equipment. The old depended on the young for economic support and security.

Today, families share all these functions with outside institutions. To get a job and provide for themselves economically, most people compete for employment in the labour market. Only a few, whose families own land or run stores or businesses, find their economic roles through the family. In old age they rely for economic security on personal savings, pensions, and assets. State-run social programs guarantee a minimum standard of life.

Gender roles in the family have also changed over time. In the 1950s and even the early 1960s, sociologists still depicted the modern family in its classic bourgeois form, organized around gender roles. Women, if they were engaged in paid employment before marriage, gave it up when children were born and focussed on child raising and homemaking. In the early 1960s, only one in ten first-time mothers continued their employment after their baby was born (Marcil-Gratton, 1988). Men worked outside the home, provided the family income, and, generally speaking, participated minimally in household chores and child care. The economic dominance of the father in the household was accompanied by a stress on father as the dominant authority, the person who dealt with the outer world and had the last word in the family.

In the 1990s less than a third of all husband-and-wife households (and only 8 percent of all households) have this sort of role division (see Table 12.2). Today, less than half of first-time mothers stop work when their child is born (Marcil-Gratton, 1988). Full-time mothering has become much less common because women's wages have become crucial to the family economy.

Values

....

The special characteristic of family life in the West (now spreading globally) is that conjugal families are broken up as each generation matures and moves away from the natal household. Families are not usually joined into economic and social units of extended kin. Each nuclear unit resides separately, is individually responsible for economic and social decisions, and is emotionally focussed inwardly.

There has been a distinct move toward equality between partners in conjugal relationships. Modern ideas, if not always practices, uphold the equality of partners in

Table 12.2

Employment Status of Husbands and Wives in Husband–Wife Families, 1991*

....

Husband only works	24.5%
Wife only works	4.0%
Both partners work	68.8%

*Figures exclude families where neither partner works.

SOURCE: *1991 Census: Families*, cat. no. 93-320 (Ottawa: Statistics Canada, 1993). Reproduced by authority of the Minister of Industry, 1994.

adult relationships. This is a marked change from the past, where the final authority of the male in the household was culturally assumed and was upheld by law and religion. In Canadian society inequality remains, but there has been a major movement toward the cultural values of gender equality. These value changes are consistently revealed in polling data. In 1954, for example, only 49 percent of Canadian men were supportive of women receiving equal pay for equal work; by 1970, 86 percent supported the principle (Boyd, 1984: 78–79).

The whole idea of arranged marriage and extensive kinship responsibility is foreign to the modern family system. Conjugal families are about intimacy, privacy, and personal emotional satisfaction. They are constructed on the foundation of individualism. Canadians decide to marry, or live with someone conjugally, because they experience intense feelings of erotic and emotional involvement: love. They look for a deeply shared relationship with their partner that they expect to provide satisfaction and security. Canadians decide to have children for similar individualistic reasons. Children are not about continuing the family name and lineage, or about social status. They are not a source of labour or security in old age. They are wanted for the emotional satisfaction they are thought to bring to their parents and other family members. The goal is personal fulfilment through the experience of commitment and love.

The individualistic focus of modern families is also expressed in value patterns that uphold relatively democratic authority. The status differences between the generations, between children and their parents, and between couples have been eroded. Changes in the last 40 years in the way children are taught in elementary schools, with a growing stress on child-centred learning, is testimony to the entirely new view of children that has taken root in modern society.

To sum up: the family today is an emotional unit, not an economic unit or social alliance. Westerners truly do, as Hugh Baker expressed in his contrast with Chinese culture, see the family as existing for the satisfaction and comfort of the individual, whereas other societies and other times have seen the family as a collective unit above the interests of individuals.

Family and Society

. . . .

The conjugal family emerged with the growth of urbanized, industrial societies, and its characteristics are shaped by that context. These societies are fast changing. There is continuous, and often rapid, rural to urban migration. Job opportunities and employment are mobile and people move frequently. In Canada, for example, households, on average, move every five years. This rapid social change and geographical mobility is not easily compatible with the complex ties of duty and obligation in consanguineal families. But conjugal families, with their compact membership and inward focus, can move easily and operate successfully in an individualistic society. Ties of affection and support are usually maintained with a limited range of close kin, but they are no longer culturally obligatory or woven into everyday life. It is easy to see how an extended family system can be placed under stress by these conditions. Extended household composition can undermine geographical mobility; extensive role demands conflict with individual participation in a competitive occupational system; values of collectivity conflict with the individualism promoted by modern cultural ideas (Parsons, 1964).

The idea that the growth of modern economies demands special characteristics in the culture and structure of family systems is a basic claim of modernization theory. The theory argues, following functionalist assumptions, that societies need to have harmony between their component parts. A culture that stresses extensive family and kinship obligations is at odds with an economy based on private enterprise and individual initiative. Wherever economic modernization takes place there is an accompanying move of consanguineal family systems towards the conjugal pattern found in already modernized western societies (Goode, 1963).

The claim that there is a general trend in this direction has been generally accepted in sociology, but it has been criticized as an over-simplification of the link between family change and economic modernization. There are societies in which traditional family systems have persisted in the presence of considerable economic modernization. In Japan, for example, economic development was achieved without a major disruption of the consanguineal family system. But Japan does now seem to be moving in the direction of something more like the family pattern of Canadians. For example, fertility rates are falling drastically. Japan has now joined most western societies in having a fertility rate lower than that needed to maintain population. Japanese divorce rates also exhibit a rising trend, coming closer to that of Canada (Eichler, 1988: 57), suggesting a lessening of the strong cultural focus on family obligations and responsibility. However, births to unmarried parents remain uncommon.

A link between change in family systems and social change is also suggested by observing the experience of non-western family systems in western societies. Canada provides a rich source of material for examining how varied family systems are influenced towards the conjugal model. The individualistic culture and social structure of the outer society often erodes consanguineal family solidarity over time. While some families will sustain authority and cultural practice for several generations, others will shed customs in a few years.

Of course, each family experience is unique in the blending of aspects of tradition and new cultural experiences and expectations. The interview in Box 12.1 gives a rich sense of this process from the perspective of two Indo-Canadian mothers. It portrays the complex blend of old and new as people resist the individualistic culture of the West.

Using a broad brush, this chapter has shown that consanguineal families, with joint property and complex obligations, are the usual foundation of non-western societies. Western societies, and those undergoing rapid economic development, develop a family system (the conjugal family) that is based not on complex ties and obligations but on the individualistic foundations of love and emotion. This individualistic foundation of the family system seems to be strongly related to the culture and social structure of the outer society.

All sociologists agree that family systems and society are deeply connected, but this is where agreement ends. The analysis of family life in modern society offered by critical perspectives is radically different from that offered by functionalists. We now explore this debate.

THE MODERN FAMILY

A Functionalist Perspective

A functionalist perspective, as demonstrated by modernization theory, views society as a system of interdependent parts constantly interacting and balancing. The family is not immune to social changes in the wider society, so it must undergo changes in values and structure to accommodate new cultural ideas and new roles.

The leading features of western society are social change, social mobility, and an individualistic ethic drawn from liberalism. In principle, access to economic opportunity is open to all through largely free education, a competitive labour market, and equal legal status for all citizens. Industrial development and the growth of extensive markets, nationally and internationally, have broken down the localized family-based

Box 12.1
A Portrait of Indo-
Canadian Families

This interview was conducted with two Indo-Canadian mothers. Amarjit was born in Kenya and has lived in Canada since 1973. Her household consists of her, her husband, three sons (8, 13, and 16) and two children of her brother-in-law.

Pammi was born in India, moved to England when she was nine, and, five years later, moved to Canada, where she has lived since 1980. She lives with her husband and two children (two years and six months).

What does family mean to you, Amarjit?
AMARJIT: Family for me would be my mother-in-law, my father-in-law, my husband, my children, my husband's brothers, and their children.
If they were all here, would they live together?
AMARJIT: Quite probably. Certainly, my husband's brothers and my parents-in-law would be living with us.
So the larger family is very important to you?
AMARJIT: Yes, it's fairly important. Whether the family lives all together or not, grandparents tend to have a very significant influence. Even though my in-laws live thousands of miles away, they have a great say in how we run our household in Victoria.
Is it the same in your family, Pammi?
PAMMI: Oh no, it is quite different. Even though family is very important to us, it doesn't have the same kind of importance when it comes to our household decisions.
Where do you think the difference between you and Amarjit comes from?
PAMMI: Personal values.
AMARJIT: Also I am a little bit older than Pammi, just a little. But there is maybe a ten or fifteen year gap, and things change a lot in fifteen years. And Pammi and her husband both came to Canada when they were both quite young. So they got a lot of their values from the Canadian society.

I'm sure that if Pammi's husband had come quite recently from India it would be different. His family responsibility would be quite similar to my husband's. Education also plays a large part, how educated your parents and grandparents were, and whether your marriage was arranged.
You mentioned arranged marriages. How does that work? Do you mind talking about that?
AMARJIT: No. My marriage was arranged and it's worked out quite well. I don't have anything to compare it with. But I am fairly happy.
How did the arranging take place?
AMARJIT: There is always a go-between. In my case my husband lived in Canada and his sister, who lived in England, had known my parents for years. She told my parents that her brother was living in Canada and asked them if they would like to meet with him to consider arranging a marriage with me. Then my parents asked me if I was ready to get married or if I wanted to study further. That was my choice, but I wanted to get married at that point. And then they met my husband and they did a good check on him. (*Laughter*). In arranged marriages
(continued)

. . . .

(continued)

a very thorough check is done that goes back generations. Then we were allowed to meet each other.

It's not the kind of thing where people are just thrown together without knowing anything about one another.

PAMMI: There's been quite an evolution from not even knowing about your spouse to actually going out and getting to know one another to a certain extent.

Then you have the right to say, "Yes, I think you made a good choice," or "No, I don't want to marry this person."

PAMMI: I think most parents these days would give their child the final say.

How do you view children in the family? Where do they fit?

AMARJIT: The way that I have been taught is that kids are so important that parents actually live through their children, in the sense that what your children do when they grow up is how the parents are judged in the community. They are that important. I am going to be measured by how my children fit into society in the coming generation. This is why it is believed that you must have children, because if you don't you really cease to exist.

Is that still a major value for you, Pammi?

PAMMI: No, I don't really see myself living through my children. Almost every day I wonder if I am acting toward my children as my parents acted toward me. If I am, I try to avoid it. I'm trying not to have any expectations of my children, except that they become good citizens of the society.

Do you think Indian parents are very strict?

AMARJIT: I think that it is traditional that you give your children a lot of independence when they are younger. It seems the opposite is true in Canadian culture. What I see here is that children are very restricted when they are younger until they are 13 or 14, then they are allowed to make their own decisions. In Indian society you let children have a great deal of freedom until they are ready to become adults. Then you set down your guidelines and rules when they are in their teens.

PAMMI: Actually, by the time you are 16 or so you should know what is expected of you.

AMARJIT: Also, your parents keep telling you, "Now you are older, you have to act in a certain way." So it becomes quite controlling by the time you are 15 or 16. Girls get it more than boys, but certainly the expectations are strong. I am sure I am doing the same thing, perhaps not to the extent my parents did, but I know I am doing it.

PAMMI: What I see in families that have immigrated to Canada are parents who assume the child knows how they expect the child to behave, and children who don't really know *what* the parents expect. The children have learned all these new ways of thinking and they have no idea what is inside their parents' heads because they haven't discussed it. That is where I see the conflict arising.

How about work? When should kids find out about work?

PAMMI: Traditionally you go to school and find a career and start working.

(continued)

(continued)
At what age would that be?
PAMMI: After you've done your university. Up until then your parents would not ask you to move out and start working. Nowadays it is the kids who want to move out. Boys are never asked to leave the house. Girls move out when they get married.
Would a child ever be expected to support himself or herself through university?
AMARJIT: No. Even if he works, that money would go to his own personal expenses. In India he would not even buy his own car or clothes. If the family were affluent they would buy him a car. If they were not so affluent they would buy him a bike. Everything comes from the parents until the child is ready to get married. Then, once the parents retire, it is the children who support the parents.
You said until they are ready to get married. Is marriage, then, the point at which children become responsible for themselves?
AMARJIT: Traditionally, when a son came out of university and was ready to start working, that was the time the parents started looking for a girl for him.
PAMMI: No time was wasted. *(Laughter).*
Do you think your children face barriers because they are not white Canadians?
PAMMI: I worry when I hear about the evils of society. Growing up in such a secure family, I have not had to face it. But I worry that my children will be vulnerable to so much these days. My main concern is that they will be protected from that somehow.
AMARJIT: I think they do face barriers because they have a different ethnic background, but I think that something my children do have is that they still belong to a community where family is still important, and they are telling me that now. And I think that is the barrier facing western society, the diminishing of family and the value of family.

SOURCE: Adapted from Joseph Schaeffer and Jim Holland, "Parental Wisdom from the East," *Island Parent Magazine* (December 1992): 14, 15, 16, 18. Reprinted with permission of *Island Parent Magazine*.

economies of the past. The family is no longer a unit of self-sufficient economic production. It is, instead, a unit of consumption. In the absence of a family economy, family ties become less obligatory: the young do not rely on the old for access to land and property; the old do not rely on the young for care and support. Weakened obligations to extended kin are functionally necessary to support geographical mobility and social mobility.

According to functionalist theory, the conjugal family offers a new system of family life that complements the demands of modern society. The ties of family are focussed inward on the self-contained unit of the couple and their children. The family is compact and mobile, and because only two generations are normally present in the household it is more suited to the rapid generational changes in knowledge, skills, and cultural ideas that are inevitable in modern society. Tradition does not hold people back from involvement in the modern world.

Some functionalist discussions of the conjugal family make the value claim that this family form is positive and progressive. Functionalist sociologist Talcott Parsons, for example, argued that a family worked better by concentrating on child raising and emotional intimacy, rather than spreading its energy over many roles. He assumed that more *specialized* social institutions fulfil a particular role more effectively than those that are all-encompassing. For example, when the family ceases to be a unit of production there is more time to focus on private life. Greater intimacy can be developed within the family. There is more time for care and play with children, more time to devote to careful socialization, and more time for the emotional closeness of the couple.

In the 1950s and 1960s, functionalists tended to assume that the most balanced form of family life (and a functionally ideal one for modern society) was a conjugal family with two heterosexual adult partners. The male partner was the sole wage earner and women did not work for significant lengths of time outside the home. Talcott Parsons claimed that modern families must satisfy two sets of functional needs. There are instrumental requirements that include generating the family income and making major economic decisions. And there are affective requirements that centre on emotional matters like caring for children and the emotional satisfaction of adults. Male and female partners both perform roles within each area, but there is gender specialization. Men are the instrumental leaders, and women the emotional leaders (Parsons and Bales, 1955).

The family was now focussed on two tasks that it was uniquely equipped to carry out: the socialization of children and the emotional support of adults. These tasks could be carried out undistracted by the multiplicity of roles that were once part of the family's activities. Most of all this new family system was positive because it provided the *individual* with love, freedom, and equality (Goode, 1963).

The assumption behind this functionalist view of the western family is that a particular type of family life is best for modern society and for individuals. This family is one that could only develop for the mass of people with the enormously increasing wealth of western capitalist societies. It arrives first in the aristocratic and upper-class families of the wealthy, but from the sixteenth and seventeenth centuries it gradually becomes a pattern that can be afforded by the growing middle class and, increasingly, in the nineteenth century, by the working class. This family has been appropriately labelled the bourgeois family, an ideal middle-class family. Women, once married, stayed home to provide housework and have children. Men worked for wages outside the home. For the middle class and well-paid working class, the home could now provide comfort and good food, moral values, early education, care, and security (Berger and Berger, 1983: 99).

The Decline of the Bourgeois Family

The principal difference between today's conjugal family and the bourgeois family is in the structure of gender roles. Although rigid role division around paid employment was apparent into the 1950s and 1960s, only 30 percent of all husband-and-wife families have such a structure today. But another gender division does persist — women continue to do most of the household and family work.

Some estimates put the additional housework and child-care work of women over men at up to 24 hours per week even among couples in which both are employed full time (National Council of Welfare, 1990: 52). A 1990 survey revealed that in 72 percent of families in which both partners work full-time, women assumed primary responsibility for meal preparation (and in 74 percent of families they also assumed responsibility for cleaning and laundry). In 86 percent of families in which the wife worked part-time, women assumed primary responsibility for meal preparation, and in 89 percent of families in which only the husband worked (Marshall, 1993: 25). Sharing tasks tends to be most common among younger, well-educated couples with fewer children. Discussions of modern families often use the term "double burden" to describe the situation of employed women: they now have outside jobs in addition to the job of family and household maintenance.

A modern functionalist view of this new family system stresses the positive features of the modern family. The conjugal family of the 1990s is said to represent an advance from the past: women now have increased opportunity and status as a result of their much more central role in the paid economy. Housework has been transformed by vacuum cleaners, modern floor finishings, washing machines, non-iron textiles, and new methods of providing for the needs of the household (i.e., buying goods and services).

Children are usually cared for by day-care services and schools, which make it possible for both adults to pursue an employment career. Family time is less about practical functions and more about togetherness, support, and the encouragement of self-development. High rates of divorce (and the ending of living-together arrangements) are an inevitable consequence of high cultural expectations of personal satisfaction from family and married life. They do not indicate that family life has been weakened, only that personal expectations are higher.

People have gained greater opportunities for personal fulfilment. Women may not yet enjoy equality in society with men, but there is a clear trend toward it. Womens' employment has promoted the equality of the sexes, and the refocussing of family roles has made it possible to retain much of the richness of bourgeois family life. This optimistic viewpoint has been greeted with a number of counter arguments, which now follow.

Conservatives and the Family

Marxism and feminism both offer critical perspectives on modern family life; but there is also a conservative viewpoint, which offers very different assumptions.

Conservatives agree in seeking a strengthening of the role of the family in individual life. They seek a family in which the individual is securely enveloped and where there is discipline and respect as well as love and affection. They hold the view that the middle-class family that spread to all classes during and after the nineteenth century remains the ideal for family life.

Conservative ideas influenced sociologists like Comte, Tonnies, and Durkheim, who all agreed that modern capitalist society weakened the family. (What they considered the "weak family" of their day modern writers now see as strong. This is a useful reminder of the limits to objectivity in sociology.) Durkheim, for example, argued that family bonds are a significant anchor for individuals, giving them a sense of belonging, of responsibility, and of moral regulation. Where family bonds are weak, individuals became anomic and egoistic. Family bonds protect individuals against suicide, Durkheim claimed, but he added that easy divorce reduces the protective strength of the family (Durkheim, 1951[1897]: 259–276). If the conjugal family is easily dissolved, its effectiveness as a system of moral regulation and social integration is weakened. Individuals need an emotional commitment to clear values and can gain this only from discipline and structure in combination with love and nurturing.

Historian Christopher Lasch (1977) echoed this attitude in a discussion that added psychological analysis. He argued that moral regulation must be deeply implanted, because modern societies have uncertain normative orders and weak external social regulation. Deep internalization of the moral order demands that the child love, as well as obey, its caregiver and socializer. Lasch was strongly committed to the idea of two-parent families, most crucially for males, and considered the presence of a father as necessary for balanced ego development and maturity.

The conservative critics of past and present argue that modern individualism and the loss of family functions and roles to other institutions dilutes family life experience. Individuals do not develop intense psychic roots in their families; they lack the deep experience of the trusts and fears, the love and anger, the commitment and security that comes from developing within a circle of intensely personal relationships.

At the foundation of these views is the assumption that a *real* family needs to have a full-time parent in the home. This bias is strenuously attacked by critical perspectives that see the relegation of women to the private world of the family and the domestic sphere as the foundation of gender inequality and the disempowerment of women.

Critical Perspectives: Marxism and Feminism

Radical critics of modern family life do not share the nostalgia of the conservatives. The most central criticism is that conservative views gloss over the effects of strongly institutionalized family life on women. Where are women in a society in which households are dependent on a male breadwinner? Advocates of the bourgeois family acknowledge that women were centred in the private realm of the home, but dismiss the idea that this diminished their status and sense of worth. In the past, they suggest, women's status was enhanced by their withdrawal from the outside work world.

A few decades ago, there *was* a dominant social attitude that it was unfortunate for women to work outside the home. When a married woman worked outside the home, it was an admission that her husband could not provide adequate support for a middle-class family structure. As a result, working women were usually accorded low status. Striking evidence of this comes from the United States, where, at the end of the nineteenth century, only 2 percent of married white women worked outside the home, while 25 percent of married Black women — in more humble economic circumstances — did so.

The "ideal family" experience looks very different when viewed from the perspective of women. Unlike the conservatives, who insist that respect and sexual equality were compatible with this sexual division of labour into the "two spheres" of domestic and paid work, the radical critics conclude that women had subordinate status in both family and society. The strong family, lauded by the conservatives, becomes inevitably a patriarchal family. An intensive family life, centred on the home, leads to a division of gender roles and women become economically and socially dependent on men.

Women who worked outside the home had low status because they were regarded as having been unable to make a "good marriage" and live the normal life for a woman as wife and mother. All working women were paid less than men for similar work because it was simply assumed that men needed a family wage, while the women needed only to support themselves or supplement their husbands' incomes. Thus the idealization of the male-headed family led to devaluation of women's work outside the home.

This family arrangement was accompanied by the entrenchment of cultural ideas that uphold segregation of women into the private world of the family as natural, desirable, and right. As a result, the socialization of women inside families with this role structure is a socialization into subordinate status in both family and society. Women have less power, fewer resources, less influence, and less status in society, and they grow up in families in which all these gender characteristics are exhibited by their mothers. At the same time, social ideas that normalize a family life with women at home create contradictions and ambiguities about the place and status of women in society. Women's access to certain careers, equal levels of pay, and equal recognition are all compromised by an ideology that upholds a male-headed family as normal and desirable.

From this perspective, the modern two-income conjugal family is a welcome development, holding out the promise of enhanced gender equality: the status of women in the family and in the society must rise. Women's status in the family and society was not always so low as it became during industrialization. The radical critics see this general subordination as being intensified by capitalism. That development is reviewed below.

Emerging Capitalism, Gender Roles, and the Family
· · · · · · · ·

In pre-industrial society the biological role of women in childbearing and mothering did not result in a complete division of gender roles. Women could, and did, combine mothering and housekeeping with work outside the home. They did a surprising range of work: plumbing, dealing in scrap, brewing and vinting beer and cider, and farming. It was also possible for men to be involved with children: as soon as they passed infancy, children simply joined in the work of adults. The concept of children as different from adults scarcely existed and there was very little stress on the idea of a private home life. As a result, gender roles were not so sharply distinguished as they later became.

In the early days of the industrial revolution, children worked alongside their parents. But, as time went on, society became increasingly sensitized to the exploitation of children, and laws restricting child labour were widely introduced. The protection of children correspondingly increased restrictions on women, because *somebody* had to look after the children displaced from the work force. The length and intensity of women's exclusive involvement with children was increased. The biological tie of women to childbearing and mothering was also very direct and insistent until very recently. The lack of effective contraception meant that women could not reliably control their fertility. Table 12.3 indicates that motherhood was certainly a major focus of women's lives until well into this century.

The ability of women to breastfeed infants was also very important in defining their roles, since breast-milk substitutes were often dangerous or unsatisfactory until the

Table 12.3
Total Fertility Rates for Women Aged 15–49, Canada, 1931–1991*
· · · · · · · ·

1931	3.20
1941	2.83
1951	3.50
1961	3.84
1971	2.19
1981	1.78
1991	1.63

*For 1981 and 1991, the figures are for the 15–44 age group.
SOURCE: For 1931 to 1971, *Historical Statistics of Canada*; for 1981 and 1991, *Fertility*, cat. no. 93-321 (Ottawa: Statistics Canada, 1993). Reproduced by authority of the Minister of Industry, 1994.

development of pablum and infant formulas in the 1900s. Consequently a social structure emerged in which there was a rigid gender division: men as income producers; women as mothers and housekeepers. Women's work, because it did not produce exchangeable commodities, lost all apparent economic value. Women spent; they did not earn. Because mothering and housekeeping were services performed in the private world of the family, they generated no income and little recognition.

Housework and mothering does, however, have economic value, and it is simply an illusion to consider these activities as somehow separate from the "real" economy. For example: eat lunch at home, and the addition to Canada's gross domestic product is the cost of the food; eat at a restaurant, and the cost is food plus service plus profit; and Canada's gross domestic product goes up another several dollars. But one has still had lunch. What is defined as production of economic value does not depend on what is done, but where it is done. Work in the home does not show up on the books. Statistics Canada estimated that if child care and household work became purchased services, the calculated gross domestic product would rise by 35–41 percent (Swinamer, 1985). More recent data from Statistics Canada suggests that, in 1992 dollars, somewhere between $211 billion and $319 billion worth of work was performed in family households, about two-thirds of it by women (Chandler, 1993). This is how much activity in production of goods and services goes on in the supposedly consumption-focussed modern household!

The absence of exchange value in housework has fundamental social effects: it undermines women's status. This perspective on housework and mothering has led some groups to advocate wages for housework. This understanding of the link between economic roles and sexual status is based on Marxist ideas (see Engels, 1942[1884]; Zaretsky, 1976). It views the private family as an economic and status trap for women. Work in the private world is unpaid, and often unrecognized, private service. Radical critics of the modern family reject entirely the view that the bourgeois family is an ideal to be striven for. A strengthening of family life and an enhanced focus on the domestic world seems inevitably associated with a lowered status for women.

Family and Individualism

Interestingly, liberal functionalists, Marxists, and feminists all advocate a loosening of the ties that bind women to family responsibility. For functionalists, freedom to compete on an equal basis in the occupational system is a guiding value. For Marxist critics, the freeing of women from disproportionate and restricting family obligations is a necessary foundation of equality. Feminist critics go beyond economic equality to advocate a transformation of the patriarchal ideology that permeates the culture.

Women's equality in the economy cannot be achieved just through the provision of day care and nurseries; there must be more equal sharing of family roles. If there is little social support for families, women will be disadvantaged in access to the higher-status jobs in society and will prepare themselves for, and accommodate themselves to, the sorts of employment that will permit part-time hours and breaks in employment. In such situations, the male spouse's work career will receive priority and attention. If women prepare for limited careers that accommodate family demands, they earn less money, achieve less status, and are partly or wholly reliant on a male income-earner. Consequently, this family structure, if only by example, socializes children of both sexes into stereotyped gender expectations and transmits the disadvantage to the next generation.

There has been a systematic tendency to pay work in which women dominate as employees considerably less than other sectors. This phenomenon can be partly understood as the result of a focussing of women's work in highly competitive areas of the economy. It is also important to note that there is a cultural tendency to evaluate what women do as being worth less than the work of men. For example, full-time women workers receive an average 71.8 percent of the average full-time male wage. This is the highest relative level yet recorded and principally reflects the harsher effect of economic recession on areas of the economy in which men predominate. Never-married women, however, earn about 99 percent of men's incomes. The relatively lower pay for women is definitely linked to family status. Table 12.4 provides further insights into women's lower position in the wage hierarchy. It clearly demonstrates the effect of children on work interruption by women and documents the negligible effect of family responsibility on the employment status of men.

Of the prime childbearing group (women aged 30–39) 61 percent had been off work for at least one year and, for over half of them, the reason was pregnancy and child care (National Council of Welfare, 1990: 47). Today, about two-thirds of women with pre-school children work outside their homes. Women's participation in the labour force has risen dramatically even in the last 30 years. In 1961, women composed 28 percent of the labour force; in 1992, the figure was 45 percent. The changes over the span of 50 years are striking: as late as 1941, only 4.5 percent of married women participated in the labour force; in 1975, it was 41.6 percent; and in 1992, it was 61 percent (Statistics Canada, 1993c). The change in the economic structure of the family has created increased economic independence for women and is obviously a primary reason for the growth of equality between adult partners.

This discussion has focussed on the economic aspects of family life because they are not just matters of economics, but of empowerment in society. Many people who work with families, write about families, and study families argue that disempowerment, especially of women, underlies serious family dysfunction — especially family violence.

Marxism and Feminism
· · · · · · · ·

The above account of radical critical perspectives on family life in society closely links Marxism and feminism. Both perspectives share the view that economic inequality between men and women, and specifically the family roles played by women, have led to pervasive inequality for women in society. In the bourgeois family, where the wife and mother stays at home to focus her work in the domestic sphere, the result is acute economic dependency and the segregation of women from the public sphere of society. This has consequences for women's social and political participation and status outside the family. In the modern conjugal family, in which a woman works outside the home, she will often be faced with working in a lower status job that can accommodate the unpredictable demands of family — illness, periods off school —

Table 12.4
Parents Not in the Labour Force by Reason for Leaving Last Job, Canada, 1991*
· · · · · · · ·

	Women	Men
Personal reasons or family responsibility	23.4%	2.2%
Lost job/Laid off	17.6%	43.8%

*Two-parent families only.
SOURCE: *Lone-Parent Families in Canada*, cat. no. 89-522E (Ottawa: Statistics Canada, 1992). Reproduced by authority of the Minister of Industry, 1994.

and with a full workload inside the home. What distinguishes feminism from Marxism is a relatively greater stress on the importance of culture, rather than just social organization, in generating and upholding the subordination of women. In particular, patriarchal ideology, a set of ideas that justify and uphold male domination over women, is seen as not just embedded in the economic dominance of men, but as pervasive throughout culture, in language, in the cultural presentation of sex, and in assumptions about temperament and intellectual and physical capacities.

Liberation and equality for women is more complicated, in the feminist perspective, than is suggested by Engels's famous statement: "The predominance of the man in marriage is simply a consequence of his economic predominance and will vanish with it automatically" (1968[1884]: 517).[1]

Some evidence to demonstrate the powerful effects of culture in the valuation of the roles of the two sexes can be found close to our present subject. Child-care workers in Canada, of whom two-thirds have post-secondary education (compared with 41 percent of the national labour force), are very low paid. A 1985 survey found that average wages in child care were 30 percent lower than for animal-care workers and farm hands. A survey reported in 1992 found that an average warehouse worker was paid 58 percent more than the average child-care worker.[2] The fact that 98 percent of child-care workers are women cannot be considered irrelevant in these relative evaluations of work.

THE FAMILY IN CRISIS

Although radical critics of the conservative idealization of family are unsupportive of the role structure of the bourgeois family, they also find dangers in a strongly privatized family life. They question the assumption that private families are naturally a healthy place for children and adults. Is a strong family necessarily a good thing? What are the realities of people's experiences in families? While many people discover warmth, support, and love in families, other people's experiences are negative and damaging. They encounter violence, psychological and sexual abuse, alienation, and frustration. An attempt to understand modern family life must inquire into these issues. Because the family is a fairly private institution, guesses and estimates must be made about some of the problems.

Intimate Violence

Canadian families are often violent places. A person is far more likely to encounter violence in the family than on the street. It is estimated that 80 percent of Canadian women who are victims of violent crime knew the accused (43 percent were spouses or ex-spouses), while only 49 percent of male victims knew the accused. While 62 percent of these female victims were victimized in their residence, this was so for only 30 percent of men (Canadian Centre for Justice Statistics, 1992a). At the most extreme level, murder, 34.2 percent of all murders in 1991 were committed by members of the victim's family (see Table 12.5). Almost 20 percent were committed by a spouse (Canadian Centre for Justice Statistics, 1992b: 2), and 54 percent of female victims were killed by a family member, while only 9 percent of male victims were killed by an intimate partner.

The killing of husbands by wives is often a response to repeated assaults on them. An Ontario study suggested that a fall in the rate of men killed by wives could be attributed to the development of shelters and the fuller use of the justice system to protect women: fewer of them were forced to kill the abusive partner.[3]

Violence in intimate couples is nearly always directed by the male against the female, but female assault on males may account for up to 10 percent of domestic vio-

Table 12.5	*Husband*	14.6%
Solved Homicide	*Wife*	4.3%
Offences (*n* = 582)	*Parent*	6.5%
by Accused–Victim	*Child*	4.1%
Relationship Type,	*Sibling*	2.9%
Canada, 1991	*Other*	1.7%
	Total family	34.2%

SOURCE: *Juristat Service Bulletin*, cat. no. 85-002, vol. 12, no. 18, p. 10 (Ottawa: Statistics Canada, 1992). Reproduced by authority of the Minister of Industry, 1994.

lence and may be even more under-reported than male assaults on females (Solicitor General, 1983).

We have good evidence that at least one Canadian woman in ten is the victim of some form of physical or psychological abuse in an intimate relationship. A 1986 survey found that 12 percent of Canadian men admitted using force against their female partners in the previous year (Lupri, 1990: 170). Acts included pushing, grabbing, or shoving their partners. Almost one in five married or cohabiting men had committed at least one act of force against their partner. Among divorced or separated men, fully 30 percent admitted to acts of force against their partners (Lupri, 1990: 171). These figures are supported by a 1992 survey of Canadian university students: 28.8 percent of women students indicated they had been sexually assaulted in the past year, and 22.3 percent reported incidents of physical abuse; 11.3 percent of men admitted being sexually abusive, and 13.7 percent acknowledged acts of physical violence (DeKeseredy and Kelly, 1993).[4]

Other data suggest a high cultural tolerance for the use of force in intimate relationships, even from those who do not practice abuse. A sample of U.S. students, for example, showed that 65 percent of boys and 57 percent of girls in junior high school thought it alright for a male to force a woman into sex after they had dated for more than six months. If the couple were married, the acceptance of rape rose to 87 percent for the boys and 79 percent for the girls.[5]

There is a pervasive cultural attitude that violent conduct between intimately related individuals is somehow not as serious as between strangers. This attitude has often been expressed by officials in the criminal justice system. In 1989, for example, a Manitoba judge remarked of a wife assault case: "How does a person admonish his wife if she goes out on the town with other people, to wit: guys, drinking, and comes home late when she should have been looking after the children or cooking, or whatever else she is expected to do? Sometimes a slap in the face is all that she needs and might not be such unreasonable force after all."[6]

While there are some very patriarchal attitudes revealed in the justice system, there is also a tendency for the courts to want to side with the preservation and support of marriages and relationships. While, in itself, this is an understandable viewpoint, it tends to lead to a minimization of the significance of intimate violence. In 1984 the solicitor general for Canada noted that:

far from being arbiters, the courts are unable to break out of the traditional belief that the family is a sacrosanct unit vital for healthy society. Conciliation is a court's primary aim and ... only the most extreme violations are able to surmount this cul-

tural context and become defined as crimes (New Brunswick Advisory Council on the Status of Women, 1989).

A recent study by the London Family Court Clinic provides evidence that a more active stance by public authorities against family violence is effective in reducing its reoccurrence. London was the first Canadian city to change the mandate of its police force to direct all officers to lay charges of assault in wife-abuse cases *regardless of the wishes of the parties involved* (London Family Court Clinic, 1991: 9). This policy change led to an astonishing rise in rates of charging for domestic assaults: from 2.7 percent of occurrences to 89 percent of occurrences! A key finding was that there was a significant reduction of violent occurrences once charges had been laid.

This suggests that the private nature of the family may increase the opportunity for perpetrators to get away with violence and be screened from social censure. It also suggests that the lack of social support for victims of violence affects its frequency and severity. This material provides reason to be sceptical of the assumption that a close, private, intimate family life is necessarily a good thing.

Family violence, of course, is not restricted to assault on adult partners. It is also directed at children and the elderly. A 1989 study in Montreal suggested that 5 percent of seniors are regularly beaten by their children and a further 10 percent suffer "psychological abuse."[7]

One of the main avenues of family violence is the sexual abuse of children. Estimates of its incidence are almost impossible to arrive at, but the more it is talked about the more reports of it come to the notice of authorities (see Rogers, 1990: 19; Committee on Sexual Offences Against Children and Youths, 1984). Children are also, of course, victims of physical violence, something officially tolerated and accepted (though normatively limited to non-injuring blows) in Canadian society. Thus, for radical critics the erosion of family autonomy by the state and the community, lamented by the conservatives, is by no means a bad thing. They feel that many families should not be able to exert largely unchecked power over vulnerable members.

Divilorce

Does a rising divorce rate present a social problem? The debate rages. Table 12.6 lists divorce rates in Canada in 1960 and 1981–90. The trend is unmistakable. Today 40

Table 12.6

Divorces per 100 Marriages, Canada, 1960–1990

1960	5.4
1981	35.4
1982	37.4
1983	37.1
1984	35.1
1985	33.7
1986	45.1
1987	50.0
1988	42.6
1989	42.3
1990	41.6

Note: The Divorce Act was first liberalized in 1968, and the number of divorces increased substantially afterward. Further restrictions were lifted in 1985.

SOURCE: *Report on the Demographic Situation in Canada,* cat. no. 91-209E, 1992 (Ottawa: Statistics Canada, 1992), p. 42. Reproduced by authority of the Minister of Industry, 1994.

Table 12.7		
Poverty Among Lone-Parent Families in Five Countries	*United States*	53.3%
	Canada	48.4%
	France	15.8%
	Sweden	5.5%
	Germany	25.5%

SOURCE: Linda McQuaig, *The Wealthy Banker's Wife* (Toronto: Penguin, 1993), p. 34. Copyright © Linda McQuaig, 1993. Reprinted by permission of Penguin Books Canada Limited.

percent of marriages will end in divorce. The median length of marriages is 10 years.[8] These figures do not include the hundreds of thousands of "divorces" of common-law marriages.

In 1991, common-law households were 11.3 percent of all couples, up from 8.3 percent reported in household surveys in 1986 (Statistics Canada, 1992a); 42 percent of these arrangements included children. Counting the termination of these types of relationships in the divorce statistics would increase the divorce rates to perhaps three-in-five of all married and equivalent-to-married relationships.

Divorce has also become the main source of a rising number of single-parent families, of which 83 percent are female headed. Poverty is common among these families (see Table 12.7). Surprisingly, the actual percentage of single-parent families in Canada has not much changed in 40 years, but the reasons for being a single parent have changed dramatically (see Table 12.8).

Why is divorce rising? The simple answer is that the pressures to stay married are weaker than the pressures to divorce or separate. Perhaps the most revealing way to think about the problem is to recognize that any intimate relationship is subject to periodic stress, but will more likely outlive those stresses if it is complexly bound together than if it rests simply on sentiment and emotion. When men and women rely on each other for economic needs, social status, and future security, this foundation is far more durable than one founded on an emotional basis. What has happened to families in modern society is that women's economic dependence has been reduced and cultural ideas have changed to promote individual satisfaction as the sole criterion for judgement of marriage. This is a very potent mix for blowing marriages apart, when considered in the context of the research of Lupri and Frideres (1981) on the normal cycle of marital satisfaction. They find that the percentages of husbands and wives who report their relationship "very satisfying" decreases with the presence of school-age children and drops dramatically when there are teenage children. The percentages rise again with retirement.

Table 12.8		1951	1991
Marital Status of Female Lone Parents, Canada, 1951 and 1991	*Single*	1.4%	19.5%
	Separated	29.3%	24.6%
	Divorced	3.3%	32.5%
	Widowed	66.0%	23.4%

SOURCE: *Canada's Lone-Parent Families*, cat. no. 93-106, and *Lone-Parent Families in Canada*, cat. no. 89-522E (Ottawa: Statistics Canada, 1992). Reproduced by authority of the Minister of Industry, 1994.

Against this cycle in the couple's attachment to each other, rising divorce rates might be seen as an index of increased opportunity to act on dissatisfaction rather than of increased marital dissatisfaction itself. The inevitable lows in the cycle of married relationships are now less likely to be worked through and are more often the trigger for divorce.

For a complex of reasons, including growing economic independence of women (70 percent of Canadian divorce petitions are initiated by women), changes to the law, the weakening of community and extended family influence, and a culture of individualism, divorce (their own or their parents') is now a part of the life cycle for a majority of Canadians (see Box 12.2). One graphic way to appreciate the impact of divorce is to see how many children experience their parents' divorce: in the 1960s about a quarter of all children would see their parents divorce prior to the child reaching 20 years of age. For children born in the late 1970s almost half will have this experience (Marcil-Gratton, 1988).

These facts can be interpreted in two ways. One might argue that they demonstrate the undermining of the institution that has always anchored individuals to the society and given them their sense of personal identity. The disruption of children's family experience through divorce may lead to poorly adjusted individuals who lack self-esteem, emotional trust, and spontaneity. This point of view was strongly advanced in a controversial American study (Wallerstein and Blakeslee, 1989). On the other hand, one might argue that ending unsatisfactory adult relationships reduces stress on children and provides a more healthy and honest atmosphere for raising them. Both views have their proponents.

Role Stress

Role stress is another reality of modern families. Today's families typically maintain two working adults, but still have to perform many of the tasks that were previously

Box 12.2
What Happens When Families Break up?

If the conjugal family is defined as the "modern" family, it is now clear that Canada has entered the era of the postmodern family. Postmodern families exhibit a variety of forms: single-parent families, families formed by combinations of two other families (the blended family), or families linked by co-operation and mutual support networks. These forms often arise from the breakdown of conjugal relationships.

Some writers have suggested that the main discontinuity between the modern and the postmodern family is found in the involvement of men. Sociologist Judith Stacey writes that if there is a family crisis today, it is primarily a *male* crisis, in which large numbers of men abandon their families or absent themselves through their work or recreational pursuits. The female bond to family continues in the new forms of single parenting and networks of kin and quasi-kin relationships.

SOURCE: Adapted from Judith Stacey, *Brave New Families in the Second North American Family Revolution, in Transition* (Ottawa: Vanier Institute of the Family, 1993).

the role of the full-time homemaker. Economic change has undermined the older family lifestyle. It has been estimated that 65 to 80 hours of work is required today to maintain the income level produced by 45 hours of work in the 1970s. If women ceased to perform paid work, there would be a doubling of the number of poor families in Canada from 7.5 to 15.9 percent.[9]

Modern market economies have a tendency to seek out new markets, to look for new possibilities for supplying goods and services. Enormous opportunity for profit is created if household production is displaced by mass-produced goods and services bought in the market place. New consumer demands are stimulated that can only be satisfied by families increasing their household income. A cycle occurs: increasing wage employment of homemakers, and increasing selling of goods and services to households. This also results in an expansion of state-supported activities to take on some of the tasks once handled by the household (day care, nurseries, and so on). Although schools have taken on many activities that were previously the responsibility of families, no market system can eliminate all the work of household maintenance and parenting. These continuing demands have created a particular intensification of the work of women (see Lowe, 1989).

The two-generation private conjugal family typical of Canada is, in historical and comparative perspective, an unusual form for human society. Its membership is narrow, its roles are narrow, and it is intensely focussed inward rather than anchored in extended kin and community. It is a private family in which members are in close interaction and have charged emotional relationships with each other. It is subject to great stress if the emotional relationships that provide its foundation break down.

The middle-class, gender-role divided family still common in Canada in the 1950s created bonds of economic interdependency as well as emotion. The changing involvement of women in the labour force undermined the separation of gender roles. The foundation of the family became much more restricted to the unstable basis of emotion. The erosion of economic dependency supported a spiralling divorce rate. Today's society is one in which family bonds in general are much more weakly constituted than in any society of the past. Usually the mother–child bond endures family and marital disruption, but almost half of Canada's children in this generation will experience part of their childhood without intimate daily contact with both of their parents.

CONCLUSION

Family life is not insulated from the outer society but is deeply connected to it. The rise of western capitalist society had effects on both the structure and values of the family system. From being an institution founded in a complex of social roles and responsibilities, the family has come to reflect the individualism of the outer society, a wage-based economy in which many necessaries of the household were purchased. Initially, industrialization pushed adult women out of employment by making it impossible for children to join in the work of adults. Women's access to power in society was very limited, since their work took place inside the unpaid private sphere of the household.

Although women's work was crucial to the economy, the location where it was performed deprived it of income-producing value. Women became almost complete economic dependants of men, and their lower status was reflected in and reinforced by laws, customs, and social ideologies. Many women attained influence, status, and power in their marriages as heads of the domestic sphere, but their roles excluded them from equal participation in the public sphere of society. Ideological claims about gender that justified and normalized this exclusion of women from the public realm became a central aspect of western culture. The gravitational pull of social life was to limit and constrain women's roles and ambitions to mothering and household management.

This framework for family life and its accompanying ideology has been shaken by two forces. First, the rising level of female participation in the labour force has been a powerful engine of social change in the status of women, but it has been achieved at the cost of an intensification of the work of employed mothers. Increased status for women has made them far less dependent on men.

Second, this economic change has been accompanied by a powerful and sustained assault on cultural ideas that assumed the naturalness of the home-focussed gender definition of femaleness. There is a widening examination of the structures and beliefs that obstruct women from true equality with men in modern society. Modern individualism has been very important here too: *self*-interest and *personal* development have been accorded a legitimacy in present-day society that was absent from societies of the past. Also, the whole definition of success and status in society is occupationally focussed: the corporate ethic of career and achievement conflicts with commitment to family. To revolt against constraint is considered healthy; to accept it leads to unhealthy self-denial.

Where does the progression of equality in the family and the stress on individual self-expression seem likely to lead? It seems that an individualistic, competitive, and socially and geographically mobile society necessarily weakens the bonds of family. People, of course, continue to maintain contacts with their parents, children, and siblings, but individuals are not fused into the family as in past times and other societies.

In addition, shared family activity inside the modern conjugal unit has diminished, largely because of the outside employment of women. This diminishment of family life is not only a matter of cultural choice; it is an economic necessity.

Economic pressures, individualism, cultural ideas denigrating obligation and elevating choice, and the breaking of old dependencies (for status, economic support, or old-age security), and their replacement by more exclusively emotional ties have all shaken the foundations of marriage and the family. In the 1990s and into the next century, divorce may well become a normal part of the life cycle. Many Canadians will be married at least twice. It will become more common for children to live in blended families or with single parents. The institutionalization of the functions of the family will increase; and the trend, already pointed to by educators, for day-care centres and schools to take wide-ranging responsibility for the social and developmental needs of children will continue.

Even if it were economically feasible to reinstate the role pattern of the middle-class, bourgeois family and increase the centrality of family in early childhood, one might doubt the rightness of a gender division that denies equality to women. Feminists have seen the glorification of domestically focussed family life as a threat to women's status and an obstruction to full equality in society. Even in societies like Sweden, with generous programs to allow *either* parent extended time out of employment for child care, it is still normal for women to take that role. Family commitment and personal choice are inevitably in tension with each other. Women have come out of relegation to the world of the private family, but the belief that the outer world (i.e., the man's world) is the most important for valuable and rewarding work has become victorious.

Modern thinking has generally turned away from proclaiming the importance of family life, because, in reality, it seems most likely to maintain its strength at the cost of female inequality. Western societies have now become the first in human history in which most children, in their formative years, spend long periods in relatively formal settings with complete strangers. Sociologists, and others, will continue to debate the consequences of changes in family life and structure as societies throughout the world develop the complex market-driven economies that underlie these profound changes in our most basic experiences as humans.

• • • • • • • •

NOTES

1. See Sargent (1981) for a comprehensive survey of the tensions between the Marxist and feminist perspectives.
2. Geoffrey York, "Child-Care Pay Near Poverty Level," *The Globe and Mail*, April 23, 1992, p. A1.
3. Sean Fine, "Women's Hostels May Shield Men," *The Globe and Mail*, June 2, 1992, p. A1.
4. This research has been the subject of criticism by other sociologists, and the figures should be used with caution. See Gartner (1993) and Fox (1993).
5. "Students Find Date Rape Acceptable," *The Globe and Mail*, May 3, 1988, p. A12.
6. "Judge Faces Panel Review for Comment on Slapping," *The Globe and Mail*, April 12, 1989, p. A10.
7. "15% of Elderly Abused by Adult Children, Study Finds," *The Globe and Mail*, May 26, 1989, p. A5. For a review of this subject, see *Report of the Standing Committee on Health and Welfare, Social Affairs, Seniors and Status of Women* (1993).
8. By the end of the 1980s, it looked as though the median length of marriage before divorce was on the increase, but it will take longer to establish a trend.
9. Geoffrey York, "Family Life: Not Enough Money, Too Much Stress," *The Globe and Mail*, January 3, 1992, p. A1.

• • • • • • • •

FURTHER READING

Andersen, Margaret L. *Thinking About Women: Sociological Perspectives on Sex and Gender*, 3rd ed. New York: Macmillan, 1993. A valuable discussion of the family, with much material on other topics raised in this chapter.

Cheal, David. *Family and the State of Theory*. Toronto: University of Toronto Press, 1991. A brief but useful review of theories of the family, discussing these in relationship to modernity.

Hudson, Joe, and Burt Galaway, ed. *Single Parent Families*. Toronto: Thompson Educational Publishing, 1993.

Popenoe, David. *Disturbing the Nest: Family Change and Decline in Modern Societies*. New York: Aldine De Gruyter, 1988. An interesting history of the family, with some useful cross-cultural comparisons. The author argues that Sweden was the first society to develop the modern conjugal family and provides a detailed analysis of the Swedish family.

Rubin, Lillian Breslow. *Worlds of Pain: Life in the Working Class Family*. New York: Basic Books, 1976. A reminder that family life, even in modern society, is also shaped by the social class of its members.

Zaretsky, Eli. *Capitalism, the Family and Personal Life*. New York: Harper Colophon, 1976. A short and engaging history of the western family since the rise of capitalism.

● ● ● ● ● ● ● ●

**STUDY
QUESTIONS**
● ● ● ● ● ● ● ●

1. What are the principal contrasts between the values and organization of consanguineal and conjugal families?

2. Explain the argument that consanguineal and conjugal families are functionally related to the types of society in which they are found.

3. Ask a friend or neighbour who comes from a non-European background how their family system in Canada has changed from the patterns usual in their traditional culture. Does their account suggest a cultural persistence or a convergence toward the family relationships (conjugal) most typical in Canadian culture?

4. To what extent does conjugal family organization in Canada socialize females into subordinate roles in society?

5. What have been some of the major social effects of changing family values and organization over the last 40 or 50 years?

6. How would you define the concept "family"? Are there conflicting definitions of the family in your community? Discuss.

7. Interview a worker from a women's refuge or crisis centre. In that person's opinion, what characteristics of the family contribute to domestic violence and abuse?

13

DEVIANCE AND SOCIETY

· · · · · · · · ·

INTRODUCTION

· · · · · · · ·

Émile Durkheim left a powerful legacy for understanding crime and deviance: the functionalist perspective. By focussing on the manner in which individuals are bonded to the society and the way in which emerging capitalism weakened the integrative mechanisms of the community, he provided the foundation for theories of crime and deviance that have been elaborated on throughout this century. From Robert Merton's work in the 1930s to John Braithwaite in the 1980s sociologists have relied on Durkheim's insight to discuss deviance. Their findings generally indicate that economic development will be accompanied by rises in crime rates.

There are several exceptions, however, which while testing Durkheim's theory really only confirm it. High rates of violence among a traditional hunting and gathering society are discussed in this chapter, as are low crime rates among two modern industrial nations: Switzerland and Japan. Each of these exceptional cases increases the understanding of crime. Finally, a consideration of very differing crime rates among welfare-state societies makes the disintegrative power of inequality of condition clear. **Symbolic interactionism**, a microperspective, provides an effective view of how those with the power to label behaviour use inequality of condition and cultural stereotypes to transform behaviour at the everyday level into crime and deviance. Understanding how crime can be considered as a social construction provides a foundation for the critical perspective, which shows how crime and violence as labels and behaviours can be used to reproduce the existing social order.

· · · · · · · ·

Order is so much taken for granted in Canada that deviation from it is a source of both curiosity and discomfort. Sociologists too, especially functionalists, have focussed so much on how order is possible in society that they consider deviation as unusual and even exceptional. However, events such as the large-scale disorder

Photo 13.1
Sociologists have focussed on order in society and assumed deviance to be unusual — so much so that large-scale disorder, such as the 1992 Los Angeles race riots, seems difficult to understand or interpret.

Joe Sohm / MASTERFILE

in Los Angeles during the race riots of 1992, the Oka crisis of 1990 in Canada, and the continuing wars and rebellions around the world make that attitude difficult to comprehend.

Sociologists, being believers in society, see humans as expressing their human qualities only in close association with others. Many, like Durkheim, have stressed the role of sociology in promoting social health and guarding against social instability and anarchy. For others, though, disorder is a reflection of resistance, of new directions, and of society's need to reshape itself.

For either point of view, understanding why people act in deviant ways — engage in conduct that departs from the social norms that apply to the individual and situation in question — is an important question. Sociologists begin by assuming that deviance is understandable as a social phenomenon. While some argue that deviance is based in individual psychological and biological differences, sociologists take their approach from Durkheim, who believed that when individual explanations had been exhausted there was still something left to explain by reference to social causes. In linking deviance to society, sociologists use the primary concepts of culture or social structure. The social component of deviance is considered a reflection of the culture and organization of society.

Durkheim believed that the individual differences predisposing people to suicide would be more or less balanced among comparable societies. Differences in the suicide rates of these societies, then, must be a reflection of concrete characteristics of the society itself (not of its members). For example, in 1991 Newfoundland had the lowest suicide rate in the country, while Quebec and Alberta had the highest rates.[1] The variation in rates interests sociologists. Similarly, Canada has a homicide rate of about 2.8 per 100 000 population, while the United States has a rate of 9.8 (*Juristat Service Bulletin*, 1991). Why? Acts of violence against women appear to be higher in some societies than in others. Why? Many similar questions arise. Sociologists answer each of them with an analysis of the social and/or cultural differences between societies.

This chapter examines the analyses of the social component of deviance to demonstrate the sociological approach. In so doing, it continues to draw a distinction between the functionalist and critical perspectives. The end of the chapter returns to the question of defining just what deviance (or crime, for that matter) is, and uses the issue to discuss symbolic interactionism, a microsociological perspective.

MODERN VERSUS TRADITIONAL SOCIETY

Throughout this book a distinction has been made between societies that reflect differences in culture and social structure: traditional versus modern, Gemeinschaft versus Gesellschaft, rural versus urban. If deviance is indeed a social phenomenon, societies of each type should display differences in the amount or kind of deviance they experience. Low rates of deviance would be forecast for societies that most closely resemble the integrated culture and social life of the Gemeinschaft community; higher rates should occur where there is more complexity in society and more opportunity to develop competing interests and values.

Durkheim's Approach to Understanding Deviance

Traditional societies appear to have lower rates of deviance than do modern societies. Criminal statistics indicate that the most modern developed nations, such as Canada, Britain, the United States, have higher overall crime rates than do developing countries. For example, using three large crime categories — crimes against the person, crimes against property, and drug- related crimes — there are about 800 offences per 100 000 persons in developing nations and 1800 per 100 000 in developed nations (Wilson and Herrnstein, 1985: 442).

Sociologists have relied heavily on Émile Durkheim in understanding the above facts. Durkheim was interested in understanding the social changes created by the emergence of modern capitalism. He was concerned that changing social organization and culture might produce social problems. Durkheim assumed in all his work that human beings are driven by insatiable appetites that can only be regulated by social forces. Society must provide them with a sense of meaning through social involvements and with a sense of discipline and moral regulation. Social problems emerge when society loses the ability to regulate individuals, and this happens when the bonds between the individual and society are weakened. Central to Durkheim's work is a concern with the relationship between the individual and society. He assumed that as society modernized this relationship was threatened, and to produce stability in modern society a new basis for integrating the individual would have to be found.

Durkheim theorized that there were two main types of suicide: egoistic and anomic. **Egoistic suicide** arises in a situation where individuals are weakly integrated into social structures (e.g., family, community, or churches). **Anomic suicide** arises in a situation where norms are weak or confused and individuals are too weakly regulated. Both of these conditions are apt to arise during modernization. (For a critique of Durkheim's assumptions, see Box 13.1.) As modern industrial societies develop, there is a disruption or disintegration of the communal bases of social life. Individuals are required to be more mobile than they were previously, reducing the obligations to extended family and community. Individuals live and work within a community of strangers to whom they have an impersonal or contractual relationship rather than a personal relationship of interdependency.

There is also an increasing differentiation of the individual from the community; people come to imagine themselves as independent and alone, without the guides of tradition and community needs. And rapid social change uproots old values and makes it unclear what norms apply to regulate conduct. Culture appears to lag behind the social realities one is faced with.

Box 13.1
Gender and Suicide

While Émile Durkheim has been central to the development of sociology, it is also clear that his theories and his use of statistics contributed to a certain vision of social order — one that marginalized women in sociology and supported traditional gender relationships.

Following the example of his nineteenth-century predecessors, Durkheim used suicide statistics as a barometer of the social health of the society. Like others, he was convinced that modernity had established the foundation for growing pathology and that this would be reflected in suicide statistics. Durkheim chose to use statistics reporting "completed" suicides when he could have chosen figures combining "completed" and "attempted" suicide. Durkheim's figures show a substantially higher suicide rate for men than for women. This remains true today. Again following the lead of others, Durkheim was prepared to argue that modernity's negative effects would be registered in the behaviour of men, not women, and that women were being protected from the destructive influence of modernity by being firmly integrated into the social relations of the traditional family. The figures for both sexes, then, are taken to be signs of his general theory that suicide rates increase as the level of social integration declines.

However, what might have happened if Durkheim had not been so wedded to his theory? If he had looked at the figures for attempted and completed suicide, he would have noticed (and he must have known this) that the suicide rates for men and women would be almost equal. So, perhaps social integration did not render women immune from suicide. Further, he did notice that men in the military had always shown a very high rate of suicide. Durkheim discussed these deaths under the heading of **altruistic suicide** (a form of self-sacrifice), when again he must have known that few of the military suicides actually registered would have fit this interpretation. They would perhaps have made more sense as examples of what Durkheim called **fatalistic suicide** — suicide deriving from excessive regulation, passions choked by oppressive discipline, and futures pitilessly blocked. This captures the situations of nineteenth-century military men as well as the positions of women enmeshed in the traditional bourgeois family.

If Durkheim had been open to looking at the statistics on women's behaviour and to understanding the situation of modern women, he might have constructed a very different theory. High suicide rates would have been linked to the most integrated societies. Then, however, modernity would not have been the villain, and suicide statistics would not have served as the barometer of this menace.

SOURCE: Adapted from Howard I. Kushner, "Suicide, Gender, and the Fear of Modernity in Nineteenth-Century Medical and Social Thought," *Journal of Social History* (1993): 461–490.

Social change and economic development lead to a disintegration of traditional structures of social involvement (such as church, family, and work guild), to a growing emphasis on individualism, and to confusion in social norms and values. These characteristics of modern life transform the relationship between the individual and society, making the regulation of individuals less certain.

Durkheim's Legacy

Robert Merton

Robert Merton, an American sociologist whose work dominated the sociology of deviance for several decades, brought the concept of normative confusion or a normative vacuum, **anomie**, to North America. Merton used the concept to build a functionalist analysis of crime and deviance. Merton began his argument with an explicit attack on Durkheim and Freud: "There persists a notable tendency in sociological theory to attribute the malfunctioning of social structure primarily to those of man's imperious biological drives which are not adequately restrained by social control" (1938: 672).

In other words, Freud and Durkheim tended to blame social disorder on the inability of society to keep the natural passions of humans under control. Merton rejected this notion of the individual as inherently evil and instead argued that the "monster" is created by society. Human appetites for wealth and power, which Durkheim assumed to be natural drives, are actually culturally created: people seek culturally derived goals. Society sets goals and also provides some direction on how these goals are to be achieved; they should be attained only by normatively approved means. Merton suggested that anomie arises where there is a disjunction between cultural goals and the normative means of attaining them. A great deal of attention can be given by society to stimulating aspirations and at the same time little attention may be given to instilling normative controls on how these goals or aspirations are achieved. Merton claimed, in fact, that if too much attention is given to stimulating aspirations, no amount of normative regulation can restrain them. This is the equivalent of having the intention to win without too much concern for the rules. Merton claimed that the United States was in that condition — the condition of anomie, where the ends justify the means.

> *The extreme emphasis on the accumulation of wealth as a symbol of success in our society militates against the completely effective control of institutionally regulated modes of acquiring a fortune. Fraud, corruption, vice, crime, in short, the entire catalogue of proscribed behaviour, becomes increasingly common* (1938: 675).

When people become convinced that material success is the source of all personal happiness, meaning, and status, it will be pursued without restraint. Merton directed attention away from biology and toward culture as one source of crime. He also provided a critique of consumer capitalism; people's desires for wealth and consumer goods may make it difficult for societal regulation to work effectively. This critique is Durkheimian in suggesting that the re-establishment of shared values and norms will reduce crime and deviance in society: social order is built on shared culture.

In this analysis, Merton focussed on culture and did not examine how social structure might affect rates of deviance: might extremes of inequality induce people toward crime? Durkheim was a critic of social inequality, arguing that extreme inequality of condition might undermine the opportunities of segments of society and would itself weaken normative regulation. Merton developed this idea in his second form of anomie, which will soon be discussed.

**The Emergence of
Youth Subculture**

· · · · · · · ·

Other authors draw attention to another effect of modernization in generating deviance: the creation of a youth culture. They suggest that economic development leads to a society in which young persons are either not required as productive workers or they must undergo extensive education and training before entering the labour market. This prolonged isolation of young people from the world of adults and adult responsibilities leads to a separate youth culture. This culture encourages a rejection of the values and the authority of adults. Since young people contribute disproportionately to the crime rate, the separation of young people and their isolation from adult culture may well be a significant crime-causing feature of modern society (Christie, 1978).

These same ideas were developed by Hartjen (1982) in analyzing the lower rate of delinquency in India, compared with mature capitalist societies. In general, he argued that several forces of social integration were still present in Indian society that reduced the likelihood of people acting in a criminal or delinquent manner. He claimed that since India is still an agriculturally based society, all family members are functionally necessary for the economic survival of the family and the community. Further, the social relationships that revolve around kin, jati (a smaller grouping within a caste), and community are still strong, so that people are firmly integrated into these networks of relations. These relationships are far more important in daily life than are occupational roles, in contrast to Canadian society. Children and young people are included in economic and social activity, so there is little sign of a youth subculture. The integration of young people into many close social and working rela-

Photo 13.2
Deviant behaviour is not always criminal. In fact, deviance includes a wide range of behaviour that departs from social norms but is not necessarily illegal. Having a tattoo, for example, is traditionally considered deviant. Some sociologists see deviance as a form of self-expression.

· · · · · · · ·

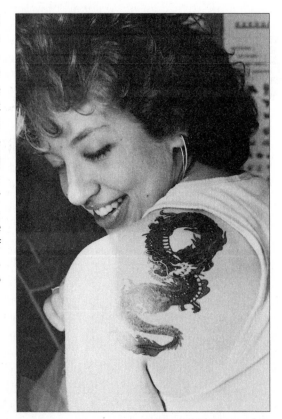

Ian Scott, Photographer

tionships with adults enables informal mechanisms of social control to influence the behaviour of youth, and as a result there is less reliance on the formal mechanisms of the law. In this analysis, too, social order rests on a shared culture. Weak integration may result in people being drawn to a subculture and socialized into an alternative lifestyle, reducing the ability of the larger society to control them.

This discussion of functionalist approaches to deviance assumes a shared normative order in which the law and other rules reflect this shared sense of order. Those who do not share it are considered potentially deviant. It can be argued that in a heterogeneous society such as Canada's there is no consensus on the normative order; rather, there may be several senses of normative order. Using drugs may mean very different things in various communities in Canada. Clearcutting the forest means one thing to loggers and a very different thing to recreational property owners. Abortion means very different things to the pro-choice movement and the pro-life movement. People learn or adopt values and meanings, which are not naturally deviant or non-deviant; perhaps they are made deviant by the way values and meanings are institutionalized through law and other social arrangements.

Shame as a Crime-Control Measure
. . . .

More recently, Braithwaite (1989) proposed a theory of crime causation, and a set of prescriptions for reducing crime in modern society, that develops these ideas. He argued for a system of crime control based on "reintegrative shaming." Shaming is the social process of "expressing disapproval which has the intention or effect of invoking remorse in the person being shamed and/or condemnation by others who become aware of the shaming" (p. 100).

Shaming is most effective when the offenders have close personal relationships in the community and concern for what people think about them. Offenders are seldom shamed by lawyers or judges, but they are shamed by their family, friends, and colleagues. Again the argument arises that crime rates are linked to the richness of social integration. Braithwaite concluded from this that the impersonality of the community's response to crime means that offenders do not adequately experience shame in the eyes of the community and do not receive its support in trying to change their personal attitudes and behaviour. Braithwaite stated that the response to offenders should aim to reintegrate them into the community after shaming. Too frequently in modern society, punishment stigmatizes and isolates the offenders. This separation undermines their attachment to society and weakens the capacity of society to control their future behaviour.

Exclusion also pushes offenders toward membership in criminal subcultures, making them even more likely to victimize the community. Societies that are "communitarian," Braithwaite suggested, are more likely to use shaming and are more successful at reintegration. Communitarianism occurs when "individuals are densely enmeshed in interdependencies which have the special qualities of mutual help and trust. The interdependencies have symbolic significance in the culture of group loyalties which take precedence over individual interests" (p. 100).

Behind all these theories about crime and delinquency in modern capitalist society are the ghosts of Gemeinschaft versus Gesellschaft, mechanical versus organic society, rural versus urban society.

Crime in Traditional Society
. . . .

Developing nations have both a higher rate, and higher absolute number, of crimes against persons than do developed nations. In developing societies, for example, crimes against the person account for 43 percent of serious crimes, while in developed nations this figure is 10 percent (Wilson and Herrnstein, 1985: 442). What does this mean?

Although this is a complicated question, sociology provides some insights. In rural area societies or close-knit communities, property crime (theft, for example) is difficult because everyone knows everyone else quite well. The close personal relationships make it difficult for people to steal from neighbours. In urban areas, relationships are much more impersonal; it is easy to steal from a stranger, and there is no relationship to perpetuate. So why is there a high rate of crimes against the person in agrarian communities?

Living in close relationships from which there is little escape tends to generate frustration, anger, and hostility. Since people cannot easily walk away from a relationship, the anger tends to erupt in acts of violence, such as an assault on the target of your anger. In modern society, people tend to live much of their lives in impersonal relationships where this kind of frustration is less likely to emerge. Further, they can always change jobs or change their circle of friends. Since family relationships are the most personal in society, it would not be surprising to find a high level of violence within the family. This tends to be confirmed by homicide statistics. In Canada in 1991, 87 percent of homicides in which the accused was identified involved suspects and victims who were known to each other; 34 percent were committed by a family member; and only 13 percent were committed by strangers (Canadian Centre for Justice Statistics, 1992b).

Crime and Modernization

Economic development and its impact on crime rates can be investigated by examining historical figures on crime in a particular society. Accurate historical statistics have been available only for a limited time, but the following general trend emerges from research in several countries. "In general, the level of crime and disorder in large cities and industrializing nations of the western world was very high in the early decades of the nineteenth century, decreased substantially during the latter part of that century, and then worsened again in the mid-twentieth century" (Wilson and Herrnstein, 1985: 408). What accounted for the high crime rate in the early part of the nineteenth century?

Although economic development and industrialization occurred at different times in most nations, the early 1800s were a period of intense development in countries such as Britain. This period was one of extreme and rapid rural–urban movement, occupational change, and dislocation of social relationships and cultural values. Sociologists argue that this intense period of development was not only associated with community disruption but with a host of social problems such as crime and delinquency. Peter Berger put it this way: "The early period of industrial capitalism in England, and probably in other western countries, exacted considerable human cost, if not in an actual decline in material living standards then in social and cultural dislocation" (1986: 41).

The early period of disruption was softened to some extent during the latter part of the nineteenth century, when governments began to develop social policies to reduce the negative effects of the market. In England, for example, policies affecting education, working conditions, sanitation, and health care were in place by 1870. Furthermore, after 1830, London, England's most important and turbulent city, had a greatly expanded and more powerful police force. To gain a further appreciation of the effects of development and cultural change, Box 13.2 discusses the effects of social dislocation on an aboriginal community in Canada.

Box 13.2
The Effects of
Economic Dislocation

> Violent gangs are terrorizing the Cree Indian reserve. Almost every weekend, there are gang-related brawls or beatings. ...
>
> In the early 1960s, Moose Lake was one of the most prosperous Indian communities in the province. The reserve, about 500 kilometers northwest of Winnipeg, was regarded as perhaps the best hunting and trapping ground in Manitoba.
>
> At that time, there were an estimated 2000 moose in the region. There were abundant supplies of fur-bearing animals. The nearby Saskatchewan River delta was one of North America's great breeding marshes for ducks and geese. A muskrat ranch was thriving, and the rich soil permitted the establishment of gardens, crops, and cattle farms.
>
> But the hunting and trapping suffered a steep decline after the construction of the Grand Rapid hydro dam, which flooded about two-thirds of the Moose Lake reserve in 1964.
>
> The muskrat ranch and the farms were destroyed. The moose population declined drastically. Many of the houses were relocated to a crowded new site where the Indians did not have room for gardens or fields. Studies found an increase in sickness in the community. ...
>
> A consultant's study in 1986 drew a direct connection between the flooding and the social problems of Moose Lake.
>
> SOURCE: Excerpted from Geoffrey York, "Terror Born of Hopelessness Plagues Manitoba Reserve," *The Globe and Mail*, October 24, 1988, p. A13. Reprinted with permission.

Developing nations can expect intense periods of dislocation and an accompanying array of social problems unless firm measures are taken to soften the effects of change. Many developing nations unfortunately have become stuck in this early period of dislocation because their economies have not been allowed to mature: they have become permanent hinterlands to distant metropolises. The actions of colonizers or mature capitalist societies have distorted the economic development of these nations, resulting in high rates of urbanization without the accompanying expansion of job opportunities. The resulting exceptionally high rates of unemployment contribute to family instability and poverty. All these conditions have been related to high crime rates.

EXCEPTIONS TO THE ABOVE TRENDS

Although there is a consistency in the above trends and general agreement on their explanation, some situations do not seem to fit the pattern. These exceptions provide further insights into the social aspects of crime and deviance.

Violence against Women

While crime is unusual in hunting and gathering or horticultural (a simple form of agriculture) societies, the Yanomamo of South America, who are forest hunter–gatherers, are an exception: they have an extremely high rate of violence against women. The social forces that generally result in high crime rates are not present in

Yanomamo society; individuals are integrated, individualism is low, and strong social bonds are present. So how can this violence toward women be understood? The first thing that is apparent about Yanomamo society is that it is one of the world's most militant societies and it is extremely masculinized; it would be difficult to find a society more imbued with male supremacy (Chagnon, 1968). Sociologists believe that societies in which warfare is common encourage male domination. Collins (1975) suggested that in societies in which there is little military threat and weapons are not well developed, there is little reason for males to organize into military groups and, generally speaking, relations between men and women are more egalitarian (Divale and Harris, 1976). In contrast, the need for well-developed militaries places an emphasis on male physical and aggressive characteristics and tends to produce high levels of male domination. In societies in which male characteristics are highly valued and institutionalized, women tend to be devalued and to occupy inferior positions in the society. Since women are devalued, men are much more likely to harm their interests and direct physical and aggressive behaviour toward them.

Although there is some evidence to suggest a link between the societal need for warfare and institutions of male domination, male domination of course does not depend on warfare. What other social conditions might lead to women being devalued and therefore becoming the target of abuse? Comparative sociology suggests that women have higher status in those societies in which they control economic resources. In hunting and gathering societies, for example, women tend to have higher status (although not equal to that of men)[2] when hunting plays a smaller part than does gathering in the life of the community. Since these activities are always sex-divided, women contribute substantially to the food resource through their gathering activities. One would expect to find more abuse of women, then, when the actual or symbolic significance of the hunt is greater. It should be noted that gender equality is perhaps more nearly attained in foraging societies than in other types of society.

The Iroquois of eastern North America were also a militaristic people, but ample evidence suggests that they did not rape captured women (Brownmiller, 1975: 142). It is perhaps important that they were a matrilineal society. In matrilineal societies, women are central to economic activity. Land is owned matrilineally, and women cultivate the land for the matrilineage. Although still not having power equivalent to men, women tend to have high status. In a patrilineal society, by contrast, land is owned and inherited through males. Although women work the land, they are producers for kinship groups organized through and dominated by men. Women in these societies tend to have lower status than do women in matrilineal societies. One might expect more abuse of women in patrilineal than in matrilineal societies.

Sanday (1981) studied rape cross-culturally by examining 95 tribal societies. She found support for the hypothesis that rape is related to male dominance. "There is considerable evidence supporting the notion that rape is an expression of a social ideology of male dominance. Female power and authority is lower in rape prone societies. Women do not participate in public decision making in these societies and males express contempt for women as decision makers" (p. 24). There was also evidence demonstrating a link between a high incidence of rape and high levels of interpersonal violence.

The transition from **horticultural societies** to **agrarian societies** — a form of society in which large plots of land are prepared and cultivated with the help of ploughs and non-human labour — brought about a significant transformation of women's roles. Agrarian society is one in which women often have the least status.

Male supremacy in agrarian societies is marked by a consistent assignment of women to inferior status. This inferior status can be found in social practices such as female infanticide; female seclusion; mutilation of sex organs; footbinding; the exile or violent punishment of women violating norms of premarital chastity or marital fidelity; and the killing of women on the death of their husbands (see Box 13.3).

Although many vestiges of agrarian attitudes and practices continue in modern industrial society, women are more integrated into the work force, have gained status, and control more resources. Two significant forms of violence toward women remain, however: rape and domestic abuse, including murder.

Canadian data suggests that domestic relations were the most common context for murders of women; 54 percent of female victims in 1991 were killed by a family member. Only 22 percent of men were killed in a similar situation, and only 8 percent of female victims and 16 percent of male victims were killed by a stranger (Canadian Centre for Justice Statistics, 1992b). Although women are less likely to be murdered

. . . .

Box 13.3
Dowry Disputes
. . . .

Six weeks ago, Ms. Rana was found hanging from a ceiling fan in the palatial New Delhi home of her husband's parents. Her father immediately charged that she had been murdered. Her in-laws insisted that she had committed suicide, but they abruptly absconded when police began to investigate.

The Rana case is one of the more publicized of India's many thousand annual dowry deaths, but its essential elements are identical to those in the unnoticed deaths of far less affluent young brides.

Ms. Rana's wealthy parents had given a stereo unit, television set and several thousand dollars in cash to her in-laws, as dowry payment for her marriage four years ago. But the two families waged a bitter and protracted wrangle over the largest element in the package: a new automobile.

... By official count, that sort of domestic hell results in a young Indian woman's death five times every day. Activist groups say the toll is much higher, perhaps as many as 10 unreported deaths for every one entered in police records.

Most of the victims are murdered, often gruesomely. The favoured way of eliminating a bride in dowry disputes is to douse her with kerosene and set her sari alight.

Since all dowry deaths are disguised as suicides or kitchen accidents, the full extent of the problem is impossible to know.

... Since 1961, India has had strict dowry prohibition laws making anyone who pays the demands liable to prosecution. Another law mandates a post mortem examination for all women who die unnaturally within seven years of marriage.

. . . .

SOURCE: Excerpted from Bryan Johnson, "Brides Die Gruesomely in Illegal Dowry Disputes," *The Globe and Mail*, January 28, 1989, p. A1. Reprinted with permission.

. . . .

than are men, they are equally likely to be victims of violent crime. Equal numbers of these crimes are classified as assaults. Women are less likely to be assaulted with a weapon than are men (Canadian Centre for Justice Statistics, 1992a).

When researchers examine the broader category of wife abuse the findings must be treated with caution because women may be reluctant to report or discuss their abuse. At the present, however, the results of victim surveys suggest that approximately 11 percent of women who live with men are abused by them in any given year (Ellis, 1987: 164).[3]

Crime in Switzerland

Switzerland presents another challenge, in that it is a highly industrialized and urban society that has a low crime rate. The theory developed above leads us to predict that Switzerland should have a crime rate comparable with other industrial nations. Does Switzerland challenge the theory? We argue that it does not; rather it confirms the above theory.

Clinard (1978) accounted for Switzerland's low crime rate in terms of the continuity of traditional forms of community integration:

With reference to urbanization, it was pointed out that urban growth has been slow, that the Swiss cities have never become extremely large, and they have no real slums. Political decentralization of the government is significant, particularly at the cantonial and communal levels. At these levels, the individual citizen plays an important role in the government, assuming greater responsibility for social and crime control measures. Contrary to the situation that exists in other European countries, firearms are readily accessible to individuals throughout the country. ...

Swiss offenders are older, in general, than are offenders in other countries ... the younger age groups conform to prescribed norms in greater proportion than they do in most West European countries. In conjunction with this conformity, along with more open communication lines between the young and the adult population, youth unrest is less in evidence. This is due, in part, to the greater participation at all age levels — for example, in numerous sports and other activities, as well as the system of national military service that systematically brings men, aged 20 to 55, together at periodic intervals, from the initial induction into the military service until the suspension of service decades later.[4]

Clinard identified several forms of integration that might contribute to the low crime rate:

- community integration around political activity;
- integration of people through sport and other activity;
- integration of men around military communities; and
- integration of young and old in similar activities (including military service).

It is also important to note that Switzerland has maintained a more traditional family form than have other European societies. The bourgeois family is still common (Popenoe, 1988).

Crime in Japan

Japan also presents a challenge to the understanding of crime. Like Switzerland, it is a highly developed society, in fact, it modernized very quickly and yet has extremely low rates of serious crime. Its crime rate may be the lowest of any developed nation.

Bayley (1976) estimated that the risk of being robbed was 208 times greater in the United States than in Japan. During 1962 and 1972, a period of rapid economic growth, serious crime in Japan *declined* by 40 percent, while London, Los Angeles, and Hamburg experienced increases of more than 50 percent.

Scholars have concluded that Japan's culture and form of social organization tend to favour compliance with the law. Japanese culture, for example, places more emphasis on obligations to the community, on interdependency, and on the reintegration of offenders into the community. Some evidence for these assertions can be found. Japanese police, for example, locate a higher percentage of offenders than do police in other western societies. This suggests that offenders are more likely to confess, to turn themselves in, or to be identified by the community. Further, offenders are prosecuted less frequently than in the West. Prosecution occurs only where the normal process of apology, compensation, and forgiveness by the victim breaks down. In the United States, 45 percent of those convicted of a serious crime serve a jail sentence; in Japan, less than 2 percent serve a prison term. In Japan 27 percent of those convicted of murder receive a suspended prison sentence (they do not go to prison) (Braithwaite, 1989: 62).

Two stories retold by Braithwaite capture something of the culture of Japan:

> The first is of two American servicemen accused of raping a Japanese woman. On Japanese legal advice, private reconciliation with the victim was secured; a letter from the victim was tabled in the court stating that she had been fully compensated and that she absolved the Americans completely. After hearing the evidence, the judge leaned forward and asked the soldiers if they had anything to say. "We are not guilty, your honor," they replied. Their Japanese lawyer cringed; it had never occurred to him that they might not adopt a repentant role. They were sentenced to the maximum term of imprisonment, not suspended.

The second story involves a Japanese woman arriving in the United States with currency she had not declared at her entry point to the country.

> It was not the sort of case that would normally be prosecuted. The law is intended to catch the importation of cash which is the proceeds of illicit activities, and there was no suggestion of this. Second, there was doubt that the woman had understood the form which required the currency declaration. After the woman left the airport, she wrote to the Customs Service acknowledging her violation of the law, raising none of the excuses or explanations available to her, apologizing profusely, and seeking forgiveness. In a case that would not normally merit prosecution, the prosecution went forward because *she had confessed and apologized*; the U.S. Justice Department felt it was obliged to proceed in the face of a bald admission of guilt.[5]

Wilson and Herrnstein (1985) also find some unique aspects of Japanese society that affect deviance rates. They identify four features of Japanese society that, they claim, help explain Japan's low crime rate: first, Japan is racially, ethnically, and culturally more homogeneous than are most western societies: second, Japan has been able to preserve village life in the neighbourhoods of its cities; third, the Japanese emphasis on solidarity and group achievement contrasts with the individualism of western nations; and finally, Japanese culture is more concerned with obligations than with rights.[6]

Switzerland and Japan appear to challenge some sociological theories about levels of societal crime, but on close analysis actually affirm them. Experience in these two societies suggests the importance of a communitarian culture and of integrating individuals into meaningful social relationships. In most western societies, capitalism has undermined community life and disrupted social relationships, and the ideology of liberalism has shifted cultural emphasis from communal values to values of individual interest and achievement.

CRIME AND THE WELFARE STATE

If social bonds and shared values reduce societal rates of deviance, one might expect to find some variation between developed societies that can be linked to their social policies. Do welfare states experience less deviance than those with minimal, if any, social programs?

In order to make sense of the research on welfare-state societies and crime rates, more must be said about the effect of capitalism on social relations and cultural values. Capitalism, left to itself, disrupts communities and undermines social relationships. Further, it promotes cultural values that emphasize individual achievement and interest. Community is weakened, and individual inequality is promoted. Inequality can be seen both in the gap between rich and poor and in the number of poor people. A large poverty class is evidence that individual citizens are marginalized. To be unemployed and poor is to be cut off from the integrating (and controlling) mechanism of employment and to be located physically and symbolically on the margin of community and social life. To be poor may result in the absence of respect and self-esteem, of the resources to maintain social relationships, and of the opportunity to participate in community affairs.

Welfare states not only develop social policies that express the importance of communal values, they provide individuals with the means to be integrated more fully into social life. This integration may be accomplished in a variety of ways such as through employment, the enhancement of self-respect, or the provision of resources such as housing and family support. One might therefore ask if there is any link between inequality, unemployment, and criminal activity.

Crime and Inequality of Opportunity

Robert Merton developed a second conception of anomie that incorporates the concept of inequality. Merton defined anomie as a state of normlessness arising from a disjunction between culturally provided goals (such as wealth and success) and the normative means available to achieve these goals. He noticed that not all members of a society have equal access to the means to achieve their culturally provided aspirations. If high levels of consumption are held out as goals that embody status, satisfaction, and personal meaning, some individuals will experience strain toward a violation of the law as a way to achieve their aspirations. Merton believed that this explained why there are higher rates of crime among the poor than among other class groups. This theory formed the basis of much social policy during the 1950s and 1960s that was intended to provide greater equality of opportunity. While focussing on the crime-causing role of marked inequality of opportunity, the theory does not comment on inequality of condition.

Merton's theory does offer an explanation of the distribution of crime; it explains that there is a higher rate of crime among the lower class because they experience more strain toward crime. Not all of the lower class commit crime, of course. In explaining why some individuals choose crime and others do not, Merton appealed to the failure of socialization. Some individuals have not sufficiently internalized the norms of control, so they find it easier to succumb to the strain toward deviance. This implies that the lower class do a poorer job of socializing their children into cultural constraints than do other classes. Here Merton is a functionalist; the family as a system of integration and formation of value consensus has failed in its task.

Crime and Inequality of Condition

● ● ● ● ● ● ● ●

Steven Box (1987) reviewed most of the research on the topics of inequality and unemployment and reached different conclusions from those of Merton. Although he confirmed the linkage of class to crime rates, he stressed the importance of specific economic causes in generating crime.

Income inequality is strongly related to criminal activity — with the exception of homicide. It should be emphasized that no existing research has produced results which contradict this. Any crime control policy which fails to recognize this finding clearly fails to get to grips with a major underlying structural factor which generates a strong motive to commit crime (p. 96).

Regarding unemployment levels, Box says:

The relationship between overall unemployment and crime is inconsistent. ... On balance the weight of existing research supports there being a weak but none the less significant causal relationship. However, properly targeted research on young males, particularly those from disadvantaged ethnic groups, which considers both the meaning and duration of unemployment ... is the only way of settling this issue (pp. 96–97).

This suggests that societies that are able to offset the effects of the market by achieving a high level of employment and reducing the extent of inequality should have lower crime rates than those that are not successful in achieving these objectives. In short, advanced welfare states should have lower crime rates than those with a minimal welfare state.

Elliott Currie (1985) examined some of these issues in relation to the United States, a society with comparatively little development of the welfare state. He concluded:

It isn't accidental, then, that among developed countries, the Unites States is afflicted simultaneously with the worst rates of violent crime, the widest spread of income inequality, and the most severe public policies toward the disadvantaged. The industrial societies that have escaped our extremes of criminal violence tend either to have highly developed public sectors with fairly generous systems of income support, relatively well developed employment policies, and other cushions against the "forces of the market," or (like Japan) to accomplish much the same ends through private institutions backed by an ethos of social obligation and mutual responsibility. By any measure we can construct, these countries have been less plagued by the extremes of inequality and economic insecurity (pp. 171–172).

Aboriginal people in Canada are the nation's most marginalized and poorest, so if Elliott is correct, they should exhibit high crime rates. For aboriginal people, the chance of being a victim of crime is almost double that of other citizens. The 1990 crime rate in aboriginal communities was 160 offences per 1000 population, compared with 92 per 1000 in all other communities. For violent offences the gap is even wider: 33.1 per 1000, compared with 9 per 1000.[7] Canadian research in 1988 revealed that 17.6 percent of homicide victims and 22.2 percent of those suspected of homicide were aboriginal Canadians (Statistics Canada, 1989), although they compose only 3 percent of the population. Can their overrepresentation in homicide statistics be attributed to their status as the most marginal and most disadvantaged of Canadians?

These findings are worth considering at a time when the welfare state is under attack and the deregulated workings of the market are being given a new importance. It is also instructive to note that of the 23 nation members of the Organization for Economic Co-operation and Development, 15 of them collect more tax revenue as a proportion of GDP than does Canada and 13 spend more on social programs (excluding education and health) than does Canada (Economic Council of Canada, 1992b: 8–9).

The preceding pages have outlined a functionalist theory of crime rates. Social change was presented as disrupting communal life or producing cultural values antithetical to co-operative behaviour. Crime, for functionalists, is often considered a cost of development, a harmful form of behaviour to be contained by social control efforts. What would a critical perspective say about this?

A CRITICAL PERSPECTIVE

A critical perspective would generally agree with what has been reported. The analysis would be extended, however, to show that the disruption of community life and the destabilization of institutions of socialization are not the natural outcomes of development or of family life. Rather, they are the result of conflict inherent in the capitalist economic system, a patriarchal society, and a society with racial intolerance and practices of exclusion. Spitzer (1975), for example, developed a Marxian theory of deviance that considered the way capitalism produces problem populations.

The competitive struggle for markets and profits in a capitalist system (especially a world system) drives a constant process of technological development that both raises productivity and tends to shift investment away from labour. This process generates unemployment and creates people who become marginal to the economic life of the community. Managers may also remove capital from a community (e.g., close a plant) in order to move investments to a community in which wages are lower or markets are closer. The globalization of the economy in the past decades has resulted in a great deal of capital mobility. The effects have included a disruption of individual lives, of family life, and of community life.

Spitzer claimed that capitalist economies inevitably generate high levels of unemployment and underemployment: large numbers of people become surplus to the needs of the economy. This surplus population becomes a social problem, and the problem increases as this population becomes larger. Meanwhile the population with the ability to consume the goods and services being produced declines. Rates of profit for the corporate sector decline. The slowing of the economy puts pressure on governments to reduce social expenditures. The reduction of unemployment payments, employment training, family support payments, and social housing increases the money available for the accumulation of capital and, by reducing corporate taxes, increases the rate of profit. Governments are often left with few options these days, since investors can quite easily move their capital to a country that does provide the conditions favourable to a higher rate of profit. Increasing unemployment, a decline in the social wage, and rising community tension can be thought of as the outcomes of policies intended to benefit the needs of capital, at the expense of the community. Property rights are favoured over social rights.

The criminal justice system in western societies devotes a great deal of time to processing members of "the problem population," those members of the society who are marginal to, even surplus to, the economic system. In Manhattan's infamous prison-courthouse complex, the Tombs, court sits 24 hours a day, dispensing with a case every five minutes. The majority of the defendants are poor and Black; many who are unable to afford bail are locked up while awaiting their trial.[8] Poverty is also common among offenders in Canada: a study of women appearing before the court in Halifax, Nova Scotia, found that 49 percent had used legal-aid lawyers, a service available only to those with incomes below the poverty line. Another 43 percent were not represented by a lawyer at all.[9]

While Spitzer identifies the consequences of class relations, feminists develop a critical perspective that identifies the consequences of gender relations. Feminists would make sense of the previously presented figures on female victims of homicide and spousal assault by referring to a patriarchal family structure and a society organized around the needs and interests of men. Rather than focussing on shared cultural values or the effects of social change, feminists draw attention to the inherent conflict between men and women in a patriarchal society.

Visible-minority status is also strongly linked to involvement with the law enforcement system. Aboriginal peoples make up approximately 3 percent of the Canadian population, but they account for 17 percent of the persons held in custody following conviction (Jackson and Griffiths, 1991: 377). Although Blacks make up 6–8 percent of the population of metropolitan Toronto, it is claimed they are substantially overrepresented in some Toronto jails.[10] In the United States, Blacks account for 11 percent of the population but 44 percent of the prison population; one study found that 42 percent of Afro-American men between the ages of 18 to 35 were enmeshed in the criminal justice system (Reiman, 1989). These figures are not easily understood in a functionalist framework, nor do they just represent the effects of economic dislocation. Rather, they must be understood in the context of a criminal justice system and a society that stigmatize people on the basis of race.

Ample evidence of pervasive racism also exists in the Canadian criminal justice system. The cases of Donald Marshall, Helen Osborne, and William Nepoose all show failures in police work and the court system that are linked to racism.[11] Between 1988 and 1992, eight Black youths were shot by the Toronto police. The dubious circumstances surrounding several of these shootings are troubling for Canadians. An inquiry into the shooting death of a Black youth by the Montreal police cited the racism of the force as an important aspect of the circumstances leading to the youth's death.[12]

A critical perspective draws attention to racist and sexist ways of organizing social life and cultural values and to the effects of economic power in transforming the social life of a community in negative ways. Critical perspectives also encourage a consideration of the processes through which crime is defined and detected and focus on the criminal behaviour of the powerful as well as the disadvantaged. Organizational crime can be defined as illegal actions carried out by a company with the intention of benefitting itself (e.g., violating environmental regulations). This is to be distinguished from white-collar crime, which is the illegal behaviour of a person in a position of trust for personal benefit (e.g., embezzlement).

Organizational Crime
· · · · · · · · ·

Critical perspectives draw attention to the gap between the formal equality promised by the law and the substantive inequality that pervades the society. They suggest that economic and social inequality leads to inequality before the law. Advocates of a critical perspective on crime question much of the early part of this chapter because they believe that the content and application of the law has a class (as well as gender and race) bias. The law, they argue, more frequently prohibits behaviour that is engaged in by the lower class than it does the behaviour of the upper class. In reply, however, Braithwaite says:

> In modern capitalist societies there are many more statutes that criminalize the behavior of corporations (anti-pollution laws, occupational health and safety laws, consumer protection laws, antitrust laws, laws to enforce compliance with standards for everything from elevators to cleaning animal cages in laboratories) than there are laws that criminalize the behavior of the poor (1989: 40–41).

But substantial bias exists in the content of the regulations and in their enforcement. Before examining this, it is worth examining whether the corporate sector does engage in a substantial amount of harmful activity.

There is more corporate crime than one might think, and some of it is very deliberate. The Ford Motor Company, for example, carefully calculated the cost of recalling cars with a faulty gas tank design, which were subject to fire and explosion on impact, compared with the cost of compensating customers for death and injury caused by this design fault. The corporation chose to compensate victims, since it was the cheaper of the two options (Reasons and Perdue, 1981: 359). Dow Chemical reportedly was advised by its research staff that the breast implants it manufactured were subject to leaking and would result in potentially serious injury to the women using them.[13] This advice was ignored. The corporate owners and politicians were warned several times of the potential for safety problems at the Westray mine in Pictou County, Nova Scotia, and questions about safety continued to be raised until the fatal explosion of May 1992 killed 26 miners.[14] In 1992, it was revealed that General Motors may have known that one of its trucks had a design fault that put the vehicle at risk of fire during a side-on collision.[15] Products that fail to meet North American standards, agricultural chemicals, pharmaceuticals, and clothing are frequently exported to Third World countries with lower standards.

In 1990, 256 claims for workplace deaths due to accidents or disease were accepted by the Ontario Workers' Compensation Board. Until 1990, the maximum fine in Ontario for a company violating health and safety regulations in the workplace was $25 000 (subsequently raised to $500 000). Non-corporate offenders who recklessly or negligently caused death would almost certainly be sentenced to jail terms. It is very rare for a corporate executive or manager to experience this punishment (see, however, Box 13.4). In addition, Canada has regulations that generally prohibit workers or their families from suing employers.

It can be argued that people are much more likely to be injured on the job, as a result of faulty safety procedures, than they are to be attacked by a street criminal. They are much more likely to lose money as a result of price fixing, fraud, and shoddy design of consumer products than they are to be robbed by a burglar or assailant. The common image of the criminal, however, is likely to be that of a lower-class individual, not of a corporate executive.

Stereotypes about what crime actually is and who is most likely to commit it are linked to the place of the justice and court system personnel in the social structure. The social similarity of judges and corporate executives perhaps helps to explain the vast difference in sentences given to rich and poor (McCormick and Greene, 1990).

Box 13.4
Tainted Blood
Supplies

In 1993, four senior administrators of France's blood supply system were found guilty of criminal charges. They had been charged with fraud and failing to assist a person in danger. Some lobby groups were pleased with this outcome, since they had been claiming that without such convictions it would appear to be acceptable to murder with impunity. The struggle revolved around the times at which senior administrators should have known that the AIDS virus could be transmitted through the blood supply system and when they took action to protect the users of blood products.

In France, approximately 45 percent of the nation's hemophiliacs became infected through blood products. There is considerable variation among nations, however. In the United States, 75 percent became infected, while in Belgium, only 7 percent did so, as did 16 percent in Sweden. In Canada, 43 percent of hemophiliacs were infected. In 1993, Canada negotiated financial compensation for those infected and established a commission of inquiry to determine how its system of blood supply failed to protect people.

Not only hemophiliacs were infected through tainted blood, of course. The gay community expressed concern that the sympathy given to those infected through tainted blood creates a moral hierarchy with the homosexual at the bottom. Many lives were lost through the slowness of government responses to educate the public.

SOURCE: Adapted from André Picard "France Makes an Example of Misdeeds," *The Globe and Mail*, September 7, 1992, p. A4.

Income tax evasion, for example, brings an average prison sentence of 1.4 months, while a robbery conviction brings an average sentence of 38.9 months (Brannigan, 1984: 108). The longest and most costly criminal case in Canada concerned the evasion of $2.2 million in income taxes. While the judge described the prosecution's case as "extremely compelling," he was not convinced beyond a reasonable doubt and acquitted the defendant.[16]

Environmental Crime

Pollution, defined as the accidental or intentional introduction of contaminants into the environment, has become a major concern for citizens as they experience the degradation of the atmosphere, land, and water. While everyone contributes to pollution, it is clear that the major polluter is the corporate sector. Industry, in the eyes of the law, has a right to pollute; it is seen by government and corporations as a cost of doing business. Regulations, however, are intended to keep pollution within "acceptable limits." These limits are often set in co-operation with industry or established on the basis of research performed by industry. Bias is inherent in the development of the regulations, but this is not the end of the story: further bias is apparent in the enforcement of environmental regulations.

In March 1989, a leaked report from Environment Canada revealed that 83 of 149 pulp mills in Canada were dumping toxic chemicals into surrounding waters at a rate and level that violated national standards. The Fraser River Task Force Report concluded from its study of this important British Columbia river that, in approximately half of the cases studied, illegal discharges were being made (MacDonald, 1991: 182). Concerning the enforcement of standards, an Ontario government commission concluded that the low rate of prosecution and the low fines imposed made it cheaper for companies to pollute than to install pollution controls. Prior to July 1992, Ontario had jailed only one person for environmental offences. George Crowe was sentenced to six months' imprisonment after being convicted of burying hazardous wastes that tainted a dozen wells. This sentence was reduced to 15 days on appeal.

The records of the federal and provincial governments are equally disappointing. A review of Environment Canada found that prior to 1986 there were no prosecutions under the Canada Water Act or the Environmental Contaminants Act, only two under the Clean Air Act, and three under the Ocean Dumping Control Act (MacDonald, 1991: 181). In recent years, governments have begun to respond to public pressure and to the escalating degradation of the environment with more onerous penalties and increased enforcement.

SYMBOLIC INTERACTIONISM

Many would challenge some of the claims made above. For example, it was stated that while Blacks make up only 6–8 percent of the population of Metropolitan Toronto, they account for a much higher proportion of some Toronto-area jails. It suggested that this high involvement with the criminal justice system was linked to poverty and the restricted opportunities of visible minorities in a society deeply influenced by racism. But critics question the whole premise of this argument and ask: do Blacks actually *commit* more crimes than non-Blacks? Or do these figures reflect greater police surveillance of the Black community and a harsher police and court response to offences?

Some people argue that Blacks do commit more crime and that the problem arises from some aspect of Black culture, from less stability in the conventional forms of family, and from greater involvement with drugs. A previous mayor of Toronto, during her election campaign, hinted quite broadly that she thought Blacks presented a crime problem in Toronto. Her successful law-and-order campaign obviously appealed to some Torontonians. The idea that Blacks are treated unfairly by the police and court system has also been rejected by some. The police force of Montreal, for example, held a mass demonstration against the suggestion by their own chief that they had not done a very good job in a case resulting in the shooting of an innocent young Black man.

Symbolic interactionism helps us understand these divergent views. It has been described as microsociology because it focusses more on the actions of individuals than on social structures. It also tends to focus on how individuals define and interpret their situation and how they give meaning to events by defining social situations through interacting with others. Symbolic interactionism enriches understanding through its focus on how individuals, in specific interactions, reproduce society.

Dorothy Smith (1975), for example, showed how a gender- differentiated society is reflected, at the micro level, through the actions of physicians. Men and women presenting themselves to their psychiatrist with the same symptoms were responded to quite differently. She noted that 48 percent of women in-patients were diagnosed as having a "neurosis" on their first admission and 6.1 percent as having "alcoholism and alcoholic disorders." The corresponding figures for men were 25 percent and 32 percent. Smith argued that the behaviours of men and women are socially structured and culturally defined and that these processes can clearly be seen in the work of the pyschiatric profession.

According to Smith, the psychiatric profession classifies and analyzes men's and women's problems differently. Psychiatrists are not identifying some objective fact in the behaviour of their patients; rather, they bring an array of typical gender-based assumptions to the diagnostic process. They have a typical picture of the alcoholic and of the neurotic. Further, they have characterizations of appropriate behaviour for women and for men; they make judgements about people's physical appearance, age, speech, and gestures. Even "objective" science is, therefore, deeply influenced by the culture and structural features of society.

The judgemental work of psychiatrists helps shape the diagnoses they arrive at for each patient. Further, the diagnoses they arrive at and the way they respond to their patients may elicit from the patients behaviour that agrees with the diagnoses. In this view, mental illness becomes a process of social definition rather than an objective property of the behaviour of individuals.

Crime may be thought to have more of an objective character than does mental illness, but for the symbolic interactionist it too is the negotiated outcome of a process. The process of charging an offender is much like the process of psychiatric diagnosis; it is not a simple and direct response to the behaviour. Police, for example, may wish to retain maximum control over the development of a case as it goes to the crown prosecutor. They can do this by choosing the particular charge carefully and perhaps by laying a number of charges. This may make it more difficult for the person to obtain bail, and this fact may influence the judge or jury in convicting or sentencing the individual. The decisions the police make, like those made by the psychiatrist, will be shaped by judgements about the character of the individual, by social stereotypes, and by assumptions about typical offenders.

The complaints about police behaviour made by Blacks across Canada are complaints about the judgemental work of the police officers. They feel they are treated unfairly because the police treat them differently, and this different treatment arises from the assumptions made about Blacks. Black parents are concerned about their children going out in the evening because they know the children will be stopped by the police, and they worry that these encounters may result in criminal or traffic charges or in violence. If the police believe that Blacks are a crime problem, do not respect authority, and are drug dealers, their intervention into the evening travels of young Blacks may to them seem like good police work. For young people, however, having been stopped by the police for no apparent cause may result in hostility to authority. The next time a police encounter occurs, the police will witness anger and retaliation and believe their initial judgement was justified. This behaviour becomes a self-fulfilling prophecy.

This kind of analysis necessitates a careful use of statistics relating to crime or deviance. Durkheim, for example, used official statistics on suicide for his research because he was convinced that suicide was an objective fact: coroners were just responding to inherent, but sometimes hidden, properties of the death. Others have shown that the classification of death as suicide involves a highly subjective process of interpretation and moral judgement (see Box 13.5). Merton assumed that the official statistics on crime showing high rates for the lower class were acceptable; others show that middle class and organizational crime is less often detected and less often punished. Police assume the high rates of arrest and incarceration of Blacks is a measure of their criminal behaviour; others suggest that focussed police activity against

Box 13.5
Is Youth Suicide
an Epidemic?

Canada has the unenviable distinction of having one of the highest suicide rates in the world for young people between the ages of 15 and 24 (UNICEF, 1993). Sixteen of every 100 000 young people end their own lives. This rate is twice that of Britain or Japan, and five times that of Italy. Only Australia and Norway have higher rates. The rate of suicide among aboriginal young people is even higher. The federal Department of Health and Welfare reports the rate for registered First Nations people as four times the national average (68 per 100 000). A British Columbia investigation that attempted to include all aboriginal people found that rates for males between the ages of 15 and 24 to be approximately 90 per 100 000 and 24 per 100 000 for females (Cooper et al., 1991).

Eglin et al. (1984), however, after an investigation of the Ontario coroner system, provide some reason to doubt whether the current high rates (still growing) are really a sign of more suicides among young people. Legal, technical, and professional changes in the coroner system have made it more difficult to hide a probable suicide and more likely that investigation will discover such a death. Further, they note that there has been a growing professionalization of suicide experts and they have focussed particularly on young people. There are now prevention programs in schools, leading parents and teachers and young people themselves to worry about the intentions of students. Further, there has been a proliferation of social and psychological supports for young people, such as crisis lines. These services leave a documentary trail that can be called upon to construct the intent of a young person in case of death.

Blacks produces much of the apparent disproportion of crime in the Black community. Behind each of these views is an assumption that criminal behaviour or suicide is a an objective event followed by an official response (a police arrest or a coroner's designation of suicide) (see Figure 13.1).

The assumption that deviant behaviour, like crime or suicide, is an objective event followed by an objective official response is open to challenge. Symbolic interactionism has shown another way to look at this relationship between behaviour and response. The two are not separated in a cause–effect relationship but are tangled together in a process of social recognition, identification, labelling, or naming. One cannot exist without the other, and the process of labelling reflects the social and cultural context in which it is done (see Figure 13.2).

What is crime, then? Is it a way of behaving (e.g., killing someone or polluting the environment), or is it just a label given to some behaviours? It's probably both. People learn quite different things by adopting each of these definitions. They can learn something about how murder is distributed in society by following the assumption that murder is an objective event; and the insights of symbolic interactionism, when combined with an analysis of power and influence, help us to understand why the many deaths resulting from asbestos fibres lodging in the lungs of workers have not been labelled as murder, although it has been known since the nineteenth century that these fibres cause cancer.

Figure 13.1
Suicide as an
Objective Event
· · · · · · · ·

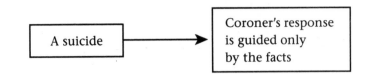

Figure 13.1
Suicide as an
Objective Event
· · · · · · · ·

CONCLUSION
· · · · · · · ·

Following Durkheim's example, this chapter demonstrated how sociologists under-stand violations of community norms by placing those violations in a societal con-text. Rates of criminal behaviour were shown to vary with social features of the com-munity. Communities that integrate individuals weakly into social life and those with a significant degree of inequality have higher rates of crime than do those that strongly integrate individuals and have a low degree of inequality. Social integration reduces crime by strengthening the social bond and increasing commitments to the social and normative order. Inequality reduces social participation and undermines the self-esteem of citizens, pushing them toward the physical and symbolic margins of the society.

Generally speaking, economic development has increased rates of criminal activity because this development is associated with some disintegration of community and an increase in the visibility of class divisions in society. This generalization is challenged by societies such as Switzerland and Japan, which have experienced modernization without the expected increase in crime. Sociologists argue that in each case the rea-son for the unexpectedly low crime rate is a high degree of social integration. Further, studies of welfare states show that those with an advanced welfare system tend to have lower rates of crime than do the others. An advanced welfare state is able to soften the effects of market economies and makes the class divisions of society less visible.

Societies also vary in the amount of violence directed against women, and this can be understood by examining the social structure of societies. Those with patriarchal values and structures are more likely to have higher rates of sexual assault and domes-tic abuse than are more egalitarian societies. Societies that have a culture of male dom-inance and glorify male physical aggression have more male violence than do those with a less masculine culture.

Functionalists tend to understand crime by focussing on the breakdown of social life. They see it as an inevitable consequence of modernization. The emergence of individualism, the rapidity of change and the increasing heterogeneity of society are all associated with a weakened ability of society to control individual behaviour. Functionalists also see some social developments as dysfunctional. For example, bar-

Figure 13.2
Suicide as a Social
Construction
· · · · · · · ·

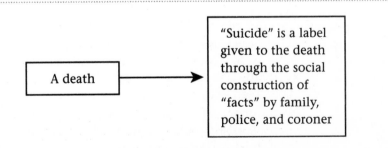

riers to opportunities increase the motivation of the deprived to engage in crime. A culture of male dominance increases crime in the society. Family instability may reduce the ability of the family to socialize children into the normative order.

A critical perspective, by contrast, tends to focus on the inherent inequalities of opportunity and condition in a particular social structure and on the way a cultural ideology legitimizes this structure. The disruption of community life brought on by modernization is not considered an inevitable consequence of development or a byproduct of social change. Rather, it is seen as a consequence of the inherent inequality of a society in which modernization is founded on capitalist free enterprise and the rights of private property. Communal disruption follows from change that is directed only by those with economic or political power. Societies in which the community itself is able to direct social change are less likely to have the same degree of disruption or the same amount of crime.[17]

Similarly, a patriarchal society is one in which women are systematically disadvantaged. Crime against women is not understood as a dysfunctional byproduct of a male culture but as an instrument of male control and an expression of devaluation. Violence and threat of violence can be understood as ways of maintaining the status quo and of getting one's way.

Critical perspectives also draw attention to the violence committed by the corporate sector in its pursuit of profit. Since big business has a closer connection to the state apparatus than do most citizens, it is not surprising that many of the acts of violence committed by business are not defined as criminal or that the enforcement of regulations governing corporations is rather weak.

The fact that many of the violent actions of business are not defined as criminal leads to a consideration of symbolic interactionism. A microperspective focussing on the interactions of individuals, this perspective shows how the social structure is reproduced through people's daily actions. In dealing with events and other individuals, people constantly interpret and define situations. They do not engage in these actions single-handedly; rather, they bring their understanding of the culture and the social structure to bear on these activities and, in so doing, act in ways that reproduce the social structure. Although people think they are dealing in an objective way with their social environment, symbolic interactionism shows that they respond through a subjective interpretation of it.

These conclusions make crime and deviance somewhat problematic, since one cannot know in advance just what will be defined as criminal or deviant or what will be responded to in a controlling fashion. What is known, however, is that the ability to criminalize others increases as social status increases and the likelihood of having a criminal "label" increases as one's social status decreases.

· · · · · · · · ·

NOTES

1. In 1991, the suicide rate for Newfoundland was 7.2 per 100 000. Alberta's was 18.14 and Quebec's 16.16. It is misleading to use figures for a single year, however, since small changes in the number of suicides can affect the rates substantially. For example, in 1991 Prince Edward Island, with a rate of 16.9, had the second-highest rate in Canada (Statistics Canada, 1993b) — not what one would expect, but there were an unusually high number of suicides that year. Similarly, Ontario had the lowest rate, again not what one might expect. It would be better to use five-year averages.

2. Leacock (1977) argues that some hunting and gathering societies have been egalitarian.

3. See W. DeKeseredey (1992) for an examination of these estimates. Some estimates are as high as 24.5 percent. A Statistics Canada survey released in 1993, however, reported that 10 percent of adult women had experienced an assault in the last year.

4. Excerpted from Marshall B. Clinard, "Implications of the Swiss Crime Rate," in Marshall B. Clinard, *Cities with Little Crime* (Cambridge: Cambridge University Press, 1978), pp. 150–151. Reprinted with the permission of Cambridge University Press.

5. Excerpted from John Braithwaite, "Shaming and the Good Society," in John Braithwaite, *Crime, Shame and Reintegration* (Cambridge: Cambridge University Press, 1989), p. 165. Reprinted with the permission of Cambridge University Press.

6. It might be noted as well that they suggest that intelligence may explain the low rate of crime in Japan. The average IQ score for Japanese citizens is approximately 10 points higher than the average in the United States. For a critique of claims about intelligence, see Chapter Seven.

7. Rudy Platiel, "Crime Against Natives Double National Level," *The Globe and Mail*, July 1, 1991, p. A4. Also see Statistics Canada (1991a) and Statistics Canada (1993d).

8. Kirk Makin, "Overworked U.S. Court Revolves Around Deals," *The Globe and Mail*, January 2, 1987, p. A8.

9. Kevin Cox "Study Links Poverty to Crimes by Women," *The Globe and Mail*, April 11, 1992, p. A5.

10. "Toronto's Lessons (II)," *The Globe and Mail*, May 7, 1992, p. A20. We should, however, be suspicious of the Canadian figures, since they are not the result of careful and systematic research.

11. For a review of the Marshall case, see M. Harris (1990); the Osborne tragedy is recounted in Priest (1989). There have been commissions of inquiry in several provinces that also document the problems that aboriginal people encounter in the justice system (see Royal Commission on Aboriginal Peoples, 1993); for the experience of Blacks, see Commission on Systemic Racism in the Ontario Criminal Justice System (1994).

12. Patricia Poirier "Cry for Help Has Been Heard," *The Globe and Mail*, May 8, 1992, p. A1.

13. "Memo Proves Manufacturer knew in 1971 Breast Implant Leaked," *Halifax Chronicle*, February 11, 1992, p. C12; Charlotte Gray, "Manufacturers, Plastic Surgeons Draw Fire at U.S. Forum on Breast Implant Issue," *Canadian Medical Association Journal* 148 (1993): 1801–1802.

14. Jennifer Wells, "The Fault Lines," *Report on Business Magazine*, December, 1992, pp. 33–52.

15. Barry Meier "Data Show G.M. Knew for Years of Risk in Pickup Trucks' Design," *New York Times*, November 17, 1992, p. A1.

16. Thomas Claridge, "Longest Court Case Produces Acquittal," *The Globe and Mail*, April 13, 1991, p. A1.

17. While it is always difficult to make cross-cultural comparisons (even more so when considering communist countries) there is evidence to suggest that Cuba was able to achieve a degree of economic development at the same time as its crime rate was reduced (Scott, 1985). In theory, at least, political power in a com-

munist country does not lie with a particular elite group; rather, efforts are made to empower the community itself.

· · · · · · · · ·

FURTHER READING

· · · · · · · · ·

Adelberg, Ellen, and Claudia Currie. *Too Few to Count.* Vancouver: Press Gang, 1987. One of the first books to address the topic of female offenders in Canada.

Box, Steven. *Recession, Crime and Punishment.* Barnes and Noble Books, 1987. This useful examination of the research on the relationship between unemployment and criminal behaviour looks at conventional, corporate, and police crime. A useful discussion of how a microperspective deepens a structural understanding of crime rates.

Braithwaite, John. *Crime, Shame and Reintegration.* New York: Cambridge University Press, 1989. An example of a recent attempt to develop a general theory of crime (including corporate crime), it bears some similarities to Durkheim.

Faith, Karlene. *Unruly Women: The Politics of Confinement and Resistance.* Vancouver: Press Gang, 1994. A feminist perspective on women and crime.

Hester, Stephen, and Peter Eglin. *A Sociology of Crime.* New York: Routledge, 1993. A clear treatment of how three quite different sociologies approach the issue of crime. Concluding that functionalism has been discredited, it focusses on a structural conflict theory, symbolic interactionism, and ethnomethodology.

Leyton, Elliott, William O'Grady, and James Overton. *Violence and Public Anxiety.* St. John's: Institute of Social and Economic Research, 1993. An engaging examination of crime in Newfoundland, with important insights for sociologists and for Canadians.

Pearons, Geoffrey. "Lawlessness, Modernity and Social Change: A Historical Appraisal." *Theory, Culture and Society* 2 (3): 15–33. Provides a powerful challenge to many of the assumptions of this chapter, and upsets the often-romantic notion that things were better in the past. For a further example of this perspective, see Olive Anderson, "Did Suicide Increase with Industrialization in Victorian England?" *Past and Present* 86: 149–173.

Schrecker, T.F. *Political Economy of Environmental Hazards.* A study prepared for the Law Reform Commission of Canada. Ottawa: Minister of Supply and Services, 1984. As the title suggests, the author takes a critical perspective to examine law and environmental crime.

Shkilnyk, A. *A Poison Stronger Than Love: The Destruction of an Ojibwa Community.* New Haven, CT: Yale University Press, 1985. A compelling description of the effects of economic and social dislocation on the lives of an aboriginal community in Ontario.

· · · · · · · · ·

STUDY QUESTIONS

· · · · · · · · ·

1. Assess the claim that functionalist explanations of deviance focus on individuals, while critical views concentrate on social forces.
2. Does the sociological study of deviance provide insight into the reasons for limited success in the rehabilitation of criminals?
3. What are some of the main reasons why statistics relating to crime and other types of deviance should not be taken at face value?
4. How does symbolic interactionism enrich an understanding of the sociology of deviant behaviour?

5. What are the features of societies with high crime rates?
6. What are the features of societies with high rates of violence against women?
7. Why might there be a high rate of deviance among young people in contemporary society?
8. Interview a person who has been publicly (or officially) labelled as a type of deviant. Have that person describe how this labelling changed his or her self-image and affected his or her relationships with others.

14 CONSUMER CULTURE

INTRODUCTION

Culture is the norms, values, and beliefs that provide people with direction and meaning. It gives them a sense of self-identity and of connection to others. In any society, culture is shaped by, and expressed in, institutional ways of doing things. Thus, in Canada, one would expect society to be shaped by the social and economic forces inherent in capitalism. From a liberal viewpoint, culture should reflect individuality and personal choice; pluralism and variety should be enhanced by free choice in a free market. But many critics suggest that modern corporate capitalism has an inherent tendency to create uniformity and homogeneity. The right of individual choice may not automatically lead to the genuine existence of choice.

Is there a conflict between the corporate ownership of national and international broadcasting and the preservation of variety? Is there even a threat to people's sense of self as a result of their emotional needs becoming linked, by advertising, to the consumption and possession of goods? Does a culture that focusses on individuals as consumers pose a threat to society? Behind these questions is a broad concern that the society has entered a cultural crisis, in which the culture no longer is able to provide meaning to individual lives or an expression of relevant social values.

This chapter concludes this book's exploration of society and demonstration of the usefulness of sociology as a vehicle for understanding. The previous seven chapters have examined the structure of key institutions of modern capitalist societies, especially Canada. This examination has contrasted the standards set by liberal social and political ideas. Although liberalism, with its emphasis on individual liberty, is a culture of promise behind every modern capitalist society, much of its promise has been unrealized. The promise of political equality among individuals has been restricted by the structure of power. The promise of a competitive economy has been frustrated by the rise of the large corporation and, in Canada, by the concentration of capital and a high degree of foreign ownership. The promise of equality of opportunity has been undermined by the class and gender dynamics of society. Finally, the promise of personal freedom has been limited by a hierarchical organization of work for intensity, efficiency, and profit that has created a deep sense of alienation among workers.

It is this gap between the promise of liberalism and the reality of social life in modern capitalist society that enables liberalism to be defined as an ideology, a set of beliefs that uphold and legitimate the present arrangement of society.

One aspect of modern society remains to be explored: the impact of modern capitalism on culture. Culture encompasses the knowledge, beliefs, and values that people learn as members of a society. They share their culture with other members of society and, to some extent, culture distinguishes them from members of other societies.

Does the structure of modern capitalist society give any special character to its culture? The promise of liberal thought is that cultural choices, like choices about other goods and services, will be protected and promoted by the free market. Individual self-expression should also be enhanced as people exercise their personal tastes and preferences. This view is closely related to the functionalist analysis of culture in modern societies and conflicts with a critical perspective. Before examining cultural production in modern societies, a brief examination of functionalist and critical perspectives is in order.

PERSPECTIVES ON CULTURE

· · · · · · · · ·

Functionalists tend to adopt a liberal view of culture in modern societies; they suggest that these societies encourage cultural pluralism. Jackson Toby saw societies becoming increasingly differentiated as they evolve and the component parts of society becoming more autonomous. This provides for a flowering of cultural variety: "Cultural systems are more autonomous in later stages of social evolution than they were earlier. Thus, it is meaningful to speak of art, science, religion, literature, music and even sociology as relatively autonomous cultural realms of modern society" (1979: 389).

If these cultural domains become autonomous, they will naturally become more separated and more differentiated, thus allowing for their independent development and distinct character. Daniel Bell (1978) also took this position when he argued that there is a growing contradiction between the values of capitalism and the values portrayed in the culture-creation agencies; there is no clear relationship between the two. According to Bell, the cultural values reflected in visual art, music, and writing are quite different from these supporting modern capitalism. He worried that a stress on personal satisfaction may undermine the values that maintain capitalist enterprise and initiative. As Max Weber might have put it, a stress on consumption as a means of satisfaction undermines the work ethic. While there is some value in this perspective, there is an alternative view. Marshall Berman (1982) captured a critical perspective:

> But what is masked here by modernists and anti-modernists alike is the fact that these spiritual and cultural movements, for all their eruptive power, have been bubbles on the surface of a social and economic cauldron that has been teeming and boiling for more than a hundred years. It is modern capitalism, not modern art and culture, that has set and kept the pot boiling — reluctant as capitalism may be to face the heat (p. 123).

This view suggests that modern culture is driven by the economic organization of society: there is a close fit between economic life and ways of cultural expression. It prompts two questions. First, does Canadian culture express variety and choice? Second, can a culture of individualism provide meaning and direction to social life? Does the image of individuals as consumers leave room for community purpose and active citizenship? This chapter examines the view that the answer to both questions is "No." It begins with two examples in which the promise of a consumer culture driven by choice has led instead to the imposition of standardization and uniformity. These examples explore a theme suggested by a Bruce Springsteen song:

> I bought a bourgeois house in the Hollywood hills
> With a trunkload of hundred thousand dollar bills
> Man came by to hook up my cable TV
> ....
> We switched 'round and 'round 'til half-past dawn
> There was fifty-seven channels and nothin' on
> ....
> So I hopped into town for a satellite dish
> I tied it to the top of my Japanese car
> I came home and I pointed it out into the stars
> A message came back from the great beyond
> There's fifty-seven channels and nothin' on

SHOPPING MALLS AND CORN!

· · · · · · · ·

What do shopping malls and corn have in common? The answer is uniformity. Margaret Visser suggests that "uniformity, disguise itself as it may behind the multiplicity of cans, boxes, bottles and cartons in our supermarkets, is a peculiarly modern curse" (1986: 55). This section explores this phenomenon and its links to the way North American society is organized.

Shopping malls became a fixture of suburban North America in the 1950s and have proliferated since. Most people visit them regularly, and communities compete to have the largest mall. There are many advantages and disadvantages to this form of retailing, but two things are of interest in this discussion. First, there is a uniformity of merchandise in shopping malls; approximately 60 percent of the stores are national retail chains, so what one sees in one community one also sees in the other. Mall owners and managers also prefer to avoid competition in accepting merchants into the mall; this ensures that each merchant maximizes profits and, by implication, that the mall owner receives maximum profit (since it frequently receives a share of the profit of individual shops in addition to receiving rents). Second, the mall is private property. Consequently, a space that more and more replaces the publicly owned street and city square falls under the control of a private owner.

Ownership permits control of the way in which space is used and to some extent control of who uses the space. Merchants are told how to display goods, and, using the law of trespass, the owner may restrict individuals who are considered disruptive or undesirable. In the United States, for example, a civil liberties group stood in a mall and handed out copies of the American Bill of Rights. They refused to leave when asked by the owner and were charged and successfully prosecuted for trespass (Kowinski, 1985: 354–359). Users of a mall are thus guaranteed a friction-free experience while shopping; everyone becomes a shopper. Some democratic rights may be infringed in the process. Citizens, while in "public," become unable to express opinions, to provide others with information, and to solicit support for social and political objectives.[2] Social life is considerably diminished. Malls present a uniformity of culture that arises from the economic organization of the space.

What about corn? Corn originated in Central America, where it has been grown for many thousands of years. Corn evolved into several hundred varieties, and the Native peoples deliberately maintained variety of corn stock by preventing the corns from mixing. Among other things, having several varieties ensures that corn will not be eliminated if any particular variety succumbs to disease or growing conditions. Things began to change, however, when North American developers and scientists became interested in corn.

> *One of the great American myths was being created and accepted with ever increasing confidence and fervour: that beauty — in corn as in everything else — is largely a matter of uniformity. Straight rows of kernels were admired, truly cylindrical cobs, absolute uniformity of colour, yellow or white. (Red corn, black, blue and the rest had long ago been eliminated as unacceptable for North Americans.)* (Visser, 1986: 47)

This uniformity not only reflected a developing cultural value; it satisfied economic needs for the maximization of output, an ease of harvest, and a reduction in the reliance on labour. Consequently, a corn cob in Saskatoon looks much like a cob of corn anywhere else in the world. There is a price to be paid for this. The absence of alternative varieties makes crops much more vulnerable to being eliminated. The genetic qualities of other types of corn that may make certain crops resistant to disease, wind, or drought become lost forever. A recent awareness of this possibility, with corn and other crops, has led to the creation of plant libraries — warehouses for the germ-plasm of plant varieties. This response itself raises several questions: do the countries from which the stock was originally taken still have access to the variety? Who owns the variety in the library? Is the variety available in the store the one with the best nutritional base? The best taste? Is freedom of choice being compromised?[3]

There is another aspect to this problem. As genetic engineering makes possible the creation of new plant stocks, it is increasingly clear that the law will make these new varieties private property. The owners of the new seeds will have an interest in reducing varieties to ensure that everyone buys and grows their seeds. Further, the new hybrid plants are typically unable to seed themselves (they do not "breed true") thus making growers totally dependent on the seed company. The Seed Savers Exchange of Iowa found that 943 open-pollinated varieties of vegetables available from seed catalogues in 1984 were no longer available in 1987. By 1991, a further 1263 varieties of seeds were dropped by the seed companies. "In addition, of the 5797 vegetable varieties available in commercial seed catalogues, 3002 are offered by only one company, with another 883 offered by only two companies" (Kneen, 1993: 82). For these reasons, there is a growing underground network cultivating heritage plants and exchanging seeds.

A UNIFORMITY OF PERSONALITY

Many critics of modern society assert that it tends to produce uniformity in the public expression of personality. Max Weber, for example, discussed the "disenchantment of the world": a culture develops that stresses systematic organizational efficiency and calculated quantifiable goals. The spiritual and mysterious element of life is diminished, and everything becomes explainable by rational analysis. Personal expression also becomes standardized, as people increasingly find their social roles in formal bureaucratic organizations:

> *When fully developed, bureaucracy also stands, in a specific sense, under the principle of* sine ira ac studio *[without ill-will and without favour]. Its specific nature,*

which is welcomed by capitalism, develops the more perfectly the more the bureau-
cracy is "dehumanized," the more completely it succeeds in eliminating from official
business love, hatred, and all purely personal, irrational, and emotional elements
which escape calculation. This is the specific nature of bureaucracy and it is
appraised as its special virtue (Gerth and Mills, 1970: 215–216).

Philip Slater, in *The Pursuit of Loneliness*, also discusses the rationalization of personality in modern, mobile societies:

Where internalization is high [in modern society] there is often a feeling that the
controls themselves are out of control — that emotion cannot be expressed when
the person would like to express it. Life is muted, experience filtered, emotion anes-
thetized or its discharge incomplete (1976: 31).

This worry about the diminishment of individuality has been a common refrain
among sociologists. David Riesman, in *The Lonely Crowd* (1950), foresaw the development of the inauthentic individual as everyone becomes increasingly subject to
fads and fashions. The result is a uniformity of individuals:

In adult life he continues to respond to these peers, not only with overt conformity,
as do people in all times and places, but also in a deeper sense, in the very quality of
his feelings. Yet, paradoxically, he remains a lonely member of the crowd because he
never comes really close to the others or to himself (p.v.).

IDEOLOGICAL A belief in the possibility of **authentic individuation** lies behind all this criticism.
INDIVIDUALISM This concept suggests that individual uniqueness is nurtured and sustained by attach-
· · · · · · · · · ment to the community, rather than by separation from it. Stanley Diamond (1974)
captured the idea in his contrast of individuation and ideological individualism.
Individuation occurs when people develop their sense of self through full participation in a well-integrated community. Their sense of who they are is fully expressed
in their social roles, since there is no expectation that people divide their private and
public identities.

Ideological individualism, on the other hand, is a reflection of a society that increasingly separates people from each other because of the replacement of natural ties of
mutual activity and involvement by contractual ties. These societies foster a commitment to individualism but only allow for the development of self within a narrow
range of human contacts. They are less tolerant of the public expression of individuality. The authentic self, therefore, is found only in private settings and intimate relationships. People find and express their individuality through family, friends, music,
books, or the leisure they choose to pursue in private. In public, especially at work,
there is considerable pressure for conformity and a muted expression of individuation.

Many examples of this pressure to assume a public personae can be found. Stern
and Shachtman (1991), in a book on how to be successful in the corporate world, suggest that it is essential to align one's thoughts and actions with the organization's
goals and strategies. They encourage individuals to carefully construct the image they
present to others so that they can successfully market themselves in their career.

The objectives of corporately driven entertainment also encourage standardization
and the elimination of personal cultural expression. In 1992, CBS television agreed
to pay David Letterman about $42 million over three years to be the host of its late-
night television show. Although this might seem expensive, they estimated that if

Letterman became a hit he could create a $20 million to $40 million profit for the corporation each year. The reason for this is that late-night shows capture a young audience, and advertisers are willing to pay more for access to this audience. It is estimated that North American teenagers spend $28 billion each year in grocery shopping for their parents and a further $12 billion on clothing for themselves. There is considerable competition among the media to capture this audience and deliver it to the advertiser. Four magazines for teenagers (*Seventeen, Sassy, Teen,* and *YM*) produce a total of about 2500 advertising pages each year.[4] These advertising pages, and indeed much of the magazines' regular content, encourage young people to commodify their self and to project a personal image taken from advertising. One's public image becomes everything, and this image is to be managed and manipulated; self becomes a commodity, and advertisers strive for a uniformity of self in order to maximize profit from fashion, cosmetics, and music.

A central feature of modern society is its pressure toward uniformity, rationalization and standardization of personality, and routinization of social life. A strong link exists between the development of uniformity and the way economic and social life is organized. This uniformity is essentially a cultural phenomenon; while the corn cob is material, the uniformity of its rows are the embodiment of cultural values. North American culture has come to uphold routinization, uniformity, and standardization. Within this development lies the potential for cultural crisis as culture becomes less reflective of individual and community life and more centred on the consumption of mass culture (see Box 14.1).

The mass media, in particular, are a powerful vehicle for cultural expression and communication. The mass media contain and express values, beliefs about the world, and convey knowledge; they are the transmitters of symbolic life. Do they reflect cultural variety and national, regional, and community life, or do they promote uniformity and standardization? Flora MacDonald, a former federal Minister of Communications, has said that uniformity is produced. She argued that the growing trend to a corporately generated global culture has aggravated the economic disadvantage of Canadian cultural industries. As a result of an "increasingly homogenized cultural product" (Canada, 1987), Canadians are exposed to cultural materials that fail to reflect Canadian experiences and social life. This problem is amplified in the following discussion.

• • • • • • • •

Box 14.1
Protecting Social
Values

• • • • • • • •

In 1990, a court in Finland banned a television advertisement for McDonald's Corp., the fast-food chain. The ad showed a boy unhappily surveying an empty apartment his parents were about to move into. His despair turns to joy when he sees a McDonald's on the other side of the street. The scene is brought to a joyful conclusion with the family eating in the restaurant.

The court said the ad exploited the loneliness of a child. It gave the impression that McDonald's products could replace friends or reduce loneliness.

• • • • • • • •

SOURCE: Adapted from "Finnish Court Bans Ad for McDonald's," *The Globe and Mail*, April 4, 1990, p. B8.

• • • • • • • •

MASS PRODUCTION AND MASS CULTURE

• • • • • • • • •

Industrialization and the techniques of mass production made it possible for goods and ideas to be produced and distributed on a mass scale. Goods once only enjoyed by the rich, who could afford to pay the artisan to produce them, could now be mass produced. Many people can now hang reproductions of the great masters on their walls and read the classics of literature in inexpensive editions while seated comfortably in reproductions of fine furniture in their living rooms. Some claim that these developments have led to the democratization of high culture: it is now available to everyone, and people have a choice. They can choose to watch an opera or a rock video, read a Harlequin romance or James Joyce, subscribe to *The Globe and Mail* or *The National Enquirer*. Likewise, the mass production of goods makes it possible to choose among a variety of goods: Levi's or designer jeans, a Honda or a BMW, Kokanee beer or Guinness stout.

Looked at this way, mass production has released people from bondage and ignorance and made possible liberation on a universal scale. The invention of the printing press, for example, the first significant development in the creation of the mass media, had important political repercussions as it made possible the dissemination of alternative ideas and opinions. One can take a less positive view, however, and be sceptical of the claims made for mass production and its effects on culture. Mass production, from this perspective, by its very nature drives out variety because everyone is encouraged to gain satisfaction from the same standardized products.

How does mass production affect artistic culture? Popular culture and artistic (or "high") culture are often contrasted, with high culture denoting the styles of thought, symbolic products, and feelings of people who are highly educated and/or enjoy high social status. Popular culture refers to the styles of thought, symbolic products, and feelings of the uneducated, or "the masses" (Gans, 1974). In addition, high culture may be considered non-commercial, heterogeneous, and non-standardized. Mass or popular culture is, by default, defined as commercial, homogeneous, and standardized. It is the product of mass production.

What impact does industrialization have on these contrasting cultures? Mass production can undermine high culture by making its products in limitless numbers and by taking control of the skill of the producer. The unique painting, sculpture, embroidery, or carving can be copied in mass quantities with industrial techniques. This is the difference between the value (economic and aesthetic) of an original work of art and that of an unlimited reproduction. While mass production may indeed democratize art, it degrades the work's artistic value and transforms its producer. The mass-produced piece becomes a commodity for mass consumption: a vulgar representation of the original. At the same time, mass production tends to squeeze out demand for the unique and original hand-crafted art work. This concern has been raised recently in Canada's North, where a factory has been established to mass produce Inuit art.

In the nineteenth century, associations of handcraft workers arose in opposition to the machine and its commodities. Countless nineteenth-century authors railed against the advent of machine production. Flaubert, for example, was passionate:

> *Let us cry against imitation silk, desk chairs, economy kitchens, fake material, fake luxury, fake pride, industrialism has developed the ugly to gigantic proportions. ... The department store has rendered true luxury difficult ... we have become fakers and charlatans* (Brantlinger, 1983: 126).

Flaubert's rallying cry very much resembles the movement that gained strength in the 1960s to reject mass culture in favour of natural foods and materials and hand-crafted products.

In modern society, a unique work of art can be copied in huge quantities with industrial techniques. Mass production, however, can undermine high culture by making its products in limitless numbers and by taking control of the skill of the producer.

. . . .

William Taufic / MASTERFILE

This critique of mass culture suggests that the varied culture maintained by artists and craftspeople gives way to cultural homogenization as the culture of the intellectual, the artist, and the artisan becomes mass produced. The marketable value of the commodity replaces the aesthetic value of the object. The value of individuality gives way to the industrial value of rational standardization. Individual preferences and the urge to self-expression no longer shape what is produced.

A second critique is more fundamental and depends on the definition of mass culture as a commercial culture. It begins by noting that the mass production of goods demands mass markets. To create these markets, culture becomes connected to commercialization and to the emergence and transmission of **consumer culture**. Christopher Lasch described the creation of mass consumption as follows:

> *Having organized mass production on the basis of the new division of labor, most realized in the assembly line, the leaders of American industry turned to the organization of a mass market. The mobilization of consumer demand, together with the recruitment of a labor force, required a far-reaching series of cultural changes. People had to be discouraged from providing for their own wants and resocialized as consumers. Industrialism by its very nature tends to discourage home production and to make people dependent on the market, but a vast effort of reeducation, starting in the 1920s, had to be undertaken before Americans accepted consumption as a way of life. As Emma Rothschild has shown in her study of the automobile industry, Alfred Sloan's innovation in marketing — the annual model change, constant upgrading of product, efforts to associate it with social status, the deliberate inculcation of a boundless appetite for change — constituted the necessary counterpart of Henry Ford's innovation in production. Modern industry came to rest on the twin pillars of Fordism and Sloanism. Both tended to discourage enterprise and independent thinking and to make the individual mistrust his own judgement, even in matters of taste (1984: 28–29).*

Lasch makes it very clear that mass production had an impact on culture — it produced consumer culture, a culture unlike that of any other society, shaped by the needs of the economy. The complexity of social life and of human nature becomes invisible, and citizens become individualized consumers.

ADVERTISING AND THE AUDIENCE

. . . .

Advertising is clearly a significant source of revenue for media corporations. Newspapers receive approximately 80 percent of their revenue from selling 50–60 percent of their space to advertisers. Magazines usually devote 60 percent of their space to advertising, and business spends approximately 60 percent of its total advertising budget on television ads. The largest buyers of Canadian advertising space in 1990 were as follows: the Government of Canada, Procter and Gamble, John Labatt, Molson Companies, General Motors, Unilever, the Government of Ontario, The Thomson Group, McDonald's Restaurants, and Bell Canada Enterprises. The total spent on advertising was $6.7 billion.

Although everyone is familiar with advertising and with shopping, few spend much time thinking about the cultural implications of these activities. For example, does the spread of consumer culture displace national cultures? Does it allow for cultural pluralism? Does it pose a threat to democracy? A starting point in exploring these questions is the observation that the stimulation of consumer demands means that the producers of goods and services must gain access to the citizens of society; they must create channels for their message. This brings about a transformation in how people are thought of by sellers of goods and services: people become an audience for the consumer message. The audience becomes a product created by the owners of the mass media, a product to be sold to the producers of goods and services. In return, the producer of the audience receives advertising dollars and other people receive the consumer message. The production of an audience has itself become a big business.[5]

Advertising has long been identified as essential to the goods-producing corporation, but more recently the production of marketable cultural materials has become a vast source of corporate profit. Large corporations have become directly interested in culture and its production and are pushing for a free market (based on liberal economic philosophy) in cultural products. The talk of "cultural industries" is a sure sign that culture has become just another product to be produced and consumed.

This tendency for cultural events to take on corporate value is nowhere more evident than in "corporate" sports. Professional sports become a vehicle for gathering an audience, and the right of access to this audience is sold to advertisers. The producers of the Super Bowl (the championship game of the National Football League in the United States) have created sufficent interest in this game that in 1993 it was broadcast live to 76 countries (an additional 25 saw it in a delayed format), with an estimated audience of 750 million people. Access to this audience does not come cheap — advertising rates were estimated at $850 000 to $900 000 per 30 second units of commercial time, translating into $50 million dollars for the company with broadcasting rights. These broadcasting rights are purchased from the football league; this clearly is big business.[6]

Having begun with big corporations producing goods and services, modern society is now witnessing the emergence of big corporations (the owners of newspapers, magazines, television stations, and radio stations) producing audiences. If media ownership is widely dispersed, people may feel that alternative messages will be available, local and regional cultures will thrive, citizen access will be possible, and the reality of their world will be reflected. What if media ownership is concentrated, however? Does concentration present a problem for society?

MEDIA OWNERSHIP

Media ownership has been a recurring concern for Canadians, evidenced by the number of royal commission investigations and inquiries that have been launched in recent years. The concern derives from the fact that large-scale societies rely heavily on communication through various media. Deciding who may have access to these instruments of communication, the nature of the message presented, and regulation of content have significant political and cultural implications. Canadians have realized two things: there is a considerable concentration of ownership of the mass media, and, uniquely, Canadian culture has increasing difficulty finding space in the "market" for cultural products.

The growing concentration of ownership was confirmed by the late Robert Maxwell, owner of one of the large international media corporations, when he said: "The communications and information industry will consolidate, in the same way as the oil, chemical and financial services industries did in their time, to the point where some ten major corporations will dominate the global market."[7] This kind of consolidation is increasingly evident in Canada (see Box 14.2).

Newspapers[8]

In 1992, Southam and Thomson controlled 50 percent of daily newspaper circulation in Canada. Torstar controlled another 10 percent.[9] There are only six communities in Canada with two daily newspapers, thus reducing competition to a minimum. In some of those communities, such as Vancouver, both newspapers are owned by the same company.

The growth of concentration in the last 40 years is apparent in the following figures, which indicate the share of national circulation held by the four largest newspaper chains: 1950, 37.2 percent; 1955, 34.3 percent; 1960, 35.7 percent; 1965, 43.6 percent; 1970, 52.9 percent; 1975, 62.7 percent; 1980, 65.1 percent; 1986, 67 percent; 1992, 71 percent. This concentration of ownership leads to a narrowing of the range of views expressed through the media. The ownership of the dominant news agency, Canadian Press, by the owners of the daily newspapers is also a force for standardization. It is estimated that one-third to one-half of the news and editorial content of newspapers comes from news agencies, with much of the continental and inter-

Box 14.2
Canada's Top Ten
Media Giants, 1992

1. Thomson Corp.
2. Quebecor Inc.
3. Maclean Hunter Ltd.
4. Southam Inc.
5. Rogers Communication Inc.
6. Torstar Corp.
7. Hollinger Inc.
8. Groupe Videotron
9. Groupe transcontinental GTC ltée
10. Canadian Broadcasting Corp.

SOURCE: *The Financial Post 500* (Summer 1993): 136. Reprinted with permission.

national news coming from American sources. With only two or three major sources of news information, the result is that journalistic voices become uniform and one point of view dominates.

Since newspapers receive approximately 80 percent of their revenue from advertising, it is clear that the interests of the advertiser can displace the goal of informing the reader. It is also evident that there is a built-in incentive for newspaper owners to increase the size of their papers to provide more space for advertising. The result is that newspaper accounts for approximately 14 percent of our garbage.[10]

Periodicals

About 65 percent of the revenue for magazines comes from advertising, and a substantial portion of this is received by a small number of publishers. A most interesting feature of this business, however, is that Canadian magazines account for about 80 percent of the subscription market, while United States publications account for 75 percent of newsstand sales. Why is this so? The two largest distributors of magazines are American and focus on the marketing of American product, thus making it hard for Canadian publications to find space on the shelf. With limited access to magazine racks, Canadian publications must rely on subscription sales.

In 1965, Canada fashioned a set of policies to protect and encourage Canadian magazines. In part this was done by denying Canadian advertisers tax deductions for advertising expenses in foreign publications. *Sports Illustrated* began to challenge these rules in 1993 by arranging to publish six of its 52 issues in Canada and to call the "new" magazine *Sports Illustrated Canada*. While the magazine would have offices in Canada and some Canadian content, it is clear that the majority of the content would be American. Further, since it would have a larger market base (all of North America), it could offer advertisers much lower costs than could Canadian magazines. Canadian magazine publishers estimate that a shift of 3 percent of Canadian advertising dollars to American magazines would completely eliminate the profits of the Canadian industry.[11]

Book Publishing

The most striking fact about book publishing in Canada is the high degree of foreign ownership. Canadian-owned publishers account for under 20 percent of domestic book sales. Foreign publishers even account for 40 percent of the sales of books published in Canada. Roughly 75 percent of all books sold in Canada are imported, and the majority of these come from the United States. Approximately 50 percent of all retail bookstore sales in Canada are made by chain stores rather than through independents. Chain stores tend to stock the same books and have contracts with the same suppliers. This reduces the choice of material for readers. Foreign firms control approximately two-thirds of the elementary and high school textbook market. Although foreign firms dominate the Canadian market, Canadian-controlled firms account for over 80 percent of new Canadian titles. They have difficulty reaching a market, however, because of the way books are distributed.

Sound Recording

In the early 1990s fourteen foreign-controlled companies took in 88 percent of revenue from sound recording sales in Canada and accounted for 79 percent of new releases. However, Canadian-controlled firms accounted for 71 percent of new Canadian-content releases.

A trend evident in the American recording industry, and also affecting other sectors, is the narrowing of the number of recordings made and an accompanying increase in promotion of a few records selected on the basis of early market tests. Not surprisingly, more profits can be made this way, although the selection available to listeners has been restricted. Foreign- controlled companies market the foreign product on a continental and international scale and have greater commercial success than do companies producing Canadian-content recordings.

Films

About 90 percent of the $1 billion in Canadian box-office revenue is generated by foreign-controlled firms. In large part, this results from the organization of distribution. Foreign distributors control 87 percent of the Canadian market and are linked by ownership or agreement with the major producers. They get exclusive rights to distribute movies. Canadian distributors are at a disadvantage because Canada is not identified as a single market but is considered part of the North American market. They cannot compete for distribution rights for popular American movies and must rely on films made by American independents or other foreign film companies. There are two primary exhibitors of movies in Canada, Famous Players and Cineplex-Odeon. These companies sign agreements with foreign distributors and may be required to give the best dates and locations to American movies, further reducing the opportunity for Canadian films to be shown. As a consequence of this structure, most of the box-office revenue generated in Canada flows out of the country rather than into the production of Canadian films.

Canadian films account for only 3 percent of Canadian theatre time — less time than domestic films in any other industrialized country. Canada is not alone in confronting the American cultural giant, however. In the early 1990s, thirteen of the fourteen top-grossing movies in Hungary were American. The most popular movie in Poland was *Indiana Jones and the Last Crusade*.[12]

Television

In 1992, Canadians watched an average of 23.3 hours of television each week. Children aged 12–17 watched an average of 17.7 hours. Television, like the film industry, is dominated by American "product." Nearly two-thirds of all the television programming that anglophone Canadians watch is American: almost all the drama and comedy they watch is American. For francophones, however, almost two-thirds of viewing time is devoted to Canadian content. Increasingly, the costs of American productions can only be recovered through international sales; in fact, American programming accounts for 75 percent of all world television sales. Popular programs (e.g., *Dallas*) are offered to foreign countries at prices far below the costs of local production, and this impedes the development of viable local productions.[13]

With the coming of the "information highway," the cable industry has gained new corporate interest, since it provides direct access to most homes in Canada. In 1994, five cable companies accounted for 65 percent of all Canadian cable subscriptions. When Rogers Communications Inc. took over Maclean Hunter Limited in 1994, this single cable company controlled 33 percent of all subscriptions.[14]

The information on corporate concentration in the media world suggests that there is a decrease in diversity of programming. Economic values encourage the elimination of competition and the homogenization of the market. Producers with a different message, different values, and different formats find it increasingly difficult to gain access to the market. While there is an increasing number of television stations (thanks to cable), radio stations, and magazines, it is not clear that these represent real choices. Each media outlet, for the most part, portrays a version of the consumer culture; it is devoted to addressing people as consumers and developing a view of the world in which consumption is a way of life. David Pearson, in assessing the debate about whether the media is becoming more homogeneous or more diverse, said:

This paradox [that it appears to be both] can only be resolved if we consider that the fragmentation occurs in areas of rather meaningless lifestyle choices, choices that are often devoid of genuine creativity, energy and idiosyncrasy. At the same time Americans are becoming more homogeneous in profoundly influential areas of ideology (1993: 19).

In the media marketplace, it is clear that the significant choices come from media outlets not driven by the corporate motive, that is, the public media. For example, the Canadian Broadcasting Corporation, community-owned radio stations, and educational television stations provide programming that differs both in content and in format from the private stations.

CULTURAL NATIONALISM
. . . .

The minimal reflection of Canadian culture in the media as a result of foreign domination presents a different but equally significant problem (see Figure 14.1). Rick Salutin summarized the problem:

Figure 14.1
The above ad, published by the Friends of Canadian Broadcasting, ran in several Canadian newspapers soliciting support for the organization.
. . . .

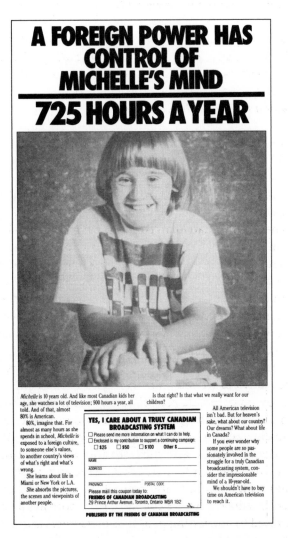

SOURCE: Reprinted with the permission of Friends of Canadian Broadcasting.

Only 3 to 5 percent of all theatrical screen time in Canada goes to Canadian films; 2 to 4 percent of video-cassette sales are Canadian titles; 97 percent of profits from films shown in Canada go out of the country, 95 percent to the United States; total prime-time broadcasting in drama and sitcoms is only 2 to 3 percent Canadian; 95 percent of English-language TV drama is non-Canadian; Canadian-owned publishers have only 29 percent of the book market; 77 percent of magazines sold here are foreign; 85 percent of record and tape sales are non-Canadian; in theatre, Canadian plays are the alternative *theatre — they are equivalent to off-Broadway, or off-off-Broadway.*[15]

For distinct societal groups or subcultures in a society, mass culture may undermine the distinctive culture of the group — the culture that holds it together and differentiates it from the surrounding population. Marx predicted the emergence of a world culture:

In place of the old wants, satisfied by the productions of the country, we find new wants, requiring for their satisfaction the products of distant lands and climes. In place of the old local and national self-sufficiency, we have intercourse in every direction, universal interdependence. And as in material, so in spiritual (geistige) *production. The spiritual creations of individual nations become common property. National one-sidedness and narrow mindedness become more and more impossible, and from the numerous national and local literatures there arises a world literature* (Marx and Engels, 1968[1848]: 38).

Marx saw this as a positive development. It may indeed have positive benefits, but it overlooks the possibility of the domination of cultural production by one nation and the trivialization of culture in the form of consumer culture (rather than world culture). Canada stands alone in terms of the weakness of its cultural production. Europeans who are beginning to experience some of the same problems refer to the Canadianization of Europe,[16] an alienation from their own cultural sovereignty (see Box 14.3).

Can Canadian identity survive in the shadow of American capitalism? Can Canadians retain control of channels of cultural communication? Can the media serve as a reflection of the culture of Canada? Some would argue that the market itself should be the determiner of these matters. If no one buys Canadian products, watches Canadian television, or reads Canadian poetry, then these things should disappear. This philosophy, however, is at odds with the history of cultural policy in Canada. Institutions such as the Canadian Broadcasting Corporation (CBC), the National Film Board, and the Canada Council, and regulations governing broadcasting are the outcome of policy fashioned to enhance and protect Canadian culture. A review of the CBC is instructive because the CBC is a major countervailing force against the homogeneity of American private broadcasting and its Canadian imitators.

During the 1920s, 80 percent of the radio programs that Canadians listened to were American. American stations had stronger signals than did Canadian stations, and some Canadian stations were affiliates of American networks. There were no Canadian networks. In 1932, following the recommendations of the Aird Commission, the Conservative government of R.B. Bennett announced the establishment of the Canadian Radio Broadcasting Commission (to become the CBC in 1936). During the parliamentary debate that took place at the time, Bennett remarked:

. . . .

Box 14.3
Canada's Youth,
Our Future

. . . .

Reginald Bibby and Donald Posterski, regular pollsters of Canada's teenagers, concluded after a 1990s study, "A good rule of thumb seems to be: all things being equal, the heroes for young Canadians are Americans." When teenagers were asked to name their three favourite TV programs, singers, movie stars, sports teams, authors, TV newspersons, politicians, and world leaders, very few Canadians made the list. Aside from politicians, those Canadians who received recognition were those who had become successful in the United States.

In a sampling of young non-Québécois Canadians, only 12 percent of the young people selected a Canadian as their favourite singer or musical group, 8 percent selected a Canadian movie star, 5 percent selected a Canadian author, 10 percent selected a Canadian television program, and 38 percent selected a Canadian professional athlete. Surprisingly, seven of ten young people said that "the CBC is important to Canada."

. . . .

SOURCE: Adapted from Reginald Bibby and Donald Posterski, *Teen Trends* (Toronto: Stoddart, 1992).

. . . .

This country must be assured of complete Canadian control of broadcasting from Canadian sources free from foreign interference or influence. Without such control, radio broadcasting can never become a great agency for the communication of matters of national concern and for the diffusion of national thought and ideas, and without such control it can never be the agency by which national consciousness may be fostered and sustained, and national unity still further strengthened (Wolfe, 1985: 105).

Clearly the CBC was created as an expression of Canadian nationalism. By the 1950s, CBC radio had been Canadianized, with the Saturday afternoon Metropolitan Opera performances being the only American program broadcast. Most Canadians would agree that CBC television has also had some success in developing and exposing Canadian content (now 90 percent of the content in prime-time hours) and provides excellent news and public affairs broadcasting. However, it still attracts a relatively small audience, carries a substantial amount of American programming, is not commercial-free (receiving 25 percent of its revenue from advertising), and, as Wolfe (1985) put it, is devoted to the sensationalized American broadcasting style of concentrating on "jolts per minute." As a competitor to American television, it has not fared well.

Many other cultural policies strive to protect and enhance Canadian culture. The National Film Board (NFB) was established in 1939; the Canadian Film Development Corporation (later Telefilm Canada) was established to assist the financing of feature films; in 1979, the Book Publishing Development Program was set up; Canadian content regulations introduced in 1971 require 30 percent of all music played on AM radio during prime time to be Canadian; only Canadians are allowed to own cable systems or radio or television stations in Canada; postal subsidies have been offered to magazines; and so on. A complete list of these attempts to resist foreign corporate domination of Canadian communication would be very long indeed. Although these policies have made some differences in stemming the inflow of American cultural material and increasing the production of Canadian cultural material, they have not satisfied cultural nationalists. Some case studies give a sense of the pressures mounted against attempts to promote a Canadian focus in cultural policy.

When Gulf and Western bought control of the book publishing firm Prentice-Hall (then a Canadian company), the purchase was subject to government review. When this review was announced,

> *U.S. diplomatic and business pressure quickly mounted. Gulf and Western told the media that if the Mulroney government blocked the takeover, it would carry out a "scorched-earth policy in Canada." In March 1986, just before the prime minister went to Washington to see President Reagan, the Canadian federal government announced that it would not block the takeover* (Warnock, 1988: 226).

In February 1987, the Canadian minister of communications proposed legislation that would prevent foreign film corporations from controlling distribution rights to movies and videos that they had not entirely financed or for which they did not own distribution rights. This was to allow Canadian film distributors an opportunity to gain some of the revenue earned from film distribution in Canada.

> *The American reaction was predictable. Jack Valenti and the MPAA (Motion Picture Association of America) began a high-pressure campaign against the legislation. He even discussed the bill with Ronald Reagan, [president of the United States and] a past president of the U.S. Screen Actors Guild. Reagan told Brian Mulroney that he did not like the legislation during their Ottawa summit in 1987. In late April a group of U.S. congressmen sent a letter to the prime minister strongly opposing the film legislation* (Warnock, 1988: 227).

The pressure continued until the legislation was held back for redrafting.[17]

Other countries have been more successful in defending their cultural industries. In the Netherlands, the bulk of radio and television broadcasting is done by membership associations — listeners' and viewers' co-operatives (Hardin, 1989: 57). In France, TV networks are allowed to purchase programming only from domestically owned distributors. Foreign investment in publishing is limited to 20 percent in a joint venture. Currently in Canada there is pressure to remove government regulations as much as possible in order to allow the free market to guide economic development; those opposed to this think the free market has already created significant cultural problems that must be met by further intervention in the market. Pierre Juneau, past president of the CBC, argued that public broadcasting (i.e., supported by public funds) would increase choice, while many Americans argue that public broadcasting interferes with the market and thus limits choice. [18]

MEDIA: PROTECTORS OF DEMOCRACY OR ENEMIES OF CHOICE?

It has been suggested that the concentration of ownership reduces the diversity of opinion presented in the media and reduces the possibility of competition from alternative voices. It presents the owners and managers of large conglomerates with an increased opportunity to promote their political and economic views. One should expect little difference of philosophy or perspective among the large media corporations, and entry to the media business becomes very costly as the acquisition activities of the large companies drive up the cost of media properties. It is estimated that start-up costs for a top-quality magazine are as high as $24 million. Those with alternative viewpoints are relegated to the back of the magazine rack and may have difficulty arranging distribution. What does all this have to do with democracy?

In a democracy it is expected that people will act as citizens; they will be well informed and able to make choices not just about toothpaste but also about social and economic policy. They will be able to assess the performance of their government and to listen to genuine debate expressing different economic and political views. Concentration of ownership already impedes the development of well-informed citizens, but Noam Chomsky, among others, argues that the selectivity of the media is more fundamental. In his research on American media, he concluded that they "train the minds of the people to a virtuous attachment to their government, and to the arrangements of the social, economic, and political order more generally." He claimed that the media are "vigilant guardians protecting privilege from the threat of public understanding and participation" (1989: 13–14). They accomplish this by the use of a double standard: not judging their own society by the criteria used to condemn others. When Armando Valladares published his account of life in a Cuban prison, for example, he gained wide media coverage in America. His publication was a vehicle for further criticisms of the communist government of Cuba and a legitimation of U.S. government policy toward Cuba. At the same time, however, Herbert Anaya, the non-governmental director of a human-rights agency in El Salvador, published a report detailing the accounts of political prisoners on their torture by U.S.-backed security forces. Did this report garner the same media attention as the reports from Cuba? No. Chomsky reported that "this material was suppressed entirely, without a word, in the national media" (p. 138). Chomsky has presented a vast number of examples of this type and his suggestion that the media can be understood as operating on a "propaganda model" makes some sense of these facts.

Chomsky suggests that the news media operate in a framework that reflects the interests of the state and powerful corporations: they naturally express a view of the world from a business perspective. Sometimes, however, there are direct attempts by government to silence the press, especially in Great Britain. When the British Broadcasting Corporation planned a TV program revealing a secret spy satellite system whose existence was unknown to Parliament, the government reacted by sending in the police to seize the tapes. When the *Observer* revealed massive waste in defence contracts by government, the paper was put on trial. In another case, the British government argued that the press should not be allowed to report proceedings in open court in Australia (the "Spycatcher" case).[19] Further, it is now illegal in Britain for any broadcasting organization to transmit an interview with anyone who supports terrorism in Northern Ireland.

Business too has the ability to censor what people read. Since business supports the majority of newspapers and magazines through advertising expenditures, this gives it a tool to influence content. By withholding advertising dollars, advertisers can penalize publishers for opinions they feel are unfriendly to business values and interests. In 1990, for example, real estate agencies "boycotted" a Kingston newspaper, *The Whig-Standard*, because it had featured an interview with the author of a book on how to sell your own home on the front of the paper's "Home" section.[20] These kinds of boycotts are more frequent than is imagined because the media itself chooses not to turn the boycott into a news story. The anticipation of the loss of advertising is the greatest censor of all.

Consider another analysis that is less specific but also raises deep concerns about the media and their role in protecting democracy. In 1988, the Supreme Court of Canada ruled that a Quebec law restricting the language used in commercial signs was a violation of the "freedom of expression" section of the Canadian Charter of Rights and Freedoms. The restriction on language was justified by the Quebec government as a means to preserve French language and culture; group rights they said must outweigh individual rights. While this case is typically thought of as evidence of French–English conflict in Canada, there is another dimension. The court judgement makes it clear that corporations (businesses) have the same rights as individuals under the Charter; like individuals, they have the right to freedom of speech. Freedom of speech is of course fundamental to the functioning of a democratic society, but is commercial free speech a protector of or threat to a democratic society? Consider two sides to this debate.

On the one hand, it might be argued that Canada's economy depends on the buying and selling of goods. In order for the market to operate in an efficient and effective manner, it is essential that buyers have as much information about what is available as possible. If sellers are able to make this information available, consumers are able to make good decisions and the best allocation of resources is achieved. Products that satisfy a need in the marketplace will thrive, and those that do not will wither. Free access to consumers makes investment in the development and production of goods worthwhile for companies, and this contributes to a dynamic and thriving economy. This view is a reflection of liberalism; it sees the right to commercial free speech as being about the provision of information and the right to obtain information. This sounds harmless enough; in fact, it even sounds beneficial. There is another view, however.

An alternative view would concentrate on the vision of social life expressed in advertising. Advertising depends on creating consumption as a way of life. A commercial vision of social life is given constitutional protection, and this vision may drive out other visions of how people might live their lives.

Commercial free speech may also reduce people's ability to act as citizens (rather than as consumers) and may diminish democratic life. For example, protecting the rights of corporations to advertise reduces the ability of the community's elected representatives to make choices. Governments may be unable to ban tobacco advertising,[21] to regulate advertising directed at children, to restrain ethnic and gender-based stereotyping, or respond to violence on television. In each case, the society would be required to rely on the forces of the market to regulate these matters. If citizens refuse to watch violent programming, violence on television will diminish.

Commercial free speech also reduces democratic life if the public debate that is central to a viable democracy is imagined as taking place between individual citizens and corporate citizens. If governments are unable to regulate corporate spending on elections or restrict corporations' ability to shape public opinion, the corporate voice will be louder than the individual voice. Treating corporations as citizens may well reduce people's ability to act like citizens.[22] The issue here is referred to as third-party advertising. The 1988 federal election in Canada (often called the free-trade election) saw a considerable increase in third-party advertising. Many large corporations contributed up to $250 000 each to support the pro–free-trade campaign. The Progressive Conservative Party was the beneficiary of this advertising and won the election. In 1993, a proposal was made by all three federal parties to limit third-party advertising to a maximum of $1000 for individuals and corporations. An earlier attempt to restrict advertising of this nature was struck down by an Alberta court as being a violation of the Canadian Charter of Rights and Freedoms. This issue is still before the courts.

To appreciate how advertising and consumer culture trivialize the world and perhaps reduce people's ability to engage in political debate, consider the following story.

The Parker Pen Company, which was in need of increased sales, began to market its pens in the late 1980s as fashionable items — "classy" gifts and tools of the powerful. It was suggested that U.S. President Ronald Reagan and Soviet leader Mikhail Gorbachev sign a nuclear arms reduction treaty with Parker pens. Mr. Reagan agreed, and the photo of the leaders signing the document became a Parker ad, under the headline: "The pen is mightier than the sword." It even ran in Moscow.[23]

CONSUMER CULTURE AND THE SEXUALIZATION OF COMMODITIES

Many social critics have argued that advertising has been successful in marketing commodities by linking them to our psychological needs and desires. The consumption of products comes to represent social status and personal achievement and is linked to needs such as love, security, and sex. Social critics argue that in capitalist societies people have become alienated from themselves and others to the extent that real and genuine needs become manipulable. There is what might be called a lack of authentic individuation, and this allows for the possibility of individual identities being linked to commodities. Herbert Marcuse put it this way:

The people recognize themselves in their commodities, they find their soul in their automobile, hi-fi set, split-level home, kitchen equipment. The very mechanism which ties the individual to his society has changed, and social control is anchored in the new needs which it has produced (1964: 9).

Marcuse went on to argue that the normal sexual feelings of viewers have been transformed into the desire to consume: there has been a **sexualization of commodities**: commodities have been linked to sex and sexuality. Sex is used to sell consumer products. How did this come about? Barbara Ehrenreich provides some insights:

The family household system has been for many millennia the primary organizer of sexual activity, but that system today is being shaken to its foundations. ... But in industrial society, in our society, millions of people from adolescents to senior citizens now live on their own. ... And sex, which for so long was organized by the family, has been undergoing rapid and enormous changes as a result. ... Sex and sexuality emerged through the 60s as crucial areas for renegotiating the relations between men and women. For heterosexual men, the emergence of mainstream explicitly sexual material — let's call it pornography — represented an expression of their withdrawal from the old family compact. ... Women could no longer get or keep men on the basis that it was a man's duty to support a household? Very well, women would learn how to be erotically pleasing and do it that way. ... From both sides, people are being sold as sex objects to each other. They're also being sold the appearances and the behaviors and the commodities that are supposed to make the personal transaction succeed. ...

It was some time in the 1950s that part of marketing strategy began to be directed toward men as individuals. Until that time, most marketing saw the home, the family, as the unit of consumption. You sold appliances, you sold big cars — stationwagons and so on. In the 1950s, you had magazines that were directed to men, and not just to the hunting and fishing type of men, that were beginning to show a different set of commodities that a man could enjoy by himself. ... And this was new, this kind of marketing directed at men and going for their wage, independent of whether they had a family or not.[24]

The sex sells the commodities, and the commodities sell the sex. An examination of almost any form of advertising will reveal a sexualization of some commodities. A

. . . .

Box 14.4
Are You Watching
Too Much TV?

. . . .

For years, U.S. statistics have been telling us that people watch, on average, more than seven hours of television a day. In fact, by the time they reach the age of 18, most children have spent more time in front of the TV than at school. As adults, the only activity which rivals TV viewing (in terms of time devoted to it) is sleeping.

As this profile of human life in the late twentieth century becomes a planet-wide characteristic, it raises grave doubts about the future of human intellect and the goal of educating children to become balanced and rounded human beings. Television erects major obstacles to that goal, both by imposing its own definitions of what a whole person is and by teaching us a way of living that accords with its own curriculum.

The overt part of television's curriculum is its programming content and its advertising. Television is a mass classroom — for adults and children alike — in which we are educated in a quite narrow range of behaviours and values. Recently people have begun to criticize the violence, sexism, and racism in many programs, the exploitation of children's needs by commercials aimed at them, the biased politics of "objective" news reporting. Also TV programs made for U.S. audiences are widely exported to developing countries. They impose a commercial culture worldwide threatening to extinguish others.

But there is another aspect of television's curriculum that is more hidden — and perhaps even more powerful — than that contained in specific programs. Just consider, for a moment, all the things a person is not doing during those seven hours they spend in front of the set each day. A whole range of leisure pursuits, hobbies, social encounters, information sources, are automatically excluded. The most powerful impact of TV's hidden curriculum is simply that of keeping people switched off from life outside the living-room.

And as more and more people tune in and switch off, so everything else has to become more like TV in order to appeal to people who have become unable to tune into anything else. In this way television sets standards for writing textbooks, editing newspapers — even for the most "effective" ways to teach in the school classroom.

Needless to say, there have been certain noticeable effects on people raised on TV over the past 40 years. Psychologists Dorothy and Jerome Singer, co-directors of the Yale University Family Television Research and Consultation Center, found that addicted TV viewers have a shortened attention span and a lack of "reflectiveness" — the ability to think, in other words. Another study, in Harvard in 1981, revealed that children learning from television showed poorer logical thinking than those who obtained their information from books. Other research, by child psychologist Dorothy Cohen, found that extensive TV viewing led to atrophy of children's imaginations.

Given this type of evidence, it is hardly surprising that TV addiction is associated with low achievement in school. A major survey of the relevant literature, carried out by the National Institute of Mental Health in the U.S., found

(continued)

> *(continued)*
> that all the research (bar just one study) agreed that television was a significant factor in failure at school.
>
> SOURCE: Joyce Nelson, "Tuned In and Switched Off," *New Internationalist* (February 1988): 14–15. Reprinted with permission.

classic example of this was the Calvin Klein advertisement for jeans featuring a teenage Brooke Shields; the significance was that she was presented in a sexually provocative pose. Many critics argue that these sexual poses are derived from the techniques of pornography; thus pornography becomes part of everyday imagery.

IS WATCHING TELEVISION GOOD FOR YOU?

Most homes now have televisions, and many people watch a number of hours of television each day. Children, it is estimated, watch 900 hours a year. It has already been pointed out that a great deal of this viewing time involves exposure to foreign programming, and for some this is a concern. Another question that could be asked is, "Whose reality is presented in the media?" When asked why so few Blacks were used in early television programming, advertisers claimed that the audience did not want to see Blacks (Tuchman, 1974). And since the advertisers did not want to lose the audience, television programming legitimated the social relations of the society; it presented a mythical world in which there were no Blacks.

In a similar fashion, television advertising does not reflect the reality of individuals who have no family to make a long-distance call to; those who do not have long, silky hair that blows in the wind; those who do not have the perfect body; and those without middle-class incomes. Media advertising tends to deal in stereotypes, and one can only wonder about the effect of this on those whose reality is a great distance from the image. If people's reality is not reflected in their culture, how can they think effectively about their condition and act in constructive ways to improve it? In this way, the media can become the "opiate of the masses" and legitimate existing social arrangements. A number of other concerns about television are discussed in Box 14.4.

The mass media can therefore be understood as one component of a cultural crisis in which culture becomes alienated and detached from individual and community life. **Mass culture** is increasingly characterized by contradiction — by a significant gap between the image and the reality of people's lives, by failure to provide space for social values and the creation of community, and finally by an inability to present and encourage the development of meaningful and fulfilled lives for individuals. It becomes artificial because it is no longer organically connected to people's real way of life.

This chapter has focussed on a vision of the public self as standardized, on the uniformity of public life and expression, and on the potential threat to citizenship and democratic life posed by the corporate control of communication. It is important to acknowledge, however, that citizens do not remain passive before these social forces. There is an active political life in Canada that attempts to resist the forces of the market, recover a sense of community, and develop a vibrant and unique Canadian culture. In their individual lives, many Canadians attempt to make choices that resist the commercialization of life. This activism was apparent in the response to an attempt to introduce television programming accompanied by commercial advertising into the classroom (see Box 11.6). Individuals are not and must not become passive: modernity can be shaped to respond to people's individual and social needs. This is explored further in the concluding chapter.

CONCLUSION

This chapter has examined the nature of mass (or popular) culture in modern society. It has been argued that the mass production of goods led to the commercialization of the instruments of cultural production and transmission and of culture itself. A consumer culture was developed.

Consumer culture was characterized as uniform and as emphasizing values of primary benefit to business. An essential aspect of this culture is a notion of the citizen as an individualized consumer. The complexity of human life, the social basis of life, diminishes as people are encouraged to shop.

This makes it difficult for a vibrant democratic system to develop, since the individual's role as citizen is trivialized (e.g., one votes for the leader who looks best on television). Further, as businesses are increasingly given "freedom of speech" rights as legal individuals, the public debate is increasingly dominated by their voice, values, and interests.

As cultural production and transmission of culture has itself become big business, there has been a growing concentration of ownership and, in many sectors of the media, a domination by American material. National cultures and diversity are replaced by the uniformity of American programming, which depicts a quite specific view of social life. This view presents the promise of liberalism (that is, of choice), but its very presence and power reduces the possibility of its fulfilment.

NOTES

1. Excerpted from Bruce Springsteen, "57 Channels (and Nothin' On)," *Human Touch*, Columbia Records. Reprinted with permission from John Landau Management.
2. Ontario has recently passed a law ensuring public access to the mall to engage in reasonable activities. This should, in principle, allow for some public expression of opinion.
3. Margaret Visser (1986) raises these questions regarding corn as well as a number of other plants. Her book is worth reading to appreciate the consequences of our way of growing food.
4. Dierdre Carmody, "Picking Teens' Pockets," *The Globe and Mail*, January 20, 1993, p. C3.
5. While we do not pursue it here, it is worth asking what the consequences are of our government being the largest spender on advertising.
6. James Christie, "NBC's Super Bowl Score: $30,000 a Second," *The Globe and Mail*, January 30, 1993, p. A21.
7. Quoted in "Media Wars," *Maclean's*, July 17, 1989, p. 27.
8. Information for this section and those following relies heavily on Frank and Durand (1993) and Canada Department of Communications (1989).
9. "Black Power," *Maclean's*, August 3, 1992, pp. 27–33.

10. "Good News from the Garbage Pile," *The Globe and Mail*, February 4, 1989, p. B1. Based on a report from the Ontario Ministry of the Environment.

11. Harvey Enchin, "Magazine Davids Need a Better Slingshot," *The Globe and Mail*, January 21, 1993, pp. B1, B10.

12. Bronwyne Drainie, "Avoiding Cultural Chernobyl," *The Globe and Mail*, March 9, 1991, p. C3.

13. For an examination of this issue, see the video "Distress Signals: The New World of Globalized Broadcasting."

14. Harvey Enchin, "Rogers Team Ready to Prove Bigger is Better," *The Globe and Mail*, September 20, 1994, p. B1.

15. Rick Salutin, "Our Cultural Air Is Being Altered," *The Globe and Mail*, November 5, 1987, p. A7.

16. Stephen Godfrey, "Who Will Rule the Waves?" *The Globe and Mail*, July 22, 1991, p. C1.

17. For further documentation of American pressure applied to Canadian governments, see Clarkson (1985). Also see Stephen Godfrey, "Behind the Big Screen," *The Globe and Mail*, March 28, 1992, pp. A1, A6.

18. "Cultural Freedom Linked to Canada's Fate," *The Globe and Mail*, January 20, 1987, p. A7.

19. These and other cases were reported in Donald Trelford, "Freedom of Press Is Vanishing from Britain," *The Globe and Mail*, May 21, 1988, p. D3.

20. Barrie Zwicker, "Where Commerce, Journalism Meet," *The Globe and Mail*, September 15, 1990, pp. D1, D8.

21. A decision by the Quebec Court of Appeal in 1993 ruled that the federal government had the right to ban all tobacco advertising, overturning a decision by the Quebec Superior Court in 1991. A decision has not yet been made by the federal Supreme Court on this matter.

22. These matters are discussed by Brian Philcox, "The Public Has a Right to Know," *The Globe and Mail*, January 16, 1989, p. A7, and by Allan Hutchinson, "Opening Pandora's Box," *Globe and Mail*, December 20, 1988, p. A7. For a fuller analysis of commercial free speech, see Schiller (1989).

23. "Parker Pen Regains Its Lost Glory to Prove It Possesses Write Stuff," *The Globe and Mail*, May 4, 1988, p. B4.

24. Extract from "Public Sex," *Ideas* series, CBC Transcripts, November–December 1983. Reprinted with the permission of CBC Radio, Ideas Transcripts.

. . . .

FURTHER READING

Canada. Department of Communications. *Vital Links: Canadian Cultural Industries.* Ottawa: Minister of Supply and Services, 1987. A clear review of the impact of global culture on Canada and a bold statement about the appropriate response. The government backed away from many of the statements in this publication, and the situation has been allowed to grow worse.

Ewen, Stuart, and Elizabeth Ewen. *Channels of Desire: Mass Images and the Shaping of American Consciousness.* New York: McGraw-Hill Book Co., 1982. A good discussion of the character and implications of the commercial culture that has developed to respond to the needs of business.

Nash, Knowlton. *The Microphone Wars: A History of Triumph and Betrayal at the C.B.C.* Toronto: McClelland and Stewart, 1994. A must-read for all Canadians.

Nelson, Joyce. *The Perfect Machine: TV in the Nuclear Age*. Toronto: Between the Lines, 1987. Nelson's essays are always informative and thought provoking.

Schiller, Herbert I. *Culture Inc.: The Corporate Takeover of Public Expression*. New York: Oxford University Press, 1989. An accessible and thought-provoking examination of corporate domination of culture.

. . . .

STUDY QUESTIONS

. . . .

1. Discuss the essential differences between a citizen and a consumer.
2. Is there a programming difference between privately owned television channels and publicly owned channels (e.g., the CBC or provincial educational networks)?
3. Does Canadian culture need protecting?
4. In your experience, how do advertisers try to get young people to be consumers?
5. We all have to become consumers. From your own experience, how is this socialization accomplished?
6. Should the government require radio stations to play Canadian music? Discuss the arguments for and against such a proposal.
7. Who owns your favourite professional sports team? Has the type of ownership changed over the years?
8. Identify your ten favourite musicians or popular songs. Discover if the musician or song is Canadian. What proportion of the ten are Canadian? Is this good or bad, in your opinion?
9. Is advertising that is directed at women different in content and style from that directed at men?

15 CONCLUSIONS

. . . .

. . . .

This book has introduced some of the key conceptual tools that sociology uses in its quest to comprehend society as a connected whole. Sociology emerged along with the transformation of western society that was associated with capitalism and the industrial revolution. Capitalism, and the constant economic and technological transformation with which it is associated, continues to recast world society. The current era is one in which scarcely any society has remained insulated from the effects of global capitalism and economic modernization.

A brief examination of three classical sociologists — Durkheim, Marx, and Weber — was presented to show how sociology responded to the rise of this modern world. Sociological concepts and debates have continued to respond to social change, and this book has outlined how modern sociologists have examined the social world, especially Canada. Substantive chapters discussed various topics — inequality, the economy, the state, work, schooling, families, deviance, and consumer culture — to show how each of these is shaped by the social forces unleashed by the rise of capitalism. The social problems that confront Canadians today have a very long history.

Two central themes in this book reflect the fundamental sociological debate about modernity. As Charles Taylor (1991) expressed it, there is an opposition of "cultural pessimism" to "cultural optimism." Does modern culture undermine community and reduce meaning in personal life? Or does it offer the promise of fulfilment and personal satisfaction?

Pessimists direct attention to the two-edged nature of the value of individualism. Individual liberty is necessary as a building block for a market economy driven by individual choices. Many praise being born into a society that values individualism, since, ideally, it removes people from the constraints of ascription, hierarchy, and legal inequality. Within limits, they can choose their values and behaviours and they can believe what they wish. This freedom reflects their becoming loosely connected to established bodies of beliefs and institutionalized ways of doing things. Now that people are free of these social constraints, and encouraged to be more self-oriented, it may become increasingly difficult to find meaningful connection to community life. Has the pursuit of individualism left them isolated and lonely and made the ties that bind them together seem more and more tenuous?

A second concern is the growing importance of instrumental rationality, what Weber called rationalization. The value given to the most efficient means for maximizing material goals has entered more and more aspects of life. While this has meant a rejection of the more "enchanted" view of the world provided through religion, the sacred, the mysterious, and the traditional, it has also meant a change in the way people look at the natural world. The natural world itself has become an object to be rationalized and exploited. In attempting to dominate nature, modern society has created a potential for the collapse of the environment. While society can fine polluters and build environmental costs into the cost of economic activity, can it return to thinking of nature as sacred or of its obligation as being one of stewardship rather than domination? While instrumental reason has allowed humanity to control many of the threats to life (disease, crop failure, and so on), it has also created a new threat — technology itself, the embodiment of instrumental rationality.

A third problem, related to the first two, concerns people's growing inability to exercise collective control over their lives. They are encouraged to think of themselves in individual terms, rather than in social terms, and in terms of instrumental rationality. Add to this a belief in the need for a free market, reduced autonomy, and creativity in the workplace because of the division of labour and the bureaucratization of activity, and the area for the genuine exercise of collective democracy is considerably reduced. The world seems out of our control, leaving people without the collective means to shape and guide society. Are they really free? Are individual consumer choices the only exercise of freedom possible, or can members of modern society identify with their local community and find ways to act in the interest of the society? Can democratic debate and democratic action survive?

In each of these areas, real tension exists between freedom and isolation, between the benefits of instrumental rationality and the high environmental costs and alienation involved, and between individual strength and community weakness. Sociologists have often emphasized the negative side of these tensions, such as the loss of freedom, the loss of meaning, and the loss of social solidarity. It is, however, possible to be more optimistic and to see capitalism and liberalism as having created the opportunity for individual self-fulfilment, the decline of the constraints of hierarchy, patriarchy, and traditional authority, and the promise of freedom of choice. This attitude, of course, is based on a liberal vision of society.

A central theme of this book is the claim that there is a contradiction between the ideals of liberal thought and the reality of modern social organization. Liberalism is an ideology because of the disjunction between its account of society and the portrait that emerges from sociological investigation. While the triumph of this ideology leads some to pessimism, others are more optimistic and believe that liberal values, actively pursued, provide a basis for satisfying social life. It is not liberalism itself that creates contemporary dissatisfaction, but the incomplete realization of a society in which there is equality of opportunity and freedom of choice.

Clearly, the goals of liberalism have not always been attained. The ideal of the free market is challenged by the growth of monopoly capitalism; the democratic ideal of participation is denied in the workplace, where control of the work process is appropriated by management; the ideal of representative democracy is challenged by the concentration of economic power and the unrepresentative nature of those elected; the ideal of equality of opportunity is denied by the presence of patriarchal authority and privilege and by the class structure of the society; the ideal of individualism creates instability in family life and ignores the gender-based constraints on women; and, finally, the ideal of pluralism is challenged by the control of the instruments of communication and by the homogenizing effect of the media as economic instruments.

These contradictions lead to the conclusion that people are not as free as they might think, nor has democracy and equality been achieved. To each of these problems it is possible to respond that liberalism provides answers if its assumptions are fully implemented. Liberalism can be advocated as a positive program to enhance equality of opportunity, restore competition, control monopoly, promote access to channels of communication, and sustain pluralism and choice.

A sociological portrait of society, as Dennis Wrong (1961) reminds us, contains an oversocialized conception of the individual. It tends to see individuals as prey for structural forces and imbued with implanted beliefs and values. But personal experience shows that people are not passive objects of modernity: they can and do create their lives and shape their society. Societies are full of individuals and groups that seek to preserve, or to construct, alternative ways of living. There is a pervasive political movement in Canada that struggles to contain and direct the forces of modernity.

Acts of resistance to modern values and social organization are manifold in modern society. They include the pursuit of eastern religions by westerners in a search for a new source of meaning in life. They include families that have decided to remove television from their homes or those who tune their sets permanently to a public broadcasting channel in order to avoid the commercials and the artificial reflection of social life. The attraction of folk-music festivals across Canada that feature "roots" music springs from the resistance to the commercial and the homogenized. Gardeners find pleasure in growing heritage seeds and preserving the diversity of the past. Some women resist having their babies in hospital and choose instead to have a home delivery in order to establish a more personal relationship with a midwife and the continuing connection to family and place.

Some perform small acts to recover a feeling of community. They choose co-operative housing, become involved in running schools, join a neighbourhood association, or delve into the traditions of their community to look for different values and ways of social life.

Ethnic roots and traditions are recovered as people seek a more enchanted connection to the social and physical world. Many Canadians are envious of the Native worldview and strive to understand their spiritual connection to the land.

There are also public and political dimensions to these acts of resistance and recovery. A national and international environmental movement attempts to place the social values of continuity and survival ahead of the instrumental rationality driving corporate decision making. World public opinion on forest preservation, marine ecology, and care of the land continues to be transformed away from a focus on exploitation. Groups like the Council of Canadians and the Friends of Public Broadcasting attempt to organize people to resist the forces of the global market, which threaten to destroy the unique communities that have been built in Canada and the values that link Canadians. Women have organized to bring great changes in the relations between the sexes and to draw closer to a society of greater gender equality. First Nations peoples move toward community recovery through the revitalization of their culture and through efforts to reassert their right to self-government. At the core of this recovery is the healing circle and the women's circle. There is an active and dynamic political life in Canada.

Others have felt pulled toward a vision of an alternative society. Socialism, with its emphasis on social values and collective action, has persisted as a utopian vision despite the triumph of modern capitalism. It has long been seen as an alternative to the dangers of individualism and the tyranny of the free market. With the collapse of communism and a thorough understanding of the harm that resulted from a society committed wholeheartedly to a single ideology, this vision of utopia has become clouded. It is not possible to ignore the assault on the freedom of the individual that communism entailed or to overlook the dangers that come with any attempt to organize a socialist society.

These societies may jeopardize individual freedom in the name of socialism as much as capitalism does in the name of the marketplace. Max Weber predicted that the collective organization of society would require a growth in centralization and rationalization even greater than occurred in modern capitalism. Few people today would advocate a revival of Soviet-style communist society. Is it possible to imagine a socialist society that preserves pluralism and choice without the foundation of individual rights to accumulate and use property? Or must ways be found to enhance social values and community within a society committed to individualism and the free market?

Might a fuller realization of the principles of liberalism bring us closer to the promise it contains? Can gender relations be transformed so that the promise of equality of opportunity comes closer for women? Can equal opportunity be brought to individuals in all class and status groups? Can an active public change the unrepresentative nature of most authority structures? Is it possible to promote diversity and debate through the mass media? Perhaps there are avenues to achieve these goals within Canadian society.

Many groups have used the principle of individual rights enshrined in the Canadian Charter of Rights and Freedoms as a tool for bringing individual freedom to various "oppressed" groups. Homosexual men and women argue for the protection of their individual rights so that they might claim spousal benefits, adopt children, and choose occupations freely without discrimination. The physically and mentally challenged demand their right to an education and to be integrated into the school classroom rather than be segregated from their peers.

Others insist on the need to return to a society modelled more closely on the vision of classical economic liberalism. They argue that much harm has resulted from restrictions on the free market and the failure to develop a market philosophy in many areas of modern social life. Some, for example, argue that individual ownership of endangered species would result in the best decisions being made regarding their future. They also argue that choice is frustrated by restrictions on competition and that this must be corrected. This may require a stronger Competition Act, reduction of the concentration of ownership, and removal of government regulations on economic activity. They believe that liberal philosophy and its commitment to individualism and freedom can be fulfilled in a capitalist society. They see a core of truth in Milton Friedman's claim that there is a strong connection between individual freedom and capitalism. It therefore becomes necessary to limit corporate concentration, government centralization, and impersonal bureaucracies, and at the same time to encourage private initiatives such as small businesses, local resource use and development, and self-reliance in order to achieve a better balance between the needs of the individual and the community.

This is the essence of the unresolved debate that has been haunting sociology for over 100 years. Can Canadians fulfil social values and build meaningful communities in a society committed to individualism and the rationality of capitalism? Or can they protect individual freedom in a society committed to satisfying social values through a collectivist economic organization? Aspects of this tension are reflected in the Canadian debate about individual rights versus collective rights. Should citizens expect to find a sense of commitment and sharing only in personal contacts and accept a rationalized public life? Or should they seek to develop community and reject this divided image of the individual? Society, after all, does colour one's whole experience of life.

· · · · · · · ·

FURTHER READING

Heilbroner, Robert. *Twenty-First Century Capitalism.* Toronto: Anansi, 1992.
Taylor, Charles. *The Malaise of Modernity.* Toronto: Anansi, 1991.

· · · · · · · ·

REFERENCES

Adams, Owen. (1990). "Divorce Rates in Canada." In C. McKie and K. Thompson, eds., *Canadian Social Trends*. Toronto: Statistics Canada and Thomson Educational Publishing.

Albert, Ethel M. (1971). "Women of Burundi." In Denise Paulme, ed., *Women of Tropical Africa*. Berkeley: University of California Press.

Anderson, Charles. (1974). *Toward a New Sociology*, 2nd rev. ed. Illinois: Dorsey Press.

Anderson, Karen. (1987). "A Gendered World: Women, Men and the Political Economy of Seventeenth Century Huron." In Heather Maroney and Meg Luxton, eds., *Feminism and Political Economy*. Toronto: Methuen.

Antoniou, A., and R. Rowley. (1986). "The Ownership Structure of the Largest Canadian Corporations, 1979." *Canadian Journal of Sociology* 11, pp. 253–268.

Ariès, Philippe. (1962). *Centuries of Childhood*. Trans. R. Baldick. New York: Random House.

Aristotle. (1948). *Politics*. Trans. E. Barker. Oxford: Oxford University Press.

Aron, Raymond. (1968). *Main Currents in Sociological Thought*. Vol. 1. Garden City, NY: Doubleday.

——— . (1970). *Main Currents in Sociological Thought*. Vol. 2. New York: Anchor.

Ashworth, W. (1962). *The International Economy Since 1850*. London: Longmans.

Axelrod, Paul. (1982). *Scholars and Dollars: Politics, Economics, and the Universities of Ontario, 1945–1980*. Toronto: University of Toronto Press.

Baer, D., E. Grabb and W.A. Johnston. (1990). "The Values of Canadians and Americans: A Critical Analysis and Reassessment." *Social Forces* 68, pp. 693–713.

Bagdkian, Ben H. (1990). *The Media Monopoly*, 3rd ed. Boston: Beacon Press.

Baker, Hugh. (1979). *Chinese Family and Kinship*. New York: Columbia University Press.

Bane, Mary Jo, and Christopher Jencks. (1976). "Five Myths about Your IQ." In N.J. Block and Gerald Dworkin, eds., *The IQ Controversy* (pp. 325–338). New York: Pantheon Books.

Barkans, John, and Norene Pupo. (1978). "Canadian Universities and the Economic Order." In R. Nelsen and D. Nock, eds., *Reading, Writing and Riches: Education and the Socio-Economic Order in North America*. Toronto: Between the Lines.

Barnett, Richard J. (1993). "The End of Jobs." *Harper's Magazine,* September, pp. 47–52.

Barrett, Michael J. (1990). "The Case for More School Days." *The Atlantic Monthly,* November, pp. 78–106.

Bayley, David. (1976). *Forces of Order: Police Behavior in Japan and the United States*. Berkeley: University of California Press.

Becker, Howard, and William Rau. (1992). "Sociology in the 1990's." *Society,* November/December.

Belenky, Mary F., B. Clinchy, N. Goldberg, and J. Tarule. (1986). *Women's Ways of Knowing*. New York: Basic Books.

Bell, D., and L. Tepperman. (1979). *The Roots of Disunity: A Look at Canadian Political Culture*. Toronto: McClelland and Stewart.

Bell, Daniel. (1973). *The Coming of Post-Industrial Society*. New York: Basic Books.

————. (1978). *The Cultural Contradictions of Capitalism.* New York: Basic Books.

Bellah, Robert, et al. (1985). *Habits of the Heart: Individualism and Commitment in American Life.* Berkeley: University of California Press.

Benedict, Ruth. (1973[1938]). "Continuities and Discontinuities in Cultural Conditioning." In Harry Silverstein, ed., *The Sociology of Youth: Evolution of Revolution.* New York: Macmillan.

Berger, Peter L. (1986). *The Capitalist Revolution: Fifty Propositions about Prosperity, Equality and Liberty.* New York: Basic Books.

Berger, Peter, and Brigitte Berger. (1983). *The War Over the Family: Capturing the Middle Ground.* New York: Anchor Press/Doubleday.

Berman, Marshall. (1988). *All That Is Solid Melts into Air: The Experience of Modernity.* New York: Viking Penguin.

Bibby, Reginald W. (1990). *Mosaic Madness: The Poverty and Potential of Life in Canada.* Toronto: Stoddart.

Bloch, Marc. (1961). *Feudal Society.* London: Routledge and Kegan Paul.

Blumberg, Paul. (1968). *Industrial Democracy: The Sociology of Participation.* New York: Shocken Books.

Bottomore, Tom, and R. Brym, eds. (1989). *The Capitalist Class: An International Study.* New York: New York University Press.

Bowen, Elenore Smith. (1964). *Return to Laughter.* Garden City, NY: Anchor Books.

Box, Steven. (1987). *Recession, Crime and Punishment.* Totowa, NJ: Barnes and Noble Books.

Boyd, Monica. (1984). *Canadian Attitudes Towards Women: Thirty Years of Change.* Ottawa: Minister of Supply and Services.

Braithwaite, John. (1989). *Crime, Shame and Reintegration.* New York: Cambridge University Press.

Brannigan, Augustine. (1984). *Crime, Courts and Corrections.* Toronto: Holt, Rinehart and Winston.

Brantlinger, Patrick. (1983). *Bread and Circuses: Theories of Mass Culture as Social Decay.* Ithaca, NY: Cornell University Press.

Braverman, Harry. (1974). *Labor and Monopoly Capitalism.* New York: Monthly Review Press.

British Columbia. Royal Commission on Education (1987–88). (1988). *A Legacy for Learners: Summary of Findings.* Victoria: Queen's Printer of British Columbia.

Brodeur, Paul. (1985). *Outrageous Misconduct: The Asbestos Industry on Trial.* New York: Pantheon Books.

Brodie, Janine. (1990). *The Political Economy of Regionalism.* Toronto: Harcourt Brace Jovanovich.

Brown, Phelps, and S. Hopkins. (1962). "Seven Centuries of the Prices of Consumables, Compared with Builder's Wage Rates." In E.C. Wilson, *Essays in Economic History.* London: Edward Arnold.

Brownmiller, Susan. (1975). *Against Our Will: Men, Women and Rape.* New York: Simon and Schuster.

Brym, Robert J., with Bonnie J. Fox. (1989). *From Culture to Power: The Sociology of English Canada.* Toronto: Oxford University Press.

Burks, Ardath. (1966). *The Government of Japan.* London: Methuen.

Canada. (1969). *Report of the Task Force on Labour Relations.* Ottawa: Queen's Printer.

————. (1972). *Foreign Direct Investment in Canada.* Ottawa: Information Canada.

————. (1978). "Report of the Royal Commission on Price Spreads (1935)." In I. Abella and D. Millar, eds., *The Canadian Worker in the Twentieth Century.* Toronto: Oxford University Press.

————. (1993). *Public Accounts of Canada.* Vol. 1. *Summary Report and Financial Statement.* Ottawa: Public Works and Government Services Canada.

Canada. Department of Communications. (1987). *Vital Links: Canadian Cultural Industries.* Ottawa: Minister of Supply and Services.

Canada Communications Group. (1992). *Education and Training in Canada.* Ottawa: Minister of Supply and Services.

Canada, Prosperity Secretariat. (1991). *Learning Well Living Well*. Ottawa: Minister of Supply and Services.

Canadian Broadcasting Corporation. (1984). *Public Sex* (from the CBC "Ideas" Series, November–December 1983). Toronto: CBC Transcripts.

Canadian Centre for Justice Statistics. (1991). "Homicide in Canada." *Juristat Service Bulletin*, Vol. 12 (18). Ottawa: Minister of Industry, Science and Technology.

———. (1992a). "Gender Differences among Violent Crime Victims." *Juristat Service Bulletin*, Vol. 12 (21). Ottawa: Minister of Industry, Science and Technology.

———. (1992b). "Homicide in Canada." *Juristat Service Bulletin*, Vol. 12 (18). Ottawa: Minister of Industry, Science and Technology.

Canadian Federation of Independent Business. (1988). *The Impact of Service Sector Growth on Employment and Earnings*. Toronto: Canadian Federation of Independent Business.

Carroll, W., J. Fox, and M. Ornstein. (1982). "The Network of Directorate Links among the Largest Canadian Firms." *Canadian Review of Sociology and Anthropology* 19, pp. 44–69.

CAW–Canada Research Group on CAMI. (1993). *The CAMI Report: Lean Production In A Unionized Auto Plant*. Willowdale, ON: CAW–Canada Research Department.

Chagnon, Napoleon A. (1968). *Yanomamo, The Fierce People*. New York: Holt, Rinehart.

Chalmers, Alan. (1991). *Science and Its Fabrication*. Minneapolis: University of Minnesota Press.

Chandler, William. (1993). "The Value of Household Work in Canada, 1992." In *National Income and Expenditure Accounts, Fourth Quarter* (pp. xxxv–xlviii). Ottawa: Statistics Canada.

Chawla, Raj K. (1990). "The Distribution of Wealth in Canada and the United States." *Perspectives on Labour and Income*. Spring.

Chodorow, Nancy. (1978). *The Reproduction of Mothering*. Berkeley: University of California Press.

Chomsky, Noam. (1989). *Necessary Illusions: Thought Control in Democratic Societies*. Toronto: CBC Enterprises.

Christie, Nils. (1978). "Youth as a Crime-generating Phenomenon." In B. Krisberg and J. Austin, eds., *Children of Ishmael*. Mayfield: Cambridge University Press.

Clark, B. (1960). "The Cooling-out Function in Higher Education." *American Journal of Sociology* 65.

Clarkson, Stephen. (1985). *Canada and the Reagan Challenge*, 2nd ed. Toronto: James Lorimer.

Clement, Wallace. (1975). *The Canadian Corporate Elite*. Toronto: McClelland and Stewart.

———. (1977). "The Corporate Elite, the Capitalist Class and the Canadian State." In L. Panitch, ed., *The Canadian State*. Toronto: University of Toronto Press.

———. (1981). *Hardrock Mining: Industrial Relations and Technological Changes at Inco*. Toronto: McClelland and Stewart.

———. (1990). "A Critical Response to 'Perspectives on the Class and Ethnic Origins of Canadian Elites.'" *Canadian Journal of Sociology* 15, pp. 179–185.

Cobban, Alfred. (1965). *A History of Modern France*. Vol. 2. Middlesex, England: Penguin Books.

Cole, G.D.H., and R. Postgate. (1961). *The Common People*. London: Methuen.

Collins, Randall. (1975). *Conflict Sociology: Toward an Explanatory Science*. New York: Academic Press.

Commission on Systemic Racism in the Ontario Criminal Justice System. (1994). *Racism Behind Bars*. Toronto: Ontario Queen's Printer.

Committee on Sexual Offences Against Children and Youths. (1984). *Sexual Offences Against Children*. 2 vols. Ottawa: Minister of Supply and Services.

Cooper, Mary, Anne Marie Karlberg, and Lorreta Adams. (1991). *Aboriginal Suicide in British Columbia: An Executive Summary*. Burnaby: B.C. Institute on Family Violence.

Coulborn, R. (1965). *Feudalism in History*. Hamden, CT: Archon Books.

Cover, J. Dan. (1993). *Sociological Investigations*. Guildford, CT: Dushkin.

Creese, Gillian, Neil Guppy, and Martin Meissner. (1991). *Ups and Downs on the Social Ladder of Success: Social Mobility in Canada*. Ottawa: Ministry of Supply and Services.

Crocker, Robert. (1990). *Science Achievement in Canadian Schools: National and International Comparisons*. Ottawa: Economic Council of Canada.

Cuff, E.C., and G.C.F. Payne. (1984). *Perspectives in Sociology*. London: Allen and Unwin.

Currie, Elliott. (1985). *Confronting Crime: An American Challenge*. New York: Pantheon Books.

Davis, Kingsley, and Wilbert E. Moore. (1945). "Some Principles of Stratification." *American Sociological Review* 10, pp. 242–249.

DeKeseredy, Walter. (1992). "Wife Assault." In V. Sacco, ed., *Deviance: Conformity and Control in Canadian Society*. Scarborough: Prentice-Hall.

DeKeseredy, Walter, and Katherine Kelly. (1993). "The Incidence and Prevalence of Woman Abuse in Canadian University and College Dating Relationships," *Canadian Journal of Sociology* 18, pp. 137–159.

Diamond, Stanley. (1974). *In Search of the Primitive*. Chicago: Transaction Books.

Dickinson, James, and Bob Russell. (1986). *Family, Economy and State*. Toronto: Garamond Press.

Divale, William, and Marvin Harris. (1976). "Population, Warfare, and the Male Supremacist Complex." *American Anthropologist* 78, pp. 521–538.

Douglas, Jack. (1967). *The Social Meaning of Suicide*. Princeton: Princeton University Press.

Dumas, J., and Y. Perron. (1992). *Marriage and Conjugal Life in Canada: Current Demographic Analysis*. Cat. no. 91-534. Ottawa: Ministry of Industry, Science and Technology.

Durkheim, Émile. (1951[1897]). *Suicide: A Study in Sociology*. New York: Free Press.

———. (1961[1902]). *Moral Education: A Study in the Theory and Application of the Sociology of Education*. Glencoe: Free Press.

———. (1962[1928]). *Socialism and Saint-Simon*. New York: Collier.

———. (1964). *The Rules of Sociological Method*. Trans. Solovay and Mueller. New York: Free Press.

———. (1984[1893]). The *Division of Labour in Society*. London: Macmillan.

Economic Council of Canada. (1989). *Legacies: Twenty-Sixth Annual Report*. Ottawa: Minister of Supply and Services Canada.

———. (1990). *Good Jobs, Bad Jobs: Employment in the Service Economy*. Ottawa: Minister of Supply and Services Canada.

———. (1991). *Employment in the Service Economy*. Ottawa: Minister of Supply and Services Canada.

———. (1992a). *Pulling Together: Productivity, Innovation, and Trade*. Ottawa: Minister of Supply and Services Canada.

———. (1992b). *The New Face of Poverty*. Ottawa: Minister of Supply and Services Canada.

Eglin, P., J. Abwunza, and W. Hallman. (1984). *Producing the "Teenage Suicide Epidemic": The Ontario Coroners System and the Suicidologists*. Waterloo, ON: Wilfrid Laurier University Research Paper Series.

Ehrenreich, Barbara. (1988). "Farewell to Work." *Mother Jones,* May.

Eichler, Margrit. (1980). *The Double Standard: A Feminist Critique of Feminist Social Science*. New York: St. Martin's Press.

———. (1988). *Families in Canada Today*. Toronto: Gage Educational.

Ellis, D. (1987). *The Wrong Stuff: An Introduction to the Sociological Study of Deviance*. Don Mills, ON: Collier-Macmillan.

Elton, G.R. (1955). *England Under the Tudors*. London: Methuen.

Emerson, Steven. (1985). *The American House of Saud*. New York: Franklin Watts.

Engels, Frederick. (1897[1845]). *Conditions of the Working Class in England in 1844*. London: George Allen & Unwin.

———. (1968[1883]). "Speech at the Graveside of Marx." In *Karl Marx and Frederick Engels: Selected Works*. London: Lawrence and Wishart.

———. (1968[1884]). "The Origin of the Family, Private Property, and the State." In *Karl Marx and Frederick Engels: Selected Works*. London: Lawrence and Wishart.

Engelstad, Diane, and John Bird. (1992). *Nation to Nation: Aboriginal Sovereignty and the Future of Canada*. Toronto: Anansi.

Erikson, Erik. (1963). *Childhood and Society*. New York: W.W. Norton.

Eyck, Erich. (1962). *The Weimar Republic*. Cambridge, MA: Harvard University Press.

Faludi, S. (1991). *Backlash*. New York: Crown.

Feuer, L. (1969). *Marx and Engels: Basic Writings on Politics and Philosophy*. London: Collins.

Firth, Raymond. (1958). *Human Types*. New York: Mentor Books.

Forrest, William G. (1966). *The Emergence of Greek Democracy*. London: World University Press.

Fox, Bonnie J. (1993). "On Violent Men and Female Victims: A Comment on DeKeseredy and Kelly," *Canadian Journal of Sociology* 18, pp. 321–324.

Fox, J., and M. Ornstein. (1986). "The Canadian State and Corporate Elites in the Post-War Period." *Canadian Review of Anthropology and Sociology* 23, pp. 481–506.

Fox, Paul. (1982). *Politics: Canada*. Toronto: McGraw-Hill.

Francis, D. (1986). *Controlling Interest: Who Owns Canada?* Toronto: Macmillan.

Frank, Jeffrey, and Michel Durand. (1993). "Canadian Content in the Cultural Marketplace." *Canadian Social Trends*, 18–21.

Freeman, Derek. (1983). *Margaret Mead and Samoa: The Making and Unmaking of an Anthropological Myth*. Cambridge, MA: Harvard University Press.

Freund, Julien. (1968). *The Sociology of Max Weber*. New York: Random House.

Fried, Morton. (1967). *The Evolution of Political Society*. New York: Random House.

Friedman, Milton. (1962). *Capitalism and Freedom*. Chicago: University of Chicago Press.

Fromm, E. (1955). *The Sane Society*. Greenwich, CT: Fawcett.

Gairdner, W.D. (1992). *The War Against the Family*. Toronto: Stoddart.

Gans, Herbert. (1974). *Popular Culture and High Culture*. New York: Basic Books.

Gardner, H. (1972). *The Quest For Mind*. New York: Alfred A. Knopf.

Gartner, Rosemary. (1993). "Studying Woman Abuse: A Comment on DeKeseredy and Kelly." *Canadian Journal of Sociology* 18, pp. 313–320.

Gaskell, Jane. (1985). "Women and Education: Branching Out." In *Towards Equity*. Ottawa: Ministry of Supply and Services.

Gerth, H., and C.W. Mills. (1970). *From Max Weber*. New York: Oxford University Press.

Giddens, Anthony. (1989). *Sociology*. Oxford: Polity Press.

——— . (1990). *The Consequences of Modernity*. Stanford: Stanford University Press.

Giere, Ronald. (1984). *Understanding Scientific Reasoning*. Fort Worth, Texas: Holt, Rinehart and Winston.

Gillies, James. (1991). "Reversing Our History: Can Canada Compete?" *Inside Guide*, June, pp. 18–19.

Goldberg, Steven. (1973). *The Inevitability of Patriarchy*. New York: William Morrow and Company.

Goode, William. (1963). *World Revolution and Family Patterns*. New York: Free Press.

Gouldner, Alvin. (1964). "Anti-Minotaur: The Myth of a Value-free Sociology." In I. L. Horowitz, ed., *The New Sociology*. New York: Oxford University Press.

Grabb, Edward G. (1990). *Theories of Social Inequality: Classical and Contemporary Theorists*, 2nd ed. Toronto: Holt, Rinehart and Winston.

Gramsci, A. (1971). *Selections from the Prison Notebooks of Antonio Gramsci*. Eds. and trans. Q. Hoare and Nowell Smith. London: Lawrence and Wishart.

Grant, Michael. (1985). *Atlas of Ancient History*. Dorset Press.

Gudeman, S. (1986). *Economics as Culture*. London: Routledge and Kegan Paul.

Gunderson, M., L. Muszynski, and J. Keck. (1990). *Women and Labour Market Poverty*. Ottawa: Canadian Advisory Council on the Status of Women.

Guppy, Neil. (1984). "Access to Higher Education in Canada." *Canadian Journal of Higher Education* 14, pp. 79–93.

Guppy, N., S. Freeman, and S. Buchan. (1987). "Representing Canadians: Changes in the Economic Backgrounds of Federal Politicians, 1965–1984." *Canadian Review of Sociology and Anthropology* 24, pp. 417–430.

Hardin, Herschel. (1974). *A Nation Unaware: The Canadian Economic Culture*. Vancouver: J.J. Douglas.

——— . (1989). *The Privatization Putsch*. Halifax: Institute for Research on Public Policy.

Harris, M. (1990). *Justice Denied: The Law versus Donald Marshall*. Toronto: Totem/Collins.

Harris, Marvin. (1975). *Cows, Pigs, Wars and Witches: The Riddles of Culture*. New York: Vintage Books.

———. (1977). *Cannibals and Kings*. New York: Vintage/Random House.

Hartjen, Clayton. (1982). "Delinquency, Development, and Social Integration in India." *Social Problems* 29, pp. 464–473.

Heilbroner, Robert L. (1989). *The Making of Economic Society*, 8th ed. Englewood Cliffs, NJ: Prentice-Hall.

Herrnstein, Richard J. (1973). *IQ in the Meritocracy*. Boston: Little, Brown.

Hobsbawm, E.J. (1969). *Industry and Empire*. London: Pelican Books.

Howard, Michael C. (1986). *Contemporary Cultural Anthropology*, 2nd ed. Toronto: Little, Brown.

Hudson, Joe, and Burt Galaway, eds. (1993). *Single Parent Families: Perspectives on Research and Policy*. Toronto: Thomson Educational.

Hunter, Alfred. (1981). *Class Tells: On Social Inequality in Canada*. Toronto: Butterworths.

Hurtig, Mel. (1991). *The Betrayal of Canada*. Toronto: Stoddart.

Innis, Harold. (1970[1930]). *The Fur Trade in Canada*. Toronto: University of Toronto Press.

Jackson, Margaret A., and Curt T. Griffiths. (1991). *Canadian Criminology*. Toronto: Harcourt Brace Jovanovich.

Jacques, Romain. (1988). *Impact of Forestry Activity on the Economy of Canada and Its Provinces: An Input-Output Approach*. Ottawa: Government of Canada, Canadian Forestry Service.

Jencks, C. (1972). *Inequality: A Reassessment of the Effect of Family and Schooling in America*. New York: Basic Books.

Kamata, Satoshi, and R. Dore. (1983). *Japan in the Passing Lane*. New York: Pantheon Books.

Karabel, J. (1976). "Community Colleges and Stratification." *Harvard Educational Review* 42, pp. 521–562.

Kaysen, Carl. (1957). "The Social Significance of the Modern Corporation." *American Economic Review* 47, pp. 311–319.

Keat, Russell, and John Urry. (1975). *Social Theory as Science*. London: Routledge and Kegan Paul.

Keller, Evelyn Fox. (1985). *Reflections on Gender and Science*. New Haven, CT: Yale University Press.

Kessler, Suzanne, and Wendy McKenna. (1978). *Gender: An Ethnomethodological Approach*. Toronto: John Wiley and Sons.

Kneen, Brewster. (1993). *From Land to Mouth: Understanding the Food System*. Toronto: NC Press.

Kosminsky, E.A. (1962). "Services and Money Rents." In E.C. Wilson, ed., *Essays in Economic History*. Vol 2. London: Edward Arnold.

Kowinski, William S. (1985). *The Malling of America*. New York: William Morrow and Company.

Krahn, Harvey. (1992). *Quality of Work in the Service Sector*. Ottawa: Minister of Industry, Science and Technology.

Krahn, Harvey, and G. Lowe. (1993). *Work, Industry and Canadian Society*, 2nd ed. Scarborough: Nelson.

Krause, W., and J. Lothian. (1989). "Measurement of Canada's Level of Corporate Concentration." *Canadian Economic Observer*, January, pp. 3.14–3.31.

Kuttner, Bob. (1983). "The Declining Middle." *The Atlantic Monthly*, July, pp. 60–72.

Lakoff, Robin T. (1990). *Talking Power: The Politics of Language*. New York: Basic Books.

Lasch, Christopher. (1977). *Haven in a Heartless World: The Family Besieged*. New York: Basic Books.

———. (1984). *The Minimal Self*. New York: W.W. Norton.

Laxer, Gordon. (1989). *Open For Business: The Roots of Foreign Ownership in Canada*. Toronto: Oxford University Press.

Leacock, Eleanor. (1977). "Women in Egalitarian Society." In R. Bridenthal and C. Koontz, eds., *Becoming Visible: Women in European History*. Boston: Houghton Mifflin.

———. (1981). *Myths of Male Dominance: Collected Articles on Women Cross-Culturally*. New York: Monthly Review.

Lenton, Rhonda. (1989). "Homicide in Canada and the U.S.A.: A Critique of the Hagan Thesis." *Canadian Journal of Sociology* 14, pp. 163–177.

Lerner, Gerda. (1986). *The Creation of Patriarchy.* New York: Oxford University Press.

Lipset, Seymour. (1986). "Historical Traditions and National Characteristics: A Comparative Analysis of Canada and the United States." *Canadian Journal of Sociology* 11, pp. 113–155.

———. (1990). *Continental Divide: The Values and Institutions of the United States and Canada.* New York: Routledge.

Lipson, E. (1945). *The Economic History of England: The Middle Ages.* London: Adam and Charles Black.

Litchfield, R. (1991). "How Our Schools Are Flunking." *Canadian Business,* February, pp. 56–65.

London Family Court Clinic. (1991). *Wife Assault as a Crime: The Perspectives of Victims and Police Officers on a Charging Policy in London, Ontario, from 1980–1990.* London, ON: London Family Court Clinic.

Lowe, Graham S. (1989). *Women, Paid/Unpaid Work, And Stress.* Ottawa: Canadian Advisory Council on the Status of Women.

Lupri, Eugen. (1990). "Male Violence in the Home." In C. McKie and K. Thompson, eds., *Canadian Social Trends.* Toronto: Thomson Educational.

Lupri, Eugen, and Jaems Frideres. (1981). "The Quality of Marriage and the Passage of Time: Marital Satisfaction over the Family Life Cycle" *Canadian Journal of Sociology* 6, pp. 283–306.

Lyotard, Jean-Francois. (1985). *The Post-Modern Condition.* Minneapolis: University of Minnesota Press.

MacDonald, Doug. (1991). *The Politics of Pollution.* Toronto: McClelland and Stewart.

MacKenzie, D. (1981). *Statistics in Britain: 1865–1930.* Edinburgh: University of Edinburgh Press.

Mackie, Marlene. (1987). *Constructing Women and Men: Gender Socialization.* Toronto: Holt, Rinehart and Winston.

MacPherson, C.B. (1962). *The Political Theory of Possessive Individualism.* Oxford: Oxford University Press.

Maille, Chantal. (1990). *Primed for Power: Women in Canadian Politics.* Ottawa: Canadian Advisory Council on the Status of Women.

Maine, Henry Sumner. (1960[1861]). *Ancient Law.* London: J. M. Dent.

Malinowski, Bronislaw. (1954[1925]). *Magic, Science and Religion.* New York: Doubleday.

Mandel, Ernest. (1969). *An Introduction to Marxist Economic Theory.* New York: Pathfinder Press.

Marchack, Patricia. (1985). "Canadian Political Economy." *Review of Canadian Sociology and Anthropology* 22 (5).

Marcil-Gratton, Nicole. (1988). *Les modes de vie nouveaux des adultes et leur impact sur les enfants au Canada.* Montreal: Université de Montréal.

Marcuse, Herbert. (1964). *One-Dimensional Man.* New York: Beacon Press.

Marr, William L., and Donald G. Paterson. (1980). *Canada: An Economic History.* Toronto: Gage.

Marshall, Katherine. (1993). "Employed Parents and the Division of Housework." *Perspectives on Labour and Income,* Autumn, pp. 23–30.

Marx, Karl. (1964). *Economic and Philosophical Manuscripts of 1844.* New York: International.

———. (1968[1845])."Thesis on Feuerbach." In *Karl Marx and Frederick Engels: Selected Works.* London: Lawrence and Wishart.

———. (1968[1859]). "Preface to a Contribution to the Critique of Political Economy." In *Karl Marx and Frederick Engels: Selected Works.* London: Lawrence and Wishart.

———. (1968[1875]). "Critique of the Gotha Program." In *Karl Marx and Frederick Engels: Selected Works.* London: Lawrence and Wishart.

———. (1954). *Capital.* Vol. 1. London: Lawrence and Wishart.

———. (1968[1852]). "The Eighteenth Brumaire of Louis Bonaparte." In *Karl Marx and Frederick Engels: Selected Works.* London: Lawrence and Wishart.

———. (1974). *Capital.* Vol. 3. London: Lawrence and Wishart.

Marx, Karl, and Frederick Engels. (1968[1848]). "Manifesto of the Communist Party." In *Karl Marx and Frederick Engels: Selected Works.* London: Lawrence and Wishart.

Maynard, Rona. (1989). "Look, Jane. Dick Can't Read." *Report on Business Magazine*, May.

Mayrand, A. (1990). *Concentration in the Canadian Financial Sector: The Situation in 1987.* Ottawa: Economic Council of Canada.

McCormick, P., and Ian Greene. (1990). *Judges and Judging.* Halifax: Formac Publishing.

McInnis, Edgar. (1969). *Canada: A Political and Social History.* Toronto: Holt, Rinehart and Winston.

McKie, Craig, and K. Thompson. (1990). *Canadian Social Trends.* Toronto: Thomson Educational.

McQuaig, Linda. (1988). *Behind Closed Doors.* Toronto: Penguin Books.

Mead, George H. (1934). *Mind, Self, and Society.* Chicago: University of Chicago Press.

Mead, Margaret. (1928). *Coming of Age in Samoa.* New York: William Morrow.

——— . (1970). *Culture and Commitment: A Study of the Generation Gap.* New York: Doubleday.

Merton, Robert K. (1938). "Social Structure and Anomie." *American Sociological Review* 3, pp. 672–682.

Michels, R. (1958[1915]). *Political Parties.* Glencoe: Free Press.

Miliband, Ralph. (1969). *The State in Capitalist Society.* London: Weidenfeld and Nicholson.

——— . (1976). *Marxism and Politics.* Oxford: Oxford University Press.

Mills, C. Wright. (1956). *The Power Elite.* New York: Oxford University Press.

——— . (1959). *The Sociological Imagination.* New York: Oxford University Press.

Mitchell, Juliet. (1974). *Psychoanalysis and Feminism.* New York: Pantheon.

Mittelstaedt, Martin. (1989). "Business Goes Global." *Report on Business Magazine*, February, pp. 72–81.

Morgan, Nicole. (1988). *The Equality Game: Women in the Federal Public Service (1908–1987).* Ottawa: Canadian Advisory Council on the Status of Women.

Murray, Charles. (1991). "Of a Conservative (Created) Caste." *Harpers*, October, pp. 17–18.

Murrell, Hywell. (1976). *Motivation at Work.* London: Methuen.

Myles, John, and Gail Fawcett. (1990). "Job Skills and the Service Economy." Ottawa: Economic Council of Canada, Working Paper no. 4.

National Council of Welfare. (1978). *Bearing the Burden, Sharing the Benefits.* Ottawa: National Council of Welfare.

——— . (1990). *Women and Poverty Revisited.* Ottawa: Minister of Supply and Services.

——— . (1993). *Welfare Incomes, 1992.* Ottawa: Minister of Supply and Services.

Naylor, R.T. (1975). *The History of Canadian Business, 1867–1914.* Vol 1. Toronto: James Lorimer.

New Brunswick Advisory Council on the Status of Women. (1989). *Male Violence in Relationships and the Justice System.* Moncton: New Brunswick Advisory Council on the Status of Women.

Newman, Peter C. (1991). *Merchant Princes.* Toronto: Penguin Books.

Newson, Janice, and H. Buchbinder. (1988). *The University Means Business: Universities, Corporations and Academic Work.* Toronto: Garamond.

Nisbet, Robert. (1966). *The Sociological Tradition.* New York: Basic Books.

——— . (1976). *Sociology as an Art Form.* New York: Oxford University Press.

Oakley, Ann. (1974). *Woman's Work: The Housewife Past and Present.* New York: Pantheon Books.

O'Connor, James. (1973). *The Fiscal Crisis of the State.* New York: St. Martin's Press.

Oderkirk, Jillian. (1993). "Educational Achievement: An International Comparison." *Canadian Social Trends*, pp. 8–12.

OECD. (1976). *Reviews of National Policies for Education: Canada.* Paris: Organization for Economic Co-operation and Development.

——— . (1989). *OECD Economic Surveys, 1988–89: Canada.* Paris: Organization for Economic Co-operation and Development.

Ogmundson, R. (1990). "Perspectives on the Class and Ethnic Origins of Canadian Elites: A Methodological Critique of the Porter/Clement/Olsen Tradition." *Canadian Journal of Sociology* 15, pp. 165–177.

Olsen, D. (1980). *The State Elite.* Toronto: McClelland and Stewart.

Ornstein, M. (1988). "Corporate Involvement in Canadian Hospital and University Boards, 1946–1977." *Canadian Review of Anthropology and Sociology* 25, pp. 363–388.

Panitch, Leo. (1977). "The Role and Nature of the Canadian State." In Leo Panitch, ed., *The Canadian State: Political Economy and Political Power.* Toronto: University of Toronto Press.

Panitch, Leo, and Donald Swartz. (1988). *The Assault on Trade Union Freedoms.* Toronto: Garamond Press.

Parsons, Talcott. (1951). *The Social System.* New York: Free Press.

———— . (1964). "The Kinship System of the Contemporary United States." In T. Parsons, ed., *Essays in Sociological Theory* (pp. 177–196). New York: Free Press.

Parsons, Talcott, and R. Bales. (1955). *Family: Socialization and Interaction Process.* New York: Free Press.

Pearson, David E. (1993). "Post-Mass Culture." *Society,* July/August, pp. 17–22.

Peitchinis, Stephen G. (1989). *Women at Work: Discrimination and Response.* Toronto: McClelland and Stewart.

Pelling, Henry. (1976). *A History of British Trade Unionism,* 3rd ed. London: Macmillan.

Phillips, Kevin. (1990). *The Politics of Rich and Poor.* New York: Random House.

Phillips, Paul, and Erin Phillips. (1993). *Women and Work.* Toronto: James Lorimer.

Piaget, Jean. (1952). *Judgement and Reasoning in the Child.* New York: Humanities Press.

Picot, G., J. Myles, and T. Wannell. (1990). *Good Jobs/Bad Jobs and the Declining Middle: 1967–1986.* Ottawa: Statistics Canada, Analytical Studies Branch, no. 28.

Popenoe, D. (1988). *Disturbing the Nest.* Chicago: Aldine De Gruyter.

Porter, John. (1965). *The Vertical Mosaic.* Toronto: University of Toronto Press.

Porter, Michael. (1991). *Canada at the Crossroads: The Reality of a New Competitive Environment.* Ottawa: Business Council on National Issues and Minister of Supply and Services.

Potter, A.M. (1955). *American Government and Politics.* London: Faber.

Pratt, Vernon. (1978). *The Philosophy of the Social Sciences.* London: Methuen.

Presthus, Robert. (1973). *Elite Accommodation in Canadian Politics.* Toronto: Macmillan.

Priest, L. (1989). *The Conspiracy of Silence.* Toronto: McClelland and Stewart.

Quasha, Solomon. (1980). *Albert Einstein: An Intimate Portrait.* Larchmont, NY: Forest.

Raymond, Janice. (1979). *The Transsexual Empire: The Making of the She-Male.* Boston: Beacon Press.

Reasons, Charles, and William D. Perdue. (1981). *The Ideology of Social Problems.* Sherman Oaks: Alfred.

Reiman, J. (1989). *The Rich Get Richer and the Poor Get Prison.* New York: Wiley.

Reiter, Rayna. (1975). *Toward an Anthropology of Women.* New York: Monthly Review Press.

Report of the Standing Committee on Health and Welfare, Social Affairs, Seniors and Status of Women. (1993). *Breaking the Silence on the Abuse of Older Canadians: Everyone's Concern.* Ottawa.

Report to the Legislature by the Ministry of Education. (1990). *The Status of Women and Employment Equity in Ontario School Boards, 1989.* Toronto: Ontario Ministry of Education.

Richardson, R. Jack. (1988). "'A Sacred Trust': The Trust Industry and Canadian Economic Structure." *Canadian Review of Anthropology and Sociology* 25, pp. 1–22.

Riddell, Craig W., ed. (1985). *Work and Pay: The Canadian Labour Market.* Toronto: University of Toronto Press.

Riesman, David. (1950). *The Lonely Crowd.* New Haven, CT: Yale University Press.

Rinehart, James W. (1987). *The Tyranny of Work,* 2nd ed. Toronto: Harcourt Brace Jovanovich.

Rogers, Rix. (1990). *Reaching For Solutions: The Report of the Special Advisor on Child Sexual Abuse in Canada.* Ottawa: Minister of Supply and Services.

Rosenthal, R., and L. Jacobson. (1968). *Pygmalion in the Classroom: Teacher Expectation and Pupils' Intellectual Development.* New York: Holt, Rinehart and Winston.

Royal Commission on Aboriginal Peoples. (1993). *Aboriginal Peoples and the Justice System.* Ottawa: Minister of Supply and Services.

Sacks, Karen. (1979). *Sisters and Wives: The Past and Future of Sexual Inequality.* Westport, CT: Greenwood Press.

Sanday, Peggy Reeves. (1981). "The Socio-Cultural Context of Rape: A Cross-Cultural Study." *Journal of Social Issues* 37, pp. 5–27.

Sanderson, Stephen K. (1988). *Macrosociology: An Introduction to Human Societies.* New York: Harper and Row.

Sargent, Lydia, ed. (1981). *The Unhappy Marriage of Marxism and Feminism.* London: Pluto Press.

Saul, John Ralston. (1988). "The Secret Life of the Branch-Plant." *Report on Business Magazine,* January, pp. 81–86.

Sayers, Janet. (1982). *Biological Politics: Feminist and Anti-Feminist Perspectives.* London: Tavistock.

Schiller, Herbert I. (1989). *Culture Inc.: The Corporate Takeover of Public Expression.* New York: Oxford University Press.

Scott, Noll. (1985). "Disappearing Desperadoes." *The New Internationalist,* December, pp. 18–21.

Segal, L. (1987). *Is the Future Female?* New York: Peter Bedrick Books.

Shkilnyk, Anastasia. (1985). *A Poison Stronger Than Love: The Destruction of an Ojibwa Community.* New Haven, CT: Yale University Press.

Shorter, Edward. (1975). *The Making of the Modern Family.* New York: Basic Books.

Sinclair, T.A. (1951). *A History of Greek Political Thought.* London: Routledge and Kegan Paul.

Slater, Philip. (1976). *The Pursuit of Loneliness: American Culture at the Breaking Point,* rev. ed. Boston: Beacon Press.

Smith, Adam. (1937[1776]). *The Wealth of Nations.* New York: Modern Library.

Smith, Dorothy. (1975). "The Statistics on Mental Illness: (What They Will Not Tell Us about Women and Why)." In D. Smith and S. J. David, eds., *Women Look at Psychiatry.* Vancouver: Press Gang.

———. (1987). *The Everyday World as Problematic: A Feminist Sociology.* Toronto: University of Toronto Press.

Smythe, Dallas W. (1981). *Dependency Road: Communications, Capitalism, Consciousness, and Canada.* Norwood, NJ: Ablex.

Solicitor General of Canada. (1983). *Seven Cities Victim Survey.* Ottawa: Ministry of Supply and Services Canada.

Spector, A. (1992). "Measuring Low Incomes in Canada." *Canadian Social Trends,* Summer, pp. 8–10.

Spitzer, S. (1975). "Toward a Marxian Theory of Deviance." *Social Problems* 22, pp. 638–651.

Statistics Canada. (1989). *Homicide in Canada, 1988.* Ottawa: Minister of Supply and Services.

———. (1990a). *A Portrait of Children in Canada.* Ottawa: Minister of Supply and Services.

———. (1990b). *Migration Between the United States and Canada.* Ottawa: Supply and Services Canada.

———. (1991a). *Crime in Aboriginal Communities: Saskatchewan 1989.* Ottawa: Centre for Criminal Justice Statistics.

———. (1991b). "Divorce." *Health Reports.* Supplement 17, Vol. 3, no. 4: Ottawa: Minister of Supply and Services.

———. (1992a). *Lone-Parent Families in Canada.* Ottawa: Minister of Industry, Science and Technology. Cat. no. 89-522.

———. (1992b). "Labour Unions 1990." *Calura.* Part II. Cat. no. 71-202.

———. (1992c). *Income Distributions by Size in Canada, 1991.* Ottawa: Ministry of Industry, Science and Technology. Cat. no. 13-207.

———. (1993a). *Aboriginal Peoples Survey 1991: Language, Tradition, Health, Lifestyle and Social Issues.* Ottawa: Minister of Industry, Science and Technology.

———. (1993b). *Causes of Death: 1991.* Ottawa: Minister of Industry, Science and Technology. Cat. no. 84-298.

———. (1993c). *Historical Labour Force Statistics 1992.* Ottawa: Minister of Industry, Science and Technology.

———. (March 1993d). *Police-Reported Aboriginal Crime in Calgary, Regina and Saskatoon.* Ottawa: Canadian Centre for Justice Statistics.

Steele, Claude M. (1992). "Race and the Schooling of Black Americans." *The Atlantic Monthly* 269, pp. 68–78.

Stern, Paul, and Tom Shachtman. (1991). *Straight to the Top.* New York: Random House.

Sunter, D. (1992). "Juggling School and Work." *Perspectives on Labour and Income*, Spring, pp. 15–21.

Sussman, M. (1974). "The Isolated Nuclear Family: Fact or Fiction?" In M. Sussman, ed., *Sourcebook in Marriage and the Family*. Boston: Houghton Mifflin.

Swinamer, J.L. (1985). "The Value of Household Work in Canada, 1981." *Canadian Statistical Review* 60 (3), pp. vi–xiv.

Sydie, R.A. (1987). *Natural Women, Cultured Men*. Toronto: Methuen.

Tannen, Deborah. (1990). *You Just Don't Understand*. New York: William Morrow.

Tanner, A. (1979). *Bringing Home Animals*. London: C. Hurst.

Taylor, A.J.P. (1965). *English History 1914–1945*. Oxford: Oxford University Press.

———. (1968). *Bismarck*. London: New English Library.

Taylor, Charles. (1991). *The Malaise of Modernity*. Toronto: Anansi.

Taylor, Frederick W. (1919). *Shop Management*. New York: Harper.

Teichova, Alice. (1990). "A Legacy of Fin-de-siècle Capitalism: The Giant Corporation." In *Fin de Siècle and Its Legacy*. M. Teich and Roy Porter, eds., Cambridge: Cambridge University Press.

Thistlewaite, Frank. (1961). *The Great Experiment: An Introduction to the History of the American People*. Cambridge: Cambridge University Press.

Tiger, L. (1969). *Men in Groups*. New York: Random House.

Toby, Jackson. (1979). "Societal Evolution and Criminality: A Parsonian View." *Social Problems* 26, pp. 386–391.

Tonnies, F. (1963[1897]). *Community and Society*. New York: Harper and Row.

Trade Union Congress. (1874). *Annual Report*. London: British Trade Union Congress.

———. (1968). *History of the T.U.C., 1869–1968*. London: General Council of the Trade Union Congress.

Trudeau, Pierre E. (1993). *Memoirs*. Toronto: McClelland and Stewart.

Tuchman, Gayle. (1974). *The TV Establishment*. Englewood Cliffs, NJ: Prentice-Hall.

Tumin, Melvin. (1953). "Some Principles of Stratification: A Critical Analysis." *American Sociological Review* 18, pp. 387–394.

Turnbull, C. (1961). *The Forest People*. New York: Simon and Schuster.

UNICEF. (1993). *Progress of Nations: The Nations of the World Ranked According to Their Achievements in Health, Nutrition, Education, Family Planning, and Progress for Women*. New York: UNICEF.

———. (1993b). *The State of the World's Children, 1993*. Oxford: Oxford University Press.

United Kingdom. (1912). *Shipping Casualties (Loss of the Steamship "Titanic")*. London: His Majesty's Stationery Office. Command 6352.

Ursel, Jane. (1986). "The State and the Maintenance of Patriarchy: A Case Study of Family, Labour and Welfare Legislation in Canada." In James Dickinson and Bob Russel, *Family, Economy and State* (pp. 150–191). Toronto: Garamond Press.

Vanier Institute of the Family. (1994). *Profiling Canadian Families*. Ottawa: Vanier Institute of the Family.

Visser, Margaret. (1986). *Much Depends On Dinner*. Toronto: McClelland and Stewart.

Wade, Wyn Craig. (1980). *The Titanic*. New York: Penguin.

Wallace, Michael, and Arne Kalleberg. (1982). "Industrial Transformation and the Decline of Craft: The Decomposition of Skill in the Printing Industry, 1931–1978." *American Sociological Review* 47, pp. 307–322.

Wallerstein, Immanuel. (1974, 1980). *The Modern World System*. Vols. 1 and 2. New York: Academic Press.

Wallerstein, Judith, and S. Blakeslee. (1989). *Second Chances: Men, Women and Children a Decade After Divorce*. New York: Ticknor and Fields.

Warnock, John W. (1988). *Free Trade and the New Right Agenda*. Vancouver: New Star.

Weber, Max. (1958[1904]). *The Protestant Ethic and the Spirit of Capitalism*. New York: Charles Scribner and Sons.

———. (1966[1947]). *The Theory of Social and Economic Organization*. New York: Free Press.

White, Burton L. (1975). *The First Three Years of Life*. New York: Avon Books.

Wilkins, Russell, Owen Adams, and Anna Branker. (1990). "Change in Mortality by Income in Urban Canada from 1971 to 1986." *Health Reports 1989* 1 (2), pp. 137–167.

Wilkins, Russell, Gregory Sherman, and P.A.F. Best. (1991). "Birth Outcomes and Infant Mortality by Income in Urban Canada, 1986." *Health Reports* 3 (1). Ottawa: Minister of Supply and Services.

Wilson, Edward O. (1975). *Sociobiology: The New Synthesis*. Cambridge, MA: Harvard University Press.

Wilson, James Q., and Richard J. Herrnstein. (1985). *Crime and Human Nature*. New York: Simon and Schuster.

Wolfe, Morris. (1985). *Jolts: The TV Wasteland and the Canadian Oasis*. Toronto: James Lorimer.

Women's Bureau, Labour Canada. (1990). *Women in the Labour Force*. Ottawa: Minister of Supply and Services.

Wrong, Dennis. (1961). "The Oversocialized Conception of Man in Modern Sociology." *American Sociological Review* 26, pp. 183–193.

Wyatt Company. (1991). *Wyatt Work Canada: The New National Benchmark on Worker Attitudes*. Vancouver: Wyatt Co.

Zakuta, L. (1964). *A Protest Movement Becalmed*. Toronto: University of Toronto Press.

Zaretsky, Eli. (1976). *Capitalism, The Family, and Personal Life*. New York: Harper Colophon Books.

Zeitlin, Maurice. (1974). "Corporate Ownership and Control: The Large Corporation and the Capitalist Class." *American Journal of Sociology* 79, pp. 1073–1119.

Ziegler, M., F. Weizmann, N. Wiener, and D. Wiesenthal. (1991). "Phillipe Rushton and the Growing Acceptance of 'Race–Science.'" In O. McKague, ed., *Racism in Canada*. Saskatoon: Fifth House.

GLOSSARY

· · · · · · · ·

· · · · · · · ·

Affinal Relationship A kinship relationship established by marriage.

Agrarian Society A society in which the main economic activity is the growing of crops. Often considered to be a more technologically advanced form of horticultural society (see below) and usually involving settled agriculture and the use of ploughs.

Alienated Labour The individual's experience of separation from the control and direction of his or her social life, especially at work. As used by Karl Marx, the concept does not require subjective feelings of alienation, but exists objectively in any structure of work organization in which work is not controlled by the worker and the product is owned by someone else.

Altruistic Suicide A suicide committed for the benefit of a society or a group; for example, self-sacrifice during wartime for military objectives.

Androcentrism A view of the world that focusses on the roles and life experiences of men and ignores or denies the separate experience of women.

Anomic Suicide Suicide resulting from a lack of normative integration. Individuals feel rootless and disconnected from guiding norms and values.

Anomie A term developed by Émile Durkheim denoting a situation in which norms become confused or weak and people lack clear guidance and social regulation.

Ascribed Status A status that arises from the inherited social position or innate characteristics of an individual. Class, caste, age, and gender statuses are examples of ascribed status.

Authentic Individuation The concept that individuals can only fully express their personality when they are intimately connected to group life, in which there is no division between private and public personal expression.

Authority Power that is recognized as legitimately exercised by individuals and institutions having a right to demand obedience.

Bilineal Descent Descent or inheritance that is determined equally through male and female blood lines.

Bourgeois Family A family system based on a private family life and in which women are separated into the domestic sphere and men act as family heads in the social and economic spheres.

Bourgeoisie The owners and controllers of the means of production in a capitalist society.

Bureaucracy A formal organization encompassing specialized roles, hierarchy, and systematic administration.

Capitalism A form of economic organization in which the means of production are privately owned and production is chiefly directed to the sale of commmodities in the marketplace.

Charismatic Authority Authority deriving from a belief in a leader's unique and inspirational powers.

Class Consciousness An understanding of class interests that arises from a grasp of the objective situation of the class in society. Its opposite is false consciousness, in which members of a social class adopt beliefs and values that serve members of other classes rather than themselves. Class consciousness is the overcoming of these false beliefs and ideologies (see below). This concept assumes that there is an appropriate, or correct, class consciousness.

Classes Categories in which individuals are placed according to their possession or non-possession of wealth or power. The ownership or non-ownership of the means of production is often used as a basis for class categories.

Class-for-Itself A social class whose members are aware of their shared social situation and of the interests that unite them: they have class consciousness.

Class-in-Itself A social class whose members share a similar social situation and commonality of interests, but who have no subjective recognition of unity.

Classless Society Found in early, and some traditional, human communities where there are no significant differences between individuals in terms of their power or possessions. Also, a socialist vision of future society in which common ownership of the means of production will eliminate all significant economic and political distinctions between individuals.

Coercion The use of force or commands to gain obedience without the consent of the individual.

Conjugal Family A nuclear family of a cohabiting couple and their dependent children in which the strongest emotions and commitments are focussed inward.

Consanguineal Family A family system of nuclear families linked through shared descent from a common ancestor. The individual nuclear families are bound into complex ties of obligation and daily activity with each other. Consanguineal families can be linked either matrilineally or patrilineally.

Consumer Culture A culture in which people are encouraged to express their status and seek emotional satisfaction through the consumption of goods and services.

Correspondence Principle The concept that the central institutions of a society will reflect common values and structural principles. Applied especially to education to suggest that schooling reflects and reproduces existing social hierarchies through both hidden and overt curricula.

Critical Perspectives A group of sociological theories, including feminism, Marxism, and political economy, which focus on the analysis of social inequality and patterns of political and social domination. Sometimes referred to as conflict theory.

Cultural Crisis A crisis occurring when a cultural system no longer is able to provide individuals with the beliefs and values that create a sense of community and shared identity with others.

Culture The knowledge, beliefs, and values that people learn as members of society through the process of socialization. Some have distinguished a separate "material culture" consisting of human artifacts like architecture, manufactured goods, and art objects. Most sociologists believe that material culture is not separable because it is a reflection of symbolic culture.

Democracy From the Greek original meaning, "rule by the people," democracy has come to mean the election of governing representatives through a competitive electoral process in which all adults have the right to participate as candidates and voters.

Deskilling The process by which division of labour and technological development has led to the reduction of the scope of an individual's work to one, or a few, specialized tasks. Work is fragmented, and individuals lose the integrated skills and comprehensive knowledge of the craftsperson.

Disenchantment of the World From Max Weber's theory of a continuing process of rationalization in modern societies. Increasingly, the older ways of understanding the world, which embody myth and magic, are replaced by practical and scientific ideas directed toward control and efficiency.

Division of Labour A process of work organization in which production is subdivided into specialized tasks.

Domination The structure of political rule, which can be exercised by coercion, but is usually found in one of three types of legitimate authority: traditional, charismatic, and rational–legal.

Egoistic Suicide Suicide that arises from an individual's weak integration into social structures, like marriage, family, and community.

Equality of Condition Equal individual possession of wealth, income, power, status, and so on; does not exist in any complex society.

Equality of Opportunity	A roughly equal individual chance to compete for economic and social rewards. Would support a situation of social mobility and create an open-class society.
Ethnic Group	A group of individuals possessing a common culture and common origins. Groups can be distinguished by physical appearance, dress, language, or cultural beliefs and behaviour.
Ethnocentrism	The belief that one's own culture is superior to all others and that alternative cultural practices are inferior and improper.
Ethnomethodology	The study of how individuals make sense of the social world; a microsociology that focusses on revealing the rules and standards that people apply to participation in social interaction.
Family of Origin (Orientation)	The (usually nuclear) family into which an individual is born. Can be more generally thought of as the intimate members of the child's immediate circle of nurturers and companions.
Family of Procreation	The family formed when a couple enter a relationship and nurture and raise a child, either natural or adopted.
Fatalistic Suicide	Suicide resulting from despair at being placed in oppressive social relationships.
Feminism	A general critical orientation to methods of social organization and cultural values that stresses their disadvantagement or exclusion of women.
Fertility Rate	The average number of children born to a population of women of child-bearing age.
Feudal Mode of Production	An economic system based on large-scale landlord ownership and the agricultural production of serfs, an unfree class of bonded labourers.
Feudalism	A political system of warrior chiefs structured in a complex web of rights and obligations between individuals. Military organization was founded on duties of military service and loyalty (vassalage) supported by a feudal system of agricultural production.
Functionalism	A sociological perspective that focusses on the mutually supportive interconnection of the principal institutions of society. Also known as structural functionalism, systems theory, the consensus perspective, or order theory.
Gemeinschaft	A model, or ideal type, of community where social bonds are direct and personal.
Gender	The cultural elaboration placed upon sexual identity that defines the norms, values, and roles considered appropriate to members of each sex.
Generalized Other	The norms and values an individual believes are held by other members of the society and to which his or her social actions are oriented.
Gesellschaft	A model, or ideal type, society in which social interaction is primarily impersonal and structured by contract, and in which individuals are self-oriented rather than collectively oriented.
Globalization	The process of international economic and cultural integration, in which individual national economies and national cultures become integrated into a worldwide system.
Hegemony	A concept associated with Antonio Gramsci, an Italian Marxist, that expresses the way that ideologies are pervasive and are reflected not only in dominant ideas but also in all major institutional areas of society.
Hidden Curriculum	The styles of thought and behaviour into which students are socialized in educational institutions. The hidden curriculum is conveyed by practices of teaching, underlying values displayed in the overt curriculum, and the organization of authority in the classroom and the institution.
Horticultural Society	A simple, and usually earlier, form of agrarian society. It is founded on the production of crops, but agriculture is small scale and often moves as land is exhausted. Hoes, rather than ploughs, are the principal technology.
Human Capital Theory	The theory that educational investment to develop individuals' skills and knowledge stimulates economic growth and creates employment opportunities.
Hunting and Gathering Society	Probably the earliest form of human society, and still found among some forest-dwelling peoples. Food and goods production comes from naturally occurring resources of plants and animals. Lack of economic and social differentiation is apparent, as is a general pattern of greater gender equality.

I George Mead's term for the spontaneous, individual component of the self. Closely related to Freud's term, *ego*. The I is the component of the self-identity that reacts to the expectations of others.

Ideology A pattern of beliefs, norms, and values that explain, justify, and uphold either existing or desired forms of social relationships.

Individualism A value system that upholds individual choice, personal freedom, and self-orientation.

Inequality of Condition *See* equality of condition.

Inequality of Opportunity *See* equality of opportunity.

Institution A typical structure of social interaction found in a society. Institutions are shaped by behavioural norms and values that remain relatively stable over time.

Kinship The web of social relationships founded on genetic, customary, or legal familial affinity.

Laissez-Faire To leave social and economic processes alone and not attempt to provide direction. A central principle of liberalism.

Legitimate Authority Authority founded in a widely held belief that individuals and institutions have the moral right to obedience.

Legitimation A set of social ideas and practices that give moral sanction to structures of power and of social relationships.

Liberalism Originally a political doctrine that asserted the innate equality of all human beings and their right to be free of all constraint except that needed to protect the exercise of freedom by others. In the later nineteenth and twentieth centuries, became associated with the idea that the state should ensure a minimal equality of opportunity.

Lumpenproletariat A disorganized poverty class displaced from the economy and dependent on charity, scavenging, and crime.

Marxism The social and political ideas associated with Karl Marx and Frederick Engels. Marxism principally focusses on economic processes and how they shape culture and social relationships. Marx advocated a socialist or communist society based on common ownership of the means of production.

Mass Culture A culture in which cultural symbols and means of social communication are directed toward large audiences and individuals are encouraged to abandon personal cultural expression.

Materialist Understanding of History A theory of historical analysis, developed by Karl Marx, that gives primary weight to economic factors, including technology and the social organization of the economy, in explaining social and intellectual change.

Matrilineal A system of reckoning family descent through the blood links of women. In such systems, a woman's descendants are her own children and a man's are his sister's children.

Me The part of self-consciousness that is shaped by culture and by the anticipated values and behaviour of others. It is a force for conformity that interacts with the individual's more ego-focussed sense of "I" (see above).

Mechanical Solidarity A state of community bonding that rests on a similarity of beliefs and values, shared activities, and ties of kinship and co-operation.

Metropolis–Hinterland Theory A theory of social and economic development that examines how economically advanced societies, through trade and colonialism, distort and retard the economic development of less developed societies and regions.

Norms Relatively precise and specific rules of behaviours established in a culture. They may be thought of as the regulations that spell out more general cultural values.

Open-Class Society A society that has only achieved status within a framework of equality of opportunity. A class situation is not transmitted generationally.

Organic Solidarity A state of social interdependency created by the specialization of roles and in which individuals and institutions become acutely dependent on others in a complex division of labour.

The basis of solidarity is abstract and may be weakened by anomie when people fail to comprehend the ties that bind them to others.

Pastoral Society A society that has an economy principally based on herd animals who range feed. Usually, pastoral societies are nomadic or make seasonal changes of location. Climate and geography prevent or restrict crop growing.

Patriarchy Social domination by men over women; pervades social institutions and cultural values.

Patrilineal A system in which family descent is reckoned through the blood links of males. A man's descendants are his own children, and women are little recognized as ancestors.

Petite Bourgeoisie A middle class of professionals and small-business people who work for themselves or own small productive facilities. Marx predicted that this class would be gradually eliminated by the consolidation of large capital under competitive forces.

Pluralism Has two central meanings. First, a theory of social change that attributes causal significance to a variety of influences. Max Weber's theory of the independent importance of cultural ideas in the development of capitalism is an example. Second, a model of political power in which it is widely dispersed and decision making is subject to the influences of a wide range of interest groups.

Polarization of Classes A process, predicted by Karl Marx, in which the middle class of petite bourgeoisie and independent craftspeople are eliminated by competitive processes and pushed into either the proletariat or the bourgeoisie. A two-class social structure emerges.

Polyandry A marriage structure in which a woman has more than one husband at one time. It is rare, but where it does occur there is sometimes fraternal polyandry, in which the husbands are brothers.

Polygamy A marriage structure in which there is more than one spouse at a time.

Polygyny A marriage structure in which men have more than one wife at one time. Widely spread in world societies, but often not practiced because of population sex-ratios and a lack of economic resources.

Post-Industrial Society Thesis The theory that modern economies have moved from a focus on goods production to a new foundation of knowledge and sophisticated services.

Power The capacity of individuals or institutions to achieve goals even if opposed by others.

Primitive Communism An imagined first human society in which all resources were owned in common, there was no concept of separate families, and individuals were completely united with the group. Has a close correspondence to some actual hunting and gathering societies.

Proletariat The social class composed of those who have no means of production of their own and who subsist by selling their labour power to a capitalist.

Protestant Ethic A set of ideas, developed as a result of the Reformation, that encourage dedication to hard work and self-advancement and offer moral justification for trade and profit seeking. Contrasts with the traditional Catholic emphasis on religious devotion and indifference to the accumulation of wealth.

Race A concept based on the assumption that human beings are classifiable into distinct biological groups. Various classification systems have been employed, based on skin colour and other physical characteristics. The concept is rejected by critics who point to the common origin of human beings and their constant historical intermingling.

Racist Ideology A belief, based on the idea of racial classification, that some human beings are biologically inferior to others.

Rational–Legal Authority Authority based on the claim that society is regulated by laws to which all individuals are subject and that have been made through a formal legal process by legitimate institutions.

Rationalization Has two key meanings in sociology. First, a cultural development in which magical and mysterious ideas about the world are replaced by those based on scientific understanding and practical calculation. Second, the process by which social institutions become oriented to the efficient achievement of specified goals.

Reflexive Role Taking A situation in which an individual's role behaviour is shaped by a consideration of the normative expectations of others.

Relative Autonomy	A theory of state power based on Marxist ideas. This perspective proposes that the state can and does play a limited independent role in the maintenance and stabilization of capitalist society. Differs from pluralism (see above) in viewing state power as strongly constrained by the ideological and structural characteristics of capitalist societies.
Role	A social position or status regulated by specific norms and behavioural expectations.
Scientific Management	A method of work organization in which management specifies a pronounced division of labour and sets out detailed instructions for the performance of the work.
Scientific Method	The experimental and research techniques, based on methods used in the natural sciences, that are employed in sociology to test hypotheses and develop theories.
Sex	The biological classification of individuals as male or female.
Sexualization of Commodities	The association of sexual feelings with the consumption of goods or services.
Shifting Agriculture	A system in which land is cleared and then cultivated until it is exhausted, at which point new land is cleared and the process restarted.
Social Mobility	A situation in which there is a lack of consistency in social class or status, either generationally or during an individual's lifetime.
Social Structure	The relatively patterned organization of social roles, power, and status found in societies and social institutions. Can be thought of both at the level of society and at the level of the individual institution.
Socialization	The process by which individuals learn and internalize the culture of their society or group. Involves the symbolic communication of language and gesture and behavioural conditioning.
State	The institution that claims the exclusive right to the exercise of legitimate force in a given territory (Max Weber). Though there are stateless "acephalous" (headless) societies, most complex societies have state systems of formal governments and administrative bureaucracies.
Status	A specific position in a social structure, often ranked according to power and social prestige.
Status Consistency/ Inconsistency	A situation in which an individual's status within different institutional hierarchies is either similar or dissimilar.
Stratification	The division of individuals into a hierarchical system based on criteria such as wealth, power, or social prestige. Class and status are the key distinctions within stratification systems.
Structural Differentiation	A situation in which social institutions previously performing a range of roles become more specialized and new institutions are created to take over the roles that have been vacated.
Subculture	A culture-within-a-culture; exists when a group within a society has different norms, values, and behaviours from other groups. Implies a degree of self-sufficiency.
Symbolic Interactionism	A microsociological theory that focusses on how individuals create and recreate society in their social interactions. Stresses the processes of interpretation and negotiation that occur when individuals orient themselves to others.
Technological Functionalism	The belief that educational systems supply society with individuals who have been educated to fill necessary roles and who have been selected on the basis of merit and ability.
Traditional Authority	Authority based on historical sanction that is upheld by religion, myth, and social practice.
Utilitarianism	The theory that only individuals are competent to maximize their satisfaction and should have individual choice. Where individuals satisfy their own self-interest, it is assumed that society as a whole achieves a maximization of satisfaction and benefits.
Values	Relatively general, emotionally charged, prescriptions of appropriate beliefs and behaviour. Can be thought of as the overarching principles that are the foundation of precise behavioural norms.

NAME INDEX

SUBJECT INDEX

level of technology in, 77, 90*n*
materialist understanding of, 108–109
modern vs. traditional, 58–59, 65, 90*n*, 127, 207, 277–78, 299–305, *see also* Traditional societies
moral order in, 127–28
organic model for, 125
pastoral/horticultural, 109, 306
postindustrial, 232–35
relation of individual to, 2–3, 27–29, 126–27, 129, 299, *see also* Durkheimian sociology; Individual(s); Social bonds; Socialization
scientific–industrial vs. theological–military, 9
simple vs. complex, 34–37
social change in, 8–9, 93
stability and dysfunction in, 15
study of, 1–3, *see also* Sociology
Sociobiology, 157
Sociology
central questions of, 7
critical perspectives, 16–17
defined, 4–5
Durkheimian, *see* Durkheimian sociology
emergence of, 7–9, 106
feminism and, 131–32
functionalist approach, 14–16
historical, 89*n*
interpretation of facts, 14, 65
Marxist, *see* Marxism
micro/macrosociology, 17
neutrality in, 10, 12, 13
perspectives on, 14–17
relation to other social sciences, 4–5
scientific principles/methods of, 10–12
Weberian, *see* Weberian sociology

Sociology of knowledge, 12
Solidarity, 131
mechanical vs. organic, 124–25
Southam, Inc., 334
Specialization, 125
Spinning, rise of capitalism, 99, 100
Sports, consumer market, 333
Sports Illustrated Canada, 335
Stability, 15
State
as abstract, 192, 193
authority of, 193
capital accumulation function, 196–97, 200
coercive function of, 196, 198
economic vs. political power, 191
foundations of power of, 193
gender and, 214–15
and globalization, 215–16
as guarantor of equality of opportunity, 198
legitimation function, 196, 197–98, 200
pluralist/functionalist view of, 204–205, 207
provider of social order, 200
as referee, 213
relative autonomy of, 213–14
stabilization of society, 199
in structural Marxism, 214–14
subjection of individual to, 129
ties to corporate sector, 205–207, 212–14
violence, 207
in Weber, 192
welfare, 197
Statistical significance, 21
Statistics, 12
crime, 14, 317–18
defined, 20
Status, 121, 136
vs. class, 151–54, 158
consistency vs. inconsistency of, 145
in Indian caste system, 139–40, 154

intelligence and, 150
occupational, 145, 150
of women, 158, 192, 285, *see also* Gender inequality
Status group(s), 154
examples of, 159
women as, 158
Stock exchange, 172
Stratification, 140
corporate ownership and, 172
in Weber vs. Marx, 154
Stratification institutions, 76
Streaming, 251
Structural differentiation, 276
Structural functionalism, *see* Functionalism
Structural integration, 125–26
Structuralism, 68*n*
Structural Marxism, 212–14
Structural mobility, 147–48
Subculture
defined, 38
ethnic groups, 52–55
multiculturalism and, 39–40
Native peoples, 52–55
women as, 64–65
youth, 302
Subsistence producers, 110
Suffrage, in Canada, 195
Suicide, 18, 19, 49*n*
altruistic, 300
anomic, 299
in Canada, 318
completed vs. attempted, 300
Durkheim's study of, 126–27, 133*n*, 299–300
egoistic, 299
fatalistic, 300
men and, 89
Native peoples and, 318
as objective event vs. social construct, 319
statistics, 317
types of, 133*n*
Super Bowl, 333
Supply-side theory, 236, 239
Surplus expropriation, 78
Surplus population, 312–13